The Routledge Handbook of Family Communication

The Routledge Handbook of Family Communication offers a comprehensive exploration and discussion of current research and theory on family interaction. Integrating the varying perspectives and issues addressed by family researchers, theorists, and practitioners, this volume offers a unique and timely view of family interaction and family relationships. With a synthesis of research on issues key to understanding family interaction, as well as an analysis of many theoretical and methodological choices made by researchers studying family communication, this Handbook serves to advance the field by reframing old questions and stimulating new ones.

The contents are comprised of chapters covering:

- theoretical and methodological issues influencing current conceptions of family;
- research and theory centering around the family life course;
- communication occurring in a variety of family forms;
- individual family members and their relationships;
- dynamic communication processes taking place in families;
- family communication embedded in social, cultural, and physical contexts.

Highlighting the work of scholars across disciplines—communication, social psychology, clinical psychology, sociology, family studies, and others—this volume captures the breadth and depth of research on family communication and family relationships. It will be of great value to researchers, theorists, and practitioners focusing on family interaction and family relationships, and also serve as a text for graduate-level coursework in family studies, family communication, relational communication, and related areas.

Anita L. Vangelisti is the Jesse H. Jones Centennial Professor of Communication at the University of Texas at Austin. Her work focuses on the associations between communication and emotion in the context of close, personal relationships.

D1300484

Routledge Communication Series
Jennings Bryant and Dolf Zillmann, Series Editors

Selected titles in Family Communication include:

Ragan, Wittenberg-Lyles, Goldsmith & Sanchez Reilly, *Communication as Comfort*

Socha & Stamp, *Parents and Children Communicating with Society*

Segrin & Flora, *Family Communication, Second Edition*

Vangelisti, *The Routledge Handbook of Family Communication, Second Edition*

The Routledge Handbook of Family Communication

Second edition

Edited by
Anita L. Vangelisti

Routledge
Taylor & Francis Group

NEW YORK AND LONDON

First published 2013
by Routledge
711 Third Avenue, New York, NY 10017

Simultaneously published in the U.K.
by Routledge
2 Park Square, Milton Park, Abingdon OX14 4RN

Routledge is an imprint of the Taylor & Francis Group, an informa business

First edition published by Routledge in 2003.

British Library Cataloguing in Publication Data
A catalogue record for this book is available from the British Library

Library of Congress Cataloging in Publication Data
Routledge handbook of family communication / edited by Anita Vangelisti.
p. cm. -- (Routledge communication series)
Rev. ed. of: Handbook of family communication / edited by
Anita L. Vangelisti. c2004.
1. Communication in families. 2. Interpersonal communication. I. Vangelisti, Anita L.
II. Handbook of family communication.
HQ519.H36 2012
302.2--dc23
2012008494

ISBN: 978-0-415-88198-2 (hbk)
ISBN: 978-0-415-88197-5 (pbk)
ISBN: 978-0-203-84816-6 (ebk)

Typeset in Goudy
by Taylor & Francis Books

Certified Sourcing
www.sfiprogram.org
SFI-00453

Printed and bound in the United States of America
by Edwards Brothers, Inc.

Contents

Contents

Preface

The family is the crucible of society. In large part, this vital social entity is defined by the way its members interact. Over the past 30 years, enormous strides have been made in our understanding of how communication affects, and is affected by, family members and their relationships. Researchers have described patterns of communication that lead to dissatisfaction in marriage (Gottman & Krokoff, 1989; Heavey, Christensen, & Malamuth, 1995), they have identified links between communication behaviors in families and certain demographic variables (Mistry, Vandewater, Huston, & McLoyd, 2002; Scaramella, Neppl, Ontai, & Conger, 2008), they have begun to unravel the meanings that family members associate with particular behaviors or experiences (Baxter et al., 2009; Leeds-Hurwitz, 2002), and they have demonstrated how the communication patterns of one generation influence the behaviors of the next (Cummings, Goeke-Morey, Papp, & Dukewich, 2002; Schudlich, White, Fleischauer, & Fitzgerald, 2011).

The second edition of *The Routledge Handbook of Family Communication* presents an analysis and synthesis of cutting edge research and theory on family interaction. This volume, like its predecessor, integrates the varying perspectives and issues addressed by researchers, theorists, and practitioners who study how family members communicate and relate to each other. As a consequence, it offers a unique and timely view of family interaction and family relationships.

Although a wide range of perspectives and issues are presented in the volume, three assumptions about families and family relationships tie the chapters together. The first is that families are systems (Minuchin, 1984). Family members and family relationships are interdependent (Kelley, 1983). They simultaneously influence, and are influenced by, each other. Change in one component of the system affects all other components. Because the various parts of family systems are interconnected, families are best conceived as "wholes" and should be studied with regard to the interrelationship of their parts (Reis, Collins, & Berscheid, 2000). Given this, it is important to examine individual members (e.g., infants, children, adolescents) in terms of the ways they relate to other members, to investigate the links between dyadic relationships (e.g., spouses, parents, siblings) and others in the family, and to examine the influences of sociocultural and historical variables (e.g., family work, media, technology) on family interaction.

The second assumption is that families are coherent (Sroufe & Fleeson, 1986). Family processes are patterned and structured. This is not to say that families are static or that they do not change. Rather, the supposition here is that the constant changes that occur in the context of families are, to some degree, organized and predictable. Family relationships and processes fluctuate in response to day-to-day pressures (e.g., economic stress), relational events (e.g., marriage), and the passage of time (e.g., aging), but the fluctuations experienced and enacted by family members are patterned. It is this patterning that allows researchers to study developmental trends in families, interactions that characterize different types of families, and responses that family members have to various social issues.

The third assumption that ties the chapters in this volume together is that families are constituted through social interaction (Caughlin, Koerner, Schrodt, & Fitzpatrick, 2011). Communication is what creates families. When family members communicate, they do more than send messages to each other—they enact their relationships. It is through communication that family members establish roles (e.g., parent or child), maintain rules (e.g., about privacy or conflict), perform functions (e.g., provide emotional or physical support), and sustain behavioral patterns (e.g., concerning media use or health). Understanding family communication processes, thus, is fundamental to understanding family members and family relationships.

The purpose of *The Routledge Handbook of Family Communication* is to analyze, synthesize, and advance existing literature. In order to capture the breadth and depth of research on family communication and family relationships, the work of scholars from a variety of disciplines—including communication, social psychology, clinical psychology, sociology, and family studies—is highlighted. The authors are internationally known scholars. They approach family interaction from a number of different perspectives and focus on topics ranging from the influence of structural characteristics on family relationships to the importance of specific communication processes. The authors were selected as contributors for this volume because they are recognized for the contributions they have made to the study of issues associated with social interaction in family relationships.

Because the *Handbook* spotlights the work of top-notch scholars, many researchers and theorists who study family interaction and family relationships will want to have this volume in their library. The ideas presented in the pages of this book offer both researchers and theorists new perspectives on extant literature as well as important theoretical and methodological recommendations for future work. Graduate students in communication, social psychology, family studies, sociology, and clinical psychology also will want to read this volume. Advanced students who study family relationships will need to know the research findings and the theories that are articulated in this book and, in many cases, will want to apply the material to their own work. Upper division undergraduate students comprise yet another audience. Many instructors who teach upper division courses will see all or part of this volume as an important addition to their current assigned reading lists. Finally, practitioners who deal with families on a regular basis will be interested in the *Handbook*. Counselors and therapists will find that the theory and research presented in the volume is extremely relevant to the work they do with individuals and families.

I am indebted to many people for their invaluable contributions to this project. This book exists only because a group of excellent authors were willing to dedicate a great deal of time, effort, and thought to writing chapters. Their work made this volume possible. My Editor, Linda Bathgate, prompted this project and kept it moving forward. Her keen awareness of the literature and her unwavering support for the *Handbook* made my work a pleasure. Kayley Hoffman and Julia Sammaritano, Linda's Editorial Assistants, made sure the project was on track and answered what must have seemed like an endless list of questions. Their knowledge and kindness both were invaluable. I also would like to thank the families, couples, and individuals who participated in the studies that are reported in this volume. Their willingness to devote their time to research gave all of us the opportunity to uncover information about family communication and family relationships that we never would have otherwise. Finally, I am grateful to, and for, my own family: John, Johnny, Erin, Abigail, and Patrick. I have learned my best and most important lessons about family communication from them.

References

Baxter, L. A., Braithwaite, D. O., Kellas, J., LeClair-Underberg, C., Lamb-Normand, E., Routsong, T., & Thatcher, M. (2009). Empty ritual: Young-adult stepchildren's perceptions of the remarriage ceremony. *Journal of Social and Personal Relationships, 26*, 467–87.

Caughlin, J. P., Koerner, A. F., Schrodt, P., & Fitzpatrick, M. A. (2011). Interpersonal communication in family relationships. In M. L. Knapp & J. A. Daly (Eds.), *The Sage handbook of interpersonal communication*, 4th edn (pp. 679–714). Los Angeles, CA: Sage.

Cummings, E. M., Goeke-Morey, M. C., Papp, L. M., & Dukewich, T. L. (2002). Children's responses to mothers' and fathers' emotionality and tactics in marital conflict in the home. *Journal of Family Psychology, 16*, 478–92.

Gottman, J. M., & Krokoff, L. J. (1989). Marital interaction and satisfaction: A longitudinal view. *Journal of Consulting and Clinical Psychology, 57*, 47–52.

Heavey, C. L., Christensen, A., & Malamuth, N. M. (1995). The longitudinal impact of demand and withdrawal during marital conflict. *Journal of Consulting and Clinical Psychology, 63*, 797–801.

Kelley, H. H. (1983). Analyzing close relationships. In H. H. Kelley, E. Berscheid, A. Christensen, J. H. Harvey, T. L. Huston, G. Levinger, E. McClintock, L. A. Peplau, & D. R. Peterson (Eds.), *Close relationships* (pp. 20–67). New York: Freeman.

Leeds-Hurwitz, W. (2002). *Weddings as text: Communicating cultural identities through ritual.* Mahwah, NJ: Lawrence Erlbaum Associates.

Minuchin, S. (1984). *Family kaleidoscope.* Cambridge, MA: Harvard University Press.

Mistry, R. S., Vandewater, E. A., Huston, A. C., & McLoyd, V. C. (2002). Economic well-being and children's social adjustment: The role of family process in an ethnically diverse low-income sample. *Child Development, 73*, 935–51.

Reis, H. T., Collins, W. A., & Berscheid, E. (2000). Attachment and the construction of relationships. In W. W. Hartup & Z. Rubin (Eds.), *Relationships and development* (pp. 51–71). Hillsdale, NJ: Lawrence Erlbaum Associates.

Scaramella, L. V., Neppl, T. K., Ontai, L. L., & Conger, R. D. (2008). Consequences of socioeconomic disadvantage across three generations: Parenting behavior and child externalizing problems. *Journal of Family Psychology, 22*, 725–33.

Schudlich, T. D. D., White, C. R., Fleischauer, E. A., & Fitzgerald, K. A. (2011). Observed infant reactions during live interparental conflict. *Journal of Marriage and Family, 73*, 221–35.

Sroufe, L. A., & Fleeson, J. (1986). Attachment and the construction of relationships. In W. W. Hartup & Z. Rubin (Eds.), *Relationships and development* (pp. 51–71). Hillsdale, NJ: Lawrence Erlbaum Associates.

Introduction

The word "family" is laden with imagery. For some, it brings to mind warm, supportive thoughts—scenes of chatty dinners, laughter-filled holidays, and comforting embraces. For others, it elicits painful memories—visions of being left alone, feeling unwanted, or being abused at the hands of a loved one. For some, the term "family" suggests a motto or a call to action—family members work hard, they stick together, or they prioritize the well-being of the group over the individual. For yet others, the word "family" embodies a set of values—values that distinguish individuals who are normal from those who are abnormal and people who are right from those who are wrong.

Although the images evoked by the term "family" vary widely, they tend to have one thing in common: they are based on, formed, and maintained through communication. Indeed, our families, and our images of families, are constituted through social interaction (Fitzpatrick, 1988; Noller & Fitzpatrick, 1993). When family members communicate, they enact their relationships. It is through communication that family members create mental models of family life and through communication that those models endure over time and across generations.

The constitutive link between communication and families is one reason that studying family communication is important. If families are created through social interaction, understanding family communication is essential to understanding family members and family relationships. This link, however, is not the only reason that scholars have focused their attention on family communication. The burgeoning literature on family interaction suggests at least three additional reasons that researchers and theorists have turned to this area as a focus of study.

First, family communication is the mechanism for most early socialization experiences. It is by observing and interacting with family members that most people learn to communicate and, perhaps more importantly, where they learn to think about communication (Bruner, 1990). From a very early age—some even argue before birth—infants engage in social interactions with their primary caregivers (Kisilevsky et al., 2003). These early interactions are the basis for what later become automated communication behaviors (Cappella, 1991). They also serve as a model for future interactions (Bowlby, 1973). By communicating with close family members, infants and children quickly learn what they should (and should not) anticipate from others. They learn how relationships function and they learn how they should behave in the context of those relationships. Indeed, communication is the means by which rules about social interaction and social relationships are established and maintained (Shimanoff, 1985). Parents use communication to teach children when they should speak, to whom they should speak, and what they should say. These rules shape the way children, and later adults, coordinate meaning with others (Pearce, 1976).

Second, communication is the vehicle through which family members establish, maintain, and dissolve their intimate relationships. People form their families through social interaction. Communication enables dating partners to meet and to evaluate the status of their relationships (e.g., Berger, Gardner, Clatterbuck, & Shulman, 1976). Individuals who are dating move toward marriage based in part on their assessments of the way they interact (Surra, Arizzi, & Asmussen, 1988). Once families are formed, members continue to relate to each other through communication. Spouses employ communication strategies to maintain their marriage (Canary & Stafford, 1992). Children's relationships with their parents and stepparents are influenced by both the amount and type of interaction that takes place in those relationships (Stafford & Dainton, 1995). The associations that adolescents have with family members mature in part because the communication patterns that characterize their relationships change (Laursen & Collins, 2009; Noller, 1995). Family relationships also are terminated using communication. Divorce is associated with particular communication patterns (e.g., Gottman, 1994) and, except in rare cases, only takes place after spouses discuss ending their relationship (Riessman, 1990).

A third reason that scholars have turned their attention to studying family communication is that communication reflects the interpersonal connections between family members. As such, it offers researchers and theorists a way to predict the quality and the course of family relationships. For instance, researchers have long argued that communication is an indicator of the quality of marital relationships. Spouses who are distressed generally express more negative effect, less positive effect, and more reciprocity of negative effect than do those who are not distressed (Margolin & Wampold, 1981; Noller, 1984; Notarius & Johnson, 1982). Further, when initial levels of satisfaction are controlled, the expression of negative effect within marriage predicts declines in satisfaction over time (Gottman & Krokoff, 1989; Huston & Vangelisti, 1991; Levenson & Gottman, 1985). In addition to reflecting the quality of particular family relationships (e.g., marriage), the communication that occurs between members of one family subsystem (e.g., parents) can influence other family members (e.g., children). Studies have demonstrated that the quality of parents' communication can affect children's problem-solving skills (Goodman, Barfoot, Frye, & Belli, 1999) as well as children's ability to relate with peers (e.g., Marcus, Lindahl, & Malik, 2001). Also, parents' tendency to engage in certain types of conflict is negatively associated with their children's adjustment (e.g., Grych, Harold, & Miles, 2003; Shelton & Harold, 2008). Perhaps because family communication patterns predict the quality of family relationships, these patterns also offer an indication of how families adapt to structural changes such as the birth of a child (Houts, Barnett-Walker, Paley, & Cox, 2008) or remarriage (Coleman, Fine, Ganong, Downs, & Pauk, 2001).

Although a case has been made here for the centrality of communication to family members and family relationships, the study of family communication is not, nor should it be, dominated only by communication researchers. Communication creates and maintains family systems—but those systems evolve through developmental stages, are comprised of many parts, and are situated in particular contexts. Scholars from a number of different fields study the developmental processes that affect family members, the components of family systems, and the contexts that influence family interaction. The study of family communication, in short, is multidisciplinary.

Multidisciplinary research—research from fields including communication, social psychology, clinical psychology, sociology, and family studies—is essential to understanding family communication because families operate as systems. The systemic nature of family relationships dictates that they be studied in terms of the associations among their parts as well as the contexts in which they are situated (Reis, Collins, & Berscheid, 2000). A clear understanding of families, thus, demands an awareness of the relationships that exist among several factors: (a) the various developmental stages of the family life course, (b) the different forms or structures of families, (c) the individuals that comprise families, (d) communication processes that take place among family members, and (e) contemporary issues and concerns that affect family relationships. The current volume is organized along these important conceptual dimensions.

In the first section of the book, both theoretical and methodological issues that influence current conceptions of the family are described. The definitional concerns raised in this section provide a foundation for examining family interaction because they set the baseline for the instantiation and evaluation of family members' behavior. For example, in Chapter 1, Glen H. Stamp and Carolyn K. Shue provide a careful analysis of the perspectives, theories, concepts, and contexts that have guided research in recent years. These authors use a pre-existing template to reflect on current research and offer a guideline for future work. Chapter 2, authored by Judith A. Feeney and Patricia Noller, focuses on the various methods that researchers use to study family interaction. Feeney and Noller not only describe the way that self-report, observational, and experimental techniques are employed, they also discuss the advantages and disadvantages associated with each of these methodologies. Feeney and Noller's discussion raises important issues that researchers need to consider in selecting methods to address their research questions and hypotheses.

In the second section, research and theory centering around the family life course is covered. Although the life course itself may be viewed as somewhat traditional—beginning with premarital relationships, progressing to marriage and parenthood, and then moving to the family relationships that characterize old age—many of the issues raised in this section challenge long-held beliefs about the ways family members interact. Chapters include material on non-traditional families and make note of the unique hurdles that individuals in these families face as they move through the life course. For instance, the influence of demographic changes on premarital relationships becomes apparent in Chapter 3. In this chapter, Jennifer S. Priem and Catherine A. Surra offer a comprehensive synthesis of recent literature on cohabitation and describe the mechanisms that explain the influence of cohabitation on the quality of premarital relationships. Priem and Surra argue that studying these mechanisms from a communication perspective provides important insights into both cohabitation and relational development.

In Chapter 4, Brian R. Baucom and Kathleen A. Eldridge examine communication in marriage. They employ a functionalist perspective to review major findings, highlight recent empirical and theoretical developments, and identify critical gaps in the literature that scholars need to address. Erin K. Holmes, Ted L. Huston, Anita L. Vangelisti, and Trey D. Guinn review and analyze work on the transition to parenthood in Chapter 5. In addition to highlighting empirical findings, these authors make special note of the ways in which the methodological choices of researchers have affected the conclusions that have been drawn concerning the influence of parenthood on marriage. In Chapter 6, Karen L. Fingerman, Kira Birditt, Jon Nussbaum, and Diana S. Ebersole look at the distinctive characteristics of midlife. They describe the content of family communication during midlife and discuss the factors that affect how middle-aged adults interact with family members. The communication of older adults is covered by Jake Harwood, Christine E. Rittenour, and Mei-Chen Lin in Chapter 7. These authors discuss some of the assumptions held by researchers who study communication and aging, review prominent theoretical perspectives, and describe studies on relationships between older adults and their family members. Harwood and his colleagues also examine work on elder abuse—an issue that has received increased attention in recent years.

The third section of the volume focuses on communication that occurs in different family forms. Some of the social interactions that people experience when they are members of divorced or single-parent families, stepfamilies, or gay/lesbian families are unique. The relationships that individuals in these, and other types of families, experience include challenges and benefits that set them apart from many who see themselves as members of an intact, biological family unit. Chapters in this section, thus, describe some of the particular communication patterns that distinguish social interaction in various types of families. Ascan F. Koerner and Mary Anne Fitzpatrick set the stage for this section by describing the communication patterns of intact families in Chapter 8. These authors provide an insightful discussion of issues associated with defining intact families, outline the theoretical "roots" of research on family communication patterns, and review studies concerning factors that influence the communication patterns of intact families. In Chapter 9, Tamara D. Afifi and Amanda Denes look at the influence of divorce and single parenthood on children using a risk and resiliency approach. They examine the communication patterns associated with both risk and resilience and offer a discussion of current trends in research and directions for future study. Dawn O. Braithwaite and Paul Schrodt focus on the communication of stepfamilies in Chapter 10. These authors review research on a broad range of issues including the developmental pathways of stepfamilies, stepfamily types, and how stepfamily members use communication to navigate the various challenges they face. In synthesizing the literature on the communication processes that typify these families, Braithwaite and Schrodt shed light on the many demands that both adults and children in stepfamilies address when they interact. In Chapter 11, Lisa M. Diamond, Kendrick A. Rith, and Molly R. Butterworth examine the family lives of individuals who are lesbian, gay, or bisexual. Diamond and her colleagues orient the chapter by discussing the terminology used to refer to these (and other) sexual minorities. They then review research on the romantic relationships and parenting practices of sexual minorities and make note of important directions for future study. In Chapter 12, Bella DePaulo offers a compelling argument concerning the families of single people who do not have children. DePaulo notes while society often suggests these individuals do not have family, they actually have close knit personal communities that include both friends and relatives and, in fact, they often are more connected with friends, siblings, and parents than those who are married. Stanley O. Gaines, Jr., Stacey L. Williams, and Kristin D. Mickelson address some of the complex issues associated with culturally diverse families in Chapter 13. They focus on supportive communication and analyze how supportive communication in families is influenced by the stigmatization associated with minority status.

Individual family members and their relationships are the centerpiece of the fourth section. The communication skills of family members, and the relational issues members must deal with, vary. Infants face one set of developmental tasks; adolescents and emerging adults face others. Mothers and fathers adopt particular roles in the family that affect the way they communicate with their children. This section describes some of the special concerns that influence the relational lives of different family members. For example, in Chapter 14, John M. Beaton, William J. Doherty, and Lisa M. Wenger review research on the parenting relationship that exists between mothers and fathers. Their careful analysis of the theoretical frameworks that have been used to examine coparenting positions them to develop a theoretical model of the factors that influence the coparenting relationship. In Chapter 15, Barbara Gruenbaum, Nicole Depowski, Kathleen E. Shaw, and Heather Bortfeld focus on infants and the interactions that take place between infants and their caregivers. These authors argue that children enter the world primed to learn language. Based on this argument, and the fact that there are learnable structures inherent in languages, Gruenbaum and her colleagues describe how interactions between infants and their caregivers support language development. Laura Stafford reviews studies on children's communication in Chapter 16. Stafford considers the social competencies of middle childhood and looks at interactions between children, their parents, and their siblings. The analysis that Stafford offers clearly demonstrates that childhood is a critical period for socialization concerning communication and interpersonal relationships. In Chapter 17, Susan Branje, Brett Laursen, and W. Andrew Collins describe the ways in which patterns of parent–child communication change over the adolescent years. These authors contextualize their discussion by reviewing theoretical accounts of relationships between adolescents and their parents and then go on to offer a nuanced description of research on changes in parent–child closeness, conflict, monitoring, and information management. Brian J. Willoughby and Jeffrey J. Arnett examine emerging adults in Chapter 18. Willoughby and Arnett look at the communication that takes place in the family relationships of emerging adults and describe the impact of that communication on individual and family development. They argue that family life course and social learning theories offer useful lenses for future study. In Chapter 19, Maria Schmeeckle and Susan Sprecher take a step back from the individuals that comprise the typical nuclear family to examine the extended family and social networks. These authors note how social networks and members of the extended family can affect couple relationships, parenting, and child outcomes. They also look at how various changes in technology can influence extended families and social networks.

The fifth section presents a sampling of the dynamic communication processes that take place in virtually any family. Because the communication that occurs in the family can be so varied, selecting the topics for this section was difficult. The processes that were ultimately included in the section were those that have received substantial attention from researchers and theorists—they definitely are not the only processes that have been studied, but the sustained attention they have received allowed the authors who wrote chapters for this section to make some important claims about the current and future state of research on family communication. In Chapter 20, John P. Caughlin, Sandra Petronio, and Ashley V. Middleton examine privacy and disclosure in families. These authors look at the use of communication in managing private information, how family members make decisions about revealing or concealing information, and the consequences of changes in privacy rules. Petronio's communication privacy management theory offers a clear organizing framework for the literature as well as a basis for making thoughtful recommendations concerning future research. In Chapter 21, Alan L. Sillars and Daniel J. Canary focus on the communication processes that occur during marital and family conflict. Research on the association between the quality of family relationships and both the amount and type of conflict is examined. The authors synthesize work on contextual factors that influence communication and that moderate associations with relational quality. They also analyze the interpretive processes that affect the meaning of conflict. Steven R. Wilson, Lisa M. Guntzviller, and Elizabeth A. Munz look at research on persuasion in Chapter 22. Although many scholars who study persuasion have neglected the family as a context for persuasive communication, those who study families have recognized that the opportunities for research in this area abound. Wilson, Guntzviller, and Munz explain how persuasive messages in family relationships have been conceptualized and, in reviewing the literature on issues such as parent–child control sequences and spouses' control attempts, offer a compelling rationale for future studies. In Chapter 23, Julie Fitness integrates empirical work on communication and emotion in families. Fitness takes a functionalist approach to emotion, reviewing literature on communication in marital and sibling relationships. She discusses the ways family members are socialized concerning emotions, the transmission of emotion climates, and the influence of emotions on family functioning. The last chapter in this section, Chapter 24, concerns the roles of stories and storytelling in families. In this chapter, Jody Koenig Kellas and April P. Trees suggest that families are constituted, in part, by stories. They argue that family members use narratives for creating individual and family identities, socializing family members, and coping with stressors.

The sixth section of the *Handbook* underlines the fact that family communication is embedded in social, cultural, and physical contexts. Because family interaction and family relationships are influenced by these contexts, a full understanding of the communication processes that take place in the family requires researchers to attend to the environmental factors and current issues that impinge on family life. For instance, in Chapter 25, Shu-wen Wang and Rena L. Repetti analyze how family members' occupational experiences affect their interpersonal well-being. Wang and Repetti look at the influence of job characteristics (e.g., work schedule) and subjective experiences (e.g., job stress) on families. They also examine the ways that family members shape the outcomes associated with job stress. In Chapter 26, Barbara J. Wilson and Kristin L. Drogos discuss the links between family communication and mass media (i.e., television, film, radio, and print). They review research on how family members use the media, describe the influence of the media on family interaction, and explain the ways family interaction can affect media experiences. Wilson and Drogos' discussion offers clear evidence concerning the central role of the media in family life. Nancy A. Jennings and Ellen A. Wartella then go on to analyze the effects of digital media technology (i.e., computers, the Internet, and video-games) on families in Chapter 27. Using family development theory and life course theory as a framework for their analysis, Jennings and Wartella illustrate the impact of technology on family relationships at different stages of development and put forth an important agenda for further research. In Chapter 28, Ashley P. Duggan and Beth A. Le Poire Molineux turn to a topic that touches many families: substance abuse. They review literature on the effects of drug and alcohol abuse on family members and discuss the association between communication and members' tendency to abuse substances. These authors employ Inconsistent Nurturing as Control theory to explain the subtle ways that family communication can sustain or deter addiction. Another sort of abuse is covered in Chapter 29. In this chapter, René M. Dailey, Carmen M. Lee, and Brian H. Spitzberg look at violence and aggression in families. They discuss some of the complexities involved in defining abuse and describe evidence concerning both the prevalence and outcomes of abuse for children and adults. Dailey, Lee, and Spitzberg also examine theories that are used to explain abuse and review prevention and intervention programs. In Chapter 30, Kory Floyd, Colin Hesse, and Perry M. Pauley discuss psychophysiology and family communication. These authors argue that studies employing psychophysiological measures can provide important information about the links between communication and well-being. Floyd and his colleagues describe principal physiological systems and note the ways these systems are associated with family communication behaviors and outcomes.

They offer practical advice for researchers who are interested in using psychophysiological methods to study family communication patterns. Chris Segrin focuses on the complex links between family communication and mental health in Chapter 31. He describes communication patterns that serve as risk factors for the development of mental-health problems and shows how mental-health problems can create or encourage pathogenic family communication. Segrin's careful analysis elucidates the associations between family interaction and mental well-being.

Finally, because the current volume includes scholarship from a variety of disciplines and a number of different theoretical perspectives, the seventh section provides a commentary emphasizing themes that tie the various chapters together. In forecasting common issues that will face families, Kathleen M. Galvin points out the concerns that those who study, treat, and work with families likely will confront in the future.

It is important to note that the chapters in this volume do not represent a complete summary of all of the topics associated with family communication. Instead, these chapters offer a synthesis of research on issues that are key to understanding family interaction as well as an analysis of many of the theoretical and methodological choices that have been made by researchers who study family communication. It is my hope that the insightful commentaries offered in each of the chapters will advance the field—both by reframing old questions and stimulating new ones.

References

Berger, C. R., Gardner, R. R., Clatterbuck, G. W., & Shulman, L. S. (1976). Perceptions of information sequencing in relationship development. *Human Communication Research, 3*, 34–39.

Bowlby, J. (1973). *Attachment and loss: Vol. 2. Separation: Anxiety and anger.* New York: Basic Books.

Bruner, J. (1990). *Acts of meaning.* Cambridge, MA: Harvard University Press.

Canary, D. J., & Stafford, L. (1992). Relational maintenance strategies and equity in marriage. *Communication Monographs, 59*, 243–67.

Cappella, J. N. (1991). The biological origins of automated patterns of human interaction. *Communication Theory, 1*, 4–35.

Coleman, M., Fine, M. A., Ganong, L. H., Downs, K. J. M., & Pauk, N. (2001). When you're not the Brady Bunch: Identifying perceived conflicts and resolution strategies in stepfamilies. *Personal Relationships, 8*, 55–73.

Fitzpatrick, M. A. (1988). *Between husbands and wives.* Newbury Park, CA: Sage.

Goodman, S. H., Barfoot, B., Frye, A. A., & Belli, A. M. (1999). Dimensions of marital conflict and children's social problem-solving skills. *Journal of Family Psychology, 13*, 33–45.

Gottman, J. M. (1994). *What predicts divorce? The relationship between marital processes and marital outcomes.* Hillsdale, NJ: Lawrence Erlbaum Associates.

Gottman, J. M., & Krokoff, L. J. (1989). Marital interaction and satisfaction: A longitudinal view. *Journal of Consulting and Clinical Psychology, 57*, 47–52.

Grych, J. H., Harold, G. T. and Miles, C. J. (2003). A prospective investigation of appraisals as mediators of the link between interparental conflict and child adjustment. *Child Development, 74*, 1176–93.

Houts, R. M., Barnett-Walker, K. C., Paley, B., & Cox, M. J. (2008). Patterns of couple interaction during the transition to parenthood. *Personal Relationships, 15*, 103–22.

Huston, T. L., & Vangelisti, A. L. (1991). Socioemotional behavior and satisfaction in marital relationships. *Journal of Personality and Social Psychology, 61*, 721–33.

Kisilevsky, B. S., Hains, S. J., Lee, K., Xie, X., Huang, H., Ye, H., Zhang, K., & Wang, Z. (2003). Effects of experience on fetal voice recognition. *Psychological Science, 14*, 220–24.

Laursen, B., & Collins, A. W. (2009). Parent–adolescent relationships during adolecence. In R. M. Lerner & L. Steinberg (Eds.), *Handbook of adolescent psychology, Vol 2*, 3rd edn (pp. 3–42). Hoboken, NJ: Wiley.

Levenson, R. W., & Gottman, J. M. (1985). Physiological and affective predictors of change in relationship satisfaction. *Journal of Personality and Social Psychology, 49*, 85–94.

Marcus, N. E., Lindahl, K. M., & Malik, N. M. (2001). Interparental conflict, children's social cognitions, and child aggression: A test of a mediational model. *Journal of Family Psychology, 15,* 315–33.

Margolin, G., & Wampold, B. (1981). Sequential analysis of conflict and accord in distressed and nondistressed marital partners. *Journal of Consulting and Clinical Psychology, 49,* 554–67.

Noller, P. (1984). *Nonverbal communication and marital interaction.* Oxford: Pergamon.

——(1995). Parent-adolescent relationships. In M. A. Fitzpatrick & A. L. Vangelisti (Eds.), *Explaining family interactions* (pp. 77–111). Thousand Oaks, CA: Sage.

Noller, P., & Fitzpatrick, M. A. (1993). *Communication and family relationships.* Englewood Cliffs, NJ: Prentice-Hall.

Notarius, C. I., & Johnson, J. S. (1982). Emotional expression in husbands and wives. *Journal of Marriage and the Family, 45,* 483–89.

Pearce, W. B. (1976). The coordinated management of meaning: A rules-based theory of interpersonal communication. In G. R. Miller (Ed.), *Explorations in interpersonal communication* (pp. 17–36). Beverly Hills, CA: Sage.

Reis, H. T., Collins, W. A., & Berscheid, E. (2000). Attachment and the construction of relationships. In W. W. Hartup & Z. Rubin (Eds.), *Relationships and development* (pp. 51–71). Hillsdale, NJ: Lawrence Erlbaum Associates.

Riessman, C. K. (1990). *Divorce talk: Woman and men make sense of personal relationships.* New Brunwick, NJ: Rutgers University Press.

Shelton, K. H. & Harold, G. T. (2008). Interparental conflict, negative parenting, and children's adjustment: Bridging links between parents' depression and children's psychological distress. *Journal of Family Psychology, 22,* 712–24.

Shimanoff, S. B. (1985). *Communication rules: Theory and research.* Beverly Hills, CA: Sage.

Stafford, L., & Dainton, M. (1995). Parent–child interaction within the family system. In T. J. Socha & G. Stamp (Eds.), *Parents, children, and communication: Frontiers of theory and research* (pp. 3–21). Hillsdale, NJ: Lawrence Erlbaum Associates.

Surra, C. A., Arizzi, P., & Asmussen, L. A. (1988). The association between reasons for commitment and the development and outcome of marital relationships. *Journal of Social and Personal Relationships, 5,* 47–63.

Part I
Family Communication Theories and Methods

1

Twenty Years of Family Research Published in Communication Journals

A Review of the Perspectives, Theories, Concepts, and Contexts

Glen H. Stamp and Carolyn K. Shue

While the above title may not be as figuratively eloquent as many of the article titles reviewed as a basis for this chapter, the title does articulate the chapter's purpose: to review family communication research published in communication journals during the past 20 years. This chapter extends the work presented in the first edition of this handbook and provides a sense of the current state of research as a backdrop for the other chapters contained within this edition.

The "theory" chapter in the first edition of *The Handbook of Family Communication* (Stamp, 2004) examined the literature in family studies so as to identify the perspectives of inquiry, theories, and concepts most commonly used within family relationships research. In order to accomplish these goals, Stamp reviewed 1,254 articles, taken from 12 journals over a 12 year timeframe. These included eight journals within the communication discipline (*Communication Monographs* [CM], *Communication Quarterly* [CQ], *Communication Studies* [CS], *Human Communication Research* [HCR], *Journal of Applied Communication Research* [JACR], *Journal of Communication* [JC], *Southern Communication Journal* [SCJ], and *Western Journal of Communication* [WJC]) and four interdisciplinary journals (*Journal of Marriage and the Family* [JMF], *Journal of Social and Personal Relationships* [JSPR], *Personal Relationships* [PR], and *Journal of Family Communication* [JFC]).

The 2004 review identified the 16 most frequently used theories in family research and over 2,000 concepts which were then organized into 28 general categories. The review also indicated that 92 percent of the articles were empiricist in orientation. Finally, a grounded theory model of family relationships was generated from the concepts identified in the literature.

The initial goals of this chapter are similar in terms of identifying perspectives of inquiry, theories, and concepts in the family literature, with three key differences. First, since the four interdisciplinary journals comprised over 90 percent of the articles reviewed for the first chapter, the focus here is narrowed to family communication research, rather than family relationships research. Second, as the first chapter examined a concentrated 12 year timeframe, the focus here is to review a longer timeframe so as to identify trends within the family communication literature. And, third, while the first chapter developed a grounded theoretical model from the data, the focus here is to use an existing template, taken from previous literature, to frame the concepts, theories, and contexts.

The specific questions guiding this inquiry are:

RQ1   How are the different research perspectives—empiricist, interpretive, and critical—represented in family communication research?

RQ2   What theories, concepts, and contexts have been investigated by family communication scholars over the past 20 years?

RQ3   What research trends can be traced across the past 20 years of family communication research?

RQ4   What do these trends tell us about the current, and future, state of family communication research?

Method

The journals analyzed in this review were the same eight communication journals used in the first handbook chapter (CM, CQ, CS, HCR, JACR, JC, SCJ, and WJC). These journals represent the national and regional journals in our discipline that have been in print since 1990 and publish family communication research. While this list is not exhaustive, it does include the major outlets for the dissemination of family communication research findings. Articles were identified through a key word search of the *Communication and Mass Media* database; family terms such as *married, spouse, parent, child, sibling,* and *family* had to appear in the title, abstract, key words, or article. To be retained for the final dataset, the articles had to be research articles that: (a) focused on family communication concepts or theories; (b) recruited a participant base indicative of the family or reflecting on their role in the family; and/or (c) reported findings that would reasonably be used in a literature review for future research. We excluded articles that were opinion pieces or literature reviews. The search resulted in 261 family communication articles published over the 20 year timeframe of 1990–2009.

To begin, we employed Bochner's (1985) definitions to code the articles by their primary research perspective—empiricist, interpretive, and critical. We recorded the frequencies for each of the perspectives as a means of presenting and analyzing research trends across the timeframes. Then, we reviewed the articles to identify the theories, concepts, and contexts investigated in the family communication research employing Graham and Shue's (2000) template as our organizing framework. Graham and Shue identified two dimensions of research, *theory/application* and *communication/relationship,* creating a four quadrant template to classify and describe research efforts. (See Table 1.2 in the Results section for a visual representation of the template and quadrants.)

The two quadrants on the left side of the communication/relationship axis contain the various theories employed in research. The upper left hand quadrant, the communication/theory quadrant, captures theories that focus on "core processes common to all communication" (Graham & Shue, 2000, p. 339) emphasizing message and perceptual processes. In contrast, the lower left hand quadrant, the relationship/theory quadrant, houses theories that explain "the role communication serves in initiating, sustaining, and dissolving social interactions" (p. 339) emphasizing relationship processes.

The two quadrants on the right side of the communication/relationship axis focus on application areas in research. The upper right hand quadrant, the communication/application quadrant, identifies the concepts, constructs, characteristics, and behaviors scholars study while the lower right hand quadrant, the relationship/application quadrant, is comprised of "the situations that serve to contextualize the study of social relationships" (p. 340). For this analysis, the relationship/application quadrant captures the varying settings related to the family (e.g., family unit, married couple, parent–child, siblings).

Following the procedures employed by Graham and Shue (2000), we reviewed the articles to identify and code the theories, concepts and contexts according to the quadrants of the template: communication/theory, relationship/theory, communication/application (construct quadrant), and relationship/application (context quadrant). Similar to the findings of Graham and Shue, articles varied in the number of theories, concepts, and contexts; consequently, one article could be represented in all four quadrants while another article could be represented in only two quadrants.

For most of the journals, we each independently coded half of the articles and then met to review each other's coding, clarify the scope of the quadrant, confirm classifications, and resolve disagreements. For particularly challenging articles or journals, we coded the articles together. During the coding process, it was necessary to make decisions about which information to retain from the articles for use in the template and trend analysis. One coding challenge we faced was inconsistencies surrounding the identification and incorporation of theories in research. Often authors would make claims that their research was grounded in theory but not reference a specific theory. In these cases, we coded the article into the concept and context quadrants only because of the lack of clear theory reference or discussion. Other authors would *list* several theories but only *discuss* one or two of the theories in the article. In these cases, we coded the articles as employing only those theories discussed in the article. Finally, there were inconsistencies in the names used to identify the theories, such as the *interactional view* (Watzlawick, Beavin, & Jackson, 1967) referred to as *relational communication*. We identified the theories employed by researchers through the theory name, theorist(s) referenced, and the author's description of the theory, and then selected the theory name most often used for inclusion in our analysis.

Another coding challenge pertained to the concept quadrant. Some authors made an argument for, and then proceeded to examine, gender differences while other authors did not address gender in the study rationale yet investigated gender differences in the results. While we recognize the importance of investigating participant and relationship characteristics, this inconsistent treatment of gender and other demographic or relationship characteristics such as age, race, and length of relationship led us to ultimately exclude these variables from the analysis.

The final coding challenge focused on the context quadrant where our coding goal was to illustrate the varied types of family relationships and family participants in communication research. To meet this goal, we had to review each methods section to determine who participated and the family relationship focused on in the analysis. For example, articles in which the authors recruited married couples to comment on marriage concepts were easy to code. Conversely, articles in which the authors recruited adults to retrospectively comment on family relationships or to project how they might communicate in a future relationship were more difficult to code. In these cases, although the participants were *adults*, we coded the context as the type of relationship investigated in the study.

After the initial coding, categories were reviewed and collapsed (i.e., "stories" and "storytelling" were combined into one "stories" category) to most accurately capture the nature of the family communication research activity across the four 5 year timeframes of 1990–94, 1995–99, 2000–4, and 2005–9. We reported the frequencies for each topic category in the template as a means of illustrating the amount of research activity associated with each theory, concept, and context. The frequencies also enabled us to statistically examine differences in the amount of research activity within each quadrant across the designated timeframes.

Results

Research Perspectives

Table 1.1 provides the overall number of articles, as well as the research perspective frequencies, across the four timeframes. The results show a statistically significant increase in the overall articles, ranging from 45 family communication articles in 1990–94 to almost twice as many (86) in 2005–9. Clearly, this incremental increase shows the rising interest, among researchers, in exploring family communication.

There has not only been a change in the number of family communication articles, but also a change in the research perspectives over time. As illustrated in Table 1.1, the percentage of articles that are empiricist in orientation have decreased over the past 20 years, while the percentage of interpretive and critical articles have increased. The change over time for the interpretive articles was also statistically significant.

Of the 261 total articles examined, 70.5 percent were empiricist in nature, 23.75 percent were interpretive, and 5.75 percent were critical. This compares to 91.87 percent empiricist, 6.46 percent interpretive, and 1.67 percent critical in the first handbook chapter. The difference can be accounted for in two ways. First, the percentages in the first chapter were heavily skewed by the inclusion of *JMF*, an interdisciplinary journal in which more than two-thirds of the examined articles were derived, and a journal that is almost exclusively empiricist in nature. Secondly, the first chapter examined a timeframe from 1990 to 2001, while this chapter analyzed 1990–2009. As indicated above, the more recent research in family communication has shifted in terms of the proportion of research perspectives within each timeframe. Communication scholars are not only conducting more family communication research, but in doing so, they are less bound to the empiricist research perspective.

Table 1.1 Research Perspective Frequencies by Timeframe

Timeframe	Empirical	Interpretive	Critical	Total Number of Articles
2005–9	59 (68.60%)*	20 (23.26%)	7 (8.14%)	86
2000–4	47 (62.67%)	26 (34.67%)	2 (2.67%)	75
1995–99	42 (76.36%)	10 (18.18%)	3 (5.45%)	55
1990–94	36 (80.00%)	6 (13.33%)	3 (6.67%)	45
Total	184 (70.50%)	62 (23.75%)	15 (5.75%)	261
Chi-Square	$\chi^2_{(3)} = 6.217$	$\chi^2_{(3)} = 16.194$	$\chi^2_{(3)} = 3.933$	$\chi^2_{(3)} = 15.950$
	$p = .1051$	$p = .0010$	$p = .2688$	$p = .0012$

* % indicates degree to which the perspective is represented in the literature for the timeframe

An example of empiricist research is the examination of stepfamily functioning, communication competence, and mental health (Schrodt, 2006). Five hundred and eighty-six stepchildren completed questionnaires measuring each of the three constructs, with the results indicating there are five different stepfamily types, each reflecting differences in both communication competence and mental health. Thompson-Hayes and Webb's (2008) work provides an example of interpretive research. Seventeen interviews were conducted with marital couples resulting in three main themes that punctuate these participants' marriage experience: a desire to remain in the marriage (commitment), a desire to grow old together (projected longevity), and outstanding characteristics (marital quality). Finally, an example of critical research is the examination of the corporate ideology of work/life (Hoffman & Cowan, 2008). Through an examination of company websites, the authors argue there is a corporate ideology that "work is the most important element in life" (p. 234), "the traditional family represents the only truly acceptable interest outside of paid work" (p. 235), and "employees bear the responsibility for maintaining this elusive 'work/life' balance" (p. 237).

Theories, Concepts, and Contexts: The Family Communication Template

The initial coding of the 261 articles resulted in 1,258 total theories, concepts, and contexts. One hundred and seven were identified as communication theories (upper left quadrant), 141 were identified as relationship theories (lower left quadrant), 717 were identified as concepts and constructs (upper right quadrant), and 293 were identified as contexts (lower right quadrant). The 1,258 initial theories, concepts, and contexts (referred to as "items" below) were then reduced to 223 specific categories, resulting in 51 communication theory categories, 42 relationship theory categories, 93 concepts and construct categories, and 37 context categories (see Table 1.2).

An examination of the 1,258 items and the 223 categories within the four quadrants reveals some interesting findings. First, by a considerable number, the application quadrants on the right side of the template contain many more family items than the theory quadrants on the left side. Indeed, 80 percent of the total items are application in orientation (1010 concepts and context items) and 20 percent are theoretical in nature (248 communication and relationship theory items).

Second, the top ten most researched categories in each quadrant collectively comprise 18 percent of the total categories (40 out of 223). However, those 40 categories account for 50 percent of the total research items (631 out of 1,258). That is, the ten most researched categories in the communication theory quadrant contain 55 items (out of 107) and each of the top ten categories in the other three quadrants contain 91 out of 141 items (relationship quadrant), 253 out of 717 items (concepts and constructs quadrant), and 232 out of 293 items (context quadrant). When one examines the top single category in each of the four quadrants (communication privacy management theory [11], dialectical theory or theory of family communication patterns [18], satisfaction [65], married couples [77]), the discrepancy in the numbers are even more striking. Four of the 223 categories (1.8 percent) account for 14 percent of the research activity (171 of the 1,258 items). These findings illustrate two seemingly opposing research outcomes: there is great diversity in theories, concepts, and contexts while also an extremely targeted research focus on a few specific theories, concepts, and contexts.

As Table 1.3 illustrates, there has been a steady, statistically significant, increase in the number of theories, concepts, and contexts investigated in the family communication

Table 1.2 Family Communication Template

COMMUNICATION

Focus: Communication Theories

Theory	Count
Activation Theory	1
Aging Theories	6
Appraisal Theory	1
Communication Accommodation	2
Personal Construct Theory	1
Accommodation Theory	6
Queer Theory	6
Communication Privacy Management Theory	11
Communication Infrastructure Theory	1
Constructivism	1
Cultivation Theory	4
Cultural Theory	2
Developmental Theories	6
Diffusion of Innovations Theory	1
Displacement Theory	2
Emotional Security Hypothesis	1
Excitation Transfer Notion	1
Face Theories	4
Feminist Theories	8
Forbidden-Fruit Theory	1
Formal Feature Theory	1
Habituation Model	1
Identity Theories	3
Impression Management Theory	1
Interpersonal Communication Motives Model	1
Language Expectancy Theory	1
Linguistics Systems Theory	1
Media Richness Theory	1
Message Production Theories	2
Message-Extrinsic/Intrinsic Perspective	1
Narrative Theory	1
Performance Theories	2
Reactance Theory	1
Risk Revelation Model	1
Script Theory	1
Self Perception Theory	1
Sensemaking Theories	2
Sensitization Model	1
Social Construction Theory	2
Social Cognitive Theory	6
Social Structural Model	1
Structuration Theory	2
Superiority Theory of Humor	1
Symbolic Convergence Theory	1
Symbolic Interactionism	8
Tainted-Fruit Theory	1
Theory of Linguistic Codes	1
Theory of Planned Behavior	1
Theory of Planning	1
Trouble Source Repair Sequence Perspective	1
Uses and Gratifications Theory	1
Whiteness Theory	2
Total	**107**

Total Categories: 51

Focus: Concepts and Constructs

Concept	Count
Abuse	8
Addiction	2
Affection	8
Aggression	3
Aging	10
Appraisals	7
Apprehension	4
Argumentativeness	4
Assertiveness	1
Attachment	9
Attitudes	6
Attraction	1
Attribution	2
Avoidance	11
Bereavement	4
Boundaries	3
Change	8
Closeness	17
Cognitions	6
Collaboration	2
Commitment	8
Competence	13
Compliance	4
Comprehension	2
Confirmation	7
Conflict	25
Contact	6
Contradictions	15
Control	19
Culture	7
Decision Making	3
Disclosure	23
Discomfort	2
Emotions	11
Empowerment	1
Expectations	2
Experience	7
Expressiveness	8
Face	3
Negotiation	8
Family Patterns	17
Feeling Caught	6
Health	13
Humor	4
Identity	20
Imagined Interactions	3
Income	2
Infidelity	3
Influence	7
Intentions	7
Interventions	6
Involvement	9
Jealousy	1
Justification	1
Liking	4
Maintenance	15
Marital Types	3
Media	9
Mediated Messages	1
Memorable Messages	1
Mental Health	8
Message Processes	29
Metaphors	2
Negative Patterns	6
Networks	4
Nonverbal	6
Outcomes	10
Parenting Style	1
Perception	4
Planning	5
Playtime	7
Protection	2
Religion	2
Rituals	7
Roles	6
Routines	9
Rules	1
Satisfaction	65
Schemata	4
Secrets	15
Self	13
Sensemaking	9
Similarity	1
Socialization	5
Stability	1
Stories	9
Structures	17
Support	13
Television	29
Trust	3
Uncertainty	6
Verbal	10
Aggression	21
Well Being	5
Work-Life	6
Total	**717**

Total Categories: 93

Table 1.2 (Continued)

THEORY		APPLICATION	
Focus: Relationship Theories		Focus: Context	
Activity Theory	1	Children	12
Adults as Gatekeepers Model	7	Children and other Family Members	2
Affectance Arousal Model	4	Daughters	1
Affection Exchange Theory	2	Divorced Families	3
Attachment Theory	1	Divorced Parents	7
Attribution Theory	4	Divorcing Couples	1
Children as Mediators Model	9	Extended Family Members	2
Circumplex Model	3	Family Unit	36
Commitment Models	2	Father–Child	2
Confirmation Theory	1	Father–Daughter	3
Conflict Theories	1	Father–Son	13
Defensiveness Model	1	Fathers	2
Dialectical Theory	2	First Marriage Families	3
Dialogism Theory	6	Grandmothers	1
Effect Models	2	Grandparent–Grandchild	9
Equity Theory	1	Husbands	1
Family Systems Theory	2	In-Laws	5
Family Violence Perspective	2	Intact Families	1
Gender Perspectives	1	Married Couples	77
Inconsistant Nurturing as Control Theory	4	Mother–Child	6
Influence Models	10	Mother–Daughter	5
Interaction Effect Model	2	Mother–Son	2
Interactional View	11	Mothers	9
Interdependence Theory	1	Older Family Members	3
Intergroup Contact Theory	2	Parent–Child	36
Interpersonal Model of Depression	1	Parents	12
Model of Aggressiveness	1	Relatives	2
Nonverbal Expectancy Violation Theory	4	Remarried Couples	1
Process Model of Blended Family Development	18	Siblings	14
Relationship Cultural Perspective	1	Single Parent Families	1
Role Theory	2	Single Parents	1
Social Relations Model	3	Stepfamilies	14
Stage Models	2	Stepmothers	1
Stress and Coping Theory	1	Stepparent–Stepchild	2
Theories of Relationship Development	2	Triads (Two Family Members and Third Party)	1
Theory of Discrimanitive Parental Solicitude	2	Widows	1
Theory of Family Communication Patterns	4	Wives	1
Theory of Marital Types	2		293
Theory of Motivated Information Management	11		
Theory of Suicide	1		
Trait/State Perspective	2		
Uncertainty Reduction Theory	1		
	141		
Total Categories: 42		Total Categories: 37	

RELATIONSHIPS

Table 1.3 Theory, Construct, and Concept Frequencies by Timeframe

Timeframe	Communication Theories	Relationship Theories	Concept	Contexts
2005–9	40	51	266	96
2000–4	34	29	189	82
1995–99	19	32	145	62
1990–94	14	29	117	53
Total: 1990–2009	107	141	717	293
Chi-Square	$\chi^2_{(3)} = 16.850$ $p = .0008$	$\chi^2_{(3)} = 9.553$ $p = .0228$	$\chi^2_{(3)} = 70.676$ $p < .0001$	$\chi^2_{(3)} = 15.437$ $p = .0015$

literature over the past 20 years. This increase can be attributed to the substantial increase in the number of family communication articles, in general, across the four time-frames. Factoring in the number of articles demonstrates that while the volume of research has increased, research still, on average, utilizes one communication or relationship theory (0.95 in 1990–94 and 1.06 in 2005–9) to explore approximately three concepts (2.6 in 1990–94 and 3.2 in 2005–9) in one context (1.18 contexts in 1990–94 and 1.1 in 2005–09).

Family Communication Theory, Concept/Construct, and Context Trends

To determine the trends in family communication research, we analyzed the data represented in each of the template quadrants in terms of volume (the most frequently researched theories, concepts, and contexts), consistency (research activity occurred across all four of the timeframes), and disproportion (research activity occurred in the earlier timeframes but not the later or vice versa). These analyses enabled us to empirically determine the theories, concepts, and contexts that have received considerable research attention from family communication scholars, the research areas that are no longer investigated, and the direction of current family research. The following discussion delineates the results of the analyses and provides a brief profile of the theories, concepts, and contexts identified.

Communication theories. The communication theory most frequently used in the family research reviewed was *communication privacy management theory* (CPM) (Petronio, 2002), n = 11. CPM explains the process of balancing information sharing and concealment in the management of relationships. According to the theory, there are metaphorical boundaries between private/concealed and public/shared information controlled and owned by individuals. Often decisions about what information is shared are guided by a rule-based management system and in response to the tension between revealing and concealing. Golish and Caughlin (2002) explained adolescents' and young adults' use of topic avoidance with their mothers, fathers, and stepparents in light of CPM processes. Adolescents use topic avoidance to regulate personal boundaries and the permeability of those boundaries vary from parents to stepparents.

Feminist theories (n = 8) were the second most frequently employed theoretical perspective in the communication quadrant. Feminist theories refer to a form of critical theory that highlights power imbalances related to gender, race, ethnicity, and class as well as women's lack of access to the male dominated public sphere of discourse (Kramarae, 1981). Buzzanell and Liu (2005) applied feminist theory to examine the discourse of women "who felt discouraged about their employment and advancement chances around the time of their maternity leaves" (p. 2). The results of their poststructuralist feminist analysis provided insights into gendered organizational practices and called into question the notion that maternity leave policies are a "gender neutral organizing process" (p. 16).

The *aging theories* category (n = 6) includes aging and communication perspectives such as the *communication predicament of aging model* (Ryan, Giles, Bartolucci, & Henwood, 1986) and the *age stereotypes in interaction model* (Hummert, Garstka, Ryan, & Bonnesen, 2004). These aging models explain how communication occurs between generations. Specifically, these models explore how such factors as cues (age, vocal, nonverbal behavior), experience, context, and stereotypes can both positively and negatively influence younger adults' communication with older adults. To gain additional insight into the utility of these models in grandparent–grandchild relationships, Anderson, Harwood, and Hummert (2005) investigated the predictors of age-adapted communication behavior such as stereotyped perceptions, relationship closeness, reciprocal self-disclosure, and age salience. The type of relationship (e.g., grandparent or acquaintance) and health of the older adult were found to be key factors in the enactment of stereotypes.

Many of the aging theories and models stem from *communication accommodation theory* (CAT; n = 6), which focuses on the processes through which interactants modify their language, vocal patterns, and nonverbal communication in response to their conversation partner (Giles, Coupland, & Coupland, 1991). The modification can result in convergence which highlights similarities in enacted behaviors or divergence which stresses distinctiveness. Rittenour and Soliz (2009) used CAT as their underlying framework to investigate the factors associated with positive and negative mother-in-law/daughter-in-law relationships. Communication factors, family of origin factors, and daughter-in-law future caregiving and contact intentions all contribute to a sense of shared family identity from the perspective of daughter-in-laws.

The final most frequently used theory, *social cognitive theory* (n = 6), was used in research across the four timeframes. The only other theory used across all four timeframes was feminist theories. Social cognitive theory assumes we learn behavior through the observation of "models" such as family members, friends, and media personalities (Bandura, 1977). Rimal and Flora (1998) examined the effectiveness of a public information campaign on the dietary behavior of children and adults finding both adult-to-child, and child-to-adult, influences. The results of their study support the need to target the entire family and not individuals as potential sources of influence when attempting to change health behaviors.

In terms of disproportional representation, aging theories, CAT, and CPM were not represented in the 1990–94 timeframe but prominently utilized in the 2000–9 timeframes. This is not surprising given when these theories were developed. The other theories that had disproportionate representation (e.g., developmental theories, face theories) were also infrequently referenced (five occurrences or less across the timeframes) in the literature.

Relationship theories. The two most commonly used relationship theories were *dialectical theory* and the *theory of family communication patterns*, each of which occurred 18 times. Dialectical theory (Baxter & Montgomery, 1996) examines the "interplay of opposing tendencies in the symbolic, not material, practices of relationship parties" (p. 14). The three most commonly occurring tensions are the dialectics of integration–separation, stability–change, and expression–nonexpression, each of which can occur as an internal dialectic (within the relationship) or an external dialectic (between the couple and someone/something else). Pawlowski (1998) examined dialectical tensions in marital relationships and found that the internal dialectic of autonomy–connection occurred most often, but the dialectic of openness–closedness was the most salient tension. In addition, the external dialectic of conventionality–uniqueness involved social networks while revelation–concealment was often used as a means to prevent a negative reaction from others.

The theory of family communication patterns (Koerner & Fitzpatrick, 2002) posits four family types based on the dimensions of conversation (the degree to which family members can talk freely and spontaneously) and conformity orientation (the degree to which families encourage or discourage uniformity of beliefs and attitudes as well as behavioral regularity). Koesten (2004) examined the relationship between family communication patterns and communication competence and found that children growing up in conversation oriented families enacted a greater variety of interpersonal skills in adult relationships than those growing up in conformity oriented families.

The next most frequently used theoretical perspective in the relationship quadrant was *family systems theory* (n = 11). Family systems theory focuses on family relationships, rather than individual characteristics. As such, factors such as interdependence, wholeness, complexity, openness, and equifinality are privileged (Galvin, Dickson, & Marrow, 2006). Schrodt, Soliz, and Braithwaite (2008) used a systems approach to examine the everyday talk and relationship satisfaction in stepchild, stepparent, and parent triads. By using the stepfamily as the unit of analysis, they determined whether relational satisfaction in everyday talk is due to actor (the propensity for a family member to engage in talk across family relationships), partner (the propensity for a family member to elicit talk across family relationships), or relationship (the propensity for a family member to talk to only one other family member) effects. Among the findings were that satisfaction between spouses is primarily due to actor effects while a child's satisfaction with the stepparent is due to relationship effects.

The *theory of marital types* was utilized ten times in the family research reviewed. According to Fitzpatrick (1988), marital couples can be categorized into three types: traditionals, who "hold conventional ideological values about relationships" and value interdependence, stability, and regularity (p. 76); independents who "hold fairly non-conventional values about relational and family life" and privilege individuality, separate spaces, and spontaneity (p. 76); and separates who "seem to hold two opposing ideological views" in that they are conventional while also valuing individual freedom (p. 76). Honeycutt and Brown (1998) examined humor in marriage and found that traditionals were higher in humor orientation than either separates or independents.

The final most referenced relationship theory was *attachment theory* (n = 9). Attachment theory developed as a means to further understand the close relationship between infants and caregivers (Bowlby, 1988). Different attachment styles include secures (confident and comfortable with others), dismissives (confident and uncomfortable with others), and fearfuls (desire close relationships but often unable to obtain them). Dainton (2007) examined the relationship between attachment style and relationship maintenance in marriage and found that spouses with a dismissive attachment style used maintenance behaviors less than those with secure attachment styles. In addition, spouses with a dismissive attachment style were less likely to value, or appreciate, the maintenance behavior of their spouse.

Attachment theory, dialectical theory, family systems theory, and the theory of family communication patterns were not only high in volume, but also consistent in usage, as each was represented at least once in each of the four timeframes. All four theories did have greater representation in the later timeframes. All four of these theories are standing the test of time and remain popular with family communication researchers.

The theory of marital types, while high in volume, was disproportionate in treatment as it was represented, with one exception, entirely from 1990–99. It appears that this theory, developed in the 1980s, is decreasing in popularity. Two other theories were also disproportionate in usage: the *interactional view* (Watzlawick, et al., 1967) and *affection exchange theory* (Floyd, 2001). The interactional view was most heavily utilized during 1990–94, with the representation tapering off in the subsequent timeframes. Cissna, Cox, and Bochner (1990) employed the interactional view in their analysis of the communicative means through which stepfamilies (re)organize into a new family structure. In contrast, affection exchange theory was only used during the 2000–9 timeframes. Floyd and Morman (2001) examined the differences in affection between fathers and sons and found more affection displayed by fathers to biological sons and adopted sons, as compared to step-sons.

Concepts and Constructs. By a substantial amount, the largest quadrant was the communication-application quadrant. In terms of volume, the following 23 concept categories were studied in at least 10 articles: *satisfaction* (n = 65), *message processes* (n = 29), *conflict* (n = 25), *disclosure* (n = 23), *verbal aggression* (n = 21), *identity* (n = 20), *control* (n = 19), *closeness* (n = 17), *mental health* (n = 17), *television* (n = 17), *contradictions* (n = 15), *maintenance* (n = 15), *family patterns* (n = 14), *self* (n = 14), *competence* (n = 13), *marital types* (n = 13), *support* (n = 13), *avoidance* (n = 11), *emotions* (n = 11), *aging* (n = 10), *health* (n = 10), *negative patterns* (n = 10), and *roles* (n = 10).

Twenty-five of the concept categories had consistent representation across the four timeframes. These include 15 of the high volume concepts (those underlined above). In addition, the following 10 concept categories, though appearing in less than 10 articles, were consistently studied across each timeframe: *attachment, commitment, contact, expectations, experience, influence, interventions, stories, trust,* and *schemata.*

Finally, 14 of the concept categories, contained in six or more articles, had disproportionate representation across the four timeframes. *Affection, aging, identity, media, self, avoidance, secrets, culture, work/life, outcomes, structure,* and *uncertainty* all were moderately or not represented in the earlier timeframes and more prominently represented in recent research. In contrast, the concepts of *abuse* and *marital types* each received more attention from family researchers in the two early timeframes.

In this data set, satisfaction was both the most frequently studied concept and the most studied concept in each of the four timeframes. Some of the subcategories making up the more general category of satisfaction were quality of contact, marital quality, and family adjustment. In much of the research, the relationship between some version of satisfaction and some other variable(s) in a particular relationship was explored. For example, recent research has examined: relationship satisfaction and family communication patterns in parent–child relationships (Zhang, 2007); relational repair message interpretation and marital satisfaction in remarried individuals (Bello, Brandau-Brown, & Ragsdale, 2008); marital and in-law satisfaction in married couples (Serewicz, Hosmer, Ballard, & Griffin, 2008); everyday talk and relationship satisfaction in stepfamilies (Schrodt, et al., 2008); and communication motives and relationship satisfaction in sibling relationships (Fowler, 2009).

Message processes was the second most frequently studied concept and included subcategories such as message types, everyday talk, communication repair, communication topics, and information processes. Heisler and Ellis (2008) examined how memorable messages from others about motherhood impacted both women's attitudes about motherhood and the construction of their identity as mothers. Other research in the message process category included the association between family communication patterns and information processing outcomes (Schrodt, Witt, & Messersmith, 2008) and address practices between married couples and their in-laws (Jorgenson, 1994).

Conflict was the third most studied concept. An example of research on conflict was the examination of the relationship between family type and conflict in family units (Koerner & Fitzpatrick, 1997). The results indicated that conflict avoidance occurs less often in pluralistic families and more often in protective and laissez faire families. In addition, there was a positive relationship between conformity orientation and conflict and a negative relationship between conversation orientation and conflict.

Regarding the concepts that were disproportionately represented in the articles, the results might be due to the incremental growth in the number of concepts across the four timeframes. However, there does appear to be increased interest in some of the areas that might not be accounted for by just a rise in overall research. For example, the concept of aging had eight of ten articles in the last ten years and none in the 1990–94 timeframe, while the concept of media had seven of nine studies, and work/life all six, in the past ten years.

Contexts. The most frequently researched family communication contexts in the past 20 years are *married couples* (n = 77), *family units* (n = 36), *parent–child* relationships (n = 36), *siblings* (n = 14), *stepfamilies* (n = 14), *father–son* relationships (n = 13), *children* (n = 12), and *parents* (n = 12). Across the four timeframes married couples, the family unit, and the parent–child relationship were consistently the top contexts studied. All the other top context areas, except for stepfamilies, also focus on individuals who make up the varying roles and relationships captured in the family of procreation. This is not surprising as these contexts also operationally represent traditional definitions of *family* from a structural approach (Koerner & Fitzpatrick, 2004) and are the ways in which most family researchers operationalize families (Fitzpatrick & Caughlin, 2002).

All of the top context areas in terms of volume except the *father–son* relationship have consistently been studied across the four timeframes. Two other context areas, *mothers* (n = 9) and *divorced parents* (n = 7), have also been a consistently studied context by family communication researchers. In regard to disproportional representation of context, *father–son* relationship research was most prominent in the 1990–94 timeframe and steadily decreased with no father–son studies in the 2005–9 timeframe. Two other context areas that have received considerable attention since 2000 are the *grandparent–grandchild* relationship (n = 9) and the *mother–child* relationship (n = 6).

There is a substantial body of research focused on married couples as participants or individuals projecting their expectations for married life. Of particular research interest are the broad outcomes of marital satisfaction (or dissatisfaction), stability (or lack thereof), and the processes that contribute to those outcomes (Fitzpatrick & Caughlin, 2002). Often married couples are compared to participants representing other relationship contexts such as engaged couples (Honeycutt & Wiemann, 1999) or even combined with other relationship contexts such as dating or cohabitating couples in the analysis of research results (Olson, 2002).

Research on the family unit has been extensive, and this analysis captures studies that ask participants to reflect in general about processes within families. For example, Schrodt (2005) asked participants to complete measures of family communication schemata and family functioning. The items on those measures asked participants to comment on "family members" (p. 375) or "our family" (p. 376). Other research on topics such as family values provide insight into the family unit context area but do not actually use family members as participants (Cloud, 1998).

The majority of dyadic research in the family of procreation setting was in the broad category of parent–child relationships. In our review, parent–child research combined responses from, or about, mothers and fathers as well as combined responses from, or about, daughters and sons (e.g., Warren, 2005). Research has, and our coding system accounted for, more specific types of parent–child dyads, such as the consistently researched mother–child relationship and the disproportionately studied father–son relationship. Mother–child studies focus on both sons and daughters collectively in the sample. For example, Wilson, Roberts, Rack, and Delaney (2008) studied mothers' interactions with their children during playtime. Sixty percent of the child participants were male while 40 percent of the child participants were female. Father–son studies, in contrast, examine the unique nature of male relationships within the family (e.g., Morman & Floyd, 1999).

In addition to the dyad, family research often focused on specific roles such as mothers, parents, divorced parents, and children. For example, there is research on how women form their expectations of motherhood (Ex, Janssens, & Korzilius, 2002), how parents transition into parenthood (Stamp, 1994), and how divorced parents negotiate co-parenting (Manusov, Cody, Donohue, & Zappa, 1994). Research on children has investigated how children perceive communication processes (Marshall & Levy, 1998), how divorce impacts children (Schrodt & Ledbetter, 2007), and how family communication processes can impact children's communication with friends (Ledbetter, 2009).

Research extending beyond the family of procreation includes studies of stepfamilies and grandparent–grandchild relationships. Although research on stepfamilies has occurred across the four timeframes, the vast majority of research has occurred since 2000. All nine articles on grandparent–grandchild relationships were published in the 2000–9 timeframe. The past decade of research on stepfamilies demonstrates evolving forms of families (e.g., Braithwaite & Baxter, 2006) while the focus on the grandparent–grandchild dyad extends intergenerational research into the family setting (e.g., Anderson et al., 2005).

Additional analysis of the *Journal of Family Communication*. The *Journal of Family Communication* (JFC) was established in 2001 and consequently did not meet the 20 year timeframe criteria of the journals selected for review. However, as a secondary analysis, we reviewed the research articles in JFC to determine their primary research perspective and to identify theories, concepts, and contexts that were not represented in the previously reviewed articles. We reviewed 85 JFC research articles; 65 percent (n = 55) of the articles were from the empiricist perspective, 34 percent (n = 29) from the interpretive perspective, and 1 percent (n = 1) from the critical perspective. JFC mirrors the national and regional communication journals in that the majority of research articles are from an empiricist perspective, but to a lesser degree, and the percentage of articles from the interpretive perspective is higher in JFC than the other journals reviewed.

Many of the most frequently researched theories, concepts, and contexts such as CPM, dialectical theory, theory of family communication patterns, satisfaction, message processes, marital couples, parent–child relationships, and the family unit were also represented in the research in JFC. The articles in JFC have, however, studied additional or provided a more nuanced investigation of some concepts and contexts, as well as employed additional theoretical perspectives. For example, research has focused on defining *family* from the perspective of participants (Edwards & Graham, 2009), the concept of *adoption* (Suter & Ballard, 2009), and more purposefully investigated the role of *culture* in the family setting (Bylund, 2003). *Step*-grandparents (Soliz, 2007), *commuter* wives (Bergen, Kirby, & McBride, 2007), *elderly* parents and their adult children

(Miller, Shoemaker, Willyard, & Addison, 2008), and same-sex families (Bergen, Suter, & Daas, 2006) were contexts explored in *JFC* articles.

As was the case in the eight reviewed journals, there was great variety in the types of theories employed by researchers publishing in *JFC*, yet many of the theories were only used in one research study. Some of the theories utilized in *JFC* that were not employed in the previously reviewed articles included the risk and resiliency model of ambiguous loss (Afifi & Keith, 2004) and social exchange theory (Ragsdale & Brandau-Brown, 2005).

Discussion and Directions for Future Research

Over the past 20 years, family communication research has steadily increased and focused on a variety of theories, concepts and contexts. Although the empiricist perspective is still the predominate approach to family communication research, research from the interpretive perspective has increased substantially and has added additional insight into the lived experience of family members. The empiricist tradition which enables the investigation of many variables in the same study has expanded our breadth of understanding. More work, however, is needed in our depth of understanding. For example, in the past 20 years satisfaction has been a concept of interest in 65 studies; however, what more do we really know about satisfaction today? What more do we need to know about satisfaction? Multi-perspective work can help us understand the complexities of concepts beyond simply measuring again the degree of a concept present in a family relationship.

As illustrated in the family communication template (Table 1.2) and similar to the findings of Graham and Shue (2000), research efforts have focused more on the right side of the communication/relationship axis, application, than on the left side of the axis, theory. The diversity of application research is both a strength and potential limitation. This diversity has added to our breadth of understanding but has also made our research somewhat fragmented. While lines of family communication research can be traced (e.g., maintenance behaviors among married couples, bereaved parents, family secrets), other researchers have explored interesting and important theories, concepts and contexts in one study but then do not develop the investigation further as evidenced by the substantial number of categories with a frequency of one or two.

This lack of commitment to a line of research is most apparent on the theory side of the quadrant. Several of the theories utilized to ground family communication research were employed in only one or two studies. Such "theory shopping" does not promote theory development in the field nor does it enable researchers to tie concepts to theories through a developed programmatic investigation. In some cases, as we reviewed and coded the articles, there seemed to be a theoretical frame that was not fully articulated, resulting in limited studies identified as using a particular approach. For example, some of the articles used stories or narratives to frame the research, but narrative theory was not developed in any systematic way, resulting in a much larger story concept category than a narrative theory category. By not including narrative theory as a foundation for the research, and then not connecting the findings back to the theory, our ability to extend the understanding of narrative theory within family communication is limited.

Building a line of research around a theory or engaging in systematic theory development will increase our understanding of the interplay between theoretical assumptions and family communication phenomena as well as promote further family communication research. This outcome can be seen in some of the most frequently utilized theoretical perspectives identified in the template. Uncertainty reduction theory, dialectical theory,

theory of family communication patterns, CAT, CPM, and affection exchange theory are all theoretical perspectives that were either developed in the communication field or embraced and advanced by communication scholars. Certainly, there is room to advance our understanding of family communication through the additional use of currently under-utilized theories such as constructivism, diffusion of innovations theory, structuration theory, and inconsistent nurturing as control theory.

Two prominent theories in the communication field that were not utilized in the 2005–9 timeframe were the theory of marital types and the interactional view. Clearly, research areas drop out of favor and scholars lose interest but there is still value in these theories. For example, Rogers (2006) argues that the interactional view applied to family interactions enables scholars to "identify specific communication behavior or patterns that lead in directions desired or toward less desired family outcomes" (p. 127). There is still more to learn from, and about, classic theories in the field.

Often the means by which theoretical and conceptual work gains attention is when the research occurs within a specific context. As family experiences in our culture evolve, so must our contextual work. Future research is needed in the areas of (1) specific family dyads beyond married couples such as mothers–sons and fathers–daughters, (2) children and other family members beyond siblings and parents, (3) single-parents and single-parent families, (4) same-sex parents, and (5) fictive kin. Over the past 20 years, we have broadened the scope of family contexts. We need to continue these efforts since, for many people, it is a specific family dyad or even fictive kin that are more influential in their lives than the primary family unit.

The purpose of this chapter was to review family communication research published in communication journals. We recognize that family communication research is published in other journals as well. Some research areas that are underrepresented in these analyses may be well-represented in other journal venues. We encourage family communication scholars to seriously consider the communication journal outlets identified in this review as a means of disseminating their work. Providing scholars with an understanding of what we currently know about the field, as well as the gaps in what has been published in the discipline, provides scholars with a foundation for their own programmatic research. We are encouraged by the breadth of past work and while we might make predictions about what might be reviewed for the third edition of the *Handbook of Family Communication*, we know we will also be surprised by some of the future family communication research directions and findings.

References

Afifi, T. D., & Keith, S. (2004). A risk and resiliency model of ambiguous loss in postdivorce stepfamilies. *Journal of Family Communication, 4*, 65–98.

Anderson, K., Harwood, J., & Hummert, M. L. (2005). The grandparent–grandchild relationship: Implications for models of intergenerational communication. *Human Communication Research, 31*, 268–294.

Bandura, A. (1977). *Social learning theory.* Englewood Cliffs, NJ: Prentice Hall.

Baxter, L. A., & Montgomery, B. M. (1996). *Relating: Dialogues and dialectics.* New York: Guilford Press.

Bello, R. S., Brandau-Brown, F. E., & Ragsdale, J. D. (2008). Attachment style, marital satisfaction, commitment, and communal strength effects on relational repair message interpretation among remarrieds. *Communication Quarterly, 5*, 1–16.

Bergen, K. M., Kirby, E., & McBride, M. C. (2007). "How do you get two houses cleaned?": Accomplishing family caregiving in commuter marriages. *Journal of Family Communication, 7*, 287–307.

Bergen, K. M., Suter, E. A., & Daas, K. L. (2006). "About as solid as a fish net": Symbolic construction of a legitimate parental identity for nonbiological lesbian mothers. *Journal of Family Communication*, 6, 201–20.

Bochner, A. P. (1985). Perspectives on inquiry: Representation, conversation, and reflection. In M. L. Knapp & G. R. Miller (Eds.), *Handbook of interpersonal communication* (pp. 27–58). Beverly Hills, CA: Sage.

Bowlby, J. (1988). *A secure base: Parent–child attachment and healthy human development*. New York: Basic Books.

Braithwaite, D., & Baxter, L. (2006). "You're my parent but you're not": Dialectical tensions in stepchildren's perceptions about communicating with the nonresidential parent. *Journal of Applied Communication Research*, 34, 30–48.

Buzzanell, P. M., & Liu M. (2005). Struggling with maternity leave policies and practices: A poststructuralist feminist analysis of gendered organizing. *Journal of Applied Communication Research*, 33, 1–25.

Bylund, C. L. (2003). Ethnic diversity and family stories. *Journal of Family Communication*, 3, 215–36.

Cissna, K. N., Cox, D. E., & Bochner, A. P. (1990). The dialectic of marital and parental relationships within the stepfamily. *Communication Monographs*, 57(1), 44–61.

Cloud, D. (1998). The rhetoric of family values: Scapegoating, utopia, and the privatization of social responsibility. *Western Journal of Communication*, 62, 387–419.

Dainton, M. (2007). Attachment and marital maintenance. *Communication Quarterly*, 55, 283–98.

Edwards, A. P., & Graham, E. E. (2009). The relationship between individuals' definitions of family and implicit personal theories of communication. *Journal of Family Communication*, 9, 191–208.

Ex, C., Janssens, J., & Korzilius, H. (2002). Young females' images of motherhood in relation to television viewing. *Journal of Communication*, 52, 955–71.

Fitzpatrick, M. A. (1988). *Between husbands and wives*. Beverly Hills, CA: Sage.

Fitzpatrick, M. A., & Caughlin, J. P. (2002). Interpersonal communication in family relationships. In M. L. Knapp & J. A. Daly (Eds.), *Handbook of interpersonal communication*, 3rd edn (pp. 726–77). Thousand Oaks, CA: Sage.

Floyd, K. (2001). Human affection exchange I: Reproductive probability of men's affection with their sons. *Journal of Men's Studies*, 10, 39–50.

Floyd, K., & Morman, M. T. (2001). Human affection exchange III: Discriminative parental solicitude in men's affectionate communication with their biological and nonbiological sons. *Communication Quarterly*, 49(3), 310–27.

Fowler, C. (2009). Motives for sibling communication across the lifespan. *Communication Quarterly*, 57, 51–66.

Galvin, K. M., Dickson, F. C., & Marrow, S. R. (2006). Systems theory: Patterns and (w)holes in family communication. In D. O. Braithwaite & L. A. Baxter (Eds.), *Engaging theories in family communication: Multiple perspectives* (pp. 309–24). Thousand Oaks, CA: Sage Publications.

Giles, H., Coupland, N., & Coupland, J. (1991). Accommodation theory: Communication, context, and consequence. In H. Giles, J. Coupland, & N. Coupland (Eds.), *Contexts of accommodation: Developments in applied sociolinguistics* (pp. 1–68). Cambridge: Cambridge University Press.

Golish, T. D., & Caughlin, J. P. (2002). "I'd rather not talk about it": Adolescents' and young adults' use of topic avoidance in stepfamilies. *Journal of Applied Communication Research*, 30, 78–106.

Graham, E. E., & Shue, C. K. (2000). Reflections on the past, directions for the future: A template for the study and instruction of interpersonal communication. *Communication Research Reports*, 17, 337–48.

Heisler, J. M. & Ellis, J. B. (2008). Motherhood and the construction of "mommy identity": Messages about motherhood and face negotiation. *Communication Quarterly*, 56, 445–67.

Hoffman, M. F., & Cowan, R. L. (2008). The meaning of work/life: A corporate ideology of work/life balance. *Communication Quarterly*, 56, 227–46.

Honeycutt, J. M., & Brown, R. (1998). Did you hear the one about? Typological and spousal differences in the planning of jokes and sense of humor in marriage. *Communication Quarterly*, 46(3), 342–52.

Honeycutt, J. M., & Wiemann, J. M. (1999). Analysis of functions of talk and reports of imagined interactions (IIs) during engagement and marriage, *Human Communication Research*, 25, 399–419.

Hummert, M. L., Garstka, T. A., Ryan, E. B., & Bonnesen, J. L. (2004). The role of age stereotypes in interpersonal communication. In J. F. Nussbaum & J. Coupland (Eds.), *Handbook of communication and aging research*, 2nd edn (pp. 91–115). Mahwah, NJ: Lawrence Erlbaum Associates.

Jorgenson, J. (1994). Situated address and the social construction of "in-law" relationships. *Southern Communication Journal, 59*, 196–204.

Koerner, A. F., & Fitzpatrick, M. A. (1997). Family type and conflict: The impact of conversation orientation and conformity orientation on conflict in the family. *Communication Studies, 48*, 59–75.

——(2002). Toward a theory of family communication. *Communication Theory, 12*, 70–91.

——(2004). Communication in intact families. In A. L. Vangelisti (Ed.), *Handbook of family communication* (pp. 177–95). Mahwah, NJ: Lawrence Erlbaum Associates.

Koesten, J. (2004). Family communication patterns, sex of subject, and communication competence. *Communication Monographs, 71*(2), 226–44.

Kramarae, C. (1981). *Women and men speaking.* Rowley, MA: Newbury House.

Ledbetter, A. M. (2009). Family communication patterns and relational maintenance behavior: Direct and mediated associations with friendship closeness. *Human Communication Research, 35*, 130–47.

Manusov, V., Cody, M., Donohue, W., & Zappa, J. (1994). Accounts in child custody mediation sessions. *Journal of Applied Communication Research, 22*, 1–15.

Marshall, L. J., & Levy, V. M. (1998). The development of children's perceptions of obstacles in compliance-gaining interactions. *Communication Studies, 49*, 342–57.

Miller, K. I., Shoemaker, M. M., Willyard, J., & Addison, P. (2008). Providing care for elderly parents: A structurational approach to family caregiver identity. *Journal of Family Communication, 8*, 19–43.

Morman, M. T., & Floyd, K. (1999). Affectionate communication between fathers and young adult sons: Individual- and relational-level correlates. *Communication Studies, 50*, 294–309.

Olson, L. (2002). Exploring "common couple violence" in heterosexual romantic relationships. *Western Journal of Communication, 66*, 104–28.

Pawlowski, D. R. (1998). Dialectical tensions in marital partners' accounts of their relationships. *Communication Quarterly, 46*(4), 396–412.

Petronio, S. (2002). *Boundaries of privacy: Dialectics of disclosure.* Albany, NY: SUNY Press.

Ragsdale, J. D., & Brandau-Brown, F. E. (2005). Individual differences in the use of relational maintenance strategies in marriage. *Journal of Family Communication, 5*, 61–75.

Rimal, R. N., & Flora, J. A. (1998). Bidirectional familial influences in dietary behavior: Test of a model of campaign influences. *Human Communication Research, 24*, 610–37.

Rittenour, C., & Soliz, J. (2009). Communicative and relational dimensions of shared family identity and relational intentions in mother-in-law/daughter-in-law relationships: Developing a conceptual model for mother-in-law/daughter-in-law research. *Western Journal of Communication, 73*, 67–90.

Rogers, L. E. (2006). Relational communication theory: An interactional family theory. In D. O. Braithwaite & L. A. Baxter (Eds.), *Engaging theories in family communication: Multiple perspectives* (pp. 115–29). Thousand Oaks, CA: Sage.

Ryan, E. B., Giles, H., Bartolucci, G., & Henwood, K. (1986). Psycholinguistic and social psychological components of communication by and with the elderly. *Language and Communication, 6*, 1–24.

Schrodt, P. (2005). Family communication schemata and the circumplex model of family functioning. *Western Journal of Communication, 69*, 359–76.

——(2006). A typological examination of communication competence and mental health in stepchildren. *Communication Monographs, 73*(3), 309–33.

Schrodt, P., & Ledbetter, A. M. (2007). Communication processes that mediate family communication patterns and mental well-being: A mean and covariance structures analysis of young adults from divorced and nondivorced families. *Human Communication Research, 33*, 330–56.

Schrodt, P., Soliz, J., & Braithwaite, D. O. (2008). A social relations model of everyday talk and relationship satisfaction in stepfamilies. *Communication Monographs, 75*(2), 190–217.

Schrodt, P., Witt, P. L., & Messersmith, A. S. (2008). A meta-analytic review of family communication patterns and their associations with information processing, behavioral, and psychosocial outcomes. *Communication Monographs, 75*, 248–69.

Serewicz, M. C. M., Hosmer, R., Ballard, R. L., & Griffin, R. A. (2008). Disclosure from in-laws and the quality of in-law and marital relationships. *Communication Quarterly, 56*, 427–44.

Soliz, J. (2007). Communicative predictors of a shared family identity: Comparison of grandchildren's perceptions of family-of-origin grandparents and stepgrandparents. *Journal of Family Communication, 7*, 177–94.

Stamp, G. H. (1994). The appropriation of the parental role through communication during the transition to parenthood. *Communication Monographs, 61*, 89–112.

———(2004). Theories of family relationships and a family relationships theoretical model. In A. L. Vangelisti (Ed.), *Handbook of family communication* (pp. 1–30). Mahway, NJ: Lawrence Erlbaum Associates.

Suter, E. A., & Ballard, R. L. (2009). "How much did you pay for her?": Decision-making criteria underlying adoptive parents' responses to inappropriate remarks. *Journal of Family Communication*, 9, 107–25.

Thompson-Hayes, M., & Webb, L. M. (2008). Documenting mutuality: Testing a dyadic and communicative model of marital commitment. *Southern Communication Journal*, 73(2), 143–59.

Warren, R. (2005). Parental mediation of children's television viewing in low-income families. *Journal of Communication*, 55, 847–63.

Watzlawick, P., Beavin, J. H., & Jackson, D. D. (1967). *Pragmatics of human communication: A study of interactional patterns, pathologies and paradoxes*. New York: Norton.

Wilson, S. R., Roberts, F., Rack, J. J., & Delaney, J. E. (2008). Mothers' trait verbal aggressiveness as a predictor of maternal and child behavior during playtime interactions. *Human Communication Research*, 34, 392–422.

Zhang, Q. (2007). Family communication patterns and conflict styles in Chinese parent–child relationships. *Communication Quarterly*, 55, 113–28.

2

Perspectives on Studying Family Communication

Multiple Methods and Multiple Sources

Judith A. Feeney and Patricia Noller

Family communication can be studied using a variety of methodologies, such as self-report, observational and experimental. In this chapter, we discuss the various ways these methodologies can be employed, and the issues related to each of them. Although we provide examples of studies using the various methodologies, we do not claim to cover the field in any comprehensive way, but rather to use illustrative examples, including some from our own work.

Research can also involve a quantitative or a qualitative perspective, although both types of data are sometimes collected in the same study. Quantitative methodologies involve individuals receiving scores—for example, on a questionnaire, as a reaction time in an experiment, or as the frequency with which a particular behavior was observed. These scores can then be analyzed statistically. In contrast, qualitative methodologies tend not to be based on numbers, and may involve intensive interviews, or content analysis of utterances or written statements. Qualitative methodologies focus on the experience of participants, often as recorded in their own words. All methods (whether basically quantitative or qualitative) have advantages and disadvantages. Hence, the key issue is the appropriateness of a methodology for answering a particular research question, and different methods may be usefully combined to provide more comprehensive analyses.

Self-Report Methodologies

Self-report methods are often used to study family communication, either alone or in combination with other methodologies. Self-report methods include questionnaires, diaries, and other experience-sampling techniques. Interviews also involve self-report, facilitated by the interviewer.

Questionnaires

Self-report questionnaires are appropriate for asking about the general or overall frequency of communication. Widely used measures of family communication include the

Communication Patterns Questionnaire (Christensen, 1988; Christensen & Sullaway, 1984), and the Conflict Resolution Styles Questionnaire (Peterson, 1990; Rands, Levinger & Mellinger, 1981). More recently, and reflecting the awareness of marriage as a significant transition point, Serewicz and Canary (2008) developed self-report scales assessing aspects of disclosure and privacy orientation by in-laws. Using both traditional and on-line methods of administration, the researchers examined associations between these scales and outcomes for the in-law relationship.

The limitations of self-report questionnaires are well known (in fact, they have been more widely acknowledged than the limitations of other methodologies such as observation). Problems include respondents' limited awareness of their own thoughts, feelings and behavior; social desirability and self-serving biases; and the difficulty respondents may experience in trying to mentally aggregate the occurrence of behavior across times and situations. Metts, Sprecher and Cupach (1991) and Ickes (2000) discuss these problems in more detail.

Some of the problems associated with self-report questionnaires can be minimized by using scales to assess the level of socially desirable responding. For example, Snyder (1979) included a measure of "conventionalization," or the tendency to portray one's relationship in an idealistic manner, in his Marital Satisfaction Inventory. Snyder found that controlling for conventionalization tended to decrease the correlations between the factors of his inventory and a measure of global marital satisfaction, but had little effect on the overall significance of these associations.

Although the limitations of self-report questionnaires are well known, the advantages are less well canvassed. For example, in contrast to other methods, questionnaires can be used to assess the frequency of behavior across different times and situations. Self-report methods are also useful for studying behavior retrospectively, and for studying behaviors that rarely occur in the laboratory.

Assessing Communication Across Times and Situations

Noller and Bagi (1985) asked adolescents and their parents about communication in the family, using the Parent–Adolescent Communication Inventory. This measure assesses communication at the level of the topics discussed (e.g., "interests," "sex problems"); communication on each topic is rated on evaluative dimensions such as frequency, self-disclosure, and satisfaction. The resulting breadth of information could not be obtained using observational methods, which usually involve a brief interaction on a relatively circumscribed topic. Similarly, Noller and Feeney (1998) employed a modification of this measure (using topics suitable for couples) to assess newlyweds' communication over 12 topics and the same evaluative scales used in the earlier study. Topics included "feelings about our relationship" and "plans for the future." These researchers were able to explore the frequency with which particular topics were discussed, and the quality of the communication around each topic.

Collecting Retrospective Data

An example of a questionnaire designed to collect retrospective data is the Parental Bonding Instrument (PBI; Parker, Tupling & Brown, 1979), which asks participants about parents' behavior toward them when they were children. The measure assesses two dimensions: care (e.g., "Spoke to me in a warm and friendly voice"), and overprotection (e.g., "Tried to control everything I did").

A major issue with retrospective data concerns validity. That is, do participants' responses really reflect what happened "back then," or do they represent subsequent reconstructions of those events? It is worth noting, however, that an individual's perception of what happened earlier in life may have a greater impact on the current situation than "the objective truth." Further, research indicates that offspring's scores on the PBI are related to parents' reports of their own parenting behavior, and to interviewers' and observers' judgments of parenting (Parker, 1983). Data also highlight the importance of perceptions of early parenting to adults' relational experiences. In one study (Feeney, Passmore, & Peterson, 2007), adults adopted during infancy reported more attachment insecurity than a comparison sample raised with both biological parents. However, self-reports of parental bonding were stronger predictors of security than was adoptive status; for both adopted and comparison groups, perceptions of parental care were particularly important.

Studying Behaviors Unlikely to Occur in the Laboratory

L. J. Roberts (2000) discussed the advantages of self-report methods for studying behaviors such as avoidance and withdrawal. These behaviors are difficult to study observationally, because demand characteristics in the laboratory context are such that individuals are unlikely to use the more obvious forms of these behaviors. For example, participants are unlikely to get up and walk out of the laboratory, and cannot resort to such techniques as turning on the television, although they may use such strategies at home.

L. J. Roberts (2000) reported on the construction of the Interaction Response Patterns Questionnaire, designed to assess different types of withdrawal and avoidance behaviors. Participants are asked to indicate how they believe their partner would respond to them when they engage in a number of different (antecedent) behaviors. The antecedent behaviors include "I criticize, blame or put my partner down" (angry withdrawal), and "When a problem comes up in our marriage, I try to get us to talk about it, share our feelings and work out a solution" (conflict avoidance). Each antecedent behavior is followed by a list of possible behavioral responses, so that partners' reactions to specific interactional contexts likely to trigger withdrawal can be assessed.

Similarly, self-report methods may be particularly useful for studying family violence, which is unlikely to occur during laboratory conversations. Hence, although laboratory paradigms can be used to compare violent and nonviolent couples in terms of arousal levels and communication patterns, the actual occurrence of violence needs to be studied using self-report. The Conflict Tactics Scales (Straus, 1979) have been widely used, and have been criticized for being too simplistic and ignoring the context of violent behavior. There is evidence, however, that those in abusive relationships are more likely to acknowledge the occurrence of violence on an anonymous questionnaire than in an interview (Szinovacz & Egley, 1995). Szinovacz and Egley also advocate collecting questionnaire data from both relationship partners, to ensure that violence is not under-reported.

Diaries

The difficulty participants may have in averaging the occurrence of a behavior across times and situations can be overcome by using a structured diary methodology. Diaries generally require participants to complete a brief report on each interaction of a particular type (e.g., with the spouse or the child), including basic information about when and where the interaction took place, along with evaluations of the communication process. The best-known versions of this methodology are based on the Rochester Interaction Record (Wheeler & Nezlek, 1977).

The major advantage of the diary method over other self-report methodologies is that the reports can be completed immediately, or at least soon after the event in question. The main limitation centers on possible reactivity; once participants are informed of behaviors to be recorded, they may change their behavior to appear more well-adjusted, or to decrease the demands of the reporting task. A further problem is that participants may not complete the diary forms regularly, or may complete them for several days at the same time. When this happens, diary data become more like retrospective data.

Noller and Feeney (1998) had newlyweds record all couple interactions lasting ten minutes or more, using diary reports based on the Rochester Interaction Record. These reports provided structural information about each interaction (e.g., time, duration, and topic), together with ratings such as initiation, disclosure, conflict and satisfaction. The ratings were used to form measures of "quantity," "quality," and "conflict," which showed significant associations with marital satisfaction. More recently, computerized daily diaries have been used to examine the extent of supportive interactions, and their effects on well-being, among couples dealing with multiple sclerosis (Kleiboer, Kuijer, Hox, Schreurs, & Bensing, 2006).

Other Experience-Sampling Techniques

Some researchers have collected diary-type data by using beepers to indicate when participants should complete a report. For example, Larson and Richards (1994) had family members report on their activities and effect at particular points in time. In this way, they could relate family members' effect to time of day and to the activity being undertaken. In another study of this type, Huston and Vangelisti (1991) used telephone calls involving a highly structured interview protocol to obtain reports of couples' socio-emotional behavior (e.g., "husband made wife laugh," "wife dominated conversation"). Such methods can help ensure that data are collected regularly, and soon after the occurrence of the relevant behavior.

Interviews

Another way of obtaining participants' perspectives on communication is to use interviews. Interviews vary in the level of structure imposed by the researcher. At the highest level of structure, interviews may not be very different from questionnaires as a methodology, except that the information being sought tends to be more immediate. At the lowest level of structure, the interview may be quite free-flowing and the interviewer may be free to pursue any issues that seem relevant.

Interviews have an advantage over questionnaires, in that the interviewer can use probes to elicit relevant information, or ask follow-up questions for clarification. For example, several groups of researchers have developed interview protocols that explore perceptions of attachment relationships, including aspects of family communication (e.g., Bartholomew & Horowitz, 1991; Main, Kaplan, & Cassidy, 1985). A potential disadvantage is that interviewers may be affected by their own biases, in terms of the questions they ask. In addition, the interviewer's nonverbal responses to the participant's answers may affect the extent to which the participant continues to be truthful, or produces socially desirable responses. This issue may be particularly critical when the information sought concerns socially undesirable or even criminal behavior (see Szinovacz & Egley, 1995, mentioned earlier).

A further disadvantage of interviews is the problem of deciding how to make sense of the data. Where the focus is on participants' experience (e.g., of violence, or family life), it may be enough to describe that experience using suitable quotations from interview transcripts. Caution is needed, however. For example, researchers need to be clear about whether examples being reported represent the modal experience of the group, or are unique to a particular participant. Just as biases can be problematic at the interview stage, they can also influence the way data are analyzed and reported.

Integrating Different Types of Self-Reports

Some researchers combine different self-report methods to provide a more comprehensive picture of family communication. For example, Noller, Feeney, Sheehan, Darlington, and Rogers (2008) examined levels and topics of conflict in divorcing and continuously married families, using questionnaires and in-depth interviews. Both methods indicated that levels of conflict remained high in divorcing families, even years after separation. While the questionnaires provided large amounts of data that could be summarized using standardized scales, the interviews allowed detailed exploration of conflict interactions and their effects on children. Similarly, Schrodt, Baxter, McBride, Braithwaite and Fine (2006) combined structured diaries and interviews, to explore the complexities of communication processes associated with post-divorce co-parenting.

Summary of Self-Report Methods

Despite the limitations of self-report methodologies, it is clear that they occupy an important place in the research arsenal of family communication scholars. Self-report methods are particularly useful for assessing communication across times and situations, for collecting retrospective data (e.g., about parent–child communication), and for assessing behaviors that rarely occur in the laboratory (e.g., violence).

Observational Methods

Observational studies of family communication involve having family members engage in an interaction and then rating or coding their behaviors. The behaviors of interest can be elicited in different ways that vary in terms of the level of structure. Free interaction, such as might occur with families in a park (Sigelman & Adams, 1990) or waiting-room (Noller, 1980a), lies at the least structured end of the dimension. Experiments that involve manipulating the environment to observe the effect on family members' behavior lie at the most structured end, and are discussed later in this chapter.

Many observational studies involve the family or couple coming into a laboratory, and engaging in an interaction that is videotaped. The topic of interaction may be specified by the researcher or chosen by the family. The content of the conversation may or may not be of primary interest; many researchers are more interested in process than in what the family talks about. These laboratory-based observational studies lie somewhere between the free-interaction situation and studies involving manipulation of variables.

Choosing a Topic

As L. J. Roberts and Greenberg (2002) noted, observational studies of couple interaction have focused primarily on conflict. Hence, we know much more about negative behavior between couples than about their positive behavior and intimate exchanges.

Many studies of couple interaction involve partners being asked to discuss a current issue in their relationship (e.g., Noller, Feeney, Bonnell, & Callan, 1994). However, Christensen and colleagues (e.g., Christensen & Heavey, 1990; Heavey, Christensen, & Malamuth, 1995) have shown that behavior in conflict interactions depends on whether the issue being discussed is raised by the husband or by the wife, particularly in terms of demanding and withdrawing behaviors. These researchers suggest that conflict processes in couples should be studied using two topics, one chosen by each partner.

Although many researchers ask couples to discuss a current relationship issue, there are problems associated with this approach. Behavioral differences found between satisfied and dissatisfied couples may be, at least partly, a function of differences in the seriousness of the problems in the two groups of couples. By contrast, conflict topics provided by the experimenter, such as the hypothetical situations used by Raush, Barry, Hertel and Swain (1974) may not be equally salient for all couples. Again, having couples engage in more than one interaction may alleviate some of these problems. For example, Robles, Shaffer, Malarkey, and Kiecolt-Glaser (2006) interviewed each couple and hence chose two or three marital issues judged likely to elicit conflict in subsequent interaction.

Focusing on Process

Where the focus of researchers is on interaction processes, they may have the videotaped interaction coded by trained coders or raters ("outsiders"), or may use the family members ("insiders") as informants about what happened in the interaction.

Outsider and Insider Data

This distinction between outsider and insider data is an important one (Olson, 1977). Outsider data are often seen as more objective and reliable, but it is important to remember that outsiders know little about the history of the relationships they observe. They may be able to describe behavior very effectively, but cannot be sure what participants are feeling, except by making assumptions about the meaning of their behavior. Further, the more interpretation coders have to engage in, the less reliable and valid are their conclusions. In their studies on demand–withdraw communication (e.g., Heavey, Christensen, & Malamuth, 1995), Christensen and his colleagues have obtained both insider data (self-reports of demanding and withdrawing behavior) and outsider data (global ratings by outsiders of couples' behavior, and coding of actual nonverbal behaviors). The advantages of this approach are discussed later in this chapter.

Coding or Rating by Outside Coders

Assessments by outsiders may involve micro-coding of each behavior, or more global ratings of the interaction. A number of coding systems are available for micro-coding interaction, particularly couple interaction. One widely used system is the Couples' Interaction Scoring System (CISS; Gottman, Notarius, & Markman, 1976), which includes codes for content (verbal) and affect (nonverbal) behavior. Affect is coded as either positive or negative, depending on whether the unit being coded contributes to a more pleasant or more unpleasant climate. A Global Rapid Couples' Interaction Scoring Scheme (RCISS; Krokoff, Gottman, & Hass, 1989) has also been developed. This scheme involves fewer coding categories, allowing for faster coding of interaction. Global scores on positivity–negativity can also be calculated for both speakers and listeners. Another commonly used system is the Marital Interaction Coding System (MICS; Weiss, Hops & Patterson, 1973), which was one of the first attempts to systematize observational coding. Several revisions have since been undertaken (the study by Robles et al., noted earlier, used a revised version of the MICS to examine links between marital conflict and stress hormones).

When behavior is coded at the micro-level, the interaction is generally divided into discrete units based on either time or events (e.g., 15-second units or the talk turn). Hence researchers can assess the types of behavior occurring, the frequency and/or duration of behaviors, and even the sequence in which behaviors occur. Important properties of coding systems include their reliability (both inter-rater and intra-rater) and their validity (the extent to which the codes reflect the interaction processes of interest).

One problem with using outside coders lies in ensuring that the coding reflects some kind of culturally shared meaning. Some researchers have tried to address this problem by using a "cultural informants" approach, which assumes that people learn the meaning and labeling of social behaviors through socialization processes (Smith, Vivian, & O'Leary, 1990). Coders and raters using this approach are not necessarily trained experts; they are asked to base their decisions on all available cues (verbal and nonverbal channels, and the context). The observers should be demographically similar to the participants, because the approach assumes that there is a common set of culturally determined rules that are applied in, for example, couple interaction. Researchers using the cultural informants approach have often relied on outsiders making global ratings, such as those utilized in the Conflict Rating System (e.g., Christensen & Heavey, 1990) to assess demanding and withdrawing behaviors.

Coding or Rating by Family Members

Where family members themselves are used as informants, a number of different strategies can be employed. Noller et al. (1994) had newlywed couples watch their videotaped conflict interaction, and describe the strategies they had used to try to influence the course of the interaction. Participants' descriptions were coded into six categories: reason, assertion, partner support, coercion, manipulation and avoidance, which were related to levels of marital satisfaction. In later re-analyses of these data, Feeney (2003) showed that scores on these strategies were also related to the attachment security of both self and spouse.

Ruzzene and Noller (1991) had partners review the videotape of their conflict interaction and make global ratings of their own and their partner's effect. Spouses also selected the three partner behaviors that had the most impact on their own feelings during the interaction, and rated the impact of these significant events. In addition, they made judgments about the partner's intention in performing that behavior; this perceived intention could be compared with the individual's self-reported intention. In a similar vein, Guthrie and Noller (1988) asked couples to identify the "emotional moments" in their interaction, and coded these for the occurrence of particular nonverbal behaviors.

These studies allowed the researchers to document patterns of interaction, and to assess their links with variables such as gender and relationship satisfaction.

Frequency Versus Sequence

Frequency data indicate whether one type of family member uses a particular behavior more or less often than others do. However, to capture the complexity of couple interaction, it may also be important to understand the sequencing of partners' behavior—that is, how an action by partner A affects partner B, how B consequently acts, how B's actions then affect A, and so on (Gottman, Markman, & Notarius, 1977; Margolin, 1988). For example, subtle differences in the communication patterns of couples in violent, compared with nonviolent relationships, may emerge only when behaviors or emotions are analyzed in terms of sequencing, rather than overall frequency. Time-series analysis can be used to investigate these issues. This method involves assessing the strength of the association between one stream of behavior (e.g., continuous assessment of heart rate) and another stream of behavior (e.g., coding of actual behavior or emotional expression).

L. J. Roberts and Krokoff (1990) used time-series analysis, and continuous ratings by trained observers, to study the conflict interactions of married couples. Their focus was on patterns of hostility and withdrawal; specifically, whether wives became hostile in response to husbands' withdrawal, or husbands' withdrawal was a response to wives' hostility. Sequential analyses have also shown the destructive effects of negative reciprocity, in which one partner's expression of displeasure follows the other partner's expression of displeasure at a rate greater than expected by chance (L. J. Roberts, 2006). As we shall see in a later section, Noller and N. D. Roberts (2002) used time-series analysis to explore the links among arousal, effect, and behavior in couples.

Focusing on Content

Sometimes, researchers are more interested in the content of the interaction, or what the family members say, than in the interaction process. In this case, researchers generally use some method of content analysis, and a qualitative approach. Many methods can be used, including asking fairly global questions about the content of the interaction, or using content analysis packages such as NUDIST or ETHNOGRAPH, which focus on patterns of word usage.

Noller, Feeney and Blakeley-Smith (2001) studied the attributions couples made about changes in their relationships. Couples were asked to discuss the three major relational "contradictions" (autonomy versus connectedness, openness versus closedness, and novelty versus predictability) highlighted by Baxter (e.g., Baxter & Simon, 1993), with a focus on describing change in those areas of their relationship. Trained coders studied the transcripts of the conversations for answers to specific questions, such as: Did the couple report change over time in that area of their relationship? What was the nature of that change? To what factors did they attribute that change? By analyzing the content of the conversations, the researchers examined how the couples experienced relational changes, and how these changes were shaped by individual, dyadic, and situational factors. Similarly, in research by Feeney and Fitzgerald (2012), the content of couples' discussions pointed to individual, dyadic, and situational factors that impacted on attempts to resolve hurtful events.

Summary of Observational Methodologies

Observational data can be used in various ways to increase our understanding of inter-action processes in couples and families. Researchers can focus on the frequency of behaviors, or the sequence in which they occur. Either the content of the interaction or the process (or both) may be of interest. The interaction can be coded or rated, either by family members or by trained coders. In addition, ratings may be either global (summarizing the entire interaction) or made at regular intervals.

Experimental Studies

In discussing research into family processes, Cummings (1995) argued that "the experimental method can make significant contributions toward explaining the bases for associations between variables, the direction of effects, and the causal relations" (p. 175). He noted that researchers have found many associations between family factors and child development, but that patterns of cause and effect need clarification. For example, marital conflict may cause children to "act out," but children's acting out behavior may also create conflict between the parents. Cummings also noted that experiments offer the advantage of assessing immediate responses in specific contexts. However, experimental methods may need to be adapted, given the sensitive nature of family problems and associated ethical issues. For example, it would be inappropriate to try to elicit violent behavior in the laboratory. Experimental studies of family communication include analog studies of marital conflict, studies of responses to hypothetical situations, and studies using the standard content methodology.

Analog Studies

Analog studies try to simulate, under controlled conditions, a situation analogous to real life. Cummings and colleagues (e.g., Cummings, Simpson, & Wilson, 1993; Cummings & Davies, 1994) were interested in children's responses to conflict between adults. They prepared videotapes that allowed them to manipulate dimensions of conflict, while avoiding the ethical issues involved in exposing children to real-life conflicts. This series of studies explored how children's reactions to inter-adult conflict are affected by such variables as parents' history of physical aggressiveness, whether the conflict is resolved or not, and whether the children have behavior problems or not. For example, El-Sheikh, Cummings, and Reiter (1996) found that children were much more negative about adults who consistently failed to resolve conflicts than about those who succeeded in resolving them.

In another application of the analog method, Noller, Atkin, Feeney, and Peterson (2006) created audiotapes of marital conflict involving four conflict styles: mutual negotia-tion, coercion, mother-demand/father withdraw, and father-demand/mother withdraw. These tapes were played to family groups consisting of mother, father and an adolescent son or daughter. For half the tapes, the conflict was child-related; for the other half, the conflict involved only the couple. Responses to the different scenarios provided inter-esting insights into marital conflict in families with adolescents. For example, family members saw mutual conflicts much more positively than other types of conflict, and mother-demand as more typical than father-demand. Further, adolescents' responses to the scenarios depended on whether conflict was child-related or not.

Responses to Hypothetical Situations

Some communication scholars ask participants to imagine themselves in particular social situations (usually described in written form), and to describe their responses to those situations. An example of an experimental study using this approach is that of Beach and colleagues (Beach, Tesser, Fincham, Johnson, & Whitaker, 1998), who asked couples to describe situations involving competition or comparison with their partner. According to the self-evaluation maintenance model, reactions to such situations depend on relative performance (whether one outperforms or is outperformed), the closeness of the other, and the relevance of the particular activity to one's self-definition. These predictions have generally been supported (e.g., Beach et al., 1998; Noller, Conway, & Blakeley-Smith, 2008).

Other researchers have used experiments involving hypothetical situations to assess the effects of adult attachment style on perceptions of relationship partners and the emotional climate of relationships. In these studies (see Mikulincer & Shaver, 2007, for a review), respondents imagine themselves in a relationship with a hypothetical partner whose attachment characteristics are manipulated by the researchers. This method also allows researchers to evaluate how participants' own attachment characteristics influence their responses to targets with different attachment styles.

Studies Using the Standard Content Methodology

Noller (1980b, 1984, 2001) used the standard content methodology, based on the work of Kahn (1970), to compare distressed and nondistressed couples in terms of their accuracy at understanding one another's nonverbal communication. Standard content methodology is ideal for this purpose, because participants use the same words to create messages with different meanings. Specifically, they are asked to create negative, neutral and positive messages, by changing the nonverbal behavior accompanying the words; their partners are then asked to "decode" the messages (that is, to say whether they are perceived to be negative, neutral or positive in tone). The validity of this methodology was supported by a laboratory study showing that much couple communication is characterized by neutral words, with the emotional tenor of the messages being conveyed by nonverbal behavior (Noller, 2001).

Summary of Experimental Methods

Experiments are not widely used in family research, but are useful for elucidating patterns of association between family communication, and variables such as family functioning and child adjustment. Relevant methods include analog studies, descriptions of hypothetical situations, and tasks involving the standard content methodology.

Studies Combining Observational and Experimental Methods

Some researchers have combined observational and experimental methods by manipulating the circumstances in which an interaction takes place, and observing the effects of manipulated variables (e.g., information about the purpose of the interaction, or instructions about how to relate to infants). For example, Stack and Arnold (1998) asked mothers to change their touch and hand gestures, and recorded the infant's responses to these changes. Similarly, Meltzoff and Moore (1979) conducted studies in which they instructed mothers to behave in particular ways, and assessed the ability of young infants to imitate their mother's behavior.

Following the work of Raush and colleagues (1974), Feeney (1998) used relationship partners as confederates, instructing one member of the couple to act distant and the other to try to reconcile. The verbal and nonverbal behaviors of participants in each of the roles were then coded, and related to dimensions of attachment security. The effects of attachment security were stronger in these interactions than in a comparison condition, in which partners were primed to experience conflict over a less threatening topic (use of shared leisure time).

In a study involving parents and their sons, Jouriles and Farris (1992) manipulated the interactions of parents by having them engage in either conflictual or nonconflictual marital interactions. The researchers examined the effects of these interactions on parents' subsequent interactions with their sons. They showed that even this relatively brief and mild manipulation affected the interactions of these nonclinical families, although fortunately (given ethical considerations), the effects dissipated over time.

Summary of Research Combining Experimental and Observational Methods

Some researchers combine observational and experimental methods, by manipulating instructions or procedures and observing the behavior elicited. Sometimes a member of the dyad or family group is used as a confederate and asked to behave in a particular way, so that researchers can study the impact of changes in behavior. This type of research may be particularly useful for studying behaviors that are unlikely to occur unsolicited in less structured interactions.

Multiple Methods and Sources

In discussing observational methodologies, we have already noted that researchers may combine insider and outsider data, and observational and experimental methods. In addition, there are other examples of family communication research using two or more approaches to data collection.

Advantages of Combining Methods

Multi-method research is increasingly popular: Nothing lends more credence to a research finding than demonstrating that the same results were found across samples and methodologies, particularly when the methodologies provide different types of information from different sources. As noted earlier, Christensen and colleagues have obtained both self-report and observational data on demand–withdraw communication; findings are generally similar across methods. For example, Noller and Christensen (see Feeney, Noller, Sheehan, & Peterson, 1999) coded the actual nonverbal behavior of couples, and related the frequency of particular behaviors to couples' ratings of demanding and withdrawing. More recently, Caughlin and Ramey (2005) conducted a comprehensive analysis of demand–withdraw in parent–adolescent dyads, using multiple measures: Demand–withdraw behavior during family members' laboratory-based discussion of conflict topics was rated by outsiders and insiders (both parent and adolescent), and insiders also provided retrospective reports of demand–withdraw over a longer (two-month) period.

Extending work on the distinction between insider and outsider data, Noller and Guthrie (1991) related this distinction to different types of data as explicated by Huston and Robins (1982). These researchers showed how the different types of data of interest to family communication researchers (subjective conditions, subjective events and interpersonal events) can be assessed using both insider and outsider data (see Table 2.1).

Noller and Roberts (2002) used multiple methods to assess conflict interaction, emotional experience, and emotional expression in couples. This study will be discussed in some detail, to highlight the advantages of the multi-method approach. Experience of emotion was assessed using self-report ratings and physiological measures; expression of emotion was assessed using outsiders' coding of behavior. Specifically, couples engaged in conflict interactions and provided continuous ratings of their subjective experience of anxiety, at the same time that their physiology was monitored. They also made global ratings of their emotional reactions using hand-held dials. After the session, trained experts coded videotapes of the interactions for behavior and affective displays. Table 2.2 shows how the various assessments used in this study fit into the categories discussed earlier; of the six categories, only outsider data on subjective conditions (which would involve outsiders rating global aspects of the relationship) were not obtained.

In this study, the researchers explored the conflict interactions using time-series analysis, relating participants' experience of anxiety to their own and their partners' behaviors (coded by outsiders). As noted earlier, examining sequence may be crucial when

Table 2.1 Integrative Framework for Describing Types of Data about Communication

Source of information	Types of information		
	Subjective conditions	Subjective events	Interpersonal events
Insider	Self reports of attitudes to, and beliefs about, the relationship	Reports of feelings, intentions etc., of self and partner	Self-reports of behavior using video, diaries etc.
Outsider	Global judgments of relationship properties (e.g., satisfaction)	Ratings and judgments of feelings, intentions, etc.	Coding of behavior by trained coders or observers

Source: Noller and Guthrie (1991)

Table 2.2 Application of integrative framework to study of couple violence

Source of information	Type of information		
	Subjective conditions	Subjective events	Interpersonal events
Insider	Self-report questionnaire measuring relationship satisfaction	Ratings of effect during interaction using hand-held dials	Reports of presence or absence of violence in the relationship
Outsider	(No measure of subjective conditions by outsiders)	Physiological responding using physiograph; ratings of affective displays by coders	Ratings of behavior by trained coders using the Couple Communication Scales

Source: Noller and Roberts (2002)

studying the conflict interactions of couples in violent relationships. These couples show greater temporal connection of behavior than those in nonviolent relationships, particularly reciprocation of negativity (e.g., Burman, Margolin, & John, 1993), suggesting that partners in violent relationships are more sensitive or reactive to each other's negative actions. Specifically, Noller and N. D. Roberts (2002) explored the effects of violence on the links between:

a   an individual's anxiety/arousal and the partner's subsequent anxiety/arousal;
b   an individual's behavior and the partner's subsequent anxiety/arousal;
c   an individual's anxiety/arousal and his or her own subsequent behavior
d   an individual's behavior and the partner's subsequent behavior.

The findings were further strengthened by using multiple measures of the extent to which one time-series could be predicted from another. For example, three measures of the extent to which females' anxiety/arousal could be predicted from the male partner's anxiety/arousal were initially created, one each for interbeat interval, skin conductance level, and self-reported anxiety. Likewise, three measures of the extent to which males' anxiety/arousal could be predicted from the female partner's anxiety/arousal were created. For each gender, the three measures of the predictability of anxiety/arousal were averaged to form an "emotional linkage" score. Thus, this final variable reflects emotional linkage between partners, as measured by a combination of self-reported anxiety and physiological arousal. Of course, combining measures in this way is only meaningful when physiological and self-report data show similar patterns of association with other variables. When such convergence exists, researchers can be confident in the reliability of summary measures and the robustness of their findings.

Multiple methods continue to be used in creative ways. For example, Verhofstadt, Buysse, Ickes, de Clercq, and Peene (2005) randomly assigned couples to a conflict condition (discussion of a marital problem) or a support condition (discussion of a personal problem). Coding by trained observers indicated that the support condition was characterized by less blame and invalidation, and by more facilitation behavior (e.g., assent). Withdrawal levels, however, were similar in both conditions. As well as using experimentation and observation, this study used questionnaires to assess on-line cognitions; in this way, the researchers assessed whether particular behaviors, as rated by outsiders, were more likely than others to have an impact on partners' on-line cognitions.

Developments in Analyzing Data from Multiple Sources

Interaction between partners is the very essence of close relationships. Hence, as we have noted, the study of family communication often involves interaction being described by two or more family members, and perhaps by outsiders as well. Because such data sets involve an event or target being described by more than one person (or more than one method), they violate the statistical assumption of independence of observations, and require special analytic techniques (Gonzalez & Griffin, 2000).

Although a comprehensive discussion of these techniques cannot be offered here, one development increasingly applied to couple data is worth noting; namely, the actor–partner interdependence model (APIM). As Kashy and Kenny (2000) discussed, relationship researchers often deal with "mixed" independent variables, such as marital intimacy; that is, variables for which variation exists both within the dyad and between dyads. For these variables, APIM analyses can be used to separate out the *actor effect* (e.g., the effect of partner A's intimacy on A's score on the outcome variable), and the *partner effect* (the effect of partner A's intimacy on B's score on the outcome variable).

A recent application of this technique is a study by Karantzas, Feeney, McCabe and Goncalves (unpublished manuscript). This study examined the role of attachment insecurity (anxiety and avoidance) and trust as predictors of conflict-centered communication. Attachment insecurity had pervasive *actor effects*, with anxiety and avoidance predicting low levels of trust for both men and women; in turn, lack of trust predicted destructive conflict-centered communication for both genders. In terms of *partner effects*, attachment anxiety was associated with partners' reports of destructive conflict-centered communication, but not with partner's trust.

These findings raise interesting questions. For example, why is attachment anxiety detrimental to the individual's (actor's) trust and to the partner's perception of communication, but not to the partner's trust? The findings probably reflect the strategies associated with attachment insecurity. For example, individuals high in attachment anxiety tend to be very dependent; they seek constant reassurance of partners' love, and monitor their behavior for signs of disaffection. Although this wary and distrustful relational style tends to be frustrating for the partner, it signals that the anxious individual values the relationship and wants it to continue; hence, distrust is unlikely to be one of the problems associated with partnering an anxious individual. More generally, this type of statistical model may clarify the ways in which relationship attitudes and behaviors impact on the individual's versus the partner's experience of interaction, and identify critical variables that shape communication patterns.

Summary and Conclusions

Research employing multiple measures can be used effectively to study the complex phenomenon that is family communication. While some excellent research has been conducted, more work is needed that combines insider and outsider data, and takes full advantage of the diverse methods available. Using multiple approaches to data collection can help offset the shortcomings of any given method, and achieve a better understanding of family communication.

References

Bartholomew, K., & Horowitz, L. M. (1991). Attachment styles among young adults: A test of a four-category model. *Journal of Personality and Social Psychology, 61*, 226–44.

Baxter, L. A., & Simon, E. P. (1993). Relationship maintenance strategies and dialectical contradiction in personal relationships. *Journal of Social and Personal Relationships, 10*, 225–42.

Beach, S. R. H., Tesser, A., Fincham, F. D., Johnson, D. J., & Whitaker, D. J. (1998). Pleasure and pain in doing well together; an investigation of performance-related affect in close relationships. *Journal of Personality and Social Psychology, 74*, 923–38.

Burman, B., Margolin, G., & John, R. S. (1993). America's angriest home videos: Behavioral contingencies observed in home re-enactments of marital conflict. *Journal of Consulting and Clinical Psychology, 61*, 28–39.

Caughlin, J. P., & Ramey, M. E. (2005). The demand/withdraw pattern of communication in parent-adolescent dyads. *Personal Relationships, 12*, 337–55.

Christensen, A. (1988). Dysfunctional interaction patterns in couples. In P. Noller, & M. A. Fitzpatrick (Eds.) *Perspectives on marital interaction* (pp. 31–52). Philadelphia, PA: Multilingual Matters.

Christensen, A., & Heavey, C. L. (1990). Gender and social structure in the demand/withdraw pattern of marital conflict. *Journal of Personality and Social Psychology, 59*, 73–81.

Christensen, A., & Sullaway, M. (1984). *Communication Patterns Questionnaire*. Available from A. Christensen, Department of Psychology, UCLA, Los Angeles, CA.

Cummings, E. M. (1995). Usefulness of experiments for the study of the family. *Journal of Family Psychology*, 9, 175–85.

Cummings, E. M., & Davies, P. T. (1994). *Children and marital conflict: The impact of family dispute and resolution*. New York: Guilford.

Cummings, E. M., Simpson, K. S., & Wilson, A. (1993). Children's responses to interadult anger as a function of information about resolution. *Developmental Psychology*, 29, 978–85.

El-Sheikh, M., Cummings, E. M., & Reiter, S. (1996). Preschoolers' responses to ongoing interadult conflict: The role of exposure to resolved versus unresolved arguments. *Journal of Abnormal Child Psychology*, 24, 665–79.

Feeney, J. A. (1998). Adult attachment and relationship-centred anxiety: Responses to physical and emotional distancing. In W. S. Rholes & J. A. Simpson (Eds.), *Attachment theory and close relationships* (pp. 189–218). New York: Guilford.

——(2003). The systemic nature of couple relationships: An attachment perspective. In P. Erdman & T. Caffery (Eds.), *Attachment and family systems: Conceptual, empirical and therapeutic relatedness* (pp. 139–63). New York: Brunner/Mazel.

Feeney, J. A., & Fitzgerald, J. R. (2012). Using emotion-focused relationship education to facilitate apology, forgiveness and relationship security following hurtful events. In P. Noller & G. Karantzas (Eds.), *Couples and family relationships: A guide to contemporary research, theory, practice and policy* (pp. 289–304). Chichester: Wiley-Blackwell.

Feeney, J. A., Noller, P., Sheehan, G., & Peterson, C. (1999). Conflict issues and conflict strategies as contexts for nonverbal behavior in close relationships. In P. Phillipot, R. S. Feldman, & E. J. Coats (Eds.), *The social context of nonverbal behavior* (pp. 348–71). Cambridge: Cambridge University Press.

Feeney, J. A., Passmore, N. L., & Peterson, C. C. (2007). Adoption, attachment and relationship concerns: A study of adult adoptees. *Personal Relationships*, 14, 129–47.

Gonzalez, R., & Griffin, D. (2000). On the statistics of interdependence: Treating dyadic data with respect. In W. Ickes & S. Duck (Eds.), *The social psychology of personal relationships* (pp. 181–213). Chichester: Wiley & Sons.

Gottman, J. M., Markman, H., & Notarius, C. I. (1977). The topography of marital conflict: A sequential analysis of verbal and nonverbal behavior. *Journal of Marriage and the Family*, 39, 461–77.

Gottman, J. M., Notarius, C. I., & Markman, H. (1976). *Couples' Interaction Scoring System (CISS)*. Department of Psychology, Champaign, IL.

Guthrie, D. M., & Noller, P. (1988). Spouses' perceptions of one another in emotional situations. In P. Noller, & M. A. Fitzpatrick (Eds.), *Perspectives on marital interaction* (pp. 153–81). Philadelphia, PA: Multilingual Matters.

Heavey, C. L., Christensen, A., & Malamuth, N. M. (1995). The longitudinal impact of demand and withdrawal during marital conflict. *Journal of Consulting and Clinical Psychology*, 63, 797–801.

Huston, T. L., & Robins, E. (1982). Conceptual and methodological issues in studying close relationships. *Journal of Marriage and the Family*, 44, 901–25.

Huston, T. L., & Vangelisti, A. (1991). Socioemotional behavior and satisfaction in marital relationships: A longitudinal study. *Journal of Personality and Social Psychology*, 61, 721–33.

Ickes, W. (2000). Methods of studying close relationships. In W. Ickes & S. Duck (Eds.), *The social psychology of personal relationships* (pp. 157–80). Chichester: Wiley & Sons.

Jouriles, E. N., & Farris, A. M. (1992). Effects of marital conflict on subsequent parent-son interactions. *Behavior Therapy*, 23, 355–74.

Kahn, M. (1970). Nonverbal communication and marital satisfaction. *Family Process*, 9, 449–56.

Karantzas, G. C., Feeney, J. A., McCabe, M., & Goncalves, C. V. (n.d.). Towards an integrative model of relationship functioning. Unpublished manuscript, Deakin University, Melbourne, Australia.

Kashy, D. A., & Kenny, D. A. (2000). The analysis of data from dyads and groups. In H. T. Reis & C. M. Judd (Eds.), *Handbook of research methods in social and personality psychology* (pp. 451–77). Cambridge: Cambridge University Press.

Kleiboer, A. M., Kuijer, R. G., Hox, J. J., Schreurs, K. M. G., & Bensing, J. M. (2006). Receiving and providing support in couples dealing with multiple sclerosis: A diary study using an equity perspective. *Personal Relationships*, 13, 485–501.

Krokoff, L. J., Gottman, J. M., & Hass, S. D. (1989). Validation of a Global Rapid Couples Interaction Scoring System. *Behavioral Assessment, 11*, 65–79.

Larson, R., & Richards, M. H. (1994). *Divergent realities: The emotional lives of mothers, fathers, and adolescents.* New York: Basic Books.

Main, M., Kaplan, N., & Cassidy, J. (1985). Security in infancy, childhood, and adulthood: A move to the level of representation. *Mongraphs of the Society for Research in Child Development, 50*, 66–104.

Margolin, G. (1988). Marital conflict is not marital conflict is not marital conflict. In R. D. Peters, & R. J. McMahon (Eds.) *Social learning and systems approaches to marriage and the family* (pp. 193–216). New York: Brunner/Mazel.

Meltzoff, A. N., & Moore, K. M. (1979). Imitation of facial and manual gestures by human neonates: Resolving the debate about early imitation. In D. Muir & A. Slater (Eds.) *Infant development; Essential readings in developmental psychology.* Malden, MA: Blackwell.

Metts, S., Sprecher, S., & Cupach, W. R. (1991). Retrospective self-reports. In B. M. Montgomery & S. Duck (Eds), *Studying interpersonal interaction* (pp. 162–78). New York: Guilford.

Mikulincer, M., & Shaver, P. R. (2007). *Attachment in adulthood: Structure, dynamics, and change.* New York: Guilford.

Noller, P. (1980a). Cross-gender effect in two-child families. *Developmental Psychology, 16*, 159–60.

——(1980b). Misunderstandings in marital communication: A study of couples' nonverbal communication. *Journal of Personality and Social Psychology, 39*, 1135–48.

——(1984). *Nonverbal communication and marital interaction.* Oxford; Pergamon.

——(2001). Using standard content methodology to assess nonverbal sensitivity in dyads. In J. A. Hall & F. Bernieri (Eds.) *Interpersonal sensitivity: Theory and measurement* (pp. 243–64). Mahwah, NJ: Lawrence Erlbaum Associates.

Noller, P., & Bagi, S. (1985). Parent-adolescent communication. *Journal of Adolescence, 8*, 125–44.

Noller, P., Atkin, S., Feeney, J. A., & Peterson, C. (2006). Family conflict and adolescents. In L. H. Turner, & R. West (Eds.) *The family communication sourcebook* (pp. 165–82). Thousand Oaks, CA: Sage.

Noller, P., Conway, S., & Blakeley-Smith, A. (2008). Sibling relationships in adolescent and young adult twin and nontwin siblings: Managing competition and comparison. In J. P. Forgas & J. Fitness (Eds.), *Social relationships: Cognitive, affective and motivational processes* (pp. 235–52). New York: Psychology Press.

Noller, P., & Feeney, J. A. (1998). Communication in early marriage: Responses to conflict, non-verbal accuracy and conversational patterns. In T. N. Bradbury (Ed.), *The developmental course of marital dysfunction* (pp. 11–43). Cambridge: Cambridge University Press.

Noller, P., Feeney, J. A., & Blakeley-Smith, A. (2001). Handling pressures for change in marriage: Making attributions for relational dialectics. In V. Manusov & J. H. Harvey (Eds.), *Attribution, communication behavior and close relationships* (pp. 153–72). Cambridge: Cambridge University Press.

Noller, P., Feeney, J. A., Bonnell, D., & Callan, V. J. (1994). A longitudinal study of conflict in early marriage. *Journal of Social and Personal Relationships, 11*, 233–52.

Noller, P., Feeney, J. A., Sheehan, G., Darlington, Y., & Rogers, C. (2008). Conflict in divorcing and continuously married families: A study of marital, parent–child and sibling relationships. *Journal of Divorce and Remarriage, 49*, 1–24.

Noller, P., & Guthrie, D. M. (1991). Methodological issues in studying communication in close relationships. In W. H. Jones & D. Perlman (Eds.), *Advances in personal relationships Vol. 3* (pp. 37–73). London: Jessica Kingsley.

Noller, P., & Roberts, N. D. (2002). The communication of couples in violent and nonviolent relationships: Temporal associations with own and partners' anxiety/arousal and behavior. In P. Noller & J. A. Feeney (Eds.), *Understanding marriage: Developments in the study of couple interaction* (pp. 348–78). Cambridge: Cambridge University Press.

Olson, D. H. (1977). Insiders' and outsiders' views of relationships: Research strategies. In G. Levinger & H. L. Raush (Eds.), *Close relationships: Perspectives on the meaning of intimacy* (pp. 115–35). Amherst, MA: University of Massachusetts Press.

Parker, G. (1983). *Parental overprotection: A risk factor in psychosocial development.* New York: Grune & Stratton.

Parker, G., Tupling, H., & Brown, L. B. (1979). A Parental Bonding Instrument. *British Journal of Medical Psychology, 52*, 1–10.

Peterson, C. (1990). Disagreement, negotiation and conflict resolution in families with adolescents. In P. Heaven & V. J. Callan (Eds.), *Adolescence: An Australian perspective.* Sydney: Harcourt, Brace, Jovanovich.

Rands, M., Levinger, G., & Mellinger, G. (1981). Patterns of conflict resolution and marital satisfaction. *Journal of Family Issues, 2*, 297–321.

Raush, H. L., Barry, W. A., Hertel, R. K., & Swain, M. E. (1974). *Communication and conflict in marriage.* San Francisco, CA: Jossey-Bass.

Roberts, L. J. (2000). Fire and ice in marital communication: Hostile and distancing behaviors as predictors of marital distress. *Journal of Marriage and the Family, 62*, 693–707.

——(2006). From bickering to battering: Destructive conflict processes in intimate relationships. In P. Noller & J. A. Feeney (Eds.), *Close relationships: Functions, forms and processes* (pp. 325–51). New York: Psychology Press.

Roberts, L. J., & Greenberg, D. R. (2002). Observational "windows" to intimacy processes in marriage. In P. Noller & J. A. Feeney (Eds.), *Understanding marriage: Developments in the study of couple interaction* (pp. 118–49). Cambridge: Cambridge University Press.

Roberts, L. J., & Krokoff, L. J. (1990). A time-series analysis of withdrawal, hostility and displeasure in satisfied and dissatisfied marriages. *Journal of Marriage and the Family, 52*, 95–105.

Robles, T. F., Shaffer, V. A., Malarkey, W. B., & Kiecolt-Glaser, J. K. (2006). Positive behaviors during marital conflict. *Journal of Social and Personal Relationships, 23*, 305–25.

Ruzzene, M., & Noller, P. (1991). Communication in marriage: The influence of affect and cognition. In F. D. Fincham & G. J. O. Fletcher (Eds.), *Cognition in close relationships* (pp. 203–33). Hillsdale, NJ: Lawrence Erlbaum Associates.

Schrodt, P., Baxter, L. A., Chad McBride, M., Braithwaite, D. O., & Fine, M. A. (2006). The divorce decree, communication, and the structuration of coparenting relationships in stepfamilies. *Journal of Social and Personal Relationships, 23*, 741–59.

Serewicz, M. C. M, & Canary, D. J. (2008). Assessments of disclosure from the in-laws: Links among disclosure topics, family privacy orientations, and relational quality. *Journal of Social and Personal Relationships, 25*, 333–57.

Sigelman, C. K., & Adams, R. M. (1990). Family interactions in public: parent–child distance and touching. *Journal of Nonverbal Behavior, 14*, 63–75.

Smith, D. A., Vivian, D., & O'Leary, K. D. (1990). Longitudinal prediction of marital discord from premarital expressions of affect. *Journal of Consulting and Clinical Psychology, 58*, 790–97.

Snyder, D. K. (1979). Multidimensional assessment of marital satisfaction. *Journal of Marriage and the Family, 41*, 813–23.

Stack, D. M., & Arnold, S. L. (1998). Changes in mothers' touch and hand gestures influence infant behavior during face-to-face exchanges. *Infant Behavior and Development, 21*, 451–68.

Straus, M. A. (1979) Measuring intrafamily conflict and violence: The conflict tactics (CT) scales. *Journal of Marriage and the Family, 41*, 75–88.

Szinovacz, M. E., & Egley, L. C. (1995). Comparing one-partner and couple data on sensitive marital behaviors: The case of marital violence. *Journal of Marriage and the Family, 57*, 995–1010.

Verhofstadt, L. L., Buysse, A., Ickes, W., de Clercq, A., & Peene, O. J. (2005). Conflict and support interactions in marriage: An analysis of couples' interactive behavior and on-line cognition. *Personal Relationships, 12*, 23–42.

Weiss, R. L., Hops, H., & Patterson, G. R. (1973). A framework for conceptualizing marital conflict, a technology for altering it, some data for evaluating it. In F. W. Clarke & L. A. Hamerlynck (Eds.), *Critical issues in research and practice. Proceedings of the Fourth Banff International Conference on Behavior Modification.* Champaign, IL: Research Press.

Wheeler, L., & Nezlek, J. (1977). Sex differences in social participation. *Journal of Personality and Social Psychology, 35*, 742–54.

Part II
Communication Across the Family Life Course

3

A Communication Perspective on Cohabitation and Contemporary Dating Relationships

Jennifer S. Priem and Catherine A. Surra

The rapid and pervasive rise in cohabitation, defined here as living with a nonmarital romantic partner, is the most substantial and influential change in contemporary dating relationships. Rates of cohabitation prior to marriage have increased from about 10 percent in the 1970s to almost 60 percent of unions formed in the mid 1990s (Bumpass & Lu, 2000). Moreover, only 12 percent of women marry in their early 20s without a prior cohabitation or nonmarital birth (Schoen, Landale, & Daniels, 2007).

Accompanying the dramatic increase in cohabitation has been a societal shift in the acceptance of cohabitation while dating. Most American young adults now view nonmarital cohabitation as acceptable (Axinn & Thornton, 2000). In fact, studies have shown that a majority of high-school seniors supported cohabitation prior to marriage (Thornton & Young-DeMarco, 2001) and that 57 percent of teens who expect to marry also plan to cohabit prior to marriage (Manning, Longmore, & Giordano, 2007). Approximately 66 percent of teenagers in one study thought that it was fine for partners to live together without being married (Flanigan, Huffman, & Smith, 2005). Taken together, current behavioral trends and perceptions in the U.S.A. suggest that cohabitation has unmistakably altered dating, marriage, and family formation and become a normative part of dating.

Given the prevalence and increased acceptance of cohabitation while dating, incorporating cohabitation into research on romantic and family relationships is crucial to understanding relationship development. The experience of cohabiting may influence the extent to which couples are able to build satisfying relationships, the trajectory of the relationship, and the outcomes associated with the relationship. To date, the majority of the research on cohabitation has been conducted by scholars in sociology, demography, and human development. The knowledge generated by this research has focused on descriptive findings about cohabitation patterns, trends, and differentials by subpopulations, such as ethnicity or social class. This information provides an important foundation for understanding cohabitation, but it leaves a gap in understanding how the experience of cohabitation influences relationship development. As Sassler (2004) stated, the absence of more extensive research on the cohabitation process "precludes the development of relationship models that might better predict union outcomes and relationship stability" (p. 502).

Communication scholars are uniquely qualified to fill the gaps in cohabitation research. As we will show, the success and progression of cohabiting relationships are highly dependent on communication processes. From making the decision to cohabit to navigating the transition to co-residence, communication is a crucial element of developing satisfying cohabiting relationships. The goals of this chapter are to highlight the importance of a communication perspective on cohabitation and suggest future avenues for research. To address our goals, we use findings from cohabitation research to draw conclusions about how cohabitation fits into relationship development. Next, we review theories that illustrate the ways in which the experience of living together may influence relationship development and quality. Then, we identify mechanisms that explain the positive and negative effects of cohabiting on relationship quality and discuss how examination of these mechanisms from a communication perspective provides unique insight into cohabitation processes. Finally, we highlight key issues to be addressed in future research on cohabitation while dating.

Understanding the Role of Cohabitation in Relationship Development

The experience of cohabitation is complex. Cohabiting couples vary in the timing of the transition to cohabitation, their reasons for deciding to live together, and how co-residence relates to conceptions of marriage and the future of the relationship.

One of the first questions to ask is: When does cohabitation occur in relationships? In a qualitative study, Sassler (2004) identified three groups of cohabitors that highlight the diversity in the timing of the transition to cohabitation. The first she called accelerated cohabitors, which constituted over half of her sample. These partners experienced a strong initial romantic attraction and moved in together within six months of dating. A second group was called tentative cohabitors, who dated seven to 12 months before moving in, had not previously lived with anyone, and were unsure whether cohabitation was right for them. The third group, purposeful delayers, dated from one to four years before sharing a residence, and had relationships that progressed slowly.

Previous research has also shown that people decide to cohabit for a variety of reasons, including testing the relationship, spending more time together, sharing financial responsibilities, and increasing convenience (Bumpass, Sweet, & Cherlin, 1991; Sassler, 2004). A study by Rhoades, Stanley, and Markman (2009) suggested that some reasons for living together may have implications for relational characteristics, such as commitment. For both cohabiting men and women, spending time together was associated with higher reports of relationship confidence and dedication. For women, but not men, living together for reasons of convenience was associated with lower reports of confidence and dedication. This preliminary research indicates that couples live together for a variety of reasons that may or may not reflect their feelings about the relationship.

The literature on cohabitation also suggests that cohabitation is not always a response to marriage plans. Nor does cohabitation always lead to marriage. The number of couples who marry without cohabiting first has continued to decline. Data from 1965 to 1974 indicated that about 10 percent of marriages were preceded by cohabitation whereas data collected between 1997 and 2001 showed that 62 percent of married individuals lived with their partner prior to marriage (Bumpass & Sweet, 1989; Kennedy & Bumpass, 2008). Although the general trend is that people who marry tend to cohabit prior to marriage, research has also shown that not all cohabitors marry. Brown and Booth (1996) reported that while as many as 75 percent of cohabitors reported plans to marry their dating partners, only about half of them actually wed. Data from the National Survey of Family Growth has shown that the proportion of individuals that marry their cohabiting partner decreased from 60 percent in 1987 to 53 percent in 1995. The proportion of cohabitors that separated within five years, regardless of whether the couple married or not, increased from 45 percent in 1987 to 54 percent in 1995 (Bumpass & Lu, 2000). Furthermore, individuals in recent cohorts of cohabitors are less likely than those in past cohorts to marry their partners, even if a pregnancy occurs (Bumpass & Lu, 2000).

Taken together, the descriptive findings about cohabitation highlight the diversity of the cohabitation experience and allow us to draw conclusions about how cohabitation fits into relationship development. More specifically, previous research suggests that cohabitation is a fluid and evolving part of dating relationships, which takes different forms and performs different functions. We expand upon each of these conclusions in the following sections.

Cohabitation as an Evolving Process

One of the most important conclusions drawn from recent cohabitation research is that, rather being an endpoint of relationship development (as it was thought to be when cohabitation was considered a substitute for marriage), for many cohabitation is a midpoint of relationship development. Sassler (2004), for example, concluded that quantitative studies have overestimated plans to marry among cohabitors, and argued that commitment continues to grow during cohabitation for many partners. Consequently, cohabitation might be best thought of as an evolving process in which daters' movement into and out of full-time, shared residential cohabitation is likely to be fluid and change as the relationship becomes more or less involved. Thus, the way cohabitation fits into the progression of dating relationships is complex, varying across couples, occurring at different stages in the relationship, and evolving in nature throughout a relationship.

In a study of noncohabiting and cohabiting daters, Priem and Surra (2011) found evidence suggesting that cohabitation while dating may be a developmental progression that parallels depth of involvement and increases in commitment to wed. These researchers examined various degrees of cohabitation while dating, including noncohabiting, quasi-cohabiting (individuals who reported living together, but maintaining separate residences), and full-time cohabiting. Results showed that increased degrees of cohabitation were associated with greater levels of involvement. Whereas most of the noncohabitors were in casual or serious dating relationships, the majority of quasi-cohabitors was seriously dating or privately committed to wed. This finding suggests that the transition from noncohabiting to part-time cohabitation may be prompted by an increase in stage of involvement from casual to serious dating. As partners become more involved, they begin to cohabit to a greater degree. Thus, cohabitation in dating relationships may be the cause or effect of increasing feelings of closeness and commitment in the relationship.

Priem and Surra (2011) also found that the degree of cohabitation was associated with differences in reports of commitment to wed. On average, noncohabitors reported a 54 percent chance of marrying their dating partners in the future; quasi-cohabitors, 65 percent; and cohabitors, 78 percent. For all three cohabitation statuses, initial chance of marriage was less when the stage of involvement was lower (e.g., casual, serious, privately committed to wed, or formally engaged). These findings further reinforce the idea that cohabitation, in this sample, evolved with growing commitment to the relationship. The results also indicate that cohabitation has the ability to influence the development of commitment to marry. To the extent that cohabitors are not certain that they will marry their partners, the experience of living together has the potential to either increase or decrease commitment to wed. Overall, the findings suggest that cohabitation may form a developmental progression that often maps well onto the development of the relationship itself.

Forms and Functions of Cohabitation While Dating

Another conclusion that can be drawn from current research is that cohabitation has different forms and functions. Form refers to the type of relationship and function refers to the tasks that the relationship performs or the provisions provided by the relationship. Two major forms of cohabitation while dating can be distinguished by the relative certainty of marriage. Each form is associated with unique functions that elucidate the various ways in which cohabitation and relationship development are interrelated.

One prominent form of cohabitation while dating is cohabitation as a prelude to marriage. In this case, cohabitation occurs when partners are seriously committed to one another or engaged formally. According to Casper and Bianchi (2002), cohabitation as a precursor to marriage was characteristic of cohabitors who have definite plans to marry and a low probability of relationship dissolution. For these individuals, cohabitation functions as an advanced stage of involvement with well-established commitment.

Another prominent form is that of cohabitation as dating. In this case, cohabitations appear to be more dating-like, in the sense that they occur earlier in the relationship and prior to the solidification of marriage or future plans. The characteristics of cohabiting relationships, in general, provide evidence that many cohabitations are entered into as part of the dating process. Like many dating relationships, cohabitating relationships tend to be rather short-lived with most ending in either termination or marriage within a few years. About 50 percent of cohabitations last a year or less and only about 10 percent last five years or more (Lichter & Qian, 2008). Moreover, the rate of dissolution of cohabitations formed by age 24 is about 52 percent (Schoen et al., 2007). For these individuals, cohabitation may serve a mate-selection function through which individuals enjoy the companionship and convenience of living together while still evaluating the suitability of their match.

Although these two forms do not encompass all cohabiting relationships, the majority of cohabiting relationships occur either as part of the mate selection process or as a prelude to marriage, rather than a substitute or alternative to marriage. Research has shown that cohabitation functions as a substitute or alternative to marriage for only about 10 percent of cohabitors (Casper & Bianchi, 2002), and they do so particularly for individuals of lower socioeconomic status (Seltzer, 2000), African Americans (Oppenheimer, 2003), and older cohabitors (King & Scott, 2005).

The different forms and functions of cohabitation have the ability to affect how relationships develops and may differentially affect or reflect relationship characteristics such as satisfaction, commitment, and relationship quality and outcomes. This is especially true for individuals who cohabit prior to the solidification of commitment. In the next section, we draw on empirical evidence and theory to understand some of the ways in which cohabitation while dating, compared to dating without cohabiting, may alter relationship development.

How Cohabitation May Influence Relationship Quality

Historically, one of the most studied topics in the cohabitation literature is how it influences relationship and marital quality. Research has focused on how cohabitation prior to marriage, compared to marriage without prior cohabitation, is associated with lower relationship quality. For example, cohabitation prior to marriage has been consistently associated with negative marital outcomes, such as lower marital quality (Kamp Dush, Cohan, & Amato, 2003), higher levels of instability (Booth & Johnson, 1988), and higher rates of marital separation and divorce (Bennett, Blanc, & Bloom, 1988). The association between premarital cohabitation and poorer marital outcomes has been termed, "the cohabitation effect."

One explanation for the cohabitation effect is that there are processes that occur during cohabitation that facilitate more negative relationship characteristics. Research has focused on the negative consequences of cohabitation; however, two relationship theories highlight the potential effects of cohabiting on couples' relationship quality: theories of commitment and interdependence.

Cohabitation and Commitment

The concept of inertia, based on commitment theories, provides an explanation for why cohabitation prior to the solidification of commitment may negatively influence later relationship quality (Stanley, Rhoades, & Markman, 2006). Stanley et al. argued that partners who live together before making a mutual decision to marry are at greater risk for marital distress because the additional constraints accrued during cohabitation promote relationship continuance regardless of dedication to the relationship. Once in a cohabiting relationship, daters engage in activities, such as sharing a lease, buying household items together, or owning a pet, that noncohabiting daters are less likely to experience. In turn, these activities increase constraints to ending the relationship regardless of cohabitors' level of personal dedication. Such cohabitors are vulnerable to the inertia effect, in which couples who would not have married end up married partly because the constraints of co-residence made leaving the relationship more difficult. Because in these cases the transition to marriage is based on constraint commitment, rather than personal dedication to the relationship, couples are more prone to later marital instability.

Consistent with this perspective, Kline et al. (2004) reported that, compared to those who cohabited after being engaged, individuals who cohabited prior to being engaged had more negative interactions and lower relationship commitment, quality, and confidence. The authors argued that the results are evidence that individuals who live together before they are engaged, a step in relationships that requires explicit commitment to the relationship, are at greater risk for negative outcomes later in their relationship.

While the theory of inertia suggests that constraints may force partners' into commitments in the absence of dedication, other data suggest that happiness, conflict, and other measures indicative of dedication to the relationship are factors that cohabiting partners weigh when deciding to wed or end the relationship. Brown (2000) found that cohabitors' transition to marriage was predicted by relationship happiness. Furthermore, negative relationship assessments, including low happiness, interaction, and conflict resolution and high disagreements, prompted cohabiting women to leave the relationship and cohabiting men to refrain from marriage. The results suggest that relationship progression from cohabitation to marriage is a function of individuals' satisfaction with the relationship, one component of dedication commitment, rather than simply due to constraints.

Cohabitation and Interdependence

Interdependence theory provides an alternative explanation for how cohabitation may positively or negatively impact commitment and relationship quality. Interdependence between partners results from the behavioral interconnections that they weave between them (Kelley et al., 1983). More diverse, frequent, and strong interconnections are associated with greater interdependence and a closer relationship. Living together while dating, compared to dating without cohabiting, undoubtedly enhances partners' interdependence. The mere fact of sharing a residence engenders greater socio-emotional and instrumental interconnections, thereby increasing both the frequency and diversity of interconnections. Sharing a residence means that partners are in closer proximity than they would be otherwise, and opportunities for coordinating and exchanging joint behaviors are increased. As a result, one partner's behavior is likely to have greater impact on the other, increasing the strength of interconnections. The greater interdependence provides opportunities for couples to get to know each other, and creates a need to coordinate routines in ways that are mutually beneficial if the relationship is to succeed.

While the experience of living together is apt to facilitate increased interdependence, the effect on relational quality is unpredictable. On the one hand, greater interdependence may increase commitment and relational quality as partners discover their compatibilities and each derives rewards from their enhanced interconnectedness. On the other hand, cohabiting may highlight incompatibilities that individuals were previously unaware of, leading to decreased commitment and relational quality.

Examples from Surra's unpublished data from a study of commitment in dating couples illustrate the ways in which the ability to adapt to the new living arrangements influence individuals' perceptions of relationship quality. In Surra's sample, cohabitation was mentioned as a reason for both increases and decreases in the chance of marriage to a partner. Some participants discussed how learning to live with their partners increased the chance of marriage because they realized they successfully live together. One participant stated:

> Moving in together was what caused it [the chance of marriage] to go up. The joint responsibilities of maintaining a place together and doing shopping together and all that kind of stuff, that goes along with, a person living. It was just kind of very worldly type stuff that we did together and did together fairly well.

Another woman discussed how living together increased the chance of marriage because it allowed the partners to get to know each other and reinforced the couple's compatibility:

> We moved in together, and he found out that I can't cook or clean, and he's still there, and we've almost killed each other a number of times, but we always work it out. I was very concerned that I would never be able to live with anybody, but, we found out that we are compatible, as far as living together goes, more than we thought, and, that we're both OK with it.

In other cases, the decision decreased the chance of marriage significantly because the inability to adapt to the new living situation was a sign that partners could not or should not get married in the future. One participant stated:

> In the five months we lived together, to me it was extremely apparent that I was more willing to adapt to his style of life than he was to adapt to my style. I began to

feel very put upon, almost as if I were a maid instead of a partner, and so at that point my feelings of having a marriage with him decreased.

Thus, while cohabitation is apt to have a strong impact on interdependence, its impact on relational quality is likely to depend on a host of other considerations beyond the fact of cohabitation itself. Given that cohabitation occurs at various levels of commitment in dating relationships and the theoretical claims that it has the potential to alter characteristics of the relationship, the question then becomes, how does cohabitation influence relationship development and quality? For example, how can cohabitors foster greater dedication commitment and reduce the potentially harmful effects of inertia? What strategies can cohabitors use to effectively manage the transition to co-residence and building interdependence? Answering these questions requires an understanding of the mechanisms and processes through which commitment, and relationship quality more generally, is built. In the next section, we use cohabitation research to identify key mechanisms through which the experience of cohabiting may influence relationship quality. We then take a communication perspective to explicate crucial insights into the effects of cohabitation on adaptive relationship development.

A Communication Perspective on Cohabitation and Relationship Quality

As of yet, communication scholars have remained silent in the discussions of cohabitation; however, it is communication scholars who are uniquely positioned to provide a micro-level examination of the processes and mechanisms that shape the cohabitation experience. In this section, we identify three factors that may substantially influence the successful development of cohabiting relationships: the process through which individuals decide to cohabit; the societal ambiguity surrounding the institution of cohabitation; and adaptation to living together. We then show the ways in which communication research may fill gaps in our current understanding of the cohabitation experience and identify key objectives for future research.

Sliding Versus Deciding and the Importance of Communication in the Decision-Making Process

According to cohabitation research, one mechanism through which living with a dating partner may exert influence on relationship quality is through a lack of discussion about the decision to cohabit. A budding line of research has begun to examine how the process of deciding to live together might influence relationship development. Cohabitation research from the 1970s (e.g., Macklin, 1978), illustrated that the transition to cohabitation is a "gradual, often unconscious, escalation of emotional and physical involvement" (p. 6). More recent descriptions focus on the degree to which the decision was "deliberate and purposeful" (Manning & Smock, 2005, p. 990). In a qualitative study about how to measure cohabitation, Manning and Smock reported that when asked how they started to live together, approximately 53 percent of participants did not describe the decision as planned. Instead, these participants described a slide into cohabitation that occurred slowly over time, without specific discussions about the implications. Participants stated, "It just happened," or "It just snuck up on me." Manning and Smock concluded that cohabitation is a state into which individuals slide rather than thoughtfully decide. Based on this research, Stanley et al. (2006) coined the term "sliding versus deciding" to describe the gradual progression into cohabitation. The assumption that arose from this line of research is that couples who "slid" into cohabitation moved in together without discussing or thinking about what the transition meant, whereas those who "decided" made the transition after discussing the new arrangement.

Although not yet empirically tested, the theory offers a variety of ways in which the decision-making process may influence relationship development and quality. Stanley et al. (2006) proposed that sliding into cohabitation without fully considering the implications of the decision increases individuals' risk for later distress due to inertia. From this perspective, discussing what the transition to co-residence means to each person and for the future of the relationship is a crucial component in the success of cohabiting relationships.

Communication research provides insight into how the decision-making process may influence the relationship quality and future outcomes of cohabitors. As currently conceptualized, sliding inherently involves a lack of communication. To the extent that individuals are deliberately avoiding discussion about the transition to co-residence, previous research on topic avoidance, or the strategic decision not to disclose information, may shed light on the detrimental effects of sliding. Research has shown that individuals avoid certain topics, such as the state of the relationship, relational rules, and negative self-disclosures, because they are considered taboo (Baxter & Wilmot, 1985) or because they are trying to protect the self or the relationship (Afifi & Guerrero, 2000). Daters may choose not to discuss the decision to cohabit for fear that the discussion will negatively impact the relationship, or out of a desire to maintain the status quo and avoid disclosing information that is face threatening. Living together may be particularly difficult to discuss because it requires a change in the status of the relationship, something that may be threatening when involvement is ambiguous, fluid, or unknown. Even in an established or committed relationship, cohabitation implies movement to a new level and it may be safer to avoid discussion of what that movement entails. Topic avoidance may reinforce relational uncertainty, leading to decreased feelings of liking, intimacy and closeness, and increased susceptibility to the negative outcomes associated with relational uncertainty.

In contrast to sliding, deciding is thought to involve active discussion of what living together means. As such, deciding requires disclosure of feelings, which may enhance intimacy and satisfaction with the relationship (Altman & Taylor, 1973). Engaging in a conversation about cohabiting may serve to define the relationship because talk serves to "project an image of the relationship as real and enduring, thereby promoting its continuance" (Sillars & Vangelisti, 2006, p. 335). Deliberations about the transition to co-residence have the potential to alter partners' perception of the relationship and their behavior toward each other. Relationship talk, including conversations about the transition to co-residence, can serve to maintain or change the relationship between individuals by influencing people's definition of the relationship and clarifying how committed or attached partners are (Baxter, 1987); however, it can also cause greater uncertainty and stress. In the context of cohabitation, conversations about moving in together may affirm the meaning of the relationship and assist in the construction of a unique relationship identity that facilitates relationship growth. Alternatively, partners may discover that their definitions of the relationship differ significantly, leading to distress and possibly dissolution.

One of the issues that future research must address to understand fully how sliding versus deciding influences the development of cohabiting relationships is how partners can manage the discussion about living together and what communication strategies are most effective in those interactions. Before pursuing this line of research, however, the first step for scholars will be to strengthen the conceptual definition of sliding versus deciding. Because sliding is a relatively new insight, the construct lacks a clear definition. First, the necessity of communication is unclear in current conceptualizations of sliding. For example, is sliding the gradual progression that cohabitors describe, starting with spending a lot of time together, to sleeping over more and more, and finally moving into a single residence; or is sliding solely a function of the lack of discussion about the implications of moving in together? Defining sliding in terms of the degree to which it is deliberate and purposeful suggests that deciding may be a function of either the discussion of what the transition means *or* careful thought about what the transition means. Thus, it is possible that people "slide" into cohabitation without discussing the transition with their partner, but having fully thought through the implications of moving in together. Further distinguishing the characteristics of sliding versus deciding would allow researchers to examine what intra-personal thought processes individuals engage in, if deliberate thought is sufficient for positive future relationship outcomes, and what communication strategies are most effective.

Ambiguity and Relational Uncertainty in Cohabiting Unions

Another mechanism through which the experience of cohabiting may influence the adaptive development of dating relationships is based on the ambiguity of cohabiting unions and the resulting relational uncertainty cohabitors endure. An abundance of research has described cohabitation as an uninstitutionalized union in the U.S.A. (see Cherlin, 2004). Compared to marriage, which is governed by consensual norms and formal laws, and dating, which has progressive relational scripts that provide clarity about the path a couple is on (Whitehead, 2002), cohabitation remains an incomplete institution (Nock, 1995). Due to the lack of institutionalization, cohabitation represents an ambiguous state that is devoid of socially accepted expectations and clear norms for what the transition means about commitment, especially for those who cohabit prior to engagement. Cohabitors are even unclear about what label to apply to their partner, presumably because of the lack of a language to describe the state of cohabiting relationships (Manning & Smock, 2005).

The ambiguity of some forms of cohabitation makes uncertainty reduction theory a relevant framework for understanding how cohabitation may influence adaptive and maladaptive relationship development. In ongoing relationships, transitions into cohabitation may influence people's relational uncertainty, which is the degree of confidence people have in their perceptions of involvement in a relationship (for review see Knobloch & Solomon, 1999). Uncertainty reduction theory posits that uncertainty is a subjective, aversive state that stems from individuals' awareness of ambiguity and an inability to predict and explain behavior (see Knobloch, 2008). The ambiguity surrounding the institution of cohabitation may lead to dyadic and individual relational uncertainty.

One study of college-aged cohabitors found that the majority of cohabitors do, in fact, experience relational uncertainty that stems from a number of sources. When asked to describe issues of relational uncertainty experienced in their cohabiting relationships, 93 percent of the 180 cohabitors sampled reported at least one relational uncertainty (Steuber & Priem, 2011). The sources of relational uncertainty documented ranged from relational sustainability and compatibility to doubts about finances, family planning, and communication. A substantial number of cohabitors referenced questions about relational norms and relational steps, which included doubts about whether participants or their partners were ready for marriage or if the relationship would progress toward marriage. Cohabitors also expressed doubts about expectations for financial responsibilities, housework, and how much time the couple should spend together.

Scholars have argued that the ambiguity surrounding the transition to cohabitation and the subsequent relational uncertainty may undermine mutual clarity about the nature of the relationship, which may, in turn, inhibit the development of a stable and committed union (Stanley et al., 2006). Communication research on relational uncertainty highlights the ways in which ambiguity and relational uncertainty in cohabiting relationships may deter adaptive relationship development in multiple ways. First, relational uncertainty enhances negative reactivity and hinders message processing. Relational uncertainty is associated with more intense experiences of negative emotions, including anger, sadness, fear, and hurt (Knobloch & Solomon, 2002, 2003). Furthermore, individuals' who experienced relational uncertainty reported more jealousy, which is associated with reduced intimacy in the relationship (Theiss & Solomon, 2008).

In addition, individuals who are unsure about their relationship lack well-defined expectations for behavior, which makes message processing more difficult. For example, relational uncertainty is associated with a decreased ability to interpret cues of intimacy and liking during interactions (Knobloch & Solomon, 2005), and may make people more critical of the messages they receive from a dating partner (Knobloch, Miller, Bond, & Mannone, 2007). Consistent with this claim, Priem and Solomon (2011a) found that individuals who reported greater partner uncertainty experienced slower recovery in the stress hormone cortisol after a supportive interaction with a dating partner, suggesting that relational uncertainty reduces the ability to capitalize on the potential stress reducing benefit of supportive messages.

Such research suggests that cohabitation prior to establishing commitment may be problematic for adaptive relationship development. The inherent ambiguity may be a catalyst for relational uncertainty, which may undermine relationship quality by enhancing negative reactions to relationship events and undercutting message processing. To the extent that relational uncertainty is a key factor in understanding the development of, and outcomes associated with, cohabitation, a crucial question for scholars to address in future research is how cohabitors manage uncertainty in ways that facilitate positive relationship development. According to uncertainty reduction theory, people seek information to reduce uncertainty, which should, in turn, enhance intimacy, liking, and similarity between partners (Berger & Calabrese, 1975). Thus, a promising line of research may be in the examination of information seeking and strategies that effectively reduce relational uncertainty.

Adapting to Co-residence and Overcoming Relational Turbulence

As discussed earlier, cohabitation is a relationship transition that requires individuals to adapt to changing levels of interdependence. Thus, partners' ability to negotiate the increasing levels of interference that stem from cohabitation may be another key mechanism for understanding how living together exerts negative or positive effects on relationship quality.

The relational turbulence model (RTM) provides a potentially advantageous framework for understanding how partners might navigate the demands of increased interdependence. According to RTM, transitions create a need to adapt to the changing interdependence, or mutually beneficial systems of behavior, in order to sustain the relationship. As couples negotiate interdependence, attempts to coordinate action sequences inevitably lead to interference, or cases where a partner's involvement makes achieving goals more difficult. The increased interference leads to relational turbulence, which is associated with intensified subjectivity wherein individuals tend to be more cognitively, emotionally, and behaviorally reactive to relationship events (for full review see Solomon & Knobloch, 2004).

One study of the RTM and perceptions of emotional support provides insight into the ways in which interference and relational turbulence may have both positive and negative effects on relationship outcomes. Priem and Solomon (2011b) found that interference was associated with both more positive and more negative perceptions of a dating partner's supportiveness. Participants who reported greater interference from their partner reported greater relational turbulence, which in turn, predicted more positive evaluations of a partner's supportive messages. Interference, however, was also directly associated with more negative evaluations of a partner's supportiveness. These results suggest that there is something unique about the ways in which a partner's hindering the accomplishment of daily tasks influences perception. On the one hand, a partner's interference causes people to feel that their relationship is stressful, which polarizes their reactions to relationship events making positive situations more positive and negative situations more negative. In the context of supportive messages, then, interference positively impacts perception. On the other hand, the direct effect of interference on perceptions of supportiveness indicates that things going on in the relationship also negatively influence how subsequent supportive interactions are perceived.

An implication of this line of research for cohabitors is that couples who are able to renegotiate interdependence and work through the turbulence associated with the transition to co-residence may reap the benefit of a stronger relationship in the future. As daters begin living together, they experience increased interference and relational turbulence that alters their perception of relationship events in negative and positive ways. Consistent with previous research, interference may make cohabitors more reactive to negative events, such as perceiving irritations as more severe and relationally threatening (Solomon & Knobloch, 2004), which over time may erode the quality of the relationship. In contrast, the ability to work through the changes affirms partners' ability to work together to solve life's problems and provide mutual support, thereby reducing uncertainty and reinforcing commitment to the relationship. As cohabitation becomes more normative, future research should identify ineffective strategies for dealing with interference that are associated with decreased relationship quality and examine how couples can manage the transition to cohabitation in a way that bolsters positive relationship development.

A Note on Methods for Studying Cohabitation

In the previous sections, we illustrated ways that the study of interpersonal communication would enhance understanding of cohabitation. In this section, we provide guidance to communication researchers who venture into the study of cohabitation.

Addressing Measurement Issues Cohabitation Research

One of the most important methodological issues is how to measure cohabitation. The perspective of cohabitation as a status, rather than a process, has created a body of research that utilizes a binary response question to measure cohabitation. For example, one of the major national surveys, the National Survey of Family Growth (NSFG) used the question, "Have you ever lived with someone whom you did not later marry?" to measure cohabitation status. Binary questions, such as this one, are problematic because they over simplify the cohabitation process and overlook the fact that for many, cohabitation develops gradually over time.

Given the diversity in the cohabitation experience, scholars have begun to acknowledge that broader definitions of cohabitation should be used to understand its role in relationship development (Knab & McLanahan, 2007; Manning & Smock, 2005). Previous research provides insight into ways in which researchers may effectively measure cohabitation. Quotations in Manning and Smock's (2005) article show that participants had a difficult time identifying when they started to cohabit, but could distinguish between when the partner moved in full-time versus when the partner stayed over every night. This suggests that even though cohabitation often occurs gradually and, therefore, lacks a clear start, the transition from part-time cohabitation to full-time cohabitation in a shared residence is meaningful. Thus, maintaining separate residences or living in a shared residence is a distinguishing feature for cohabitors that can be used when measuring cohabitation.

Other research has endorsed the use of subjective and behavioral measures to capture more fully the cohabitation experience (see Knab & McLanahan, 2007). The Fragile Families survey, for example, includes a more objective question, "How many nights per week do you spend the night together?" and a more subjective categorical question, "Are you and—living together?" with options being "all/most of the time," "some of the time," "rarely," or "never."

Priem and Surra (2011) also used a method of measuring cohabitation while dating that provides greater nuance. Participants were asked to choose one of five categorical options provided that best described the status of their relationship. From that data, the authors created three groups: noncohabitors, quasi-cohabitors, and cohabitors. Individuals who reported they were dating and living in separate residences were labeled as *noncohabitors*. The term *quasi-cohabitor* was used for participants who reported either "living together 3–4 nights, but keeping separate residences," or "living together every night, but keeping separate residences." *Cohabitors* included individuals who reported "living together with both partners' possessions in one residence." This method of measuring cohabitation retains the assumption that a central distinguishing factor in cohabitation is the sharing of a residence, and makes a distinction between those living together part of the time and not at all.

Embracing Repeated Measurement and Diversity in Sampling to Study Cohabitation

As noted previously, most research on cohabitation has come from large-scale surveys with national representative samples. Commenting on the limited set of methods used to study cohabitation, Stanley et al. (2006) lamented "the fact that a vast number of studies published on the cohabitation effect are from a single, now aging data set (the National Survey of Families and Households)" and the "general dearth of longitudinal methods with sufficient sensitivity and quality of measurement" (pp. 499–500). While communication scholars have much to offer the study of cohabitation theoretically, the methods used to study it will be demanding. The study of cohabitation and its role in relationship development is best achieved by means of repeated measurement of diverse samples of cohabiting individuals at different levels of involvement. As we have demonstrated, cohabitation is a fluid state, something that typically develops gradually and that individuals enter in steps, with occasional falls backwards, before living together full-time in one residence. Because of the fluid nature of cohabitation and its uncertain place in relationship development, studies are needed in which frequent, repeated measurements are taken to match assessments of quality against changes in cohabitation or the evolution of decisions to begin or end cohabitations.

Likewise, sampling will be challenging in the study of cohabitation. One advantage of large national surveys is that they make it possible to tease out the diverse forms and functions of cohabitation in different subpopulations. Such surveys have consistently shown that cohabitation varies greatly by race, immigrant status, social class, and other variables (for a review see Greenland & Smock, in press). Yet the large majority of research on dating relies almost exclusively on college-student samples or samples in which the characteristics of the partners are not described (Surra et al., 2007). In the context of cohabitation, reliance on a college-student sample is less desirable because the effects associated with cohabitation are known to vary by demographic characteristics. In order to study cohabitation, communication scholars will need to use samples more broadly selected from the community-at-large.

Evolving as a Key for Future Research

As noted previously, American views and their practice of cohabitation have changed drastically. As cohabitation becomes more institutionalized, norms surrounding it will develop, and the associations between cohabitation and relationship outcomes will change. These changes will require that scholars' thinking about, and research on, cohabitation also evolve.

One way that research on cohabitation can evolve is by acknowledging the changing nature of cohabitation and building from previous research and theory in new cohorts and samples. Research surrounding the cohabitation effect highlights the need for testing old assumptions with new data. Although it seemed as though the negative effects of cohabitation on marriage were undeniable in early research on cohabitation, the rapid changes in cohabitation has led scholars to question the relevance of the cohabitation effect in contemporary relationships. Smock (2000) stated that newer findings provide, "strong indications that cohabitation is changing," and that "the inverse relationship between premarital cohabitation and marital stability is diminishing. The effect, if any, is trivial for recent birth cohorts" (p. 13), For example, Teachman (2003) found that for women, cohabiting with their future spouse is not associated with a higher risk of marital dissolution. Schoen (1992) found that the negative association between cohabitation and marital stability largely disappears as cohabitation becomes increasingly common.

Regardless of whether or n͏͏ ͏ ͏͏͏ cohabitation effect is weakening in more recent cohorts (a fact that remains highly debated), the shifts in findings underscore one of the most important points for future research. Trends in cohabitation continue to change. As cohabitation while dating reaches normative status, it will become more institutionalized. Researchers must continue to test old assumptions using new data to keep up with changing trends. This includes not only using new analysis techniques and sampling from a diverse range of groups, as discussed earlier, but also being aware of the assumptions that have been made in early research and testing the validity of old assumptions with more recent cohorts of cohabitors.

Conclusion

In this chapter, we argued that communication scholars need to incorporate the study of cohabitation into their research in order to shed light on the development of romantic relationships. We have drawn from research on cohabitation and communication to demonstrate the ways in which the two now separate bodies of work might be integrated to inform one another. For communication scholars cohabitation is rife with several fruitful avenues of research that are fundamental to the discipline. Potential areas of study include the role of communication in sliding into or deciding to cohabit, particularly how threatening discussions and the need to avoid them figure into cohabitation decisions. Another offshoot of cohabitation research is how partners who are living together renegotiate interdependence to work through the turbulence associated with the transition and the identification of effective strategies for dealing with relational ambiguity and interference from a partner. Research on these topics and others will inform scholars and lay persons alike on how couples can manage cohabitation in a way that bolsters positive relationship development.

References

Afifi, W. A., & Guerrero, L. K. (2000). Motivations underlying topic avoidance in close relationships. In S. S. Petronio (Ed.), *Balancing the secrets of private disclosures* (pp. 165–80). Mahwah, NJ: Lawrence Erlbaum Associates.

Altman, I., & Taylor, D. (1973). *Social penetration: The development of interpersonal relationships.* New York: Holt, Rinehart & Winston.

Axinn, W. G., & Thornton, A. (2000). The transformation in the meaning of marriage. In L. J. Waite (Ed.), *The ties that bind: Perspectives on marriage and cohabitation* (pp. 147–65). New York: Aldine de Gruyter.

Baxter, L. A. (1987). Cognition and communication in the relationship process. In R. Barnett, R. McGhee, & D. Clarke (Eds.), *Accounting for relationships* (pp. 192–212). London: Methuen.

Baxter, L. A., & Wilmot, W. W. (1985) Taboo topics in close relationships. *Journal of Social and Personal Relationships, 2,* 253–69.

Bennett, N. G., Blanc, A. K., & Bloom, D. E. (1988). Commitment and the modern union: Assessing the link between premarital cohabitation and subsequent marital stability. *American Sociological Review, 53,* 127–38.

Berger, C. R., & Calabrese, R. J. (1975). Some explorations in initial interactions and beyond: Toward a developmental theory of interpersonal communication. *Human Communication Research, 1,* 99–112.

Booth, A., & Johnson, D. R. (1988). Premarital cohabitation and marital success. *Journal of Family Issues, 9,* 255–72.

Brown, S. L. (2000). Union transitions among cohabitors: The significance of relationship assessments and expectations. *Journal of Marriage and Family, 62,* 833–46.

Brown, S. L., & Booth, A. (1996). Cohabitation versus marriage: A comparison of relationship quality. *Journal of Marriage and Family, 58,* 668–78.

Bumpass, L. L., & Lu, H. (2000). Trends in cohabitation and implications for children's family contexts in the United States. *Population Studies, 54,* 29–41.

Bumpass, L. L., & Sweet, J. A. (1989). National estimates of cohabitation. *Demography, 26,* 615–25.

Bumpass, L. L., Sweet, J. A., & Cherlin, A. J. (1991). The role of cohabitation in declining rates of marriage. *Journal of Marriage and the Family, 53,* 913–27.

Casper, L. M., & Bianchi, S. M. (2002). *Continuity and change in the American family.* Thousand Oaks, CA: Sage.

Cherlin, A. J. (2004). The deinstitutionalization of American marriage. *Journal of Marriage and Family, 66,* 848–61.

Flanigan, C., Huffman, R., & Smith, J. (2005). Teens' attitudes toward marriage, cohabitation, and divorce, 2002. Science Says. Washington, DC: National Campaign to Prevent Teen Pregnancy.

Greenland, F. R., & Smock, P. J. (in press). Living together unmarried: What do we know about cohabiting families? In G. Peterson & K. Bush (Eds.), *Handbook on marriage and family*, 3rd edn. New York: Springer.

Kamp Dush, C. M., Cohan, C. L., & Amato, P. R. (2003). The relationship between cohabitation and marital quality and stability: Change across cohorts? *Journal of Marriage and Family*, 65, 539–49.

Kelley, H. H., Berscheid, E., Christensen, A., Harvey, J. H., Huston, T. L, Levinger, G., et al. (1983). *Close relationships*. New York: Freeman.

Kennedy, S., & Bumpass, L. (2008). Cohabitation and children's living arrangements: New estimates from the United States. *Demographic Research*, 19, 1663–92.

King, V., & Scott, M. (2005). A comparison of cohabiting relationships among older and younger adults. *Journal of Marriage and Family*, 67, 271–85.

Kline, G. H., Stanley, S. M., Markman, H. J., Olmos-Gallo, P. A., St. Peters, M., Whitton, S. W., et al. (2004). Timing is everything: Pre-engagement cohabitation and increased risk for poor marital outcomes. *Journal of Family Psychology*, 18, 311–18.

Knab, J. T., & McLanahan, S. (2007). Measuring cohabitation: Does how, when, and who you ask matter? In S. L. Hofferth & L. M. Casper (Eds.), *Handbook of measurement issues in family research* (pp. 19–34). Mahwah, NJ: Lawrence Erlbaum Associates.

Knobloch, L. K. (2008). The content of relational uncertainty within a marriage. *Journal of Social and Personal Relationships*, 25, 467–95.

Knobloch, L. K., Miller, L. E., Bond, B. J., & Mannone, S. E. (2007). Relational uncertainty and message processing in marriage. *Communication Monographs*, 74, 154–80.

Knobloch, L. K., & Solomon, D. H. (1999). Measuring the sources and content of relational uncertainty. *Communication Studies*, 50, 261–78.

——(2002). Intimacy and the magnitude and experience of episodic relational uncertainty within romantic relationships. *Personal Relationships*, 9, 457–78.

——(2003). Responses to changes in relational uncertainty within dating relationships: Emotions and communication strategies. *Communication Studies*, 54, 282–305.

——(2005). Relational uncertainty and relational information processing. Questions without answers? *Communication Research*, 32, 349–88.

Lichter, D. T., & Qian, C. (2008). Serial cohabitation and the marital life course. *Journal of Marriage and Family*, 70, 861–78.

Macklin, E. (1978). Nonmarital heterosexual cohabitation. *Marriage and Family Review*, 1, 3–12.

Manning, W. D., & Smock, P. J. (2005). Measuring and modeling cohabitation: New perspectives from qualitative data. *Journal of Marriage and Family*, 67, 989–1002.

Manning, W. D., Longmore, M. A., & Giordano, P. C. (2007). The changing institution of marriage: Adolescents expectations to cohabit and to marry. *Journal of Marriage and Family*, 69, 559–75.

Nock, S. L. (1995). A comparison of marriages and cohabiting relationships. *Journal of Family Issues*, 16, 53–76.

Oppenheimer, V. K. (2003). Cohabiting and marriage during young men's career development process. *Demography*, 40, 127–49.

Priem, J. S., & Solomon, D. H. (2011a). Relational uncertainty and cortisol responses to hurtful and supportive messages from a dating partner. *Personal Relationships, Special Issue: Mind-body Connections in Personal Relationships*, 18, 198–223.

——(2011b). Relational turbulence, perceptions of enacted support, and emotional improvement. Paper presented at the annual meeting of the National Communication Association, New Orleans, LA.

Priem, J. S., & Surra, C. A. (2011). Cohabitation, involvement and trajectories of commitment to wed. Paper presented at the annual meeting of the National Council on Family Relations, Minneapolis, MN.

Rhoades, G. K., Stanley, S. M., & Markman, H. J. (2009). Couples' reasons for cohabitation: Associations with individual well-being and relationship quality. *Journal of Family Issues*, 30, 233–58.

Sassler, S. (2004). The process of entering into cohabiting unions. *Journal of Marriage and Family*, 66, 491–505.

Schoen, R. (1992). First unions and the stability of first marriages. *Journal of Marriage and Family*, 54, 281–84.

Schoen, R., Landale, N. S., & Daniels, K. (2007). Family transitions in young adulthood. *Demography*, 44, 807–20.

Seltzer, J. A. (2000). Families formed outside of marriage. *Journal of Marriage and the Family*, 62, 1247–68.

Sillars, A. L., & Vangelisti, A. L. (2006). Communication: Basic properties and their relevance to relationship research. In A. L. Vangelisti & D. Perlman (Eds.), *Handbook of personal relationships* (pp. 332–51). Cambridge: Cambridge University Press.

Smock, P. J. (2000). Cohabitation in the United States: An appraisal of research themes, findings, and implications. *Annual Review of Sociology*, 26, 1–20.

Solomon, D. H., & Knobloch, L. K. (2004). A model of relational turbulence: The role of intimacy, relational uncertainty, and interference from partners in appraisals of irritations. *Journal of Social and Personal Relationships*, 21, 795–816.

Stanley, S. M., Rhoades, G. K., & Markman, H. J. (2006). Sliding vs. deciding: Inertia and the premarital cohabitation effect. *Family Relations*, 55, 499–509.

Steuber, K. R., & Priem, J. S. (2011). *Ambiguity in cohabiting partnerships: The content and similarity of partners' reports of relational uncertainty*. Paper presented at the annual meeting of the National Communication Association, New Orleans, LA.

Surra, C. A., Boettcher-Burke, T. M. J., Cottle, N. R., West, A. R., & Gray, C. R. (2007). The treatment of relationship status in research on dating and mate selection. *Journal of Marriage and Family*, 69, 207–21.

Teachman, J. (2003). Premarital sex, premarital cohabitation, and the risk of subsequent marital dissolution among women. *Journal of Marriage and Family*, 65, 444–55.

Theiss, J. A., & Solomon, D. H. (2008). Parsing the mechanisms that increase relational intimacy: The effects of uncertainty amount, open communication about uncertainty, and the reduction of uncertainty. *Human Communication Research*, 34, 625–54.

Thornton, A., & Young-DeMarco, L. (2001). Four decades of trends in attitudes toward family issues in the United States: The 1960s through the 1990s. *Journal of Marriage and Family*, 63, 1009–37.

Whitehead, B. D. (2002). *Why there are no good men left: The romantic plight of the new single woman*. New York: Broadway.

4

Marital Communication

Brian R. Baucom and Kathleen A. Eldridge

From the earliest days of behavioral research on romantic relationships, communication behavior has held a central place and served a defining role in the study of married couples. A tremendous amount of effort has been devoted to describing the ways that married couples interact and the implications of those interaction behaviors and patterns for individual and relational functioning. Historically, negative communication during conflict has received the lion's share of theoretical and empirical attention. There is growing recognition that a broad spectrum of negative and positive behaviors and a diversity of interaction contexts have important, unique, and interactive effects on marital functioning and stability. Recent efforts have focused on elucidating and empirically validating new models of adaptive communication patterns and refining our understanding of dysfunctional communication patterns. This chapter presents a theoretical framework for integrating the large body of work on marital communication, provides an integrative review of major research findings on communication behavior in marriage with particular emphasis placed on recent developments, and suggests directions for future research.

Theoretical Perspectives

Marital communication has been a central area of research in numerous disciplines for several decades. As a result of the widespread interest in, and diverse motivation for, studying marital communication, a large number of theories and models have been advanced to identify the most salient aspects of marital communication. Marital communication figures prominently in social exchange theory (Thibaut & Kelley, 1959), social learning theory (Skinner, 1938), family systems theories (e.g., Bowen, 1966; Minuchin, 1974), attachment theory (Bowlby, 1969), and the vulnerability-stress-adaptation model (Karney & Bradbury, 1995) to name but a few. Each of these theories identifies specific sets of intra- and interpersonal variables that give rise to different forms of communication and additionally specifies mechanisms by which communication affects relationship functioning. Despite this variability, they all agree that marital communication is one of, if not the, most important correlates of relationship satisfaction and stability. All of these theories have been used to make enormously valuable discoveries in, and contributions to, the field of marital communication. We attempt to provide a unifying framework for the large body of theoretical and empirical study of marital communication by adopting a trans-theoretical, functionalist perspective that organizes forms of marital communication in terms of their impact on relationship satisfaction and stability.

We organize marital communication into two broad categories: appetitive (i.e., rewarding) and aversive processes (i.e., punishing). In using the terms appetitive and aversive processes, we are referring to communication behaviors that distinguish satisfied couples from distressed couples with appetitive processes occurring at higher levels in satisfied couples and aversive processes occurring at higher levels in distressed couples. It is important to note that this organizational scheme is not meant to imply that distressed couples only engage in aversive processes nor that satisfied couples solely engage in appetitive processes. Rather, we are suggesting that, on balance, satisfied couples engage in relatively more appetitive processes than aversive processes and vice versa for distressed couples. Similar to social exchange theory's supposition that relationship satisfaction is largely determined by the ratio of rewards to costs in a relationship, low levels of aversive processes are assumed to be insufficient for marital satisfaction in and of themselves; they must co-occur with moderate to high levels of appetitive processes in order for marital satisfaction to be likely. Thus, this scheme is also consistent with Weiss and Heyman's (1997, p. 17) keen observation that "marital harmony is not just the absence of whatever it is that dissatisfied couples do."

This organizational system is a very close adaptation of Gable and Reis' (2001) two dimensional model of relationship processes. Gable and Reis (2001) propose that relationship processes can be classified by a two dimensional space defined by appetitive and aversive axes. Consistent with their model, we conceptualize appetitive and aversive processes as distinct and orthogonal processes rather than as extremes of a single bipolar scale of behavior (see Gable & Reis, 2001 for a review of distinct appetitive and aversive systems in numerous psychological domains). Indirect support for this view of appetitive and aversive processes comes from recent research which suggests that distressed and satisfied couples appear to be both quantitatively and qualitatively different from one another (Whisman, Beach, & Snyder, 2008), perhaps in part because they engage in different communication processes. The main distinction between the organizational scheme used in this chapter and Gable and Reis' two dimensional model is that whereas Gable and Reis consider a wide array of functional domains (including relationship outcomes as well as physical and mental health) for defining appetitive and aversive processes, we define forms of marital communication as appetitive or aversive solely based on their association with relationship satisfaction. In many cases, the two systems would result in the same classification; however, there are some instances when the two systems may disagree. For example, inhibiting the impulse to respond in kind when a partner has behaved in a hurtful manner (i.e., editing; Gottman, Notarius, Gonso, & Markman, 1976) is a form of behavioral accommodation associated with higher levels of relationship satisfaction. However, editing also involves suppression of negative emotional expression, which is associated with adverse physiological sequelae (Gross & Levenson, 1993; Butler, Egloff, Wilhelm, Smith, Erickson, & Gross, 2003). Though we do not mean to imply that the physiological consequences of suppression are not important, we weigh relationship outcomes more heavily and consider editing to be an appetitive process. In the next section, we use this scheme to review major appetitive and aversive communication behaviors linked to relationship satisfaction and highlight recent discoveries related to these communication behaviors.

Recent Findings in Marital Communication

In order to focus our review of empirical findings on communication behaviors associated with relationship satisfaction and stability, we chose to only discuss studies where the majority of participants were married couples, data on relationship satisfaction or stability was available, and couples had not received a couple-based intervention as part of their participation in the study.

Aversive Behaviors and Processes

General Negativity

A large number of specific negative communication behaviors have been linked to relationship distress and an increased risk for divorce during lab-based relationship problem discussions. This list includes, but is not limited to, high levels of defensiveness, stubbornness, negative emotions (such as anger, sadness, etc.), complaining, withdrawal, contempt, criticism, domineeringness, and belligerence (Carstensen, Gottman, & Levenson 1995; Gottman & Krokoff, 1989; Gottman & Levenson, 1992; Gottman, 1993). Aversive behavior in the lab also has been linked to aversive behavior at home. Gottman and Krokoff (1989) found higher levels of husbands' negativity at home to be associated with higher levels of lab-based husband negativity and higher levels of wife defensiveness and withdrawal, and higher levels of wives' negativity at home to be associated with lower levels of husbands' lab-based positivity. These findings demonstrate the importance of general negative behavior and suggest that negative behavior seen during lab-based studies is meaningfully similar to negative behavior at home.

Though there is support for behavioral consistency in home- and lab-based settings in general, behavioral variability across the two settings also appears to have important implications for couple functioning. Gottman and Driver (2005) found very little evidence for behavioral consistency of specific hostile and withdrawing responses to vulnerable disclosures during dinner time conversation and during lab-based conflict discussions. Rather, husband's hostile behavior during dinner predicted husband's withdrawing during conflict. In addition to showing that negative behavior varies within a couple depending on the setting and the type of interaction, the study authors suggest that these findings demonstrate the link between every day routine interactions and long-standing, unresolved couple conflict.

Negative Reciprocity

In an attempt to better understand why distressed couples engage in so many more negative behaviors than satisfied couples, researchers have sought to identify negative behavioral sequences characteristic of distressed couples. These efforts have largely focused on two cycles, negative reciprocity and the demand–withdraw interaction pattern (described in the next section). Negative reciprocity refers to a cycle of behavior where a negative communication from one spouse increases the likelihood of a subsequent negative behavior from the other spouse. In other words, negative reciprocity is a chain of negative communication between spouses that occurs not simply because both spouses are generally negative but rather because they are each responding to the other's negativity with negativity of their own. Negative reciprocity consistently distinguishes distressed couples from nondistressed couples, as well as couples who eventually divorce from couples who remain married over time across a variety of cultures including the U.S.A., England, and Germany (Filsinger & Toma, 1989; Gottman, et al., 1977; Hooley & Hahlweg, 1989) and across the developmental life span of young adult, middle-aged, and older adult couples (Carstensen, Gottman, & Levenson, 1995). These results have been replicated using laboratory-based conflict discussions (e.g., Hooley & Hahlweg, 1989) and daily diary methods (Margolin, 1981).

As is clear from the long list of negative behaviors in which distressed couples engage, there are many possible ways that distressed couples could engage in negative reciprocity. Gottman (1993) decomposed general negative reciprocity into three different forms: avoidant, hostile, and hostile–detached. Avoidant couples were characterized by lower levels of complaint, criticism, disgust, and contempt, higher levels of withdrawal, and less entrenched negative reciprocity relative to hostile and hostile–detached couples. Significantly lower levels of engaged listening behavior distinguished hostile–detached couples from hostile couples, and hostile–detached couples engaged in more contempt and displayed more disgust than did hostile couples. Both hostile–detached and hostile couples were significantly more likely to have considered divorced or to have divorced over the course of a year than were avoidant couples or couples who did not engage in significant levels of negative reciprocity. These findings demonstrate the value of decomposing broad categories of negative behaviors into meaningfully different subtypes since different forms of negative reciprocity are differentially associated with marital functioning.

Distressed couples not only engage in negative reciprocity during conflict but also during interactions where one spouse is seeking support from the other. Pasch, Bradbury, and Davila (1997) linked a greater tendency to engage in negative reciprocity during social support interactions to lower relationship satisfaction and found that when wives were seeking support from husbands, both husbands and wives were more likely to reciprocate negative behaviors when husbands were higher in negative affectivity (i.e., the dispositional tendency to experience and express negative emotion). Their findings make several unique contributions to the understanding of negative reciprocity. First, these findings generalize the link between negative reciprocity and relationship functioning by showing that there is a consistent association between the two variables in both conflictual and supportive interactions. Second, husband's negative affectivity predicted negative sequences initiated by both husbands and wives but only during interactions where wives were seeking support from husbands. As is also highlighted by the research on the demand–withdraw interaction pattern described below, variation in negative behavior appears to be particularly sensitive to which spouse has determined the topic being discussed.

Demand–Withdraw Interaction Pattern

The demand–withdraw interaction pattern is a specific form of negative reciprocity where one partner, the demander, nags, criticizes, or complains in an attempt to create change within the relationship while the other partner, the withdrawer, avoids, quickly terminates, or minimally participates during discussion of a requested change (Christensen, 1987). A large number of studies document that distressed couples engage in the demand–withdraw interaction pattern at higher levels than do nondistressed couples. This finding holds true for couples from a wide variety of cultures and countries of origin including Australia, Brazil, Germany, the Netherlands, Pakistan, Switzerland, Taiwan, and the U.S. and in studies using a variety of methodologies including self-report, observational, and daily diary measures of demand–withdraw behavior (see Eldridge & Baucom, in press for a review).

Husbands and wives tend to assume particular behavioral roles when engaging in the demand–withdraw interaction pattern. Wives tend to demand more than husbands, husbands withdraw more than wives, and wives tend to take on a demanding role and husbands tend to take on a withdrawing role during discussions of relationship change desired by wives (e.g., Vogel & Karney, 2003). Findings related to behavioral roles during discussions of husband desired changes are mixed. Some studies fail to find differences in husbands' and wives' tendencies to take on either demanding or withdrawing roles (e.g., Vogel & Karney, 2003) while other studies find husbands to be more likely to take on a demanding role and wives to be more likely to take on a withdrawing role (e.g., Klinetob & Smith, 1996). Regardless of when it occurs, the wife demand–husband withdraw pattern is more highly associated with concurrent relationship dissatisfaction than is the husband demand–wife withdraw pattern, although both are associated with decreased levels of satisfaction (e.g., Heavey et al., 1993).

Recent work has refined long-standing models of the individual, societal, and contextual variables relevant for demand–withdraw behavior. Individual difference models are based on differences in enduring characteristics between spouses. The *escape conditioning* model (Gottman & Levenson 1988) suggests that men are more likely to withdraw during conflict than women because men tend to experience higher levels of aversive arousal during interpersonal conflict than women.[1] Withdrawing is viewed as a means to reduce aversive arousal. Despite a consistent link between higher overall levels of demand–withdraw behavior and higher levels of aversive arousal for both spouses, there is currently little conclusive empirical support for the specific hypotheses of the escape conditioning model. The findings most supportive of the escape conditioning model come from Denton et al. (2001) who linked higher levels of withdrawing behavior to greater systolic blood pressure reactivity. In contrast, Baucom (2010) found demanders to exhibit higher levels of aversive arousal than withdrawers using a vocal measure of arousal. This collection of findings suggests that while it is clear that there is an association between demand–withdraw behavior and aversive arousal, the escape conditioning model may need to be modified to better account for the nature of the association. One possible modification comes from Baucom (2010), who suggests that the specific emotions associated with the aversive arousal are likely to be important. Arousal associated with approach oriented emotions like anger is likely to be associated with demanding, whereas arousal associated with avoidance oriented emotions like fear or anxiety is likely to be associated with withdrawing. Indirect support for this possibility comes from findings linking higher levels of withdrawing behavior to higher levels of anxiety (Heavey et al., 1993). Another individual difference model, the *gender role socialization* model (e.g., Sagrestano et al. 2006), suggests that women's tendency to demand may be a reflection of socialization experiences that encourage a relationship focus and relationship maintaining behaviors, whereas men's tendency to withdraw may be a reflection of socialization experiences that reward independence and autonomy. There is substantial empirical support for this model with numerous studies linking higher levels of desired closeness to higher levels of demanding behavior (e.g., Christensen, 1987).

The *social structure* model (Sagrestano et al. 2006) focuses on the impact of social and cultural factors, such as gendered norms for power, status, and acceptable behavior. In groups where men are given greater power and typically hold more high status positions than women, men are assumed to be able to use that greater power and status to structure marriage so that it is maximally beneficial for themselves even if that comes at the expense of their wives. Women are likely to make efforts to restructure a particularly imbalanced marriage (demands) so that it offers them more benefits, and men are likely to resist those efforts (withdraw) to maintain the status quo.

Rehman and Holtzworth-Munroe (2006) conducted an important test of the social structure model by examining demand–withdraw behavior in three groups of couples from cultures with varying levels of patriarchy, (White couples living in the U.S.A., immigrant Pakistani couples living in the U.S.A., and Pakistani couples living in Pakistan). White U.S. couples engaged in higher levels of wife demand–husband withdraw than both groups of Pakistani couples, and both Pakistani groups engaged in higher levels of husband demand–wife withdraw than White U.S. couples. An additional contribution of this study is that it examined two types of demands, unassertive and aggressive, and found cross-spouse patterns to vary depending on the level of patriarchy. Consistent with previous findings, American wives exhibited significantly more aggressive demands than their husbands but Pakistani couples engaged in the opposite pattern with husbands aggressively demanding more than their wives. Finally, when Pakistani wives did demand, they were significantly more likely to do so using unassertive demands than aggressive demands, while the converse was true for White U.S. wives. The study authors suggest that high levels of both structural patriarchy (differential access to education and employment) and ideological patriarchy (little flexibility in gendered expectations for marital roles) typical in Pakistani culture may result in a sense of resignation in Pakistani women that may be driving their tendency to demand less and to use less direct forms of demanding.

In contrast to the macrolevel focus of the social structural model, the *conflict structure* model (Heavey et al., 1993) focuses on immediate qualities of an interaction. One spouse (the requestor) seeking change that cannot occur without agreement from the other (the requestee) determines patterns of demand–withdraw behavior and establishes a structure where the requestor is more likely to demand in pursuing change while the requestee is more likely to withdraw in preventing change or preserving the status quo. Eldridge and colleagues (Eldridge, Sevier, Jones, Atkins, & Christensen, 2007) provided an important extension of the conflict structure model by examining demand–withdraw behavior during interactions where the target of change was the partner (during discussions of desired relationship change) and the self (during discussions of desired personal change). Across relationship change and personal change discussions, both spouses assumed a withdrawing role significantly more often when they were the target of change. These results not only strengthen support for the conflict structure model but also extend its generalizability to include conflictual discussions about relationship change as well as supportive interactions about self-change.

The recently proposed *multiple goals* model (Caughlin & Scott, 2010) builds on the conflict structure model by drawing a distinction between primary and secondary goals in interactions. Primary goals are the "what" of the interaction and refer to the task oriented objectives such as creating change or maintaining stability within the relationship, whereas secondary goals are the "how" of the interaction and refer to the style a spouse uses in pursuit of a desired primary goal. For example, a spouse's primary goal may be increased autonomy with a secondary goal of not appearing disinterested or invalidating. Importantly, the multiple goals model predicts that both spouses' primary and secondary goals will change minute to minute during interaction as well as over longer periods of time as a marriage develops and changes.

As with subtypes of negative reciprocity, recent research has identified subtypes of demanding behaviors that have different implications for relationship functioning. One example of this research is the Rehman and Holtzworth-Munroe (2006) study discussed earlier that found significant differences in wives' use of aggressive and unassertive demands in highly patriarchal cultures relative to wives in less patriarchal cultures. Another example is the work of Mitnick and colleagues (Mitnick, Heyman, Malik, & Smith Slep, 2009) who examined the impact of specific forms of change requests on the likelihood of a resistant response and on relationship satisfaction. When wives requested that husbands decrease a behavior, husbands requested that wives increase a behavior, or either spouse placed the burden of change solely on the other, the responding spouse was significantly more likely to withdraw than to indicate a willingness to continue discussing the issue. Conversely, when wives placed the burden of change on the couple, husbands were significantly less likely to withdraw in response. Finally, wives were more satisfied to the extent that they used more specific requests, and requests with the burden of change placed on the couple. Continuing this work by further identifying subtypes of demanding and withdrawing behavior is an important avenue for future research.

Appetitive Behaviors and Processes

General Positivity

Despite the theoretical importance given to appetitive behavior for relationship functioning, substantially less attention has been devoted to documenting and understanding the positive ways that married couples communicate. Though interest in positive communication behavior is exponentially increasing, additional investigation of appetitive communication processes remains a pressing need for future research. To date, it is well documented that satisfied couples and stably married couples show more affection, interest in their partners, positive emotion (such as joy), humor, and validation than distressed couples and couples who ultimately divorce (Carstensen, Gottman, & Levenson, 1995; Gottman & Levenson, 1992). In a logical extension of the work linking higher levels of these appetitive behaviors to increased marital satisfaction and stability, recent findings also demonstrate that declines in positive communication behavior over time are a significant risk factor for marital distress and divorce (Huston, Caughlin, Houts, Smith, & George, 2001; Markman, Rhoades, Stanley, Ragan, & Whitton, 2010).

Similar to the study of negative marital communication, much of what is known about positive marital communication is based on interactions recorded in laboratory settings. One exception to this general pattern is the work of Driver and Gottman (2004) who examined positive behaviors during a standard lab-based conflict resolution task and during a dinner time conversation. Couples that engaged in more humorous behavior during the laboratory conflict interaction also engaged in more playfulness and were more enthusiastic during dinner time conversations. Consistent with the findings of Gottman and Driver (2005), dinner time behavior more strongly predicted conflict behavior than vice versa. The study authors suggest that these findings demonstrate the importance of daily positive behaviors and highlight the need for additional research on the contribution of attempts to positively connect to long-term marital stability.

Age effects are one major area of active research on positive marital behavior. In general, findings are inconsistent across studies and there has yet to be a prospective study of marital communication in middle and older adulthood. Some studies find positive behaviors to occur at different rates and to be differentially related to relationship outcomes across the life span. For example, Carstensen, Gottman, and Levenson (1995) found older adult couples to engage in higher levels of affection than middle adult couples, and Pasupathi, Carstensen, Levenson, and Gottman (1999) found that higher levels of listener interest distinguished satisfied from unsatisfied couples only during middle age but not during older age. In contrast, other studies fail to find age differences in the levels of positive behaviors or differential effects of positive behavior on relationship functioning in young adult and older adult marriages (e.g., Schmidt, Kliegel, & Shapiro, 2007; Smith, Berg, Florsheim, Uchino, Pearce, Hawkins, Henry, Beveridge, Skinner, & Olsen-Cerny, 2009). Additional research on age effects on positive behavior and the implications of positive behaviors across the life span is needed given the divergence of existing findings. Prospective, longitudinal studies would be particularly valuable as they would allow for disentangling cohort and age effects.

Social Support Behavior

Another very active area of current scholarship on positive marital communication is social support behavior (e.g., Burleson & MacGeorge, 2002; Cutrona et al., 2005; Gaines, Williams, & Mickelson, Chapter 13 of this volume). The study of marital social support is a broad, interdisciplinary endeavor that encompasses numerous aspects of support including cognition (support schema/perceptions), internal and external resources (supportive relationships/networks), and behavior (supportive transactions; Pierce, Sarason, Sarason, Joseph, & Henderson, 1996). In keeping with the focus of this chapter, we restrict our discussion to the impact of social support behavior, defined as "specific communicative behavior enacted by one party with the intent of benefitting or helping another" (Burleson & MacGeorge, 2002, p. 386), on relationship functioning.

Determining the qualities and characteristics of effective support behavior has been one major area of focus in research on the effects of social support on marital outcomes. One key difference between the study of social support and the study of general positive marital communication is that social support behavior is studied most often within the context of an external or an individual stressor, such as a medical illness, rather than within the context of a relationship stressor. Because of the wide diversity of stressors that spouses could experience, there are numerous reasons for seeking support and many different kinds of support that can be given in response. The optimal matching model (Cutrona & Russell, 1990) served as the conceptual basis for many early studies that sought to understand the interaction of stress characteristics and support provision. This model proposes that received support will be most effective when it matches the demands of the stressor and that the controllability of the stressor is one factor that determines what kind of support is most effective. Action-facilitating support encourages problem-focused coping and should be most effective with controllable stressors, whereas nurturant support encourages emotion focused coping and should be most effective with uncontrollable stressors.

Within the optimal matching model, there are two categories of action-facilitating support (informational and instrumental) and three categories of nurturant support (emotional, esteem, and network support). A recent investigation of the factor structure of social support behavior provided mixed support for these five proposed categories of behavior. Four factors (emotional, informational, tangible, and physical support) emerged for men and women, and these factors were stable over time (Barry, Bunde,

Brock, & Lawrence, 2009). These results provide strong empirical support for differentiating types of marital support behavior but also suggest the need to revise the specific categories of support to include physical support.

Further important refinements of the optimal matching model incorporate the concept of sensitive support provision. Sensitive support provision refers to the ability of one spouse to provide the kind and amount of support desired by the other spouse independent of the characteristics of the stressor. Consistent with this notion, spouses rate one another to be more sensitive when their partner provides them with the kind of support they desire, are more satisfied when they receive the kind of support they desire, and perceived spousal sensitivity mediates the association between matched desired support/support provision and relationship satisfaction (Cutrona, Shaffer, Wesner, & Gardner, 2007). Social desirability does not explain these associations, so it is not the case that more agreeable individuals perceive their spouses as being more sensitive and are also more satisfied with their marriages (Dehle, Larsen, & Landers, 2001). Additionally, spousal sensitivity explains unique variance in marital satisfaction not accounted for by the overall amount of social support behavior (Lawrence, Bunde, Barry, Brock, Sullivan, et al., 2008). Finally, some forms of insensitive support provision are more detrimental to relationship satisfaction than others. Higher levels of over- and underprovision of support are both uniquely associated with lower levels of relationship satisfaction, but the magnitude of these effects were stronger for overprovision than underprovision of support (Brock & Lawrence, 2009).

While it is clear that more sensitive support provision is consistently linked to greater relationship satisfaction, less is known about the mechanisms that promote sensitivity. One possibility comes from the work of Verhofstadt, Buysse, Ickes, Davis, and Devoldre (2008) examining the role of emotional similarity and empathic accuracy on support provision. Greater similarity of spouses' emotional experience was associated with provision of more emotional support and less negative support, and greater empathic accuracy was associated with provision of more instrumental support and less negative support. While these findings are not directly related to perceived spousal sensitivity, they suggest that spouses' ability and willingness to provide beneficial support is greater to the extent that they are experiencing a similar affective state to their partner and that they are correctly able to infer what their partner is thinking and feeling.

The relationship enhancement model (Cutrona et al., 2005) incorporates these revisions to the optimal matching model and offers a current framework for conceptualizing the impact of social support on relationship functioning. Similar to the concept of sensitive support provision, supportive behaviors are thought to be beneficial to the extent that they are perceived to be consistently available from a spouse who is motivated by kindness, love, and commitment. Supportive behavior improves relationship satisfaction and stability by increasing the level of trust in the relationship, or the expectation that one's partner will be responsive to one's future needs. Higher levels of trust improve relationship functioning through behavioral mechanisms, such as decreased monitoring of the spouse, and cognitive mechanisms, such as a greater tendency to make benevolent attributions for negative partner behaviors. This model offers a compelling conceptual framework for future research on supportive marital behavior.

Mixed Effects of Receiving Support

One of the fascinating findings in the broader social support literature is that receiving social support frequently does not lead to positive outcomes and occasionally leads to negative outcomes. Though a number of explanations for this effect have been proposed, the most promising one is that awareness of receiving support may lower one's self-esteem. Bolger and colleagues provide evidence for this explanation in two studies of couples where one spouse was preparing to take the bar exam. In the final days leading up to the bar exam, Bolger, Zuckerman, and Kessler (2000) found that anxiety and depression increased on days after participants reported receiving support from their partners and that depression decreased on days after partners reported providing support. Interestingly, the days when spouses showed the greatest benefit of support provided by their partners was on days when they were not aware that their partners had provided support. Bolger and colleagues interpret these findings to indicate that invisible support, or support that spouses are not aware of receiving, may be particularly beneficial because it quells a source of distress without costs to self-esteem. In the second study, Gleason and colleagues (Gleason, Iida, Shrout, & Bolger, 2008) further analyzed the effects of giving and receiving support on negative mood and feelings of closeness with one's spouse in the same sample. For most couples, receiving more support was associated with feeling closer to one's spouse but also to increased negative mood; additionally, individuals who showed the greatest increase in closeness also showed the lowest increase in negative mood. However, a minority of spouses experienced increased closeness and decreased negative mood when receiving support, and a very small number of spouses experienced decreased closeness and increased negative mood when receiving support. These results are the first empirical evidence of the heterogeneity of the effects of receiving support and clearly demonstrate the importance of considering couple-level differences in the study of marital communication.

Combined Effects of Appetitive and Aversive Behaviors

A small but growing number of studies are tackling the difficult task of examining the combined effects of social support and conflict behaviors on relationship functioning. In one of the earliest of these studies, Pasch and Bradbury (1998) found both lower levels of negative communication behaviors enacted during couple conflict and higher levels of positive support behaviors enacted during supportive interactions to be uniquely associated with higher levels of relationship satisfaction over time. Sullivan et al. (2010) recently replicated and extended these findings by examining links between changes in communication behaviors and relationship outcomes for the same couples ten years later. Higher initial levels of positive and lower levels of negative support behaviors were generally predictive of higher levels of relationship satisfaction and a reduced likelihood of divorce or separation 10 years later, and almost all of these significant associations were significantly mediated by longitudinal changes in negative effect during conflict. To the extent that spouses were more supportive initially, these same spouses showed smaller longitudinal increases in negative behavior that were in turn associated with higher levels of marital satisfaction ten years later. These findings demonstrate the importance of both appetitive and aversive behaviors for relationship functioning and offer an initial glimpse into how both types of behavior influence one another over time. Furthering this integrative work is one of the main challenges facing marital communication researchers today.

Summary

Of all of the communication behaviors and patterns that have been investigated, five stand out as consistently differentiating satisfied couples from distressed couples across cultures and age. Distressed couples are generally more negative and engage in higher levels of negative reciprocity and demand–withdraw behavior than do satisfied couples, and satisfied couples are generally more positive and engage in more sensitive and more helpful social support behaviors than do distressed couples. Numerous theories and models exist for explaining why and how couples engage in these patterns, and recent revisions both validate and refine most of these models. However, the vast majority of our evidence base comes from separate studies of each type of behavior. The main challenge facing the field of marital communication today is to integrate these separate lines of research and discover how, why, and to what extent, appetitive and aversive processes are related to one another across interpersonal contexts and settings.

Directions for Future Research

The rapid pace of development in, and expanding focus of, marital communication research is generating a rich and nuanced empirical basis for understanding the role of spousal communication in marital functioning. Of the many on-going threads of discovery, recent developments in marital communication point to the need for further investigation of two fundamental questions in particular. One, how do appetitive and aversive processes interact with one another? Two, how can we best understand variability in these processes both within and between couples? The first of these questions speaks to the search for a unifying framework while the second question asks us to reexamine assumptions about the nature of behavioral consistency.

Recent research on social support goes a long way towards addressing the historical gap in attention paid to appetitive and aversive behavior. The similar and overlapping conceptual models driving this research generally include a concept similar to closeness, intimacy, or trust as a central mechanism linking vulnerable disclosure and empathic responding to relationship functioning (e.g., Cutrona et al., 2005). Additionally, some of these models hypothesize that aversive behaviors and relationship distress are at least partially the result of repeated, failed attempts to create closeness, intimacy, or trust (e.g., Gottman & Driver, 2005). However, concepts such as closeness are not only the domain of appetitive processes. For example, the gender socialization model of demand–withdraw behavior identifies desired closeness as a key component in this aversive cycle. It is therefore likely that desired closeness and behaviors involved in the modulation of closeness jointly contribute to both appetitive and aversive processes.

One class of closeness regulating behaviors that is likely to be involved in both appetitive and aversive processes is avoidance oriented behaviors such as withdrawal, minimization, and denial. Two primary functions of these behaviors for a conversation are down-regulation of the seriousness or intensity of the issue being discussed and bringing the discussion of the current issue to a close. At times, such an effect may be a desirable outcome. For example, well timed avoidance, such as withholding unimportant complaints (see Roloff & Ifert, 2000 for a review) or mutual agreement to declare a topic taboo (Roloff & Ifert, 1998), can be an effective strategy for avoiding unnecessary conflict and preventing emotional wounds. However, avoidant behaviors also make closeness very difficult, if not impossible, to achieve or maintain. Poorly timed and excessively frequent avoidant behaviors are therefore likely to play a role in both ineffective and insensitive support provision and in escalating aversive processes like demand–withdraw and negative reciprocity.

It is very likely that there are a number of other shared determinants of appetitive and aversive processes beyond avoidant behaviors and other shared factors beyond desired and experienced closeness. One method for beginning to look for these factors is to consider what makes marital relationships unique from other types of relationships and therefore drives the communication of spouses. Processes such as feeling heard, understood, appreciated, and accepted are some of the core components of marital relationships (Christensen & Jacobson, 2000), and behaviors that encourage or inhibit these experiences of oneself vis-à-vis one's spouse are likely to contribute to both appetitive and aversive processes. This line of reasoning suggests that vulnerable disclosure, empathic responding, and affirming and valuing statements as well as their counterparts blame, denial, and judgmental and devaluing statements are likely involved in both appetitive and aversive processes.

The notion that there may be fundamental processes and shared behaviors involved in both appetitive and aversive processes means that some assumptions about the nature of behavioral consistency are in need of empirical examination. Researchers and theorists have long argued that spouses develop unique ways of responding to one another that are functionally consistent even if they are behaviorally variable across setting and interaction context (see Surra & Ridley, 1991, for a review). The effect of topic on demand–withdraw behavior is a good example of this phenomenon. When discussing relationship change desired by the wife, a couple may engage in a strong wife demand–husband withdraw pattern that reverses when discussing relationship change desired by the husband. From Eldridge et al. (2007) we know that it is likely that these same spouses will engage in strongly gendered demand–withdraw roles when seeking social support from one another but that those roles will likely be opposite from what they were during conflict. Thus, the same husband and wife engage in both demanding and withdrawing behaviors to different degrees depending on what they are talking about and do so in a manner that consistently prevents or inhibits closeness. We are aware of no current confirming or conflicting evidence regarding this type of functional consistency combined with behavioral variability for negative escalation, social support, or any other appetitive process.

There is also no current evidence examining behavioral consistency in both appetitive and aversive processes across multiple settings and interaction contexts. Recent work (e.g., Sullivan et al., 2010) clearly demonstrates that aversive behavior during conflict and supportive behavior during social support interactions are related, but it is currently unknown how supportive and aversive processes are related to one another during a single type of interaction (i.e., either during conflict or during supportive interactions) and how supportive and aversive processes are related to one another across different types of interactions (i.e., how supportive processes during conflict are related to aversive processes during social support interactions). We hypothesize that behavioral variability between couples functions differently from variability within couples, such that well-functioning couples consistently engage in more constructive and fewer destructive processes than distressed couples, and that well-functioning couples engage in more behavioral variability across conflictual and supportive interactions than distressed couples. Within-couple behavioral variability is likely to be the sign of an adaptable marriage. Different situations require different behavioral responses and happily married couples likely have a wider array of behavioral options that allow them to appropriately respond to unique challenges while also maintaining and preserving a sense of closeness, intimacy, and trust than do distressed couples. Indirect support for this hypothesis comes from findings linking greater behavioral rigidity to lower levels of relationship satisfaction (Eldridge et al., 2007) but the specific hypothesis advanced here is in need of empirical investigation across a wide range of appetitive and aversive processes assessed during supportive and conflictual interactions conducted in laboratory and real world settings.

As the recent developments reviewed above demonstrate, there are many unturned stones that have the potential to clarify long-standing questions and to open up new avenues of exploration in the study of marital communication. Interdisciplinary study of marital communication provides rich and nuanced answers to these questions not achievable without the variety of empirical foci that exist across psychology, communication studies, and family studies. This diversity of perspective and thought makes the literature on marital communication scientifically compelling and socially relevant and will continue to drive important empirical developments in the future.

Note

1 Later work on gender differences in physiological reactivity to interpersonal conflict contradicts this aspect of the escape conditioning model by showing that women tend to be more physiologically reactive than men (Kiecolt-Glaser & Newton, 2001).

References

Barry, R., Bunde, M., Brock, R., & Lawrence, E. (2009). Validity and utility of a multidimensional model of received support in intimate relationships. *Journal of Family Psychology, 23*, 48–57.

Baucom, B. (2010). Power and arousal: New methods for assessing couples. In K. Hahlweg, M. Grawe-Gerber, & D. Baucom (Eds.), *Enhancing couples: The shape of couple therapy to come* (pp. 171–84). Cambridge, MA: Hogrefe.

Bolger, N., Zuckerman, A., & Kessler, R. (2000). Invisible support and adjustment to stress. *Journal of Personality and Social Psychology, 79*, 953–61.

Bowen, M. (1966). The use of family theory in clinical practice. *Comprehensive Psychiatry, 7*, 345–74.

Bowlby, J. (1969). *Attachment and loss: Vol. I. Attachment.* New York: Basic Books.

Brock, R. & Lawrence, E. (2009). Too much of a good thing: Underprovision versus overprovision of partner support. *Journal of Family Psychology, 23*, 181–92.

Burleson, B. R., & MacGeorge, E. L. (2002). Supportive communication. In M. L. Knapp, J. A. Daly, & G. R. Miller (Eds.), *Handbook of interpersonal communication*, 3rd edn (pp. 374–424). Thousand Oaks, CA: Sage.

Butler, E. A., Egloff, B., Wilhelm, F. H., Smith, N. C., Erickson, E. A., & Gross, J. J. (2003). The social consequences of expression suppression. *Emotion, 3*, 48–67.

Carstensen, L., Gottman, J., & Levenson, R. (1995). Emotional behavior in long-term marriage. *Psychology and Aging, 10*, 140–49.

Caughlin, J. P., & Scott, A. M. (2010). Toward a communication theory of the demand/withdraw pattern of interaction in interpersonal relationships. In S. W. Smith & S. R. Wilson (Eds.), *New directions in interpersonal communication research* (pp. 180–200). Thousand Oaks, CA: Sage.

Christensen, A. (1987). Detection of conflict patterns in couples. In K. Hahlweg & M. J. Goldstein (Eds.), *Understanding major mental disorder: The contribution of family interaction research* (pp. 250–65). New York: Family Process Press.

Christensen, A., & Jacobson, N. (2000). *Reconcilable differences.* New York: Guilford Press.

Cutrona, C. E., & Russell, D. (1990). Type of social support and specific stress: Toward a theory of optimal matching. In I. G. Sarason, B. R. Sarason, & G. R. Pierce (Eds.), *Social support: An interactional view* (pp. 319–66). New York: Wiley.

Cutrona, C. E., Russell, D. W., & Gardner, K. A. (2005). The relationship enhancement model of social support. In T. A. Revenson, K. Kayser, & G. Bodenmann (Eds.), *Couples coping with stress* (pp. 3–23). Washington, DC: American Psychological Association.

Cutrona, C., Shaffer, P., Wesner, K., & Gardner, K. (2007). Optimally matching support and perceived spousal sensitivity. *Journal of Family Psychology, 21*, 754–58.

Dehle, C., Larsen, D., & Landers, J. (2001). Social support in marriage. *The American Journal of Family Therapy, 29*, 307–24.

Denton, W. H., Burleson, B. R., Hobbs, B. V., Von Stein, M. & Rodroguez, C. P. (2001). Cardiovascular reactivity and initiate/avoid patterns of marital communication: A test of Gottman's psychophysiologic model of marital interaction. *Journal of Behavioral Medicine, 24*, 401–21.

Driver, J., & Gottman, J. (2004). Daily marital interactions and positive affect during marital conflict among newlywed couples. *Family Process, 43*, 301–14.

Eldridge, K. A., & Baucom, B. (in press). Couples and consequences of the demand-withdraw interaction pattern. In P. Noller & G. Karantzas (Eds.), *Positive pathways for couples and families: Meeting the challenges of relationships.* Chichester: Wiley–Blackwell.

Eldridge, K. A., Sevier, M., Jones, J., Atkins, D. C., & Christensen, A. (2007). Demand–withdraw communication in severely distressed, moderately distressed, and nondistressed couples: Rigidity and polarity during relationship and personal problem discussions. *Journal of Family Psychology, 21*, 218–26.

Filsinger, E., & Toma, S. (1989). Behavioral antecedents of relationship stability and adjustment: A five-year longitudinal study. *Journal of Marriage and the Family, 50*, 785–95.

Gable, S., & Reis, H. T. (2001). Appetitive and aversive social interaction. In J. H. Harvey & A. E. Wenzel (Eds.), *Close romantic relationship maintenance and enhancement* (pp. 169–94). Mahweh, NJ: Lawrence Erlbaum Associates.

Gleason, M., Iida, M., Shrout, P., & Bolger, N. (2008). Receiving support as a mixed blessing: Evidence for dual effects of support on psychological outcomes. *Journal of Personality and Social Psychology, 94*, 824–38.

Gottman, J. (1993). The roles of conflict engagement, escalation, and avoidance in marital interaction: A longitudinal view of five types of couples. *Journal of Consulting and Clinical Psychology, 61*, 6–15.

Gottman, J., & Driver, J. (2005). Dysfunctional marital conflict and everyday marital interaction. *Journal of Divorce & Remarriage, 43*, 63–77.

Gottman, J. M., & Krokoff, L. J. (1989). The relationship between marital interaction and marital satisfaction: A longitudinal view. *Journal of Consulting and Clinical Psychology, 57*, 47–52.

Gottman, J. M., & Levenson, R. W. (1988). The social psychophysiology of marriage. In P. Noller & M. A. Fitzpatrick (Eds.), *Perspectives on marital interaction* (pp. 182–200). Clevedon: Multilingual Matters.

Gottman, J., & Levenson, R. (1992). Marital processes predictive of later dissolution: Behavior, physiology, and health. *Journal of Personality and Social Psychology, 63*, 221–33.

Gottman, J., Markman, H., & Notarius, C. (1977). The topography of marital conflict: A sequential analysis of verbal and nonverbal behavior. *Journal of Marriage and the Family, 39*, 461–77.

Gottman, J., Notarius, C., Gonzo, J., & Markman, H. (1976). *A couple's guide to communication.* Champaign, IL: Research Press.

Gross, J. J., & Levenson, R. W. (1993). Emotional suppression: Physiological, self-report, and expressive behavior. *Journal of Personality and Social Psychology, 64*, 970–86.

Heavey, C. L., Layne, C., & Christensen, A. (1993). Gender and conflict structure in marital interaction: A replication and extension. *Journal of Consulting and Clinical Psychology, 61*, 16–27.

Hooley, J., & Hahlweg, K. (1989). The marriages and interaction patterns of depressed patients and their spouses: Comparison of high and low EE dyads. In M. J. Goldstein, I. Hand, & K. Hahlweg (Eds.), *Treatment of schizophrenia: Family assessment and intervention* (pp. 85–95). Berlin: Spring-Verlag.

Huston, T. L., Caughlin, J. P., Houts, R. M., Smith, S. E., & George, L. J. (2001). The connubial crucible: Newlywed years as predictors of marital delight, distress, and divorce. *Journal of Personality and Social Psychology, 80*, 237–52.

Karney, B. R., & Bradbury, T. N. (1995). The longitudinal course of marital quality and stability: A review of theory, methods, and research. *Psychological Bulletin, 118*, 3–34.

Klinetob, N. A., & Smith, D. A. (1996). Demand–withdraw communication in marital interaction: Tests of interpersonal contingency and gender role hypotheses. *Journal of Marriage and the Family, 58*, 945–57.

Lawrence, E., Bunde, M., Barry, R., Brock, R. L., Sullivan, K. T., Pasch, L. A., et al. (2008). Partner support and marital satisfaction: Support amount, adequacy, provision and solicitation. *Personal Relationships, 15*, 445–63.

Margolin, G. (1981). Behavior exchange in distressed and nondistressed marriages: A family cycle perspective. *Behavior Therapy, 12*, 329–43.

Markman, H. J., Rhoades, G. K., Stanley, S. M., Ragan, E., & Whitton, S. (2010). The premarital communication roots of marital distress: The first five years of marriage. *Journal of Family Psychology, 24*, 289–98.

Minuchin, S. (1974). *Families and family therapy.* Cambridge, MA: Harvard University Press.

Mitnick, D. M., Heyman, R. E., Malik, J., & Smith Slep, A. M. (2009). The differential association between change request qualities and resistance, problem resolution, and relationship satisfaction. *Journal of Family Psychology, 23*, 464–73.

Kiecolt-Glaser, J. K., & Newton, T. L. (2001). Marriage and health: His and hers. *Psychological Bulletin, 127*, 472–503.

Pasch, L., & Bradbury, T. (1998). Social support, conflict, and the development of marital dysfunction. *Journal of Consulting and Clinical Psychology, 66*, 219–30.

Pasch, L. A., Bradbury, T. N., & Davila, J. (1997). Gender, negative affectivity, and observed social support behavior in marital interaction. *Personal Relationships, 4*, 361–78.

Pasupathi, M., Carstensen, L., Levenson, R., & Gottman, J. (1999). Responsive listening in long-married couples: A psycholinguistic perspective. *Journal of Nonverbal Behavior, 23*, 173–93.

Pierce, G. R., Sarason, B. R., Sarason, I. G., Joseph, H. J., & Henderson, C. A. (1996). Conceptualizing and assessing social support in the context of the family. In G. R. Pierce, B. R. Sarason, & I. G. Sarason (Eds.), *The handbook of social support and the family* (pp. 3–23). New York: Plenum Press.

Rehman, U. S. & Holtzworth-Munroe, A. (2006). A cross-cultural analysis of the demand–withdraw marital interaction: Observing couples from a developing country. *Journal of Consulting and Clinical Psychology, 74*, 755–66.

Roloff, M. E., & Ifert, D. (1998). Antecedents and consequences of explicit agreements to declare a topic taboo in dating relationships. *Personal Relationships, 5*, 191–205.

Roloff, M. E., & Ifert, D. E. (2000). Conflict managements through avoidance: Withholding complaints, suppressing arguments, and declaring topics taboo. In S. S. Petronio (Ed.), *Balancing the secrets of private disclosure* (pp. 151–64). Mahwah, NJ: Lawrence Erlbaum Associates.

Sagrestano, L. M., Heavey, C. L., & Christensen, A. (2006). Individual differences versus social structural approaches to explaining demand–withdraw and social influence behaviors. In K. Dindia & D. J. Canary (Eds.), *Sex differences and similarities in communication* (pp. 379–95). Mahweh, NJ: Lawrence Erlbaum Associates.

Schmidt, M., Kliegel, M., & Shapiro, A. (2007). Marital interaction in middle and old age: A predictor of marital satisfaction? *International Journal of Aging and Human Development, 65*, 283–300.

Skinner, B. F. (1938). *The behavior of organisms: An experimental analysis*, New York: Appleton-Century-Crofts.

Smith, T., Berg, C., Florsheim, P., Uchino, B., Pearce, G., Hawkins, M., Henry, N., Beveridge, R., Skinner, M., & Olsen-Cerny, C. (2009). Conflict and collaboration in middle-aged and older couples: I. Age differences in agency and communion during marital interaction. *Psychology and Aging, 24*, 259–73.

Sullivan, K., Pasch, L., Johnson, M., & Bradbury, T. (2010). Social support, problem solving, and the longitudinal course of newlywed marriage. *Journal of Personality and Social Psychology, 98*, 631–44.

Surra, C. A., & Ridley, C. A. (1991). Multiple perspectives on interaction: Participants, peers, and observers. In B. Montgomery & S. Duck (Eds.), *Studying interpersonal interaction* (pp. 35–55). New York: Guilford Press.

Thibaut, J. W., & Kelley, H. H. (1959). *The social psychology of groups*. Oxford: Wiley.

Verhofstadt, V., Buysse, A., Ickes, W., Davis, M., & Devoldre, I. (2008). Support provision in marriage: The role of emotional similarity and empathic accuracy. *Emotion, 8*, 792–802.

Vogel, D. L., & Karney, B. R. (2003). Demands and withdrawal in newlyweds: Elaborating on the social structure hypothesis. *Journal of Social and Personal Relationships, 19*, 685–701.

Weiss, R. L., & Heyman, R. E. (1997). Marital interaction. In W. K. Halford & H. Markman (Eds.), *Clinical handbook of marriage and marital interaction* (pp. 13–35). New York: Wiley.

Whisman, M., Beach, S., & Snyder, D. (2008). Is marital discord taxonic and can taxonic status be assessed reliably? Results from a national, representative sample of married couples. *Journal of Consulting and Clinical Psychology, 76*, 745–55.

5

On Becoming Parents

Erin K. Holmes, Ted L. Huston,
Anita L. Vangelisti, and Trey D. Guinn

There can be no doubt that parenthood produces changes in the lives of mothers and fathers. New parents become true experts on things like strollers, car seats, bottles, diapers, and late night feedings. Not only does everyday life change for mothers and fathers as they add more tasks to their seemingly full list of family chores, the activities that make up their marital relationship change. The transformations in a couple's lifestyle, particularly the changing climate of their marital relationship, have sparked much scholarly debate. Historically, academic writing concerned with the introduction of a baby into a family emphasized its strong negative impact (although occasionally a researcher such as Russell, 1974, would come forward to propose that parenthood brings forth compensating gratifications). LeMasters' (1957) classic article declared that new fathers and mothers were unprepared for and overwhelmed by the "crisis" accompanying the arrival of a child. His thesis aroused strong public interest in this issue. Almost a dozen years later, as LeMasters (1970) noted, his conclusion continued to be put forth in national magazines and major newspapers. Longitudinal studies initiated in the early 1980s, however, began to create cracks in this monolithic negative view of the impact of parenthood on marriage. As scholars examined correlates of the direction and extent of change in satisfaction following the birth of a child, they increasingly recognized that parenthood may enhance, undermine, or have little effect on other marriages (Lawrence, Rothman, Cobb, Rothman, & Bradbury, 2008; Shapiro, Gottman & Carrere, 2000; Twenge, Campbell, and Foster, 2003).

In this chapter we present a framework that researchers can use to address the adaptations spouses make when they become parents. We consider both research design and other methodological issues that have undermined research in this area. Our central concern will be on the impact of primiparous parenting on marital well-being, but we will also discuss the process of becoming a parent, focusing on the adjustments partners make as they incorporate a child into their life together. We organize our discussion around our own longitudinal study of couples, some of whom became parents, and examine how marriages and lifestyles change when couples have their first baby. As we move from how having a baby affects various facets of married life, we place our findings in the context of the larger body of research, showing both the contribution of our own research as well as its limitations.

Research Design and Methodological Considerations

On Establishing Parenthood as a Causal Agent

Research on the transition to parenthood has implemented successively more sophisticated strategies for establishing the role parenthood plays in marital life. Cook and Campbell (1979) identify three hallmarks of causal explanation that can be used to characterize the evolution of work on the transition to parenthood. The first criterion for establishing causality is showing that the presumed cause (parenthood) covaries with its putative effect (marital quality). Cross-sectional studies comparing parents and nonparents meet this criterion (e.g., Figley, 1973; Miller, 1976). Cross-sectional studies that find parents less happily married than nonparents are, however, marked by three problems. First, couples who become parents may differ in satisfaction independent of their parental status. The lesser satisfaction of couples who become parents may have been present prior to parenthood. Lawrence et al. (2008) discovered that couples who became parents reported lower marital quality than those who were voluntarily childless, but that couples who planned their pregnancies had higher pre-pregnancy satisfaction and that planning slowed husbands' postpartum declines in satisfaction. The purported differences associated with parenthood may actually reflect partners' values and expectations for parenthood which, as Helms-Erickson (2001) suggests, are critical aspects of timing and life course transitions.

Second, having children encourages unhappy couples to stay married out of the belief that divorce would put their children at risk (Glenn, 1998; Previti & Amato, 2004). The stability of their union is not, however, a function of their marital happiness, thus any group of parents is likely to include unhappy couples (Waite & Lillard, 1991; Waite, Browning, Doherty, Gallagher, Luo, & Stanley, 2002).

Third, couples who become parents may differ from nonparents in other ways including, but not limited to, their own attitudes and desires toward parenting, their expectations for either joy or misery as a parent, and their feelings of adequacy or inadequacy as a caregiver (Curran, Hazen, & Mann, 2009; Rholes, Simpson, Blakely, Lanigan, & Allen, 1997). A cross-sectional comparison of married couples who are parents with those who are nonparents would include sets of couples who were married at different ages and who have been married different lengths of time. Even with changing demographic trends suggesting that women are bearing their first children at older ages than they have in the past 40 to 50 years (Waldrop, 1994), the parent group is likely to be younger and married for a shorter length of time than the nonparent group, and these factors, rather than parenthood status alone, may account for group differences in marital satisfaction or marital stability (Huston & Vangelisti, 1995; Moore & Waite, 1981).

Cook and Campbell's (1979) second criterion for proving causal significance is establishing the temporal precedence of the putative cause. With data gathered from couples before and after becoming parents, longitudinal designs establish the temporal precedence of parenthood as the putative cause. In the most common longitudinal design, a single group of couples, in which the wives are pregnant, is followed from before to after the births of the children. These studies often (Belsky, Lang, & Rovine, 1985; Cowan et al., 1985; Feldman & Nash, 1984; Ruble, Fleming, Hackel, & Stangor, 1988; Tomlinson, 1987), although not invariably (Cox, Paley, Burchinal, & Payne, 1999; Meyerowitz & Feldman, 1966; Waldron & Routh, 1981; Wallace & Gotlib, 1990), report linear declines in marital well-being from before to one year after childbirth. Although the designs used in most longitudinal investigations provide information that was unavailable in earlier cross-sectional studies, they have at least three limitations (Cook & Campbell, 1979). First, couples about to become parents may, as a consequence of their pregnancies, be temporarily happier with their marriages; thus changes in marital satisfaction may reflect regression toward the mean (regression effects).

Second, as couples settle into marriage, their satisfaction may decline over time regardless of whether they become parents (maturation effects). This is important because a sizable proportion of couples become parents during the first few years of marriage, a period over which declines in satisfaction are normative (see Glenn, 1998). Third, the before/after design used in the studies that investigate the impact of parenthood on marriage, coupled with the participants' awareness of the general purposes of the investigation, may affect the data (testing effects).

The third criterion for establishing causality is the exclusion of alternative explanations for the putative cause–effect relationship (Cook & Campbell, 1979). The use of a comparison group of couples who do not make the transition to parenthood provides one way of eliminating alternative explanations such as maturation effects. The few studies that have included comparison groups of couples who have not made the transition over the same period provide little support for the idea that parenthood produces a linear decline in marital satisfaction. For example, couples become less satisfied with their marriages over time, regardless of whether they become parents (e.g., Cowan & Cowan, 1988; Doss, Rhoades, Stanley, & Markman, 2009; Lawrence et al., 2008; MacDermid, Huston, & McHale, 1990; McHale & Huston, 1985; Ryder, 1973). Further, one may find steeper declines for women who transition to parenthood within the first six years of marriage (Shapiro, Gottman, & Carrere, 2000), a buffering effect for parents who planned their pregnancies and had higher pre-pregnancy marital satisfaction (Lawrence, et al., 2008), steeper declines in marital happiness as the result of destructive conflict and active avoidance, and discrete groups of couples with varying degrees of stability and change including increases in marital satisfaction and marital happiness over time (Anderson, Van Ryzin, & Doherty, 2010; Belsky & Hsieh, 1998; Kamp Dush, Taylor, & Kroeger, 2008). Only through continued inclusion of both parent and nonparent groups can one come to solid conclusions about the complex effects of parenthood on marriage.

Temporal Aspects of the Impact of Parenthood on Marriage

Practical considerations have led most researchers to gather data on one or two occasions within a year after childbirth from couples who have become parents. Because the processes through which parenthood affects marital well-being are poorly understood, social scientists have given little attention to the timing of marital assessments. Kelly and McGrath (1988) argue that researchers need to incorporate temporal parameters into their conceptualization of causal agents and to articulate the hypothesized temporal path created by the putative cause. They describe a variety of ways an event, X (e.g., child-birth), might affect an outcome, Y (e.g., marital satisfaction).

Figures 5.1a and 5.1b portray parenthood as creating an immediate effect that persists over time in the first case and fades in the second. Research that uses data gathered from parents soon after childbirth assumes parenthood has an almost immediate impact. Much of the research on the transition to parenthood, even that of a longitudinal nature, reports data gathered from new parents on only one or two occasions relatively

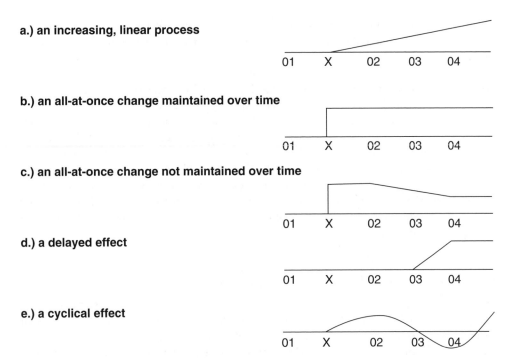

a.) an increasing, linear process

01   X   02   03   04

b.) an all-at-once change maintained over time

01   X   02   03   04

c.) an all-at-once change not maintained over time

01   X   02   03   04

d.) a delayed effect

01   X   02   03   04

e.) a cyclical effect

01   X   02   03   04

Figure 5.1

soon after the birth of the first child. As a consequence, the studies may pick up short-term fluctuations in satisfaction, but may fail to detect more slowly emerging effects of parenthood. Thus, although the literature on the transition to parenthood tends to characterize parenthood as a "crisis," it is unclear whether the crisis and its effects dissipate over time as couples reconcile differences and grow together as a result of the crisis (Figure 5.1b) or whether the marital patterns instigated by the crisis become ongoing and create long-lasting change in marital well-being (Figure 5.1a).

Figure 5.1c suggests another possible pattern. Here, the effect of parenthood on marital satisfaction increases gradually over time. For example, if parenthood increases stress and conflict in marriage (Hill, 1949; LeMasters, 1957), the impact of the conflictual and negative patterns may cumulate with time and erode satisfaction. On the other hand, parenthood may bring with it a sense of elation that might be reflected in a short-lived upswing in satisfaction, followed by a decline (see Miller & Sollie, 1980; Wallace & Gotlib, 1990). Figure 5.1d, in contrast, shows parenthood as having a delayed or "sleeper" impact on marriage. The influence of parenthood on marital satisfaction may surface years later, for example, as a consequence of spouses' having very different religious values or ideas about child rearing.

Finally, Figure 5.1e shows a cyclical pattern reflecting modulations in spouses' marital satisfaction over time. Marital satisfaction contains both a relatively stable trait-like component and a state-like element that resonates to the vicissitudes of day-to-day life (Robins, 1990). If the cyclical pattern of spouses' satisfaction is similar across couples, different conclusions might be reached about the impact of parenthood, depending on the timing of measurement. Parenthood could create highs and lows in the lives of couples, but the timing of these highs and lows may be largely idiosyncratic. If the pattern is not timed similarly across couples the effects of parenthood are likely to be masked.

We have referred to findings above that reflect multiple possibilities about the temporal aspects of the transition to parenthood, and highlight one recent study that helps us better understand the changes in marital quality for parents over time. Doss et al. (2009) studied couples over the first eight years of marriage and questioned whether and how parenthood undermines marital quality. These researchers found that parents and nonparents demonstrated similar amounts of decline in relationship functioning, but that the change occurred suddenly following the birth of the baby for parents, and more gradually for nonparents. Also, a number of variables influenced parents' post-birth relational functioning including a history of parental divorce (for mothers), having a baby more quickly following marriage (for fathers), the sex of the baby, and couples' conflict management skills.

Links Among Parenthood, Marital Patterns, and Satisfaction

Parenthood marks a transition for couples, but that transition begins before the physical birth of the child (Cowan, 1991). Pregnancy itself can strengthen couples' feelings of togetherness (Feeney et al., 2001), increase a wife's sense of her husband's care for her (Holmes, Duncan, Bair, & White, 2007), increase a man's potential to develop generativity (Hawkins & Dollahite, 1997), or provide the couple with new leisure opportunities (e.g., buying materials for baby, planning for baby's future, choosing baby's names, and attending birthing classes together; Claxton & Perry-Jenkins, 2008). Pregnancy can also introduce a new life course transition for women as they consider the place their new childcare responsibilities fit in their current career goals (Holmes, Erickson, & Hill, in press). These considerations suggest that parenthood "as a cause" can be viewed in a number of different ways. Following Cook and Campbell (1979), parenthood can be taken as a "macro" event that sets in motion a number of other adjustments of a macro nature (e.g., changes in spouses' labor force participation or economic well-being) that may affect marital satisfaction. According to Cook and Campbell, macro events may also set in motion other, more specific, events—referred to as "micromediational" events—that affect the satisfactoriness of the marriage. Thus, for example, parenthood may be the root cause of alterations in the division of household labor, sleep deficits (Medina, Lederhos, & Lillis, 2009), increases in the amount of stress spouses experience, or decreases in the opportunity for spouses to pursue enjoyable leisure activities—any of which may undermine partners' sense of satisfaction with their marriage. It is critical to identify how parenthood affects the day-to-day lives of marital couples and to pinpoint which of these changes make differences in how spouses come to feel about each other and their marriage. Parenthood may be a "big change" for many couples, but whether it is an unwelcome change for marriage is another matter.

The PAIR Project as a Context for Studying the Impact of Parenthood on Marriage[1]

We organize our discussion of the transition to parenthood around our longitudinal study of newlyweds because the study has several design strengths that are unusual in research in this area. First, by gathering systematic diary data from couples we were able to explore in considerable depth the impact of having a baby on a great many aspects of married life, including the roles played by the husband and the wife, their companionship, their sexual behavior in the marriage, expressions of affection, the degree to which they were irritable with each other, their leisure patterns, their love, and their satisfaction with their marriage. Second, we were able to compare the earlier courtship and marital patterns of couples who became parents with those of childless couples, making it possible for us to discover whether parents differ from nonparents before they have a child with regard to various features of their marriages. Third, the comparison over time of couples who became parents with those who do not made it possible for us to determine whether it is parenthood, rather than the passage of time, that accounts for changes in the quality of marriage. Fourth, we could examine the influence of the timing of parenthood on aspects of the marriage. Fifth, participants were not sensitized to the nature of the study. The issue of parenthood was never identified as a focal point of the research, nor was the timing of births used to determine data collection periods. This study is limited, like most longitudinal studies of parenthood, to the period of time during which the transition takes place, but does not consider longer-term ramifications of parenthood for marriage relationships. Unlike most research, which generally focuses on a group of couples as they become parents, we were able to compare couples who had children at different points in the marriage with those who were childless at these times. We were thereby in a position to determine whether parenthood hastens the loss of romance, as others have suggested, or whether previous researchers were mistaken and that such a loss, if it occurs, is part of the ordinary waning of romance as marriage progresses.

We initially gathered data two months after couples were wed. The second and third phases of data collection took place 14 months and 26 months into marriage. The initial sample, drawn from marriage license records in four counties in central Pennsylvania, consisted of 168 first-time married couples, 129 of whom stayed married and were followed across all three phases of the study. We collected detailed diary data on three occasions that were spaced a year apart, beginning when couples were newlyweds, so we could see how marriages unfolded and how becoming parents affected the couples' marriages and their lifestyle. It is important to note here that because "newlywed" data were gathered about two months into marriage, with the next two data collections occurring at 14 months and 26 months, the couples who made the transition to parenthood did so between two and 26 months of their wedding.

How Parenthood Affects Married Life

Parenthood is generally thought to nudge marriages away from "loving companionships" toward more "working partnerships." We examined division of labor, spousal leisure and companionship, and socioemotional behavior to assess the ways in which parenthood affects the day-to-day life of couples, including whether the division of labor becomes more traditionalized, whether spouses' companionship is reduced, and whether marriages become less affectionate or more conflict ridden over time.

The Expansion of Work at Home

Figure 5.2 uses PAIR project data to illustrate alterations in couples' lifestyle that accompany parenthood (Huston & Vangelisti, 1995; MacDermid et al., 1990). Before

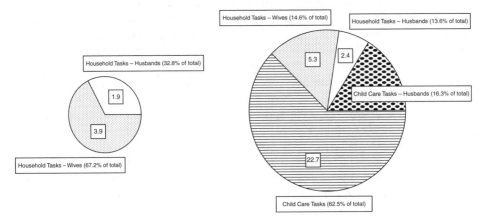

Figure 5.2

parenthood, we see that wives do 67.2 percent of the chores (an average of 3.9 chores a day), leaving husbands with the remaining 32.8 percent of the chores (an average of 1.9 chores a day). The arrival of a child produces a six-fold increase in the number of family-related activities performed on an average day, from 5.8 tasks completed per day before parenthood to 36.2 tasks per day after parenthood. New mothers increase their household tasks to 5.3 tasks on average per day and accumulate another 22.7 childcare tasks. New fathers also increase their participation in household tasks to 2.4 per day and accrue an average of 5.9 childcare tasks. One can see the great expansion of the couples' workload in the home after they become parents, particularly as new mothers, dramatically increase their involvement in childcare tasks (see also Cowan et al., 1985; Ruble et al., 1988). Fathers' responsibilities grow as they become involved in childcare tasks, but the escalation of their duties is clearly more modest than those of mothers.'

Though inequity in the amount of work women and men do at home still exists, and though women's perceptions of inequity in housework contribute to their dissatisfaction (Dew & Wilcox, 2011), empirical evidence shows that women often do not perceive the uneven division of labor as unfair. Indeed, one study showed that women will complete up to two-thirds of household work before they feel a sense of unfairness in the division of labor and that men will complete roughly 36 percent of family work when they begin to sense the load landing unjustly on them (Lennon & Rosenfeld, 1994). Grote, Naylor, and Clark (2002) explored women's and men's sense of fairness in family work across the transition to parenthood. Women's perceptions of equity are linked to the pleasure they get out of performing household and childcare tasks, while men's enjoyment for these tasks does not consistently predict their reports of satisfaction with the division of labor. Further the most consistent predictor of a husband's sense of fairness was his sense of competency at family work combined with his wife's sense of his competence in performing household and childcare activities. The more husbands thought their wives viewed them as competent, the more husbands contributed to both housework and childcare. The sense of competence of wives, either as they perceived it or as their spouses perceived it was unrelated to how wives felt about the division of family tasks. Finally, mothers' perceptions that fathers' were good at family work were linked with reports that their husband actually did more housework and childcare.

Other findings suggest that fairness in the division of household labor may not play as significant a role in predicting marital quality as previously suggested. In particular, the work that couples do to maintain the quality of their relationships, coined emotion work, has been identified as a stronger predictor of marital satisfaction (Lawrence, et al., 2008; Wilcox & Nock, 2006; Goldberg & Perry-Jenkins, 2004). Although couples generally divide tasks unequally, with most of the burden given to women, some women report fairness in the division if they feel appreciated and cared for emotionally (Wilcox & Nock, 2006).

Work Roles and Childcare

Most wives in the U.S.A. work outside the home—even when they are mothers of young children (U.S. Bureau of Census, 2011). Indeed for some mothers the loss of their work role outside the home contributes to a decline in relational satisfaction (Keizer, Dykstra, & Poortman, 2010). For others, a mismatch between one's ideal and actual employment (e.g., desiring full-time work but staying home, or desiring to stay home but working full time) increases depression across the first three years of the transition to parenthood (Holmes et al., in press).

Despite a cultural ideal that includes employment for mothers, working wives who become mothers experience what some have called a cultural contradiction between a high mothering identity and a calling for career (Elgar & Chester, 2007; Giele, 2008; Johnston & Swanson, 2007). As a result, in addition to creating a unique mothering identity, contemporary women must also determine a worker identity that "justifies their decision to work or not to work outside the home" (Johnston & Swanson, 2007, p. 448). While men's labor force participation continues to remain more stable than women's through the transition to parenthood, cultural contradictions in men's identities as "breadwinner" and "caregiver" also exist (Henwood & Procter, 2003).

Comparisons between data from the past decade or so with earlier data from the 1970s and 1980s suggest that fathers in intact families have increased accessibility to their children, boosted direct engagement with their children (Yeung, Sandberg, Davis-Kean, & Hofferth, 2001), and enhanced father–son relationship quality (Morman & Floyd, 2002). Thus, while the breadwinner role for men is still a strong cultural ideal, the highly involved "new father" who, like his wife, is immersed in his child's life in the effort to meet his child's emotional, psychological, relational, and spiritual needs is also becoming more prevalent (Brotherson & White, 2007).

Though it may be possible for some mothers and fathers to act out both scripts, for most there is an inherent contradiction (Holmes, Baumgartner, Marks, Palkovitz, & Nesteruk, 2010). For instance, Deutsch (1999) found that the couples were overtly committed to allocating equivalent resources to work inside and outside of the home, but they often contradicted their values in practice. Couples in her sample grappled with the personal ideal that splitting work evenly among partners was the best alternative for fairness in families because they continued to feel an internal pull to act on traditional norms regarding the division of labor.

In our own research, when husbands worked and wives were the primary caregivers, fathers rarely stepped forward to help with their child, unless they felt confident they knew what they are doing (McHale & Huston, 1984) and unless they experienced stronger than average feelings of love for their wife (Crouter, Perry-Jenkins, Huston & McHale, 1987). The tendency of any spouse—whether traditional or egalitarian—to engage in more childcare activity in part depends on their perceived skills (McHale & Huston, 1984). Fathers who feel skilled with regard to parenting are more involved in child-oriented activities than are those who feel unskilled (Bonney, Kelley, & Levant, 1999; Hudson, Elek, & Fleck, 2001). Even fathers' perception of their skill prior to the birth of the baby is linked to their involvement over the transition to parenthood (Barry, Smith, Deutsch, & Perry-Jenkins, 2011). Fathers who feel competent about performing childcare tend to have wives who are more satisfied with their relationship (Biehle & Mickelson, 2011). It is also interesting to note that paternal competence in infant care is mediated by men's marital satisfaction, such that the more satisfied a father is with his marriage before the transition to parenthood, the more competent he will be after the transition (Bonney et al., 1999; Cowan & Cowan, 1987). Further, a close, confiding marriage before the transition to parenthood continues to breed men's sense of paternal skill with their infants during the first six months postpartum (Cox, Owen, Lewis, & Henderson, 1989).

For fathers in our sample, perceived skill in childcare is a relatively stable trait. It does not significantly change when they become parents (McHale & Huston, 1984)—husbands who feel skilled at childcare before becoming fathers also tend to feel skilled afterward. In an exploration of men's transition to fatherhood, Strauss and Goldberg (1999) emphasize not only the general continuity between men's early caregiving competence and later competence, but also the match between their ideal roles and their actual roles. Those who were more able to achieve their ideal roles felt competent and satisfied as fathers, often being more inclined to be involved in childcare tasks. Although husbands' and wives' role preferences are not related to each other before they become parents, afterward, mothers' expressivity (defined in terms of: warmth in relations with others, gentleness, ability to devote self completely to others, kindness, awareness of others' feelings, etc.) and their perceived skill are inversely related to fathers' preferences for being involved in childcare. The more expressive mothers are, and the more skilled they perceive themselves to be in terms of childcare, the less their husbands prefer to engage in childcare activities (see also Cook, Jones, Dick, & Singh, 2005; Genesoni & Tallandini, 2009; Habib & Lancaster, 2010).

In addition to examining perceived skill, scholars continue to become more attuned to the ways mothers influence father involvement (prior to the transition to parenthood and much after). For example, some mothers may serve as "gatekeepers" to fathers' relationships with their children by regulating fathers' involvement either as gate openers (mothers whose beliefs and attitudes encourage father involvement in family work) or as gate closers (mothers whose beliefs and attitudes hinder father involvement) (Allen & Hawkins, 1999; Cannon, Schoppe-Sullivan, Mangelsdorf, Brown, & Sokolowski, 2008; McBride, Brown, Bost, Shin, Vaughn, & Korth, 2005). Whether undermining or supportive, mothers control fathers' active involvement with their children (Gaunt, 2008; Herzog, Umana-Taylor, Madden-Derdich, & Leonard, 2007; Sano, Richards, & Zvonkovic, 2008; Schoppe-Sullivan et al., 2008), fathers' parenting behaviors (Cannon, et al., 2008; McBride, et al., 2005), and fathers' accessibility to their children (McBride, et al., 2005), sometimes limiting men's involvement in childcare tasks (Fagan & Barnett, 2003; McBride et al., 2005).

From our own data, it appears that the changing role preferences of wives influence husbands' involvement with their children. The associations between wives' role-related characteristics and their husbands' activities are stronger than the associations between husbands' characteristics and their own activities. Although husbands who are more expressive tend to believe that they are more skilled in terms of childcare, husbands' expressivity does not by itself predict their tendency to engage in child-oriented activities. Wives' role preferences (measured after they become mothers), however, predict husbands' involvement with their children. Wives who prefer their husbands to be involved in childcare after they become parents tend to have husbands who engage in more child-oriented activities (McHale & Huston, 1984). As we will see below, however, husbands' greater involvement in childcare does not always bode well for the marriage.

Balancing Career and Family Life

Many new parents have to juggle the demands of two jobs and their new babies. Forty-three percent of those we interviewed found themselves in such a situation. The total work burden was rarely equally balanced between the parents when both partners worked for pay outside the home. All told, in such situations fathers took on a fourth of the childcare and household responsibilities. By the second year of the child's life, working mothers were employed an average of 30 hours a week for pay while performing 26 household and childcare tasks. Their husbands worked 34 hours a week for pay, while performing about five household and childcare tasks (Smith & Huston, 2004). Since there was a strong correlation between the number of tasks performed and the total amount of time devoted to them, we can use the number of tasks and the time spent in tasks interchangeably. The imbalance of the household work would have been even greater had employed mothers not cut back on the number of tasks they took on compared to the mothers who did not work outside the home (Crouter, Perry-Jenkins, Huston, & McHale, 1987). The dual-earner couples generally chose efficiency (e.g., one parent caring for the child—mostly the mother—while the other engaged in another activity) over companionship (e.g., both parents spending time together with the child). Another adaptation parents created to manage career and home life included differing work hours between father and mother. For three-fourths of the dual-earner parents, one partner might work daytime hours, with the other working in the evening, or on the overnight shift.

In our research we did not ask dual-earner couples *why* they chose one form of childcare arrangement rather than another. Johnson (2000) found that couples generally leave childcare decisions up to the mother, rather than jointly considering the merits of alternative solutions. According to Johnson, mothers' ideas about the importance of family-care, the availability of kin to provide such care, cost considerations, and quality of care play important roles in childcare decisions.

Working mothers usually wanted their husbands to be more involved in childcare than the husbands tended to be. Indeed, employed mothers in our sample discovered that securing help from their employed husbands could carry significant costs. When the fathers assisted them, they often did so with obvious reluctance, offering clear signs that they believed they were being exploited, saddled with chores that were not included in their job description. The more fathers in dual-earner marriages were involved with childcare, the more they complained, criticized, and otherwise showed dissatisfaction toward their wives. Furthermore, fathers in dual-earner marriages who behaved more negatively tended to be less satisfied with the division of childcare tasks and also less in love with their wives. Conversely, fathers in dual-earner marriages who were less involved with their children (with regard to both childcare and leisure activities) were more in love with their wives. Research suggests that more recent generations of parents experience greater declines in satisfaction than prior generations (Twenge, Campbell, & Foster, 2003) and that the division of labor is a primary source of conflict among new parents (Kluwer, 2010).

Does Parenthood Undermine Romance and Lead to Conflict?

Spouses' increased childcare responsibilities restrict the amount of time they have to be with each other as a couple. Not surprisingly, the amount of time husbands and wives pursue leisure activities together as a couple decreases once they become parents (Claxton & Perry-Jenkins, 2008). The disenchantment new parents express with the limited amount of time they now spend together reflects in part the fact that they pursue fewer activities that they both enjoy. Even when parents do engage in leisure together, they often have to keep a sharp eye on the child.

The extent to which mothers, in particular, spend time with their child doing leisure activity comes to rival time they spend in leisure with their husbands alone as a pair (Crawford & Huston, 1993). Fathers and children pursue relatively few leisure activities together without the mother also involved. Having a baby allows mothers to spend more time doing leisure activities that they like, and less leisure time in activities they dislike, while the reverse is true for new fathers. New fathers' leisure time shifts from activities with friends or time in solitary activities toward less enjoyable family and home-centered pursuits. This constricted freedom may produce a feeling of being hemmed in by fatherhood. Indeed, Claxton and Perry-Jenkins (2008) found that men who participated in more independent leisure activities before the birth of their baby reported less love and more conflict in their marriage one year later.

Our data indicate that the disquiet that fathers feel about changes in their social life does not undermine their overall feelings of marital satisfaction or weaken their expressed love for their wives—or their wives for them. Nor does the reduced amount of time couples have alone together affect such feelings. This may be explained, in part, by their recognition that such changes are an inevitable part of parenthood. They may also be sustained by a feeling of pride. Their production of a child anchors them in the mainstream of the culture, and is an achievement regarded as praiseworthy.

Aside from leisure pursuits, parents in our sample spend less time talking together than do nonparents (McHale & Huston, 1985). Given the centrality of communication to spouses' marital satisfaction, this reported decrease in partners' time together would not seem to bode well for the quality of their marriage. When we examined the parents' affectionate expressions toward one another we found that parenthood has little impact on the relationship. Though new parents may spend less time conversing, they are no less affectionate with each other than couples who do not yet have children (MacDermid et al., 1990). New parents seem to make the most of their limited time together. Furthermore, the data show that for some couples, the amount of affection that husbands express toward their wives actually increases during the transition to parenthood (McHale & Huston, 1985). New parents said "I love you" to each other as often as nonparents; they also tried to make one another laugh, hugged and kissed each other, shared their feelings, and did something nice for each other about as often as nonparents (MacDermid et al., 1990). Parents and nonparents also were equally involved in talking about their personal needs and trying to work out their problems. As suggested by Cowan and Cowan (1988), parents may be able to communicate more effectively with one another, knowing that they have less time to interact with each other.

While sexual intercourse was curtailed during the later stages of pregnancy and during the postpartum period, declines in sexual activity among new parents were otherwise no greater than the abatement of nonparents' sexual behavior. At times new parents had to be creative about sex, and even then things sometimes didn't go as planned; however, they recognized these changes as part of their own decisions regarding childbearing, not just as a result of the presence of their child.

The parent and nonparent groups were equally likely to bicker, argue, criticize, or turn down each other's sexual overtures—either before or after the birth of a child. Because negativity is a particularly sensitive barometer of spouses' marital satisfaction (Huston & Vangelisti, 1991; Karney & Bradbury, 1997), this finding lends further credence to describing the arrival of a child as changing couple's lifestyles rather than producing a "crisis" in their marriages. What takes place is largely a shift in lifestyle rather than diminishing affection resulting from more restricted schedules and greater tension.

Conclusions and Directions for Future Research

The birth of a baby clearly has an impact on marital behavior patterns and individual identity. Spouses change the way they organize their instrumental tasks and leisure time. Wives' face new questions about establishing a maternal identity that also include career identity. Husbands face new questions about being both a "good provider" and a nurturant caregiver. Husbands engage in fewer of the leisure activities they enjoy, but may also find satisfaction in competence at parenting tasks. The responsibilities that accompany childcare limit the amount of time spouses have to spend together as a couple. Accordingly, parents report spending less time in conversation than do nonparents. Although new parents change many of their behavioral patterns, the socioemotional aspects of their interaction do not differ from those of nonparents. Because socioemotional behavior is an important predictor of spouses' relational satisfaction, the lack of difference in this domain of marriage for parents and nonparents suggest that parenthood, per se, need not encourage decreases in spouses' marital satisfaction and love. Data from the PAIR project support this claim.

Having noted that parents do not differ from nonparents in terms of the way they evaluate the quality of their marriages in the PAIR project, it is important to acknowledge that the changes that accompany parenthood are more easily managed by some than others.

Our efforts to trace the multiple ways parenthood affects marriage and to identify the conditions under which parenthood affects satisfaction fits into a new, emerging paradigm that seeks to create a richer, more balanced portrait of the transition to parenthood. Researchers are poised, we believe, to recognize that parenthood includes greater opportunities as well as problems, and that the overall effect of parenthood on marriage reflects the operation of a number of causal dynamics.

Future research in this vein ought to study the potential differences between working-class and middle-class couples. Researchers further need to expand work on the transition to parenthood to include unwed mothers and fathers because first-time parenthood increasingly takes place outside of marriage. Nearly 40 percent of births in the U.S. are to unwed mothers and fathers (U.S. Center for Disease Control, 2011). Scholars are beginning to examine the influence of families and social networks on the relational world of unmarried parents (England & Edin, 2009; Hofferth & Goldscheider, 2010; McLanahan, 2009). Increasing research on the larger sociocultural context of the transition to parenthood, including particularly race and ethnicity, will largely impact our understanding of the transition to parenthood and its effects on parents and their relationships.

Acknowledgment

This research was supported by grants from the National Science Foundation (SBR-9311846) and National Institute of Mental Health (MH-33938), Ted L. Huston, principal investigator.

Note

1 PAIR stands for Processes of Adaptation in Intimate Relationships. The acronym captures our interest in studying how couples adapt or adjust to one another as they move through their life together. Readers interested in learning more about the results should consult the project website: www.utexas.edu/research/pair.

References

Allen, S. M., & Hawkins, A. J. (1999). Maternal gatekeeping: Mothers' beliefs and behaviors that inhibit greater father involvement in family work. *Journal of Marriage and the Family, 61*(1), 199–212.

Anderson, J. R., Van Ryzin, M. J., & Doherty, W. J. (2010). Developmental trajectories of marital happiness in continuously married individuals: A group-based modeling approach. *Journal of Family Psychology, 24*(5), 587–96.

Barry, A. A., Smith, J. Z., Deutsch, F. M., & Perry-Jenkins, M. (2011). Fathers' involvement in child care and perceptions of parenting skill over the transition to parenthood. *Journal of Family Issues, 32*, 1500–21.

Belsky, J., & Hsieh, K.-H. (1998). Patterns of marital change during the early childhood years: Parent personality, coparenting, and division-of-labor correlates. *Journal of Family Psychology, 12*, 511–28.

Belsky, J., Lang, M. E., & Rovine, M. (1985). Stability and change in marriage across the transition to parenthood: A second study. *Journal of Marriage and the Family, 47*, 855–65.

Biehle, S. N., & Mickelson, K. D. (2011). Preparing for parenthood: How feelings of responsibility and efficacy impact expectant parents. *Journal of Social and Personal Relationships, 28*, 668–83.

Bonney, J. F., Kelley, M. L., & Levant, R. F. (1999). A model of fathers' behavioral involvement in child care in dual-earner families. *Journal of Family Psychology, 13*, 401–15.

Brotherson, S., & White, J. (2007). *Why fathers count.* Harriman, TN: Men's Studies Press.

Cannon, E. A., Schoppe-Sullivan, S. J., Mangelsdorf, S. C., Brown, G. L., & Sokolowski, M. S. (2008). Parent characteristics as antecedents of maternal gatekeeping and fathering behavior. *Family Process, 47*(4), 501–19.

Claxton, A., & Perry-Jenkins, M. (2008). No fun anymore: Leisure and marital quality across the transition to parenthood. *Journal of Marriage and Family, 70*, 28–43.

Cook, J. L., Jones, R. M., Dick, A. J., & Singh, A. (2005). Revisiting men's role in father involvement: The importance of personal expectations. *Fathering: A Journal of Theory, Research, and Practice about Men as Fathers, 3*(2), 165–78.

Cook, T., & Campbell, D. T. (1979). *Quasi-experimentation: Design and analysis issues for field settings.* Chicago, IL: Rand McNally,

Cowan, C. P., & Cowan, P. A. (1987). Men's involvement in parenthood: Identifying the antecedents and understanding the barriers. In P. W. Berman & F. A. Pedersen (Eds.), *Men's transitions to parenthood: Longitudinal studies of early family experience* (pp. 45–171). Hillsdale, NJ: Lawrence Erlbaum Associates.

Cowan, C. P., Cowan, P. A., Heming, G., Heming, G., Garrett, E., Coysh, W. S., Curtis-Boles, H., & Boles, A. J. (1985). Transitions to parenthood: His, hers, and theirs. *Journal of Family Issues, 6*, 451–81.

Cowan, P. A. (1991). Individual and family life transitions: A proposal for a new definition. In P. A. Cowan & M. Hetherington (Eds.), *Family transitions* (pp. 3–30). Hillsdale, NJ: Lawrence Erlbaum Associates.

Cowan, P. A., & Cowan, C. P. (1988). Changes in marriage during the transition to parenthood: Must we blame the baby? In G. Michaels & W. Goldberg (Eds.), *The transition to parenthood: Current theory and research* (pp. 114–54). Cambridge: Cambridge University Press.

Cox, M. J., Owen, M., Lewis, J., & Henderson, V. K. (1989). Marriage, adult adjustment, and early parenting. *Child Development, 60*, 1015–24.

Cox, M. J., Paley, B., Burchinal, M., & Payne, C. C. (1999). Marital perceptions and interactions across the transition to parenthood. *Journal of Marriage and the Family, 61*, 611–25.

Crawford, D. W., & Huston, T. L. (1993). The impact of the transition to parenthood on marital leisure. *Personality and Social Psychology Bulletin, 19*, 39–46.

Crouter, A. C., Perry-Jenkins, M., Huston, T. L., & McHale, S. M. (1987). Processes underlying father involvement in dual-earner and single-earner families. *Developmental Psychology, 23*, 431–40.

Curran, M., Hazen, N., & Mann, T. (2009). Representations of marriage and expectations of parenthood: Predictors of supportive coparenting for first-time parents. *Parenting, 9*, 101–22.

Deutsch, F. (1999). *Having it all: How equally shared parenting works.* Cambridge, MA: Harvard University Press.

Dew, J., & Wilcox, W. B. (2011). If momma ain't happy: Explaining declines in marital satisfaction among new mothers. *Journal of Marriage and Family, 73*, 1–12.

Doss, B. D., Rhoades, G. K., Stanley, S. M., & Markman, H. J. (2009). The effect of the transition to parenthood on relationship quality: An 8-year perspective study. *Journal of Personality and Social Psychology, 96*, 601–19.

Elgar, K., & Chester, A. (2007). The mental health implications of maternal employment: Working versus at-home mothering identities. *Australian e-Journal for the Advancement of Mental Health, 6*(1), 1–9.

England, P., & Edin, K. (2009). *Unmarried couples with children.* New York: Russell Sage Foundation.

Fagan, J., & Barnett, M. (2003). The relationship between maternal gatekeeping, paternal competence, mothers' attitudes about the father role, and father involvement. *Journal of Family Issues, 24*, 1020–43.

Feeney, J. A., Hohaus, L., Noller, P., & Alexander, R. P. (2001). *Becoming parents: Exploring the bonds between mothers, fathers, and their infants.* Cambridge: Cambridge University Press.

Feldman, S. S., & Nash, S. C. (1984). The transition from expectancy to parenthood: Impact of the firstborn child on men and women. *Sex Roles, 11*, 61–78.

Figley, C. R. (1973). Child density and the marital relationship. *Journal of Marriage and the Family, 35*, 272–82.

Gaunt, R. (2008). Maternal gatekeeping antecedents and consequences. *Journal of Family Issues, 29*(3), 373–95.

Genesoni, L., & Tallandini, M. A. (2009). Men's psychological transition to fatherhood: An analysis of the literature, 1989–2008. *Birth, 36*(4), 305–18.

Giele, J. Z. (2008). Homemaker or career woman: Life course factors and racial influences among middle class Americans. *Journal of Comparative Family Studies, 39*(3), 393–411.

Glenn, N. D. (1998). The course of marital success and failure in five American 10-year marriage cohorts. *Journal of Marriage and the Family, 60*, 569–76.

Goldberg, A. E., & Perry-Jenkins, M. (2004). Division of labour and working-class women's well-being across the transition to parenthood. *Journal of Family Psychology, 18*(1), 225–36.

Grote, N. K., Naylor, K. E., & Clark, M. S. (2002). Perceiving the division of family work to be unfair: Do social comparisons, enjoyment, and competence matter? *Journal of Family Psychology, 16*, 510–22.

Habib, C., & Lancaster, S. (2010). Changes in identity and paternal-fetal attachment across a first pregnancy. *Journal of Reproductive and Infant Psychology, 28*(2), 128–42.

Hawkins, A. J., & Dollahite, D. C. (Eds.) (1997). *Generative fathering.* Thousand Oaks, CA: Sage.

Helms-Erickson, H. (2001). Marital quality ten years after the transition to parenthood: Implications of the timing of parenthood and the division of housework. *Journal of Marriage and Family, 63*, 1099–110.

Henwood, K., & Procter, J. (2003). The "good father": Reading men's accounts of paternal involvement during the transition to first-time fatherhood. *British Journal of Social Psychology*, 42(3), 337–55.

Herzog, M. J., Umana-Taylor, A. J., Madden-Derdich, D. A., & Leonard, S. A. (2007). Adolescent mother's perceptions of fathers' parental involvement: Satisfaction and desire for involvement. *Family Relations*, 56(3), 244–57.

Hill, R. (1949). *Families under stress: Adjustment to the crises of ward and separation and reunion*. New York: Harper.

Hofferth, S. L., & Goldscheider, F. (2010). Family structure and the transition to early parenthood. *Demography*, 47, 415–37.

Holmes, E. K., Erickson, J. J., & Hill, E. J. (in press). Doing what she thinks is best: Maternal psychological well-being and attaining desired work situations. *Human Relations*.

Holmes, E. K., Baumgartner, J., Marks, L. D., Palkovitz, R., & Nesteruk, O. (2010). Contemporary contradictions and challenges facing married fathers and mothers. In K. S. Pearlman (Ed.), *Marriage: Roles, stability, and conflict* (pp. 157–71). Hauppage, NY: Nova Science.

Holmes, E. K., Duncan, T., Bair, S., & White, A. (2007). How mothers and fathers help each other count. In S. E. Brotherson, and J. M. White (Eds.), *Why fathers count* (pp. 43–58). Harriman, TN: Men's Studies Press.

Hudson, D. B., Elek, S., & Fleck, M. (2001). First-time mothers' and fathers' transition to parenthood: Infant care self-efficacy, parenting satisfaction, and infant sex. *Issues in Comprehensive Pediatric Nursing*, 26, 5–6.

Huston, T. L., & Vangelisti, A. L. (1991). Socioemotional behavior and satisfaction in marital relationships: A longitudinal study. *Journal of Personality and Social Psychology*, 61, 721–33.

——(1995). How parenthood affects marriage. In M. A. Fitzpatrick & A. Vangelisti (Eds.), *Explaining family interactions* (pp. 147–76). Thousand Oaks, CA: Sage.

Johnson, E. M. (2000). The child care and employment decision-making process of expecting parents. Unpublished doctoral dissertation, The University of Texas at Austin.

Johnston, D. D., & Swanson, D. H. (2007). Cognitive acrobatics in the construction of worker-mother identity. *Sex Roles*, 57(5): 447–59.

Kamp Dush, C. M., Taylor, M. G., & Kroeger, R. A. (2008). Marital happiness and psychological well-being across the life course. *Family Relations*, 57(2), 211–26.

Karney, B. R., & Bradbury, T. N. (1997). Neuroticism, marital interaction, and the trajectory of marital satisfaction. *Journal of Personality and Social Psychology*, 72, 1075–92.

Keizer, R., Dykstra, P. A., & Poortman, A. R. (2010). The transition to parenthood and well-being: The impact of partner status and work hour transitions. *Journal of Family Psychology*, 24, 429–38.

Kelly, J. R., & McGrath, J. E. (1988). *On time and method*. Newbury Park, CA: Sage.

Kluwer, E. S. (2010). From partnership to parenthood: A review of marital change across the transition to parenthood. *Journal of Family Theory and Review*, 2, 105–25.

Lawrence, E., Rothman, A. D., Cobb, R. J., Rothman, M. T., & Bradbury, T. N. (2008). Marital satisfaction across the transition to parenthood. *Journal of Family Psychology*, 22, 41–50.

LeMasters, E. E. (1957). Parenthood as crisis. *Marriage and Family Living*, 19, 352–55.

——(1970). *Parents in modern society: A sociological analysis*. Homewood, IL: Dorsey.

Lennon, M. C., & Rosenfeld, S. (1994). Relative fairness and the division of housework: The importance of options. *American Journal of Sociology*, 100, 506–31.

MacDermid, S. M., Huston, T. L., & McHale, S. M. (1990). Changes in marriage associated with the transition to parenthood: Individual differences as a function of sex-role attitudes and changes in the division of household labor. *Journal of Marriage and the Family*, 52, 475–86.

McBride, B. A., Brown, G. L., Bost, K. K., Shin, N., Vaughn, B., & Korth, B. (2005). Paternal identity, maternal gatekeeping, and father involvement. *Family Relations*, 54, 350–72.

McHale, S. M., & Huston, T. L. (1984). Men and women as parents: Sex role orientations, employment, and parental roles with infants. *Child Development*, 55, 1349–61.

——(1985). The effect of the transition to parenthood on the marriage relationship: A longitudinal study. *Journal of Family Issues*, 6, 409–33.

McLanahan, S. (2009). Fragile families and the reproduction of poverty. *The ANNALS of the American Academy of Political and Social Science*, 621, 111–31.

Medina, A. M., Lederhos, C. L., & Lillis, T. A. (2009). Sleep disruption and decline in marital satisfaction across the transition to parenthood. *Families, Systems, & Health*, 27(2), 153–60.

Meyerowitz, J. H., & Feldman, H. (1966). Transition to parenthood. *Psychiatric Research Reports*, 20, 78–84.

Miller, B. C. (1976). A multivariate developmental model of marital satisfaction. *Journal of Marriage and the Family*, 38, 643–57.

Miller, B. C., & Sollie, D. L. (1980). Normal stresses during the transition to parenthood. *Family Relations*, 29, 459–65.

Moore, K. A., & Waite, L. J. (1981). Marital dissolution, early motherhood and early marriage. *Social Forces*, 60, 20–40.

Morman, M. T., & Floyd, K. (2002). A "changing culture of fatherhood": Effects on closeness, affection, and satisfaction in men's relationships with their fathers and their sons. *Western Journal of Communication*, 66, 395–411.

Previti, D., & Amato, P. R. (2004). Why stay married? Rewards, barriers, and marital stability. *Journal of Marriage and Family*, 65(3), 561–73.

Rholes, W. S., Simpson, J. A., Blakely, B. S., Lanigan, L., & Allen, E. A. (1997). Adult attachment styles, the desire to have children, and working models of parenthood. *Journal of Personality*, 65, 357–85.

Robins, E. (1990). The study of interdependence in marriage. In F. D. Fincham & T. Bradbury (Eds.), *The psychology of marriage: Basic issues and applications* (pp. 59–86). New York: Guilford Press.

Ruble, D. N., Fleming, A. S., Hackel, L. S., & Stangor, C. (1988). Changes in the marital relationship during the transition to first time motherhood: Effects of violated expectations concerning the division of labor. *Journal of Personality and Social Psychology*, 55, 78–87.

Russell, C. S. (1974). Transition to parenthood: Problems and gratifications. *Journal of Marriage and the Family*, 36, 294–302.

Ryder, R. G. (1973). Longitudinal data relating marriage satisfaction and having a child. *Journal of Marriage and the Family*, 35, 604–6.

Sano, Y., Richards, L. N., & Zvonkovic A. M. (2008). Are mothers really "gatekeepers" of children? Rural mothers' perceptions of nonresident fathers' involvement in low-income families. *Journal of Family Issues*, 29(12), 1701–23.

Schoppe-Sullivan, S. J., Cannon, E. A., Brown, G. L., Mangelsdorf, S. C., & Sokolowski, M. S. (2008). Maternal gatekeeping, coparenting quality, and fathering behavior in families with infants. *Journal of Family Psychology*, 22(3), 389–98.

Smith, S. E., & Huston, T. L. (2004). How and why marriages change over time: Shifting patterns of companionship and partnership. In R. Conger (Ed.), *Continuity and change in family relations: Theory, methods, and empirical findings* (pp. 145–80). Mahwah, NJ: Lawrence Erlbaum Associates.

Shapiro, A. F., Gottman, J. M., & Carrere, S. (2000). The baby and the marriage: Identifying factors that buffer against decline in marital satisfaction after the first baby arrives. *Journal of Family Psychology*, 14(1), 59–70.

Strauss, R., & Goldberg, W. A. (1999). Self and possible selves during the transition to fatherhood. *Journal of Family Psychology*, 13, 244–59.

Tomlinson, P. S. (1987). Spousal differences in marital satisfaction during the transition to parenthood. *Nursing Research*, 36, 239–43.

Twenge, J. M., Campbell, W. K., & Foster, C. A. (2003). Parenthood and marital satisfaction: A meta-analytic review. *Journal of Marriage and Family*, 65, 574–83.

U.S. Bureau of Census (2011). *Statistical abstract of the United States*. Washington, DC: U.S. Government Printing Office.

U.S. Center for Disease Control (2011). *National vital statistics reports*,59(3). http://www.cdc.gov/nchs/data/nvsr/nvsr59/nvsr59_03.pdf?loc=interstitialskip.

Waite, L. J., Browning, D., Doherty, W. J., Gallagher, M., Luo, Y., & Stanley, S. M. (2002). *Does divorce make people happy? Findings from a study of unhappy marriages*. New York: The Institute for American Values.

Waite, L. J., & Lillard, L. A. (1991). Children and marital disruption. *American Journal of Sociology*, 96, 930–53.

Waldron, H., & Routh, D. K. (1981). The effect of the first child on the marital relationship. *Journal of Marriage and the Family*, 43, 785–88.

Waldrop, J. (1994). What do working women want? *American Demographics*, 16, 36–37.

Erin K. Holmes, Ted L. Huston, Anita L. Vangelisti, and Trey D. Guinn

Wallace, P. M., & Gotlib, I. H. (1990). Marital adjustment during the transition to parenthood: Stability and predictors of change. *Journal of Marriage and the Family, 52,* 21–29.

Wilcox, W., & Nock, S. (2006). What's love got to do with it? Equality, equity, commitment, and women's marital quality. *Social Forces, 84*(3), 1321–45.

Yeung, J. W., Sandberg, J. F., Davis-Kean, P. E., & Hofferth, S. L. (2001). Children's time with fathers in intact families. *Journal of Marriage and Family, 63*(1), 136–54.

6

Generational Juggling

Family Communication at Midlife

Karen L. Fingerman, Kira Birditt,
Jon Nussbaum, and Diana S. Ebersole

Adulthood, like a good story, has a beginning, middle, and an end. Like many stories, however, the beginning and the end of adulthood are more clearly explicated than the middle. Although the start of adulthood in most Western societies does not involve a formal ceremony, there are definable indicators of this period of life. As a matter of course, in general, young adults complete schooling, search for paid work, find mates, and start new families (Furstenberg, 2010). Likewise, late adulthood includes physical and social markers such as retirement, an intensification of ties to family, chronic disease, and physical decline. But, what are the characteristics of midlife, and how do these characteristics shape family communication? What occurs in the middle years of adult family life that differentiates it from the beginning and the end?

This chapter examines the ways in which family communication patterns are distinct at midlife. Other chapters in this volume address relationships that pepper middle-aged adults' lives—middle-aged adults communicate with romantic partners, children, and extended family. They engage in conflict resolution, attend reunions, build new relationships, and maintain friendships. In this chapter, however, we consider characteristics of middle adulthood that may contribute to family communication. Middle-aged adults bring perspectives to their relationships based on their prior experiences and their current developmental goals. Finally, families are systems with dynamic processes; middle-aged adults respond to interactions with other family members in their communications (Fingerman & Bermann, 2000).

We first describe aspects of middle-aged adults' family life and the roles they occupy as well as their developmental goals and experiences. Then, we address two questions about family communication in midlife:

1 What is the content of family communication for middle-aged individuals?
2 What factors determine how middle-aged individuals communicate with family members?

Finally, we devote attention to topics in this area ripe for future research. As the population grows older, the middle years of adulthood become increasingly discrete and increasingly important for family functioning. Scholarly work in this area has only begun to investigate what is happening to individuals within families at midlife.

Characteristics of Midlife

Individual differences are rampant at midlife. Middle-aged adults manifest variation on nearly every issue of interest to family scholars: marital status, presence and age of children, physical health, career development, grandparenting roles, ties to family of origin and their own aging parents, leisure time, and personal style of communication. Indeed, treatises on midlife development commonly begin with disclaimers about the vast diversity evident at this period of life (e.g., Lachman, 2001; Staudinger & Bluck, 2001). Add to these considerations macrolevel differences with regard to gender, socioeconomic status, and ethnicity, and the question arises, should we even attempt to describe commonalities of midlife communication?

In fact, convergent experiences exist at midlife, just as they exist in infancy, adolescence or old age. People communicate in different ways based on their accumulated life experiences, who they are communicating with, their available time and energy, and the roles or social positions they occupy; these factors vary systematically by age (Nussbaum, Pecchioni, Robinson, & Thompson, 2000). In the following section, we first describe the social contexts in which middle-aged adults function and then consider psychological goals that middle-aged adults share.

Social Contexts of Midlife Communication

Popular culture often describes midlife as a period of increasing demands from others, as "life in the middle" with regard to social and work pressures. To assess the challenges middle-aged adults face, we pulled together national data regarding the roles and demands middle-aged adults confront in their daily lives in comparison to younger and older adults. Table 6.1 provides a summary of this information (see table footnotes for citations). This table is intended as a heuristic rather than as precise information about the activities of middle-aged adults. For example, published reports of the percentages of adults who have children over the age of 18 and who have living parents include data from the 1980s (e.g., Rossi & Rossi, 1990; Sweet, Bumpass, & Vaughn, 1988). Instead, we used data from the more recent National Survey of Midlife Development (MIDUS) study to estimate these probabilities (Radler & Ryff, 2010). For some activities, we could not obtain precise information for all age categories. When data were available for a wider age range than used in the table, we repeated numbers across columns (e.g., physical disability rates for individuals aged 20 to 34 and 35 to 44 in the table reflect reported disability rates for individuals aged 20 to 44). We describe three general aspects of this table:

1 the family relationships middle-aged adults have;
2 the other social roles in which they are embedded;
3 the task demands in which family communication takes place.

Family Ties at Midlife

The term "midlife" is highly descriptive with regard to family ties—it is literally a period in the middle of the family. A study of individuals aged 13 to 99 revealed that middle-aged

Table 6.1 Competing Demands at Midlife: Proportions of Individuals Fitting Each Category by Age Group

	Age					
	20–34	35–44	45–54	55–64	65–74	75+
Health status						
Has a physical disability[a]	.11	.11	.19	.30	.40	.64
Limitation in activity[b]	.07	.07	.13	.20	.25	.42
4+ healthcare appointments in past year[c]	.32	.32	.38	.45	.57	.65
Had major depression in past year[d]	.03	.03	.02	.02	.01	.01
Social engagement						
Working for pay[e]	.70	.77	.75	.60	.25	.07
Enrolled in school[f]	.19	.04	.02	.00	.00	.00
Community activity 2+ hours a week[g]	.62	.64	.56	.51	.47	.32
Exercises at least 3 times a week[i]	.36	.36	.32	.32	.26	.18
Uses the Internet[h]	.91	.84	.86	.78	.61	.42
Uses internet social media[h]	.74	.55	.47	.36	.21	.08
Family roles						
Married[j]	.91	.77	.77	.68	.65	.76
Widowed[j]	.01	.02	.04	.05	.16	.99
Children in home under 18[j]	.32	.40	.23	.04	.01	.00
Children aged 18–24 in home[j]	.00	.13	.56	.27	.02	.00
Children over 18[k]	.00	.26	.62	.77	.74	.74
Has grandchildren[l]	.03	.33	.33	.79	.81	.81
Grandmother regularly helps with grandchildren[m]	–	–	.54	.45	.29	–
Has a living mother[k]	.71	.69	.55	.30	.09	–
Has a living father[k]	.61	.51	.31	.10	.01	–
Providing care for spouse[n]	.01	.03	.05	.05	.07	.07
Providing care for aging parent[n]	.05	.10	.11	.11	.06	.01
Total U.S. population in year 2008 in 1,000s	61,991	42,501	44,372	33,686	20,123	18,747

Source:
[a] U.S. Bureau of the Census (2005). *Survey of income and program participation, June-September 2005*. Retrieved from http://www.census.gov/hhes/www/disability/sipp/disable05.html

[b] National Center for Health Statistics (2006–7). *Activity limitation caused by chronic conditions among working-age adults*. Retrieved from http://www.cdc.gov/nchs/data/hus/hus09.pdf#fig14

[c] National Center for Health Statistics (2010). *Health, United States*. Retrieved from http://www.cdc.gov/nchs/data/hus/2010/091.pdf

[d] National Center for Health Statistics (2005–6). *Depression among adults 18 years of age and over by sex and age: United States*. Retrieved from http://www.cdc.gov/nchs/data/hus/hus09.pdf#fig12

[e] Bureau of Labor Statistics (2010). *Labor force statistics from the current population survey*. Retrieved from http://www.bls.gov/cps/cpsaat3.pdf

[g] Gallup Organization (1990). *Giving and volunteering in the United States: Findings from a national survey*. Washington, DC: Independent Sector.

[h] Pew Internet & American Life Project (2010). December 2010: *Social side of the internet* [Data file]. Retrieved from http://www.pewinternet.org/Shared-Content/Data-Sets/2010/December-2010-Social-Side-of-the-Internet.aspx

[i] U.S. Bureau of the Census (2008). *Statistical abstracts of the United States*. Retrieved from http://www.census.gov/compendia/statab/2011/tables/11s0208.pdf.

[k] O. G. Brim, P. B. Baltes, L. L. Bumpass, P. D. Cleary, D. L. Featherman, W. R. Hazzard & R. A. Shweder (2011). *National survey of midlife development in the United States* (MIDUS), 1995–96. ICPSR02760-v7. Ann Arbor, MI: Inter-university Consortium for Political and Social Research.

[l] M. E. Szinovacz (1998). Grandparents today: A demographic profile. *The Gerontologist, 38*, 37–52.

[m] N. Baydar & J. Brooks-Gunn (1998). Profiles of grandmothers who help care for their grandchildren in the United States. *Family Relations, 47*, 385–93.

[n] N. F. Marks (1996). Caregiving across the lifespan. National prevalence and predictors. *Family Relations, 45*, 27–36.

adults had more living family members than did younger or older adults (Fingerman & Birditt, 2003). Middle-aged adults have ties to family members in generations above them (e.g., parents), generations below them (e.g., children and grandchildren), and their own generation (e.g., partner, siblings, and cousins). Younger adults have ties to their family of origin, but are generally in the process of finding mates and having children. By contrast, at the end of life, older adults have often lost their parents and may have outlived their spouses, siblings, and even some of their children.

Obviously, there is considerable diversity in middle-aged adults' family ties. For example, high divorce rates, alternative lifestyles, and decisions during early adulthood leave a high proportion of adults unpartnered at midlife. The presence and ages of children also varies. Some individuals who had children early in life are showing pictures of grandchildren to co-workers at midlife, whereas other individuals who had children in their 30s or 40s are organizing play dates for their toddlers, and still other individuals enjoy evenings out on the town in the absence of ties to children. Nonetheless, midlife tends to be the period when individuals of all backgrounds have the greatest number of close family ties (Antonucci & Akiyama, 1987; Fingerman & Birditt, 2003; Lang, 2004).

Middle-aged adults not only *have* more family members, they are more engaged with these family members than are younger or older adults. Young adults are interested in fostering new ties to people outside the family (Charles & Carstensen, 2010) and are unlikely to take on family demands. At the same time, however, young adults turn to their middle-aged parents for advice about their careers, schooling, and even love affairs, generating family work for this generation (Fingerman, Miller, Birditt, & Zarit, 2009). Likewise, by late life, many older adults have lost members of their own generation and turn to middle-aged children, nieces, or nephews for assistance or comfort (Wolff & Kasper, 2006).

Midlife is a period during which relationships with others tend to become salient and responsibilities for other individuals increase (Erikson, 1963). Multiple individuals across generations often depend upon the middle generation for emotional, physical, and financial support at various times and in crises (Fingerman et al., 2010; Grundy & Henretta, 2006). Middle-aged adults talk with members of generations above and below them. They assist young adult offspring, take pride in nieces, nephews, and care for grandchildren. With older family members, they discuss their own careers, children, grandchildren, the older adult's health and daily happenings, and long-time family friends and traditions. They are likely to be in communication with their siblings and cousins.

With regard to more intense caregiving, middle-aged adults are sometimes falsely referred to as "the sandwich generation" in reference to finding themselves "sandwiched" between generations. Thirty years ago, Brody (1981) warned that a significant percentage of middle-aged women would find themselves "sandwiched" in the overwhelming role of managing multiple family responsibilities. Nonetheless, social scientists do not find evidence for such "sandwiching" when they study families at midlife (Putney & Bengtson, 2001; Williams & Nussbaum, 2001). For the most part, the nearly impossible task of simultaneously caring for an older parent and a misbehaving teen in the same house is quite rare. The common place pattern is for middle-aged adults to have young adult offspring and aging parents. Research shows that middle-aged adults provide considerable support to their grown children, and the frequency of such help has increased over the past two decades (Fingerman, Cheng, Tighe, Birditt, & Zarit, 2012; Fingerman et al., 2010). Indeed, even when middle-aged adults engage in caregiving for their aging parents, they continue to support grown children, albeit to a lesser extent (Fingerman et al., 2010; Grundy & Henretta, 2006). These studies have led researchers to use the term "pivot generation" to describe middle-aged adults' attention to generations above and below them.

Furthermore, as can be seen in Table 6.1, over a third of middle-aged adults have children in their homes, and a third of them have grandchildren. Of those middle-aged adults who have grandchildren, the majority of these grandparents provide at least some care for them. Further, although information is not available concerning the age distribution of grandparents who are raising their grandchildren full-time, data from a national study indicated that their mean age is 59 (Fuller-Thomson, Minkler, & Driver, 1997). As such, a sizable group of middle-aged adults serve as surrogate parents for their grandchildren.

In short, the family context of midlife reflects a vast accumulation of ties from prior stages of life. Middle-aged adults retain ties to their families of origin, their spouse or romantic partner, their family of procreation, and often reap the benefits of grown children's ventures to create their own families. Middle-aged adults also have the stamina to foster new ties and build on existing relationships. The resulting family network provides multiple venues for communication. Middle-aged adults also often feel torn in many directions as they attempt to meet the needs of multiple family members.

Nonfamilial Demands at Midlife

Although they deal with multiple family roles, middle-aged adults also confront multiple demands outside the family (Goodman & Crouter, 2009). Some demands may impede the processes of family communication (by drawing middle-aged adults away from family) and may also generate the substance of that communication. Middle-aged adults are likely to talk about extrafamilial issues, such as work and civic activities, with family members.

For example, at the individual level, functional ability contributes to the nature of family communication. As can be seen in Table 6.1, most middle-aged adults are in good health and confront few physical difficulties getting around or communicating with loved ones. At the same time, limitations in daily activities increase around age 45, as do visits to doctors. By age 55, this shift is even more dramatic. As such, middle-aged adults must devote time and energy to their own health care in ways that younger adults (who rebound quickly from life's physical demands and a night of partying) do not. From this perspective, the capacity to communicate remains intact at midlife, but the content of communication may become more health focused (Hay et al., 2009; Wright, 2009).

Further, as can be seen in Table 6.1, family communication at midlife occurs in concurrence with demands from work and leisure activities. Research examining American's use of time indicates that parents of small children face the greatest demands on their use of time. For middle-aged adults who have small children, family communication must take place in the harried context of children's demands and schedules. Many middle-aged adults have passed this stage of hands-on childrearing, however, and have greater latitude in the use of their time on a day-to-day basis. Yet, middle-aged adults commonly confront increasing task demands at work and from multiple generations of family members who turn to them in periods of crisis. Indeed, data from the American Time Use Study collected from 2003 to 2007 found that adults aged 35 to 54 average 508 minutes a day devoted to work, family care, and household tasks, and adults aged 55 to 64 continue to average 454 minutes of such work. It is only after age 65 that work-type activities drop off (Bianchi, 2010).

As will be discussed, middle-aged adults also often take on tasks associated with maintaining ties to a variety of family members, such as holiday celebrations and special occasions. As such, we liken family communication at midlife to a juggling act: Middle-aged adults must keep a hand out to keep many interactive balls in the air simultaneously.

Content of Communication with Family Members at Midlife

Communication research often focuses on the expression of information rather than on the content of information. From a developmental perspective, what people talk about is important. Midlife is a time of numerous familial roles such as spouse, parent, child, sibling, and possibly grandchild and grandparent. At the same time, individuals encounter new responsibilities in their careers and civic lives. Individuals find themselves engaged in the most diverse set of communicative encounters of their lives, ranging from appropriate curfew times for the children, to bathroom wallpaper decisions with a spouse, to organizing the family reunion, to decisions about parental health care. At no time in life is the content of communication more diverse and thus more challenging for the individuals involved.

Social Contexts and the Content of Family Communication at Midlife

As mentioned previously, family communication at midlife partially reflects the complicated social situations in which middle-aged adults are embedded and the multiple roles they juggle. The question arises—how does the diverse content of these interactive lives relate to the construction and management of specific familial roles? At midlife, individuals are faced with maintaining several different, and at times contradictory, relational roles. For instance, they are simultaneously a parent who must raise children and a child who must manage an ever-changing power dynamic with a parent. The middle-aged adult must exhibit appropriate controlling and dominant behavior with adolescent children while indicating respect and submission with parents. The children may observe this submissive behavior and attempt to take advantage. At the same time, the middle-aged adults' parents may view the controlling behavior toward their grandchildren and attempt to interject their opinions on child rearing. The middle-aged adult must respond with appropriate communication across parties—juggling multiple roles simultaneously.

An additional challenge that adults face at midlife concerns the choice as to whether particular topics should or should not be communicated to a specific individual, to numerous individuals, or to no family members. Midlife presents the individual with an overwhelming number of conversation options. It is not unreasonable to imagine that certain familial relationships are appropriate for certain conversations, whereas other relationships would be threatened if not destroyed by a similar conversation. For example, a divorced, middle-aged woman might talk with her teenage daughter about the daughter's desire to date a young man in her class at school, to her mother about the loneliness of being unpartnered, but to neither party about her own sexual behavior. Similarly, a husband and wife might discuss financial problems with one another, but seek to hide these problems from grown children and aging parents.

There is little doubt that middle-aged adults are aware of their conversational choices and the effects that these choices have upon the family members with whom they interact. The juggling act of maintaining appropriate conversational boundaries adds to the complexities of family ties at midlife. Middle-aged adults not only find themselves in multiple family roles but also must possess an understanding of the parameters of those roles that help determine what and with whom they communicate if their communication is to be successful.

Content Reflecting Middle-Aged Adults' Psychological Development

Features of psychological development may also contribute to what middle-aged adults talk about with family members. Middle-aged adults tend to demonstrate greater cognitive complexity, stability of the self, and more mature coping styles than do younger or older adults (Diehl, Youngblade, Hay, & Chui, 2011; Labouvie-Vief, Hakim-Larson, & Hobart, 1987). These features of individual development contribute to a more sophisticated pattern of communication and to greater control over the content of that communication. For example, observational studies of middle-aged women talking with their adolescent children and with their mothers reveals that the middle-aged adult does most of the talking, regardless of the family partner (Lefkowitz & Fingerman, 2003; Lefkowitz, Kahlbaugh, & Sigman, 1996). Further, the content of those communiqués tends to involve the middle-aged adult's efforts to guide other family members, to provide advice or input into their behaviors (Fingerman, 2000).

The emotional qualities of relationships at midlife also tend to be complex. Carstensen and her colleagues have argued that individuals focus on emotional goals in relationships as they approach the end of life. Older adults select relationships that are most rewarding and describe their relationships in more positive terms than do younger adults (Carstensen, Isaacowitz, & Charles, 1999; Charles & Carstensen, 2010). Yet, middle-aged adults tend to view their relationships in more complicated emotional terms than do older or younger adults. For example, middle-aged adults are both more positive and more negative about their parents and their children than are younger or older adults; they may see nuances of the strengths and weaknesses of these family members in any given encounter (Fingerman, 2000; Fingerman & Hay, 2004). Middle-aged adults may also talk more about the "other" rather than the "self" in family communication based on both social contexts and psychological processes at midlife. From a theoretical perspective, Erikson (1950) initially argued that midlife is a period of generativity, a time during which individuals increasingly derive rewards from assisting and guiding younger people. Subsequent research suggests middle-aged adults are also likely to nurture individuals in their own generation and generations above them (Stewart & Vandewater, 1998). For example, in one study, middle-aged women were asked to describe what they enjoy about their aging mothers and their grown daughters. Middle-aged women reported that conversations about everyday events were a source of pleasure in both relationships. The women enjoyed conversations about the daughter's decisions at school, romantic ties, and her children (if she had them). With their mothers, they talked about daily events, friends, or the larger family network in which both women were invested (Fingerman, 2000).

As an extension of generativity, middle-aged adults may engage in conversations aimed at protecting other family members. A series of studies have found that adults of all ages engage in protective communication behaviors when they perceive time remaining with another person as limited (Fingerman & Charles, 2010). This theoretical premise extends to middle-aged adults' behaviors with their family members. Studies suggest middle-aged offspring worry about their parents' future health needs long before the parents incur actual needs for care (Cicirelli, 1988; Fingerman, Hay, Kamp Dush, Cichy, & Hosterman, 2007). Further, middle-aged grandparents worry about their grandchildren's home environments more than do older grandparents (though older grandparents worry more about their grandchildren overall; Fingerman, 1998). Middle-aged adults are likely to communicate these concerns to other family members in their efforts to nurture them or to contribute to their growth.

Finally, by midlife, gender differences in family communication notable in the early years of adulthood may become muted (Huyck, 1999). Men and women alike may value their relationships, and the content of communication may focus increasingly on efforts to connect to family members. Gerontologists have argued that an older woman in the family often serves as the "kinkeeper" who rallies family members to celebrations and reunions (Troll, 1988). Yet, it is middle-aged adults who are the "kinkeepees," the individuals who respond to the kinkeeper's efforts by attending such festivities and bringing along their spouses, children, and other relatives (Fingerman, 2001). As grown children leave home and return to visit, men and women alike may become invested in fortifying ties, organizing family structure, and bridging relationships. In sum, from both a theoretical and a practical perspective, the content of middle-aged adults' family conversations may focus on the details of keeping the family going.

Communication Styles at Midlife

In addition to considering *what* middle-aged adults communicate within families, we might ask, how do they communicate it? Williams and Nussbaum (2001) argued that middle-aged adults must develop a complex set of communicative behaviors to simultaneously meet the disparate needs of multiple generations of family members. Family communication is often difficult under the most perfect conditions. Numerous studies (see Williams & Nussbaum, 2001, for a review) have shown middle-aged adults face distinct challenges, however, as they interact with family and nonfamily members of differing ages. The general issues surrounding competent family communication encompass use of language, cognitive processing ability, stereotypes that may result in misjudged accommodations to the conversational partner, and general skills that are required to send and receive messages. Yet, middle-aged adults face particular demands in these processes. Middle-aged adults must develop sophisticated approaches to communication given their need to interact with multiple partners of different ages. These partners have specific familial roles, a wide range of cognitive abilities, differing interactive styles, and may or may not possess the necessary skills to manage an effective conversation at times. Furthermore, middle-aged adults must adjust their communication styles to facilitate family unity.

Middle-aged adults' communication styles may reflect their social contexts and their psychological development. From a contextual perspective, they must simultaneously serve as listeners and communicators in their family relationships, while processing what is taking place. To illustrate this point, a young child wishes to communicate her desire to go to the park to her parents. Appropriate to her age, she is not concerned with her parents' desires, whether going to the park conflicts with her older brother's desire for help with his homework, or drawing the larger family together (e.g., her mother's need to telephone the child's grandmother). Middle-aged adults possess the capacity to consider others' needs. At times, their own needs may dominate their concern, but middle-aged adults often turn outward to balance the needs of other family members.

As a result, middle-aged adults must "analyze the audience" as they juggle; they must determine what each family member wants and understands. This task requires specific skills to communicate with an appropriate style and intensity for each family member. Furthermore, middle-aged adults not only are concerned with communication in each of their multiple relationships (e.g., with spouse, parent, child) but also are concerned *across* these ties. Midlife communication styles may reflect a desire to unify the family or at least to handle multiple relationships.

Middle-aged adults' positions in the family may also diminish their likelihood of confronting other family members in an aggressive manner. Rook (1995) argued that certain family ties, such as long-term marriage, parenting, and caring for an aging parent, entail enduring responsibilities. Such responsibilities may curtail negative behaviors and even negative feelings. Similarly, an experimental study asked adults of different ages to indicate how they would react to social transgressions committed by older and younger social partners. Participants were considerably less likely to confront an older adult than a younger adult committing the exact same faux pas (Miller, Fingerman, & Charles, 2009). In midlife, adults may increasingly mute their responses as their family members grow older.

Furthermore, psychological processes such as the ability to regulate emotions may contribute to individuals' ways of dealing with interpersonal problems (Birditt, Fingerman, & Almeida, 2005). Birditt and Fingerman (2005) asked individuals how they handled problems they experienced in their close and problematic relationships. They found that older adults were more likely to use avoidant strategies (e.g., doing nothing) to solve the problems than were younger people (who used confrontational means of handling problems more often). Bergstrom and Nussbaum (1996) reasoned that younger and middle-aged adults might differ in their strategies for dealing with interpersonal conflict in general. Results from their investigation point toward more cooperative conflict management as individuals grow older. For the most part, in their study, younger adults were found to be more aggressive and competitive in their style of conflict, whereas older adults were more conciliatory in working out a solution that benefited both family members.

In sum, as middle-aged adults find themselves in positions of increasing responsibility and authority, they may be more likely to take charge of family communication. In this regard, middle-aged adults may attempt to direct conversation, ask questions, include multiple family members' perspectives, and adjust their conversational style to the needs of the other family members. Of course, such communication may be more an ideal than a reality. Research suggests middle-aged spouses may still engage in overt confrontation when they are upset with one another (Carstensen, Gottman, & Levenson, 1995; Story et al., 2007), and middle-aged parents may still engage in conflict with their adolescent children (Laursen & Collins, 1994; Laursen, Coy, & Collins, 1998). Furthermore, because middle-aged adults may be forced to focus so much on other people, they feel cast into a role of listener or director rather than that of communicator. Their ability to communicate their own needs may become stifled. Nonetheless, most middle-aged adults rise to the occasion and deal with family communication issues successfully.

Suggestions for Future Research

Scientific methodology by definition involves addressing unanswered questions, but we know considerably more about family communication at some periods of life than at others. Many questions about family communication in midlife warrant investigation. For example, in comparison to assessments of family ties in childhood and young childhood, researchers have relied on a limited set of methodologies to examine communication between middle-aged adults and their family members.

Future studies might seek to ascertain information about basic questions such as:

1 With whom do middle-aged adults communicate most frequently in the family?
2 What contexts require communication with different family members?
3 What is the content of communication?

With regard to the first question given the demands involved with growing children and adolescents, certain middle-aged adults may have the majority of their interactions with their children. Other middle-aged adults may have a much broader and more multigenerational family interaction pattern. For still other middle-aged adults, the oft-cited increase in marital satisfaction when children leave the nest (Gorchoff, John, & Helson, 2008) may reflect more time to communicate with a romantic partner and friends outside the family.

Certain contexts, of course, may be stressful. Middle-aged adults typically are involved with their siblings, particularly when it comes to care and support of aging parents (Suitor, Sechrist, Plikuhn, Pardo, & Pillemer, 2008). Alternately, one of the middle-aged daughters may take over care of the parents, talking primarily to her spouse about the stress incurred (Stephens, Townsend, Martire, & Druley, 2001). These difficult contexts for communication often occur with little time for planning or preparation. The siblings may have communication skills or relationship patterns allowing them to work together to assist in the aging parent, or they may experience discord and conflict. Other contexts of midlife communication are more positive. Family celebrations that surround activities such as first holy communions, bar mitzvahs, graduations, and marriages bring families together to celebrate (Fingerman, Buckser, & Turiano, 2009). These life events offer ample opportunities for family members to contact one another, share experiences, and to maintain high levels of family solidarity. Further, the content of family communication is an empirical indicator of what issues are most important to the family and which family members are involved in managing these issues. The persistence of certain content can also indicate how well middle-aged adults are managing family problems. If communication consistently focuses on stressful issues, does this indicate that the family may be dysfunctional?

Do topics of family discussion change across middle adulthood? We know little about normal changes in the content of communication across a typical day, a week, a year, or across the entirety of midlife. Scant evidence suggests young adults talk about themselves and their goals, and expect family members to be interested in these topics (Fingerman, 2000). Middle-aged adults are less intrigued with their own development. Middle-aged adults are the workers who keep the family running. As a result, are middle-aged adults confined to talking with family members about tasks that must be accomplished in daily life? Further, given demands on middle-aged adults, few individuals have time for the deep friendships characteristic of younger adulthood. How do middle-aged adults nurture their sense of art, creativity, and leisure within the family?

Midlife adults must also adapt to changing communication technologies utilized by adolescents, younger adults, and by an increasing number of older adults (Ledbetter, 2010; Mesch, 2006). On-line social networking and text messaging are challenging face-to-face communication as the preferred method with which to not only gather information, but to start, maintain, and end relationships (see Table 6.1). Midlife parents often must utilize Facebook to discover what their teenage children are doing. How do communication technologies affect communication patterns of midlife adults who attempt to stay actively engaged within the lives of their children and their parents is an area rich for future investigations. In addition, very little is known about how communication content changes or how communication effectiveness is enhanced when interacting on some form of communication technology.

In addition to these questions, future research should use diverse methodologies to tap the nonverbal aspects of family communication at midlife. The questions above prioritize the study of verbal communication. Yet, effective family communication involves sending and interpretations of nonverbal communication as well. The interpretation of messages depends upon such factors as the intensity, passion, timing, gestures, eye behavior, touch, and paralanguage of communication. Observational studies of middle-aged adults that have incorporated analysis of nonverbal behavior are notably sparse. Prior observational studies have focused on how middle-aged parents communicate with their adolescent children (Flannery, Montemayor, & Eberly, 1994; Grotevant & Cooper, 1985; Lefkowitz et al., 1996; Smetana, Yua, Restrepo, & Braeges, 1991). Indeed, most observational studies of marital couples focus on newlyweds (e.g., Cobb, Davila, & Bradbury, 2001; Hawkins, Carrere, & Gottman, 2002). Few studies have focused on communication with other family members at midlife such as parents or spouse (for exceptions see Carstensen, Gottman, & Levenson, 1995; Cichy, Lefkowitz, & Fingerman, in press; Lefkowitz & Fingerman, 2003; Story et al., 2007).

Communication scholars must consider macrolevel influences on family communication involving middle-aged adults. Investigators might also consider how changes in family structures over the past 50 years have altered family communication. For example, several excellent, recent studies have investigated the impact of divorce, remarriage, and stepfamilies upon familial communication (King, 2009; Soliz, 2007). Further, middle-aged adults must communicate not only with family members but also with outside parties *about* family members. Parents in some contexts may have greater ease in communicating with their children's teachers, peers, or after-school providers than parents in other contexts (Bronfenbrenner & Morris, 2006).

Increasing outside pressures (work, commute, geographic moves) pull people away from family ties at midlife. Technological advances over the past 50 years have rendered communication by phone or email everyday occurrences within families, regardless of distance. Likewise, car and air travel have become easier and less expensive over the past 50 years (long waits, traffic delays, and detours notwithstanding), potentially altering the ways in which family members communicate and the primacy of family in individuals' lives (Cotten, McCullough, & Adams, 2011; Fingerman, 2009). Family no longer holds the center stage on the social world that it might have in foregone eras.

In summary, scholars have only begun to examine how middle-aged adults communicate with family members. It is clear that families are strengthened by the work of middle-aged adults in bridging members of many generations. It is also clear that middle-aged adults respond to family members by juggling multiple demands and needs. Future research must focus on understanding how this act is accomplished with such apparent ease for an audience of so many.

Acknowledgement

Karen L. Fingerman was supported by "The Psychology of Intergenerational Transfers," grant R01AG02776 from the National Institute of Aging while writing this chapter.

Karen L. Fingerman, Kira Birditt, Jon Nussbaum, and Diana S. Ebersole

References

Antonucci, T. C., & Akiyama, H. (1987). Social networks in adult life and a preliminary examination of the convoy model. *Journal of Gerontology, 42,* 519–27.

Baydar, N., & Brooks-Gunn, J. (1998). Profiles of grandmothers who help care for their grandchildren in the United States. *Family Relations, 47,* 385–93.

Bergstrom, M. J., & Nussbaum, J. F. (1996). Cohort differences in interpersonal conflict: Implications for older patient-younger care provider interaction. *Health Communication, 8,* 233–45.

Bianchi, S. M. (2010). Family change and time allocation in American families. Focus on workplace flexibility, November. Retrieved from http://workplaceflexibility.org/images/uploads/program_papers/bianchi-family_change_and_time_allocation_in_american_families.pdf.

Birditt, K. S., & Fingerman, K. L. (2005). Do we get better at picking our battles? Age differences in descriptions of behavioral reactions to interpersonal tensions. *Journals of Gerontology: Psychological Sciences, 60B,* 121–28.

Birditt, K. S., Fingerman, K. L., & Almeida, D. (2005). Age and gender differences in reactions to daily interpersonal stressors. *Psychology and Aging, 20,* 330–40.

Brim, O. G., Baltes, P. B., Bumpass, L. L., Cleary, P. D., Featherman, D. L., Hazzard, W. R., & Shweder, R. A. (2011). *National survey of midlife development in the United States* (MIDUS), 1995–96 (Computer file). ICPSR02760-v7. Ann Arbor, MI: Inter-university Consortium for Political and Social Research.

Brody, E. M. (1981). Women in the middle and family help to older people. *The Gerontologist, 21,* 451–71.

Bronfenbrenner, U., & Morris, P. A. (2006). The bioecological model of human development. In W. Damon (Ed.), *Handbook of child psychology,* 6th edn (Vol. I, pp. 793–825). New York: Wiley.

Bureau of Labor Statistics (2010). *Labor force statistics from the current population survey.* Retrieved from http://www.bls.gov/cps/cpsaat3.pdf.

Carstensen, L. L., Gottman, J. M., & Levenson, R. W. (1995). Emotional behavior in long-term marriage. *Psychology and Aging, 8,* 301–13.

Carstensen, L. L., Isaacowitz, D., & Charles, S. T. (1999). Taking time seriously: A theory of socioemotional selectivity. *American Psychologist, 54,* 165–81.

Charles, S. T., & Carstensen, L. L. (2010). Social and emotional aspects of aging. *Annual Review of Psychology, 61,* 383–409.

Cichy, K. E., Lefkowitz, E. S., & Fingerman, K. L. (in press). Conflict engagement and conflict disengagement during interactions between adults and their parents. *Journal of Gerontology: Psychological Sciences.*

Cicirelli, V. G. (1988). A measure of filial anxiety regarding anticipated care of elderly parents. *The Gerontologist, 28,* 478–82.

Cobb, R. J., Davila, J., & Bradbury, T. N. (2001). Attachment security and marital satisfaction: The role of positive perceptions and social support. *Personality and Social Psychology Bulletin, 27,* 1131–43.

Cotten, S. R., McCullough, B. M., & Adams, R. G. (2011). Technological influences on social ties across the lifespan. In K. L. Fingerman, C. Berg, J. Smith, & T. C. Antonucci (Eds.), *Handbook of lifespan development* (pp. 649–74). New York: Springer.

Diehl, M., Youngblade, L. M., Hay, E. L., & Chui, H. (2011). The development of self-representations across the life span. In K. L. Fingerman, C. A. Berg, T. C. Antonucci, & J. Smith (Eds.), *The handbook of lifespan development* (pp. 613–48). New York: Springer.

Erikson, E. H. (1950). *Childhood and society.* New York: Norton.

——(1963). *Childhood and society,* 2nd edn. New York: Norton.

Fingerman, K. L. (1998). Tight lips: Aging mothers' and their adult daughters' responses to interpersonal tensions in their relationship. *Personal Relationships, 5,* 121–38.

——(2000). "We had a nice little chat": Age and generational differences in mothers' and daughters' descriptions of enjoyable visits. *Journals of Gerontology: Psychological Sciences, 55,* 95–106.

——(2001). *Aging mothers and their adult daughters: A study in mixed emotions.* New York: Springer.

——(2009). Consequential strangers and peripheral ties: The importance of unimportant relationships. *Journal of Family Theory and Review, 1,* 69–82.

Fingerman, K. L., & Bermann, E. (2000). Applications of family systems theory to the state of adulthood. *International Journal of Aging and Human Development, 51,* 5–29.

Fingerman, K. L., & Birditt, K. S. (2003). Do age differences in close and problematic family networks reflect the pool of available relatives? *Journals of Gerontology: Psychological Sciences, 58,* 80–87.

Fingerman, K. L., Buckser, A., & Turiano, N. A. (2009). Holidays and relationships. In H. T. Reis & S. K. Sprecher (Eds.), *Encyclopedia of human relationships*. Thousand Oaks, CA: Sage.

Fingerman, K. L. & Charles, S. T. (2010). It takes two to tango: Why older people have the best relationships. *Psychological Science, 19*, 172–76.

Fingerman, K. L., Cheng, Y. P., Tighe, L., Birditt, K. S., & Zarit, S. (2012). Relationships between young adults and their parents. In A. Booth, S. L. Brown, N. Landale, W. Manning & S. M. McHale (Eds.), *Early adulthood in a family context* (pp. 59–85). New York: Springer.

Fingerman, K. L., & Hay, E. L. (2004). Intergenerational ambivalence in the context of the larger social network. In K. Luescher & K. Pillemer (Eds.), *Intergenerational ambivalence: New perspectives on parent–child relations in later life* (pp. 133–52). Belgium: Elsevier/JAI Press.

Fingerman, K. L., Hay, E. L., Kamp Dush, C. M., Cichy, K. E., & Hosterman, S. (2007). Parents' and offspring's perceptions of change and continuity when parents experience the transition to old age. *Advances in Life Course Research, 12*, 275–306.

Fingerman, K. L., Miller, L. M., Birditt, K. S., & Zarit, S. (2009). Giving to the good and the needy: Parental support of grown children. *Journal of Marriage and Family, 71*, 1220–33.

Flannery, D. J., Montemayor, R., & Eberly, M. B. (1994). The influence of parent negative emotional expression on adolescents' perceptions of their relationship with their parents. *Personal Relationships, 1*, 259–74.

Fuller-Thomson, E., Minkler, M., & Driver, D. (1997). A profile of grandparents raising grandchildren in the United States. *The Gerontologist, 37*, 406–11.

Furstenberg, F. F., Jr. (2010). On a new schedule: Transitions to adulthood and family change. *Future of the Child, 20*, 67–87.

Gallup Organization (1990). *Giving and volunteering in the United States: Findings from a national survey*. Washington, DC: Independent Sector.

Goodman, W. B., & Crouter, A. C. (2009). Longitudinal associations between maternal work stress, negative work–family spillover, and depressive symptoms. *Family Relations, 58*, 245–58.

Gorchoff, S. M., John, O. P., & Helson, R. (2008). Contextualizing change in marital satisfaction during middle age: An 18-year longitudinal study. *Psychological Science, 19*, 1194–2000.

Grotevant, H. D., & Cooper, C. R. (1985). Patterns of interaction in family relationships and the development of identity exploration in adolescence. *Child Development, 56*, 415–28.

Grundy, E., & Henretta, J. C. (2006). Between elderly parents and adult children: A new look at the "sandwich generation." *Aging & Society, 26*, 707–22.

Hay, J., Shuk, E., Zapolska, J., Ostroff, J., Lischewski, J., Brady, M. S., & Berwick, M. (2009). Family communication patterns after melanoma diagnosis. *Journal of Family Communication, 9*, 209–32.

Hawkins, M. W., Carrere, S., & Gottman, J. M. (2002). Marital sentiment override: Does it influence couples' perceptions? *Journal of Marriage and Family, 64*, 193–201.

Huyck, M. H. (1999). Gender roles and gender identity in midlife. In S. L. Willis & J. D. Reid (Eds.), *Life in the middle: Psychological and social development in midlife* (pp. 209–32). San Diego, CA: Academic Press.

King, V. (2009). Stepfamily formation: Implications for adolescent ties to mothers, nonresident fathers, and stepfathers. *Journal of Marriage and Family, 71*, 954–69.

Labouvie-Vief, G., Hakim-Larson, J., & Hobart, C. J. (1987). Age, ego level, and the lifespan development of coping and defense processes. *Psychology and Aging, 2*, 286–93.

Lachman, M. E. (Ed.) (2001). *Handbook of midlife development*. New York: Wiley.

Lang, F. R. (2004). Regulating personal relationships across the lifespan: Individuals as proactive producers of their social world. In F. Lang & K. L. Fingerman (Eds.), *Growing together: Personal relationships across the lifespan* (pp. 341–67). Cambridge: Cambridge University Press.

Laursen, B., & Collins, W. A. (1994). Interpersonal conflict during adolescence. *Psychological Bulletin, 115*, 197–209.

Laursen, B., Coy, K. C., & Collins, A. (1998). Reconsidering changes in parent–child conflict across adolescence: A meta-analysis. *Child Development, 69*, 817–32.

Ledbetter, A. M. (2010). Family communication patterns and communication competence as predictors of online communication attitude: Evaluating a dual pathway attitude. *Journal of Family Communication, 10*, 99–115.

Lefkowitz, E. S., & Fingerman, K. L. (2003). Positive and negative emotional feelings and behaviors in the aging mother and adult daughter relationship. *Journal of Family Psychology, 17*, 607–17.

Lefkowitz, E. S., Kahlbaugh, P., & Sigman, M. D. (1996). Turn-taking in mother-adolescent conversations about sexuality and conflict. *Journal of Youth and Adolescence, 25,* 307–21.

Marks, N. F. (1996). Caregiving across the lifespan: National prevalence and predictors. *Family Relations, 45,* 27–36.

Mesch, G. S. (2006). Family relations and the Internet: Exploring a family boundaries approach. *Journal of Family Communication, 6,* 119–38.

Miller, L. M., Fingerman, K. L., & Charles, S. (2009). Perceptions of social transgressions in adulthood. *Journal of Gerontology: Psychological Sciences, 64,* 551–59.

National Center for Health Statistics (2010). *Health, United States.* Retrieved from http://www.cdc.gov/nchs/data/hus/2010/091.pdf.

——(2005–6). *Depression among adults 18 years of age and over by sex and age: United States.* Retrieved from http://www.cdc.gov/nchs/data/hus/hus09.pdf#fig12.

——(2006–7). *Activity limitation caused by chronic conditions among working-age adults.* Retrieved from http://www.cdc.gov/nchs/data/hus/hus09.pdf#fig14.

Nussbaum, J. F., Pecchioni, L. L., Robinson, J. D., Thompson, T. L. (2000). *Communication and aging,* 2nd edn. Mahwah, NJ: Lawrence Erlbaum Associates.

Pew Internet & American Life Project (2010). December 2010: Social Side of the Internet [Data file]. Retrieved from http://www.pewinternet.org/Shared-Content/Data-Sets/2010/December-2010-Social-Side-of-the-Internet.aspx.

Putney, N. M., & Bengtson, V. L. (2001). Families, intergenerational relationships, and kinkeeping in midlife. In M. E. Lachman (Ed.), *Handbook of midlife development* (pp. 528–70). New York: Wiley.

Radler, B. T. & Ryff, C. D. (2010). Who participates? Accounting for longitudinal retention in the MIDUS national study of health and well-being. *Journal of Aging and Health, 22,* 307.

Rook, K. S. (1995). Support, companionship, and control in older adults' social networks: Implications for well-being. In J. F. Nussbaum & J. Coupland (Eds.), *Handbook of communication and aging research* (pp. 437–64). Mahwah, NJ: Lawrence Erlbaum Associates.

Rossi, A. S., & Rossi, P. H. (1990). *Of human bonding: Parent–child relations across the life course.* New York: Aldine de Gruyter.

Smetana, J. G., Yua, J., Restrepo, A., & Braeges, J. L. (1991). Adolescent–parent conflict in married and divorced families. *Developmental Psychology, 27,* 1000–10.

Soliz, J. (2007). Communication predictors of shared family identity: Comparison of grandchildren's perceptions of family-of-origin grandparents and stepgrandparents. *Journal of Family Communication, 7,* 177–94.

Staudinger, U., & Bluck, S. (2001). A view on midlife development from lifespan theory. In M. E. Lachman (Ed.), *Handbook of midlife development* (pp. 3–39). New York: Wiley.

Stephens, M. A. P., Townsend, A. L., Martire, L. M., & Druley, J. A. (2001). Balancing parent care with other roles: Interrole conflict of adult daughter caregivers. *Journal of Gerontology: Psychological Science, 56,* P24–P34.

Stewart, A. J., & Vandewater, E. (1998). The course of generativity. In D. P. McAdams & E. de St. Aubin (Eds.), *Generativity and adult development: Psychosocial perspective on caring for and contributing to the next generation* (pp. 75–100). Washington, DC: American Psychological Association Press.

Story, T. N., Berg, C. A., Smith, T., Beveridge, R., Henry, N. A., & Pearce, G. (2007). Positive sentiment bias in middle and older married couples. *Psychology and Aging, 22,* 719–27.

Suitor, J. J., Sechrist, J., Plikuhn, M., Pardo, S. T., & Pillemer, K. (2008). Within-family differences in parent–child relations across the life course. *Current Directions in Psychological Science, 17,* 334–38.

Sweet, J., Bumpass, L., & Vaughn, C. (1988). *The design and content of the National Survey of Families and Households* (Working Paper No. 1). Center for Demography and Ecology, University of Wisconsin.

Szinovacz, M. E. (1998). Grandparents today: A demographic profile. *The Gerontologist, 38,* 37–52.

Troll, L. E. (1988). New thoughts on old families. *The Gerontologist, 28,* 586–91.

U.S. Bureau of the Census (2005). *Survey of income and program participation, June-September 2005.* Retrieved from http://www.census.gov/hhes/www/disability/sipp/disable05.html.

——(2008). *Statistical abstracts of the United States.* Retrieved from http://www.census.gov/compendia/statab/2011/tables/11s0208.pdf.

Williams, A., & Nussbaum, J. F. (2001). *Intergenerational communication across the lifespan.* Mahwah, NJ: Lawrence Erlbaum Associates.

Wolff, J. L., & Kasper, J. D. (2006). Caregivers of frail elders: Updating a national profile. *The Gerontologist, 46,* 344–56.

Wright, P. J. (2009). Father–child sexual communication in the United States: A review and synthesis. *Journal of Family Communication, 9,* 233–50.

7

Family Communication in Later Life

Jake Harwood, Christine E. Rittenour,
and Mei-Chen Lin

The study of communication in older adulthood has grown exponentially in the past 20 years. From a small body of pioneering work in the late 1980s and early 1990s, the field now boasts a large cadre of active researchers, numerous textbooks, courses at a large number of universities, and broad recognition as a valid area of study. Family is as central in older adulthood as any other period of the lifespan. Older adults are often recognized as grandparents and great-grandparents, but they are also parents, spouses, children, and even grandchildren. They are sometimes the stereotypical storehouses of family history and sage advice, but they communicate in a myriad of other ways within families. They are caregivers and care-recipients within families, but their contributions to family life extend beyond their roles in the caregiving process.

In this chapter we discuss areas of family communication in later life in which there is research and theory. We begin with some broad coverage of the communication and aging literature so as to give context for the family-specific work. This discussion includes principles shared by most researchers in the area and widely used theories. Subsequently, the bulk of the chapter is organized by relationship, with sections on spouses, siblings, adult children, and grandchildren. We close with a section on elder abuse and some concluding comments.

Three pieces of "set-up" are merited at the outset. First, researchers in this area are often asked "what counts" as old? Age is a continuum, and there is no clear demarcation for who is "old" and who is not. However, much of the research focuses on 65 as a convenient cut-off, and this chapter will do likewise. Second, the word "elderly" is used extensively to describe the populations we are addressing. As scholars concerned with communication processes, we avoid this word. It has strong associations with frailty, dependency, and illness, and is subject to the depersonalizing, homogenizing article ("*the* elderly"). As a result, we use (and recommend) the terms "older people" or "older adults," or more specific descriptors (e.g., "65- to 75-year-olds"). Third, different cultures place different values on aging, have diverse family structures within which older people are embedded, and consider family cohabitation differently. In this chapter, we attempt to incorporate such cultural concerns. However, we cannot do full justice to cultural issues given space limitations, and the fact that most research is from North America and Northern Europe.

Underlying Principles

The communication and aging literature has been driven by some broad underlying principles concerning human aging. Most communication and aging scholars accept that age brings decline in certain aspects of functioning, which in turn has consequences for communication behavior (e.g., hearing and memory problems influence communication in ways that cannot be ignored). Most scholars, however, understand this decline with some qualifications. First, we assume that *some* of that decline has a social etiology grounded in attitudes about old age. If older adults are forgetful, we ask if this is influenced by a lifetime of hearing jokes about older adult forgetfulness, exchanging birthday cards playing on ideas of memory loss, and hearing and making age-related attributions for forgetfulness. Full review of negative attitudes about old age is not appropriate here, but we direct the reader to important work by Hummert (2010) and Levy (2009).

Second, we assume that there are appropriate and successful compensations for many areas of decline (e.g., hearing aids, memory aids, increased use of social networks). The extent to which such compensations are adopted (or not) is itself a social and communicative process worthy of study. Third, we acknowledge a distinction between "normal" and "pathological" aging; declines associated with conditions such as Alzheimer's disease (AD) or other dementias are qualitatively different from, and more devastating than, normal changes expected in old age. For example, memory challenges faced in normal aging tend to be grounded in short term memory, and often result in linguistic difficulties with complex grammatical constructions (Kemper, Kynette, & Norman, 1992). In contrast, communication problems associated with AD largely relate to long-term memory problems. While grammar is retained, people with AD lose the ability to retrieve words and concepts as the disease progresses (Kemper & Mitzner, 2001).

Fourth, we assume that older adulthood is a diverse period in the lifespan (something underlined by the normal-pathological distinction just outlined). Merely the diversity in *age* among older adults is remarkable. The 30-year difference between a 67-year-old and a 97-year-old carries with it profound implications for human functioning, social roles, and family position. Add to this, diversity in socioeconomic status, health, culture, gender, marital status, and the like, and the resulting picture is extreme heterogeneity.

Fifth, many scholars acknowledge that some declines in cognitive and communicative processes uncovered in the lab are small and not particularly influential in daily life. While older adults score somewhat lower on a backwards digit span, for instance, the implications of this for daily functioning are minimal. Sixth, almost all scholars in this area would emphasize that there are *positive* changes and continued development in old age. Knowledge continues to be accumulated, which translates to continued growth in vocabulary and areas of social skills. Older adults are also happier than younger people (Yang, 2008). Amidst generally negative attitudes about aging, these positives can get lost. It is critical that we remain cognizant of benefits and improvements that come with old age in our research agendas, and avoid becoming driven by stereotypical negative assumptions.

Theoretical Perspectives

Many theoretical perspectives have been invoked in the study of family communication in later life, a few of which we summarize here. Much research emerges from an "intergroup" approach to intergenerational relations, focusing on how we deal with each other as group members rather than individuals. This involves perspectives such as social identity theory and self-categorization theory (Giles, Reid, & Harwood, 2010), which treat social categorization as an inevitable and natural process, albeit one with sometimes unfortunate consequences. This work acknowledges the family as an important social category, while also describing how family members treat one another in terms of other social categories (notably age).

Communication accommodation theory (CAT) has been a powerful force behind much communication and aging research, including work on the family (Giles, Coupland, & Coupland, 1991). CAT describes how people adjust communication to their partner. Early versions focused on adjusting speech so as to be more similar to the partner's speech style (converging). Later incarnations focused on intergroup manifestations of communication adjustments at multiple levels of discourse (e.g., adjusting discourse stylistics or topics). A particular focus has been placed on how younger people adjust their speech to accommodate perceptions of older adults' hearing (e.g., speaking louder), cognitive abilities (e.g., using simplified speech to accommodate cognitive decline), or social mores (e.g., avoiding controversial topics to accommodate "old-fashioned" values). The communication predicament of aging model has described how such adjustments contribute to dissatisfying intergenerational communication, and to reinforcing pernicious stereotypes of aging (Ryan, Giles, Bartolucci, & Henwood, 1986). On the flipside, the communication *enhancement* model has focused on how appropriate and person-centered accommodations to older adults can facilitate intergenerational communication (Ryan, Meredith, & MacLean, 1995). Also important in this area is intergroup contact theory (Allport, 1954; Harwood, 2010), which suggests that contact with members of other social groups (in this context, older adults) improves attitudes about those groups.

Beyond the intergroup, socioemotional selectivity theory suggests that certain social and psychological processes in later life are driven by lifespan position (specifically the perception of time "left" at different ages: Carstensen, 1992). Older adults' time horizon grows more limited than younger people's. As this occurs, their approach to interpersonal relations shifts from a focus on "acquiring" friends to enhancing the quality of existing relationships. Thus, they emphasize interactions with existing contacts, and become less interested in meeting new people. Socioemotional selectivity theory has been applied to marriage, depression, and marital conflict in later life (Harper & Sandberg, 2009).

Attachment theory originally aimed to understand interaction patterns between infants and their primary caregivers, and personality development as a result of these patterns (Ainsworth & Bowlby, 1991). According to the theory, children formulate attachment styles based on experiences with primary caregivers and these styles frame relationships *across the lifespan*. Research has examined associations between attachment styles and many relational phenomena (e.g., Guerrero & Bachman, 2006). Cicirelli (1983) found that adult children's attachment styles influence how they discuss caregiving arrangements.

Other perspectives such as intergenerational stake (Giarrusso, Stallings, & Bengtson, 1995), communication privacy management theory (Petronio, 2002), and relational dialectics theory (Baxter, 2004) may also generate fruitful insights on late life family communication. We now move to discuss key family relationships in older adulthood.

Spousal Communication

As a relationship frequently regarded as the beginning of a family (see Chapter 4 of this handbook), husband-wife bonds are a fruitful area for communication and aging research. However, communication-based studies of marriage in later life remain scarce, with most research appearing in other disciplines (e.g., social psychology, gerontology). We discuss a few caveats before diving into the existing literatures. First, terms such as *long-term marriages*, *older couples*, and *marriage in older couples*, have been used interchangeably. Their emphasis on relationship length versus person age complicates interpretations of study results, particularly when researchers fail to distinguish between first versus later marriages. Second, most studies on late-life marriage are cross-sectional in design. This illustrates meaningful differences between middle-aged and older couples, but longitudinal studies are needed to understand differences between relational history, cohort, or individual maturation effects (Levenson, Carstensen, & Gottman, 1993). Third, sampling techniques are a concern in this research. Solicitation in churches and senior centers might yield samples that are happier or more functional than the population (Sporakowski & Axelson, 1984).

Mirroring trends in younger populations, the bulk of older marriage studies reveal that marriage is beneficial (Gilford, 1986). Older married people have more social support available than those who are not married. They are physically healthier (Palmore, 1981) and happier (Altergott, 1985) than unmarried individuals. Consistent with other marriage research, men are particularly benefited by staying married: retired men rely on wives' social networks rather than building their own and are more likely than wives to receive spousal care (Keicolt-Glaser & Newton, 2001).

Cross-sectional studies suggest a curvilinear trend of relations across the lifespan, with middle-aged couples experiencing more conflict and negative emotions than other age groups (Sillars & Zietlow, 1993). Compared with middle-aged couples, older couples enjoy their marriage more, have fewer conflicts with their spouses, and continue to communicate affection sexually and nonsexually (Gott & Hinchliffe, 2003). Dickson and Walker (2001) found that older (versus younger) men were more emotionally expressive and willing to discuss their relationship with their wives. These findings disconfirm stereotypes of aging as decline, suggesting that benefits of intimate relationships are sustained or increased with age.

To explain heightened satisfaction in older marriages, Levenson et al. (1993) showed that older couples are less likely than middle-aged couples to argue over children. Instead, older couples shift to conversing about good memories from their children's past and current events in children's and grandchildren's lives. Children's marriages create new potential stressors with the introduction of children-in-law and potential disagreements over grandchildren (Morr Serewicz, 2006), and couples transition from spending the majority of time with younger family members to more time with each other, and become more emotionally interdependent (Arp & Arp, 1996). For couples who have been married a long time, awareness of each other's behaviors and dispositions contribute to their success. Older couples have a "been there, done that" mentality which yields a more relaxed attitude toward spousal interactions. Older adults also find ways to prevent conflicts from escalating. Levenson et al. (1993; Carstensen, Gottman, & Levenson, 1995) showed older couples expressing more positive and less negative effect during conflict.

Reciprocity of social support also affects quality of marriage among older couples (Goodman, 1999), as is the case in all marriages. However, in older adult marriages support is more likely to be manifested in more life-altering behaviors such as full-time caregiving. Though providing this support can be emotionally and physically draining for the caregiver (Mui, 1995), this strain is often tempered by the support of caregivers' friends or family (Scharlach, Li, & Dalvi, 2006) and particularly the care-receiving spouse (Dorfman, Holmes, & Berlin, 1996). Edwards and Noller (1998) found that a direct communication style by autonomous caregivers was associated with the receiver's satisfaction. Conversely, caregivers who used patronizing talk created conflict and negative effect for their spouse. Caregiving is often viewed with a negative lens, but (consistent with other forms of support) it yields benefits for both provider and receiver.

Just as marital satisfaction is linked to physical and psychological health, ample evidence links poor marital quality to depression (Harper & Sandberg, 2009). Communication between distressed individuals and their spouses is negative in both content and manner, which causes negative emotions in both partners (Kahn, Coyne, & Margolin, 1985). Negative communication such as criticism is associated with marital conflict, frustration, hostility, negative evaluation of one's spouse and the marriage, reduced intimacy between spouses, and depression. A vicious cycle may ensue, wherein both partners jointly create and reinforce marital dissatisfaction and problematic mental well-being (Segrin & Flora, 2011). Sandberg, Miller and Harper (2002) show that depressed couples demonstrate an inability to resolve conflicts or engage in empathetic communication. Such findings reflect a dyadic etiology for depression (Coyne, 1976), within which negative effects are stronger for relationally closer couples (Tower & Kasl, 1995).

Unsurprisingly, the loss of a spouse takes a heavy toll on the widow(er), particularly when it occurs at a younger age (Arp & Arp, 1996). Bergstrom and Holmes (2000) asked widows to offer advice to other widows, revealing prominent themes of staying active, spending time with family, and celebrating the qualities of the lost spouse. Such suggestions provide support for activity theory perspectives on aging (that successful aging is a product of remaining active: Atchley, 1999), and further discredit ideas pertaining to functional disengagement in old age. Though widowhood is difficult, particularly for men, bonds with children and siblings tend to grow stronger as they provide social support to buffer the effects of the loss (Anderson, 1984).

Parent–Adult Child Communication

While most parent–child research focuses on childrearing (see Chapter 5), recent work acknowledges that this relationship has important implications for families beyond the early years of life. Value transmission is a prominent parenting practice in older adulthood, particularly as it concerns memorable messages about aging (Holladay, 2002) and communicating beliefs about death (Cicirelli, 2001). Common themes include an emphasis on maintaining family relationships, working to maintain youth and youthful appearances, and embracing old age.

Upward (child to parent) influence is prevalent in the literature only in the context of caregiving. Though many older parents are the *providers* rather than the recipients of financial and emotional support (Lye, 1996), adult children increasingly provide care for their aging parents (Walker, Pratt, & Eddy, 1995). Caregiving brings benefits such as increased closeness with the parent (Koerner, Kenyon, & Shirai, 2009), pride, feelings of being needed, and joy in repayment for care received during youth (Lawton, Moss, Kieban, & Glicksman, 1991). These benefits are linked to the parents' communication of appreciation and affection to their children (Blieszner & Shifflett, 1989). Koerner and colleagues (2009) found that support from spouse, caregiver agreeableness and extroversion, and support from other family members also predict caregiver benefits.

The strains of caregiving receive greater attention in the research and include emotional stress and physical ailments (Cicirelli, 1983; Walker et al., 1995), financial loss, threats to occupation, time away from family/spouse, ethical dilemmas in providing support for parents instead of own children (Koenig, 2004), and a decline in marital satisfaction

(Sparks Bethea, 2002). These strains, though common, should be reduced with improvements to communication between parent, child, and the surrounding family system. One promising avenue here is the role of humor in these contexts, given its demonstrated utility in alleviating caregiving-related strain (Sparks Bethea, Travis, & Pecchioni, 2000; Wanzer, Sparks, & Frymier, 2009). Communication scholars should identify the communicative, relational, and personal factors associated with balancing the burdens and benefits of this complex relationship.

In the task of improving the communication surrounding adult children's care of aging parents, we might begin by assessing family discussions about caregiving. Such conversations occur infrequently; although parents (Blieszner & Mancini, 1987) and children (Pratt, Schmall, & Wright, 1987) perceive these discussions as important, the tendency is to avoid. Fowler and Fisher (2009) show that discussions are more likely when children endorse shared autonomy and parents endorse independent autonomy, have fears about aging, and expect future care needs. Given that shared autonomy is associated with joint decision-making and that independent autonomy is linked to making decisions alone, these predictors suggest that dyads more likely to discuss caregiving might also be least likely to agree. Fowler and Afifi's (2011) research suggests that children's sense of urgency about care needs determines whether or not discussions occur, and most adult children feel little sense of urgency. These studies suggest a need to balance increasing people's sense of urgency about discussing these issues, while avoiding perpetuating stereotypes of aging and dependency.

Researchers are also exploring the process and content of parent–child decision-making about eldercare. In their assessment of mother–daughter discussions, Pecchioni and Nussbaum (2000) showed that mothers' and daughters' endorsement of paternalism was associated with the daughters talking more during these discussions. Furthermore, while half of the dyads were relatively egalitarian, approximately 20 percent of the conversations involved daughters' dominating the conversation, speaking for the mother and overlooking or undermining the mother's desires.

Sibling Communication

Despite the fact that siblings are often long-lasting, resilient, and intimate bonds in the lives of older adults, family research tends to overlook these bonds (Gold, 1989). Older adulthood is a time for strong sibling bonds (Goetting, 1986). While some sibling relationships maintain closeness throughout their lifespan, others experience turning points surrounding siblings' ties to parents, spouses, and children. Due to changes in responsibilities and potential dislike for a siblings' spouse (Allan, 1977), marriage is associated with a decrease in sibling closeness that is restored when marriages experience distress (Felson, 1983), or dissolve as a result of divorce or the death of the spouse (Spicer & Hampe, 1975). Similarly, the death of, or distance from parents enhances sibling bonds due to the reduction in phenomena such as sibling rivalry (Felson, 1983). Siblings share experiences such as peer groups, power within the family system, religious and cultural orientations, and often geographic closeness (Harwood, 2007). Of course, not all siblings grow close in older adulthood, with some siblings expressing indifference or hostility toward each other (Gold, 1989).

Certain communication behaviors that negatively affect commitment, trust, and liking, are less frequent in middle and older adulthood than among younger siblings (e.g., verbal aggression: Myers & Goodboy, 2006). In older adulthood, siblings are less likely to communicate as a means of providing counsel or as an escape, tending to communicate more for positivity and to establish family connections (Fowler, 2009; Goodboy, Myers, & Patterson, 2009). Gold (1989) presents a typology of sibling relationships varying in terms of feelings (Gold, Woodbury, & George, 1990): intimate (closeness beyond obligation; best friends), congenial (deep friendship that peaks in stressful times), loyal (bond grounded in shared background rather than personal connection), apathetic (indifference and absence), and hostile (feelings of resentment, disgust, and avoidance). Future research could employ this typology to examine communicative trends across various sibling relationships, including those that are less positive.

Grandparent–Grandchild Communication

Images and rhetorics of grandparenthood have become closely associated with perceptions of aging in the family context. Such images are largely positive, which contrasts with the rather negative broader social discourse surrounding aging. The grandparent role offers a focus on nurturing that fits well with an established stereotype of older people as low in competence but high in warmth (Cuddy, Norton, & Fiske, 2005). The grandparent–grandchild relationship is for most people the "first, most frequent, and most enduring" (Harwood, 2007, p. 111) source of intergenerational communication in their lives. Increasing numbers of grandchildren have multiple grandparents who live well into the grandchildren's adulthood; the majority of recent work has focused on relational issues for grandchildren who are college-age (Soliz, Lin, Anderson, & Harwood, 2005).

Closeness and Distance

Overall, research shows that grandparent relationships are more intimate when the parties live closer together, when the grandparent is young, when the grandparent is healthy, and when the grandparent is a maternal grandmother (Harwood, 2007). Closer relationships are also more likely when women in the middle generation have a good relationship with the grandparent (Fingerman, 2004). In terms of communication *medium*, telephone (Harwood, 2000) and email (Holladay & Seipke, 2007) positively influence the quality of grandparenting relationships. Face-to-face communication in the grandparent relationship may occur more often in groups (e.g., family gatherings), and hence contribute less directly to intimacy. Telephoning or emailing is a more direct one-to-one communication connection that symbolizes targeted caring and relational commitment. In terms of communication content, accommodating behaviors, self-disclosure, and social support are all associated with positive grandparent–grandchild relationships (Harwood, 2007), as is true in many relationships. Similarly, predictable forms of relational maintenance behaviors are associated with positive grandparenting relationships (Mansson, Myers, & Turner, 2010).

Grandparents serve a symbolic function in the family context, representing the past and supporting ideas of family tradition and identity, while also representing family continuity and stability. This symbolic role is apparent in communication patterns. Storytelling between grandparents and grandchildren is frequent (see Chapter 24)—particularly from grandmothers to grandchildren (Nussbaum & Bettini, 1994). Stories often relate to family issues and serve to reinforce family identity (Kornhaber & Woodward, 1981). The symbolic function is also apparent in themes that emerge in grandparents' communication *about* the relationship. Notably, the theme of "pride" is apparent in grandparents' communication about their grandchildren (Harwood & Lin, 2000), reflecting the awareness and pleasure in the continuity of the family that grandchildren represent.

Grandparent–grandchild communication is not always characterized by undifferentiated positivity. Kam and Hecht (2009) discuss how grandchildren sometimes behave inconsistently with their personal identities when communicating with their grandparents (e.g., avoiding topics). Interestingly, Mansson et al. (2010) demonstrate that "openness" is the least commonly used relational maintenance strategy exercised by grandchildren, supporting the idea of felt-constraint in this relationship. Younger adults also report "biting their tongue" in communication with other older people (Williams & Garrett, 2002), demonstrating that some more general intergenerational communication issues extend to the grandparent–grandchild relationship, and are not buffered by shared family status (but see Anderson, Harwood, & Hummert, 2005).

Another area in which grandparent–grandchild communication reflects broader intergenerational communication issues is in terms of painful self-disclosure. Older adults disclose unpleasant life events (e.g., bereavement, illness) more than young people (Coupland, Coupland, Giles, & Henwood, 1988). Fowler and Soliz (2010) find that grandparents also disclose such events to grandchildren; grandchildren's discomfort in dealing with such disclosures is associated with more negative evaluations of the relationship.

Complex Family and Cultural Roles

Custodial relationships present a challenge to traditional grandparenting roles (Fuller-Thomson, Minkler, & Driver, 1987). Physical strain, less time for friends and spouse, decreased privacy, and financial loss represent challenges to custodial grandparents (Kolomer & McCallion, 2005). Grandparents also must help children manage emotional distress resulting from their parents' absence. Successful strategies for this include involving grandchildren in the local community, acknowledging parents' absence, and focusing on "effective communication" (Gibson, 2005). Grandparents also work to shield their grandchildren from parents' misfortunes or failures (Silverstein & Ruiz, 2006). The role shifts and stigmas surrounding custodial care sometimes overshadow important benefits of custodial grandparenting. Custodial grandparents get a second chance in the parent role, and also experience enhanced life purpose and a sense of pride (Kolomer & McCallion, 2005).

Grandparents provide support to grandchildren during parental divorce (Cogswell & Henry, 1995), including serving in complex roles. Soliz (2008) describes a peacekeeper role, wherein grandparents maintain a relationship with their child's former spouse and encourage positive perceptions of that individual in grandchildren.

Grandparent roles and behaviors are, of course, culturally patterned and distinct. Sandel, Cho, Miller, and Wang (2006) examined grandmothering in Taiwan and the U.S.A., demonstrating distinct patterns whereby advice-giving (to daughters and daughters-in-law) and disciplining of grandchildren were viewed as normative in Taiwan. In contrast, Euro-American grandmothers were more likely to view themselves as playmates to the grandchildren (Lin & Harwood, 2003). Culture also carries implications for language. In immigrant families, grandparent and grandchild may lack a common language, and they become reliant on the middle generation to serve as linguistic "brokers." Ng and He (2004) describe how such brokering can both enhance and constrain the grandparent–grandchild relationship. Weisskirch (2006) notes that language brokering is often associated with a sense of pride. This work illustrates some of the benefits of examining grandparenting tri-generationally (Miller-Day, 2004). An additional dynamic that can occur in immigrant families is when the grandchild performs translation services for the grandparent (e.g., in service settings such as physicians' offices: Greenhalgh, Robb, & Scambler, 2006). Such phenomena are more likely to occur when grandparent and grandchild cohabitate, which enhances the likelihood that the grandchild will speak the grandparent's language (Ishizawa 2004). Grandchildren are more likely to maintain the family of origin language when parents encourage such maintenance, which they often do to retain communication between grandparent and grandchild (Park & Sarkar, 2007). In the case of threatened languages, grandparents are often critical to the transmission of such languages to grandchildren, and play a central role in protecting some languages from extinction via a tri-generational transmission pattern (Nolan, 2008).

As should be clear, scholars are beginning to examine complex identities in the grandparenting context (e.g., Soliz, Thorson, & Rittenour, 2009). Families are complex and evolving structures; today's families challenge our theories as we pay more attention to gay couples; multiracial, multilingual or multinational families; step-families; families with adopted children; and single-parent families. In all of these cases, the important consequences extend beyond the parents and the children to other generations, and the implications for identities in the grandparent–grandchild relationship merit study.

Technology

Technology offers new routes for grandparent–grandchild contact, including new forms of play between grandparents and grandchildren (see Chapter 27). Some data indicate that older adults are particularly drawn to games that bring them together with their grandchildren (Mubin, Shahid, & Mahmud, 2008). Boomers are more likely to play computer games with their grandchildren rather than with their children, including on-line games with geographically distant grandchildren (Pearce, 2008). Grandchildren are often early adopters of technology who teach parents and grandparents (Aarsand, 2007), resulting in interesting identity and role shifts. There are also interesting research avenues here in terms of culture, with preliminary work showing how older generations help to structure grandchildren's learning of cultural constructs (Kenner, Ruby, Jessel, Gregory, & Arju, 2008). Technology offers numerous means by which geographical distance can be overcome, both via media already described (e.g., telephone, email) and also newer and emerging media (Vetere, Davis, Gibbs, Francis, & Howard, 2006).

Intergroup Contact

A small body of research examines whether the grandparent–grandchild relationship has broader implications for grandchildren's perceptions of older people and aging in general. Harwood, Hewstone, Paolini, and Voci (2005) demonstrate such a connection, showing that the link is mediated by specific communication behaviors (notably self-disclosure and accommodative behaviors). Soliz and Harwood (2003) demonstrate that having multiple and *diverse* grandparents predicts perceptions of older adult heterogeneity (thinking that all older people are not the same). One important issue here is the boundary of the family unit and if the grandparent is viewed as peripheral to the core family. Soliz (2007) compared step-grandparents with family-of-origin grandparents, finding that specific predictors of shared family identity were shared across grandparent types (e.g., grandchildren with better step-grandparent relationships were more likely to perceive a shared family identity with them). This contributes to the idea that family represents a "common ingroup" to which grandchildren and grandparents can subscribe; achieving the perception of belonging to the same family is one way to transcend intergenerational boundaries (Soliz & Harwood, 2006).

Elder Abuse and Family Communication

Beyond specific family relationships, communication researchers have begun to examine family dynamics surrounding abuse of older adults. Elder abuse has been treated as a crime since the 1990s but its prevalence is not fully recognized nor is enough research being done. Elder abuse is "any knowing, intentional or negligent act by a caregiver or any other person that causes harm or a serious risk of harm to someone over 65 years of age" (National Center on Elder Abuse, 2004, para 2), including physical assault, emotional harm, verbal aggression, and financial exploitation, as well as sexual abuse (Burgess, Prentky, & Dowdell, 2000). The media downplay elder abuse, focusing instead on child and spouse abuse (Payne, Appel, & Kim-Appel, 2008; see Chapter 29 for overview of abuse in the family).

A large proportion of elder abuse is perpetrated by family members—particularly husbands and adult sons (Krienert, Walsh, & Turner, 2009). Family members experience significant caregiving stress and simultaneously benefit from trust and often complete control in these relationships; a combination of factors that can precipitate abuse (Thompson, Buxton, Gough, & Wahle, 2007).

Giles and Helmle (2011) proposed a model of elder abuse and communication to address ten different bi-lateral communicative pathways between abusee, abuser, their social/family networks, and institutional networks. For instance, negative age stereotypes (Hummert, 2010) and communication schemas (Harwood, McKee, & Lin, 2000) can lead family caregivers to dismiss messages from the aging parent or misjudge his/her communication competence and hence fail to attend to his/her needs. Similarly, in links between family/friends networks and the abusee, abusees face the dilemma of whether and to whom they can disclose the abuse—such disclosure being a communicative privacy dilemma (Petronio, 2002). Disclosure is influenced not only by complex relational issues, but also by the cognitive state of the abusee (Schofield & Mishra, 2004), and the stereotyping and stigma associated with being abused (Quinn & Tomita, 1986). This discussion focuses on family caregivers as perpetrators of the crime; equally common is when the perpetrators are nursing home residents or staff. In such contexts, older adults are isolated from the community and family and their relationships with their families may greatly influence if and how they can reveal these criminal activities (Giles & Helmle, 2011).

Conclusion

This chapter has illustrated the richness and complexity of family communication in older adulthood. Beyond the stereotype of grandma in her rocking chair telling stories about the good old days, there are dynamic life-and-death issues surrounding family relationships among older adults. Communication helps us explain why older adults have positive relationships and it provides for some of the most meaningful experiences of late life. Communication also generates and perpetuates negative myths about aging which can influence even the most intimate interpersonal relationships. It is in this tension that we find the fascination in studying family communication in later life.

References

Aarsand, P. A. (2007). Computer and video games in family life. *Childhood: A Global Journal of Child Research, 14,* 235–56.

Ainsworth, M. D. S., & Bowlby, J. (1991). An ethological approach to personality development. *American Psychologist, 46,* 331–41.

Jake Harwood, Christine E. Rittenour, and Mei-Chen Lin

Allan, G. (1977). Sibling solidarity. *Journal of Marriage and the Family, 39,* 177–84.

Allport, G. W. (1954). *The nature of prejudice.* Cambridge, MA: Addison-Wesley.

Altergott, K. (1985). Marriage, gender and social relations in later life. In W. A. Peterson & J. Quadagno (Eds.), *Social bonds in later life* (pp. 51–70). Beverly Hills, CA: Sage.

Anderson, K., Harwood, J., & Hummert, M. (2005). The grandparent–grandchild relationship: Implications for models of intergenerational communication. *Human Communication Research, 31,* 268–94.

Anderson, T. B. (1984). Widowhood as a life transition. *Journal of Marriage and the Family, 46,* 105–14.

Arp, D., & Arp, C. (1996). *The second half of marriage.* New York: Zondervan.

Atchley, R. C. (1999). Continuity theory, self, and social structure. In C. D. Ryff & V. W. Marshall (Eds.), *Families and retirement* (pp. 145–58). Newbury Park, CA: Sage.

Baxter, L. A. (2004). Distinguished scholar article: Relationships as dialogues. *Personal Relationships, 11,* 1–22.

Bergstrom, M. J., & Holmes, M. E. (2000). Lay theories of successful aging after the death of a spouse. *Health Communication, 12,* 377–406.

Blieszner, R., & Mancini, J. A. (1987). Enduring ties: Older adults' parental role and responsibilities. *Family Relations, 36,* 176–80.

Blieszner, R., & Shifflett, P. A. (1989). Affection, communication, and commitment in adult-child caregiving for parents with Alzheimer's disease. In J. A. Mancini (Ed.), *Aging parents and adult children* (pp. 231–43). Lexington, MA: Lexington Books.

Burgess, A., Prentky, R., & Dowdell, E. (2000). Sexual predators in nursing homes. *Journal of Psychosocial Nursing, 38,* 26–35.

Carstensen, L. L. (1992). Social and emotional patterns in adulthood: Support for socio-emotional selectivity theory. *Psychology and Aging, 7,* 331–38.

Carstensen, L. L., Gottman, J. M., & Levenson, R. W. (1995). Emotional behavior in long-term marriage. *Psychology and Aging, 10,* 140–49.

Cicirelli, V. G. (1983). Adult children's attachment and helping behavior to elderly parents. *Journal of Marriage and the Family, 45,* 815–23.

——(2001). Personal meanings of death in older adults and young adults in relation to their fears of death. *Death Studies, 25,* 663–83.

Cogswell, C., & Henry, C. S. (1995). Grandchildren's perceptions of grandparental support in divorced and intact families. *Journal of Divorce and Remarriage, 23,* 127–50.

Coupland, N., Coupland, J., Giles, H., & Henwood, K. (1988). Elderly self-disclosure: Interactional and intergroup issues. *Language & Communication, 8,* 109–33.

Coyne, J. C. (1976). Toward an interactional description of depression. *Psychiatry, 39,* 28–40.

Cuddy, A., Norton, M., & Fiske, S. (2005). This old stereotype: The pervasiveness and persistence of the elderly stereotype. *Journal of Social Issues, 61,* 267–85.

Dickson, F. C., & Walker, K. L. (2001). The expression of emotion in later-life married men. *Qualitative Research Reports in Communication, 2,* 66–71.

Dorfman, L. T., Holmes, C. A., & Berlin, K. L. (1996). Wife caregivers of frail elderly veterans. *Family Relations, 45,* 46–55.

Edwards, H., & Noller, P. (1998). Factors influencing caregiver–care receiver communication and its impact on the well-being of older care receivers. *Health Communication, 70,* 317–41.

Felson, R. B. (1983). Aggression and violence between siblings. *Social Psychology Quarterly, 46,* 271–85.

Fingerman, K. L. (2004). The role of offspring and in-laws in grandparents' ties to their grandchildren. *Journal of Family Issues, 25,* 1026–49.

Fowler, C. (2009). Motives for sibling communication across the lifespan. *Communication Quarterly, 57,* 51–66.

Fowler, C., & Afifi, W. A. (2011). Applying the theory of motivated information management to adult children's discussions of caregiving with aging parents. *Journal of Social and Personal Relationships, 28,* 507–35.

Fowler, C., & Fisher, C. L. (2009). Attitudes toward decision making and aging, and preparation for future care needs. *Health Communication, 24,* 619–30.

Fowler, C., & Soliz, J. (2010). Responses of young adult grandchildren to grandparents' painful self-disclosures. *Journal of Language and Social Psychology, 29,* 75–100.

Fuller-Thomson, E., Minkler, M., & Driver, D. (1987). A profile of grandparents raising grandchildren in the United States. *The Gerontologist, 37,* 406–11.

Giarrusso, R., Stallings, M., & Bengtson, V. L. (1995). The "intergenerational stake" hypothesis revisited. In V. L. Bengtson, K. W. Schaie, & L. M. Burton (Eds.), *Adult intergenerational relations* (pp. 229–96). New York: Springer.

Gibson, P. A. (2005). Intergenerational parenting from the perspective of African American grandmothers. *Family Relations, 54*, 280–97.

Giles, H., Coupland, J., & Coupland, N. (1991). Accommodation theory: Communication, context, and consequence. In H. Giles, J. Coupland, & N. Coupland (Eds.), *Contexts of accommodation* (pp. 1–68). Cambridge: Cambridge University Press.

Giles, H., & Helmle, J. (2011). Elder abuse and neglect: A communicative framework. In A. Duszak & U. Okulska (Eds.), *Language, culture and the dynamics of age* (pp. 223–52). Berlin: Mouton de Gruyter.

Giles, H., Reid, S., & Harwood, J. (Eds.) (2010). *The dynamics of intergroup communication.* New York: Peter Lang.

Gilford, R. (1986). Marriages in later life. *Generations, 10*, 16–20.

Goetting, A. (1986). The developmental tasks of siblingship over the life cycle. *Journal of Marriage and Family, 48*, 703–14.

Gold, D. T. (1989). Sibling relationships in old age: A typology. *International Journal of Aging and Human Development, 28*, 37–51.

Gold, D. T., Woodbury, M. A., & George, L. K. (1990). Relationship classification using grade of membership analysis. *Journal of Gerontology, 45*, 543–51.

Goodboy, A. K., Myers, S. A., & Patterson, B. R. (2009). Investigating elderly sibling types, relational maintenance, and lifespan affect, cognition, and behavior. *Atlantic Journal of Communication, 17*, 140–48.

Goodman, C. C. (1999). Reciprocity of social support in long-term marriage. *Journal of Mental Health and Aging, 5*, 341–57.

Gott, M., & Hinchliffe, S. (2003). How important is sex in later life? The views of older people. *Social Science and Medicine, 56*, 1617–28.

Greenhalgh, T., Robb, N., & Scambler, G. (2006). Communicative and strategic action in interpreted consultations in primary health care: A Habermasian perspective. *Social Science & Medicine, 63*, 1170–87.

Guerrero, L. K., & Bachman, G. F. (2006). Associations among relational maintenance behaviors, attachment styles categories, and attachment dimensions. *Communication Studies, 57*, 341–61.

Harper, J. M., & Sandberg, J. (2009). Depression and communication processes in later life marriages. *Aging and Mental Health, 13*, 546–56.

Harwood, J. (2000). Communication media use in the grandparent–grandchild relationship. *Journal of Communication, 50*, 56–78.

——(2007). *Understanding communication and aging: Developing knowledge and awareness.* Thousand Oaks, CA: Sage.

——(2010). The contact space: A novel framework for intergroup contact research. *Journal of Language and Social Psychology, 29*, 147–77.

Harwood, J., Hewstone, M., Paolini, S., & Voci, A. (2005). Grandparent–grandchild contact and attitudes towards older adults. *Personality and Social Psychology Bulletin, 31*, 393–406.

Harwood, J., & Lin, M-C. (2000). Affiliation, pride, exchange and distance in grandparents' accounts of relationships with their college-age grandchildren. *Journal of Communication, 50*, 31–47.

Harwood, J., McKee, J., & Lin, M-C. (2000). Younger and older adults' schematic representations of intergenerational communication. *Communication Monographs, 67*, 20–41.

Holladay, S. J. (2002). "Have fun while you can," "You're only as old as you feel," and "Don't ever get old!": An examination of memorable messages about aging. *Journal of Communication, 52*, 681–97.

Holladay, S., & Seipke, H. (2007). Communication between grandparents and grandchildren in geographically separated relationships. *Communication Studies, 58*, 281–97.

Hummert, M. L. (2010). Communicating across generations. In H. Giles, S. Reid, & J. Harwood (Eds.), *Dynamics of intergroup communication* (pp. 41–52). New York: Peter Lang.

Ishizawa, H. (2004). Minority language use among grandchildren in multigenerational households. *Sociological Perspectives, 47*, 465–83.

Kahn, J., Coyne, J. C., & Margolin, G. (1985). Depression and marital conflict: The social construction of despair. *Journal of Social and Personal Relationships, 2*, 447–62.

Kam, J., & Hecht, M. (2009). Investigating the role of identity gaps among communicative and relational outcomes within the grandparent–grandchild relationship. *Western Journal of Communication, 73*, 456–80.

Keicolt-Glaser, J. K., & Newton, T. L. (2001). Marriage and health: His and hers. *Psychological Bulletin, 127*, 472–503.

Kemper, S., & Mitzner, T. L. (2001). Language production and comprehension. In J. E. Birren & K. W. Schaie (Eds.), *Handbook of the psychology of aging*, 5th edn (pp. 378–98). San Diego, CA: Academic Press.

Kemper, S., Kynette, D., & Norman, S. (1992). Age differences in spoken language. In R. West & J. Sinnot (Eds.), *Everyday memory and aging* (pp. 138–54). New York: Springer-Verlag.

Kenner, C., Ruby, M., Jessel, J., Gregory, E., & Arju, T. (2008). Intergenerational learning events around the computer. *Language & Education: An International Journal, 22*, 298–319.

Koenig, T. L. (2004). From the woman's viewpoint: Ethical dilemmas confronted by women as informal caregivers of frail elders. *Families in Society: The Journal of Contemporary Human Services, 85*, 236–42.

Koerner, S. S., Kenyon, D. B., & Shirai, Y. (2009). Caregiving for elder relatives: Which caregivers experience personal benefits/gains? *Archives of Gerontology and Geriatrics, 48*, 238–45.

Kolomer, S. R., & McCallion, P. (2005). Depression and caregiver mastery in grandfathers caring for their grandchildren. *International Journal of Aging and Human Development, 60*, 283–94.

Kornhaber, A., & Woodward, K. L. (1981). *Grandparents/grandchildren: The vital connection.* Garden City, NY: Anchor Press/Doubleday.

Krienert, J. L., Walsh, J. A., & Turner, M. (2009). Elderly in America: A descriptive study of elder abuse examining National Incident-Based Reporting System (NIBRS) data, 2000–2005. *Journal of Elder Abuse & Neglect, 21*, 325–45.

Lawton, M. P., Moss, M. S., Kieban, M. H., & Glicksman, A. (1991). A two-factor model of caregiving appraisal and psychological well-being. *Journal of Gerontology, 46*, 181–89.

Levenson, R. W., Carstensen, L. L., & Gottman, J. M. (1993). Long-term marriage: Age, gender, and satisfaction. *Psychology and Aging, 8*, 301–13.

Levy, B. (2009). Stereotype embodiment: A psychosocial approach to aging. *Current Directions in Psychological Science, 18*, 332–36.

Lin, M-C., & Harwood, J. (2003). Predictors of grandparent–grandchild relational solidarity in Taiwan. *Journal of Social and Personal Relationships, 20*, 537–63.

Lye, D. N. (1996). Adult child–parent relationships. *Annual Review of Sociology, 22*, 79–102.

Mansson, D., Myers, S., & Turner, L. (2010). Relational maintenance behaviors in the grandchild-grandparent relationship. *Communication Research Reports, 27*, 68–79.

Miller-Day, M. A. (2004). *Communication among grandmothers, mothers, and adult daughters.* Mahwah, NJ: Lawrence Erlbaum Associates.

Morr Serewicz, M. C. (2006). Getting along with the in-laws: Relationships with parents-in-law. In K. Floyd & M. Morman (Eds.), *Widening the family circle* (pp. 101–28). Thousand Oaks, CA: Sage.

Mubin, O., Shahid, S., & Mahmud, A. (2008). Walk 2 win: Towards designing a mobile game for elderly's social engagement. ACM *Proceedings of the 22nd Annual British HCI Conference*, Liverpool, England. Retrieved from http://www.bcs.org/upload/pdf/ewic_hc08_v2_paper3.pdf.

Mui, A. C. (1995). Multidimensional predictors of caregiver strain among older persons caring for frail spouses. *Journal of Marriage and the Family, 57*, 733–40.

Myers, S. A., & Goodboy, A. K. (2006). Perceived sibling use of verbally aggressive messages across the lifespan. *Communication Research Reports, 23*, 1–11.

National Center on Elder Abuse (2004). *Frequently asked questions: What is elder abuse?* Retrieved from http://www.ncea.aoa.gov/NCEAroot/Main_Site/FAQ/Questions.aspx.

Ng, S. H., & He, J. A. (2004). Code-switching in tri-generational family conversations among Chinese immigrants in New Zealand. *Journal of Language and Social Psychology, 23*, 28–48.

Nolan, S. J. (2008). School and extended family in the transmission and revitalisation of Gallo in Upper-Brittany. *Journal of Multilingual & Multicultural Development, 29*, 216–34.

Nussbaum, J. F., & Bettini, L. (1994). Shared stories of the grandparent–grandchild relationship. *International Journal of Aging and Human Development, 39*, 67–90.

Palmore, E. (1981). *Social patterns in normal aging: Findings from the Duke longitudinal study.* Durham, NC: Duke University Press.

Park, S. M., & Sarkar, M. (2007). Parents' attitudes toward heritage language maintenance for their children and their efforts to help their children maintain the heritage language. *Language, Culture and Curriculum, 20*, 223–35.

Payne, B. K., Appel, J., & Kim-Appel, D. (2008). Elder abuse coverage in newspapers. *Journal of Elder Abuse & Neglect, 20*, 265–75.

Pearce, C. (2008). The truth about baby boomer gamers: A study of over-forty computer game players. *Games and Culture, 3*, 142–74.

Pecchioni, L. L., & Nussbaum, J. F. (2000). The influence of autonomy and paternalism on communicative behaviors in mother–daughter relationships prior to dependency. *Health Communication, 12*, 317–38.

Petronio, S. (2002). *Boundaries of privacy: Dialects of disclosure*. Albany, NY: SUNY Press.

Pratt, C., Schmall, V., & Wright, S. (1987). Ethical concern of family caregivers to dementia patients. *The Gerontologist, 27*, 632–38.

Quinn, M. J., & Tomita, S. K. (1986). *Elder abuse and neglect*. New York: Springer.

Ryan, E. B., Giles, H., Bartolucci, G., & Henwood, K. (1986). Psycholinguistic and social psychological components of communication by and with the elderly. *Language and Communication, 6*, 1–24.

Ryan, E. B., Meredith, S. D., & MacLean, M. J. (1995). Changing the way we talk with elders: Promoting health using the communication enhancement model. *International Journal of Aging and Human Development, 41*, 89–107.

Sandberg, J. G., Miller, R. B., & Harper, J. M. (2002). A qualitative study of marital process and depression in older couples. *Family Relations, 51*, 256–64.

Sandel, T., Cho, G., Miller, P., & Wang, S. (2006). What it means to be a grandmother: A cross-cultural study of Taiwanese and Euro-American grandmothers' beliefs. *Journal of Family Communication, 6*, 255–78.

Scharlach, A., Li, W., & Dalvi, T. B. (2006). Family conflict as a mediator of caregiver strain. *Family Relations, 55*, 625–35.

Schofield, M. J., & Mishra, G. D. (2004). Three year health outcomes among older women at risk of elder abuse. *Quality of Life Research, 13*, 1043–52.

Segrin, C., & Flora, J. (2011). *Family communication*. New York: Routledge.

Sillars, A. L., & Zietlow, P. H. (1993). Investigations of marital communication and lifespan development. In N. Coupland & J. F. Nussbaum (Ed.), *Discourse and lifespan identity* (pp. 237–61). Newbury Park, CA: Sage.

Silverstein, M., & Ruiz, S. (2006). Breaking the chain: How grandparents moderate the transmission of maternal depression to their grandchildren. *Family Relations, 55*, 601–12.

Soliz, J. (2007). Communicative predictors of a shared family identity: Comparison of grandchildren's perceptions of family-of-origin grandparents and stepgrandparents. *Journal of Family Communication, 7*, 177–94.

——(2008). Intergenerational support and the role of grandparents in post-divorce families. *Qualitative Research Reports in Communication, 9*, 72–80.

Soliz, J., & Harwood, J. (2003). Perceptions of communication in a family relationship and the reduction of intergroup prejudice. *Journal of Applied Communication Research, 31*, 320–45.

——(2006). Shared family identity, age salience, and intergroup contact: Investigation of the grandparent–grandchild relationship. *Communication Monographs, 73*, 87–107.

Soliz, J., Lin, M.-C, Anderson, K., & Harwood, J. (2005). Friends and allies: Communication in grandparent–grandchild relationships. In K. Floyd & M. Mormon (Eds.), *Widening the family circle* (pp. 65–79). Newbury Park, CA: Sage.

Soliz, J., Thorson, A., & Rittenour, C. (2009). Communicative correlates of satisfaction, family identity, and group salience in multiracial/ethnic families. *Journal of Marriage and Family, 71*, 819–32.

Sparks Bethea, L. (2002). The impact of an older adult parent on communicative satisfaction and dyadic adjustment in the long-term marital relationship. *Journal of Applied Communication Research, 30*, 107–25.

Sparks Bethea, L., Travis, S. S., & Pecchioni, L. L. (2000). Family caregivers' use of humor in conveying information about caring for dependent older adults. *Health Communication, 12*, 361–76.

Spicer, J. W., & Hampe, G. D. (1975). Kinship interaction after divorce. *Journal of Marriage and the Family, 37*, 113–19.

Jake Harwood, Christine E. Rittenour, and Mei-Chen Lin

Sporakowski, M. J., & Axelson, L. V. (1984). Long-term marriage: A critical review. *Lifestyles of the Elderly, 7*, 76–93.

Thompson, E. H., Buxton, W., Gough, P. C., & Wahle, C. (2007). Gendered policies and practices that increase older men's risk of elder mistreatment. *Journal of Elder Abuse & Neglect, 19*, 129–51.

Tower, R. B., & Kasl, S. V. (1995). Depressive symptoms across older spouses and the moderating effect of marital closeness. *Psychology and Aging, 10*, 625–38.

Vetere, F., Davis, H., Gibbs, M. R., Francis, P., & Howard, S. (2006). A magic box for understanding intergenerational play. *CHI Extended Abstracts*, 1475–81.

Walker, A. J., Pratt, C. C., & Eddy, L. (1995). Informal caregiving to aging family members: A critical review. *Family Relations, 44*, 402–11.

Wanzer, M. B., Sparks, L., & Frymier, A. B. F. (2009). Humorous communication within the lives of older adults. *Health Communication, 24*, 128–36.

Weisskirch, R. (2006). Emotional aspects of language brokering among Mexican American adults. *Journal of Multilingual & Multicultural Development, 27*, 332–43.

Williams, A., & Garrett, P. (2002). Communication evaluations across the lifespan: From adolescent storm and stress to elder aches and pains. *Journal of Language and Social Psychology, 21*, 101–27.

Yang, Y (2008). Social inequalities in happiness in the United States, 1972 to 2004: An age-period-cohort analysis. *American Sociological Review, 73*, 204–26.

Part III
Communication in Various Family Forms

8

Communication in Intact Families

Ascan F. Koerner and Mary Anne Fitzpatrick

Writing about communication in intact families is an interesting challenge because intact ostensibly describes the structure of a family, but it also carries connotations of normalcy and normative functioning that rarely are articulated. Consequently, we start this chapter by discussing what we, and others, mean by saying a family is intact. Then we describe types of family functioning that are most closely associated with structural intactness and how structural intactness is related causally to family functioning. Finally, we will discuss how structural intactness might affect families' habitual ways of communicating in their mundane, day-to-day interactions, that is, their family communication patterns. We conclude the chapter with a look at the future of research on intact families.

Intact Families: Multiple Levels of Meaning

Defining Intact Families

Historically, social scientists and other family researchers have used three distinct perspectives to define family (Wamboldt & Reiss, 1989). *Structural* definitions are based on the presence or absence of certain family members or roles and allow for distinctions between, for example, families of origin, families of procreation, single-parent families, families headed by homosexual parents, as well as step, adopted, and extended families. *Psychosocial task* definitions are based on whether groups of people accomplish certain tasks together, such as maintaining a household, educating their children, and providing emotional and material support to one another. Finally, *transactional* definitions are based on whether groups of intimates through their behaviors generate a sense of family identity with emotional ties and a shared experience of a history and a future (for detailed discussions, see Fitzpatrick & Caughlin, 2002).

Intact, customarily defined as meaning whole or unbroken, when applied to families initially suggested a structural definition of family, which focuses on who is part of a family and who is missing, respectively. Examples include nuclear family, adopted family, single-parent family, and intergenerational family, to name a few. As to who is part of a family, one could argue that the presence of at least one child is a necessary condition for a group of individuals to be a family. As far as the adults are concerned, because two adults of opposite sex are required for the conception of the child and humans have a tendency to form enduring dyadic relationships with their procreational partners that are often socially sanctioned in the form of marriage, one could argue that the presence of a married or otherwise committed adult couple that are the parents of the children in the family is the other necessary condition that defines family. From a structural perspective then, an intact family can be very narrowly defined as a couple of heterosexual adults in a committed relationship and their biological children (i.e., the nuclear family). It is also possible to expand structural definitions to include others, such as adopted and step children, other relatives such as grandparents, aunts, uncles and cousins, and biologically unrelated individuals, such as a homosexual partner of a parent, boy and girlfriends, neighbors, and others.

Because of its connotation of wholeness and unbrokenness, to define intact families from the other two perspectives is more difficult and less intuitive. From the psychosocial task perspective, intactness could mean that families are those who accomplish their respective psychosocial tasks, while from the transactional perspective, it could mean that families are those who create a sense of permanence and interdependence of their relationships. While there are many psychosocial tasks that families can and do accomplish, among the most central and therefore most defining tasks for families are the raising and socialization of children, or parenting, and providing emotional and instrumental support for one another. Thus, intact from these perspectives can be defined as engaging in the parenting of children in the context of enduring, interdependent, and supportive interpersonal relationships. In other words, intactness of families from these perspectives is largely defined in terms of its functioning.

This observation is of more than semantic importance, because when researchers and laypersons alike think and write about families, they usually define families from all three distinct perspectives simultaneously, so that notions of structure, transactions, and psychosocial tasks are conflated (Fitzpatrick & Caughlin, 2002). They do so necessarily because any definition based upon only one of the three perspectives does not adequately capture the entire theoretical concept of "family." For example, a group consisting of a married couple and their biological children might meet a structural definition of family, but if the parents do not talk to their children regularly and, as a consequence, the group neither develops a shared identity nor adequately socializes its children, it clearly lacks some fundamental attributes of a family. Similarly, a household of two single fathers who raise their children together may lack a mother and thus do not meet the structural definition of family, yet it clearly provides the core functions of a family: parenting and social support. In other words, it is impossible to define family exclusively from only one of the three perspectives and, in practice, families are defined from all three perspectives simultaneously. As a consequence, intact becomes a term with multiple layers of meaning when applied to families.

One reason "intact" is a difficult term when applied to families is because intact most directly refers to structure, so that structurally intact often is equated with accomplishing its psychosocial and transactional functions. This is the case even if the connection between structure and function is only implied and not explicitly stated, especially because structure and function are theoretically independent. Neither the psychosocial task definition nor the transactional definition of family require structural intactness; they only require that the family group fulfills certain functions. At the same time, structural definitions do not require any functioning either. At least theoretically, structurally defined families do not need to function well, and functionally defined families do not need to be structurally intact. Thus, implicitly assuming that structurally intact families function well can obfuscate the real causal factors for family functioning, especially in cases where structure is used as an indicator of the quality of functioning, as in many studies that compare intact with nonintact families.

Structurally Intact Families in American Society

Although much has been made of the decline of the structurally intact family in contemporary America, according to the last census, the vast majority of children (71 percent) are still living in families headed by two heterosexual adults. Of children in these families, 78 percent live with both their biological parents, 19 percent live in families with a stepparent, and 3 percent live in families headed by two unmarried adults (Fields, 2001). Thus, the structurally intact family headed by two adults is still the predominant family form in North American society, and understanding the communication in the structurally intact family is therefore of great importance for scholars and lay persons interested in family communication, as well as those interested in public policy.

In addition, as we have argued above, the nuclear, structurally intact family often is perceived by the general public as the most natural and therefore normative way for families to be, and for parents to raise their children. Although less likely to make the same argument explicitly, family scholars frequently seem to imply the same when they focus their attention on investigating families that are not structurally intact (e.g., single-parent families) or structurally different (e.g., families headed by same sex parents) and more or less explicitly use structurally intact families as the standard to compare other types of families to. Despite the implication that communication in intact families is normative and how it functions is well researched and understood, it is actually neither fully understood nor is its functioning not interesting. Quite the opposite! Far from being a homogenous group exhibiting similar behaviors that lead to predictably positive outcomes for families, individual family members, and society at large, intact families exhibit a wide range of communication behaviors that are associated with both positive and negative outcomes for families and their members. In addition, there is no single pattern of family communication that is equally beneficial for every family. In fact, as our own research on family communication patterns over the past decades has shown, different families function quite well employing very different communication patterns. At the same time, the different family communication patterns do not result in uniform outcomes for all families. Each family communication pattern has distinct strengths and weaknesses for families and individual family members.

Thus, there is no easy way to describe family communication in structurally intact families. Rather, understanding of communication of structurally intact families requires consideration of different types of intact families, each characterized by their own, unique communication patterns and appreciation of the particular strengths and weaknesses of each pattern. To this end, we will first review research on the association between intactness and family functioning before briefly reviewing family communication patterns theory and how communication patterns define different types of families. Then, we will show the profound effects that family communication patterns have on various outcomes for families, and conclude with a review of factors that link family structure and family communication patterns.

Family Structural Intactness and Functioning

Despite theoretically being independent from one another, there is empirical evidence (Biblarz & Stacey, 2010) that suggest that structurally intact families often do function better than structurally nonintact families, although the causes of better functioning are not necessarily found in the structure itself. Rather, they often happen to be associated with structural intactness for other reasons. For example, in structurally intact families, the bond between parents and children is often stronger and more intimate because it is not interrupted by stressful events that often characterize nonintact families, such as parental divorce or death (Noller & Fitzpatrick, 1993). Similarly, structurally intact families often experience less conflict and stress than families where the parents are divorced, separated, or widowed (Gano-Phillips & Fincham, 1995). Furthermore, structurally intact families usually have more economic and social resources available to them (Gringlas & Weinraub, 1995; Kissman & Allen, 1993). While none of these factors is deterministic in regard to family functioning, combined they can give structurally intact families significant advantages over nonintact families and thus create what might be most accurately called a mediated relationship between structural intactness and functioning.

Linking Structure and Function

The variables that mediate the relationship between structural intactness and family functioning operate at different psychological and sociological levels and through a number of different processes. Although communication in its broadest definition is probably involved in all of them, as interpersonal communication scholars, we are most interested in those that connect structure and functioning primarily through interpersonal communication and relationship processes. Consequently, we will briefly acknowledge other factors that are associated with measures of family functioning, such as child adjustment and individual well-being, but do not consider them further in this chapter other than to remind ourselves and our readers to keep them in mind as potentially alternative explanations for the associations between structural intactness and family functioning.

Distal Causes of Family Functioning

External Factors

Probably most important among these factors that do not directly involve communication is the economic advantages that a family headed by a married couple has over a single parent household. Being in a single parent household is the single largest contributor to child poverty in the U.S.A. (Brown, 2010; Manning & Brown, 2006) with children of single parents being about five times more likely to grow up in families below the poverty line than children of married and cohabiting parents (Manning & Brown, 2006). Not only do these households benefit from the material contributions of two adults that often both work for pay, but married and cohabiting parents are usually older, better educated, and therefore have access to better educational and other social resources than single parent households. Thus, they live in a socio-economic space that advantages their children over that of single parent households.

Another set of external factors that favors structurally intact families but whose impact is difficult to quantify is the socio-cultural space that these families occupy. Although social acceptance of alternative family forms has increased significantly over the past 30 years, most social and cultural institutions are geared toward structurally intact families. Schools and daycare providers often have hours that accommodate families with either one parent working part-time or with two working parents with flexible schedules, but not single parents with full eight-hour work days. Similarly, many extracurricular or after school activities, such as athletics or music classes, require parents to accompany their children but do not provide supervision or a safe space for their siblings. As a consequence, social institutions are often geared to the needs and capabilities of structurally intact families. This creates barriers for the use of these institutions by nonintact families and deprives their children of the advantages these institutions can deliver to the children. Again, it is difficult to quantify the precise impact that these social institutions have on child adjustment or other measurers of family functioning, but it is quite obvious to us that their overall effect on families is positive and that, at least in contemporary U.S. society, structurally intact families have easier access to these institutions.

Relational and Communication Factors

Other advantages that structurally intact families have over structurally nonintact families are rooted not as much in societal context, but are related to interpersonal processes and family communication more directly. One such important aspect of structurally intact families that differentiates them from structurally nonintact families is the stability of the parental (i.e., usually marital) relationship. Because under most circumstances children cannot and do not leave their parents, it is primarily the stability of the parents' relationship that determines whether or not a family is structurally intact. Infrequently, the stability is determined by external factors, such as death, military deployment, or imprisonment of a spouse, for example, but most frequently the stability of the parental relationship is determined by its quality.

An enduring parental relationship suggests that parents of structurally intact families have more satisfying intimate relationships than adults in nonintact families, which generally has a positive effect on their own life satisfaction, and, by extension, also positively affects their relationships with their children as well (Gano-Phillips & Fincham, 1995; Noller & Fitzpatrick, 1993). In addition, couples in high quality relationships are able to provide each other with emotional and instrumental support in stressful or challenging situations (Cutrona, 1996). As a consequence, parents in structurally intact families more often can rely on each other for emotional support, especially in situations where the stress results from parenting or from difficult relationships with the children. This is particularly important, because the attentive, warm, and supportive parenting most associated with positive child outcomes is difficult to perform for parents who experience difficulties in their relationships with their children and assign responsibility for the difficulties to the children. In these situations, having a partner intervene on behalf of the parent or take over parenting responsibilities can be tremendously beneficial, not only for the parent, but for the quality of the parent–child relationship as well.

In contrast, parents in structurally nonintact families often lack such supportive relationships with another adult, and if they have one, they often perceive it to be less important than their relationships with their children (Burrell, 1995). Consequently, these parents often are emotionally overly dependent on their children, which makes them relatively less powerful in their relationship with their children than parents in structurally intact families. In other words, the power dynamics between parents and children often are vastly different in structurally intact and nonintact families. Parents in structurally intact families are relatively more powerful and influential in regard to family communication behaviors compared to parents in nonintact families and thus are able to better provide parental discipline and monitoring of children's behaviors

(Baumrind, 1991), both of which correlate positively with child adjustment outcomes (Steinberg, 2001).

In addition to being less dependent on their relationships with their children for their own psychological well-being, parents in structurally intact families also often are better at allowing their children to develop secure attachment (Nair & Murray, 2005). Attachment security is very much a function of parents' ability to function as both a secure base for exploration as well as a safe haven during stress for their children (Bowlby, 1969, 1973, 1988); abilities that are enhanced when the adults themselves are in satisfying and supportive adult partnerships (Davies & Cummings, 1998) and do not experience negative life events such as separation and divorce (Waters, Merrick, Treboux, Crowell, & Albersheim, 2000). Children's secure attachment to their parents, in turn, has been shown to have positive effects on children's mental health and psychosocial adjustment (Davies & Cummings, 1998), and these positive effects seem to endure well into adulthood (Repetti, Taylor, & Seeman, 2002).

Genetic Factors

Finally, another potential advantage of structurally intact families over nonintact families is the genetic relationship between parents and children, which often is greater in structurally intact families. The quality of parent–child relationships and children's acceptance of, and compliance with, parental discipline often is a function of their perceptions of parent's intentions. Parents sometimes make their intentions explicit, for example, by explaining them to their children, but frequently the children have to rely on attributions they make about their parents' behaviors to deduce their intentions. Because there is a genetic component to cognitive information processing and to underlying attitudes and beliefs, genetically related individuals, such as biological parents and children, should be able to make more accurate attributions about their intentions. In addition, these attributes should be more sympathetic and understanding (Rueter & Koerner, 2008). In a study testing this reasoning by comparing the adjustment of adopted to biological children, Rueter and Koerner found that adopted children that are low in conversation orientation are at a three- to five-times increased risk for externalization problems as compared to biological children. Because there was no difference in the externalization behaviors of adopted and biological children of families high in conversation orientation, Rueter and Koerner interpreted these findings to suggest that genetic relatedness between parents and children is a protective factor that can compensate for poor family communication.

Proximal Causes of Family Functioning

The demonstrated empirical correlation between structural intactness and functioning seems to suggest that little real harm is done by equating one with the other, even if done only implicitly. From a theoretical perspective, however, it is important to recognize the definitional independence of the two concepts and to focus on those underlying variables that causally connect structure and functioning. From a practical and public policy perspective, knowledge of the real reasons that structural integrity and function are associated is paramount.

A good example is the public discussion of the importance of structurally intact families for child adjustment and well-being, and in particular the singular importance of fathers for families. The two most recent presidents, Bush and Obama, have publicly endorsed the importance of fathers for families and children and have referred to research showing better adjustment of children of married parents as compared to children of single-parent children as evidence for their position. Furthermore, both administrations have devoted significant public resources to encourage more fathers to marry, or to stay married to, the mothers of their children. However, a recent meta-analysis by Biblarz and Stacey (2010) that compared families headed by same and opposite sex parents and single-parent families found that essentially all of the positive effects that have been ascribed to the presence of fathers in families are a statistical artifact. Specifically, Bibarz and Stacey argued that past research on the role of fathers compared married to single-parent families and confounded the effects of fathers with those of dual parents. When they separated the effects of number and sex of parents and compared families headed by two parents with one another, they found that there was no advantage for the children in terms of their adjustment to having opposite sex parents. In fact, families headed by lesbian parents seemingly outperformed mixed sex couples on a number of child outcome variables and families headed by two homosexual men were largely indistinguishable in that regard from families headed by heterosexual couples. Biblarz and Stacey concluded that there are real advantages for families that stem from having two parents that bring their economic and social resources to the family and their children, but that the sex of the parents is not one of those important resources.

Summary

To summarize, even though labeling a family as intact is ostensibly a statement about the structure of a family, it often implies a well-functioning family as well. Furthermore, there are pragmatic reasons for why structurally intact families do function comparatively better than structurally nonintact families. In addition to having the benefit of two adults that provide material and interpersonal resources to the family, structurally intact families are less likely to experience the stress and strain inherent in deteriorating parental relationships. In addition, parents in structurally intact families tend to readily provide social support to one another and also have relatively more power in their relationships with their children and therefore have relatively more influence on family communication behaviors than parents in nonintact families. These parents also are better at raising securely attached children, and finally they are better understood by their children due to shared genes. While these factors are not necessarily attributes exclusive to structurally intact families, they tend to be positively correlated with structural intactness, and because they are associated with better functioning, suggest that structural intactness has a positive effect on family functioning, albeit a mediated one.

Family Transactional/Psychosocial Task Intactness and Functioning

In the preceding sections, we discussed the associations between structural intactness and family functioning. A similar discussion of the association of transactional/psychosocial task intactness and family functioning is not quite possible. Not only is the meaning of intactness when applied to a transactional/psychosocial task definition of family somewhat unclear, but as we argued above, the transactional nature of family interaction and the psychosocial tasks that define family are closely intertwined with, if not defined by, the core functions of families. Consequently, any attempt to associate transactional/psychosocial task intactness with functioning is at danger of being tautological.

Parenting as Family Function

Despite this danger, it seems to us that a look at the type of psychosocial tasks that families accomplish and the transactional processes involved in accomplishing those tasks is informative. As the review of the research on structural intactness has shown, one outcome by which family functioning is typically evaluated is how well their children are adjusted, which in the studies reviewed was usually defined in terms of social performance or psychological well-being. This suggests at least two qualitatively different types of functions that families are expected to perform and by which they are judged. One function is to socialize children so that they become socially competent and successfully perform in their respective social roles. The other is that children (and parents) achieve a certain degree of psychological well-being that is indicated by them exhibiting satisfaction with their lives and relationships, self-esteem, and a general sense of happiness.

That there are two distinct functions that families are expected to fulfill for their children suggest that there also are two distinct processes or sets of processes that families employ to achieve these two functions. One process teaches children how to be socially successful by making them aware of social expectations of others and by instructing them how to manage these expectations and relationships. This process is externally oriented toward social relationships and is concerned with social norms and rules and adherence to them. One could say that this process is fundamentally about compliance with social rules and norms. The other process makes the children self-confident and happy with themselves. This process is internally oriented toward acceptance and love of self and is concerned with the child's self-esteem. One could argue that this process is fundamentally about love and acceptance.

From the psychosocial task and the transactional perspectives then, intactness can be defined as the presence of parental love, expressed as warmth and support, and parental discipline, expressed as clearly communicated expectations for behavior and sanctions for behaviors that violate those expectations. This view is supported by researchers who study parenting, such as Steinberg (2001), who argues that the most consistent findings of parenting research over the last three decades have been that warm and firm parenting that is responsive to children's needs for autonomy is most likely to be associated with child adjustment. It is also supported by researchers such as Baumrind (1968, 1991), who consistently has found that authoritative parenting, that is, parenting that combines parental warmth with parental discipline, is superior in terms of child outcomes to warmth without discipline (permissive parenting), discipline without warmth (authoritarian parenting), and parenting that ignores the children all together (neglecting parenting).

Family Communication Patterns in Intact Families

As argued above, to the extent that families foster a family communication climate that at the same time is warm and supportive and provides firm guidance for children, they can be considered intact from the psychosocial tasks and the transactional perspectives. Thus, theories of family communication that are concerned with intact families need to account for the communication processes that are associated with warmth and support and with firm guidance, respectively. Family communication patterns theory (Koerner & Fitzpatrick, 2002, 2006; Koerner, 2007) is such theory, which is why it deserves closer examination here.

Family communication patterns describe families' fairly stable and thus predictable ways of communicating with one another. These habitual ways of communication allow researchers to distinguish between different types of families and are predictive of a number of important family processes and psychosocial outcomes for families and individual family members, especially children.

Family communication patterns emerge from the process by which families create and share social reality. Thus, they are inextricably linked to the most basic social functioning of the family. Specifically, family communication patterns result from the process of co-orientation without which human interaction in general, and family communication in particular, would not be possible. The process of co-orientation and its role in creating social reality was described in detail by McLeod and Chaffee and their colleagues (1972, 1973; Kim 1981). Co-orientation occurs when two or more persons focus on and evaluate the same object in their social or material environment and are aware of their shared focus.

In dyads and groups, co-orientation results in two distinct cognitions for each person involved. The first cognition is a perception of the observed object, and second cognition is a representation of the other person's perception of the same object. These distinct cognitions determine three attributes of the co-oriented dyad or group: agreement, accuracy, and congruence. *Agreement* refers to similarity between the two or more persons' perceptions of the object. *Accuracy* refers to the similarity between one person's representation of the other persons' perception and the other persons' actual perception of the object. Finally, *congruence* refers to the similarity between one person's own perception of the object and the same person's representation of the other persons' perceptions of the object. These three attributes of the dyad or group are linearly dependent on one another such that the state of any two determines the state of the third, such that a dyad or group that has accuracy and congruence also is in agreement.

Families and other social groups that are co-oriented are not necessarily in agreement, however. They do not necessarily share a social reality. Social reality is shared only when the family is co-oriented and has agreement, accuracy, and congruence (McLeod & Chaffee, 1972). There are psychological and pragmatic factors, however, that favor congruence and accuracy (Koerner, 2007), respectively, and because of the linear dependency between congruence, accuracy, and agreement described above, also agreement. As a consequence, co-orientation in families usually leads to a shared social reality. The processes of co-orientation that establish that shared social reality, however, are the communication processes that determine family communication patterns.

Co-orienting Communication in Families

Family members can achieve shared social reality in two distinct ways. One way is for individuals to discern another family member's attitude about an object and to adopt that attitude. In other words, they can conform to other family members. Because this process emphasizes the relationships between family members over their relationships to the concept, McLeod and Chaffee (1972) called this process *socio-orientation*. The other way to achieve a shared social reality is for families to discuss the object of co-orientation and its role in the family's social reality and thus arrive at a shared perception of the object. Because this process emphasizes how family members conceptualize the objects over their interpersonal relationships, McLeod and Chaffee called this process *concept-orientation*.

Concept orientation and socio-orientation, however, are not only important because they describe the processes by which families arrive at a shared social reality. They are important because they underlie the communication behaviors and practices of families and therefore are associated with a large number of important outcomes for families that on the surface have nothing to do at all with the creation of social reality. Much in the same way as social groups develop and maintain a particular grammar, syntax, and vocabulary in their language, family members create and maintain their shared social reality every time they say or do anything within the context of the family. Every family interaction contributes to how a family constructs its reality, even though individual family members engage in these interactions for ostensibly entirely different reasons.

Of particular importance for the study of families is the fact that families develop preferences for how they achieve a shared social reality that become habitual (Reiss, 1981). Some families prefer socio-orientation to concept-orientation, whereas other families prefer concept-orientation to socio-orientation. Yet other families make ample use of both strategies, and some families do not use either strategy particularly frequently.

Family Communication Patterns Theory

The two processes of co-orientation have important effects on the behavior of family members. Recognizing this, Fitzpatrick and Ritchie (1994; Ritchie, 1991, 1997; Ritchie & Fitzpatrick, 1990) reconceptualized McLeod and Chaffee's (1972, 1973) socio- and concept-orientation by placing a greater emphasis on the communication behaviors typical of the two orientations. Thus, concept-orientation became conversation orientation because the communication behavior typical of concept-orientation emphasizes family discussions. Similarly, socio-orientation became conformity orientation because the communication behavior typical of socio-orientation emphasizes conformity within families.

Conversation Orientation

The first dimension of family communication, conversation orientation, is defined as the degree to which families create a climate where all family members are encouraged to participate in unrestrained interaction about a wide array of topics. In families on the high end of this dimension, family members freely, frequently, and spontaneously interact with each other without many limitations in regard to time spent in interaction and topics discussed. These families spend a lot of time interacting with each other and family members share their individual activities, thoughts, and feelings with each other. In these families, activities that the family plans to engage in and decisions that affect the family are discussed within the family. Conversely, in families at the low end of the conversation orientation dimension, members interact less frequently with each other and there are only a few topics that are openly discussed with all family members. There is less exchange of private thoughts, feelings, and activities. In these families, activities are not discussed in great detail and not everybody is involved in family decisions.

Associated with high conversation orientation is the belief that open and frequent communication is essential to an enjoyable and rewarding family life. Families holding this view value the exchange of ideas, and parents holding this belief see frequent communication with their children as the main means to educate and to socialize them. Conversely, families low in conversation orientation believe that open and frequent exchanges of ideas, opinion, and values are not necessary for the function of the family or for the education and socialization of children.

From this description of conversation orientation, it should be apparent that conversation orientation is also associated with perceptions of a warm and supportive family climate and warm and supportive parent–child relationships. Because conversation orientation values individuals and their perceptions and perspectives, it leads to communication that is affirmative of individuals and therefore perceived as warm and supportive. Thus, while conversation orientation originates with families' needs to inhabit a shared social reality, how it is implemented affects parent–child relationships and family communication climates in ways that are profoundly important for child adjustment and well-being.

Conformity Orientation

The second dimension of family communication is conformity orientation. Conformity orientation refers to the degree to which family communication stresses a climate of homogeneity of attitudes, values, and beliefs. Families on the high end of this dimension are characterized by interactions that emphasize a uniformity of beliefs and attitudes. Their interactions typically focus on conflict avoidance and adherence to social rules and norms, with obedience to parents being among the most important ones. In inter-generational exchanges, communication in these families reflects obedience to parents and other adults and authority figures. Families on the low end of the conformity orientation dimension are characterized by interactions that focus on heterogeneous attitudes and beliefs, as well as on the individuality of family members and their independence from their families. In inter-generational exchanges, communication reflects the equality of all family members, e.g., children are usually involved in decision making (Koerner & Cvancara, 2002).

Associated with high conformity orientation is the belief in what might be called a traditional family structure. In this view, families are cohesive and hierarchical. Family members favor their family relationships over relationships external to the family and they expect that resources such as space and money are shared. Families high in conformity orientation believe that individual schedules should be coordinated to maximize family time and they expect family members to subordinate individual interests to those of the family. Parents are expected to make the decisions for the family and the children are expected to act according to their parents' wishes. Conversely, families low in conformity orientation do not believe in a traditional family structure. Instead, they believe in less cohesive and hierarchically organized families. Families on the low end of the conformity dimension believe that relationships outside the family are equally important as family relationships, and that families should encourage the individual growth of individual family members, even if that leads to a weakening of the family structure. They believe in the independence of family members, they value personal space, and they subordinate family interests to personal interests.

From this description of conformity orientation, it should be apparent that conformity orientation is also associated with perceptions of parental guidance and the teaching of social norms and expectations. Because conformity orientation emphasizes compliance with others' expectations, it leads to communication that is regulating behaviors and makes social rules and norms explicit and therefore perceived as firm and providing guidance. Thus, while conformity orientation originates with families' needs to inhabit a shared social reality, how it is implemented also affects parent–child relationships and family communication climates in ways that are profoundly important for child adjustment and well-being.

Interdependence of Conversation and Conformity Orientation

The effects that these two core dimensions of communication in families have on actual family communication are often dependent on one another. That is, rather than having main effects on family communication, these two dimensions frequently interact such that the impact of conformity orientation on family outcomes is moderated by the degree of conversation orientation of the family, and vice versa. The impact of conformity orientation is especially sensitive to the degree of conversation orientation in a family. Generally speaking, guidance and expectations that are expressed and enforced without warmth and support are perceived as coercive, undermining one's autonomy, and ultimately as belittling or disaffirmation of self. Conversely, guidance and expectations that are provided in a warm and supportive environment are perceived as helpful, enabling of autonomy, and ultimately affirming of self. Therefore, to predict the influence of family communication patterns on family outcomes, it is rarely sufficient to investigate only one dimension without assessing the other dimension as well (Koerner & Fitzpatrick, 2002). Because the two dimensions of conformity orientation and conversation orientation interact consistently with one another, in effect they create four family types that differ from each other in qualitative ways.

Consensual families are high in both conversation and conformity orientation. Their communication is characterized by a tension between pressure to agree and to preserve the existing hierarchy within the family, on the one hand, and an interest in open communication and in exploring new ideas, on the other hand. That is, parents in these families are interested in their children and what the children have to say, but at the same time also believe that they, as the parents, should make final decisions for the family and for the children. They resolve this tension by listening to their children and by spending time and energy in explaining their decisions to their children in the hope that their children will understand and adopt the reasoning, beliefs, and values behind the parents' decisions. Children in these families usually learn to value family conversations and tend to adopt their parents' values and beliefs. In these families, conflict is generally regarded as negative and harmful to the family, but because unresolved conflict is perceived as potentially threatening to the relationships within the family, these families also value and engage in conflict resolution (Koerner & Fitzpatrick, 1997).

Parenting in these families is warm and supportive, but parents also provide firm guidance to their children. The parenting corresponds to Baumrind's (1968) authoritative style. Accordingly, children in these families are usually well adjusted. Communicatively speaking, these families are intact.

Pluralistic families are high in conversation orientation but low in conformity orientation. Communication in pluralistic families is characterized by open, unconstrained discussions that involve all family members. Parents in these families do not feel the need to be in control of their children or to make all their decisions for them. This parental attitude leads to family discussions where opinions are evaluated based on the merit of arguments rather than on which family members supports them. That is, parents are willing to accept their children's opinions and to let them participate equally in family decision making. Because of their emphasis on the free exchange of ideas and the absence of overt pressure to conform or to obey, these families openly address their conflicts with one another, are low in conflict avoidance, engage in positive conflict resolution strategies, and most often resolve their conflicts. Children of these families learn to value family conversations and, at the same time, learn to be independent and autonomous, which fosters their communication competence and their confidence in their ability to make their own decisions.

Parenting in these families is warm and supportive, but parents fail to provide firm guidance to their children. The parenting corresponds to Baumrind's (1968) permissive style. Although children in these families are often well adjusted, because of the relative lack of parental guidance, how well they do depends on their personality and social intelligence. Thus, for children that have deficits in these areas, growing up in pluralistic families can be associated with poor adjustment and related outcomes. Communicatively, these families are less intact than consensual families.

Protective families are low on conversation orientation and high on conformity orientation. Communication in protective families is characterized by an emphasis on obedience to parental authority and by little concern for conceptual matters or for open communication within the family. Parents in these families believe that they should be making the decisions for their families and their children, and they see little value in explaining their reasoning to their children. Conflict in protective families is perceived negatively because these families place great emphasis on conformity and little value on open communication (Koerner & Fitzpatrick, 1997). Family members are expected not to have any conflicts with one another and to behave according to the interests and norms of the family. Because communication skills are not valued and not practiced much, these families often lack the necessary skills to engage productively in conflict resolution. Children in protective families learn that there is little value in family conversations and to distrust their own decision making ability.

Parenting in these families is cold and often coercive, consisting of insistence for obedience with little concern for explanation or for the autonomy needs of the child. The parenting corresponds to Baumrind's (1968) authoritarian style and children are less well adjusted. Communicatively, the families are less intact than consensual families.

Laissez-faire families are low in both conversation orientation and conformity orientation. Their communication is characterized by few and usually uninvolving interactions among family members that are limited to a small number of topics. Parents in laissez-faire families do believe that all family members should be able to make their own decisions, but unlike parents in pluralistic families, they have little interest in their children's decisions and do not value communicating with them very much. Most members of laissez-faire families are emotionally uninvolved in their families. Laissez-faire families value neither conformity nor communication very much. As a result, they do not experience their families as constraining their individual interests, and incidents of colliding interests and thus conflicts are rare. These families also do not engage much in conversation with one another and therefore also tend to avoid conflict. Children of these families learn that there is little value in family conversation and that they have to make their own decisions. Because they do not receive much support from their parents, however, they come to question their decision making ability.

Parenting in these families is uninvolved and often neglectful and fails to provide either warmth or guidance. The parenting corresponds to Baumrind's (1968, 1991) neglecting style and children are most likely to be poorly adjusted. Communicatively, the families are the least intact.

Conclusion

Structurally intact families are still by far the most frequent type of family in North American society and the vast majority of American children grow up in these families. In addition, structurally intact families are used by researchers and lay people alike as a sort of norm to compare other types of families against, although this is usually done implicitly rather than explicitly. For these reasons, structurally intact families deserve our continued attention and research. Only when we know how structurally intact families communicate and understand why this communication often is associated with superior functioning can we use this knowledge to aid all families in improving their functioning.

In this chapter, we have made the distinction between structural intactness and the functional intactness implied by definitions of family based on psychosocial tasks and transactional approaches. Because families are usually defined from all three perspectives simultaneously, structural intactness and functioning are often conflated, which leads to the unstated assumption that structurally intact families are also highly functional. While there is empirical evidence for an association between structural intactness and functioning, the reasons for this association are not necessarily causal, but often are spurious or mediated, and not all of them are associated with interpersonal communication. We highlighted some of the relational and communication variables that appear to causally connect structure and function. Among them are that the parent–child relationships in structurally intact families are often more stable and supportive than those in nonintact families. In addition, structurally intact families are more likely to foster secure attachment in children, and parents are less emotionally dependent and consequently more powerful in their relationships with their children, which enables them to parent more resourcefully than parents in nonintact families. Finally, there is initial evidence that suggests that the genetic relatedness in structurally intact families can compensate for inadequate communication; an advantage that these families have over nonintact families.

As far as the communication that characterizes functionally intact families is concerned, we have argued that two processes are essential: love and discipline. We have further argued that family communication patterns theory (FCPT) is a theory that conceptualizes two communication practices that can be associated with parental warmth and support and parental guidance and discipline, respectively: conversation orientation and conformity orientation. Not only does FCTP identify the communication processes most closely associated with child adjustment and well-being, by linking them to the functional need for families to create a shared social reality, it provides an explanation for the origin of the communication behaviors as well. To our knowledge, this sets FCTP apart from other theories of family communication that describe communication behaviors and link them to outcomes, but that fails to explain the origin of the communication behaviors in the first place.

Future Directions

In this chapter, we have reviewed and synthesized a large amount of research on family communication, but very little of that was explicitly on intact families. In fact, one could argue that intactness as an attribute of families and variable of relevance to family communication is largely ignored, at least by communication scholars. As we have argued, while there clearly is an association between intactness and functioning, this association is primarily implicit and assumed rather than explicitly investigated and theorized about. Thus, one obvious avenue for future research is to conceptualize intactness as a variable in its own right and to develop theories that explain how intactness and family functioning relate. In this chapter, we have made some preliminary attempts along this vein, but much more theoretical work could and needs to be done in this regard.

Another important area that needs more attention than it currently receives is the question of what exactly constitutes family functioning and whose outcomes we should consider. The research that we reviewed defined family functioning primarily in terms of child outcomes. Although consistent with a conceptualization of family that has child rearing at its core, this perspective completely ignores the outcomes family relationships and family communication have for the parents. Because family relationships are also central to parents' lives, they should have significant influence on how parents fare as well. In addition, because parents do have a greater degree of autonomy than children in regard to how they communicate in families, how well family functions for them in turn probably affects how well they parent their children, and how well they allow family to function for their children as well. Thus, we see research on the impact of family communication on parent outcomes as another promising and fruitful avenue of future research.

References

Baumrind, D. (1968). Child care practices anteceding three patterns of preschool behavior. *Genetic Psychology Monographs, 75,* 43–88.

——(1991). Effects of authoritative parental control on child behavior. *Child Development, 37,* 887–907.

Biblarz, T. J. & Stacey, J. (2010). How does the gender of parents matter? *Journal of Marriage and Family. 72,* 3–22.

Bowlby, J. (1969). *Attachment and loss:* Vol. I: *Attachment.* New York: Basic Books.

——(1973). *Attachment and loss:* Vol. II: *Separation, anxiety and anger.* New York: Basic Books.

——(1988). *A secure base: Clinical applications of attachment theory.* London: Routledge.

Brown, S. L. (2010). Marriage and child well-being: Research and policy perspectives. *Journal of Marriage and Family, 72,* 1059–77.

Burrell, N. A. (1995). Communication patterns in step families. In M. A. Fitzpatrick & A. Vangelisti (Eds.), *Explaining family interactions* (pp. 290–309). Thousand Oaks, CA: Sage.

Cutrona, C. E. (1996). *Social support in couples: Marriage as a resource in times of stress.* Thousand Oaks, CA: Sage.

Davies, P. T., & Cummings, E. M. (1998). Exploring children's emotional security as a mediator of the link between marital relations and child adjustment. *Child Development, 69,* 124–39.

Fields, J. (2001). *Living arrangements of children: Fall 1996.* Washington, DC: U.S. Census Bureau.

Fitzpatrick, M. A., & Caughlin, J. P. (2002). Interpersonal communication in family relationships. In M. L. Knapp & J. A. Daly (Eds.), *Handbook of interpersonal communication,* 3rd edn (pp. 726–77). Thousand Oaks, CA: Sage.

Fitzpatrick, M. A., & Ritchie, L. D. (1994). Communication schemata within the family: Multiple perspectives on family interaction. *Human Communication Research, 20,* 275–301.

Gano-Phillips, S., & Fincham, F. D. (1995). Family conflict, divorce, and children's adjustment. In M. A. Fitzpatrick & A. Vangelisti (Eds.), *Explaining family interactions* (pp. 206–31). Thousand Oaks, CA: Sage.

Gringlas, M., & Weinraub, M. (1995). The more things change: Single parenting revisited. *Journal of Family Issues, 16,* 29–52.

Kim, H. S. (1981). Coorientation and communication. In B. Dervin & M. J. Voigt (Eds.), *Progress in communication sciences* (Vol. VII, pp. 31–54). Norwood, NJ: Ablex.

Kissman, K., & Allen, J. A. (1993). *Single parent families.* Newbury Park, CA: Sage.

Koerner, A. F. (2007). Social cognition and family communication: Family communication patterns theory. In D. Roskos-Ewoldsen & J. Monahan (Eds.), *Communication and social cognition: Theory and methods* (pp. 197–216). Mahwah, NJ: Lawrence Erlbaum Associates.

Koerner, A. F., & Cvancara, K. E. (2002). The influence of conformity orientation on communication patterns in family conversations. *The Journal of Family Communication, 2,* 132–52.

Koerner, A. F., & Fitzpatrick, M. A. (1997). Family type and conflict: The impact of conversation orientation and conformity orientation on conflict in the family. *Communication Studies, 48,* 59–75.

——(2002). Understanding family communication patterns and family functioning: The roles of conversation orientation and conformity orientation. *Communication Yearbook, 26,* 37–69.

——(2006). Family communication patterns theory: A social cognitive approach. In D. O. Braithwaite & L. A. Baxter (Eds.) *Engaging theories in family communication: Multiple perspectives* (pp. 50–65). Thousand Oaks, CA: Sage.

Manning, W. D., & Brown, S. L. (2006). Children's economic well-being in married and cohabiting parent families. *Journal of Marriage and Family, 68,* 345–62.

McLeod, J. M., & Chaffee, S. H. (1972). The construction of social reality. In J. Tedeschi (Ed.), *The social influence process* (pp. 50–59). Chicago, IL: Aldine-Atherton.

——(1973). Interpersonal approaches to communication research. *American Behavioral Scientist, 16,* 469–99.

Nair, H., & Murray, A. (2005). Predictors of attachment security in preschool children from intact and divorced families. *Journal of Genetic Psychology, 166,* 245–63.

Noller, P., & Fitzpatrick, M. A. (1993). *Communication in family relationships.* Englewood Cliffs, NJ: Prentice Hall.

Reiss, D. (1981). *The family's construction of reality.* Cambridge, MA: Harvard University Press.

Repetti, R. L., Taylor, S. E., & Seeman, T. E. (2002). Risky families: Family social environments and the mental and physical health of offspring. *Psychological Bulletin, 128,* 330–66.

Ritchie, D. L. (1991). Family communication patterns: An epistemic analysis and conceptual reinterpretation. *Communication Research, 18,* 548–65.

Ritchie, L. D., & Fitzpatrick, M. A. (1990). Family communication patterns: Measuring interpersonal perceptions of interpersonal relationships. *Communication Research, 17,* 523–44.

Rueter, M. A., & Koerner, A. F. (2008). The effect of family communication pattern on adopted adolescent adjustment. *Journal of Marriage and Family 70,* 715–27.

Steinberg, L. (2001). We know some things: Parent–adolescent relationships in retrospect and prospect. *Journal of Research on Adolescence, 11,* 1–19.

Wamboldt, F., & Reiss, D. (1989). Task performance and the social construction of meaning: Juxtaposing normality with contemporary family research. In D. Offer & M. Sabshin (Eds.), *Normality: Context and theory* (pp. 2–40). New York: Basic Books.

Waters, E., Merrick, S., Treboux, D., Crowell, J., & Albersheim, L. (2000). Attachment security in infancy and early adulthood: A twenty-year longitudinal study. *Child Development, 71,* 684–89.

9

Divorced and Single-Parent Families

Risk, Resiliency, and the Role of Communication

Tamara D. Afifi and Amanda Denes

The rise in divorced and single-parent families represents one of the most profound changes in the American family in the past four decades (Amato, 2005; Usdansky, 2009). As a result of this change, there has been an outpouring of interest from researchers over the potential "deterioration" of the American family and its effects on children. The impact of family structure on children has arguably been one of the most well researched areas in the social sciences, generating two thousand research articles on divorce between 2000 and 2009 alone (Amato, 2010).

Despite the wealth of research on divorce and single parenthood, less is known about how the American people feel about these changes to the traditional family form. To address this issue, Usdansky (2009) conducted a content analysis of attitudes toward divorce and single parenthood in popular magazines ($N = 474$) and scholarly research articles ($N = 202$) published between 1900 and 1998. She found that critical attitudes toward divorce in both the scholarly articles and popular press magazines plunged during this time, not due to an increase in favorable opinions about divorce, but as a result of a "virtual disappearance of normative debate" (Usdansky, 2009, p. 209). As Usdansky speculates, the absence of debate may reflect an ambivalent acceptance of divorce, perhaps as a result of weakening family values and norms in favor of individual choice and personal happiness or varied feelings about the benefits and consequences of divorce for children. These same opinions, however, were not shared with regard to nonmarital childbearing, which scholars and the lay public equally criticized throughout the century (Usdansky, 2009). One possible explanation for the more critical attitude toward single parenting is that while Americans are relatively ambivalent about divorce, they simultaneously place a high value on marriage, and single parenthood represents the antithesis of marriage (Cherlin, 2009).

To better understand why these attitudes exist, we take a closer look at what researchers have found regarding the impact of divorce and single parenthood on children using a risk and resiliency approach. In particular, we focus on communication patterns that promote risk and resilience in divorced and single-parent families. Communication is the foundation of a family because it is the means through which family members construct and maintain their relationships with each other (Whitchurch & Dickson, 1999). As such, it is often the catalyst for positive and negative change in families. We conclude with a discussion of current trends and possible directions for future research.

Effects of Divorce and Single Parenthood on Children

Impact of Divorce on Children

Determining the precise impact of divorce on children is a difficult task because it depends upon a host of complex circumstances (see Amato, 2010). Most research suggests that divorce can have short-term and long-term effects on children. Some of the short-term effects of divorce on children include a decline in their standard of living, less quality and quantity of time spent with parents, internalizing problems (e.g., anxiety, stress, depression, lower self-esteem), externalizing problems (e.g., aggression, delinquency, acting out in school), poorer academic achievement, changes in residences and schools, and greater fears of abandonment (e.g., Burt, Barnes, McGue, & Iacono, 2008; Strohschein, 2005; Sun & Li, 2002). Divorce can have long-term effects as well. Children whose parents divorce tend to have a greater fear of commitment in romantic relationships, are more likely to get divorced themselves, have greater psychological and economic difficulties, obtain less education, have insecure attachments, and experience more strained relationships with their parents (especially fathers) than those whose parents remain married (Amato, 1996; Amato & Sobolewski, 2001; Li & Wu, 2008; Sun & Li, 2010; Yu, Pettit, Lansford, Dodge, & Bates, 2010). Even though many of these effects may dissipate over time, there is evidence that for some individuals, the negative effects of divorce linger into adulthood (Amato, 2010).

The scholarly debate that has continued for years concerns the exact size of these effects and their long-term nature. Earlier studies by Wallerstein (e.g., Wallerstein & Blakeslee, 1989; Wallerstein & Kelly, 1980) suggested that most children suffered from long-term, debilitating effects of divorce. Other scholars like Popenoe (1993) have argued that divorce has strongly contributed to the demise of the American family. Most research, however, tends to take more of a "moderate" and multi-faceted approach. An important shift in thinking came with Hetherington (e.g., Hetherington, 1999, 2003) and Booth and Amato's (e.g., 1994, 2001) research on divorce, which tends to assume a risk and resiliency approach. Hetherington's research suggests that children vary considerably in their responses to divorce, with some fairing quite well and potentially benefiting from being removed from a tumultuous family environment and others suffering from long-term difficulties (Hetherington, 2003). Most of this variance is due to contextual factors, such as the age and gender of the child and parent, the number of stressors and transitions the child experiences, how long it has been since the divorce, whether remarriage is involved, and the communicative patterns that characterize the parents' post-divorce relationship and the parent–child relationship.

Amato and colleagues' research (e.g., Amato & Afifi, 2006; Amato, Loomis, & Booth, 1995; Amato & Sobolewski, 2001; Booth & Amato, 1994, 2001) has been instrumental in demonstrating the impact of divorce on children (see Amato, 2010 for a more extensive review). With their longitudinal data set that spans generations, Amato and Booth have found that one of the most important predictors of how well children function after divorce is the degree of interparental conflict. In fact, research has found that even though divorce still has a direct influence on children's well-being (Riggio, 2004), inter-parental conflict is probably more important than divorce in predicting children's psychological well-being and parent–child relationship quality (Amato & Afifi, 2006; Jekielek, 1998). As Amato and his colleagues (2001; Amato & Sobolewski, 2001; Booth & Amato, 2001) note, children whose parents have a conflicted marriage and who remain married may have poorer psychological well-being than children whose parents have a conflicted marriage and divorce. Amato et al. (1995) also found that children whose parents had a high conflict marriage and divorce were better off after the divorce. By contrast, children whose parents had little conflict in their marriage prior to the divorce were worse off if their parents divorced. Hetherington (1999, 2003), however, argues that much of the long-term effects of divorce dissipate *if* conflict between former spouses is kept at a minimum.

Two meta-analyses conducted by Amato have been foundational for delineating the impact of divorce on children. Amato and Keith (1991) first conducted a meta-analysis of 92 studies that compared children of divorce with children of first marriage families on measures of well-being. In general, they found that divorce is associated with lower well-being for children. As the authors also emphasize, however, the effect sizes were small (with the average effect size being .14 of a standard deviation) and were smallest with more recent and more methodologically and statistically sophisticated studies. Amato (2001) then updated the aforementioned meta-analysis with another analysis of 67 studies published in the 1990s, finding similar effects for children of divorce on academic achievement, psychological well-being, conduct, and social relationships. Interestingly, the gap for children of divorced and married parents across these variables was smallest during the 1980s and *increased* again during the 1990s (with an average effect size of-.29). In other words, children today might be *more* affected by their parents' divorce than previous generations. Amato argues that there are two primary explanations for why this trend exists. First, couples are divorcing for different reasons. In the 1970s and 1980s, couples were likely to get divorced when it was a highly discordant relationship. In the 1990s and today, however, couples are more likely to get divorced in the quest for personal happiness, even if there is little or no conflict in the marriage, which may be more damaging to children because is disrupts their schemata for marriage and commitment. A second account for the rise in effect sizes during the 1990s could be that the gap in economic well-being became even wider between children of single parents and children of married parents, contributing to more significant effects of divorce on children in that era.

Impact of Single Parenthood on Children

Although much of the research on single parenthood is subsumed under the research on divorce, scholars have also examined the impact of growing up with only one parent on children regardless of divorce. Most of this research shows that, on average, children who grow up in single-parent homes are disadvantaged on a variety of behavioral, psychological, and cognitive outcomes, as well as financial attainment compared to children who grow up in two-parent households (O'Connor, Dunn, Jenkins, Pickering, & Rasbash, 2001; Riala, Isohanni, Jokelainen, Jones, & Isohanni, 2003). Research has also found that children who are raised by single parents are more likely to engage in risky behaviors, including increased use of drugs and alcohol and earlier sexual activity, than children raised by two parents (Barrett & Turner, 2006; Griffin, Botvin, Scheier, Diaz, & Miller, 2000; Wagner et al., 2010).

Research has long shown that children from single-parent homes are educationally disadvantaged, both in their likelihood of completing high school as well as attending college (e.g., Barton, 2006). Single parents are less able to provide support and monitor their child's academic behavior, resulting in lower academic achievement and higher drop out rates (Jeynes, 2002). Astone and MacLanahan (1991) found that children from single-family households reported that their parents helped less with homework and, more generally, were less supervised at home. Parents' own behavior often influences children's behavior and similarly, parents' educational aspirations for their children often influence the children's school outcomes (Astone & MacLanahan, 1991).

While research suggests that single parenthood negatively affects children's well-being, research also indicates that the type of single-parent family matters and that not all single-parent families should be considered synonymous. Hill (1986) analyzed different types of single-parent families and found that, compared to two-parent households, single-parent families on average spent more time transitioning between stages of stability. However, he found that the addition of a child when single parents remarry required even greater transitions and periods of family disorder than those who did not remarry. He also discovered that widowed mothers who remarry are the least likely to divorce compared to other single parents who remarry and first-marriage couples. What Hill's study and other research (e.g., Jablonska & Lindberg, 2007) shows is that finer distinctions among single-parent families are required.

Research has also differentiated between single-mother and single-father homes. Because single mothers are more economically disadvantaged than single fathers (Grall, 2009), it has been suggested that children from single-father homes should experience certain benefits due to their higher SES status. Amato and Keith (1991) found that children in father-custody homes exhibited fewer problems than children in mother-custody homes. This finding contradicted early work that found that children in father-custody homes, though having the highest SES, had the worst health outcomes (i.e., Hanson, 1986). Some scholars have argued that because of inherent gender and sex roles of men and women, a single mother and a single father naturally have different strengths in their parenting. For example, research has found that single mothers are better than single fathers at socializing their children and providing interpersonal communication skills, while single fathers are better than single mothers at providing economic and practical skills (Downey, 1994). To test this individualist perspective, Downey, Ainsworth-Darnell, and Dufur (1998) used a national data set to compare well-being of children from single-mother versus single-father households. Overall, they found that single mothers from nearly all backgrounds were disadvantaged compared to single fathers (single fathers had more prestigious occupations, higher income, and more education). Despite the disadvantages faced by single mothers, children from such homes had better outcomes than children from single-father homes, though these differences were small. Along six indicators of poor behavior, only two showed that children raised by fathers were significantly less well behaved than those raised by mothers. Overall, Downey et al. conclude that few differences exist between single mothers and single fathers.

Single fathers are also becoming more involved in their children's lives than any other time in history. Amato, Meyers, and Emery (2009) found that between the 1970s and 2000s, the percentage of uninvolved dads (those who had not seen their children or paid child support in a year) decreased from 35 percent to 22 percent, while the amount of involved dads (those who see their child once a week and pay child support) increased from 8 percent to 26 percent. As single fathers continue to become more involved in their children's lives, the effects of single parenthood on children may change as well.

Why Divorce and Single Parenthood Can Place Children at Risk and the Role of Communication

Divorce, Risk, and Communication Patterns

There are numerous reasons why divorce can place children at risk for maladaptation. When a divorce occurs, parents and children experience a cascade of stressors. Afifi, Hutchinson, and Krouse (2006) identified 15 of the top stressors that parents and adolescents experience during a divorce, some of which included interparental conflict, finances, moving, loneliness, and loss of friendships. Most of these stressors directly or indirectly impact parents' communication with each other and their children. Many times, the communication patterns themselves are the primary source of the stress.

One of the most pressing stressors for parents and children when undergoing a divorce is interparental conflict. Most research on divorce focuses solely on the short-term effects of divorce, but longitudinal research is essential because processes like interparental conflict are often present long before and after a divorce occurs (Amato, 2010; Yu et al., 2010). Researchers also need to delineate the specific aspects of conflict that are healthy and unhealthy. Too much conflict and never seeing one's parents engage in conflict can both be poor models of conflict management for children. Amato and DeBoer (2001) found that young adults who never saw their parents' divorce coming were the worst off psychologically and had the most difficulty with commitment in their own romantic relationships. Research suggests that interparental conflict that is prolonged, intense, concerns the children, and makes children feel enmeshed in it, tends to be particularly harmful (Booth, 1999). More specifically, when children feel caught between their parents' conflict or get put in the middle of their parents' disputes, it can increase children's anxiety, depressive symptoms, and weaken their relationship with their parents (Afifi, 2003; Afifi & Schrodt, 2003; Buchanan, Maccoby, & Dornbusch, 1991; Hetherington, Cox, & Cox, 1982; Schrodt & Afifi, 2007). Because children love their parents, it produces cognitive dissonance when they are forced to defend their loyalty to both of them. Unfortunately, children often eventually side with one parent over the other in an effort to reduce the dissonance.

Research has examined the communication patterns that predict children's feelings of being caught and how children respond behaviorally when these feelings surface. Children feel caught when they act as messengers of information or mediators between their parents, feel the need to defend loyalties, and when their parents disclose negative information about each other, engage in demand–withdraw patterns, or have difficulties with conversation and conformity orientation (Afifi & Schrodt, 2003; Schrodt & Afifi, 2007; Schrodt & Ledbetter, 2007; Buchanan et al., 1991). When children feel caught between their parents, their first instinct is to engage in avoidance (Afifi, Afifi, Morse, & Hamrick, 2008). They might use avoidance behaviors or avoid talking about their parents' relationship as a way to escape or minimize their parents' conflict, not make their parent feel bad, or preserve their relationships with their parents. Children also sometimes model their parents' conflict behaviors by becoming aggressive in response to their feelings of being caught or they may directly confront their parents about their feelings when they get older and develop more communication competence (Afifi & Schrodt, 2003). While feeling caught is more common in divorced families, it can also occur in first marriage families (Afifi & Schrodt, 2003; Schrodt & Ledbetter, 2007). In fact, these feelings may dissipate in children of divorce approximately ten years after the divorce, but they may linger in children whose parents are still married because they are unable to escape the conflict (Amato & Afifi, 2006).

Parents' conflict and stress can also spill onto their children through the parents' divorce disclosures. As Koerner and others (e.g., Glenwick & Mowrey, 1986; Koerner et al., 2004) have found, parental disclosures regarding intimate, private, or sensitive information, like finances, ill feelings toward the other parent, and personal worries, increase children's anxiety. When former spouses have unsettled emotions with each other and their social networks decline after a divorce, they might confide in their children as a way to fill their need for support (Greeff & Van Der Merwe, 2004). These disclosures can result in emotional parentification whereby a child provides emotional support to a parent in a peer-like relationship (Jurkovic, Thirkeild, & Morrell, 2001). Divorce disclosures tend to be particularly problematic when parents disclose inappropriate information about each other. These types of disclosures are predictive of children's diminished mental and physical health and feelings of being caught (e.g., Afifi et al., 2008; Afifi & McManus, 2010; Koerner, Wallace, Lehman, & Raymond, 2002).

Not all parental divorce disclosures are harmful, however, and some can actually promote psychological well-being and facilitate parent–child bonds. Children need information about the divorce and related topics (e.g., the parents' new dating partners) to reduce their uncertainty (Ferguson & Dickson, 1995; Thomas, Booth-Butterfield, & Booth-Butterfield, 1995). Some scholars (e.g., Arditti, 1999; Thomas et al., 1995; Westberg, Nelson, & Piercy, 2002) suggest that parental divorce disclosures may enhance adolescents' psychological well-being and closeness with their parents. For instance, Koerner, Jacobs, and Raymond (2000) argued that talking about meaningful issues related to the divorce may promote cohesive bonds between custodial parents and adolescents while simultaneously helping both the parent and the child cope with the divorce. Arditti also found in her interviews with college-age daughters that when the daughters assumed a more powerful role in the family after the divorce, they appreciated the greater intimacy and disclosures with their mothers that followed.

Although the bonds between children and custodial mothers can become more cohesive after a divorce because they are coping with their loss together, there are substantial changes in interaction between children and custodial parents, in general, that occur in the years following a divorce that can be detrimental to children (Tein et al., 2000; Wolchik et al., 2000). When custodial parents are stressed because of the divorce, they often show less affection and warmth and administer more inconsistent parenting (Hetherington et al., 1982; Tein et al., 2000; Wallerstein & Kelly, 1980). This diminished ability to parent is associated with children's post-divorce adjustment problems (Koerner, Jacobs, & Raymond, 2000).

Divorce also makes it incredibly difficult for non-custodial parents, who must learn new maintenance strategies to foster cohesive relationships with their children (Lamb, 1999; Yu et al., 2010). Research indicates that both the quantity and quality of contact with the nonresidential parent are important for maintaining close relationships with children after a divorce (Lamb, 1999). When adolescents are closer and more involved with their residential and nonresidential fathers, they tend to have less delinquency, fewer depressive symptoms, higher self-esteem, and better grades (Booth, Scott, & King, 2009; Mitchell, Booth, & King, 2009).

The research on the intergenerational transmission of divorce also suggests that parents may transfer their interpersonal skill deficiencies to their children. Amato (1996) found that parents' interpersonal skills was a stronger mediator of the association between the parents' divorce and their adult children's divorce than contextual variables (e.g., age at divorce, cohabitation, income) or divorce attitudes. If the parents have interpersonal problems, such as anger, jealousy, criticism, infidelity, dogmatism, and passive aggressiveness, their adult children may model these skills in their own marriages. Parents' divorce may increase the risk that their children get divorced because of the parents' tendency to model skill deficits.

Single Parenthood, Risk, and Communication Patterns

While many of the same factors that place children at risk for divorce exist with single parenthood, there are unique characteristics of the structure of a single-parent family that can hinder the ways that parents communicate with their children. These characteristics revolve around three issues:

1 economic hardship;
2 stress overload and the lack of another parent to buffer the stress;
3 diminished parenting.

Economic Hardship

Many of the cognitive and behavioral differences for children of single-parent families and children of two-parent families are thought to be due to economic hardship. For example, while 12.5 percent of the overall population lives in poverty, this percentage nearly doubles to 24.6 percent for custodial single parents (Grall, 2009). In 2007, 27 percent of custodial mothers and 12.9 percent of custodial fathers fell below the poverty line (Grall, 2009). Children of single mothers are also more likely than children in other family types to be poor in adulthood and eventually become single parents themselves (McLanahan & Booth, 1989). When a family is experiencing financial hardship, it can unleash a multitude of stressors, which then increases the propensity for conflict, parental depression, and difficulty parenting (McLanahan & Sandefur, 1994). A lack of economic resources in and of itself is not necessarily problematic. It becomes problematic when parents perceive it as stressful and it affects their interactions with each other and their children (Amato, 2005).

Several studies have found drastic decreases in the differences between single-parent and two-parent homes when controlling for SES (e.g., McLanahan & Sandefur, 1994; McLanahan, Astone, & Marks, 1991). For example, after controlling for SES, McLanahan and Sandefur (1994) found that nearly half the differences between one-parent and two-parent homes disappeared. However, they still found that single parents spent less time helping children with homework, overseeing activities, and meeting with teachers and visiting their children's school. Similarly, McLanahan et al. (1991) found that when holding SES constant, single-parent households and step-parent households had similar effects on educational outcomes. Astone and MacLanahan (1991) found that in stepfamilies, children reported less involvement with homework, but their reports of parent supervision mimicked two-parent families. These researchers point out that such a finding may show that increases in SES through remarriage may moderate some of the behavioral and educational difficulties of divorce, but not all of them. In general, studies have shown that children in stepfamilies have similar outcomes to single-parent families and worse out-comes than families with two continuously married parents (Amato, 2005).

Stress Overload and the Lack of Another Parent to Buffer the Stress

According to stress theory, changes in family structure can be stressful because these changes often propel other changes in family organization, rules, roles, and parenting behaviors (Carlson & Corcoran, 2001). Single parents and their children often undergo a number of changes, including a divorce or death, changes in residences and schools, a decrease in household income, the parent potentially working multiple jobs, and a decrease in the size of the parents' social networks. These transitions tend to become even harder when the single parent then remarries (Hetherington, 1999). While a step-parent can and often does provide a good parental role model for children, these bonds take time to develop. There is an increasing amount of research that shows that the number of transitions a child experiences is an important predictor of well-being (Booth, 1999). When children's home life is unstable, they are more likely to disengage from it and gravitate toward negative peer influences, making them more susceptible to drug and alcohol use, risky sexual behaviors, and delinquency (Carlson & Corcoran, 2001).

Single parenthood can be stressful because single parents are managing multiple stressors alone for sustained periods of time. Unlike two-parent homes, in single-parent families there is often not another parent to help buffer the stress. Single parents also tend to be more likely than married parents to suffer from depression and anxiety (Anderson, 2008; McLanahan & Booth, 1989). Single parents who become socially iso-lated, often as the result of a divorce, tend to be at risk for the psychological effects of the stress of single parenthood (Usdansky & Wolf, 2008).

The accumulation of stressors, combined with a lack of spousal and social support, can weaken single parents' coping mechanisms. For instance, divorce and single parenting may affect parents' self-control or ability to effectively regulate their emotions. As Baumeister, Vohs, & Tice (2007) contends, self-control is like a scarce resource or energy reserve that can become depleted through repeated use, resulting in "numbness" or baseline levels of coping. The stressors of divorce and single parenthood may overwhelm or deplete parents' cognitive and emotional resources, leaving them emotionally unavailable for their children which, in turn, can affect their parental monitoring, affection, and awareness of their child's feelings. As Hartos and Power (2000) found, single mothers were aware of only about half of their adolescents' stressors, but adolescents and mothers who were in more agreement about the adolescents' stressors had fewer family problems and more parental monitoring.

When parents are stressed, their stress can spill over onto their children through their verbal and nonverbal communication (Larson & Almeida, 1999). For example, Larson and Gillman (1999) randomly collected survey data throughout the day with beepers from single mothers and their adolescents. They found that when mothers were anxious and angry, their children were anxious and angry. Parents' anxiousness and anger had stronger contagion effects on their children when the parents were highly stressed and used psychological control with their children. Given the many stressors that single parents experience, stress contagion effects can be quite important.

Diminished Parenting

As we suggested above, the stress of single parenthood is believed to largely affect children's well-being through diminished parenting. Perhaps because they are emotionally and cognitively exhausted from the various stressors they face, single parents tend to administer more inconsistent and harsh punishment (e.g., spanking), monitor their children less, and are more permissive (Amato, 2005; Bulcroft, Carmody, & Bulcroft, 1998). Although some research suggests that there are few effects of family structure on parental monitoring for pre-adolescent children, most research shows that single parents are less likely to supervise their adolescents' behavior (Bulcroft et al., 1998). As a result, adolescents from single-parent families tend to have more delinquency problems and engage in more risky behaviors than adolescents from two-parent families, but when parental monitoring increases, these problems are reduced (Griffin et al., 2000; Wagner et al., 2010). Single mothers who also work outside the home have been shown to be particularly susceptible to poor care-giving (Berger, 2004), perhaps due to the demands of balancing work and family.

More recent research has shown that the type of difficulties children can encounter when they grow up in single parent homes needs to be more clearly delineated. Lanza et al. (2010) found that urban youth who have at least an average amount of warmth and affection, social support, and consistency in parenting are at low risk for externalizing problems like aggression, but are still at risk for poor academic achievement. Rather than accumulative risks, these authors argue that scholars need to assess the types of risks children are exposed to in single-parent families and how it differentially affects their well-being. In particular, research is necessary that can determine how various communication patterns within the family, and how they might interact with the type of school and neighborhood environment, affect different aspects of a child's attitudes and behaviors.

As is the case with divorce, single parents in general also run a greater risk of instrumental parentification (e.g., children caring for the house, caring for siblings and other family members, and contributing to household income) and emotional parentification (Jurkovic, 1997) than other parents. For example, single parents may communicate with their children about the financial difficulties they experience, or issues they have with the non-custodial parent. Koerner et al. (2000) examined disclosure between single mothers and their daughters and found that most mothers in their sample had disclosed information about both finances and their former husbands (their daughters' fathers). Interestingly, however, they found that mothers did not disclose about finances because they perceived their children as "equals," but rather because they believed that making their child financially aware was part of their parenting responsibilities. Regardless of intent, Koerner et al. found that disclosures in both of these domains were positively associated with daughter's psychological distress.

What Factors Promote Resilience in Divorced and Single-Parent Families?

Just as parents' communication skill deficits predict maladaptation in divorced and single-parent families, communication competencies can buffer some of the adverse effects. In particular, researchers have found that high amounts of parental warmth, affection, and social support, as well as access to larger social networks, moderate the association between stressors and mother–adolescent relationships in divorced and single-parent families (e.g., Wagner et al., 2010; Wolchik et al., 2000). Research has also shown that when both parents are involved in their children's life, risky behaviors do not increase in single-parent families (Garis, 1998). In addition, Griffin et al. (2000) found that eating dinner together was associated with less aggression and delinquency in youth in single-parent families. Rituals like dinner not only provide stability and monitoring, but they allow a family to build cohesion through talk. Despite the challenges in single-parent homes, children from such homes report that they spend more time talking to their parents than children from two-parent homes (Astone & MacLanahan, 1991). While this talk can sometimes result in emotional parentification, it can also facilitate incredibly meaningful, cohesive relationships, as well as reduce children's uncertainty about a host of topics, including their parents' dating behaviors (Ferguson & Dickson, 1995).

Communal coping is another way that divorced and single-parent families can build strength in the face of adversity. Communal coping involves dyads or groups of people who face similar stressors actively addressing a stressor as "our problem and our responsibility" (Lyons et al., 1998). While communal coping can be ineffective if parents' verbally ruminate about their stressors and displace their own stress onto their children, when families resolve their stressors as a group, it often builds collective coping efficacy (Afifi et al., 2006).

One often overlooked factor that may promote resilience in post-divorce families is forgiveness. Forgiveness is associated with better psychological well-being, less conflict and anger toward one's ex-spouse, and more effective co-parenting after divorce (Bonach & Sales, 2002). Moreover, clinical interventions have shown that former spouses can be taught how to forgive, which can enhance their mental health (e.g., Rye et al., 2005). As part of this process, former spouses must also successfully renegotiate their attachments with each other from spouses to co-parents, uncoupling while remaining committed to their family (Graham, 1997, 2003). As Masheter (1997) argues, the healthiest ex-spouse relationships are those that are high in friendship, low in hostility, and low in preoccupation. Given that divorced parents are co-parenting more than ever before and positive co-parenting consists of trust, fairness, and good faith (Braithwaite, McBride, & Schrodt, 2003; Schrodt, Baxter, McBride, Braithwaite, & Fine, 2006), it is important to examine how forgiveness can facilitate this process.

While research has explored many of the negative effects of children being raised in single-parent households, only recently have scholars turned their attention to the characteristics that help to make a healthy single-parent family. One challenge facing single-parent families is how the parent can effectively balance work and family. One possibility is to use a work–family fit approach, where emphasis is placed on how work and family domains enhance each other. For example, Kirchmeyer (1992) found more positive spillover between nonwork and work domains than negative spillover. Organizations that offer flexible work schedules and other policies that are family friendly, as well as encourage communication about one's family, probably help buffer some of the stress of single parenthood because they it make being a single parent more manageable and less isolating.

Trends and Directions for Future Research

There are numerous directions for future research related to divorce and single parenthood that involve communication. One important trend in the research on family structure is biology. The vast majority of the research on the impact of divorce on children has relied on self-reports, but it is important to assess how divorce affects children's physiological stress responses. Thus far, a handful of studies have found that young adults who experienced as a child severe separation or loss of a parent as a result of divorce, had lower cortisol levels upon wakening (or cortisol awakening responses) (Bloch, Peleg, Koren, Aner, & Klein, 2007; Meinlschmidt & Heim, 2005) and lower pre-task and post-task cortisol levels (Kraft & Luecken, 2009; Tyrka et al., 2008). Cortisol is a hormone that is released by the hypothalamic-pitutary-adrenocortical (HPA) system when the body is stressed. The release of cortisol is a natural and healthy response to stress, but abnormally high, low, or irregular levels of cortisol can be indicative of maladaption. However, these were young adults who experienced rather severe divorce circumstances or an artificial stress-inducing task in the laboratory.

Whether adolescents experience over or under activation of their hypothalamic-pitutary-adrenocortical (HPA) and sympathic nervous systems (SNS) may have more to do with interparental conflict and other communication skills than divorce. To test this assumption, Afifi, Granger, Aldeis, Joseph, & Denes (2012) asked adolescents and parents to talk about something stressful related to the parents' relationship and measured the adolescents' HPA axis (measured by salivary cortisol) and SNS (measured by salivary alpha-amylase or sAA) responses to their parents' communication skills (i.e., social support, communication competence, and interparental conflict). One of the primary findings from this study was that regardless of whether the parents were married or divorced, the adolescents and young adults whose parents were communicatively skilled were able to down regulate or recover quickly after the discussion task. However, children whose parents were still married and lacked communication skills had more rapid and erratic response patterns for sAA and greater difficulty recovering from the interaction with their parent than children of divorce whose parents lacked these skills.

Researchers also have begun to examine how single-parent life contributes to allostatic load. Allostatic load refers to the "wear and tear" on a body caused by stress (McEwen, 2001). When individuals experience an accumulation of different life stressors, their allostatic load tends to increase, making it difficult for the body to maintain a state of homeostasis (or allostasis). This stress can slowly erode the body's stress response system, resulting in greater susceptibility to disease. Single parents often have worse health compared to other adults, which could partially be explained by the allostatic load they experience due to an influx of stressors (Johner, 2007).

Another under-researched area of single-family life involves parents' sexual identity. Bigner and Jacobsen (1989) found that gay fathers followed less traditional parenting roles, focused less on being economic providers, and were more nurturing than heterosexual fathers. Gay fathers also tend to be stricter and more responsive to children's needs than nongay fathers (Bigner & Jacobsen, 1992). Studies of lesbian mothers have largely found positive outcomes for children. Green et al. (1986) looked at differences between the children of single lesbian mothers and single heterosexual mothers. They found no significant differences between the two groups of children regarding their sexual identity, popularity, or social adjustment. While the research on single gay fathers and lesbian mothers is limited, exploring the positive communication behaviors in such families is a worthwhile endeavor.

Additional research that examines divorce from a global perspective also is necessary. Too often divorce is viewed from a Western lens, as "his and her" divorce, seemingly regardless of extended kin, norms, or group influences. In cultures that are more collectivistic or where the family is given precedence over the individual and where power within the family is hierarchical, extended family may become stakeholders in other family members' decisions regarding marriage and divorce (Afifi et al., 2012). After a divorce, certain family members may also bridge the two families together for the sake of the children, even if the former spouses would rather not see each other. In essence, divorce may "look different" in different cultures.

Ultimately, the most important to children's outcomes is the quality of parenting received (Amato, 2005). Regardless of whether there is one parent or two parents or the parents are divorced or married, it is ultimately the quality of the parenting that is the most important factor in determining children's well-being. Children thrive when healthy relationships are established within and across families, with communication at the crux of these relationships.

References

Afifi, T. D. (2003). "Feeling caught" in stepfamilies: Managing boundary turbulence through appropriate communication privacy rules. *Journal of Social and Personal Relationships, 20*, 729–55.

Afifi, T. D., Afifi, W. A., Morse, C., & Hamrick, K. (2008). Adolescents' avoidance tendencies and physiological reactions to discussions about their parents' relationship: Implications for post-divorce and non-divorced families. *Communication Monographs, 75*, 290–317.

Afifi, T. D., Granger, D., Aldeis, D., Joseph, A., & Denes, A. (2012). *The Influence of Divorce and Parents' Communication Skills on Adolescents' and Young Adults' Stress Reactivity and Recovery.* Manuscript submitted for publication.

Afifi, T. D., Hutchinson, S., & Krouse, S. (2006). Toward a theoretical model of communal coping in post-divorce families and other naturally occurring groups. *Communication Theory, 16*, 378–409.

Afifi, T. D., & McManus, T. (2010). Divorce and adolescents' physical and mental health and parental relationship quality. *Journal of Divorce and Remarriage, 51*, 83–107.

Afifi, T. D., & Schrodt, P. (2003). "Feeling caught" as a mediator of adolescents' and young adults' avoidance and satisfaction with their parents in divorced and non-divorced households. *Communication Monographs, 70*, 142–73.

Amato, P. R. (1996). Explaining the intergenerational transmission of divorce. *Journal of Marriage and the Family, 58*, 628–40.

——(2001). Children of divorce in the 1990s: An update of the Amato and Keith (1991) meta-analysis. *Journal of Family Psychology, 15*, 355–70.

——(2005). The impact of family formation change on the cognitive, social, and emotional well-being of the next generation. *Future of Children, 15*, 75–96.

——(2010). Research on divorce: Continuing trends and new developments. *Journal of Marriage and Family, 72*, 650–66.

Amato, P. R., & Afifi, T. D. (2006). Feeling caught between parents: Adult children's relations with parents and subjective well-being. *Journal of Marriage and Family, 68*, 222–35.

Amato, P. R., & DeBoer, D. D. (2001). The transmission of marital instability across generations: Relationship skills or commitment to marriage? *Journal of Marriage and the Family, 63*, 1038–51.

Amato, P. R., & Keith, B. (1991). Parental divorce and the well-being of children: A meta-analysis. *Psychological Bulletin, 110*, 26–46.

Amato, P. R., Loomis, L., & Booth, A. (1995). Parental divorce, marital conflict, and offspring well-being during early adulthood. *Social Forces, 73*, 895–915.

Amato, P. R., Meyers, C. E., & Emery, R. E. (2009). Changes in nonresident father–child contact from 1976 to 2002. *Family Relations, 58*, 41–53.

Amato, P. R., & Sobolewski, J. M. (2001). The effects of divorce and marital discord on adult children's psychological well-being. *American Sociological Review, 66*, 900–21.

Anderson, L. S. (2008). Predictors of parenting stress in a diverse sample of parents of early adolescents in high-risk communities. *Nursing Research, 57*, 340–50.

Arditti, J. A. (1999). Rethinking relationships between divorced mothers and their children: Capitalizing on family strengths. *Family Relations, 48*, 109–19.

Astone, N. M., & MacLanahan, S. S. (1991). Family structure, parental practices and high school completion. *American Sociological Review, 56*, 309–20.

Barrett, A. E., & Turner, R. J. (2006). Family structure and substance use problems in adolescence and early adulthood: Examining explanations for the relationship. *Addiction, 101*, 109–20.

Barton, P. E. (2006). The dropout. *Educational Leadership, 63*, 14–18.

Baumeister, R. F., Vohs, K. D., & Tice, D. M. (2007). The strength model of self-control. *Current Directions in Psychological Science, 16,* 351–55.

Berger, L. M. (2004). Income, family structure, and child maltreatment risk. *Children and Youth Services Review, 26,* 725–48.

Bigner, J. J. & Jacobsen, R. B. (1992). Adult responses to child behavior and attitudes toward fathering: Gay and nongay fathers. *Journal of Homosexuality, 23,* 99–112.

Bigner, J. J., & Jacobsen, R. B. (1989). The value of children to gay and heterosexual fathers. *Journal of Homosexuality, 18,* 163–72.

Bloch, M., Peleg, I., Koren, D., Aner, H., & Klein, E. (2007). Long-term effects of early parental loss due to divorce on the HPA axis. *Hormones & Behavior, 51,* 516–23.

Booth, A. (1999). Causes and consequences of divorce: Reflections on recent research. In Ross Thompson and Paul Amato (Eds.), *The postdivorce family: Children, parenting, and society* (pp. 29–48). Thousand Oaks, CA: Sage.

Booth, A., & Amato, P. R. (1994). Parental marital quality, parental divorce, and relations with parents. *Journal of Marriage and the Family, 56,* 21–34.

——(2001). Parental predivorce relations and offspring postdivorce well-being. *Journal of Marriage and the Family, 63,* 197–212.

Booth, A., Scott, M. E., & King, V. (2009). Father residence and adolescent problem behavior: Are youth always better off in two-parent families? *Journal of Family Issues, 31,* 585–605.

Bonach, K., & Sales, E. (2002). Forgiveness as a mediator between post divorce cognitive processes and coparenting quality. *The Journal of Divorce and Remarriage, 38,* 1050–2556.

Braithwaite, D. O., McBride, M. C., & Schrodt, P. (2003). "Parent teams" and the everyday interactions of co-parenting in stepfamilies. *Communication Reports, 16,* 93–111.

Buchanan, C. M., Maccoby, E. E., & Dornbusch, S. M. (1991). Caught between parents: Adolescents' experience in divorced homes. *Child Development, 62,* 1008–29.

Bulcroft, R. A., Carmody, D., & Bulcroft, K. A. (1998). Family structure and patterns of independence giving to adolescents. *Journal of Family Issues, 19,* 404–35.

Burt, S., Barnes, A., McGue, M., & Iacono, W. (2008). Parental divorce and adolescent delinquency: Ruling out the impact of common genes. *Developmental Psychology, 44,* 1668–77.

Carlson, M. J., & Corcoran, M. E. (2001). Family structure and children's behavioral and cognitive outcomes. *Journal of Marriage and Family, 63,* 779–92.

Cherlin, A. J. (2009). The origins of the ambivalent acceptance of divorce. *Journal of Marriage and Family, 71,* 226–29.

Downey, D. B. (1994). The educational performance of children in single-mother and single-father families: Interpersonal or economic deprivation? *The Journal of Family Issues, 15,* 129–47.

Downey, D. B., Ainsworth-Darnell, J. W., & Dufur, M. J. (1998). Sex of parent and children's well-being in single-parent households. *Journal of Marriage and the Family, 60,* 878–93.

Ferguson, S. M. & Dickson, F. (1995) Children's expectations of their single parents' dating behavior: A preliminary investigation of emergent themes relevant to single parent dating. *Journal of Applied Communication Research, 23,* 1–17.

Garis, D. (1998). Poverty, single-parent households, and youth at-risk behavior: An empirical study. *Journal of Economic Issues, 32,* 1079–105.

Glenwick, D., & Mowrey, J. (1986). When parent becomes peer: Loss of intergenerational boundaries in single-parent families. *Family Relations, 35,* 57–62.

Graham, E. E. (1997). Turning points and commitment in post-divorce relationships. *Communication Monographs, 64,* 350–68.

——(2003). Dialectic contradictions in postmarital relationships. *Journal of Family Communication, 3,* 193–214.

Grall, T. S. (2009). *Custodial mothers and fathers and their child support: 2007.* Current Population Reports. Washington, DC: U.S. Census Bureau.

Greeff, A. P. & Van Der Merwe, S. (2004). Variables associated with resilience in divorced families. *Social Indicators Research, 68,* 59–75.

Green, R., Mandel, J. B., Hotvedt, M. E., Gray, J., & Smith, L. (1986). Lesbian mothers and their children: A comparison with solo parent heterosexual mothers and their children. *Archives of Sexual Behavior, 15,* 167–84.

Griffin, K., Botvin, G., Scheier, L., Diaz, T., & Miller, N. (2000). Parenting practices as predictors of substance use, delinquency, and aggression among urban minority youth: Moderating effects of family structure and gender. *Psychology of Addictive Behaviors, 14*, 174–84.

Hanson, S. M. H. (1986). Healthy single-parent families. *Family Relations, 35*, 125–32.

Hartos, J. L., & Power, T. G. (2000). Relations among single mothers' awareness of their adolescents' stressors, maternal monitoring, mother-adolescent communication, and adolescent adjustment. *Journal of Adolescent Research, 15*(5), 546–63.

Hetherington, E. M. (1999). Should we stay together for the sake of the children? In E. M. Hetherington (Ed.), *Coping with divorce, single parenting, and remarriage: A risk and resiliency perspective* (pp. 93–116). Mahwah, NJ: Lawrence Erlbaum Associates.

——(2003). Social support and the adjustment of children in divorced and remarried families. *Childhood, 10*, 217–36.

Hetherington, E. M., Cox, M., & Cox, R. (1982). Effects of divorce on parents and children. In M. E. Lamb (Ed.), *Nontraditional families: Parenting and child development* (pp. 233–59). Hillsdale, NJ: Lawrence Erlbaum Associates.

Hill, R. (1986). Life cycle stages for types of single-parent families: Of family development theory. *Family Relations, 35*, 19–29.

Jablonska, B., & Lindberg, L. (2007). Risk behaviors, victimization, and mental distress among adolescents in different family structures. *Social Psychiatry Epidemiology, 42*, 656–63.

Jekielek, S. (1998). Parental conflict, marital disruption and children's emotional well-being. *Social Forces, 76*, 905–36.

Jeynes, W. (2002). *Divorce, family structure, and the academic success of children.* Binghamton, NY: Haworth.

Johner, R. L. (2007). Allostatic load: Single parents, stress-related health issues, and social care. *Health & Social Work, 32*, 89–94.

Jurkovic, G. J. (1997). *Lost childhoods: The plight of the parentified child.* Mazel, PA: Brunner.

Jurkovic, G. J., Thirkeild, A., & Morrell, R. (2001). Parentification of adult children of divorce: A multidimensional analysis. *Journal of Youth and Adolescence, 30*, 245–58.

Kirchmeyer, C. (1992). Perceptions of nonwork-to-work spillover: Challenging the common view of conflict-ridden domain relationships. *Basic and Applied Social Psychology, 13*, 231–49.

Koerner, S. S., Jacobs, S. L., & Raymond, M. (2000). When mothers turn to their adolescent daughters: Predicting daughters' vulnerability to negative adjustment outcomes. *Family Relations, 49*, 301–9.

Koerner, S. S., Wallace, S., Lehman, S. J., Lee, S., & Escalante, K. A. (2004). Sensitive mother-to-adolescent disclosures after divorce: Is the experience of sons different from that of daughters? *Journal of Family Psychology, 18*, 46–57.

Koerner, S. S., Wallace, S., Lehman, S. J., & Raymond, M. (2002). Mother-to-daughter disclosure after divorce: Are there costs and benefits? *Journal of Child and Family Studies, 11*, 469–83.

Kraft, A. J., & Luecken, L. J. (2009). Childhood parental divorce and cortisol in young adulthood: Evidence for mediation by family income. *Psychoneuroendocrinology, 34*, 1363–69.

Lamb, M. E. (1999). Non-custodial fathers and their impact on the children of divorce. In R. A. Thompson & P. Amato (Eds.), *The post-divorce family: Research and policy issues* (pp. 105–125). Thousand Oaks, CA: Sage.

Lanza, S., Rhoades, B., Nix, R., & Greenberg, M. (2010). Modeling the interplay of multilevel risk factors for future academic and behavior problems: A person-centered approach. *Development and Psychopathology, 22*, 313–35.

Larson, R., & Almeida, D. M. (1999). Emotional transmission in the daily lives of families: A new paradigm for studying family process. *Journal of Marriage and Family, 61*, 5–20.

Larson, R., & Gillman, S. (1999). Transmission of emotions in the daily interactions of single mother families. *Journal of Marriage and the Family, 61*, 21–37.

Li, J. C., & Wu, L. L. (2008). No trend in the intergenerational transmission of divorce. *Demography, 45*, 875–83.

Lyons, R. F., Mickelson, K., Sullivan, J. L., & Coyne, J. C. (1998). Coping as a communal process. *Journal of Social and Personal Relationships, 15*, 579–607.

Masheter, C. (1997). Healthy and unhealthy friendship and hostility between ex-spouses. *Journal of Marriage and the Family, 59*, 463–75.

McEwen, B. S. (2001). Plasticity of the hippocampus: adaptation to chronic stress and allostatic load. *Annals of the New York Academy of Science, 933,* 265–77.

McLanahan, S. S., Astone, N. M., & Marks, N. F. (1991). The role of mother-only families in reproducing poverty. In A. C. Husten (Ed.), *Children in poverty* (pp. 51–78). Cambridge: Cambridge University Press.

McLanahan, S., & Booth, K. (1989). Mother-only families: Problems, prospects, and politics. *Journal of Marriage and the Family, 51,* 557–80.

McLanahan, S. S., & Sandefur, G. (1994). *Growing up with a single parent: What hurts, what helps?* Cambridge, MA: Harvard University Press.

Meinlschmidt, G., & Heim, C. (2005). Decreased cortisol awakening response after early loss experience. *Psychoneuroendocrinology, 30,* 568–76.

Mitchell, K. S., Booth, A., & King, V. (2009). Adolescents with nonresidential fathers: Are daughters more disadvantaged than sons? *Journal of Marriage and Family, 71,* 650–62.

O'Connor, T., Dunn, J., Jenkins, J., Pickering, K., & Rasbash, J. (2001). Family settings and children's adjustment: differential adjustment within and across families. *British Journal of Psychiatry, 179,* 110–15.

Popenoe, D. (1993). American family decline 1960–90: A review and appraisal. *Journal of Marriage and the Family, 55,* 527–42.

——(1999). Can the nuclear family be revived? *Society, 36,* 28–30.

Riala, K., Isohanni, I., Jokelainen, J., Jones, P. B., & Isohanni, M. (2003). The relationship between childhood family background and educational performance, with special reference to single-parent families: A longitudinal study. *Social Psychology of Education, 6,* 349–65.

Riggio, H. R. (2004). Parental marital conflict and divorce, parent–child relationships, social support, and relationship anxiety in young adulthood. *Personal Relationships, 11,* 99–114.

Rye, M. S., Wei, P., Shogren, K. A., Pargament, K. I., Yingling, D. W., & Ito, M. (2005). Can group interventions facilitate forgiveness of an ex-spouse? A randomized clinical trial. *Journal of Consulting and Clinical Psychology, 73,* 880–92.

Schrodt, P., & Afifi, T. (2007). Communication processes that predict young adults' feelings of being caught and their associations with mental health and family satisfaction. *Communication Monographs, 74,* 200–28.

Schrodt, P., Baxter, L. A., McBride, M. C., Braithwaite, D. O., & Fine, M. (2006). The divorce decree, communication, and the structuration of co-parenting relationships in stepfamilies. *Journal of Social and Personal Relationships, 23,* 741–59.

Schrodt, P., & Ledbetter, A. M. (2007). Communication processes that mediate family communication patterns and mental well-being: A mean and covariance structures analysis of young adults from divorced and non-divorced families. *Human Communication Research, 33,* 330–56.

Strohschein, L. (2005). Parental divorce and child mental health trajectories. *Journal of Marriage and Family, 67,* 1286–300.

Sun, Y., & Li, Y. (2002). Children's well-being during parent's marital disruption process: A pooled time-series analysis. *Journal of Marriage and Family, 64,* 742–62.

——(2010). Postdivorce family stability and changes in adolescents' academic performance: A growth-curve model. *Journal of Family Issues, 30,* 1527–55.

Tein, J., Sandler, I. N., & Zautra, A. J. (2000). Stressful life events, psychological distress, coping, and parenting of divorced mothers: A longitudinal study. *Journal of Family Psychology, 14,* 27–41.

Thomas, C. E., Booth-Butterfield, M., Booth-Butterfield, S. (1995). Perceptions of deception, divorce disclosure, and communication satisfaction with parents. *Western Journal of Communication, 59,* 228–46.

Tyrka, A., Wier, L., Price, L., Ross, N., Anderson, G., Wilkinson, C., & Carpenter, L. (2008). Childhood Parental Loss and Adult Hypothalamic-Pituitary-Adrenal Function. *Biological Psychiatry, 63,* 1147–54.

Usdansky, M. L. (2009). A weak embrace: Popular and scholarly depictions of single-parent families, 1900–98. *Journal of Marriage and Family, 71,* 209–25.

Usdansky, M. L., & Wolf, D. A. (2008). When child care breaks down. *Journal of Family Issues, 29,* 1185–210.

Wagner, K., Ritt-Olson, A., Chou, C., Pokhrel, P., Duan, L., Baezconde-Garbanati, L., Soto, D., & Unger, J. (2010). Associations between family structure, family functioning, and substance use among Hispanic/Latino adolescents. *Psychology of Addictive Behavior, 24,* 98–108.

Wallerstein, J., & Blakeslee, S. (1989). *Second chances: Men, women, and children a decade after divorce.* Boston, MA: Houghton Mifflin.

Wallerstein, J. S., & Kelly, J. B. (1980). *Surviving the breakup: How parents and children cope with divorce.* New York: Basic Books.

Westberg, H., Nelson, T. S., & Piercy, K. W. (2002). Disclosure of divorce plans to children: What the children have to say. *Contemporary Family Therapy, 24,* 525–44.

Whitchurch, G. G., & Dickson, F. C. (1999). Family communication. In M. Sussman, S. K. Stinmetz, & G. W. Peterson (Eds.), *Handbook of marriage and the family* (pp. 687–704). New York: Plenum Press.

Wolchik, S. A., Wilcox, K. L., Tein, J-Y., & Sandler, I. N. (2000). Maternal acceptance and consistency of discipline as buffers of divorce stressors on children's adjustment problems. *Journal of Abnormal Child Psychology, 28,* 87–102.

Yu, T., Pettit, G., Lansford, J., Dodge, K., & Bates, J. (2010). The interactive effects of marital conflict and divorce on parent-adult children's relationships. *Journal of Marriage and Family, 72,* 282–92.

10

Stepfamily Communication

Dawn O. Braithwaite and Paul Schrodt

Stepfamilies are one growing family form that represents both opportunities and challenges to the members who live in them, the professionals who work with them, and the scholars who study them. Defined as families in which "at least one of the adults has a child (or children) from a previous relationship" (Ganong & Coleman, 2004, p. 2), stepfamilies represent one of the more difficult family forms to index and study. Earlier estimates suggested that about one-third of U.S. children would spend at least part of their lives as stepchildren (Bumpass, Raley, & Sweet, 1995), and more recently, Stewart (2007) reported that 15 percent of children under the age of 18 currently live in a married stepfamily. In fact, stepfamily membership is underrepresented in national data sets as stepfamily members' time is often split between households and an increasing number of stepfamilies are cohabiting outside of marriage (Teachman & Tedrow, 2008). In addition, children in any given household may be the product of different adult relationships, and thus, many stepfamilies spring from multiple marriages and cohabiting relationships, creating changing and fluid boundaries.

Whatever challenges exist to estimating the incidence of stepfamilies, social scientists agree that they are a prevalent and growing family type that is often misunderstood and understudied. Until recent years, stepfamily scholarship as a whole tended toward what Ganong and Coleman (1994; 2004) labeled a "deficit-comparison" approach, as stepfamilies were compared against intact families, and their differences from the traditional family archetype were most often evaluated negatively. Making an effort to move beyond a deficit approach, one key question researchers have addressed involves the ways stepfamilies are qualitatively similar and distinct from intact, first-marriage families. While scholars have necessarily focused on challenges stepfamilies face, some are also examining communication behaviors that promote growth and resilience in stepfamilies (e.g., Afifi, 2008; Golish, 2003).

The broad interdisciplinary contributions to the study of stepfamilies are a strength of the available empirical and clinical work (Ganong & Coleman, 2004). More recently, family communication scholars have sought to understand the central role of communication in the formation and enactment of stepfamily relationships. While scholars across disciplines study communication variables relevant to stepfamily processes, scholars with a central focus on stepfamily communication are contributing work that centers communication as the primary, constitutive social process by which relationships are formed and enacted (cf. Baxter, 2004). Central to family communication scholarship is the recognition that families are discourse dependent, meaning that all families form and negotiate expectations and identities via interaction (Galvin, 2006). From this perspective, all families are discourse dependent. However, families that depart from cultural norms, as is the case with stepfamilies, are even more dependent on interaction to define and legitimate themselves as family and negotiate boundaries and expectations for those inside and outside the family. In essence, those who study family communication enlighten the discourses and processes by which families interact and negotiate relationships and expectations of what it means to be a family.

In this chapter, we review research on stepfamily communication and advance a set of claims that can be made about stepfamily interaction, as well as a set of new directions that future scholars can take to advance the recent proliferation of stepfamily scholarship that has emerged over the last two decades.

Communication and Stepfamily Development

One of the fundamental questions to emerge from the growing body of stepfamily scholarship is whether or not stepfamilies develop and function in qualitatively distinct ways from first-marriage families. As Cherlin argued (Cherlin, 1978; Cherlin & Furstenberg, 1994), the "incompletely institutionalized" status of stepfamilies fosters uncertain expectations and ambiguity regarding the proper use of kinship terms (Kellas, LeClair-Underberg, & Normand, 2008), the appropriate role of stepparents in children's lives (Fine, Coleman, & Ganong, 1998; Schrodt, 2006a), and the permeability of stepfamily boundaries as family members negotiate the rights, obligations, and communication processes associated with family membership, maintenance, and functioning (Braithwaite, Olson, Golish, Soukup, & Turman, 2001; Schrodt & Braithwaite, 2010; Sweeney, 2010). Despite the uncertainties and ambiguities of stepfamily formation, some researchers and family clinicians view stepfamilies as developing along one linear, developmental path, where stepfamily relationships form based on prescriptive, chronological stages (e.g., Papernow, 2008). As Baxter, Braithwaite, and their colleagues have argued (Baxter, Braithwaite, & Nicholson, 1999; Braithwaite et al., 2001), however, these developmental stage models are limiting because they oversimplify the developmental process and fail to recognize the tremendous within-group variability that exists among stepfamilies.

Thus, in response to developmental stage models, communication scholars have undertaken efforts to examine the interpersonal behaviors that contribute to different stepfamily developmental pathways and/or stepfamily types. For example, Baxter et al. (1999) used retrospective interviews to identify different types of turning points that stepfamily members experience during the first four years of re-configuration. Their analysis revealed 15 primary types of turning points, ranging from actual physical events such as "changes in household configuration" and "holidays/special events," to relational turning points such as "conflict," "quality time," and "family crisis," among others. These researchers then provided a depiction of changes in "feeling like a family" that included five different trajectories of the first four years of stepfamily development. The *accelerated* trajectory reflected a pattern of quick and sustained movement toward higher levels of feeling like a family. The *declining* trajectory began with a high level of feeling like a family, but quickly declined to very low levels of feeling like a family by the end of the four-year period. The *stagnating* trajectory started and ended with relatively low levels of feeling like a family, whereas the *prolonged* trajectory reflected stepfamilies in which movement toward feeling like a family progressed gradually over a longer period of time. Finally, the *high-amplitude turbulent* trajectory reflected stepfamilies that experienced a "roller-coaster" effect, with rapid increases and decreases in levels of feeling like a family (Baxter et al., 1999).

Not only did each of the trajectories, or developmental pathways, differ in terms of the frequency of different types of turnings points, but stepfamily members from each of the five developmental pathways experienced different processes of interacting and forming appropriate roles and boundaries (Braithwaite et al., 2001). Using the same data set, Braithwaite et al. (2001) found that an accelerated trajectory occurred when stepfamily members adopted the conventional, nuclear family model with its prescribed rules and family norms. Stepfamily members who identified with a declining trajectory, however, experienced an initial degree of closeness that quickly diminished due to false expectations of needing to have an "instant family." Stepfamilies that were successful in their ability to feel like a family developed and maintained flexible boundaries between households, whereas stepfamilies that were unable to successfully negotiate their family ties had boundaries that "became extremely rigid and impermeable, demarcating bloodlines and generations" (Braithwaite et al., 2001, p. 241). Overall, Braithwaite et al. (2001) found that families that let their bonds and roles within the family develop naturally, rather than adhering to the myths of "instant family" and "instant love" (Visher & Visher, 1993), were better able to establish close relationships over time.

Recently, Pryor (2008) argued that it may be time to move away from framing stepfamilies as incomplete institutions because the continued use of this "negative phrase" may (a) contribute to stigmatization within the scholarly community, and (b) maintain a scholarly focus on stepfamily deficits rather than on sources of strength and resiliency. Consistent with Pryor's (2008) position, Golish (2003) used family systems theory and research on coping and resiliency to examine the communication strengths that differentiated strong stepfamilies from those struggling with the developmental process. Her results identified seven primary challenges facing stepfamilies regardless of their strength:

1 "feeling caught";
2 regulating boundaries with a noncustodial family;
3 ambiguity of parental roles;
4 "traumatic bonding";
5 vying for resources;
6 discrepancies in conflict management styles;
7 building solidarity as a family unit.

The communicative tactics used to manage these challenges, however, differed according to the strength of the stepfamily, as strong stepfamilies reported using everyday talk, more openness, communicating clear rules and boundaries, engaging in family problem solving, spending time together as a family, and promoting a positive image of the noncustodial parent more so than stepfamilies that were struggling with the developmental process.

Finally, Schrodt (2006a, 2006b, 2006c) surveyed more than 580 stepchildren from four different states on their perceptions of stepfamily functioning (i.e., dissension, avoidance, involvement, flexibility, and expressiveness) and their relationship with their primary stepparent (in terms of positive regard, parental authority, and affective certainty). Using these dimensions of stepfamily life, he identified five different types of stepfamilies for which significant differences in stepchildren's communication competence and mental health symptoms emerged. First, *bonded* stepfamilies were characterized by low levels of dissension and avoidance and relatively high levels of stepfamily involvement, flexibility, and expressiveness. Second, *functional* stepfamilies were characterized by moderately high levels of stepfamily involvement, flexibility, and expressiveness, as well as moderately low levels of dissension and avoidance. What distinguished bonded from functional stepfamilies was the level of parental authority stepchildren granted their stepparent, with stepchildren from bonded stepfamilies granting much more parental authority to the stepparent than those from functional stepfamilies. Whereas *ambivalent* stepfamilies were characterized by slightly above-average levels of dissension and avoidance and slightly below-average levels of involvement, flexibility, and expressiveness, both *evasive* and *conflictual* stepfamilies were characterized by high levels of dissension and avoidance and relatively low levels of involvement and flexibility, with the primary difference between the final two types being levels of stepfamily expressiveness. Importantly, Schrodt (2006c) demonstrated that stepchildren from all five stepfamily types differed in terms of communication competence and mental health symptoms, such that those from bonded and functional stepfamilies were more likely to report higher competence for themselves, their mother, and their primary stepparent, as well as fewer mental health symptoms, than those from ambivalent, evasive, and conflictual stepfamilies.

Collectively, then, Baxter and Braithwaite's research (Baxter et al., 1999; Braithwaite et al., 2001) on stepfamily developmental trajectories, Golish's (2003) research on stepfamily communication strengths, and Schrodt's (2006a, 2006b, 2006c) program of research on stepfamily functioning and types demonstrate the variability that exists within and between different kinds of stepfamilies. As Banker and Gaertner (1998) noted, however, the more stepchildren perceive their stepfamily as one group, the more they perceive their stepfamily as being harmonious, which stresses the importance of developing and managing healthy boundaries during the process of becoming a stepfamily. Two key factors that influence the successful negotiation and maintenance of healthy boundaries within stepfamilies are how family members respond to dialectical tensions and feelings of triangulation, as well as how they negotiate their own and other family members' roles within the stepfamily. Thus, in the next two sections, we review empirical research on these topics before turning our attention to more recent research on coparental communication in stepfamilies.

Stepfamily Discourses and Challenges

Beyond understanding how stepfamilies develop, scholars have focused on how discourse creates, reflects, and changes stepfamily relationships. Summarized broadly, stepfamily communication scholars have centered their work on (a) dialectical approaches, (b) stepfamily rituals, and (c) conflict and/or loyalty binds that emerge when different stepfamily members feel caught in the middle.

First, scholars have employed dialectical approaches to understand the central tensions and challenges confronting stepfamily members in various stepfamily roles. For instance, Cissna, Cox, and Bochner (1990) interviewed remarried couples and identified the dialectic of the marital and parental relationships in the stepfamily. They described challenges remarried couples faced negotiating the dual tasks of communicating to the children the solidarity of the marriage and the authority of the stepparent. Taking the perspective of the stepchildren, Baxter et al. (2004) examined their discourse and identified three contradictions that infused stepchildren's talk about the stepparent–stepchild relationship: a desire for emotional closeness and distance with their stepparent, a desire for the stepparent to be open with them while simultaneously wanting to maintain privacy, and a desire for parenting from stepparents while simultaneously resisting their parenting efforts. Braithwaite and Baxter (2006) then examined stepchildren's interaction with their non-residential parent, and ironically, identified two similar dialectical contradictions. Specifically, the young adult stepchildren in their study recalled wanting parenting and openness from their nonresidential father or mother, yet at the same time, they identified many difficulties in these attempts and equally strong desires for nonparenting and privacy.

Second, scholars have sought to understand stepfamily challenges reflected in stepfamily members' interaction and negotiation of family rituals. Braithwaite, Baxter, and Harper (1998) studied stepfamily members' accounts of interacting and navigating rituals in the first four years of stepfamily life. During this time, some old pre-stepfamily rituals drop out, some are adapted and brought into the stepfamily, and some rituals are created anew in the stepfamily. These scholars concluded that rituals were successful in the new stepfamily to the extent that they spoke to and honored both the old and new families. Most recently, Baxter et al. (2009) interviewed young adult stepchildren about the remarriage rituals of their parent and stepparent. Regardless of parental attempts (or not) to involve them in the wedding, most stepchildren found the marriage ritual empty. The exception was when children perceived that the remarriage ritual reflected the creation of a family and not just the creation of the marital relationship.

In addition to the dialectical tensions and family rituals that underscore the discourse dependency of stepfamilies, a third line of inquiry has centered on stepfamily conflict and the feelings of triangulation that so often plague stepfamily relationships. For example, Coleman, Fine, Ganong, Downs, and Pauk (2001) identified the main sources of conflict as primarily constituting challenges in negotiating internal and external stepfamily boundaries. They described the strategies stepfamily members used to interact and negotiate conflict, and all but one strategy involved communication centrally—going to counseling, holding family meetings, establishing family rules, compromising, parental dispute mediation, and/or withdrawing/leaving.

Likewise, scholars have examined how various stepfamily members experience and interact when they feel "caught in the middle" in the family. For example, Weaver and Coleman (2010) examined the difficulties that mothers face when caught between their children and the stepfather. When conflicts arose, mothers engaged in one of four protective behaviors, all of which were communicative in nature and included gatekeeping, mediating, interpreting, and defending the child(ren)'s actions. Afifi (2003) identified several behaviors that exacerbated young adult stepchildren's feelings of being caught between their divorced parents, including being the recipient of inappropriate disclosures about the divorce, being elevated to the role of peer or confidant, and being asked to mediate and/or act as a messenger. Afifi and Schrodt (2003) found that the effects of divorce on adolescent and young adult children's topic avoidance and relational satisfaction with their parents were mediated by feelings of being caught, which were a function of their parents' demand–withdraw patterns and communication competence. Schrodt and Afifi (2007) then examined interparental conflict behaviors that heightened children's feelings of triangulation, and found that parents' aggression, demand–withdraw patterns, and negative disclosures were positively associated with young adult children's feelings of being caught. Such feelings, in turn, were inversely associated with children's reports of family satisfaction and mental health.

Building on these lines of research, Braithwaite and colleagues (2008) brought stepchildren together in focus groups and identified competing tensions that characterized what it means to be caught in the middle. On one hand, stepchildren did not want to be caught between their parents, and yet at the same time, they wanted to have relevant information and to be *centered* in their parents' attention. They found that stepchildren interact in ways to maintain a relationship with both parents and manage information disclosed to them. The stepchildren in their study offered advice to parents on how to communicate in ways that kept children in their desired centered position. Given that feelings of triangulation and many of the other challenges that arise in stepfamilies are associated with particular stepfamily roles or confusion over roles, we review this literature in the section to follow.

Communication and Stepfamily Roles

Perhaps the most important and challenging task associated with becoming a stepfamily involves (re)negotiating family roles. Not surprisingly, the stepparent role has received the lion's share of scholarly attention thus far, due in part to the ambiguities and uncertainties associated with how best to enact such a role in children's lives (Fine et al., 1998; Fine, Ganong, & Coleman, 1997, 1999; Ganong, Coleman, Fine, & Martin, 1999; Schrodt, 2006a; Schrodt, Soliz, & Braithwaite, 2008). As Ganong and Coleman (1994, 2004) noted, the stepparent–stepchild relationship is typically considered to be the most challenging and stressful relationship in stepfamilies. Contrary to other personal relationships that are freely chosen by relational partners, step-relationships are often involuntary, leaving very little motivation for stepchildren and stepparents to develop close ties (Ganong et al., 1999). In an effort to address the challenges of creating and sustaining healthy stepparent–stepchild bonds, Fine, Ganong, Coleman, and their colleagues advanced a program of research examining some of the fundamental issues inherent to stepparent relationships (e.g., Fine et al., 1997, 1998, 1999; Ganong et al., 1999). In essence, the basic question concerned whether or not the stepparent should have an active or inactive role in the stepchildren's lives (Fine et al., 1998). For instance, Fine and Kurdek (1994) found that remarried couples expected stepparents to be less active in childrearing than parents, whereas in earlier studies, parents and stepparents reported that stepparents should share equally in childrearing responsibilities (Giles-Sims, 1984). In more recent research, Craig and Johnson (2011) explored the role strain that childless stepmothers face as they desire to have a more active role in their stepchildren's lives, yet face tremendous resistance from biological mothers. Thus, a considerable amount of variability exists in research on stepparent role expectations and enactments.

Some scholars contend that the stepparent should do no more than try to build a friendship with the stepchild(ren), whereas others (e.g., Hetherington, 1999) have found that the long-term benefits of having the stepparent act as a parent outweigh the short-term benefits of having the stepparent simply act as a friend. In their program of research, Fine et al. (1998, 1999) found different perceptions of the stepparent role between adults and children in the stepfamily system. Children were more likely than parents or stepparents to indicate that they preferred the stepparent to function as a friend rather than as a parental figure. Adults were generally more likely to discuss the stepparent role with each other, however, than they were to discuss this role with their stepchildren. This, in turn, led to little consistency in perceptions of parenting behaviors (i.e., warmth and control behaviors) for stepparents among family members, an unfortunate consequence given that consistency in perceptions of the stepparent role was positively associated with stepfamily members' interpersonal adjustment (Fine et al., 1998).

Schrodt (2006a) recently argued that viewing the stepparent relationship in terms of the positive regard that stepparents establish with their stepchildren, the parental authority that stepchildren grant their stepparents (if any), and the degree to which stepparents and stepchildren discuss their feelings and their relationships with each other may be more useful in the long run than trying to fit the stepparent into some pre-existing role or label, such as "parent" or "friend." Indeed, liking is considered among scholars and clinicians to be an important factor in stepparent–stepchild bonding (Visher & Visher, 1996). For instance, Ganong et al. (1999) explored the strategies that stepparents used to develop and maintain affinity with their stepchildren, and found three relatively distinct patterns of affinity-seeking and affinity-maintaining strategies among stepparents in their sample: *nonseeking* stepparents, *early affinity-seeking* stepparents, and *continuous affinity-seeking* stepparents. Not surprisingly, stepparents who were genuinely interested in establishing and maintaining close relationships with their stepchildren and continued their efforts well beyond the formation of the stepfamily (i.e., continuous affinity-seeking stepparents) were more likely to have stepchildren who reciprocated affinity-seeking efforts and developed close stepparent–stepchild relationships.

In addition to affinity-seeking behaviors, communication scholars have compared patterns of topic avoidance, everyday talk, and relational satisfaction in stepparent–stepchild relationships with other parent–child relationships. Golish (2000) investigated adolescents' and young adults' use of topic avoidance and its association with relational satisfaction and the parenting style of the stepparent. She found that the more satisfied children were with their mother, father, stepmother, stepfather, and stepfamily overall, the less avoidance they were likely to use in each of these respective relationships. More importantly, Golish reported that stepchildren's avoidance patterns with their stepparents varied as a function of the stepparent's parenting style, with authoritarian stepparenting producing a positive association with avoidance and a negative association with satisfaction, and with both permissiveness and authoritativeness producing an inverse association with avoidance.

Golish and Caughlin (2002) then compared the types of topics avoided across different types of parent–child relationships. In general, adolescents and young adults in their sample engaged in the most topic avoidance with their stepparents (regardless of stepparent sex), followed by their fathers, and then their mothers in descending order of frequency. Their participants also identified several commonly avoided topics, including talking about the other parent/family, deep conversations, and money (e.g., child support payments), as well as frequently reported reasons for avoidance that included self-protection, relationship protection, and conflict avoidance. In support of their findings, Schrodt et al. (2007) compared patterns of everyday talk across parent–child, stepparent–child, and nonresidential parent–child relationships and found that children engaged in different kinds of everyday talk (e.g., small talk, catching up, recapping the day's events, etc.) more frequently with residential parents than with residential stepparents or nonresidential parents. However, only two notable differences emerged in stepchildren's everyday talk with residential stepparents and nonresidential parents, such that stepchildren engaged in more love talk with nonresidential parents than with stepparents, but engaged in more small talk with stepparents than with nonresidential parents. Moreover, Schrodt et al. (2008) provided evidence of dyadic reciprocity in everyday talk and relational satisfaction for stepparents and stepchildren, such that stepparents who engaged in more everyday talk with their stepchildren were more likely to have stepchildren who reported being satisfied in their relationship with their stepparent.

The work of these scholars demonstrates the centrality of interpersonal communication to family members' negotiations of the stepparent role. The issue of whether or not the stepparent should function as a "parent," however, is not the only issue facing stepfamily

Dawn O. Braithwaite and Paul Schrodt

members as they (re)negotiate their various roles within the stepfamily system. (Non)residential parents and (step)children must also navigate their own uncertainties and ambivalence during the process of becoming a stepfamily. For instance, Coleman, et al. (2001) found that residential parents (e.g., residential mothers) often wrestle with a "guard and protect" ideology with their new spouse or partner, in which the biological parent errs on the side of guarding and protecting their children's interests in any disputes that may arise with the stepparent. At the same time, residential parents who have experienced divorce may also be managing tremendous tensions and/or resentment toward their former spouses (Graham, 1997, 2003), particularly in stepfamilies where both ex-spouses are involved in the coparenting of children (Braithwaite, McBride, & Schrodt, 2003; Schrodt, Baxter, McBride, Braithwaite, & Fine, 2006).

Nonresidential parents are perhaps even more likely to experience stress and tension as they negotiate access and coordinate visitations with their ex-spouses and their ex-spouses' new partners (i.e., the stepparents). Researchers have demonstrated that remarriage is associated with less frequent coparental interaction (Maccoby & Mnookin, 1992), less reported parenting support from the former spouse, and more negative attitudes about the other parent (Christensen & Rettig, 1995), as well as diminished visitation with the children (Wolchik & Fenaughty, 1996). As Braithwaite and Baxter (2006) reported, stepchildren experience tremendous ambivalence and contradictions in relationships with their nonresidential parents. Such tensions and contradictions may constitute a primary source of the distancing that often occurs between nonresidential parents and their children in stepfamilies (cf. Schrodt et al., 2007), as stepchildren attempt to reconcile loyalty divides (cf. Amato & Afifi, 2006).

Moreover, (step)children may also be navigating tremendous role ambiguity in their relationships with other members of the family system, including stepparents, nonresidential parents, and/or stepsiblings. Baxter et al. (2004) discovered, for example, that stepchildren struggle with the tension of wanting both a one-parent authority system in which the residential parent alone enacts discipline in the family, and a two-parent authority system in which the parent and stepparent enact discipline as a couple. Speer and Trees (2007) recently examined stepchildren's autonomy and connection-seeking behaviors with their stepparents, and found that perceptions of stepparents' warmth behaviors were positively associated with stepchildren's role clarity, which in turn was positively associated with connection-seeking behaviors and family satisfaction.

Although scholars have tended to focus on members within the stepfamily household and nonresidential parents, extended family relationships are largely understudied in the stepfamily literature. Children from divorced families often have little say in the amount of contact and the relationships they have with their extended family members, yet many of these important relationships may be diminished or threatened altogether during the development of a new stepfamily (Ganong & Coleman, 2004). For instance, researchers have identified the important role grandparents may play in children's adjustment post-divorce, such that grandparents may be uncertain how to best enact this role and may experience barriers to interacting with their grandchildren, especially when children do not reside with a parent (Soliz 2008). DiVerniero (2011) interviewed stepchildren about interaction with their nonresidential parent's family members. She focused on how the children and extended family accommodated their communication toward one another and discovered that stepchildren and their extended family members employed discourse management strategies, particularly topic avoidance, as they sought to converge or maintain their relationship with the nonresidential family. For

168

example, stepchildren often avoided talking about positive interactions with a stepparent that they perceived would be uncomfortable for their grandparents or other extended family members. Stepchildren also wanted to avoid opening the door for their relatives to express negative information that would make the child feel uncomfortable.

One theme springing from the literature is that in-group/out-group distinctions are inherent to the process of (re)negotiating family roles within stepfamily systems. In addition, questions regarding family membership often revolve around issues of physical and psychological ambiguity in stepfamilies. Drawing on national survey data, Stewart (2005) found that boundary ambiguity (a) is much more prevalent in stepfamilies than in two-parent families, (b) is more prevalent in certain types of stepfamilies, such as those with nonresident stepchildren and/or those that are more structurally complex (i.e., both adults bringing children from previous unions as opposed to only one adult), and (c) is negatively associated with the quality of the couple's relationship and the stability of the union, but only from the perspectives of wives or female partners. Further, Stewart found greater role ambiguity among nonresidential parents than among residential parents, and more recently, she identified a litany of problems that can occur when stepfamily members disagree about what type of stepfamily they belong to (e.g., a traditional family or not) (Stewart, 2007). Given that boundary ambiguity has been linked to both family conflict and adjustment problems for stepfamily members (Gosselin & David, 2007), Stewart's findings call particular attention to role performance in stepfamilies, including the various ways in which ex-spouses and their new partners negotiate their coparenting relationships post-divorce. Thus, in the next section of this chapter, we review recent research on coparental communication in stepfamilies before concluding our chapter with new directions for researchers.

Coparental Communication in Stepfamilies

Perhaps no other family experience is simultaneously more rewarding and more challenging than coparenting children (see Beaton, Doherty, & Wenger, Chapter 14, this volume). A coparenting relationship exists "when at least two individuals are expected by mutual agreement or societal norms to have conjoint responsibility for a particular child's well-being" (Van Egeren & Hawkins, 2004, p. 166). Coparental communication, in turn, refers not to the individual attempts of a parent to guide and direct the behaviors and activities of his or her child, but to the interaction patterns that emerge as one coparent supports and/or undermines the parenting attempts of his or her partner. Adamsons and Pasley (2006) argued that coparental communication should be conceptualized and studied as distinct from other interparental interactions because of the potential unique effects that coparenting may have on family member outcomes. For example, researchers have demonstrated that coparenting in first-marriage families is more predictive of parents' and children's adjustment than is general marital quality, that coparenting accounts for variance in parenting and child outcomes after controlling for individual parent characteristics, and that coparenting is more predictive of marital quality than marital quality is of coparenting (Feinburg, Kan, & Hetherington, 2007; Schoppe-Sullivan, Mangelsdorf, Frosch, & McHale, 2004).

Although the coparenting relationship is central to family functioning, to date, coparenting relationships within stepfamily households have received scant attention. In the two most recent decades in review on stepfamilies, for example, Coleman et al. (2000) and Sweeney (2010) summarized empirical research on remarriage and stepfamily relationships from more than 900 publications over the last 20 years. Ironically, research on coparental communication in stepfamilies was missing altogether from both reviews. In an effort to address this void in the stepfamily literature, Braithwaite, Schrodt, and their colleagues (Braithwaite et al., 2003; Schrodt et al., 2006) examined communication patterns among coparents in stepfamilies (including residential parents, stepparents, and nonresidential parents) using time diaries and in-depth interviews. In their first report using diary data, Braithwaite et al. (2003) found that the coparents in their sample had a moderate level of interaction that was characterized as being very "business-like" and focused primarily on the children. In their second report using follow-up interviews, Schrodt et al. (2006) investigated the various ways in which parents and stepparents communicated about the meaning of the divorce decree within their coparenting relationships. They found that issues of trust, fairness, and good faith were fundamentally tied to how remarried couples used the divorce decree to facilitate or hinder the coparenting actions of nonresidential parents.

Extending these earlier efforts, Schrodt and Braithwaite (2011; Schrodt, 2010, 2011; Schrodt, Miller, & Braithwaite, 2011) then conducted a series of studies exploring the associations among supportive and (non)antagonistic coparental communication, relational satisfaction, and mental health among various coparenting dyads within the stepfamily. In their first report, Schrodt and Braithwaite (2011) found that residential parents' and stepparents' coparental communication quality (i.e., supportive and nonhostile) positively predicted their own (but not their partners') satisfaction and mental health. Couples' relational satisfaction, in turn, mediated the effects of parents' and stepparents' supportive coparental communication on their own mental health symptoms. In fact, after controlling for relational satisfaction, a suppressor effect emerged whereby parents' coparental communication with their partners produced an *inverse*, partner effect on stepparents' mental health. As Schrodt and Braithwaite (2011) reasoned, stepparents may experience stress and ambivalence as they are called upon to help raise their spouse's offspring. In one sense, being called upon to act as a parent may help a residential stepparent feel more like a member of the family, and yet in a completely different sense, such reliance on the stepparent in raising the (step)children may foster a heightened sense of stress and ambivalence as he or she navigates role uncertainties and expectations.

Not only must residential parents and stepparents navigate the challenges associated with coparenting children, but remarriages occur and are maintained under the watchful eyes of a third party who holds a vested interest in the quality and stability of the stepfamily system, namely the former spouse (or partner) (Ganong, Coleman, & Hans, 2006). Given this finding, Schrodt (2010) examined couples' coparental communication with nonresidential parents as a predictor of residential parents' and stepparents' satisfaction and mental health. Specifically, his results revealed that stepparents' coparental communication (i.e., supportive and cooperative) with nonresidential parents positively predicted their satisfaction with their current partners (i.e., with residential parents). Likewise, stepparents' coparental communication with nonresidential parents reduced their own mental health symptoms, but *positively* predicted their partner's mental health symptoms (i.e., indicating poorer mental health for residential parents). Consequently, Schrodt's (2011) results highlight the stress and ambivalence that residential parents may experience as they manage the tensions associated with having their current relational partner coparent with their ex-spouse.

Having discovered the ambivalence that both residential parents and stepparents feel as they coparent together, as well as with the nonresidential parent, Schrodt et al. (2011) tested the effects of supportive and antagonistic coparental communication on ex-spouses' relational satisfaction in stepfamilies. Consistent with their first two reports, Schrodt et al.

(2011) found that ex-spouses' supportive and antagonistic coparental communication predicted their own (but not their ex-spouse's) relational satisfaction. More importantly, nonresidential parents' supportive and antagonistic coparental communication with the residential stepparent predicted their own satisfaction with their ex-spouse, as well as their ex-spouses' satisfaction with them. In essence, their findings further demonstrated the interdependence of coparenting relationships in stepfamilies, as supportive coparental communication between nonresidential parents and their ex-spouse's new partner (i.e., the stepparent) predicted meaningful variance in relational satisfaction for both ex-spouses.

In their recent review of stepfamily research, Schrodt and Braithwaite (2010) argued that one of the defining characteristics that distinguishes stepfamilies from other family forms is the (dys)functional ambivalence inherent to stepfamily life. Although ambivalence is likely to characterize (to greater or lesser degrees) each of the dyadic relationships that exist within stepfamily systems, perhaps no relationship is filled with greater ambivalence than the relationship that emerges between a residential stepparent and his or her partner's ex-spouse (i.e., the nonresidential parent). Not only are these two adults faced with the awkwardness and tension associated with having (or having had) a common relational partner, but most residential stepparents and nonresidential parents are brought together (if at all) by their common (and at times, competing) interests in coparenting children. To further explore these issues, Schrodt (2011) investigated coparental communication and relational satisfaction in residential stepparent/nonresidential parent dyads. He found that although some stepparents and nonresidential parents may avoid contact altogether when it comes to the children, those who do communicate with each other in ways that are understanding and supportive of each other's parenting attempts are likely to enhance the satisfaction that both adults feel in their coparenting relationship. More importantly, Schrodt discovered that nonresidential parents' coparental communication with their ex-spouses (i.e., with residential parents) predicted meaningful variance in stepparents' satisfaction with the nonresidential parent. To the extent that stepparents and nonresidential parents learn to cooperate with each other and work together with the residential parent in childrearing activities, such efforts may ease the stress and anxiety that comes from enacting a new role with a former (or current) partner's new (or former) partner.

Taken together, Schrodt and Braithwaite's (2011; Schrodt, 2010, 2011; Schrodt et al., 2011) investigations of coparental communication, relational satisfaction, and mental health in stepfamilies illustrate the importance of supportive and cooperative coparental communication to the relational and personal well-being of adult family members, as well as the interdependence that exists among various adult dyads within the stepfamily system. Margolin, Gordis, and John (2001) proposed that coparental communication may act as a risk mechanism in family systems, mediating the relationships between marital quality and parenting, and children's adjustment. Thus, examining the degree to which coparental communication mediates the effects of witnessing interparental conflict on children's emotional and mental well-being represents one of several future directions researchers might take as they seek to further our understanding of communication and stepfamily functioning.

Conclusions and Future Directions

As evidenced by this review, scholars have made great strides in recent years toward understanding the centrality of communication in stepfamily development, in navigating dialectical tensions and loyalty binds, enacting new roles, and developing healthy and satisfying coparental relationships. While stepfamilies share some commonalities with first-marriage families, they are qualitatively distinct from them as well. For example, Schrodt and Braithwaite (2010) identified three sources of functional ambivalence that demonstrate their uniqueness, including role ambivalence, emotional ambivalence, and communicative ambivalence. Scholars will do well when they seek to understand step-families in their own right and the discourses that shape and test them. Researchers will continue to confront the complexities of studying stepfamilies and, in so doing, develop more nuanced understandings of stepfamily communication and increasingly sophisticated models of interaction that account for multiple family members' perspectives.

Scholars also need to continue to devote more attention to understudied relationships in stepfamilies. For example, stepsibling relationships and extended stepfamily networks warrant further investigation, as do cohabiting stepfamilies given that these families are on the rise and are increasingly functioning as two-parent families (Manning, 2006). The fluidity of cohabiting families provides an inherent challenge for stepfamily members, as they test the boundaries and bonds that stepfamilies experience and negotiate. Communica-tion scholars can contribute an understanding of the discourses of cohabiting stepfamilies and the influences of these relationships for those inside and outside the stepfamily boundary. In addition, scholars need to pay attention to stepfamilies across the lifespan (Ganong & Coleman, 2004), as there has been little focus on family communication beyond the stepfamily's formative years or stepfamily experiences during childhood.

There will be continued debate regarding the role of the stepparent. Some scholars eschew the idea that the stepparent should enact a parental role in the stepchild's life, whereas others (e.g., Hetherington, 1999) argue that the long-term benefits of having the stepparent act as a parent may outweigh any short-term difficulties associated with such a move. At a minimum, scholars have reached a general consensus that the stepparent role represents one of the key features (if not the key feature) distinguishing the step-family from other family forms, and we advocate research that continues to examine how stepparents interact and navigate the stepfamily system.

While stepfamily research has long been the purview of social scientists, a number of scholars interested in family communication are adopting a critical turn in their work. For example, Baxter (2010) has taken relational dialectical theory in a critical direction, arguing for a focus on discourses that are centered and those that are marginalized. This represents a potentially fruitful research direction for stepfamily communication scholars, especially those seeking to understand the experiences of stepchildren whose agency is most often limited as their parents separate, divorce, and enter into stepfamily relationships, bringing children along, often reluctantly, into new territory.

Finally, we encourage researchers to increase efforts focused on understanding stepfamily strengths, moving toward more sophisticated theoretical explanations of stepfamily inter-action and functioning that favor resiliency and coping processes. Family communica-tion scholars are well positioned to enhance our understanding of stepfamilies as they interact to form, legitimize, and enact stepfamily life.

References

Adamsons, K., & Pasley, K. (2006). Coparenting following divorce and relationship dissolution. In M. A. Fine & J. H. Harvey (Eds.), *Handbook of divorce and relationship dissolution* (pp. 241–61). Mahwah, NJ: Lawrence Erlbaum Associates.

Afifi, T. D. (2003). "Feeling caught" in stepfamilies: Managing boundary turbulence through appropriate communication privacy rules. *Journal of Social and Personal Relationships, 20,* 729–55.

——(2008). Communication in stepfamilies: Stressors and resilience. In J. Pryor (Ed.), *The international handbook of stepfamilies: Policy and practice in legal, research, and clinical environments* (pp. 299–320). Hoboken, NJ: John Wiley & Sons.

Afifi, T. D., & Schrodt, P. (2003). "Feeling caught" as a mediator of adolescents' and young adults' avoidance and satisfaction with their parents in divorced and non-divorced households. *Communication Monographs, 70*, 142–73.

Amato, P. R., & Afifi, T. D. (2006). Feeling caught between parents: Adult children's relations with parents and subjective well-being. *Journal of Marriage and Family, 68*, 222–35.

Banker, B. S., & Gaertner, S. L. (1998). Achieving stepfamily harmony: An intergroup-relations approach. *Journal of Family Psychology, 12*, 310–25.

Baxter, L. A. (2004). Relationships as dialogues. *Personal Relationships, 11*, 1–22.

——(2010). *Voicing relationships: A dialogic approach.* Thousand Oaks, CA: Sage.

Baxter, L. A, Braithwaite, D. O., Bryant, L., & Wagner, A. (2004). Stepchildren's perceptions of the contradictions in communication with stepparents. *Journal of Social and Personal Relationships, 21*, 447–67.

Baxter, L. A., Braithwaite, D. O., Kellas, J., LeClair-Underberg, C., Lamb-Normand, E. Routsong, T., Thatcher, M. (2009). Empty ritual: Young-adult stepchildren's perceptions of the remarriage ceremony. *Journal of Social and Personal Relationships, 26*, 467–87.

Baxter, L. A., Braithwaite, D. O., & Nicholson, J. H. (1999). Turning points in the development of blended families. *Journal of Social and Personal Relationships, 16*, 291–313.

Braithwaite, D. O., & Baxter, L. A. (2006). "You're my parent but you're not": Dialectical tensions in stepchildren's perceptions about communicating with the nonresidential parent. *Journal of Applied Communication Research, 34*, 30–48.

Braithwaite, D. O., Baxter, L. A., & Harper, A. M. (1998). The role of rituals in the management of dialectical tensions of "old" and "new" in blended families. *Communication Studies, 48*, 101–20.

Braithwaite, D. O., McBride, M. C., & Schrodt, P. (2003). "Parent teams" and the everyday interactions of co-parenting in stepfamilies. *Communication Reports, 16*, 93–111.

Braithwaite, D. O., Olson, L., Golish, T., Soukup, C., & Turman, P. (2001). Developmental communication patterns of blended families: Exploring the different trajectories of blended families. *Journal of Applied Communication Research, 29*, 221–47.

Braithwaite, D. O., Toller, P., Daas, K., Durham, W., & Jones, A. (2008). Centered but not caught in the middle: Stepchildren's perceptions of dialectical contradictions in the communication of co-parents. *Journal of Applied Communication Research, 36*, 33–55.

Bumpass, L., Raley, R. K., & Sweet, J. A. (1995). The changing character of stepfamilies: Implications of cohabitation and nonmarital childbearing. *Demography, 32*, 425–36.

Cherlin, A. (1978). Remarriage as an incomplete institution. *American Journal of Sociology, 84*, 634–50.

Cherlin, A., & Furstenberg, F. F. (1994). Stepfamilies in the United States: A reconsideration. *Annual Review of Sociology, 20*, 359–81.

Christensen, D. H., & Rettig, K. D. (1995). The relationship of remarriage to post-divorce co-parenting. *Journal of Divorce & Remarriage, 24*, 73–88.

Cissna, K. N., Cox, D. E., & Bochner, A. P. (1990). The dialectic of marital and parental relationships within the stepfamily. *Communication Monographs, 57*, 44–61.

Coleman, M., Fine, M. A., Ganong, L. H., Downs, K., & Pauk, N. (2001). When you're not the Brady Bunch: Identifying perceived conflicts and resolution strategies in stepfamilies. *Personal Relationships, 8*, 55–73.

Coleman, M., Ganong, L., & Fine, M. (2000). Reinvestigation remarriage: Another decade of progress. *Journal of Marriage and the Family, 62*, 1288–307.

Craig, E. A., & Johnson, A. J. (2011). Role strain and online social support for childless stepmothers. *Journal of Social and Personal Relationships, 28*, 868–87.

DiVerniero, R. D. (2011). Stepchildren's perceptions of accommodation with their nonresidential parent's family. Unpublished manuscript.

Feinburg, M. E., Kan, M. L., & Hetherington, E. M. (2007). The longitudinal influence of coparenting conflict on parental negativity and adolescent maladjustment. *Journal of Marriage and Family, 69*, 687–702.

Fine, M. A., Coleman, M., & Ganong, L. H. (1998). Consistency in perceptions of the step-parent role among step-parents, parents, and stepchildren. *Journal of Social and Personal Relationships, 15*, 811–29.

Fine, M. A., Ganong, L. H., & Coleman, M. (1997). The relation between role constructions and adjustment among stepfathers. *Journal of Family Issues, 18,* 503–25.

——(1999). A social constructionist multi-method approach to understanding the stepparent role. In E. M. Hetherington (Ed.), *Coping with divorce, single-parenthood, and remarriage: A risk and resiliency perspective* (pp. 273–94). Mahwah, NJ: Lawrence Erlbaum Associates.

Fine, M. A., & Kurdek, L. A. (1994). Parenting cognitions in stepfamilies: Differences between parents and stepparents and relations to parenting satisfaction. *Journal of Social and Personal Relationships, 11,* 95–112.

Galvin, K. (2006). Diversity's impact on defining the family: Discourse-dependence and identity. In L. H. Turner & R. West (Eds.), *The family communication sourcebook* (pp. 3–19). Thousand Oaks, CA: Sage.

Ganong, L. H., & Coleman, M. (1994). *Remarried family relationships.* Thousand Oaks, CA: Sage.

——(2004). *Stepfamily relationships: Development, dynamics, and interventions.* New York: Kluwer Academic/Plenum.

Ganong, L., Coleman, M., Fine, M., & Martin, P. (1999). Stepparents' affinity-seeking and affinity-maintaining strategies with stepchildren. *Journal of Family Issues, 20,* 299–327.

Ganong, L., Coleman, M., & Hans, J. (2006). Divorce as prelude to stepfamily living the consequences of redivorce. In M. A. Fine & J. H. Harvey (Eds.), *Handbook of divorce and relationship dissolution* (pp. 409–34). Mahwah, NJ: Lawrence Erlbaum Associates.

Giles-Sims, J. (1984). The stepparent role: Expectations, behavior, and sanctions. *Journal of Family Issues, 5,* 116–30.

Golish, T. D. (2000). Is openness always better?: Exploring the role of topic avoidance, satisfaction, and parenting styles of stepparents. *Communication Quarterly, 48,* 137–58.

——(2003). Stepfamily communication strengths: Understanding the ties that bind. *Human Communication Research, 29,* 41–80.

Golish, T. D., & Caughlin, J. P. (2002). "I'd rather not talk about it": Adolescents' and young adults' use of topic avoidance in stepfamilies. *Journal of Applied Communication Research, 30,* 78–106.

Gosselin, J., & David, H. (2007). Risk and resilience factors linked with the psychosocial adjustment of adolescents, stepparents and biological parents. *Journal of Divorce & Remarriage, 48*(1/2), 29–53.

Graham, E. E. (1997). Turning points and commitment in post-divorce relationships. *Communication Monographs, 64,* 351–67.

——(2003). Dialectic contradictions in postmarital relationships. *Journal of Family Communication, 3,* 193–214.

Hetherington, E. M. (1999). Family functioning and the adjustment of adolescent siblings in diverse types of families. *Monographs of the Society for Research in Child Development, 64* (4, Serial No. 259), 1–25.

Kellas, J. K., LeClair-Underberg, C., & Normand, E. L. (2008). Stepfamily address terms: "Sometimes they mean something and sometimes they don't." *Journal of Family Communication, 8,* 238–63.

Maccoby, E. E., & Mnookin, R. H. (1992). *Dividing the child: Social and legal dilemmas of custody.* Cambridge, MA: Harvard University Press.

Manning, W. (2006). Cohabitation and child well-being. *Gender Issues, 23,* 21–34.

Margolin, G., Gordis, E. B., & John, R. S. (2001). Coparenting: A link between marital conflict and parenting in two parent families. *Journal of Family Psychology, 15,* 3–21.

Papernow, P. L. (2008). A clinician's view of "stepfamily architecture": Strategies for meeting the challenges. In J. Pryor (Ed.), *The international handbook of stepfamilies: Policy and practice in legal, research, and clinical environments* (pp. 423–54). Hoboken, NJ: Wiley.

Pryor, J. (Ed.). (2008). *The international handbook of stepfamilies: Policy and practice in legal, research, and clinical environments.* Hoboken, NJ: Wiley.

Schoppe-Sullivan, S. J., Mangelsdorf, S. C., Frosch, C. A., & McHale, J. L. (2004). Associations between coparenting and marital behavior from infancy to the preschool years. *Journal of Family Psychology, 18,* 194–207.

Schrodt, P. (2006a). The Stepparent Relationship Index: Development, validation, and associations with stepchildren's perceptions of stepparent communication competence and closeness. *Personal Relationships, 13,* 167–82.

——(2006b). Development and validation of the Stepfamily Life Index. *Journal of Social and Personal Relationships, 23,* 427–44.

——(2006c). A typological examination of communication competence and mental health in stepchildren. *Communication Monographs*, 73, 309–33.

——(2010). Coparental communication with nonresidential parents as a predictor of couples' relational satisfaction and mental health in stepfamilies. *Western Journal of Communication*, 74, 484–503.

——(2011). Stepparents' and nonresidential parents' relational satisfaction as a function of coparental communication in stepfamilies. *Journal of Social and Personal Relationships*, 28, 983–1004.

Schrodt, P., & Afifi, T. D. (2007). Communication processes that predict young adults' feelings of being caught and their associations with mental health and family satisfaction. *Communication Monographs*, 74, 200–28.

Schrodt, P., Baxter, L. A., McBride, M. C., Braithwaite, D. O., & Fine, M. (2006). The divorce decree, communication, and the structuration of co-parenting relationships in stepfamilies. *Journal of Social and Personal Relationships*, 23, 741–59.

Schrodt, P., & Braithwaite, D. O. (2010). Dark clouds with silver linings: The (dys)functional ambivalence of stepfamily relationships. In W. R. Cupach & B. H. Spitzberg (Eds.), *The dark side of close relationships II* (pp. 243–68). New York: Routledge.

——(2011). Coparental communication, relational satisfaction, and mental health in stepfamilies. *Personal Relationships*, 18, 352–69.

Schrodt, P., Braithwaite, D. O., Soliz, J., Tye-Williams, S., Miller, A., Normand, E. L., & Harrigan, M. M. (2007). An examination of everyday talk in stepfamily systems. *Western Journal of Communication*, 71, 216–34.

Schrodt, P., Miller, A. E., & Braithwaite, D. O. (2011). Ex-spouses' relational satisfaction as a function of coparental communication in stepfamilies. *Communication Studies*, 62, 272–90.

Schrodt, P., Soliz, J., & Braithwaite, D. O. (2008). A social relations model of everyday talk and relational satisfaction in stepfamilies. *Communication Monographs*, 75, 190–217.

Soliz, J. (2008). Intergenerational support and the role of grandparents in post-divorce families: Retrospective accounts of young adult grandchildren. *Qualitative Research Reports in Communication*, 9, 72–80.

Speer, R. B., & Trees, A. R. (2007). The push and pull of stepfamily life: The contribution of stepchildren's autonomy and connection-seeking behaviors to role development in stepfamilies. *Communication Studies*, 58, 377–94.

Stewart, S. D. (2005). Boundary ambiguity in stepfamilies. *Journal of Family Issues*, 26, 1002–29.

——(2007). *Brave new stepfamilies: Diverse paths toward stepfamily living*. Thousand Oaks, CA: Sage.

Sweeney, M. M. (2010). Remarriage and stepfamilies: Strategic sites for family scholarship in the 21st century. *Journal of Marriage and Family*, 72, 667–84.

Teachman, J., & Tedrow, L. (2008). The demography of stepfamilies in the United States. In J. Pryor (Ed.), *The international handbook of stepfamilies: Policy and practice in legal, research, and clinical environments* (pp. 3–29). Hoboken, NJ: Wiley.

Van Egeren, L. A., & Hawkins, D. P. (2004). Coming to terms with coparenting: Implications of definition and measurement. *Journal of Adult Development*, 11, 165–78.

Visher, E. B., & Visher, J. S. (1993). Remarriage families and stepparenting. In F. Walsh (Ed.), *Normal family processes*, 2nd edn (pp. 235–53). New York: Guilford.

——(1996). *Therapy with stepfamilies*. New York: Brunner/Mazel.

Weaver, S. E., & Coleman, M. (2010). Caught in the middle: Mothers in stepfamilies. *Journal of Social and Personal Relationships*, 27, 305–26.

Wolchik, S. A., & Fenaughty, A. M. (1996). Residential and nonresidential parents' perspectives on visitation problems. *Family Relations*, 45, 230–37.

11

The Family Relationships of Sexual Minorities

Lisa M. Diamond, Kendrick A. Rith, and Molly R. Butterworth

Introduction

After decades of invisibility, the unique family experiences of lesbian, gay, and bisexual (collectively denoted *sexual minority*) individuals are finally receiving systematic attention. Whereas much early research on this population focused on *individual*-level dynamics and challenges, such as identity development and mental health, the past several decades have witnessed an explosion of research on their *interpersonal* experiences. These studies have broadened our knowledge of the sexual-minority life course and have advanced our understanding of the processes through which sexual orientation shapes day-to-day interpersonal functioning. The present chapter reviews the state of contemporary research on the family experiences of sexual-minority individuals, focusing on their romantic relationships and parenting practices.

First, however, some clarifications bear mention. Throughout this chapter we refer to "sexual-minority" (instead of "gay/lesbian/bisexual") individuals and families. *Sexual minority* denotes any individual with same-sex attractions or relationships, and we use this term because not all individuals with same-sex attractions and/or relationships identify as lesbian, gay, or bisexual: In fact, the *majority* of such individuals do not (Laumann, Gagnon, Michael, & Michaels, 1994; Mosher, Chandra, & Jones, 2005). Similar findings have emerged from surveys conducted in other countries (Wichstrom & Hegna, 2003) and in studies of adolescents (Garofalo, Wolf, Wissow, Woods, & Goodman, 1999). Despite the diversity of these individuals' experiences, one thing they undeniably share is that their same-sex attractions and relationships place them outside conventional norms prescribing uniform and universal heterosexuality, potentially exposing them to self-stigmatization, denigration by others, and lack of public acknowledgement of their relationships. This is why they are considered *sexual minorities*. In this chapter we will review what is known about the specific processes and mechanisms through which an individual's sexual-minority status shapes his/her family dynamics and functioning, calling attention to the most important areas for future research.

Same-Sex Romantic Relationships

Sexual-minority individuals have long been stereotyped as unable and/or unwilling to pursue long-term relationships, but research resoundingly contradicts this view. Between

40 and 60 percent of gay men and 50 and 80 percent of lesbians are partnered (reviewed in Peplau & Spalding, 2000), and the majority of lesbian–gay–bisexual individuals would like the option of formalizing such relationships through same-sex marriage (Kaiser Foundation, 2001). In fact, recent representative data reveal that 27 percent of the country's 581,000 cohabiting same-sex couples *consider* themselves spouses, even if U.S. law does not (National Center for Family & Marriage Research, 2010). Research shows that same-sex couples meet, fall in love, and maintain their relationships through the same processes as do heterosexual couples, and that they show notable similaries regarding communication, conflict resolution, and levels of intimacy, autonomy, equality, and mutual trust (Conley, Roesch, Peplau, & Gold, 2009; Kurdek, 2004; Roisman, Clausell, Holland, Fortuna, & Elieff, 2008; Solomon, Rothblum, & Balsam, 2005). They have even been found to fight about the same core issues: finances, affection, sex, criticism, and household tasks (Kurdek, 2004; Solomon et al., 2005), and to show similar levels of physiological reactivity to conflict (Gottman et al., 2003; Roisman et al., 2008). Also, as with heterosexual couples, same-sex couples with higher levels of overall relationship satisfaction report higher levels of sexual satisfaction (Deenen, Gijs, & van Naerssen, 1994; Kurdek, 1991). What, then, *distinguishes* same-sex from heterosexual couples? First, their social stigmatization and invalidation introduces persistent strain that may erode relationship quality and commitment (Green, 2008; Lehmiller & Agnew, 2006). Second, "combining" two individuals of the same gender produces distinctive dynamics regarding communication, intimacy, and sexuality.

Lack of Formal Recognition for Same-Sex Relationships

Recent debates over same-sex marriage have provided a "natural experiment" for examining the effects of social marginalization on the functioning of same-sex couples. Studies have consistently found that same-sex couples who have the opportunity to formalize their relationships experience numerous benefits, whereas those living in areas that specifically forbid same-sex marriage show poorer well-being. For example, a number of recent studies have directly compared same-sex cohabiting couples in "civil unions" to same-sex cohabiting couples *without* civil unions, and also to the married heterosexual siblings of civil union couples (Solomon, Rothblum, & Balsam, 2004; Solomon et al., 2005; Todosijevic, Rothblum, & Solomon, 2005). These couples started out quite similar to each other on overall satisfaction or functioning, yet a three-year follow-up assessment found that the same-sex couples in civil unions were less likely to have broken up than same-sex couples who had not pursued civil unions (Balsam, Beauchaine, Rothblum, & Solomon, 2008). These findings support the notion that *barriers to dissolution* play a key role in influencing couples' attitudes about, and motivations to deal with, hurdles in their relationships (Kurdek, 1998), although it is also important to consider self-selection effects. Specifically, couples who eventually sought civil unions may have started out with greater overall levels of commitment than couples who did not eventually seek civil unions.

Even in highly committed and satisfied couples, relationship formalization can have additional positive effects. Same-sex couples report that formalizing their relationships makes them feel more "real" (Lannutti, 2007) and Solomon and colleagues (Solomon et al., 2005) found that 54 percent of same-sex couples reported increased love and commitment to one another after having had a civil union. One question awaiting future research is whether these benefits would also accrue to same-sex couples pursuing other means of formally acknowledging their relationships, such as naming one another as insurance beneficiaries and/or legal heirs, purchasing property together, giving one another power of attorney, legally taking the same last name, or merging finances (Badgett, 1998; Beals, Impett, & Peplau, 2002; Suter & Oswald, 2003). Such investigations call for careful attention to the specific *mechanisms* through which relationship formalization relates to relationship functioning, and in this respect it is important to distinguish between *symbolic* and *legal* formalization. Fingerhut (2010) found that couples who had formalized their relationships *symbolically* (through commitment ceremonies or weddings with no legal bearing) reported greater life satisfaction and relationship satisfaction, whereas those who formalized their relationships *legally* (through registered domestic partnerships) reported greater investments in their relationship. This suggests that symbolic formalization has particularly strong implications for personal and moral aspects of commitment, whereas legal formalization has relatively stronger implications for structural aspects of commitment (M. P. Johnson, 1999). Importantly, some same-sex couples choose not to pursue symbolic formalization because they believe that rituals such as commitment ceremonies lack meaning if they do not have legal standing (Reczek, Elliott, & Umberson, 2009).

Both symbolic and legal formalization appear to play a role in reducing what Green (2008) has called "relational ambiguity," or the lack of standard cultural "rules" by which partners can gauge the progress and future status of their relationship. Green notes that heterosexual marriage involves a set of cultural expectations that guide partners' behavior, such as cohabitation, pooled property and finances, and caring for one another in times of illness. Without the clear demarcation of *marriage*, same-sex couples must make such decisions on a case-by-case basis, and must openly and repeatedly revisit questions about whether their relationship is "serious" enough to warrant certain commitments and sacrifices (such as giving up a job opportunity, allowing elderly parents to share the household, etc). In some cases, same-sex couples cannot even identify a reliable marker of when their relationship *began* (Reczek et al., 2009). Hence, pursuing either symbolic or legal formalization may help to decrease relational ambiguity and create a set of shared expectations about the status and future of the relationship.

Relationship formalization may also help to buffer couples from the day-to-day stress of social marginalization. Fingerhut (2010) found that the association between internalized homophobia and psychosocial adjustment was attenuated among individuals who had legally or symbolically formalized their relationship. Similarly, Riggle, Rostosky, and Horne (2010) found that same-sex couples in legally recognized relationships reported significantly less psychological distress than those in committed—but not legally recognized—relationships. This does not, however, suggest that formal recognition for same-sex relationships would provide a "magic buffer" against the stress of social stigmatization. In their study of same-sex couples who entered into civil unions in Vermont, Todosijevic and colleagues (2005) found that many of these couples continued to struggle with familial rejection of their relationship. Similarly, Eskridge and Spedale (2006) noted that same-sex married couples in Denmark and other Scandinavian countries (which have significantly more accepting attitudes toward same-sex sexuality than does the U.S.A.) continue to confront daily prejudice and social rejection. The often-vociferous debates over same-sex marriage have been observed to take a notable toll on same-sex couples' views of themselves and their relationships (Rostosky, Riggle, Horne, & Miller, 2009).

This raises the broader question of how same-sex couples' formalization practices are related to their *other* familial ties. As argued by Cohler and Hammack (2007), sexual-minority individuals live "linked lives," such that *all* of their social relationships are intrinsically interbraided. Accordingly, the decision to legally formalize a same-sex relationship has "ripple effects" across the couple's entire social network. Same-sex couples who decide to formalize their relationship enter into a protracted period of relationship re-negotiation with *all* of their important social ties, which may be extended over many years (Smart, 2007). Currently, we understood little about how these renegotiations unfold, particularly in cases where close friends and family members express ambivalence, confusion, or even hostility regarding same-sex sexuality, and this is a key area for future research. Smart (2007) notes that marriage is a "fateful moment" during which sexual-minority individuals must confront, make sense of, and potentially resolve complicated family ties. Yet marriage is obviously not the only such "fateful moment:" Consider, for example, the *dissolution* of a long-term same-sex relationship: Do the parents of sexual-minority individuals treat such changes as equivalent to a conventional heterosexual divorce, or do they inadvertently discount the emotional ramifications? When same-sex couples have children, how does the grandparents' behavior depend on the circumstances of the child's birth (i.e., adoption, surrogacy, birth) and on the status of their child as a biological versus nonbiological parent? These are some of the questions that deserve substantive attention in future research.

Gender-Related Dynamics in Couple Functioning

Of course, the signature characteristic of same-sex couples is that both partners have the same gender role and same history of gender-related socialization, and this similarity appears to facilitate smoother day-to-day communication, support, and negotiation (Gottman et al., 2003; Roisman et al., 2008; Stacey & Biblarz, 2001). Similarity in day-to-day experiences also appears to facilitate relationship functioning: For example, one study found that lesbian women suffering from PMS (Premenstrual Syndrome) reported high levels of responsiveness, understanding, open communication, and responsibility-sharing by their female partners, which contrasts notably with the findings from research on *heterosexual* women, who typically report that male partners fail to understand, support, or validate their symptoms (Ussher & Perz, 2008).

Although both male–male and female–female couples appear to benefit from gender similarity at the level of day-to-day communication and functioning, female–female couples appear to have an additional advantage owing to women's relationally oriented socialization (Choderow, 1978; Jordan, 1987). Women are encouraged from an early age to seek and to prioritize high levels of connectedness and intimacy within their close interpersonal ties (Cross & Madson, 1997), and as a result they tend to surpass men with respect to interpersonal sensitivity, empathy, emotional awareness, and emotional expressivity, especially in their romantic relationships (Barrett, Lane, Sechrest, & Schwartz, 2000; Thomas & Fletcher, 2003). In contrast, men are socialized to emphasize autonomy, independence, and self-reliance, which has historically been observed to interfere with intimacy and expressiveness in their romantic ties (reviewed in Green, Bettinger, & Zacks, 1996).

Consequently, lesbian couples tend to exhibit more emotional connectedness, cohesion, and intimacy than gay male or heterosexual couples (Green et al., 1996; Kurdek, 1998; Zacks, Green, & Marrow, 1988), greater capacity for mutual empathy (Ussher & Perz, 2008), more egalitarianism and more shared and flexible decision-making (Green et al., 1996; Matthews, Tartaro, & Hughes, 2003), and more adaptability in dealing with emotional needs and household tasks (Connolly, 2006). Observational research has found that they show more effective patterns of conflict resolution characterized by more positive emotional tone and more effective negotiation (Metz, Rosser, & Strapko, 1994; Roisman et al., 2008). Initially, investigators critiqued the heightened connectedness of female–female couples as evidence of problematic "fusion" or "merger" (Burch, 1986; Hill, 1999), yet more recent work indicates that female–female couples manage to *balance* emotional expressiveness and sharing with boundary-setting and autonomy (Ackbar & Senn, 2010; Ussher & Perz, 2008).

Importantly, there is more evidence for interpersonal *strengths* in female–female couples than for interpersonal *deficits* in male–male couples. Initially, researchers expected that because men are socialized to value independence and autonomy over connectedness and intimacy, male–male couples would be characterized by distance and disengagement (Kresten & Bepko, 1980). Yet this does not appear to be the case. Most studies detect no differences (or trivial differences) between levels of support, intimacy, cohesion, and satisfaction between male–male and male–female couples (Kurdek, 2001, 2004, 2006; Means-Christensen, Snyder, & Negy, 2003), and in many cases male–male relationship functioning appears to *surpass* that of male–female couples (Green et al., 1996; Kurdek, 2006).

The one area in which male–male couples appear distinctive is sexual exclusivity: Male–male couples are more likely than either male–female or female–female couples to report engaging in extra-dyadic sexual activity, usually with the explicit knowledge of their partner (see also Bonello, 2009; Solomon et al., 2004). This is commonly attributed to the fact that men are socialized to separate sex from love more easily than are women, making it possible for two men in a committed, enduring bond to mutually agree that extradyadic sexual activity does not threaten their emotional commitment to one another (reviewed in Bonello, 2009). Such couples explicitly distinguish *emotional* monogamy from *sexual* monogamy (Adam, 2006; LaSala, 2004), and often negotiate guidelines to ensure that extradyadic sex does not lead to romantic attachment (for example, forbidding one another from having extradyadic sex with the same person more than once). A number of studies have compared relationship functioning and satisfaction in sexually monogamous versus nonmonogamous male–male couples, and have found no significant differences in satisfaction or stability (reviewed in Bonello, 2009). The exceptions were couples who had difficulty communicating effectively about their respective needs and desires, especially desires to renegotiate the "rules" around their arrangement, and couples in which one partner explicitly violated the rules (Bonello, 2009). Overall, the literature on nonmonogamy demonstrates the importance of treating salient differences between same-sex and heterosexual couples *not* as evidence of dysfunction, but instead as potentially adaptive strengths.

Overall, then, the factors that make same-sex romantic relationships different from other-sex romantic relationships appear to have far more to do with gender than with sexual orientation. Sexual-minority and heterosexual individuals do not go about the processes of forming and maintaining romantic ties all that differently from one another, but *men and women* do, and such differences are echoed and magnified in same-sex couples. Before leaving the topic of romantic relationships, however, it bears reiterating that over the course of their lives, the majority of sexual-minority individuals will have romantic relationships with *other-sex* as well as same-sex partners. For many sexual minorities, these relationships are most likely to take place in adolescence and young adulthood, before they have developed a sexual-minority identity and before they have had opportunities to meet potential same-sex partners. Among sexual-minority individuals with nonexclusive (i.e., bisexual) attractions, alternating between other-sex and same-sex partners may remain a consistent pattern over the life course. One fascinating, unanswered question is how such individuals perceive and experience similarities and differences between their interactions with same-sex versus other-sex romantic partners, particularly regarding gender-related patterns of thought and behavior. This is clearly an area in which greater attention to the distinctive, underinvestigated experiences of bisexual men and women has particular potential to advance our understanding of romantic relationship dynamics more generally.

Parenting

Perhaps one of the most fascinating changes in the lesbian–gay–bisexual community over the past 20 years has been the increasing number—and increasing visibility—of same-sex couples raising children, sometimes called the "gayby boom" (S. M. Johnson & O'Connor, 2002). Census data reveal that 24 percent of same-sex couples have a child under 18 in the home (this figure is larger—34 percent—among female–female couples, Gates & Ost, 2004). Historically, simply possessing a same-sex sexual orientation was enough to disqualify an individual from "fitness" for parenthood in the eyes of society (Clarke, 2002; Golombok, 2000). Yet studies have increasingly demonstrated that same-sex parents show equal or even *higher* levels of parental involvement, time spent with children, warmth, affection, shared decision-making, shared childcare, and overall satisfaction with their parenting roles than heterosexual couples (Dunne, 2000; Fulcher, Sutfin, & Patterson, 2008; Golombok et al., 2003).

Numerous dynamics within the household appear to predict the parenting skills of same-sex parents. One important consideration is biological relatedness. Studies of female–female households have consistently found that the mother who gave birth to the child tends to take on a stronger parenting role and to develop a closer tie to the child, even when parents consciously strive for egalitarian parenting roles and practices (Bos, van Balen, & van den Boom, 2007; Dundas & Kaufman, 2000; S. M. Johnson & O'Connor, 2002). Biblarz and Savci (2010) argued that these trends suggest that lesbians are just as vulnerable as are heterosexuals to the societal ideology of "biologism," which implicitly posits biological parents as more "authentic" parents. Numerous studies demonstrate that nonbiological mothers in same-sex couples often are not acknowledged as "real" mothers by their friends, families, and society at large (reviewed in Bergen, Suter, & Daas, 2006). One manifestation of this phenomenon is the lack of language to refer to the nonbiological mother in a same-sex parenting couple. On one hand, the lack of a widely agreed-upon term (such as "co-mother," "second mother," or "nonbiological mother") might be viewed as socially and politically progressive, since it decouples the social role of mothering from the biological act of childbirth (Dunne, 2000). On the other hand, however, the lack of a linguistic category may impede nonbiological mothers' development of the unique and powerful social identity as "mother" (Hequembourg & Farrell, 1999).

Several studies have found that lesbian couples adopt a variety of symbolic strategies and practices to formalize the parenting role of the nonbiological mother, such as settling on distinctive address terms for children to use for each mother (such as "Mommy" and "Mama," or "Mama B" and "Mama P"), incorporating the nonbiological mother's last name into the child's last name, avoiding references to biological relatedness in the household, and assigning critical childcare tasks (such as feeding and bathing) to the nonbiological mother (Bergen et al., 2006; Hequembourg & Farrell,

1999). In the absence of formal legal recognition for the nonbiological mother (which is only available through second-parent adoption, an option that is unavailable to same-sex parents in many states) these strategies play an important role in creating both a public and private sense of family. Additionally, they may promote relationship stability, given that large discrepancies between co-mothers' parenting roles have been associated with jealousy, dissatisfaction, and greater risks for dissolution (Chrisp, 2001; Sullivan, 2004). One important question for future research is whether these linguistic practices are less common and carry less import in geographical regions that grant more protections and legal rights for same-sex couples.

The small amount of research conducted on gay male parents who have children through surrogacy provides no evidence that the father who donated the sperm takes a larger day-to-day parenting role, or is considered a more "authentic" father (Bergman, Rubio, Green, & Padron, 2010). This may reflect the fact that (1) the process of bearing and nursing a child takes considerably more time and physical effort than donating sperm, creating a more substantial discrepancy between the parenting role of the biological and nonbiological mother than between the roles of a biological and nonbiological father; (2) there is much more extensive cultural and historical ideology about the "natural bond" established between mothers and their children during the processes of birth and nursing, which may lead biological mothers and their families to *expect* that they will be more involved with, and more emotionally connected to, the child. One key question for future research is whether the differences that have been observed between biological and nonbiological mothers will diminish as society becomes progressively more accustomed to alternative family forms and structures. Recent data suggest that approximately 90 percent of gay and lesbian adolescents report that they would like to have children (D'Augelli, Rendina, Sinclair, & Grossman, 2006/7). By the time this "next generation" of sexual-minority parents begins rearing children, they may have developed substantially different and more flexible ideologies about the role of gender and biology in parenting.

Adjustment of Children in Same-Sex Households

Considerable research has investigated whether being raised in a same-sex household has repercussions for a child's psychological adjustment, sexual or gender identity, and social relationships, and has found no significant effects (Patterson, 2002). Children and adolescents raised by same-sex couples show no elevations in psychological problems, school difficulties, or behavioral problems (Bos et al., 2007; Golombok et al., 2003; Wainright, Russell, & Patterson, 2004); they show no problems with respect to quality of family interaction or parent–child relationships (Perry et al., 2004), no differences regarding peer relationships, peer acceptance, and the size of their friendship networks (Wainright & Patterson, 2008), no significant problems with self-esteem, anxiety, or depression (Vanfraussen, Ponjaert-Kristoffersen, & Brewaeys, 2003; Wainright et al., 2004), no differences in rates of delinquency, school connectedness, or school performance (Wainright & Patterson, 2006; Wainright et al., 2004). Altogether, evidence clearly indicates that it is the presence of *two high-quality* parents, rather than a parent of each gender, that has the strongest influence on child development (Golombok et al., 2003; Wainright et al., 2004).

Gender identity development in the children of same-sex parents has been a persistent concern: Critics of same-sex parenting have argued that children raised by two women or two men will fail to internalize appropriate gender roles and identities, either because of their observation of an "abnormal" relationship between their parents or the absence of both female and male adult role models in the household on a day-to-day basis (reviewed in Clarke, 2002; Golombok, 2000; Stacey & Biblarz, 2001). Early studies investigating this question were hampered by reliance on fairly limited measures of gender identity, which primarily focused on children's interest in conventionally masculine versus feminine activities and occupations (reviewed in Stacey & Biblarz, 2001). More recent research has adopted more sophisticated conceptualizations of gender identity (for example Egan & Perry, 2001) which focus on the child's subjective experience of comfort in his/her gender, experiences of pressure to conform to gender stereotypes, and attitudes about the relative value of his/her own versus the other gender. Research using these more sophisticated assessments has found that children of lesbian families, compared to those raised in heterosexual families, experience *less* pressure to conform to gender stereotypes and are less likely to view the other gender as superior to their own (Bos & Sandfort, 2010).

Interestingly, parents' household labor appears to be one of the mechanisms through which the children of lesbian parents develop their ideas about gender identity and gender roles. A study comparing the children of lesbian and heterosexual parents (Fulcher et al., 2008) found a strong association between parents' division of household labor and their children's gender stereotypes. Specifically, in *both* lesbian and heterosexual households, children whose parents divided household labor unequally reported more gender-stereotypical occupational preferences. This is particularly notable given that Fulcher and colleagues (2008) also found (similar to many other studies) that lesbian parents endorsed more flexible gender roles for their children. Clearly, children attend to what their parents *do*, and not simply what they *say*, when it comes to household gender roles When women are observed doing "all" the housework (even if there is another woman in the household doing fairly little), this provides a potent message to young children about women's roles as homemakers.

Perhaps the most controversial focus of inquiry is the sexual orientation of children raised in same-sex households, despite consistent evidence that practically all of the children of lesbians and gay men grow up to identify as heterosexual (Golombok et al., 2003; Patterson, 2004). However, longitudinal research has shown that in young adulthood, girls raised by lesbian mothers are significantly more likely than girls raised by heterosexual parents to consider and to experiment with same-sex relationships, regardless of heterosexual identification (Golombok & Tasker, 1996). Notably, however, the heightened same-sex exploration of girls raised by same-sex parents does *not* apparently lead such girls to identify as lesbian. It is possible that such a trajectory of heterosexual development, in which individuals have the freedom and familial support to *question* their sexuality instead of simply presuming their own heterosexuality by default, may actually prove adaptive, potentially leading to a greater sense of sexual self-determination and autonomy. Clearly, we need additional longitudinal research on such questions.

Conclusions and Future Directions

Perhaps the most significant weakness of extant research on the family relationships of sexual minorities is that it has addressed only a small fraction of the sexual-minority population. As noted in the beginning of this chapter, most individuals with same-sex attractions and relationships do *not* openly identify as gay, lesbian, or bisexual, and yet the vast majority of research on same-sex romantic relationships and same-sex parenting has been conducted with lesbian–gay–bisexual-identified men and women. We do not yet know whether and how individuals' decisions about sexual identification influence their family ties. Historically, it was presumed that sexual-minority individuals who chose not to label their sexual identities were still struggling with the sexual questioning process, or suffered from internalized homophobia, and yet we now know that this is not the case (Diamond, 2008). In many cases, individuals choose not to label their sexual identities because they have sexual attractions and relationships with *both* men and women, and may not know about, or feel comfortable with, the term "bisexual." It bears noting that whereas bisexual individuals were once thought to be relatively uncommon, we now know on the basis of several random representative studies, conducted in the U.S. and internationally, that individuals with bisexual attractions and relationships *far* outnumber individuals with exclusively same-sex attractions and relationships (Garofalo et al., 1999; Laumann et al., 1994). Despite this fact, the identity category of "bisexual" has been much slower to receive cultural legitimacy than the categories of "gay," and is frequently misunderstood and denigrated even within lesbian–gay communities (Mohr & Rochlen, 1999; Mulick & Wright, 2002; Ochs, 1996; Rust, 1995). Researchers must strive to identify and recruit bisexual individuals and to assess how their nonexclusive attractions and relationships have shaped their interpersonal experiences across the life course.

Ethnic and socioeconomic diversity is also an important issue: Although the majority of published research focuses on white, middle-class parents, Census data reveal that ethnic-minority same-sex couples are more likely to have children than white same-sex couples (by a factor of 2 among women and by a factor of 4 among men, reviewed in Gates & Romero, 2009). Although only 24 percent of individuals in same-sex couples are ethnic minorities (Romero, Baumle, Badgett, & Gates, 2007), fully 40 percent of same-sex couples raising children are ethnic minorities, and 50 percent of the *children* of same-sex couples are ethnic minorities. Another important issue is income: Same-sex couples with children have lower median household incomes (approximately $46,000) than heterosexual cohabiting couples raising children (approximately $60,000) and married heterosexual couples raising children (approximately $75,000, Romero et al, 2007). This is all the more striking given that cohabiting male–male couples *without* children generally have higher median incomes than heterosexual couples (National Center for Family & Marriage Research, 2010). Furthermore, same-sex couples raising children are approximately twice as likely to be receiving public assistance as married couples with children, across all ethnic groups (although their rates of public assistance pale in comparison to those of unmarried heterosexual households with children, Gates & Romero, 2009). Despite these notable demographic trends, very little research on same-sex parenting has specifically addressed issues of ethnicity and social class, and this remains among the most important areas for future research.

Another chronic weakness is the lack of attention to gay–bisexual *fathers* (with some notable exceptions, such as Bergman et al., 2010; Golombok & Tasker, 2010). Given that sexual-minority women have historically been more likely to parent than sexual-minority men, this imbalance is understandable. Yet as the number of male–male parenting households continues to increase, it will become increasingly important to investigate whether and how gender-related dynamics create substantially different parenting practices among male–male versus female–female and male–female couples (paralleling the investigations reviewed above on *couple* functioning in these three types of dyads). The *child's* gender must also be taken into account. Some studies have found that lesbian parents report greater comfort raising daughters than sons (Chrisp, 2001; Dundas & Kaufman, 2000), and that lesbians with daughters report higher-quality mother–child interactions than do lesbians with sons (Vanfraussen, Ponjaert Kristoffersen, & Brewaeys, 2003). Such findings raise provocative questions about the degree to which male–male and female–female couples may be guided in their parenting decisions by different implicit assumptions about the "nature" of male versus female children. Notably, such assumptions have a long and stubborn history: Courts have historically treated the legal rights of same-sex parents quite differently depending on the gender of the parents *and* the child, reflecting long-standing cultural expectations about what female and male children *need*, and what female and adult parents are capable of *providing* (Rosky, 2009). Clearly, we need additional research investigating the potentially unique ways in which male–male and female–female parents interact with male and female children, and such gendered patterns of parenting emerge and unfold over time.

Another intriguing area for future research concerns "alternative" family arrangements and practices, such as maintaining separate residences from a primary partner (Hess & Catell, 2001), maintaining long-standing ties with ex-lovers (Weinstock, 2004), pursuing multiple and/or nonmonogamous partnerships (Munson & Stelboum, 1999; West, 1996), developing romantic, emotionally primary, but nonsexual relationships (Rothblum & Brehony, 1993), or forgoing "primary" ties altogether in favor of "chosen families" of close friends (Nardi, 1999; Weinstock & Rothblum, 1996). We know little about the prevalence of these practices and their implications for day-to-day family processes. Yet greater attention to these phenomena has the potential to advance researchers' understanding of the psychological and behavioral mechanisms through which adaptive interpersonal ties are crafted, managed, and maintained over the life course.

In conclusion, it bears emphasizing that perhaps the single most defining characteristic of sexual-minority individuals' family relationships is that they have no single defining characteristic. Sexual-minority individuals are as diverse as the American population more generally, with similarly diverse family practices and processes. Hence, future research must go beyond simply testing for differences between sexual-minority and heterosexual individuals, and should instead attempt to reveal the specific interpersonal *processes and mechanisms* through which individuals' status as a sexual minority shapes the formation, functioning, and long-term development of their closest interpersonal ties. Such research has the potential to greatly advance our understanding of the diversity and complexity of the sexual-minority life course.

References

Ackbar, S., & Senn, C. Y. (2010). What's the confusion about fusion? Differentiating positive and negative closeness in lesbian relationships. *Journal of Marital and Family Therapy, 36,* 416–30.

Adam, B. D. (2006). Relationship innovation in male couples. *Sexualities, 9,* 5–26.

Badgett, M. V. L. (1998). The economic well-being of lesbian, gay, and bisexual adults' families. In C. Patterson & A. R. D. Augelli (Eds.), *Lesbian, gay, and bisexual identities in families: Psychological Perspectives* (pp. 231–48). Oxford: Oxford University Press.

Balsam, K. F., Beauchaine, T. P., Rothblum, E. D., & Solomon, S. E. (2008). Three-year follow-up of same-sex couples who had civil unions in Vermont, same-sex couples not in civil unions, and heterosexual married couples. *Developmental Psychology, 44,* 102–16.

Barrett, L. F., Lane, R. D., Sechrest, L., & Schwartz, G. E. (2000). Sex differences in emotional awareness. *Personality & Social Psychology Bulletin, 26,* 1027–35.

Beals, K. P., Impett, E. A., & Peplau, L. A. (2002). Lesbians in love: Why some relationships endure and others end. *Journal of Lesbian Studies, 6,* 53–63.

Bergen, K. M., Suter, E. A., & Daas, K. L. (2006). "About as solid as a fish net": Symbolic construction of a legitimate parental identity for nonbiological lesbian mothers. *Journal of Family Communication, 6,* 201–20.

Bergman, K., Rubio, R. J., Green, R.-J., & Padron, E. (2010). Gay men who become fathers via surrogacy: The transition to parenthood. *Journal of GLBT Family Studies, 6*, 111–41.

Biblarz, T. J., & Savci, E. (2010). Lesbian, gay, bisexual, and transgender families. *Journal of Marriage & the Family, 72*, 480–97.

Bonello, K. (2009). Gay monogamy and extra-dyadic sex: A critical review of the theoretical and empirical literature. *Counselling Psychology Review, 24*, 51–65.

Bos, H. M. W., & Sandfort, T. G. M. (2010). Children's gender identity in lesbian and heterosexual two-parent families. *Sex Roles, 62*, 114–26.

Bos, H. M. W., van Balen, F., & van den Boom, D. C. (2007). Child adjustment and parenting in planned lesbian-parent families. *American Journal of Orthopsychiatry, 77*, 38–48.

Burch, B. (1986). Psychotherapy and the dynamics of merger and lesbian couples. In T. S. Stein & C. J. Cohen (Eds.), *Contemporary perspectives on psychotherapy with lesbians and gay men* (pp. 57–72). New York: Plenum.

Choderow, N. (1978). *The reproduction of mothering*. Berkeley, CA: University of California Press.

Chrisp, J. (2001). That four letter word—sons: Lesbian mothers and adolescent sons. *Journal of Lesbian Studies, 5*, 195–209.

Clarke, V. (2002). Sameness and difference in research on lesbian parenting. *Journal of Community & Applied Social Psychology, 12*, 210–22.

Cohler, B. J., & Hammack, P. L. (2007). The psychological world of the gay teenager: Social change, narrative, and "normality." *Journal of Youth and Adolescence, 36*, 47–59.

Conley, T. D., Roesch, S. C., Peplau, L. A., & Gold, M. S. (2009). A test of positive illusions versus shared reality models of relationship satisfaction among gay, lesbian, and heterosexual couples. *Journal of Applied Social Psychology, 39*, 1417–31.

Connolly, C. M. (2006). A feminist perspective of resilience in lesbian couples. *Journal of Feminist Family Therapy, 18*, 137–62.

Cross, S. E., & Madson, L. (1997). Models of the self: Self-construals and gender. *Psychological Bulletin, 122*, 5–37.

D'Augelli, A. R., Rendina, H. J., Sinclair, K. O., & Grossman, A. H. (2006/7). Gay and lesbian youths' aspirations for marriage and raising children. *Journal of LGBT Issues in Counseling, 1*, 77–98.

Deenen, A. A., Gijs, L., & van Naerssen, A. X. (1994). Intimacy and sexuality in gay male couples. *Archives of Sexual Behavior, 23*, 421–31.

Diamond, L. M. (2008). *Sexual fluidity: Understanding women's love and desire*. Cambridge, MA: Harvard University Press.

Dundas, S., & Kaufman, M. (2000). The Toronto Lesbian Family Study. *Journal of Homosexuality, 40*, 65–79.

Dunne, A. (2000). Opting into motherhood: Lesbians blurring the boundaries and transforming the meaning of parenthood and kinship. *Gender & Society, 14*, 11–35.

Egan, S. K., & Perry, D. G. (2001). Gender identity: A multidimensional analysis with implications for psychosocial adjustment. *Developmental Psychology, 37*, 451–63.

Eskridge, W. N., & Spedale, D. R. (2006). *Gay marriage: For better or for worse? What we've learned from the evidence*. Oxford: Oxford University Press.

Fingerhut, A. W. (2010). Relationship formalization and individual and relationship well-being among same-sex couples. *Journal of Social and Personal Relationships, 27*, 956–69.

Fulcher, M., Sutfin, E., & Patterson, C. (2008). Individual differences in gender development: Associations with parental sexual orientation, attitudes, and division of labor. *Sex Roles, 58*, 330–41.

Garofalo, R., Wolf, R. C., Wissow, L. S., Woods, E. R., & Goodman, E. (1999). Sexual orientation and risk of suicide attempts among a representative sample of youth. *Archives of Pediatrics and Adolescent Medicine, 153*, 487–93.

Gates, G. J., & Ost, J. (2004). *The gay and lesbian atlas*. Washington, DC: Urban Institute.

Gates, G. J., & Romero, A. P. (2009). Parenting by gay men and lesbians: Beyond the current research. In H. E. Peters & C. M. K. Dush (Eds.), *Marriage and family: Perspectives and complexities* (pp. 227–43). New York: Columbia University Press.

Golombok, S. (2000). *Parenting: What really counts*. London: Routledge.

Golombok, S., Perry, B., Burston, A., Murray, C., Mooney-Somers, J., Stevens, M., et al. (2003). Children with lesbian parents: A community study. *Developmental Psychology, 39*, 20–33.

Golombok, S., & Tasker, F. (1996). Do parents influence the sexual orientation of their children? Findings from a longitudinal study of lesbian families. *Developmental Psychology, 32*, 3–11.

——(2010). Gay fathers. In M. E. Lamb (Ed.), *The role of the father in child development* (pp. 319–40). Hoboken, NJ: John Wiley & Sons.

Gottman, J. M., Levenson, R. W., Swanson, C., Swanson, K., Tyson, R., & Yoshimoto, D. (2003). Observing gay, lesbian and heterosexual couples' relationships: Mathematical modeling of conflict interaction. *Journal of Homosexuality, 45,* 65–91.

Green, R.-J. (2008). Gay and lesbian couples: Successful coping with minority stress. In M. McGoldrick & K. V. Hardy (Eds.), *Re-visioning family therapy: Race, culture, and gender in clinical practice,* 2nd edn (pp. 300–10). New York: Guilford Press.

Green, R.-J., Bettinger, M., & Zacks, E. (1996). Are lesbian couples fused and gay male couples disengaged? Questioning gender straightjackets. In J. Laird & R.-J. Green (Eds.), *Lesbians and gays in couples and families: A handbook for therapists* (pp. 185–230). San Francisco, CA: Jossey-Bass.

Hequembourg, A., & Farrell, M. P. (1999). Lesbian motherhood: Negotiating marginal-mainstream identities. *Gender & Society, 13,* 540–57.

Hess, J., & Catell, P. (2001). Dual dwelling duos: An alternative for long-term relationships. In B. J. Brothers (Ed.), *Couples, intimacy issues, and addiction* (pp. 25–31). New York: Haworth Press, Inc.

Hill, C. A. (1999). Fusion and conflict in lesbian relationships? *Feminism and Psychology, 9,* 179–85.

Johnson, M. P. (1999). Personal, moral, and structural commitment to relationships: Experiences of choice and constraint. In J. M. Adams & W. H. Jones (Eds.), *Handbook of interpersonal commitment and relationship stability* (pp. 73–87). Dordrecht: Kluwer Academic.

Johnson, S. M., & O'Connor, E. (2002). *The gay baby boom: The psychology of gay parenthood.* New York: New York University Press.

Jordan, J. V. (1987). *Clarity in connection: Empathic knowing, desire and sexuality.* Wellesley, MA: Stone Center, Wellesley College.

Kaiser Foundation (2001). *Inside-out: Report on the experiences of lesbians, gays and bisexuals in America and the public's view on issues and policies related to sexual orientation.* Menlo Park, CA: Kaiser Foundation.

Kresten, J., & Bepko, C. S. (1980). The problem of fusion in lesbian relationships. *Family Process, 19,* 277–89.

Kurdek, L. A. (1991). Sexuality in homosexual and heterosexual couples. In K. McKinney & S. Sprecher (Eds.), *Sexuality in close relationships* (pp. 177–91). Hillsdale, NJ: Lawrence Erlbaum Associates.

——(1998). Relationship outcomes and their predictors: Longitudinal evidence from heterosexual married, gay cohabiting, and lesbian cohabiting couples. *Journal of Marriage and the Family, 60,* 553–68.

——(2001). Differences between heterosexual-nonparent couples and gay, lesbian, and heterosexual-parent couples. *Journal of Family Issues, 22,* 727–54.

——(2004). Are gay and lesbian cohabiting couples really different from heterosexual married couples? *Journal of Marriage & Family, 66,* 880–900.

——(2006). Differences between partners from heterosexual, gay, and lesbian cohabiting couples. *Journal of Marriage and Family, 68,* 509–28.

Lannutti, P. J. (2007). The influence of same-sex marriage on the understanding of same-sex relationships. *Journal of Homosexuality, 53,* 135–57.

LaSala, M. C. (2004). Extradyadic sex and gay male couples: Comparing monogamous and nonmonogamous relationships. *Families in Society, 85,* 405–12.

Laumann, E. O., Gagnon, J. H., Michael, R. T., & Michaels, F. (1994). *The social organization of sexuality: Sexual practices in the United States.* Chicago, IL: University of Chicago Press.

Lehmiller, J. J., & Agnew, C. R. (2006). Marginalized relationships: The impact of social disapproval on romantic relationship commitment. *Personality and Social Psychology Bulletin, 32,* 40–51.

Matthews, A. K., Tartaro, J., & Hughes, T. L. (2003). A comparative study of lesbian and heterosexual women in committed relationships. *Journal of Lesbian Studies, 7,* 101–14.

Means-Christensen, A. J., Snyder, D. K., & Negy, C. (2003). Assessing nontraditional couples: Validity of the Marital Satisfaction Inventory-Revised with gay, lesbian, and cohabiting heterosexual couples. *Journal of Marital and Family Therapy, 29,* 69–83.

Metz, M. E., Rosser, B. R. S., & Strapko, N. (1994). Differences in conflict-resolution styles among heterosexual, gay, and lesbian couples. *Journal of Sex Research, 31,* 293–308.

Mohr, J. J., & Rochlen, A. B. (1999). Measuring attitudes regarding bisexuality in lesbian, gay male, and heterosexual populations. *Journal of Counseling Psychology, 46,* 353–69.

Mosher, W. D., Chandra, A., & Jones, J. (2005). *Sexual behavior and selected health measures: Men and women 15–44 years of age, United States, 2002.* Advance data from vital and health statistics, no. 362. Hyattsville, MD: National Center for Health Statistics.

Mulick, P. S., & Wright, L. W., Jr. (2002). Examining the existence of biphobia in the heterosexual and homosexual populations. *Journal of Bisexuality, 2,* 45–64.

Munson, M., & Stelboum, J. P. (Eds.) (1999). *The lesbian polyamory reader: Open relationships, non-monogamy, and casual sex.* New York: Haworth Press.

Nardi, P. M. (1999). *Gay men's friendships.* Chicago, IL: University of Chicago Press.

National Center for Family & Marriage Research (2010). *Same-sex couple households in the U.S., 2009,* FP.10.08, from http://ncfmr.bgsu.edu/pdf/family_profiles/file87414.pdf.

Ochs, R. (1996). Biphobia: It goes more than two ways. In B. A. Firestein (Ed.), *Bisexuality: The psychology and politics of an invisible minority* (pp. 217–39). Thousand Oaks, CA: Sage Publications, Inc.

Patterson, C. J. (2002). Lesbian and gay parenthood. In M. H. Bornstein (Ed.), *Handbook of parenting.* Vol. III: *Being and becoming a parent,* 2nd edn (pp. 317–38). Mahwah, NJ: Lawrence Erlbaum Associates.

——(2004). Gay fathers. In M. E. Lamb (Ed.), *The role of the father in child development,* 4th edn (pp. 397–416). New York: John Wiley & Sons.

Peplau, L. A., & Spalding, L. R. (2000). The close relationships of lesbians, gay man, and bisexuals. In C. Hendrick & S. S. Hendrick (Eds.), *Close relationships: A sourcebook* (pp. 111–23). Thousand Oaks, CA: Sage.

Perry, B., Burston, A., Stevens, M., Golding, J., Golombok, S., & Steele, H. (2004). Children's play narratives: What they tell us about lesbian-mother families. *American Journal of Orthopsychiatry, 74,* 467–79.

Reczek, C., Elliott, S., & Umberson, D. (2009). Commitment without marriage: Union formation among long-term same-sex couples. *Journal of Family Issues, 30,* 738–56.

Riggle, E. D. B., Rostosky, S. S., & Horne, S. G. (2010). Psychological distress, well-being, and legal recognition in same-sex couple relationships. *Journal of Family Psychology, 24,* 82–86.

Roisman, G. I., Clausell, E., Holland, A., Fortuna, K., & Elieff, C. (2008). Adult romantic relationships as contexts of human development: A multimethod comparison of same-sex couples with opposite-sex dating, engaged, and married dyads. *Developmental Psychology, 44,* 91–101.

Romero, A. P., Baumle, A. K., Badgett, V. L., & Gates, G. J. (2007). *Census snapshot: The United States.* Los Angeles, CA: The Williams Institute.

Rosky, C. (2009). Like father, like son: Homosexuality, parenthood, and the gender of homophobia. *Yale Journal of Law and Feminism, 20,* 257–355.

Rostosky, S. S., Riggle, E. D. B., Horne, S. G., & Miller, A. D. (2009). Marriage amendments and psychological distress in lesbian, gay, and bisexual (LGB) adults. *Journal of Counseling Psychology, 56,* 56–66.

Rothblum, E. D., & Brehony, K. A. (Eds.) (1993). *Boston marriages.* Amherst, MA: University of Massachusetts Press.

Rust, P. C. R. (1995). *Bisexuality and the challenge to lesbian politics: Sex, loyalty, and revolution.* New York: New York University Press.

Smart, C. (2007). Same-sex couples and marriage: Negotiating relational landscapes with families and friends. *The Sociological Review, 55,* 671–86.

Solomon, S. E., Rothblum, E. D., & Balsam, K. F. (2004). Pioneers in partnership: Lesbian and gay male couples in civil unions compared with those not in civil unions and married heterosexual siblings. *Journal of Family Psychology, 18,* 275–86.

——(2005). Money, housework, sex, and conflict: Same-sex couples in civil unions, those not in civil unions, and heterosexual married siblings. *Sex Roles, 52,* 561–75.

Stacey, J., & Biblarz, T. J. (2001). (How) does the sexual orientation of parents matter? *American Sociological Review, 66,* 159–83.

Sullivan, M. (2004). *The family of woman: Lesbian mothers, their children, and the undoing of gender.* Berkeley, CA: University of California Press.

Suter, E. A., & Oswald, R. F. (2003). Do lesbians change their last names in the context of a committed relationship? *Journal of Lesbian Studies, 7,* 71–83.

Thomas, G., & Fletcher, G. J. O. (2003). Mind-reading accuracy in intimate relationships: Assessing the roles of the relationship, the target, and the judge. *Journal of Personality and Social Psychology, 85,* 1079–94.

Todosijevic, J., Rothblum, E. D., & Solomon, S. E. (2005). Relationship satisfaction, affectivity, and gay-specific stressors in same-sex couples joined in civil unions. *Psychology of Women Quarterly*, *29*, 158–66.

Ussher, J. M., & Perz, J. (2008). Empathy, egalitarianism and emotion work in the relational negotiation of PMS: The experience of women in lesbian relationships. *Feminism & Psychology*, *18*, 87–111.

Vanfraussen, K., Ponjaert-Kristoffersen, I., & Brewaeys, A. (2003). What does it mean for youngsters to grow up in a lesbian family created by means of donor insemination? *Journal of Reproductive and Infant Psychology*, *20*, 237–52.

Vanfraussen, K., Ponjaert Kristoffersen, I., & Brewaeys, A. (2003). Family functioning in lesbian families created by donor insemination. *American Journal of Orthopsychiatry*, *73*, 78–90.

Wainright, J. L., & Patterson, C. J. (2006). Delinquency, victimization, and substance use among adolescents with female same-sex parents. *Journal of Family Psychology*, *20*, 526–30.

——(2008). Peer relations among adolescents with female same-sex parents. *Developmental Psychology*, *44*, 117–26.

Wainright, J. L., Russell, S. T., & Patterson, C. J. (2004). Psychosocial adjustment, school outcomes, and romantic relationships of adolescents with same-sex parents. *Child Development*, *75*, 1886–98.

Weinstock, J. S. (2004). Lesbian ex-lover relationships: Under-estimated, under-theorized and under-valued? In J. S. Weinstock & E. D. Rothblum (Eds.), *Lesbian ex-lovers: The really long-term relationships* (pp. 1–8). Binghamton, NY: The Harrington Park Press/The Haworth Press, Inc.

Weinstock, J. S., & Rothblum, E. D. (Eds.) (1996). *Lesbian friendships: For ourselves and for each other*. New York: NYU Press.

West, C. (1996). *Lesbian polyfidelity*. San Francisco, CA: Bootlegger Publishing.

Wichstrom, L. & Hegna, K. (2003). Sexual orientation and suicide attempt: A longitudinal study of the general Norwegian adolescent population. *Journal of Abnormal Psychology*, *112*, 144–51.

Zacks, E., Green, R.-J., & Marrow, J. (1988). Comparing lesbian and heterosexual couples on the Circumplex Model: An initial investigation. *Family Process*, *27*, 471–84.

12

Single, No Children

Who Is Your Family?

Bella DePaulo

After his election in 2008, President Barack Obama nominated a single woman with no children, Janet Napolitano, to be the Secretary of Homeland Security. Commenting on Napolitano's qualifications, Pennsylvania Governor Ed Rendell declared her to be "perfect"—"because for that job, you have to have no life. Janet has no family. Perfect. She can devote, literally, 19–20 hours a day to it" (Collins, 2008).

About a year into her time as Homeland Security Director, Napolitano was called early in the morning when a passenger on a flight headed to Detroit, Michigan, turned out to have a bomb concealed in his underwear. It was Christmas Day, 2009, and the director was at the home of her brother (Kornblut, 2010).

Yet neither Napolitano's brother nor her sister seem to come to mind when people such as Ed Rendell think about Janet Napolitano's life. There are shorthand words and phrases used to refer to single people with no children—they are "alone," they "don't have anyone" (DePaulo, 2006). Those ways of thinking and speaking render invisible all of the important people in the lives of singles with no children, including their family and their friends (DePaulo, 2011b).

In this chapter, I will draw from the available research literature to show that single people with no children have families and do family-type things. They have personal communities that typically include friends and relatives. They have "social convoys" that provide shared experiences, continuity, and a sense of identity. Singles with no children are in some ways even more interconnected with other people such as friends, siblings, parents, and neighbors than are individuals who are married. Perceptions of who counts as family have not kept up with the realities of how people actually live their lives. As I will document in the next section, the number of single people, and of adults with no children, has been climbing for decades, so perhaps our understandings of those demographic juggernauts will soon begin to catch up.

Adults Who Are Not Married and Adults with No Children: Two Demographic Groups on the Rise

In 1970, 37.5 million Americans, 18 and older, were unmarried—they were divorced or widowed or had always been single. They comprised 28.3 percent of the population

(Saluter & Lugaila, 1998). Their numbers have grown steadily. The 2009 data from the American Community Survey reported 106.4 million unmarried Americans—45.8 percent of the population (U.S. Census Bureau, 2009). Of the 106.4 Americans who were not married in 2009, 65.4 million of them had never been married.

As more Americans are living single, so, too are more Americans—both unmarried and married—living with no children. A Pew Research Center report (Livingston & Cohn, 2010) compared the number of women, ages 40 to 44, who had never had children in 1976 and 2008. In 1976, only 580,000 women in that age range, or 10 percent, had never given birth. By 2008, the number jumped to 1.9 million, or 18 percent. Adding births after age 44, as well as nonbiological children, would increase the number of women with children at both points in time, but would not change the historical trend toward not having any children at all. The same Pew report found that the percentage of women who had never had children was especially high for those who had always been single—56 percent, compared to 13 percent among those who were currently or previously married, for the 2008 data.

Although much of the research I will describe focuses on Americans and does not report separate results for different racial or ethnic groups, the key demographic changes are widespread. For example, the trend toward having no children is characteristic of Blacks, Hispanics, and Asians, as well as White Americans (Livingston & Cohn, 2010). One of the many demographic shifts contributing to the growing number of single people is the rising age at which people first marry, among those who do marry. United Nations data from 128 countries indicate that this is a global phenomenon (United Nations, 2009). It is strongest, to be sure, in countries classified as "developed," but it is also evident in many "developing" countries.

Conceptualizing Family in the Lives of Singles with No Children

If you are single with no children, who is your family? In the next several sections, I will approach that question from a variety of perspectives. The meaning of family of origin is straightforward, so I will begin there. Then I will ask whether there are defining attributes of family. Next, I will discuss the performative perspective, known as "doing" family, and I will ask whether singles with no children do family-type things. Another approach is to set aside the family terminology, and simply ask adults to name and describe the important people in their lives. Perhaps family is whoever people say it is; I'll consider that, too. Finally, I'll review what nonprofessionals say when asked who counts as family.

Families of Origin

In 2007, the *Journal of Family Issues* devoted the October and November issues to research and theory about people who have no children. In their introduction to the special issues, Pearl Dykstra and Gunhild Hagestad (2007) said:

> It is common to hear young adults being asked, "Do you have a family?" and responding, "not yet." Seldom does the person who posed the question follow up with the query, "So you have no parents, no brothers and sisters, no aunts and uncles, and no cousins?" We tend to disregard the fact that everyone is someone's child, and the parent–child ties from the family of orientation may last for more than 60 years!
>
> (p. 1281)

191

Family of origin. That's the first answer to the question, "Single, no children: Who's your family?" Later in this chapter, I will address the question of just how much contact singles maintain with their parents and siblings, compared to married people.

Are There Defining Criteria for "Family"?

When people in contemporary American society ask other adults about their families, they do not expect to hear about families of origin. What they are really asking is whether the adult stands at the helm of a nuclear family. In white middle-class America of the 1950s, a unit comprised of a married mother and father and their minor children was the dominant household form. Now, however, there are fewer households comprised of mom, dad, and the kids, than of single people living solo (Klinenberg, 2012).

In the 1950s, few scholars saw that coming. As Scanzoni (2001) noted:

> The accepted wisdom was that the post-World War II nuclear family style was the culmination of a long journey—the end point of changes in families that had been occurring for several hundred years. Accordingly, that style was commonly regarded as the standard—the gauge against which all other forms of families were measured and found wanting.
>
> (p. 688)

There was a name that the sociologist Talcott Parsons (1965) gave to the nuclear family form: "the normal American family." Dorothy Smith (1993) used the term "Standard North American Family" (SNAF), but she saw the construct as ideological rather than descriptive. Here is her definition of SNAF:

> It is a conception of the family as a legally married couple sharing a household. The adult male is in paid employment; his earnings provide the economic basis of the family-household. The adult female may also earn an income, but her primary responsibility is to the care of husband, household, and children. Adult male and female may be parents (in whatever legal sense) of children also resident in the household.
>
> (p. 52)

The expectation that the husband will work and the wife will primarily take care of him, the kids, and the home has diminished over time. Still, other components of this conceptualization of family still dominate popular definitions. The U.S. Census Bureau, for example, defines family as "*a group of two people or more* (one of whom is the householder) *related by birth, marriage, or adoption and residing together*." (The householder is the person "in whose name the housing unit is owned or rented.")

The Census Bureau definition counts as family more than just the "married with children" groups. A group of just two people can be included—a married couple, for instance, or one parent and a child. Unmarried couples, though, would not count. If the Census Bureau had used the word "blood" instead of "birth," then two siblings living together would count as family, but since the key term is "birth," the sibs are excluded. There is no room in this definition of family for single adults with no children.

Twenty-first-century scholars are not so narrow in their views of who counts as family. An unmarried, cohabiting conjugal couple is sometimes regarded as family, even if the couple is comprised of two men or two women. Adding children strengthens their claim to family status but not having children does not disqualify them.

Even the criterion of sharing a household is not as defining as it once was. In divorced and single-parent families, one parent sometimes lives in a different household than a child, but the parent and the child still consider one another to be family. Growing numbers of couples have commuter marriages or "live apart together" (Levin, 2004), either because they want their separate household spaces, or because obstacles such as far-flung jobs keep them apart. Members of transnational immigrant families live not just in different households but in different countries. Still, they are family.

So far, here are the criteria for family that are unnecessary, at least according to some important formulations. First, a family does not need to include children. Second, a family does not need to include two adults (single-parent families count). Third, when there are two adults in a family, they do not need to be married (cohabiting couples count). Fourth, the two adults do not need to consist of a man and a woman (two women count, as do two men). Fifth, a family does not need to include two adults in a conjugal relationship. Finally, the family members do not need to live under the same roof.

"Doing" Family: What Do Families Do?

An entirely different approach to defining family sets aside structural considerations and instead asks what families do. Weeks, Heaphy, and Donovan (2001), for example, suggested that "it is less important whether we are *in* a family than whether we *do* family-type things ... We live family rather than dwell within it" (p. 38).

There is no one set of functions of family that scholars have agreed upon as definitive. The ones I will describe below have been culled from a variety of writings. The claim that families perform certain functions is sometimes more of an ideal or an aspiration than a reality. The functions may also be regarded as possibilities—people can tap into their families for these purposes when they need to, but they do not necessarily engage with their families in all of these ways in their everyday lives.

When families are defined by whether they do family-like things, then many people more commonly regarded as friends become redefined as family. In a later section, I will make the case that we should not completely merge our notions of friends and family, as the two contribute in distinct ways to our lives.

Care for Those Who Cannot Care for Themselves

A nationally representative sample of British adults answered the question, "Do you currently or have you ever regularly looked after someone, for at least three months, who is sick, disabled or elderly?" The author (Henz, 2006) reported results separately for marital status and parental status. Both single men and single women were more likely to have provided such care than were married men or women. Parental status did not matter for men unless they had a child younger than seven years old—those men were less likely to care for the sick, disabled, or elderly than were men who had no children. For women, those who had two or more children were less likely to provide care than women with no children or just one child.

Results from a nationally representative sample of Americans (Heymann, 2000) were reported only according to parental status. Participants kept a diary every day for a week of their experiences as workers and caregivers. On the key measures of cutting back on paid employment in order to care for others, Heymann found that adults with no children took cutbacks for children such as nieces and nephews. In fact, they were just as likely to take time off to care for those categories of children as were adults with their own children under the age of 18. Adults with no children were more than three times as likely to take time off from work to care for parents. Participants also reported cutting back on work hours to care for adults who were not their parents; 46 percent of adults without children did so, compared to just 13 percent of adults with minor children.

In short, single people and adults with no children are doing at least their fair share—and sometimes more—of caring for people who cannot care for themselves. Qualitative research supports that conclusion, too (e.g., Simpson, 2003). Of course, adults with no children take no time off to care for their own children since they do not have any, but they are just as likely as parents to cut back on work hours to care for other children such as nieces and nephews.

Socialize the Young

In his book on aunts and uncles as the forgotten kin, Milardo (2010) notes that singles with no children are among those most actively involved as aunts and uncles. Others, too, have observed that single adults are often closer to their nieces and nephews than are married adults (e.g., Connidis, 2001; Rubinstein, Alexander, Goodman, & Luborsky, 1991).

McAdams and de St. Aubin (1992) took a different approach to evaluating the roles of different categories of adults in socializing children. Drawing from Erik Erikson's notion of generativity, a concern with "establishing and guiding the next generation," the authors developed a scale to measure that concern. It included items such as, "I try to pass along the knowledge that I have gained through my experiences" and "I have a responsibility to improve the neighborhood in which I live."

Married people scored no higher on the generativity scale than single people did. Parental status made little difference for women. Only among men did parents score higher than adults with no children.

On this criterion of doing family-type things, as on the previous one, single people clearly qualify. They are often important figures in the lives of relatives such as nieces and nephews. In formal roles as teachers, counselors, and more, and in their informal interactions, single men and single women, including single women with no children, are just as concerned and involved with guiding the next generation as married people are.

Share Experiences and Create a Sense of Continuity and Identity

Single people with no children have shared experiences and a sense of continuity and identity with their families of origin, both nuclear and extended. Parents, siblings, grandparents, cousins, aunts and uncles, nieces and nephews all have the potential to contribute to the sense of rootedness that can be central to the experience of family.

A sense of an interpersonal history does not come from a natal family alone. Life-span scholars, such as Antonucci and her colleagues (Antonucci & Akiyama,1995; Kahn & Antonucci, 1980), have shown that people have "social convoys"—networks of people who provide continuity over the course of a lifetime. The convoys are not static; particular people, or categories of people such as friends and family members, can become more or less important over time, or even fall out of the inner circles of a person's life. Still, there is enough constancy amidst the change to provide an enduring sense of continuity and identity.

Exchange Emotional, Practical, and Material Support

"Doing" family is not just a matter of being there—or having someone there for you—in times of dependency or crisis. The family experience, at least in its ideal form, also includes routine exchanges of interest in one another's lives and help with even the small challenges of everyday life. In this section, I'll first review the place of siblings in the lives of singles with no children. Then I'll assess singles' exchanges with their parents. Finally, I'll evaluate the role in singles' lives of friends, neighbors, and community members.

Siblings. Some of the best data on American sibling relationships come from the National Survey of Families and Households (NSFH), a national sample of Americans 19 and older who were interviewed in 1987–88 and again in 1992–94. Participants were asked about their contacts with their siblings, including visits, phone calls, and written communications. (The surveys took place before the ubiquity of cell phones and email.) They answered questions about giving and receiving help with transportation, repairs, chores, advice, and child care. They also indicated how close they were with their siblings and how well they got along.

Data from the first wave of interviews (1987–88) were reported by Spitze and Trent (2006), who focused on adults from two-child families. They found that "siblings are central to the lives of adults; most sibling relationships involve frequent contact and positive feelings" (p. 977). On the average, siblings visited one another three times a month, and also phoned or wrote three times a month—except when the sibs were sisters, who averaged five calls or letters per month. More than 75 percent of the men said they got along with their sibling, and more than 80 percent of the women said that they did.

The siblings who were single (defined as having no spouse or partner) did more to maintain ties with their siblings than those who were married. (Singles are more likely to live with a sibling [Gerstel & Sarkisian, 2006; Wenger et al., 2007], but the authors excluded from their analyses those singles who were sharing a household.) The single participants visited their sibling more often, called more often, and wrote more often. They also tended to participate more frequently in helping exchanges, but only a few of those effects were significant. Whether or not a person had children made almost no difference in the extent to which the siblings gave or received help. What mattered more to those exchanges was living close to the sibling.

Gerstel and Sarkisian (2006) reported results from the 1992–94 wave of data. They looked more closely at marital status, adding the category of previously married to the analyses. Again, they found that the participants who had always been single were more likely than the currently married participants to visit their siblings and to call and write them. The previously married maintained levels of contact that were in between the single and the currently married. The adults who had always been single also provided more emotional support and practical assistance to their siblings than either the currently married or the previously married participants did.

The findings from each of the individual waves of data are suggestive, but fall short of answering the question of whether married people are less involved with their siblings *because* they are married, or whether the results can be explained in some other way. Short of randomly assigning people to stay single or get married or divorced, the best approach is to follow the same people over time to see whether they become more or less connected with their siblings as their marital status changes. That's what White (2001) did, in her analyses of the changes in contact between the first and second waves of the NSFH data collection. She found that people who got married had significantly less contact with their siblings than they had when they were single, and that people whose marriages dissolved had significantly more contact with their siblings than they did when they were married. Whether the participants had children did not seem to matter.

White (2001) also reported on the overall trajectory of sibling relationships in adulthood. During the early adult years, siblings become somewhat more geographically distant from one another, and their contacts decrease modestly as well. These measures of connection stabilize when adults reach their 30s and remain consistent throughout later life. Giving and receiving help from siblings generally decreases over the course of the adult years, but then increases after the age of 70 for people with siblings nearby. When marital status is considered, the involvement with siblings is greater for those who are single—especially those who have always been single.

Parents. Similar to the results for sibling ties, research on relationships with parents also shows that single people are at least as likely—and sometimes more likely—to invest time and effort in their intergenerational relationships. In a study of more than 1,900 young adults (ages 18 to 34) from the Netherlands, for instance (Bucx, van Wel, Knijn, & Hagendoorn, 2008), singles had more face-to-face contact with their parents than married or cohabiting people did. There were no differences by marital or relationship status in the frequency of telephone or email contacts.

Drawing from several national samples of Americans, Gerstel and Sarkisian (2007) also found greater intergenerational support and connection for singles than married people. In fact, single people exchanged more help with just their own parents than married people exchanged with their parents and parents-in-law combined.

Friends, neighbors, and community. Data from the NSFH are again relevant to the question of whether single adults maintain more active contacts and more mutually supportive relationships with friends and neighbors than married people do.

Gerstel and Sarkisian (2006) reported the results from that survey, along with another national sample from the 2004 wave of data of the General Social Survey. Consistent with the results for connections with siblings and parents, the findings from the two surveys showed that singles are more likely to socialize with friends and neighbors than are currently married people, with the previously married in between. Adults who had always been single were also more likely than the currently married or previously married to exchange emotional support and practical assistance with friends and neighbors.

The Wisconsin Longitudinal Study has followed thousands of students who graduated from Wisconsin high schools in 1957. As adults in their 50s and 60s, the participants were twice asked whether they had given each of various kinds of help to each of various categories of people over the past month (Kahn, McGill, & Bianchi, 2011). (Marital status categories were not analyzed separately by parental status.) Across all kinds of help to friends, neighbors, and coworkers, a greater percentage of the always-single men and women provided help than the previously married, the currently married in their first marriages, or the currently married in their second (or later) marriages. In fact, it was the currently married in their first marriage who always provided the lowest rates of helping to nonkin. The kinds of help that the always-single adults were more likely than adults of other marital statuses to provide to friends, neighbors, and coworkers included transportation, errands, and shopping; housework, yard work, repairs, or other work around the house; and advice, encouragement, or moral or emotional support.

There are other studies of the place of friends in the lives of singles, though these investigations did not specifically assess different kinds of exchanges. The importance of friends to women who have always been single was documented several decades ago in

Simon's (1987) study of 50 ever-single American women, ages 65 to 105, who were born near the turn of the 20th century. Simon found that only one of the 50 women was socially isolated. The other 49 had a total of 47 friends they were in touch with daily, and 98 more they connected with once or twice a week. A more recent study of a random sample of older American women (Carr, 2008) showed that those who had always been single and those who were previously married spent more time with friends than did the currently married women.

Friends are also important to single men and women younger than 65. Surveying a nationally representative sample of nearly 3,000 adults from the Netherlands, Kalmijn (2003) asked participants to name up to five of their best friends, not counting children or conjugal partners. The hypothesis was that across the life course, the number of friends would decrease. The study, though, was cross-sectional. Singles were compared with various groups such as people who were cohabiting or married without children, couples who did have children, and empty-nesters. The role of friends did in fact diminish across the various categories. Singles, for example, reported an average of four close friends, whereas empty-nesters reported about three. The number of monthly contacts decreased, too, from about 13 or 14 for the singles to about five or six for the empty-nesters.

In a study of more than 10,000 Australian women, ages 73–78 (Cwikel, Gramotnev, & Lee, 2006), the authors set out to learn whether the women who had always been single and had no children would be particularly disadvantaged in later life. For example, would they be socially isolated? Quite the contrary. Compared to married or previously married women, with or without children, the always-single women with no children were especially likely to provide volunteer services. They were also active participants in social groups.

Who Are the Important People in the Lives of Singles with No Children?

Another approach to the study of family in the lives of singles with no children is to set aside the use of "family" terminology and the quest for evidence of the kinds of functions that families are believed to serve and instead answer this question: "Who are the important people in the lives of singles with no children?" One methodology involves showing people a set of concentric circles, and asking them to locate the most important people in the innermost circle, and the next most important people in the other circles (e.g., Fiori, Antonucci, & Cortina, 2006; Spencer & Pahl, 2006; Wenger, Dykstra, Melkas, & Knipscheer, 2007). Another is to ask particular questions that seem especially significant—for instance, "Is there a person with whom you can really share your private feelings and concerns?" and "Looking back over the last six months, who are the people with whom you discussed matters that are important to you?" (Hampton, Sessions, & Ja Her, 2011; Marks, 1996). These are similar to some of the questions about the exchange of emotional support reviewed in the section on family functions (above), except that they focus specifically on particularly personal or consequential matters. Still other researchers (e.g., Roseneil, 2004) conduct in-depth interviews to learn about the people who matter most to their interviewees.

When they were 53 or 54 years old, more than 6,000 people from the Wisconsin Longitudinal Study were asked about their kin and nonkin confidants (Marks, 1996). The kin (nonkin) questions were: "Is there a person in your family (friend outside your family) with whom you can really share your private feelings and concerns?" Married

197

people—who could name their spouse in response to the question about family members—named more kin confidants than did the people who had always been single. However, the always-single men and women (taken together) named nonsignificantly more nonkin confidants than the currently married people did, and the always-single women named significantly more nonkin confidants than the currently married women did.

In 2008, a national sample of 2,512 American adults was asked, "Looking back over the last six months, who are the people with whom you discussed matters that are important to you?" (Hampton, Sessions, & Ja Her, 2011). The total number of confidants did not differ between those who were married or living with a partner and everyone else. However, the single participants were significantly more likely than the married or cohabiting people to name at least one nonkin confidant.

Results were not reported separately for singles with no children in either of the two studies of confidants (Hampton et al., 2011; Marks, 1996). However, parental status was considered, and in neither study did it predict the total number of confidants or the number of kin or nonkin confidants.

The most comprehensive study of the interpersonal ties of single people with no children was based on data from adults 65 and older from nine nations: Australia, Finland, Germany, Israel, Japan, the Netherlands, Spain, the U.K. and the U.S. (Wenger et al., 2007). For six of those countries (Australia, Finland, the Netherlands, Spain, the U.K. and the U.S.), the authors were able to map out the social networks of singles with no children, to see if they were the sorts of restricted networks that might leave them vulnerable in later life.

The two most limited network types they documented were the *local self-contained* and *private restricted* support networks. The local self-contained network describes a home-centered lifestyle, with the individual reaching out to neighbors when necessary. The private restricted network is typical of married couples who have little local support. Among those who do have kin nearby, some have *local family dependent* networks, in which they rely on those relatives for help when they need it. The last two types of support networks include friends as important sources of support. In the *locally integrated* networks, there are kin nearby, and the individual relies on them as well as friends and neighbors for support. People with locally integrated networks also tend to be involved in local community groups. Finally, in the *wider community focused* support networks, individuals do not have kin nearby, but they maintain contact with the kin they do have. Their friends and local voluntary groups are their key sources of everyday support.

With five kinds of support networks, six countries, and 12 marital/parental combinations to consider (men without children, women without children, mothers, and fathers, each subcategorized as always-single, previously married, or currently married), the results were complex. Still, certain patterns were discernible across the countries, except for Australia. Adults with no children tended to have the most restricted networks—either local self-contained or private restricted. Women who had always been single and had no children were a big exception. These women often had the kinds of support networks in which friends were important—either locally integrated networks (in which local kin and neighbors were also important) or wider community focused networks (in which women without any local kin maintained ties with friends and local voluntary groups). Australia is the exception in that both the men and the women who had always been single were likely to have local self-contained networks, and among the other marital/parental status groups, the wider community focused network was more commonplace than it was in other countries.

A more intensive qualitative approach to the study of the social embeddedness of people living outside of marriage and nuclear family was pursued by Roseneil and Budgeon (2004). Their focus was on people not living with a conjugal partner. They interviewed 53 people, ages 25 through 60, for as long as 2.5 hours each. The participants came from three different kinds of localities in the U.K.: a conventional small town, an unconventional small town, and a multi-ethnic inner city. Results showed that "far from being socially isolated, solitary individuals who flit from one unfulfilling relationship to another, most of the people we interviewed were enmeshed in complex networks of intimacy and care, and had strong commitments and connections to others ... very few showed any yearning to be part of a conventional couple or family. Of those with partners, almost all had chosen not to live together" (Roseneil, 2004, p. 413).

Getting to Choose: Is Family Whoever You Say It Is?

In the past several sections, I've taken indirect approaches to the question of who counts as family. I described some of the functions most often attributed to families, and asked whether they apply to the lives of singles with no children. I also reviewed studies in which participants were asked, in different ways, to name the people who are important to them.

But what about a more direct approach? Why not simply ask people, "Who is your family," and let them decide who qualifies?

In her influential book, *Families We Choose: Lesbians, Gays, Kinship*, Weston (1991) documented ways in which gays and lesbians created families of their own, sometimes in the context of being rejected by their families of origin after coming out as lesbian or gay. "Rather than being organized through marriage and child rearing," Weston noted, "most chosen families are characterized by fluid boundaries, eclectic composition, and relatively little symbolic differentiation between erotic and nonerotic ties" (p. 206).

A decade later, Weeks et al. (2001) continued the study of what they called "families of choice and other life experiments." They described those families as "flexible, informal and varied, but strong and supportive networks of friends and lovers, often including members of families of origin. They provide the framework for the development of mutual care, responsibility and commitment" (p. 4). Families of choice can include people of different ages, including children; biological kin as well as friends, lovers, and ex-lovers; and they can reach across several households. People who had romantic partners, as well as those who did not, described people they regarded as their families.

Families of choice, Weston (1991) notes, are not just "substitutes" for families of origin. Many lesbians and gays who experienced no ostracism from their families of origin still created families of choice. Not all of the people she interviewed, though, used the language of family to refer to the important people in their lives; some lesbians and gays used the word "family" only in the more conventional ways.

In the Eyes of Others: Who Counts as Family?

So far, I have asked who counts as family according to scholars and official organizations (such as the Census Bureau) and I have also reviewed individual people's responses to the question of who they count as family in their own lives. Still missing is the point of view that is often particularly significant in everyday life—what everyone else believes. What is the conventional wisdom of our time?

In 2010, the Pew Research Center released a report titled, "The decline of marriage and rise of new families" (Taylor, 2010). It begins with this overview:

> Over the past 50 years, a quiet revolution has taken place in this country. Decades of demographic, economic, and social change have transformed the structure and composition of the American family. The pre-eminent family of the mid 20th century—mom, dad, and the kids—no longer has the stage to itself. A variety of new arrangements have emerged, giving rise to a broader and evolving definition of what constitutes a family.
>
> *(p. 1)*

Among the many questions the Pew researchers asked the national sample of 2,691 American adults was, "What is a family?" Participants did not provide their own answers. Instead, they were read a list of possibilities, and were asked whether they considered each one a family. Every arrangement they asked about that included either a married couple or children was viewed as a family by more than half of the participants. Those arrangements were *married couple with children* (viewed as a family by 99 percent), *married couple without children* (90 percent), *single parent with children* (88 percent), *unmarried couple with children* (80 percent), and *same-sex couple with children* (63 percent). The two arrangements viewed as family by fewer than half of the participants were *same-sex couple without children* (45 percent) and *unmarried couple without children* (43 percent).

The fact that so many different arrangements counted as family to so many Americans was cited as evidence for the report's opening claim that the definition of family is evolving and becoming broader. That's an important point. But notice what is missing from the list of arrangements that participants were asked about. No one was asked whether a pair of siblings living together for decades, whose lives were as interdependent as a married couple's in every way except for the sex, counted as family. No one was asked whether a household of people who *chose* to live together, in an arrangement not considered as temporary, counted as family, regardless of the number of people, their ages, or their marital or parental statuses. No one was asked whether a single person living solo, when considered along with the convoy of people who have been part of that person's life for years or even decades, qualifies as family.

Participants in the Pew survey were also given an opportunity to be judgmental. For each of seven increasing trends, they were asked whether the trend was a bad thing for society, a good thing, or if it doesn't make much difference. Only 29 percent said that the *increasing number of women not ever having children* was a bad thing. The only trend that fewer people disparaged as a bad thing was the *increase in people of different races marrying each other* (14 percent). Just one of the seven trends was deemed bad for society by more than half of the participants: 69 percent described the *increase in the number of single women having children* that way. (The other trends and their "bad thing" percentages were *people living together without being married*, 43; *unmarried couples raising children*, 43; *gay/lesbian couples raising children*, 43, and *mothers of young children working outside the home*, 37.) Missing from the list of growing trends that participants were asked about were the increase in the number of single people and the increase in the number of people living solo.

The unmarried participants in the Pew survey were less likely than the married ones to say that the increases in the various family forms were bad for society. They were also more open-minded when asked which particular arrangements counted as family.

Perhaps even more indicative of future trends, the youngest participants were the least likely to believe that the growing variety of family types was bad for society.

Reconsidering: Should We Really Count Friends as Family?

The research I've reviewed affirms the importance of friendship in people's lives, perhaps particularly in the lives of singles with no children. When people claim friends as family, they may be doing something that Western societies too often fail to do—acknowledging the significance of friends. "Family" sometimes has such a sentimentalized, and even revered, status that including friends under that protective umbrella may seem like a gracious and honorable thing to do.

Yet friends are not the same as family, and they are not the same as a conjugal partner. Ideally, a friend does not presume to be "The One" or "the one and only" emotionally significant person in your life. Friends are not supposed to be greedy that way—they usually expect to be part of a network that will probably include other friends.

When we refer to our friends as family, we risk marginalizing friendship by making it less salient. That's just one of the unintended consequences. Trimberger (2005) described some of the others:

> Using family terms for nonkin relationships, however, reinforces the invisibility of care provided by friendship networks and contributes to the insecurity that those with weak family ties feel. We obscure the manner in which a network of friends can provide care without taxing individual friends or family members ... The strength of friendship networks—and their ability to promote community—rests on their separateness from family and cohabitation.
>
> *(p. 249)*

Hertz and Ferguson (1997) made similar points in their discussion on the strengths of the networks of single mothers:

> By parceling out these various aspects (the physical work, the caring work, the emotional work, etc.) across a wide network of people, these mothers spread the "risk" of losing a key player (like a husband) as well as safeguarding against anyone feeling overtaxed or burned out.
>
> *(p. 206)*

Often the power of friendship inheres in the fact that we are not limited to just one friend. Some potentially important contributions to the research literature are compromised by the failure to appreciate that. For example, Pahl and Pevalin (2005) wanted to know about the relative significance of friends compared to kin (not including a spouse) across the life course. But they asked participants to name only the one person "you can best share your private feelings and concerns with" (p. 440). They found that single people were more likely than married people to name a friend, and that the older participants were more inclined than the younger ones to name a relative. Those results are important, but cannot tell us what we need to know about the actual place of friendship in our lives. The kinds of studies in which people are invited to map out the relative closeness of all of the important people in their lives are better suited for showing where friends really do stand, compared to everyone else.

Another important way that friendship differs from family is in the sense of obligation linked with the two relationship types. Family members, by prevailing norms, more often feel obligated to help when help is needed. Of course, that doesn't mean that they will always provide such help. Friendship, in contrast, is not a relationship defined by feelings of obligation. Western friendships typically exist because two people like each other and enjoy each other's company. Rarely are people friends only grudgingly, because they think they "should" be. In his poem, "Death of the hired man," Robert Frost said, "Home is the place where, when you have to go there, They have to take you in." Perhaps friendship is the place where, when you want to go there, they *want* to take you in.

Research is likely to be misleading when it does not recognize the different roles of obligation and liking in our relationships with family and friends. In the Pew study of the rise of new families (Taylor, 2010), for instance, participants were asked, "Suppose someone you know had a serious problem and needed either financial help or caregiving. How obligated would you feel to provide assistance if that person were your –," with the blank filled in with nine different categories of people. The percent who said they would feel "very obligated" to help (rather than somewhat obligated, not too obligated, or not obligated) was lowest for the category of *best friend* (39 percent). (The other categories, and percentages who felt obligated, were: *parent*, 83; *grown child*, 77; *grandparent*, 67; *brother or sister*, 64; *spouse or partner's parent*, 62; *grown stepchild*, 60; *stepparent*, 55; and *step or half sibling*, 43.)

The Pew report claimed that the relative rankings of obligation were "evidence of the value that people place on relationships" (p. 45). But obligation is the wrong metric for assessing the value of friendships. It may not even be the best predictor of whether people really will provide help, though that remains to be determined.

A Look Toward the Future

For decades, Western societies have been changing in ways that are bringing single adults and adults with no children to the forefront. Yet there is little consideration of what family means to singles with no children (DePaulo, 2011a). When participants in national surveys (such as the Pew surveys) are asked whether various sets of people count as family, the kinds of living arrangements relevant to singles with no children are not even represented.

That is likely to change. Scholars such as Barry Wellman who have studied changes in social networks over time and around the globe argue that "in some societies, there may be a turn away from the household to the individual as the basic personal networking unit" (Wellman, 2007). The phenomenon is called "networked individualism." Although singles living solo are especially likely to fit that description, others qualify too. To quote Wellman (2007) again, "The emerging picture is of 'networked individuals' operating somewhat autonomously out of 'networked households' (Wellman, 2001; Kennedy and Wellman, 2007)." Even in contemporary nuclear families, experiences are not shared as much as they once were. Instead, individual family members sit in front of their own computers surfing their own favorite sites, watching their own preferred shows, and communicating with their own friends. There are individual cell phones rather than a family phone, and individual cars in families who can afford them. For married couples, the evidence is not just anecdotal. A study comparing couples in the year 2000 to those from 20 years previously showed that the couples from 2000 were less likely than the ones from 1980 to work on projects around the house together, go out together, visit friends together, or even to eat together (Amato, Booth, Johnson, & Rogers, 2007).

In the opening years of the 21st century, we are still accustomed to asking people about their families. Maybe in the decades to come, it will not be just the phone companies who instead ask, "Who's in your network?"

References

Amato, P. R., Booth, A., Johnson, D. R., & Rogers, S. J. (2007). *Alone together: How marriage in America is changing*. Cambridge, MA: Harvard University Press.

Antonucci, T. C., & Akiyama, H. (1995). Convoys of social relations: Family and friendships within a life span context. In R. Bliezner & V. H. Bedford (Eds.), *Handbook of aging and the family* (pp. 355–71). Westport, CT: Greenwood Press.

Bucx, F., van Wel, F., Knijn, T., & Hagendoorn, L. (2008). Intergenerational contact and the life course status of young adult children. *Journal of Marriage and Family*, 70, 144–56.

Carr, D. (2008). The desire to date and remarry among older widows and widowers. *Journal of Marriage and Family*, 66, 1051–68.

Collins, G. (2008). One singular sensation. *New York Times*, December 4.

Connidis, I. A. (2001). *Family ties and aging*. Thousand Oaks, CA: Sage.

Cwikel, J., Gramotnev, H., & Lee, C. (2006). Never-married childless women in Australia: Health and social circumstances in older age. *Social Science & Medicine*, 62, 1991–2001.

DePaulo, B. (2006). *Singled out: How singles are stereotyped, stigmatized, and ignored, and still live happily ever after*. New York: St. Martin's Press.

——(2011a). Living single: Lightening up those dark, dopey myths. In W. R. Cupach & B. H. Spitzberg (Eds.), *The dark side of close relationships II* (pp. 409–39). New York: Routledge.

——(2011b). *Singlism: What it is, why it matters, and how to stop it*. Charleston, SC: DoubleDoor Books.

Dykstra, P. A., & Hagestad, G. O. (2007). Roads less taken: Developing a nuanced view of older adults without children. *Journal of Family Issues*, 28, 1275–310.

Fiori, K. L., Antonucci, T. C., & Cortina, K. S. (2006). Social network typologies and mental health among older adults. *Journal of Gerontology: Series B*, 61, P25–P32.

Gerstel, N., & Sarkisian, N. (2006). Marriage: The good, the bad, and the greedy. *Contexts*, 5, 16–21.

——(2007). Intergenerational care and the greediness of adult children's marriages. In T. J. Owens & J. J. Suitor (Eds.), *Intergenerational relations across the life course: Advances in life course research* (Vol. XII, pp. 153–88). San Diego, CA: JAI Press.

Hampton, K. N., Sessions, L. F., & Ja Her, E. (2011). Core networks, social isolation, and new media: Internet and mobile phone use, network size, and diversity. *Information, Communication, & Society*, 14, 130–55.

Henz, U. (2006). Informal caregiving at working age: Effects of job characteristics and family configuration. *Journal of Marriage and Family*, 68, 411–29.

Hertz, R., & Ferguson, F. I. T. (1997). Kinship strategies and self-sufficiency among single mothers by choice: Postmodern family ties. *Qualitative Sociology*, 20, 187–209.

Heymann, J. (2000). *The widening gap: Why America's working families are in jeopardy—and what can be done about it*. New York: Basic Books.

Kahn, J. R., McGill, B. S., & Bianchi, S. M. (2011). Help to family and friends: Are there gender differences at older ages? *Journal of Marriage and Family*, 73, 77–92.

Kahn, R. L., & Antonucci, T. C. (1980). Convoys across the life course: Attachment, roles, and social support. In P. B. Baltes & O. C. Brim (Eds.), *Life-span, development, and behavior* (pp. 254–83). New York: Academic Press.

Kalmijn, M. (2003). Friendship networks over the life course: A test of the dyadic withdrawal hypothesis using survey data. *Social Networks*, 25, 231–49.

Kennedy, T. L. M., & Wellman, B. (2007). The networked household. *Information, Communication, & Society*, 10, 645–70.

Klinenberg, E. (2012). *Going solo: The extraordinary rise and surprising appeal of living alone*. New York: Penguin Press.

Kornblut, A. E. (2010). DHS Secretary Janet Napolitano winning over heavyweights with her persona. *Washington Post*, April 22.

Levin, I. (2004). Living apart together: A new family form. *Current Sociology, 52*, 223–40.

Livingston, G., & Cohn, D. (2010, June). Childlessness up among all women; down among women with advanced degrees. Pew Research Center, Social and Demographic Trends Report.

Marks, N. F. (1996). Flying solo at midlife: Gender, marital status, and psychological well-being. *Journal of Marriage and the Family, 58*, 917–32.

McAdams, D. P., & de St. Aubin, E. (1992). A theory of generativity and its assessment through self-report, behavioral acts, and narrative themes in autobiography. *Journal of Personality and Social Psychology, 62*, 1003–15.

Milardo, R. M. (2010). *The forgotten kin: Aunts and uncles.* Cambridge: Cambridge University Press.

Pahl, R., & Pevalin, D. J. (2005). Between family and friends: a longitudinal study of friendship choice. *British Journal of Sociology, 56*, 433–50.

Parsons, T. (1965). The normal American family. In S. M. Farber, P. Mustacchi, & R. H. L. Wilson (Eds.), *Man and civilization: The family's search for survival* (pp. 31–50). New York: McGraw-Hill.

Roseneil, S. (2004). Why we should care about friends: An argument for queering the care imaginary in social policy. *Social Policy & Society, 3*, 409–19.

Roseneil, S., & Budgeon, S. (2004). Cultures of intimacy and care beyond "the family": Personal life and social change in the early 21st century. *Current Sociology, 52*, 135–59.

Rubinstein, R. L., Alexander, B. B., Goodman, M., & Luborsky, M. (1991). Key relationships of never married, childless older women: A cultural analysis. *Journal of Gerontology: Social Sciences, 45*, S270–S277.

Saluter, A. F., & Lugaila, T. A. (1998). Marital status and living arrangements: March 1996. Census Bureau Current Population Reports, Document P20–496.

Scanzoni, J. (2001). From the normal family to alternate families to the quest for diversity with interdependence. *Journal of Family Issues, 22*, 688–710.

Simon, B. L. (1987). *Never married women.* Philadelphia, PA: Temple University Press.

Simpson, R. (2003). Contemporary spinsters in the new millennium: Changing notions of family and kinship. London School of Economics, Gender Institute. New Working Papers Series.

Smith, D. E. (1993). The Standard North American Family: SNAF as an ideological code. *Journal of Family Issues, 14*, 50–65.

Spencer, L., & Pahl, R. (2006). *Rethinking friendship: Hidden solidarities today.* Princeton, NJ: Princeton University Press.

Spitze, G., & Trent, K. (2006). Gender differences in adult sibling relations in two-child families. *Journal of Marriage and Family, 69*, 977–92.

Taylor, P. (2010). The decline of marriage and rise of new families. Pew Research Center, Social and Demographic Trends Report, November.

Trimberger, E. K. (2005). *The new single woman.* Boston, MA: Beacon Press.

United Nations (2009). *Demographic yearbook 2006.* New York: United Nations.

U.S. Census Bureau (2009). 2009 American Community Survey 1-Year Estimates. Table B12002: Sex by Marital Status by Age for the Population 15 Years and Over. Retrieved from http://www.census.gov/acs/www.

Weeks, J., Heaphy, B. & Donovan, C. (2001), *Same sex intimacies: Families of choice and other life experiments.* London: Routledge.

Wellman, B. (2001). Physical space and cyberspace: the rise of personalized networks. *International Urban and Regional Research, 25*, 227–52.

——(2007). The network is personal: Introduction to a special issue of *Social Networks. Social Networks, 29*, 349–56.

Wenger, G. C., Dykstra, P. A., Melkas, T., & Knipscheer, K. C. P. M. (2007). Social embeddedness and late-life parenthood: Community activity, close ties, and support networks. *Journal of Family Issues, 28*, 1419–56.

Weston, K. (1991). *Families we choose: Lesbians, gays, kinship.* New York: Columbia University Press.

White, L. (2001). Sibling relationships over the life course: A panel analysis. *Journal of Marriage and Family, 63*, 555–68.

13

Support Communication in Culturally Diverse Families

The Role of Stigma

Stanley O. Gaines, Jr., Stacey L. Williams,
and Kristin D. Mickelson

To mark a person implies that [a] deviant condition has been noticed and recognized as a problem in [an] interaction or [in a social or personal] relationship. To stigmatize a person generally carries a further implication that the mark has been linked by an attributional process to dispositions that discredit the bearer, i.e., that "spoil" [the bearer's] identity.

Edward Jones, Amerigo Farina, Albert Hastorf, Hazel Markus, Dale Miller,
and Robert Scott, *Social Stigma: The Psychology of Marked Relationships* (1984, p. 8)

Support Communication in Culturally Diverse Families: The Role of Stigma

Ethnic minority groups are societally defined groups that exist as psychological and/or numerical minorities, and whose members presumably share biological and/or cultural heritage (Markus, 2008). Although religious and national minority groups clearly are defined by culture, racial minority groups (which psychologists have tended to regard as defined by biology; Fairchild, Yee, Wyatt, & Weizmann, 1995; Yee, Fairchild, Weizmann, & Wyatt, 1993) similarly are defined by culture (Jones, 1997). In turn, culturally diverse families are defined by the presence of one or more family members who are members of racial, religious, or national minority groups within a given society (Gaines, 1997).

According to Erving Goffman (1963), stigmatization toward members of ethnic minority groups not only can affect those individuals but also can affect the individuals' families. Within the U.S.A. and other Western nations, majority group members as well as minority group members in interracial marriages often are acutely aware of the transmission of stigmatization throughout entire families (Gaines & Ickes, 2000). However, the transmission of stigmatization can occur in all families in which one or more members belong to racial, religious, or national minority groups (Gaines, 2001).

In the present chapter, we draw upon Goffman's (1959, 1963) symbolic interactionist theory in examining support communication within culturally diverse families. We pay particular attention to Goffman's (1963) concept of stigma as applied to members of ethnic minority groups and as applied to their families. Moreover, we focus on specific forms of support communication (following Mickelson & Williams, 2008; Williams & Mickelson, 2008) that members of ethnic minority groups may use to obtain social support from family members and, thus, counteract the potentially negative effects of stigmatization. In addition, we consider the utility of Claude Steele's (1997) concept of stereotype threat in explaining the potential lack of generalizability of support communication processes across ethnic (and especially racial) groups.

Goffman's Symbolic Interactionist Theory: A Theoretical Point of Departure for Understanding Stigma and Support Communication within Culturally Diverse Families

Symbolic interactionist theories generally are based on the premise that individuals in social contexts are like actors on stages, striving to convince audience members to accept individuals' performances as authentic (Stryker & Statham, 1985). In *The Presentation of Self in Everyday Life*, Erving Goffman (1959) not only embraced this general premise but also argued that individuals often possess considerable flexibility in the manner in which they engage in impression management. However, in *Stigma: Notes on the Management of Spoiled Identity*, Goffman (1963) contended that when individuals in social contexts are stigmatized, those individuals are likely to find it difficult (if not impossible) to persuade audience members to perceive them as they would like to be perceived. Taken as a whole, Goffman's (1959, 1963) version of symbolic interactionist theory—which is as relevant to modern-day mediated communication as it is to traditional interpersonal communication (Smith, 2007)—presents a stark contrast between (a) idealized social interaction involving nonstigmatized individuals as actors, and (b) actual social interaction involving stigmatized individuals as actors.

Especially relevant to the present chapter is Goffman's (1963) conclusion that when families consist of one or more members of ethnic minority groups, *all* family members are stigmatized. At first glance, such a conclusion offers little hope for the long-term survival of culturally diverse families. Regarding families with one or more members from religious and/or national minority groups, individual members might experience pressure from several sources (e.g., strangers, acquaintances, friends, other family members) to convert and/or to become naturalized citizens. Regarding families with one or more members from racial minority groups, individual members (who generally lack the option of changing their racial group memberships) might experience pressure to exit the families via separation or divorce; such an option typically would be available only to spouses or to unmarried, cohabiting romantic partners (see also Meisenbach, 2010, for a contemporary critique of Goffman's emphasis on individuals' defensive responses to stigmatization).

Identity as a Property of Interaction in Goffman's Symbolic Interactionist Theory

One of the great ironies of Goffman's *Stigma: Notes on the Management of Spoiled Identity* (1963) is that Goffman did not offer a specific definition of identity. For our purposes, *identity* can be understood as "the definitions that are created for and superimposed on the self" (Baumeister, 1997, p. 682). In turn, *self* can be understood as "the direct feeling [that] each person has of privileged access to his or her own thoughts and feelings and sensations" (Baumeister, 1997, p. 681).

In many psychological theories of identity—most notably Erik Erikson's (1950, 1968) ego psychology—identity is conceived as a property of the individual. However, in many sociological theories of identity—most notably Erving Goffman's (1959, 1963) symbolic interactionist theory—identity is conceived as a property of interaction (Cote, 2006). Unlike Erikson, Goffman emphasized society (via social roles) and social and personal relationships (via face-to-face interaction) as the primary shapers of individuals' identity.

How do society, social relationships, and personal relationships combine to shape individuals' identity? As Goffman (1963) observed, society is especially adept at informing individuals as to the social groups (e.g., racial, religious, and national groups) to which they do or do not belong; social relationships (which typically involve little or no emotional intimacy) are especially adept at informing individuals as to who they are in the eyes of members of outgroups; and personal relationships (which typically involve considerable emotional intimacy; Duck, 1999) are especially adept at informing individuals as to who they are in the eyes of members of individuals' ingroups. Through years-long processes of immersion in social roles and in social interaction with ingroup and outgroup members, individuals acquire a sense of who they are, and in relation to whom (Cote, 2006).

Implications of Goffman's Symbolic Interactionist Theory for Ethnic Minority Group Members' Receipt of Social Support

Goffman's (1963) symbolic interactionist theory suggests that members of ethnic minority groups are most likely to receive social support from ingroup members (most likely family and friends who tend to view the individual favorably), less likely to receive social support from outgroup members (most likely strangers and acquaintances who tend to view the individual unfavorably), and still less likely to receive social support from societal institutions (faceless in themselves but controlled primarily by members of ethnic majority groups, most likely strangers and acquaintances who tend to view the individual unfavorably), unless those institutions are required by law to provide social support (Jones, 1997). One mechanism by which members of ethnic minority groups provide social support to each other appears to be ingroup members' overt and/or covert communication to each other as follows: "You are who you say you are, and I accept who you are." This tendency on the part of racial minority ingroup members to minimize or eliminate the discrepancy between social actors' *virtual social identity* (i.e., the identity that perceivers believe to be true of actors) and social actors' *actual social identity* (i.e., the identity that actors believe to be true of themselves; Goffman, 1963) has been documented in experimental research by Garcia, Hallahan, and Rosenthal (2007) regarding initial meetings between strangers of the same race; African American and Latino pairs displayed greater actor-perceiver agreement than did European American pairs.

This is not to say that all ingroup members will automatically provide social support toward members of ethnic minority groups, or that all outgroup members will automatically withhold social support from members of ethnic minority groups. For example, some European American wives in interracial marriages report that their own parents have rejected them (especially if those wives have borne children in those marriages); whereas the most reliable sources of social support come from African Americans, not only within spouses' families, but also within the wider African American community (Porterfield, 1978; Rosenblatt, Karis, & Powell, 1995). Nevertheless, interracial marriages and families remain the exception for European Americans, African Americans, and Latinas/os (though not necessarily for Asian Americans or Native Americans; Gaines & Ickes, 2000).

A Case in Point: Stigma and Support Communication among Asian-Descent Immigrants in the U.S.A.

A review of the literature on stigma and support communication within culturally diverse families reveals that this area has not received much attention from researchers, especially with regard to large-scale, quantitative studies. Much of the relevant literature focuses on social support and social networks among Asian-descent immigrants in the U.S.A. (e.g., Thomas & Choi, 2006; Xu & Burleson, 2001; Yeh, Okubo, Ma, Shea, Ou, & Pitue, 2008). A consistent theme emerging from these studies is the role that social network members can (but do not always) play in mitigating the stigmatization that many Asian-descent immigrants experience upon arrival in the U.S.A. Not only are Asian-descent immigrants members of a racial minority group (thus possessing a *discredited* stigma that outsiders can detect without talking to stigmatized persons); but they also are members of a national minority group (thus possessing a *discreditable* stigma that is not immediately visible but that outsiders can detect once they talk to stigmatized persons; Goffman, 1963).

Yeh et al. (2008) examined links among cultural interactions, acculturation, family obligations, language use, and social support among adolescent Chinese immigrants in the U.S.A. These researchers assessed sources of social support (i.e., significant others, family members, and friends), rather than content areas of social support. Thus, it is not clear how the immigrants sought or received social support, let alone what social network members actually said or did to provide support. Nevertheless, Yeh et al. found that Chinese immigrants' level of social support received from friends in particular (and not level of social support received from significant others or from family members) was significantly and negatively related to the immigrants' concerned about intercultural competence.

Thomas and Choi (2006) examined links between acculturative stress and social support among 10- to 20-year-old Korean and Indian immigrants in the U.S.A. Like Yeh et al. (2008), Thomas and Choi (2006) distinguished among sources of social support (i.e., friends, parents, religious organizations, social organizations, and cultural associations), rather than content areas of social support. As was the case with Yeh et al.'s study, it is not clear from Thomas and Choi's study how social network members communicated support to the immigrants. Nonetheless, Thomas and Choi found that social support from parents in particular was a significant negative predictor of the immigrants' acculturative stress.

Finally, Xu and Burleson (2001) examined gender, culture, and support type on perceptions of spousal social support among native-born American university students and native-born Chinese university students; all students were married and were living in the U.S.A., though (unlike the native-born American students) none of the native-born Chinese students had lived in the U.S.A. longer than five years. Unlike Yeh et al. (2008) or Thomas and Choi (2006), Xu and Burleson (2001) distinguished among content areas of social support (i.e., emotional, esteem, network, tangible, and informational). As was the case with the Yeh et al. and Thomas and Choi studies, Xu and Burleson's study did not specify what spouses did or said to convey support. Nevertheless, Xu and Burleson detected a "support gap" such that American as well as Chinese wives obtained significantly lower emotional support and esteem support from their spouses than did husbands; in addition, Chinese wives (but not American wives) obtained significantly less network support from their spouses than did husbands.

Stigma Versus Perceived Stigma Among Members of Ethnic Minority Groups and Culturally Diverse Families

Perhaps relevant here is a distinction in the stigma literature on stigma versus perceived stigma. The former refers to the stigmatized mark itself or the unfair treatment one might receive for having the stigmatized mark. By contrast, perceived stigma is a stigmatized individual's perception of holding the stigmatized mark. This self-perception or self-stigma has been discussed in relation to individuals with mental illness and other stigmatizing conditions (Corrigan, Watson, & Barr, 2006).

In the case of ethnic minority status or being a member of a culturally diverse family, one could report stigma as well perceived stigma—that is, the unfair treatment by others, the anticipated unfair treatment by others and the resultant self-beliefs. Perceived stigma has been discussed previously as the internalization of negative stereotyping or treatment by the public (presumably nonstigmatized) of those holding a stigmatizing mark. Internalization of stigma or perceived stigma has been the focus of prior literature in a variety of contexts (e.g., homosexuality, Herek, Gillis, & Cogan, 2009; sexual assault, Rife & Williams, under review), and has shown associations with negative psychosocial correlates, including relational ones (e.g., social constraints, Lewis, Derlega, Clarke & Kuang, 2006; lower support availability, Mickelson, 2001; Mickelson & Williams, 2008).

Despite the apparent hopelessness that pervades much of Goffman's (1963) symbolic interactionst theory with regard to stigmatization of members of ethnic minority groups within culturally diverse families, Goffman did observe that individuals and families need not passively accept society's verdict regarding devaluation of ethnic minority group members (Gaines, 2001). For example, individuals from ethnic minority groups often seek and receive social support from social network members who can empathize with the plight of those individuals (i.e., "the own") or from social network members who can sympathize with the plight of those individuals (i.e., "the wise"; Goffman, 1963, p. 31). The skill with which many members of ethnic minority groups obtain social support from social network members might explain why members of ethnic minority groups generally score far higher on self-esteem scales and on other measures of psychological well-being than their objective circumstances would lead one to predict (see Crocker, Major, & Steele, 1998). Indeed, research has shown that identifying with the stigmatized group—that is, having a positive group identity is related to better outcomes (Sellers, Caldwell, Schmeelk-Cone, & Zimmerman, 2003). This resilience may be due to the supportive context that similar others provide to a stigmatized individual faced with unfair treatment or the threat of it.

How do we make sense of the seemingly opposing outcomes among stigmatized groups and enhance the positive outcomes of stigmatized relationships? In the following section we consider literature on social support dynamics, perceived stigma and identity to explain possible support and communication processes in culturally diverse individuals and families.

Reconciling the Opposing Outcomes: Considering Perceived Stigma and Support Dynamics

Barbee and Cunningham (1995) in their sensitive interaction system theory (SIST) state that support encounters reflect a dynamic between the individuals involved in the exchange. That is, the social support outcome—or level or quality of social support—is not dependent solely on the actions of the support provider, but rather also depends upon the method of support seeking employed by the support recipient (or seeker). The specific strategies or activation used by support seekers can, in part, determine the responsiveness of the support network. Specifically, direct (e.g., asking for support, disclosure of problem) versus indirect (e.g., nondisclosure, seeking the network to be close but not stating there is a specific problem, appearing sad or distressed but not stating why) support seeking strategies can lead to supportive (solace, solve) or unsupportive (escape, dismiss) network responses, respectively (Barbee & Cunningham, 1995).

In recent research, this theory has been applied to stigmatized individuals as support seekers. Derlega, Winstead, Oldfield, and Barbee (2003), for example, examined the SIST in a sample of individuals with HIV—a group that holds a concealable stigma, and one that might even reflect multiple stigma due to the association of HIV with deviant sexual behavior. This work has shown evidence that direct forms of support seeking are linked with more positive or supportive responses from the support network.

Subsequent research has examined these patterns in relation to explicit reports of perceived stigma and fear of social rejection. In trying to manage others' perceptions of the self, individuals who perceive stigma might approach their network members for support in ways that would presumably minimize social rejection or negative support responses. The extent to which individuals perceive stigma may be connected to their expectations and subsequently their behaviors within social exchanges. Stigmatized individuals may fear rejection and uncertainty about how others view them (Goffman, 1963).

Negative Support Exchanges Involving Members of Ethnic Minority Groups and Culturally Diverse Families

Of course, receipt of rejecting behaviors from others is a reality in the lives of the stigmatized in general (Dovidio, Major, & Crocker, 2000), as illustrated by work on discrimination and unfair treatment (Kessler, Mickelson, & Williams, 1999). Among members of ethnic minority groups and culturally diverse families in particular, strategies for approaching the network in ways to avoid social rejection might include less direct and more indirect methods to get comfort. In turn, indirect support seeking behaviors might inadvertently evoke an undesired, unsupporting network response; whereas direct support seeking behaviors might evoke a desired, supportive network response (and, perhaps, inhibition of unsupportive network response).

Indeed, work involving both women in poverty (Mickelson & Williams, 2008) and women experiencing abuse (Williams & Mickelson, 2008), has shown that increased levels of perceived stigma (i.e., shame, embarrassment, or unfair treatment from others) are linked with greater fears of anticipated social support rejection. In turn, individuals perceiving stigma use more indirect strategies to gain support from friends and family (see Figure 13.1), and consequently, reported more negative support responses from the support network (see Figure 13.2). By contrast, use of direct seeking strategies was related to reports of more positive responses from the network (Williams & Mickelson, 2008).

Thus, individuals who perceive stigma appear to report some difficulties in their support network exchanges including fear or social support rejection and unsupportive network responses to their attempts to seek support. But does this work apply to racial minorities and those in culturally diverse families? That is, do they perceive stigma and encounter negative support exchanges?

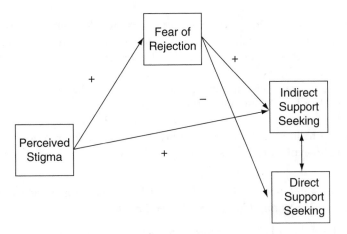

Figure 13.1 Hypothesized Links among Perceived Stigma, Fear of Support Rejection, and Indirect and Direct Support Seeking for Stigmatized Persons
Source: Adapted from S. Williams & Mickelson, 2008, p. 500.

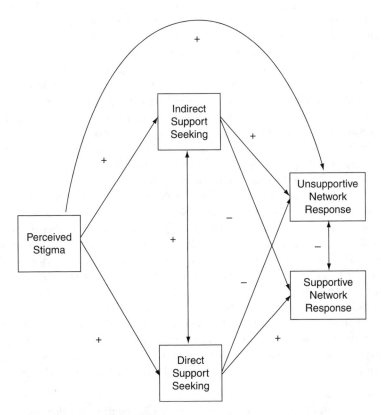

Figure 13.2 Hypothesized Links among Perceived Stigma, Indirect Support Seeking, Direct Support Seeking, Unsupportive Network Response, and Supportive Network Response for Stigmatized Persons
Source: Adapted from S. Williams & Mickelson, 2008, p. 504.

The idea that racial minorities might perceive stigma including self-stigma is supported by the work of some on the internalization of racial stereotypes, or internalized racism (Taylor, 1990; D. Williams & Williams-Morris, 2000). Taylor (1990) has argued that Blacks may internalize the racism that is rampant in U.S. culture and endorse the stereotypes of Blacks. Taylor and his colleagues have found this internalization to be linked with negative psychosocial as well as health outcomes (Butler, Tull, Chambers, & Taylor, 2002; Taylor, 1990). As well, Williams and his colleagues have argued that one mechanism by which racism can come to impact Blacks' mental health is via this internalized racism process, perhaps helping to explain racial disparities (e.g., D. Williams & Williams-Morris, 2000).

The Role of Concealability of Stigma in Support Exchanges Among Members of Ethnic Minority Groups and Culturally Diverse Families

Given the findings that Blacks can internalize racism or stigma, we might extrapolate to indicate they can also encounter fears of social rejection as well as a tendency toward indirect support seeking strategies, followed by unsupportive responses from their network. Yet, one might argue the generalizability of the work on perceived stigma and support exchanges to racial minorities and culturally diverse families due to the concealable nature of the stigmas that were investigated in the prior examples. As Goffman (1963) pointed out, those with concealable stigmas are managing information and not impressions of others. Concealable stigmas (or discreditable stigma, as outlined by Goffman) have their own unique set of psychosocial processes due to the vigilance and cognitive salience that can pervade daily life (Quinn & Chaudoir, 2009).

Importantly, similar findings of negative support related exchanges have been shown with more visible stigmas, such as the perceived stigma reported by parents of children with special needs. Stigma related to special needs children not only is a more visible stigma, but also is associative in nature. Research on this population has revealed parents' perceived stigma linked to increased negative interactions with the support network and decreased support availability from them (Mickelson, 2001).

Yet, equally possible to the idea that culturally diverse families encounter negative social exchanges like the ones we describe, is that the visibility of the stigmatized characteristic (i.e., race) creates a situation divergent from the one elaborated. Racial minorities perhaps more often encounter direct experiences with stigma or anticipated stigma and less often with internalized or self-stigma. Indeed, although some work has shown that racial minorities can internalize stereotypes (as illustrated by the work of Taylor, 1990), a large literature supports the resilience of racial minorities to the negative stereotypes. By having a strong sense of group identity (Sellers, Caldwell, Schmeelk-Cone, & Zimmerman, 2003), minorities and culturally diverse families may overcome the potential harmful effects—bypassing self-stigma. Indeed, other theoretical work on stigma argues that seeing the membership in the stigmatized group as central to one's identity can be protective, contributing to positive outcomes such as self-esteem (Crocker & Major, 1989). For example, unfair treatment can be attributed to the stigmatized group rather than to the self.

The Role of Strength of Group Identity in Support Communication Processes Among Members of Ethnic Minority Groups and Culturally Diverse Families

If low self-stigma and strong group identity are related to better self-related outcomes, might they also be linked to reduced likelihood of negative support dynamics? It could be that those holding a stigma but who have low levels of self-stigma and strong group identity use fewer indirect strategies for seeking social support. As a result, support exchanges might be protected because it is the indirect seeking that has been linked with negative support outcomes. Indeed, perceived stigma is not a monolithic construct. Different psychosocial processes are associated with subtypes of perceived stigma. For example, Mickelson and Williams (2008) in their sample of women in poverty showed that there are separate mechanisms linked to self-stigma and to experienced stigma.

This distinction between self-stigma and experienced stigma has been made by others (Corrigan, Watson, & Barr, 2006; Watson, Corrigan, Larson, & Sells, 2007) from whom we draw important theory on stigma. In a sample of women in poverty, results showed that self-stigma, or the internalization of negative stereotypes and unfair treatment resulting in a negative self-image (shame, embarrassment, thinking the self is inferior to others), is linked with impaired self-esteem and fear of support rejection, whereas experienced stigma, or the actual reports of unfair treatment or social exclusion, is linked with not only fear of support rejection, but also lower perceived support availability (Mickelson & Williams 2008). This study did not examine the support seeking dynamics of the SIST. However, one might imagine differences in interpersonal exchange based on type of perceived stigma and type of stigma that elicits the perception of stigma. The resulting model is shown in Figure 13.3.

How might the support communication dynamic look for racial minorities and culturally diverse families, whose stigmas are not only visible but can be associative and moderated by a strong and protective group identity? Current understanding based on the above reviewed literature highlights that support and communication exchanges for

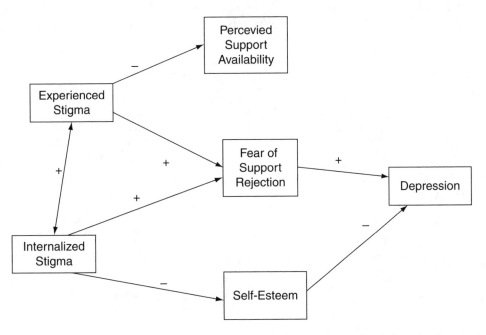

Figure 13.3 Hypothesized Links among Experienced Stigma, Internalized Stigma, Perceived Support Availability, Fear of Support Rejection, Self-Esteem, and Depression among Stigmatized Persons
Source: Adapted from Mickelson & S. Williams, 2008, p. 910.

racial minorities and culturally diverse families might depend on the level that they perceive stigma, report self/internalized stigma, report strong group identity (or that the group membership is central to their identity), interact with similarly stigmatized or nonstigmatized others, and use direct or indirect support strategies in their communications.

A model showing these general factors that contribute to support communication dynamics is shown in Figure 13.4. As depicted, individuals and families who identify strongly with their ethnic group would be buffered by the potentially negative experiences of experienced stigma (discrimination, anticipated unfair treatment) and thus report more support availability, more direct support seeking and more positive support outcomes given that they fear less support rejection. In addition, those with strong identification would report less internalized stigma thereby reducing the likelihood of using indirect support seeking strategies which are linked with unsupportive outcomes from support network members, again given that they fear less support rejection. Psychosocial outcomes of self-esteem and depression would be protected as a parallel process. This figure presents a cohesive model representing support communications in culturally diverse families, while previous literature has supported the hypothesized relationships individually or in parts. Further, this combined model has yet to be tested empirically. Thus, this model is intended to provide impetus for future collaborative work between researchers studying stigma and personal relationship and communication processes.

The Role of Stereotype Threat in Support Communication Processes Among Members of Ethnic Minority Groups and Culturally Diverse Families

So far, we have focused on stigma as the primary construct that was derived from Erving Goffman's (1959, 1963) symbolic interactionism theory. In turn, Claude Steele's (1997)

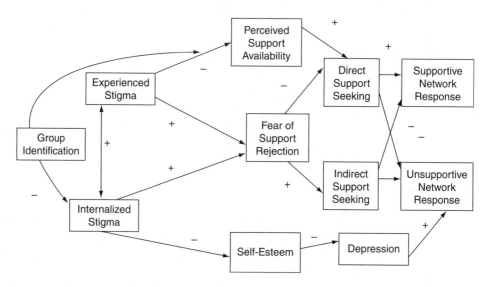

Figure 13.4 Hypothesized Links among Ethnic Group Identification, Perceived Stigma, Fear of Support Rejection, Perceived Support Availability, Indirect and Direct Support Seeking, Psychosocial Variables, and Network Response to Understand Support Communication in Culturally Diverse Families

construct of *stereotype threat* (i.e., the anxiety and, potentially, impaired performance that result from stigmatized individuals' belief that they will be evaluated in a domain where members of their group historically have been expected to perform poorly) was derived from Goffman's construct of stigma. Stereotype threat has been invoked as a reason for women's poorer performance on mathematics tests, relative to the performance of men (Carr & Steele, 2009; Pronin, Steele, & Ross, 2004; Spencer, Steele, & Quinn, 1999), and as a reason for African-descent Americans' poorer performance on academic tests in general, relative to the performance of European-descent Americans (Blascovich, Spencer, Quinn, & Steele, 2001; Deaux, Bikmen, Gilkes, Ventuneac, Joseph, Payne, & Steele, 2007; Steele & Aronson, 1995). In addition, stereotype threat might help explain why African-descent Americans rely on their kin networks and are less likely to seek professional help (or to continue seeking such help over time) for mental health difficulties than are European-descent Americans (Brown et al., 2010)—decisions that could place even greater demands on African-descent Americans' families as social support networks over the long term.

As the literature on stereotype threat indicates, African-descent Americans are keenly aware of the negative societal stereotypes that depict them as intellectually deficient (Crocker, Major, & Steele, 1998). Moreover, negative societal stereotypes characterize African-descent Americans as *personally* deficient, not just intellectually deficient (White & Parham, 1990). Among those African-descent Americans who are contemplating whether to seek psychological help, the stigma that accompanies their status as members of one devalued group (i.e., African-descent Americans) may be complemented by a stigma that accompanies their potential status as members of another devalued group (i.e., clients in therapy; Brown, et al., 2010). Just as individual African-descent Americans may be wary of entering academic settings in which their intellectual performance can be interpreted as reflecting negatively upon African-descent Americans as a group, so too may individual African-descent Americans be wary of entering clinical or counseling settings in which their social performance can be interpreted as reflecting negatively upon African-descent Americans as a group. It should not be surprising, therefore, that individual African-descent Americans tend to seek family members, rather than mental health professionals, for psychological assistance.

Stacey Williams and Kristin Mickelson (2008) suggested that the negative impact of stereotype threat on stigmatized persons' behavior in academic settings parallels the negative impact of anticipated social rejection on stigmatized persons' tendency to engage in behaviors that are likely to bring about actual social rejection. We are not aware of any published empirical studies examining the links between these two processes. Nevertheless, even if the two processes operate independently, knowledge of social-psychological processes that involve stereotype threat may help social scientists understand communication processes that involve other aspects of stigmatization among African-descent Americans.

Generalizability of Stereotype Threat and Support Communication Processes Across Members of Various Racial Minority Groups

The literature on stereotype threat implies that the same social-psychological processes that characterize the stigmatization of African-descent Americans (constituting 13 percent of the U.S. population; Humes et al., 2011) also characterize members of other so-called racial minority groups (Crocker, Major, & Steele, 1998). However, such a conclusion may be premature. The stigmatization of African-descent Americans is unique and includes such historical events as enslavement, segregation, and enduring discrimination (Gaines &

Reed, 1994, 1995; Reed & Gaines, 1997). Thus, it is not clear whether the role of stereotype threat in support communication processes can be generalized from African-descent Americans to members of other so-called racial minority groups.

Consider the plight of Asian-descent Americans. Unlike African-descent Americans, Asian-descent Americans (constituting 5 percent of the U.S. population; Humes et al., 2011) are often stereotyped *positively* as the "model minority" regarding academic performance (see Crocker, Major, & Steele, 1998). In and of itself, stereotype threat would not be expected to place the same burden upon individual Asian-descent Americans or their families as it would upon African-descent Americans or their families. Nevertheless, unlike African-descent Americans, Asian-descent Americans are *more* likely to suffer from low self-esteem than are European-descent Americans (Chan & Mendoza-Denton, 2008). This apparent paradox might be explained by the fact that Asian-descent Americans are negatively stereotyped in the social and athletic domains, but not in the academic domain (Mendoza-Denton, Kahn, & Chan, 2008). Ironically, some Asian-descent Americans may find it more difficult to seek (if not to obtain) social support from their own families than do African-descent Americans, out of concern that they will not live up to their families' academic expectations.

Next, consider the plight of Latinas/os. Technically, Latinas/os (constituting 16 percent of the U.S. population; Humes et al., 2011) do not constitute a race. Nevertheless, Latinas/os often are treated individually and collectively as distinct racially from non-Hispanic Blacks and from non-Hispanic Whites (Roth, 2010). Moreover, although anti-Hispanic stereotypes might not be as negative or as pervasive as are anti-Black stereotypes, the stereotype of Latinas/os as intellectually deficient is comparable to the stereotype of African-descent Americans as intellectually deficient (Dixon & Rosenbaum, 2004). Many Latinas/os may experience stigmatization and stereotype threat; and many Latinas/os may find it difficult to seek or to maintain help from mental health professionals, thus placing further strain upon their families as social support networks.

Generalizability of Stereotype Threat and Support Communication Processes Across Members of Various National Minority Groups

The terms "race" and "ethnicity" often are treated as if they are interchangeable (Phinney, 1996). However, as Goffman (1963) pointed out, race represents only one component of individuals' ethnicity. A second important component of ethnicity is individuals' nationality. As it turns out, individuals' native-born versus foreign-born status and individuals' race covary: More than 90 percent of African-descent Americans and more than 90 percent of European-descent Americans were born within the U.S.A.; whereas 60 percent of Latinas/os and fewer than 35 percent of Asian-descent Americans were born in the U.S.A. (Grieco, 2010).

Among African-descent Americans, the native-born/foreign-born distinction carries important implications for individuals' susceptibility to stereotype threat and, hence, for the burdens than African-descent Americans' families must bear as social support networks. For example, African-descent Americans who were born in West Indian nations generally seem to be less susceptible to stereotype threat than are African-descent Americans who were born in the U.S.A. (Deaux, 2006). Moreover, first-generation African-descent Americans having roots in the West Indies tend to be less susceptible to stereotype threat than are second-generation African-descent Americans having roots in the West Indies (Deaux et al., 2007).

Since the passage of immigration reform legislation in 1965, most immigrants to the U.S.A. (currently 13 percent of the U.S. population; Grieco, 2010) have come from Asian or Latin American nations (Deaux, 2008). However, immigrants from Asian nations typically are regarded as legal immigrants; whereas immigrants from Latin American nations (especially from Mexico) typically are regarded as illegal immigrants, regardless of the veracity of such assumptions (Guyll, Madon, Prieto, & Scherr, 2010). Stereotype threat may be especially problematic for those Latinas/os who are perceived as having relocated to the U.S.A. illegally. To the extent that language barriers prevent many Latinas/os from seeking help from mental health professionals, stereotype threat may loom ever larger as a burden for Latinos' families as social support networks.

Generalizability of Stereotype Threat and Support Communication Processes Across Members of Various Religious Minority Groups

A third major component of ethnicity that Goffman (1963) identified alongside race and nationality is individuals' religion. The U.S. Census has never included a question on individuals' religion (Schultz, 2006). Thus we cannot state percentages of individuals from specific religious groups with any certainty. Nevertheless, we can speculate as to the degree that individuals from particular religious minority groups are more, versus less, likely to be susceptible to stereotype threats and consequent burdens to individuals' families as support networks.

In the post-9/11 era, Muslims have emerged as arguably the most negatively stereotyped religious minority group within the U.S.A. (although Muslims were stereotyped negatively before 9/11; Kalkan, Layman, & Uslander, 2009). Indeed, within the U.S.A., Muslims are stereotyped as lower in both warmth and competence than are Christians (Fiske, Cuddy, Glick, & Xu, 2002). The anti-Muslim stereotype is similar to anti-Hispanic and anti-Black stereotypes. As such, it is likely that Muslims will find it difficult to seek or to obtain help from mental health professionals and will lean upon their families as social support networks—no small task, given that some Muslim families are subjected to intense scrutiny by non-Muslim majorities in their communities (Post & Sheffer, 2007).

In contrast to Muslims, Jews are stereotyped in largely positive terms within the U.S.A. (Reyna, 2000). In fact, within the U.S.A., Jews are stereotyped as higher in competence (albeit lower in warmth) than are Christians (Fiske, Cuddy, Glick, & Xu, 2002). The pro-Jewish stereotype is similar to the pro-Asian American stereotype. As such, individual Jewish persons may not be susceptible to stereotype threat (at least within academia) but nonetheless may find that their own families place such high emphasis on achievement that any admission of difficulty might be viewed as tantamount to failure.

Closing Remarks

Discussed above, Goffman (1959, 1963) contended that in social contexts stigmatized individuals find it difficult to persuade audience members to perceive them as they would like to be perceived. As we have seen from the present chapter, and like other stigma researchers have stated, stigma influences social interactions and "the psychological and social consequences of stigma involve the responses both of the perceivers and of stigmatized people themselves" (Dovidio, Major, & Crocker, 2000, p. 5). Evidence is accumulating that direct support seeking communication strategies in social exchanges with close others appear to enhance positive, supportive, outcomes in interpersonal interactions.

Yet, admittedly, direct disclosure of support needs most likely is not the preferred method for use with acquaintances, strangers, or others with whom interactions are wrought with outcome uncertainty. Instead, perhaps essential is a simple awareness that indirect methods of communication are not effective. It may be an unfortunate responsibility on the part of the stigmatized that some encounters will not have positive outcomes but that these exchanges with nonstigmatized others could be the exposure needed to effect change in negative attitudes (exposure to stigmatized individuals can assist in creating more accepting cultural attitudes toward the stigmatized; Pettigrew, 1998; see also Allport, 1954). Such action on the part of the stigmatized might in part reflect what Crocker and colleagues refer to as an ecological approach to social exchanges as opposed to one involving the ego (Crocker & Garcia, 2009; Migacheva, Crocker, & Tropp, 2011) and may be one resulting in better outcomes in the end.

Indeed reviews of research on intergroup contact reveal that intergroup contact is helpful in having a positive impact on the nonstigmatized or those exposed to minority individuals, but may be more difficult on the stigmatized or minorities given the threat and perception of prejudice and discrimination within the exchange (e.g., Tropp, 2006). Moreover, enhancing the support exchanges with close others could serve to buffer individuals in the face of difficult encounters with others; "the extent to which stigmatized partners receive love and esteem from significant others may enable stigmatized partners to maintain high levels of self-esteem, despite the ever-present possibility that a given social situation will bring negative stereotypes to bear upon the nature of interactions between stigmatized target persons and nonstigmatized as well as stigmatized perceivers" (Gaines, 2001, pp. 126–27).

References

Allport, G. W. (1954). *The nature of prejudice*. Reading, MA: Addison-Wesley.

Barbee, A. P., & Cunningham, M. R. (1995). An experimental approach to social support communications: Interactive coping in close relationships. In B. R. Burleson (Ed.), *Communication yearbooks* (Vol. XVIII, pp. 381–413). Thousand Oaks, CA: Sage.

Baumeister, R. F. (1997). Identity, self-concept, and self-esteem: The self lost and found. In R. Hogan, J. Johnson, & S. Briggs (Eds.), *Handbook of personality psychology* (pp. 681–710). San Diego, CA: Academic Press.

Blascovich, J., Spencer, S., Quinn, D., & Steele, C. (2001). African-Americans and high blood pressure: The role of stereotype threat. *Psychological Science, 12*, 225–29.

Brown, C., Conner, K. O., Copeland, V. C., Grote, N., Beach, S., Battista, D., & Reynolds, C. F. (2010). Depression stigma, race, and treatment seeking behavior and attitudes. *Journal of Community Psychology, 38*, 350–68.

Butler, C., Tull, E. S., Chambers, E. C., & Taylor, J. (2002). Internalized racism, body fat distribution, and abnormal fasting glucose among a African-Caribbean women in Dominica, West Indies. *Journal of the National Medical Association, 94*, 143–48.

Carr, P. B., & Steele, C. M. (2009). Stereotype threat and inflexible perseverance in problem solving. *Journal of Experimental Social Psychology, 45*, 853–59.

Chan, W. Y., & Mendoza-Denton, R. (2008). Status-based rejection sensitivity among Asian Americans: Implications for psychological distress. *Journal of Personality, 76*, 1317–46.

Corrigan, P. W., Watson, A. C., & Barr, L. (2006). The self-stigma of mental illness: Implications for self-esteem and self-efficacy. *Journal of Social and Clinical Psychology, 25*, 875–84.

Cote, J. (2006). Identity studies: How close are we to developing a social science of identity? An appraisal of the field. *Identity, 6*, 3–25.

Crocker, J. & Garcia, J. A. (2009). Downward and upward spirals in intergroup interactions: The role of self-motivations. In T. D. Nelson (Ed.), *Handbook of stereotyping, prejudice and discrimination* (pp. 229–45). Hillsdale, NJ: Lawrence Erlbaum Associates.

Crocker, J., & Major, B. (1989). Social stigma and self-esteem: The self-protective properties of stigma. *Psychological Review*, 96, 608–30.

Crocker, J., Major, B., & Steele, C. (1998). Social stigma. In D. Gilbert, S. T. Fiske, & G. Lindzey (Eds.), *Handbook of social psychology*, 4th edn (Vol. II, pp. 504–53). Boston, MA: McGraw-Hill.

Deaux, K. (2006). A nation of immigrants: Living our legacy. *Journal of Social Issues*, 62, 633–51.

——(2008). To be an American: Immigration, hyphenation, and incorporation. *Journal of Social Issues*, 64, 925–43.

Deaux, K., Bikmen, N., Gilkes, A., Ventuneac, A., Joseph, Y., Payne, R. & Steele, C. (2007). Becoming American: Stereotype threat effects in Black immigrant groups. *Social Psychology Quarterly*, 70, 384–404.

Derlega, V. J., Winstead, B. A., Oldfield, E. C., & Barbee, A. P. (2003). Close relationships and social support in coping with HIV: A test of Sensitive Interaction Systems Theory. *AIDS and Behavior*, 7, 119–29.

Dixon, J. C., & Rosenbaum, M. S. (2004). Nice to know you? Testing contact, cultural, and group threat theories of anti-black and anti-Hispanic stereotypes. *Social Science Quarterly*, 85, 257–80.

Dovidio, J. F., Major, B., & Crocker, J. (2000). Stigma: Introduction and overview. In T. F. Heatherton, R. E. Kleck, M. R. Hebl, & J. G. Hull (Eds.), *The social psychology of stigma* (pp. 1–28). New York: Guilford Press.

Duck, S. (1999). *Relating to others*, 2nd edn. Buckingham: Open University Press.

Erikson, E. H. (1950). *Childhood and society*. New York: Norton.

——(1968). *Identity: Youth and crisis*. New York: Norton.

Fairchild, H. H., Yee, A. H., Wyatt, G. E., & Weizmann, F. (1995). Readdressing psychology's problem with race. *American Psychologist*, 50, 46–47.

Fiske, S. T., Cuddy, A. J. C., Glick, P., & Xu, J. (2002). A model of (often mixed) stereotype content: Competence and warmth respectively follow from perceived status and competition. *Journal of Personality and Social Psychology*, 82, 878–902.

Gaines, S. O., Jr. (1997). *Culture, ethnicity, and personal relationship processes*. New York: Routledge.

——(2001). Coping with prejudice: Personal relationship partners as sources of socioemotional support for stigmatized individuals. *Journal of Social Issues*, 57, 113–28.

Gaines, S. O., Jr. & Ickes, W. (2000). Perspectives on interracial relationships. In W. Ickes & S. Duck (Eds.), *The social psychology of personal relationships* (pp. 55–78). Chichester: John Wiley & Sons.

Gaines, S. O., Jr. & Reed, E. S. (1994). Two social psychologies of prejudice: Gordon W. Allport, W. E. B. Du Bois, and the legacy of Booker T. Washington. *Journal of Black Psychology*, 20, 8–28.

——(1995). Prejudice: From Allport to Du Bois. *American Psychologist*, 50, 96–103.

Garcia, S. M., Hallahan, M., & Rosenthal, R. (2007). Poor expression: Concealing social class stigma. *Basic and Applied Social Psychology*, 29, 99–107.

Goffman, E. (1959). *The presentation of self in everyday life*. Garden City, NY: Doubleday.

——(1963). *Stigma: Notes on the management of spoiled identity*. Englewood Cliffs, NJ: Prentice-Hall.

Grieco, E. M. (2010). *Race and Hispanic origin of the foreign-born population in the United States: 2007*. Washington, DC: U.S. Census Bureau.

Guyll, M., Madon, S., Prieto, L., & Scherr, K. C. (2010). The potential roles of self-fulfilling prophecies, stigma consciousness, and stereotype threat in linking Latino/a ethnicity and educational outcomes. *Journal of Social Issues*, 66, 113–30.

Herek, G. M., Gillis, J. R., & Cogan, J. C. (2009). Internalized stigma among sexual minority adults: Insights from a social psychological perspective. *Journal of Counseling Psychology*, 56, 32–43.

Humes, K. R., Jones, N. A., & Ramirez, R. R. (2011). *Overview of race and Hispanic origin: 2010*. Washington, DC: U.S. Census Bureau.

Kalkan, K. O., Layman, G. C., & Uslander, E. M. (2009). "Bands of others"? Attitudes toward Muslims in contemporary American society. *Journal of Politics*, 71, 847–62.

Kessler, R. C., Mickelson, K. D., & Williams, D. (1999). The prevalence, distribution, and mental health correlates of perceived discrimination in the United States. *Journal of Health and Social Behavior*, 40, 208–30.

Jones, E. E., Farina, A., Hastorf, A. H., Markus, H., Miller, D. T., & Scott, R. A. (1984). *Social stigma: The psychology of marked relationships*. New York: Freeman.

Jones, J. M. (1997). *Prejudice and racism*, 2nd edn. New York: McGraw-Hill.

Lewis, R. J., Derlega, V. J., Clarke, E. G., & Kuang, J. C. (2006). Stigma consciousness, social constraints, and lesbian well-being. *Journal of Counseling Psychology*, 53, 48–56.

Markus, H. R. (2008). Pride, prejudice, and ambivalence: Toward a unified theory of race and ethnicity. *American Psychologist*, 63, 651–70.

Meisenbach, R. J. (2010). Stigma management communication: A theory and agenda for applied research on how individuals manage moments of stigmatized identity. *Journal of Applied Communication Research*, 38, 268–92.

Mendoza-Denton, R., Kahn, K., & Chan, W. Y. (2008). Can fixed views of ability boost performance in the context of favorable stereotypes? *Journal of Experimental Social Psychology*, 44, 1187–93.

Mickelson, K. D. (2001). Perceived stigma, social support, and depression. *Personality and Social Psychology Bulletin*, 27, 1046–56.

Mickelson, K. D., & Williams, S. L. (2008). Perceived stigma of poverty and depression: Examination of interpersonal and intrapersonal mediators. *Journal of Social and Clinical Psychology*, 27, 903–30.

Migacheva, K., Crocker, J., & Tropp, L. (2011). Focusing beyond the self: Goal orientations in intergroup relations. In L. R. Tropp & R. K. Mallett (Eds.), Moving beyond prejudice reduction: Pathways to positive intergroup relations (pp. 99–115). Washington, DC: American Psychological Association.

Pettigrew, T. F. (1998). Intergroup contact theory. *Annual Review of Psychology*, 49, 65–83.

Phinney, J. S. (1996). When we talk about American ethnic groups, what do we mean? *American Psychologist*, 51, 918–27.

Porterfield, E. (1978). *Black & White mixed marriages: An ethnographic study of Black-White families.* Chicago, IL: Nelson-Hall.

Post, J. M., & Sheffer, G. (2007). The risk of radicalization and terrorism in U.S. Muslim communities. *Brown Journal of World Affairs*, 13, 101–12.

Pronin, E., Steele, C. M., & Ross, L. (2004). Identity bifurcation in response to stereotype threat: Women and mathematics. *Journal of Experimental Social Psychology*, 40, 152–68.

Quinn, D. M., & Chaudoir, S. R. (2009). Living with a concealable stigmatized identity: The impact of anticipated stigma, centrality, salience, and cultural stigma on psychological distress and health. *Journal of Personality and Social Psychology*, 97, 652–66.

Reed, E. S. & Gaines, S. O., Jr. (1997). Not everyone is "different-from-me": Toward an historico-cultural account of prejudice. *Journal of Black Psychology*, 23, 245–74.

Reyna, C. (2000). Lazy, dumb, or industrious: When stereotypes convey attribution information in the classroom. *Educational Psychology Review*, 12, 85–110.

Rosenblatt, P. C., Karis, T. A., & Powell, R. D. (1995). *Multiracial couples: Black & White voices.* Thousand Oaks, CA: Sage.

Roth, W. D. (2010). Racial mismatch: The divergence between form and function in data for monitoring racial discrimination of Hispanics. *Social Science Quarterly*, 91, 1288–311.

Schultz, K. M. (2006). Religion as identity in postwar America: The last serious attempt to put a question on religion in the United States Census. *Journal of American History*, 93, 359–84.

Sellers, R. M., Caldwell, C. H., Schmeelk-Cone, K. H., & Zimmerman, M. A. (2003). Racial identity, racial discrimination, perceived stress, and psychological distress among African American young adults. *Journal of Health and Social Behavior*, 44, 302–17.

Smith, R. A. (2007). Language of the lost: An explication of stigma communication. *Communication Theory*, 17, 462–85.

Spencer, S. J., Steele, C. M., & Quinn, D. M. (1999). Stereotype threat and women's math performance. *Journal of Experimental and Social Psychology*, 35, 4–28.

Steele, C. M. (1997). A threat in the air: How stereotypes shape the intellectual identities and performance of women and African-Americans. *American Psychologist*, 52, 613–29.

Steele, C. M., & Aronson, J. (1995). Stereotype threat and the intellectual test performance of African-Americans. *Journal of Personality and Social Psychology*, 69, 797–811.

Stryker, S., & Statham, A. (1985). Symbolic interaction and role theory. In G. Lindzey & E. Aronson (Eds.), *Handbook of social psychology*, 3rd edn (Vol. I, pp. 311–78). New York: Random House.

Taylor, J. (1990). Relationship between internalized racism and marital satisfaction. *Journal of Black Psychology*, 16, 45–53.

Thomas, M., & Choi, J. B. (2006). Acculturative stress and social support among Korean and Indian Immigrant adolescents in the United States. *Journal of Sociology and Social Welfare*, 33, 123–43.

Tropp, L. R. (2006). Stigma and intergroup contact among members of minority and majority status groups. In S. Levin and C. van Laar (Eds.), *Stigma and group inequality: Social psychological perspectives* (pp. 171–91). Mahwah, NJ: Lawrence Erlbaum Associates.

Watson, A. C., Corrigan, P. W., Larson, J. E., & Sells, M. (2007). Self-stigma in people with mental illness. *Schizophrenia Bulletin, 33*, 1312–18.

White, J. L., & Parham, T. A. (1990). *The psychology of Blacks: An African American perspective*, 2nd edn. Englewood Cliffs, NJ: Prentice-Hall.

Williams, S. L., & Mickelson, K. D. (2008). A paradox of support seeking and rejection among the stigmatized. *Personal Relationships, 15*, 493–509.

Williams, D. R., & Williams-Morris, R. (2000). Racism and mental health: The African American experience. *Ethnicity and Health, 5*, 243–68.

Xu, Y., & Burleson, B. R. (2001). Effects of sex, culture, and support type on perceptions of spousal social support: An assessment of the "support gap" hypothesis in early marriage. *Human Communication Research, 27*, 535–66.

Yee, A. H., Fairchild, H. H., Weizmann, F. & Wyatt, G. E. (1993). Addressing psychology's problem with race. *American Psychologist, 48*, 1132–40.

Yeh, C. J., Okubo, Y., Ma, P.-W. W., Shea, M., Ou, D., & Pitue, S. T. (2008). Chinese immigrant high school students' cultural interactions, acculturation, family obligations, language use, and social support. *Adolescence, 43*, 776–90.

Part IV
The Relational Communication of Family Members

14

Mothers and Fathers Coparenting Together

John M. Beaton, William J. Doherty,
and Lisa M. Wenger

The coparenting relationship between mothers and fathers is a central feature of family life, however, the coparenting relationship was mostly ignored by family scholars and researchers until at least the mid 1990s. The construct of "coparenting" was usually synonymous with postdivorce coparenting and confined to the study of conflict and cooperation across households. It is only in the past 15 years that both family theory and research directly assessing multiple dimensions of coparenting has exploded.

One explanation for the neglect of coparenting (at least outside of divorced families) is that the field is just beginning to absorb family systems theories concepts that are prominent in family therapy. Whereas family researchers in psychology and interpersonal communication were invested in dyadic formulations of family relationships (e.g., husband–wife, parent–child), family therapists have long focused on triadic interactions, claiming that the triad is the minimal unit needed for understanding family communication (Bowen, 1976; Minuchin, 1974). Triads allow for examining the influence of one relationship, such as the mother–father relationship, on a third member of the family, such as a child. A triadic analysis also illuminates how one relationship affects another, such as how the marital relationship affects the father–child relationship. Beyond family therapists, it is only in the past 15 years that family researchers have studied coparenting dynamics intentionally. Even less theory and research has focused on how mothers and fathers coparent multiple children who have relationships with one another (polyadic relationships).

Why did triadic, family systems models become appealing to family researchers only during the 1990s? We note that this was the decade of powerful research findings on the negative impact of marital and coparental conflict on parent–child relations and children's well-being in intact families (see review by Erel & Burman, 1995) and of parallel findings in studies of postdivorce families. Beyond the empirical findings, we believe that scholars became disenchanted with the over simplifications of dyadic models of family communication and decided to take the plunge into family systems theory by trying to operationalize heuristically interesting ideas that family therapists had observed but never measured. Jay Belsky (1981) and Patricia Minuchin (1985) were early theoretical leaders in this integration of developmental and family systems theories.

More recently, scholars have provided innovative theoretical models about coparenting in an effort to guide future research and intervention (e.g., Doherty & Beaton, 2004; Feinberg, 2003; McHale, 2007a; McHale, Kuersten-Hogan, & Rao, 2004). Yet, with the exception of Doherty and Beaton (2004), marital status has not been used as a central theoretical construct and research variable in coparenting relationships. This is surprising because there is a consensus that positive marital relationships typically lead to more effective coparenting and increased parental involvement, especially for fathers (Burney & Leerkes, 2010; Furstenberg & Cherlin, 1991; Isacco, Garfield, & Rogers, 2010; Morril, Hines, Mahmood, & Cordova, 2010; Van Egeren, 2004). It appears that marriage has been assumed in this literature, and that this assumption has led to less robust theorizing about how the structure of the coparenting relationship (married, cohabiting, romantic but not living together, never-married and broken up, and divorced) affects coparenting dynamics and child outcomes. This chapter will offer a broad framework for coparenting that includes marital status as a fundamental variable. The outline of this chapter follows its purposes: to summarize contemporary research on coparenting within heterosexual families, to delineate theoretical frameworks that can be fruitful for understanding the coparenting relationship, to offer a theoretical model of factors influencing coparenting, and to suggest innovative areas for further research.

Review of Coparenting Research

Although Belsky (1981) did not explicitly focus on coparenting in the early 1980s, he proposed that parenting was influenced by multiple systems: parent, marital, and child subsystems. He argued that the marital relationship was the most important support system for parents. That is, in order to understand the influence of parenting on child development, consideration must be given to the marital relationship. In later work, Belsky (1984) developed a pioneering theoretical framework to study how parenting was multidetermined by parents' developmental histories, personalities, marital relations, employment characteristics, social networks, and individual child characteristics. This framework set the stage for future theory and research that focused on both dyadic and triadic relationships.

Lewis, Owen, and Cox (1988) were among the first researchers to study both dyadic and triadic relationships: the marital relationship, mother–child relationship, the father–child relationship, and the mother–father–child relationship. They discovered that the parents' positive marital quality prenatally predicted higher levels of parental investment at three months and one year following birth. Although Lewis et al. did not focus specifically on the coparenting relationship, their research was the first of many other studies that would investigate how marital relationships influence parental involvement (see Erel & Burman, 1995). Philip and Carolyn Cowan (1999) investigated how marital relationships impact coparenting over time. In a 10-year longitudinal intervention study, the Cowans followed couples expecting their first child. They found that declining marital satisfaction measured at three time periods (pregnancy and when the child was 1.5 and 3.5 years old) was associated with low warmth in mother–child and father–child interactions at age 3.5.

An important distinction that has emerged in the field is between the coparenting relationship and the couple relationship (which almost always has been the marital relationship, given the samples used). Numerous studies have shown how supportive coparenting has positive outcomes for child development beyond the quality of the marital relationship. McHale (1997, 2007b) was a pioneer in studying coparenting distinct from marital and parent–child relationships. Previous research primarily focused on coparenting within the marital relationship, and measures were comprised of marital satisfaction items as opposed to triadic coparenting items. In assessing triadic interactions, he found that increased marital distress leads to more hostile/competitive parenting and imbalances of mother and father involvement. Moreover, the interplay between the quality of the marital relationship and a child's gender affected parental involvement. In the face of marital distress, boys were more likely to encounter hostile/competitive coparenting, whereas girls were more likely to encounter larger discrepancies in coparental involvement. McHale's research on the coparental relationship set the foundation for further research in this area.

Belsky, Crnic, and Gable (1995), with a sample of mothers, fathers, and their toddler boys, discovered that parents with similar individual psychological attributes had more positive coparenting relationships. The more mothers and fathers differed on characteristics of introversion and extraversion, the more likely they were to engage in unsupportive coparenting behaviors. Furthermore, Belsky et al. discovered that coparenting dynamics and whole-family dynamics played distinctive roles in the development of behavioral inhibition in children, beyond the child's temperament, individual parenting, individual parent well-being, and marital quality.

McHale and Rasmussen (1998) found that family warmth during infancy was associated with men's positive coparenting practices (self-reported) when the child was age 3, which in turn were linked to fewer internalizing and aggressive behaviors in preschool. In a breakthrough study, McHale, Lauretti, Kuersten-Hogan, and Rasmussen (2000) did observational assessments of both dyadic (parent–child) and triadic (mother–father–child) interactions. This was one of the first studies to investigate potential differences in how parents behave in these two contexts. The authors discovered that maternal and paternal behaviors within parent–child dyadic observations are very different from maternal and paternal behaviors within whole-family dynamics.

As momentum on coparenting research increased, new researchers were drawn to the area, and theoretical discussions increased. Margolin, Gordis, and John (2001) proposed a model of coparenting based on three dimensions: conflict between parents, cooperation between parents, and triangulation (a condition that occurs when a parent forms a coalition with a child that undermines the other parent). Margolin et al. found that coparenting dynamics were a function of a child's age, parents' gender, and a child's gender. Between married parents of preadolescents they observed marital conflict discussions concerning a child-related topic. They divided couples along the categories of hostility/defensiveness and agreeableness/problem solving. Couples who were more agreeable and displayed more problem-solving skills scored higher on total coparenting. In a follow-up study of their longitudinal sample, Cowan and Cowan (2003) began to focus more explicitly on coparenting using an observational coding system to study parents' interaction style in the presence of a child. Their results indicated that when parents showed displeasure with one another in the form of anger and disagreement, children showed higher levels of externalizing and internalizing behaviors in first grade.

More recently, McHale and Rotman (2007) followed mothers, fathers, and their first child from pregnancy through the toddler years. They found that positive prebirth expectations among both parents during pregnancy were associated with high levels of coparenting solidarity at 12 months, and for fathers this association was also evident at 30 months postbirth. In addition, Brown, Schoppe-Sullivan, Mangelsdorf, and Neff (2010) studied coparenting and parental sensitivity with 3.5 month old infants, and later assessed parental attachment at age one. They found that positive coparenting at 3.5 months was later associated with father–child secure attachments. Finally, in a meta-analysis with 59 studies, Teubert and Pinquart (2010) concluded that coparenting plays an important role in predicting positive child outcomes, even after accounting for mother's and father's parenting practices and marital health.

In summary, a growing body of research demonstrates the importance of coparenting relationships in families and the value of a triadic approach to studying families. Prominent conceptualizations of the coparenting relationship focus on the dimensions of conflict, cooperation, and triangulation with a child. Evidence is mounting that the coparenting dynamics have effects on child development and adjustment beyond the effects of individual parenting practices and that each parent behaves differently in and out of the presence of the other. Research findings also highlight the importance of building strong prenatal coparenting relationships early on between mothers and fathers (particularly for fathers), and the need for researchers to account for issues of child's gender, age of child, and multiple children.

Theoretical Frameworks

Until recently, coparenting research has been more descriptive than theory driven, with the literature concentrating on characterizing coparenting patterns, developing assessment tools, and examining influences on children's adjustment. Both Feinberg (2003) and McHale et al. (2004) have developed innovative theoretical frameworks to guide coparenting research and intervention. Feinberg's comprehensive ecological framework focuses on coparenting as the central mediating and moderating factor that influences individual parental characteristics, parenting practices, and child factors. By contrast, McHale et al.'s coparenting framework highlights the importance of considering coparenting structure, coparenting definitions, and specific comprehensive assessment tools needed to measure coparenting dynamics accurately. McHale et al.'s framework also makes important links between coparenting and adult development. Finally, both Feinberg and McHale et al. advocate for more research with diverse family systems, both in terms of racial diversity, and coparenting relationships beyond mother-father dyads (e.g., grandparents, teen parents, single parents, gay and lesbian parents). From our perspective, the majority of McHale et al.'s and Feinberg's assumptions are rooted in four foundational theoretical frameworks. Next we briefly discuss these four theoretical frameworks that can shed light on the coparental relationship. We will conclude this section by presenting an updated theoretical framework (see Doherty & Beaton, 2004) based on these four theoretical frameworks to guide research and intervention on factors that influence the coparental relationship.

Social constructionism seems an ideal fit for understanding the coparental relationship. As developed by Berger and Luckman (1966) and a variety of symbolic-interactionist scholars, social constructionism emphasizes the shared construction of a social reality by the participants in a relationship. From this perspective, social roles are created through ongoing interaction and through the negotiation of mutual expectations in the context of broader cultural norms. A social constructionist view of coparenting would stress how the creation of a couple's coparental relationship begins from the first time they discuss children and parenting. The negotiation process becomes more intense when they are expecting their first child together, and a negotiated coparenting relationship is set in motion quickly after the baby is born. Some aspects of coparenting may be openly negotiated, such as who will work more for pay and who will stay home more with the child, whereas other aspects are decided implicitly, as in situations where both assume the mother's preeminence as a child care expert and the father's auxiliary role. From a social constructionist standpoint, when researchers observe a couple interacting with their child in the laboratory, they are witnessing the public demonstration of a coparenting relationship that has been worked out over many interactions and will continue to be worked out over time.

Family systems theoretical frameworks have served as a principal framework for much of the coparenting research. As articulated by Bowen (1976), Minuchin (1974), and others, family systems theory focuses on multiple simultaneous interactions in the family, with particular reference here to the triangular relationship consisting of the parents and a child. As mentioned earlier, family systems theory allows the researcher to focus on triadic interactions, not just the dyadic interactions that are the forte of social constructionism. It also can illuminate the ways in which parents develop complementary or competitive relationships with each other. The work of Bowen also points to the influence of each parent's family of origin on current coparental dynamics.

Family development theoretical frameworks are important for understanding coparenting over time. As articulated by Aldous (1978), and Hill and Mattessich (1979), family development theories emphasize the changing structures and roles in the family as members grow older and the family undergoes important transitions. From this perspective, the developmental tasks of coparenting differ considerably depending on the family's life stage, from coparenting an infant to coparenting an adult child, and the number of children in a family. And of course, children in the family might be at considerably different developmental stages, requiring complex coordination of coparenting roles, with, say, one parent being more central to the younger child and the other parent being more central to the older child. Researchers have just begun to tap into the complexities of coparenting from a family life cycle perspective.

Human ecology theoretical frameworks focus on the interdependent web of personal, familial, and community influences on human development and functioning (Bronfenbrenner, 1979). Whereas the previous three frameworks emphasize intrafamilial dynamics, ecological frameworks concentrate on the niches within which children and families function, from the surrounding community systems to the broader societal and environmental systems. From this perspective, coparenting plays out in a complex ecology of social and economic influences. Using an ecological framework, Doherty, Kouneski, and Erickson (1998) summarized research showing that fathering is influenced more strongly by ecological factors than mothering is. Coparenting researchers have looked at the influence of the marital relationship and childhood factors on the coparenting relationship, but have only begun to examine the influence of broader ecological factors (see Feinberg, 2003).

A Theoretical Framework of Influences on the Coparental Relationship

Integrating elements of the four frameworks discussed previously, we have developed a model of influences on coparenting (see Figure 14.1). The focal point of the model is the triadic mother–father–child relationship, with the lines connecting the three participants representing how they mutually construct the coparenting relationship through ongoing systemic interaction and negotiation of roles. The bidirectional arrows represent how individual factors in the model influence each other in a reciprocal manner. Because the marital status of the parents is such an important context for coparenting, we include this

John M. Beaton, William J. Doherty, and Lisa M. Wenger

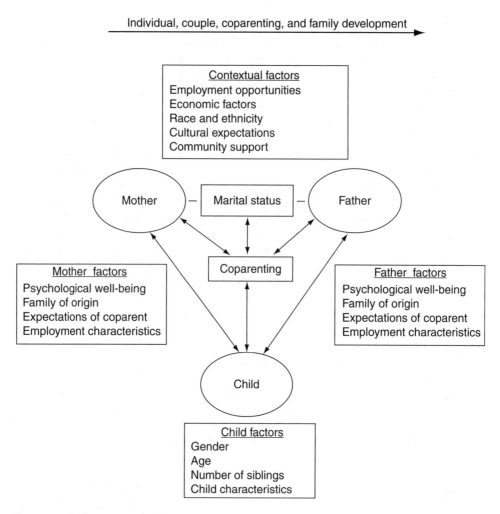

Individual, couple, coparenting, and family development

Contextual factors
Employment opportunities
Economic factors
Race and ethnicity
Cultural expectations
Community support

Mother — Marital status — Father

Coparenting

Mother factors
Psychological well-being
Family of origin
Expectations of coparent
Employment characteristics

Father factors
Psychological well-being
Family of origin
Expectations of coparent
Employment characteristics

Child

Child factors
Gender
Age
Number of siblings
Child characteristics

Figure 14.1 Influences on the Coparental Relationship

variable within the triangle itself, indicated by dashes rather than by a straight line because obviously not all mothers and fathers are married to each other. The straight lines indicate the coparenting relationship, which in turn is influenced by whether or not the parents are married. For simplicity's sake, we omit cohabitating relationships, which vary considerably in commitment from a functional marriage-like relationship to a transitory relationship of convenience.

Outside the triangle are depicted several categories of influences on the coparental relationship: individual factors in the mother and father, child factors, mother–father relationship factors, and broader ecological factors. The top line in the model depicts the arrow of time, which stands for the developmental process of the individuals involved, the evolving couple, the family and coparenting system, and the changing nature of the ecological influences. In this theoretical framework, we attempt to capture key elements of the four frameworks outlined previously as they help us understand the dynamics of coparenting relationships. We offer the theoretical framework for heuristic purposes as a guide to further research and intervention. For some domains of the theoretical framework, there is considerable research evidence for the influence of the variables (e.g., mothers' expectations about fathering), whereas for other domains there is relatively little at this time.

The Impact of Marital Status

As discussed before, variation in marital status and family structure are invisible in most theoretical frameworks of coparenting. One reason may be that most of the research on coparenting has been done by psychologists who focus on process and quality issues but not the more sociological variable of family structure. The main case for looking at marital status comes from compelling evidence that father involvement is tied to the endurance of the relationship bond with the mother. In the absence of a marriage, father bonds and coparenting quality are at risk over time. The Fragile Families Study and Child Well-Being Survey of Low-Income Urban Parents found that married fathers also reported higher levels of coparental support and father involvement than unmarried fathers (Isacco, Garfield, & Rogers, 2010). In another study using the same data set with unmarried fathers, Edin, Tach, and Mincy (2009) discovered that not only did father involvement decline when the couples broke up, but by the time the child had reached age five, one-third of nonresident fathers had completely lost contact with their child. While divorced fathers tend to coparent more and stay more involved with their children than nonmarried fathers, the trend is still towards less contact with the child (and therefore less coparenting with the mother) over time (Seltzer, 2000). Furstenberg and Cherlin (1991) argued that for many men, fatherhood and marriage are "a package deal." Not marrying the mother or divorcing the mother signals to these men that active fathering and coparenting are optional. Mothers may also internalize this cultural norm and lower their expectations of active fathering and coparenting after the break up of the couple relationship (Doherty et al., 1998).

Studies of nonmarital fathers suggest their involvement must be seen in the light of the coparenting relationship, not just as a dyadic variable. When nonresidential fathers exercise authoritative parenting and cooperate with the mother, child well-being is positively affected (Amato & Gilbreth, 1999; Marsiglio, Amato, Day, & Lamb, 2000). Both of these factors must be in place: positive authoritative parenting and positive coparenting in the form of payment of child support and cooperative child rearing. In other words, both healthy dyadic and triadic functioning—parenting and coparenting—need to be present for the well-being of children. And both of these forms of functioning are affected by the marital status of the parents.

More research is needed on coparenting in noncommitted cohabiting relationships, which we believe would be intermediate in quality between married and couples with severed relationships. Of course, cooperative coparenting is possible outside of an intact couple relationship, and such coparenting relationships aid children's development. But the severing of the intimate couple bond strikes a blow to the coparental relationship by creating diverging and sometimes competitive interests between the parents when it comes to parenting. Only a minority of couples are likely to overcome these obstacles well enough to have coparenting relationships that are high in harmony and cooperation and low in competition, hostility, and triangulation. A complete theoretical framework of coparenting requires attention to the influence of marital status on coparental dynamics.

Contextual Factors

With the exception of Feinberg's (2003) ecological framework about coparenting and Conger and Conger's (2002) contextual framework about farm families, little attention has been paid to the influence of factors outside of the family on coparenting. However, there is considerable research from the literature on work–family balance and from the fathering literature. In making use of the fathering literature, we are working from the assumption that factors that influence fathers' involvement with their children have at least indirect effects on the coparenting relationship.

In his ecological framework of coparenting, Feinberg (2003) notes that positive social support can strengthen coparenting relationships. Furthermore, financial pressure and work stress can have a negative impact on marital and coparenting functioning. For instance, Conger and Conger's (2002) contextual framework, based on their longitudinal study of farm families in the Midwest, showed how economic hardship is related to family well-being. The authors offered supportive evidence for an ecological framework demonstrating how economic hardship leads to economic pressure, which impacts coparenting through two sources: increased parent emotional distress and increased interparental conflict–withdrawal patterns. Both of these latter factors lead in turn to disrupted parenting and then to poorer child and adolescent adjustment. This research was replicated in a study of over 400 two-parent African American families (Conger et al., 2002).

Another important contextual factor in coparenting is employment. Parents face increasing challenges in balancing work, parenting, and family time (see Daly, 2001). Recent decades have witnessed an increase in dual earning families and in jobs requiring shift work, combined with a dramatic increase of employment opportunities for women (see Bianchi, 2000). In addition, the 1990s saw a dramatic increase in the number of temporary jobs with few benefits (Seccombe, 2000). The increase in temporary jobs has the potential to put more emotional strain on parents, and as Conger and Conger (2002) have found, makes it harder for mothers and fathers to coparent effectively. Furthermore, coparental strain can be the result of the total number of work hours per family increasing (Perry-Jenkins, Repetti, & Crouter, 2000), specifically in the managerial, professional, and technical occupations (Daly, 2001). These employment-related factors present challenges for contemporary parents to negotiate their coparenting roles when both parents are breadwinners at the same time that traditional cultural norms call for mothers to work a "second shift" when they come home (Hochschild, 1989).

As noted earlier, research on father involvement can be examined through a "coparenting lens" to show how shifts in father involvement influence coparenting. When fathers are less involved with their children because of contextual forces, there is less balance in the coparental relationship, and there may be more conflict and triangulation. The research reviewed by Doherty et al. (1998) is quite clear: father involvement is influenced by a variety of contextual factors, especially employment opportunities and other economic factors, and this influence is stronger for fathers than for mothers. Doherty et al. (1998) suggest that cultural norms are stricter about the centrality and the endurance of the mother–child dyad, no matter what is taking place outside the relationship. Father–child relationships, on the other hand, are seen as requiring men's success as breadwinners and protectors in the public sphere and therefore may require a greater level of support from external contexts. Fathers may withdraw from responsible fathering and coparenting as a result of contextual factors, unless their own individual level of devotion to fathering is strong and resilient.

Unfortunately, even with the explosion of coparenting theory and research over the past 15 years, there still has been little research investigating how race and ethnicity influence coparenting dynamics. One study conducted by Cabrera, Shannon, and La Talliade (2009) with Mexican American families concluded that couple conflict (mothers and fathers were asked about the quality of their couple relationship) was the strongest predictor of coparenting conflict. In another study with African American families, Brody, Flor, and Neubaum (1998) showed that harmonious interactions between parents who shared responsibilities for child rearing had positive outcomes for children. McHale et al. (2004) argue that the definition of coparenting as including a biological father and a biological mother needs to be expanded for different ethnic groups. Extended kin networks are very common with African American, Mexican American, Latino, American Indian, and Asian American families. For example, Kurrien and Vo (2004) studied South and Southeast Asian families and discovered that extended family members play valuable coparenting roles, often in dyadic coparenting relationships with mothers who are the primary caregivers. Clearly there is still a need for more research about how various ethnic groups coparent their children, keeping in mind that this may involve members of extended kin networks and "fictive" kin.

Another contextual factor in the model, broad cultural expectations, can influence how parents are involved with their children and how they coparent. In his historical studies, LaRossa (1997) has documented how cultural norms wax and wane over time for how fathers should be involved with their children, and implicitly, how fathers and mothers should coparent. The emergence in the 1970s of the expectation for cooperative labor and delivery of babies, with fathers actively participating in the process, is an example of how cultural norms influence coparenting practices. More research on cultural expectations about coparenting needs to be done.

Mother Factors

Numerous studies have shown that mothers' expectations about father involvement have a direct influence on how fathers are involved with their children, and thus, indirectly, on the kind of coparenting relationship mothers have with the father (Maurer, Pleck, & Rane, 2001). In general, research suggests that mothers' expectations for fathers' behavior are more influential than fathers' own expectations for their own behavior. For example, Van Egeren and Hawkins (2004) concluded that lower levels of maternal support for fathers in their paternal roles leads to lower levels of paternal competence. Furthermore, Schoppe-Sullivan, Brown, Cannon, Mangelsdorf, and Sokolowski (2008) discovered that maternal encouragement was positively correlated with increased father involvement, even when controlling for the quality of the coparental relationship and fathers' views about their paternal roles.

Mother's work experience is also a contributor to coparenting, beyond ways we discussed earlier. Women seem to be happier at home and work when they have flexible workplace options, they are supported in their jobs by their partners, and they can afford high-quality daycare (Arendell, 2000). Mothers tend to experience more work–family tension than fathers, since mothers are more likely to be interrupted at work about a family issue than are fathers (Perry-Jenkins et al., 2000). Notably, Galinsky's (1999) interviews with children indicate that it is not women entering the workforce that has negative effects on children, but the degree of work stress experienced by both mothers and fathers that affects children's well-being. This body of research has implications for the study of coparenting, because mothers' experiences of work–home stress might influence their expectations about father involvement and the coparenting relationship, and because fathers' cooperation or lack of cooperation with mothers' expectations might be an important source of coparental conflict.

Father Factors

We have argued that the large literature on father involvement supports the idea that more involved fathers are more active coparents. Studies also clearly demonstrate a positive association between fathers' psychological well-being and their involvement with their children (Bronte-Tinkew, Horowitz, & Carrano, 2010; Pleck, 1997). Fathers who feel competent about themselves as parents are more involved with their children and adolescents (Lamb, Pleck, Charnov, & Levine, 1985; Pleck, 1997). For example, two recent studies using the Fragile Families and Child Well-Being Survey (a diverse sample of nationally representative of unmarried and married fathers) found that fathers' mental health (levels of depression and anxiety) was the strongest predictor of positive coparenting support (Isacco, Garfield, & Rogers, 2010), and higher levels of paternal stress were correlated with lower levels of supportive coparenting (Bronte-Tinkew et al., 2010).

A father's sense of psychological well-being may also be connected to his family of origin experiences. Studies based on fathers' retrospective reports of childhood have shown how secure attachments for fathers are associated with securely attached infants (e.g., Cowan & Cowan, 1999; Steele, Steele, & Fongay, 1996). For example, Steele and colleagues (1996), with a sample of married couples and their 18-month-old children, found that both mothers' and fathers' secure attachments in adulthood predicted infants' secure attachment. By contrast, studies have also shown that some men who experienced little affection from their own fathers compensate for this negative family of origin experience by being highly affectionate with their own children (Beaton & Doherty, 2007). As well, Snarey (1993), in a 35-year longitudinal study, showed how men who experienced distant fathers during their childhood were more involved with the social emotional development of their adolescent children. Therefore, both negative and positive family-of-origin experiences can lead to fathers being more involved with their children and being more active coparents.

On the other hand, research needs to be conducted to examine the possible offsetting influence of father involvement on coparenting, such as increased conflict between parents. Clearly more research is needed that investigates fathers' expectations of maternal involvement in coparenting, especially as it relates to mothers' participation in the paid labor force. As mentioned before, father's employment characteristics play a significant role in father involvement. Fathers who lose their job generally struggle emotionally, and this adversely affects their involvement with their children (Pleck, 1997). In addition, greater work flextime and profamily policies are associated with more father involvement. Furthermore, research indicates that mothers' work schedules have more effect on father involvement than fathers' work schedules, because fathers are more involved with their children when mothers enter the paid workforce (Pleck, 1997). Researchers can examine how fathers' employment situations influence their everyday coparenting practices with mothers.

Child Factors

Recently, researchers have discovered how child factors play a pivotal role in influencing supportive coparenting. We suggest four areas that might be especially fruitful: gender, age, number of siblings, and child characteristics (e.g., temperament). With regard to gender, Brown et al. (2010) found that boys formed stronger attachments with both parents than girls when higher levels of supportive coparenting were reported by parents. In another study McHale (1995) examined how the interplay between the quality of the marital relationship and a child's gender can affect parental involvement. He found that when the parents are in marital distress boys are more likely to encounter hostile competitive coparenting, whereas girls are more likely to encounter larger discrepancies in coparental involvement. This is not to suggest that fathers are not just as enamored with their girls as with their boys, but that during marital conflict men may draw closer to sons in a triangle with their wives (McHale et al., 2002). A child's gender seems to influence father involvement more than mother involvement. Fathers tend to be more involved with their sons, especially when their sons get older, perhaps because fathers identify more easily with their older sons (Pleck, 1997). These gender patterns may have especially important implications for coparenting dynamics in families with adolescents.

We also suggest that age of the child and number of children bear attention as influences on coparenting. Coparenting young children may require more physical labor from parents, and more "tag-team" coparenting, whereas older children may require more difficult decision making by coparents. The number of siblings, and the need to divide parenting attention among them, may also be an important influence on coparenting practices. Coalitions between children might influence coparenting just as a coalition between a parent and a child does. As mentioned previously, little theory or research has examined coparenting relationships with multiple children. Different children present different challenges in parenting and coparenting.

Finally, there has been a dramatic increase in research on how child characteristics, primarily child's temperament, influence coparenting. Burney and Leerkes (2010) discovered that an infant's temperament at six months predicts mothers' and fathers' supportive coparenting practices. For both mothers and fathers, coparenting was affected by the infant's reactivity. Fathers reported more negative coparenting with a reactive infant when there was a poor marital relationship. Mothers reported a more negative coparenting relationship with a reactive infant only if they could not comfort the infant easily or if they were not satisfied with the division of parenting duties. Cook, Schoppe-Sullivan, Buckley, and Davis (2009), with a sample of mothers, fathers, and preschoolers found that couples who had children with higher levels of negative effect also demonstrated more behaviors that negatively influenced effective coparenting. Finally, Davis, Schoppe-Sullivan, Mangelsdorf, and Brown (2009) followed mothers, fathers, and their infants during the infant's first year of life. For fathers, challenging infant temperament issues at 3.5 months were linked to a decrease in cooperative coparenting over the first year of life, measured at 13 months. These findings indicate that child characteristics, like temperament, play a critical role in promoting positive coparenting, and that mothers and fathers are affected in different ways by child characteristics. Researchers are only beginning to understand how individual child characteristics affect mother's and father's parenting practices, coparenting relationship, and marital health.

Future Directions in Coparenting Research

Here we summarize some of the gaps in the current research on coparenting and propose new areas for research investigation, and future intervention. First, with the exception of Feinberg, Kan, and Hetherington (2007), the vast majority of research related to coparenting focuses on the pregnancy through toddler years and particularly neglects coparenting relationships during adolescence and young adulthood. Feinberg and colleagues followed mothers and fathers and their adolescents for a three-year period. They found that coparenting conflict in raising adolescents was a key variable in predicting higher levels of marital conflict, and that coparenting conflict was associated with higher levels of parental negativity and adolescent problems. This gap in adolescent coparenting research is especially important to close because, as Margolin et al. (2001) note, coparenting may become harder as children get older. Parents tend to cooperate more when children are young and disagree more about parenting when children become adolescents. More research is needed with older children even beyond adolescence/young adulthood, as more children are living longer at home (or leaving home and returning again); therefore, many mothers and fathers are coparenting their children for many more years than in the recent past. In addition, research needs to follow families over time to study how the coparenting relationship evolves as the family develops, from parenting in the infant years through parenting in the young adult years.

Second, researchers are only starting to investigate how children participate in socially constructing the coparenting relationship. The bidirectional nature of parent–child relationships has long been a focus of the literature on child development, with children seen as playing an active role in shaping dyadic parent–child interactions. The same case can be made for triadic interactions. For example, Fivaz-Depeursinge, Lopes, Python, and Favez (2009) have shown in a number of longitudinal studies how cues from infants have a direct impact on triadic interactions, as well as on mothers' and fathers' responses to infants. Further research is needed that looks at how children influence coparental interactions, including accounting for children's gender, age of child, and multiple children. For example, research is needed on why fathers seem to place more importance on their relationships with their sons, and whether this increases over time as sons become adolescents. Father involvement (and therefore his part of the coparenting team) seems to be more susceptible to fluctuations depending on children's gender and age, than does mother involvement. As mentioned, virtually no research exists about coparenting multiple children. Family therapists have known for years that the more individuals involved in the family, the more complex the family dynamics and interactions.

Third, as noted earlier, there has been little research that focuses on coparenting among diverse cultural and racial groups, and family forms. As much as theorists have advocated for coparenting research with diverse samples over the past 10 years, the overwhelming majority of coparenting research samples are still comprised of white, middle class, married mothers and fathers. The rise in interracial marriages and parenting also presents an opportunity to expand our understanding of the roles of race and ethnicity in coparenting, both at the nuclear family level and at the extended family and community levels. Furthermore, many children are being raised in homes with one parent, and often there are other important family and community members who function as coparents (e.g., grandparents). This is often the case with generational extended kin networks that are common within racially diverse families. In addition, many children are now spending substantial time in stepfamilies and there is a need for expanding coparenting research to this complex family form. Indeed, coparenting research could be enriched by comparing findings across biological, stepfamily, never-married, and postdivorce family structures in order to tease out what is core to successful coparenting across contexts and what is dependent on family structure. Finally, research is in needed on coparenting with gay and lesbian families, an increasingly visible group of families.

Fourth, there is limited empirical evidence in our theoretical framework in the area of contextual factors, such as employment, cultural expectations for parental roles, and community support (see Feinberg, 2003). For example, in our increasingly busy world, more research is needed that studies how both mothers' and fathers' work schedules affect parental involvement. In addition, more research is needed about evolving cultural expectations for marriage and parental involvement, and subsequently how these expectations affect supportive coparenting relationships. Furthermore, community expectations and support for effective coparenting can have a dramatic impact on family well-being.

Beyond these straightforward next steps in coparenting research, we offer ideas for bolder steps in terms of intervention for both mothers and fathers early on in the development of their coparenting relationship. Since marital status is a strong predictor for effective coparenting, early intervention that focuses on both the marital and coparenting relationship including both mothers and fathers is critical. In the last 10 years there have been a few successful coparenting interventions that we are aware of (see Doherty, Erikson, & LaRossa, 2006; Feinberg, Jones, Kan, & Goslin, 2010), and an innovative coparenting intervention that has focused on teen fathers (see Fagan, 2008). As mentioned earlier, more research is needed with culturally and racially diverse families, and therefore, obviously more intervention is needed as well. The results from two recent research studies with the Fragile Families and Child Well-Being Study were clear that marital status and income are important predictors of supportive coparenting for fathers (Edin, Tach, & Mincy, 2009; Isacco, Garfield, & Rogers, 2010). Interventions need to be developed for mothers and fathers from diverse family backgrounds. Finally, interventions need to be developed that focus beyond the pregnancy and toddler years that specifically target the adolescence and young adulthood years. The explosion of coparenting theory and research over the past 15 years has laid the foundation for effective coparenting interventions focused on helping families across the lifespan engage in supportive coparenting relationships.

References

Aldous, J. (1978). *Family careers: Developmental change in families.* New York: Wiley.

Amato, P. R., & Gilbreth, J. G. (1999). Nonresident fathers and children's well-being: A meta-analysis. *Journal of Marriage and the Family, 61,* 557–73.

Arendell. T. (2000). Conceiving and investigating motherhood: The decade's scholarship. *Journal of Marriage and the Family, 62,* 1192–207.

Beaton, J. M., & Doherty, W. J. (2007). Fathers' family of origin relationships and attitudes about father involvement from pregnancy through first year postpartum. *Fathering: A Journal of Theory, Research and Practice about Men as Fathers, 5*(3), 236–45.

Belsky, J. (1981). Early human experience: A family perspective. *Developmental Psychology, 17,* 3–23.

——(1984). The determinants of parenting: A process model. *Child Development, 55,* 83–96.

Belsky, J., Crnic, K., & Gable, S. (1995). The determinants of coparenting in families with toddler boys: Spousal differences and daily hassles. *Child Development, 66,* 629–42.

Berger, P. L., & Luckman, T. (1966). *The social construction of reality: A treatise in the sociology of knowledge.* New York: Doubleday.

Bianchi, S. M. (2000). Maternal employment and time with children: Dramatic change or surprising continuity. *Demography, 37,* 401–14.

Bowen, M. (1976). Theory in the practice of psychotherapy. In P. Guerin (Ed.), *Family therapy: Theory and practice (pp. 42–90).* New York: Gardner Press.

Brody G. H., Flor, D. L., & Neubaum, E. (1998). Coparenting processes and child competence among rural African-American families. In M. Lewis & C. Feiring (Eds.), *Families, risk, and competence (pp. 227–44).* Mahwah, NJ: Lawrence Erlbaum Associates.

Bronfenbrenner, U. (1979). *The ecology of human development: Experiments by nature and design.* Cambridge, MA: Harvard University Press.

Bronte-Tinkew, J., Horowitz, A., & Carrano, J. (2010). Aggravation and stress in parenting: Associations with coparenting and father engagement among resident fathers. *Journal of Family Issues, 31,* 525–55.

Brown, G. L., Schoppe-Sullivan, S. J., Mangelsdorf, S. C., & Neff, C. (2010). Observed and reported supportive coparenting as predictors of infant-mother and infant-father attachment security. *Early Child Development and Care, 180,* 121–37.

Burney, R. V., & Leerkes, E. M. (2010). Links between mothers' and fathers' perceptions of infant temperament and coparenting. *Infant Behavior & Development, 33,* 125–35.

Cabrera, N. J., Shannon, J. D., & La Talliade, J. J. (2009). Predictors of coparenting in Mexican American families and links to parenting and child social emotional development. *Infant Mental Health, 30*(5), 523–48.

Conger, R. D., & Conger, K. J. (2002). Resilience in Midwestern families: Selected findings from the first decade of a prospective, longitudinal study. *Journal of Marriage and Family, 64,* 361–73.

Conger, R. D., Wallace, L. E., Sun, Y., Simons, R. L., McLoyd, V. C., & Brody, G. H. (2002). Economic pressure in African American families: A replication and extension of the Family Stress Model. *Developmental Psychology, 38,* 179–93.

Cook, J. C., Schoppe-Sullivan, S. J., Buckley, C. K., & Davis, E. F. (2009). Are some children harder to coparent than others? Children's negative emotionality and coparenting relationship quality. *Journal of Family Psychology, 23,* 606–10.

Cowan, P. A., & Cowan, C. P. (1999). *When partners become parents: The big life change.* Mahwah, NJ: Lawrence Erlbaum Associates.

——(2003). Normative family transitions, normal family processes, and healthy child development. In F. Walsh (Ed.), *Normal family processes,* 3rd edn (pp. 424–59). New York: Guilford Press.

Daly, K. J. (2001). Deconstructing family time: From ideology to lived experience. *Journal of Marriage and Family, 63,* 283–95.

Davis, E. F., Schoppe-Sullivan, S. J., Mangelsdorf, S. C., & Brown, G. L. (2009). The role of infant temperament in stability and change in coparenting across the first year of life. *Parenting: Science and Practice, 9,* 143–59.

Doherty, W. J., Kouneski, E. F., & Erickson, M. F. (1998). Responsible fathering: An overview and conceptual framework. *Journal of Marriage and the Family, 60,* 277–92.

Doherty, W. J., & Beaton, J. M. (2004). Mothers and fathers parenting together. In A. L. Vangelisti (Ed.), *Handbook of family communication* (pp. 269–86). Mahwah, NJ: Lawrence Erlbaum Associates.

Doherty, W. J., Erikson, M. F., & LaRossa, R. (2006). An intervention to increase father involvement and skills with infants during the transition to parenthood. *Journal of Family Psychology, 20,* 438–47.

Edin, K., Tach, L., & Mincy, R. (2009). Claiming fatherhood: Race and dynamics of paternal involvement among unmarried men. *Annals of the American Academy of Political and Social Science, 621,* 149–77.

Erel, O., & Burman, B. (1995). Interrelatedness of marital relations and parent–child relations: A meta-analytic review. *Psychological Bulletin, 118,* 108/132.

Fagan, J. (2008). Randomized study of a prebirth coparenting intervention with adolescent and young fathers. *Family Relations, 57,* 309–23.

Feinberg, M. E. (2003). The internal structure and ecological context of coparenting: a framework for research and intervention. *Parenting: Science and Practice, 3*(2), 95–131.

Feinberg, M. E., Kan, M. L., & Hetherington, E. M. (2007). The longitudinal influence of coparenting conflict on parental negativity and adolescent maladjustment. *Journal of Marriage and Family, 69,* 687–702.

Feinberg, M. E., Jones, D. E., Kan, M. L., & Goslin, M. C. (2010). Effects of family foundations on parents and children: 3.5 years after baseline. *Journal of Family Psychology, 24,* 532–42.

Fivaz-Depeursinge, E., Lopes, F., Python, M., & Favez, N. (2009). Coparenting and toddler's interactive styles in family coalitions. *Family Process, 48*(4), 500–16.

Furstenberg, F. F., & Cherlin, A. J. (1991). *Divided families: What happens to children when parents part.* Cambridge, MA: Harvard University Press.

Galinsky, E. (1999). *Ask the children: What America's children really think about working parents.* New York: William Morrow.

Hill, R., & Mattessich, P. (1979). Family development theory and life span development. In P. Baltes & O. Brim (Eds.), *Life span development and behavior* (Vol. II, pp. 161–204). New York: Academic Press.

Hochschild, A. R. (1989). *The second shift: Working parents and the revolution at home.* New York: Viking.

Isacco, A., Garfield, C. F., & Rogers, T. E. (2010). Correlates of coparental support among married and nonmarried fathers. *Psychology of Men and Masculinity, 11*(4), 262–78.

Kurrien, R. & Vo, E. D. (2004). Who is in charge? Coparenting in South and Southeast Asian families. *Journal of Adult Development, 11*(3), 207–19.

Lamb, M. E., Pleck, J., Charnov, E. L., & Levine, J. A. (1985). Paternal behavior in humans. *American Zoologist, 25,* 883–94.

LaRossa, R. (1997). *The modernization of fatherhood: A social and political history.* Chicago, IL: University of Chicago Press.

Lewis, J. M., Owen, M. T., & Cox, M. J. (1988). The transition to parenthood: III. Incorporation of the child into the family. *Family Process, 27,* 411–21.

Margolin, G., Gordis, E. B., & John, R. S. (2001). Coparenting: A link between marital conflict and parenting in two-parent families. *Journal of Family Psychology, 15,* 3–21.

Marsiglio, W., Amato, P., Day, R. D., & Lamb, M. E. (2000). Scholarship on fatherhood in the 1990s and beyond. *Journal of Marriage and the Family, 62,* 1173–91.

Maurer, T. W., Pleck, J. H., & Rane, T. R. (2001). Parental identity and behavior: A contextual model. *Journal of Marriage and Family, 63,* 394–403.

McHale, J. P. (1995). Coparenting and triadic interactions during infancy: The roles of marital distress and child gender. *Developmental Psychology, 31,* 985–96.

——(1997). Overt and covert coparenting processes in the family. *Family Process, 36,* 183–201.

——(2007a). When infants grow up in multiperson relationship systems. *Infant Mental Health Journal, 28,* 370–92.

——(2007b). *Charting the bumpy road of coparenthood: Understanding the challenges of family life.* Washington, DC: Zero to Three Press.

McHale, J. P., Kuersten-Hogan, R., & Rao, N. (2004). Growing points for coparenting theory and research. *Journal of Adult Development, 11*(3), 221–34.

McHale, J. P., Lauretti, A., Kuersten-Hogan, R., & Rasmussen, J. L. (2000). Parental reports of coparenting and observed coparenting behavior during the toddler period. *Journal of Family Psychology, 14,* 220–36.

McHale, J., Lauretti, A., Talbot, J., & Pouquette, C. (2002). Retrospect and prospect in the psychological study of coparenting and family group process. In J. McHale & W. Grolnick (Eds.), *Retrospect and prospect in the psychological study of Families* (pp. 127–65). Mahwah, NJ: Lawrence Erlbaum Associates.

McHale, J. P., & Rasmussen, J. L. (1998). Coparental and family group-level dynamics during infancy: Early family precursors of child and family functioning during preschool. *Development and Psychopathology, 10,* 39–59.

McHale, J. P., & Rotman, T. (2007). Is seeing believing? Expectant parents' outlooks on coparenting and later coparenting solidarity. *Infant Behavior & Development, 30,* 63–81.

Minuchin, S. (1974). *Families and family therapy.* Cambridge, MA: Harvard University Press.

Minuchin, P. (1985). Families and individual development: Provocations from the field of family therapy. *Child Development, 56,* 289–302.

Morril, M. I., Hines, D. A., Mahmood, S., & Cordova, J. V. (2010). Pathways between marriage and parenting for wives and husbands: The role of coparenting. *Family Process, 49,* 59–73.

Perry-Jenkins, M., Repetti, R. L., & Crouter, A. C. (2000). Work and family in the 1990s. *Journal of Marriage and the Family, 62,* 981–1017.

Pleck, J. H. (1997). Paternal involvement: Levels, sources, and consequences. In M. L. Lamb (Ed.), *The role of the father in child development* (pp. 66–104). New York: Wiley.

Schoppe-Sullivan, S. J., Brown, G. L., Cannon, E. A., Mangelsdorf, S. C., & Sokolowski, M. (2008). Maternal gatekeeping, coparenting quality, and fathering behavior in families with infants. *Journal of Family Psychology, 22,* 389–98.

Seccombe, K. (2000). Families in poverty in the 1990s: Trends, causes, consequences, and lessons learned. *Journal of Marriage and the Family, 62,* 1094–113.

Seltzer, J. A. (2000). Child support and child access: Experiences of divorced and nonmarital families. In J. T. Oldham & M. S. Melli (Eds.), *Child support: The next frontier* (pp. 69–87). Ann Arbor, MI: University of Michigan Press.

Snarey, J. (1993). *How fathers care for the next generation: A four-decade study.* Cambridge, MA: Harvard University Press.

Steele, H., Steele, M., & Fongay, P. (1996). Associations among attachment classifications of mothers, fathers, and their infants. *Child Development, 67,* 541–55.

Teubert, D., & Pinquart, M. (2010). The association between coparenting and child adjustment: A meta-analysis. *Parenting Science and Practices, 10*(4), 286–307.

Van Egeren, L. A. (2004). The development of the coparenting relationship over the transition to parenthood. *Infant Mental Health Journal, 25*(5), 453–77.

Van Egeren, L. A., & Hawkins, D. P. (2004). Coming to terms with coparenting: Implications of definition and measurement. *Journal of Adult Development, 11*(3), 165–78.

15

Infant Communication

Barbara Gruenbaum, Nicole Depowski,
Kathleen E. Shaw, and Heather Bortfeld

Introduction

We know that a great deal of language development takes place in the first year of life. During this initial period, infants are immersed in the ambient language(s), which—coupled with a dynamic period of neural development—drives rapid and robust language learning. A key factor in this process is the infant's own active elicitation of responses from his or her caregivers. This communicative give-and-take helps create for the infant an environment rich in linguistic structure, which is fundamental for language development to take place. In this chapter, we will review data that highlight the dynamic nature of caregiver–child interaction and how such interaction supports language learning. Specifically, we will discuss the degree to which children enter the world primed to learn the ambient language(s), the learnable structures that are inherent in languages, and how communicative interaction between caregivers and infants potentiates and supports infants' learning of these structures.

Infants Start Learning *In Utero*

Strict interpretations of language development as completely experience driven or completely innately guided have softened in recent years, concomitant with emerging evidence suggesting that, although the biological basis for learning about language is in place and at work much earlier in development than was previously thought, changes in the environment have substantial effects on language outcome as well. Indeed, there is evidence that environmental tuning is at work in utero. This work highlights how biology and environment have already combined prenatally to set the process of language learning in motion.

Research focused on prenatal infants, while difficult to conduct, has been important to our emerging understanding of how exposure to sound in the womb gives babies a head start with language. The womb acts as a low-pass filter for sounds in the mother's environment, including the voices of those around her and her own. Furthermore, where others' voices will vary in intensity depending on where they are relative to the mother, the mother's own voice is present for the developing fetus at a relatively constant volume and with more clarity than other voices, given the internal nature of the source of that voice (e.g., mother's vocal folds, articulators). This means that, in addition to the external voice, internal bone and membrane conduction supplements the signal, providing infants with a relatively robust and consistent source of speech input. How this signal interacts with the maturation of the infant's auditory system is important to informing our understanding of what infants have already learned about language when they enter the world.

Using changes in the fetal heart rate as their dependent measure, Lecanuet and colleagues (1995) obtained some of the first physiological data to suggest that fetal hearing occurs before 28 gestational weeks. In fact, the fetus appears to respond to sound at 22 gestational weeks (Hepper & Shahidullah, 1994) and habituates to repeated sounds around 32 gestational weeks (Morokuma et al., 2004). Moreover, as infants near term, their sensitivity to more complex auditory stimuli improves, allowing them to perceive variations in music (Kisilevsky et al., 2004) and to differentiate between familiar and novel rhymes (DeCasper et al., 1994). Thus, the concept of "experience," rather than strictly referring to information available to the infant postnatally, implies a currently unknown threshold in prenatal auditory processing as well. Needless to say, this has not simplified theoretical debates about the degree to which nature and nurture come into play in early language development; it has only served to push the focal age for this debate earlier. But these data represent an important advance in our understanding of the toolkit with which infants enter the world.

With the understanding that birth is not the initial point at which infants are exposed to environmental sounds, behavioral researchers have capitalized on measures of infant attention to establish whether and which prenatal experiences underlie postnatal perceptual biases. This work has made it clear that fetal exposure to sound instills infants with a variety of sensitivities once in their postnatal world. For example, newborns can discriminate speech from nonspeech when played forwards, though not backwards (Ramus et al., 2000). In terms of language specific characteristics, neonates prefer their native one over another, unfamiliar language (Moon, Panneton-Cooper, & Fifer, 1993), can distinguish between stress patterns of different multisyllabic words (Moon et al., 1993), and can categorically discriminate lexical versus grammatical words (Shi, Werker, & Morgan, 1999). Finally, three-day-olds are sensitive to word boundaries (Christophe et al., 1994), can distinguish between two rhythmically dissimilar languages (Mehler et al., 1988; Nazzi, Bertoncini, & Mehler, 1998; Ramus et al., 2000), and can differentiate between good and poor syllable forms (Bertoncini & Mehler, 1981). These represent just a sampling of the findings demonstrating that mechanisms available prenatally position neonates to successfully navigate the earliest stages of the language learning process.

Preference for Maternal Speech

The preceding highlights how prenatal exposure to sound shapes infants' biases for particular structural characteristics of speech; infants likewise have been prepared to respond to social aspects of the signal. The best example of this is that neonates, who have been processing a wealth of maternal speech prenatally, have a strong preference for stimuli presented in their mother's voice once born. DeCasper and Fifer (1980) found that, three days after being born and even given only minimal postnatal maternal contact, an infant's sucking response was greater when it produced the maternal voice over another female's voice. Not only do neonates prefer their mother's voice over that of another woman, but familiarity with that voice interacts with the learning of speech structure.

For example, DeCasper and Spence (1986) found that prenatal exposure to maternal speech influenced other forms of postnatal auditory preferences. In their study, the researchers asked women to read a passage aloud each day during the last six weeks of their pregnancy. After the infants were born, they were tested using an operant-choice procedure to see whether they preferred the familiar passage over a novel passage. Results indicated that the infants did, indeed, find the familiar passage more reinforcing, while the control group demonstrated no specific preference for one or the other passage.

This preference for mother over other manifests in utero as well. Kisilevsky and colleagues (2003) investigated the ability of human fetuses to recognize their own mother's voice over the voice of an unfamiliar woman. The researchers placed a loudspeaker at about 10 cm above the mother's abdomen and played three stimulus trials, each beginning with silence, continuing with a voice (either that of the mother or unfamiliar woman) and, again, ending with silence. Results showed that fetal heart rates increased for the mother's voice but decreased for the unfamiliar woman's voice relative to the baseline established during the silent segment of each trial. This finding clearly demonstrates that infants can differentiate between the mother's voice and that of a stranger while still in the womb. Finally, DeCasper and colleagues found that fetuses 37 weeks old differentially responded to nursery rhymes that their mothers had recited daily for the previous four weeks (DeCasper et al., 1994). In other words, the mother's voice serves to stimulate not only maturation of the fetal auditory system, but also rudimentary social biases that will serve as the foundation for normal postnatal emotional development.

Interestingly, although newborns will work harder (by sucking more) to elicit maternal voices over another female's voice, they will not alter their patterns of sucking to elicit paternal voices over another male's voice. Using an operant choice procedure, DeCasper and Prescott (1984) tested newborns to determine whether they would prefer the father's voices to that of other males. The data revealed no specific preferences, one way or the other. Subsequent studies by the same researchers revealed that the infants could discriminate between the voices but that the voices apparently lacked reinforcing value, thus failing to elicit differential sucking. Similarly, in another study, young infants did not show a change in heart rate after hearing the father's voice but did after hearing the mother's voice (Ockleford et al., 1988); this lack of heart rate change was not due to an inability to discriminate among male voices. Overall, infants appear to prefer their mother's voice to that of a female stranger, yet they do not appear to prefer the voices of their fathers (Ward & Cooper, 1999) relative to that of a male stranger. These and other findings add support to the notion that early preferences for speech are specific to the mothers' vocalizations. Although one might assume that the father's voice is a relatively high frequency stimulus for the developing fetus, at least in most cases, the combination of frequency and source robustness of the mother's voice appears to give this particular auditory signal precedence over all other acoustic stimuli that are available to the infant prenatally.

Mothers Produce—and Infants Prefer—Infant-Directed Speech

Although infants initially prefer maternal vocalizations over all others, additional work has revealed that this preference is, in large part, driven by the exaggerated intonation with which maternal vocalizations are typically produced. Indeed, in an important early study, Mehler and colleagues (1978) found that 30-day-old infants only preferred their mothers' vocalizations over an unfamiliar woman's if the mothers' voices were properly intoned. If the mothers spoke with a flat intonation, infants showed no difference in their preference for their own mother's voice relative to the vocalizations of the female stranger. But mothers typically do speak in an animated manner when addressing their infants, a form of speech often referred to as "motherese" (Newport, 1975). It is precisely this bias on the part of mothers, as well as infants' preference for it, that has made motherese, or infant-directed speech, one of the focal areas of research for understanding infant communication.

Infant-directed speech is characterized by a variety of prosodic cues, such as exaggerated stress and pitch changes. These appear to help infants locate phrase boundaries (Jusczyk, 1997), decode syntactic structures of sentences (Morgan & Demuth, 1996), and come to a primitive form of semantic differentiation (Mehler et al., 1988). Researchers posited that the exaggerated pitch contours in infant-directed speech are useful to language development precisely because they attract and hold attention, improve sound localization, and improve awareness of contrast and coherence (Fernald & Simon, 1984). Indeed, behavioral data from infants over the first year of life support this theory. For example, prosodic cues are among the first that infants use to distinguish between languages (Cutler, Dahan & van Donselaar, 1997), thus allowing them to differentiate native from nonnative speech at birth. Moreover, infants can distinguish low-pass filtered infant-directed speech from similarly filtered adult-directed speech (Cooper & Aslin, 1994) in the first month of life. And, since boundaries of prosodic units are also often word boundaries, infants can use prosody to at least begin to segment fluent speech (Christophe & Dupoux, 1996). Thus prosody, particularly infant-directed prosody, makes speech salient. As such, it is an early and important contributor to language learning.

We have highlighted that the mother's voice is something infants come into the world recognizing and preferring. Interestingly, the infant-directedness of speech interacts with the familiarity of a speaker's voice. For example, if mothers' voices were somewhat intoned, then one-month-olds preferred the mother's voice over that of an unfamiliar woman regardless of whether they were speaking directly to the infant or to another adult (Cooper et al., 1997). However, this lack of preference between infant-directed speech and adult-directed speech is unique to maternal vocalizations. When the same researchers replaced the maternal vocalizations with vocalizations of unfamiliar women, infants then preferred the infant-directed speech over the adult-directed speech. Why is it that infants prefer infant-directed over adult-directed speech among strangers, but display no preference between the two when their mothers are the ones doing the speaking? The reason may be due to the fact that early in infancy, infants process their own mothers' voices differently than the voices of strangers. One view is that, since the mothers' vocalizations are so crucial to the developing infant, preference for her voice overrides preference for infant-directed speech. In other words, infants allocate more attentional resources towards their mothers' speech as a function of the emerging emotional bonds between them (Purhonen et al., 2004).

Infants' preferences for these two forms of speech—the mother's voice in particular and infant-directed speech in general—interact to orient them from an early age towards important sensory information in their environment. As infants gain experience post-natally, they develop a significant preference for maternal infant-directed speech over all other acoustic information. This is because when infants are about four months old their mothers begin to increase their use of exaggerated—infant-directed—speech. They increase the pitch of their voices and expand its range and variability over time. And they repeat themselves, a lot. Infants likewise are attracted to these properties, quickly learning to listen when their mothers' attention is on them, thereby gaining experience from the interaction. They thus begin to show a significant preference for maternal infant-directed speech over maternal adult-directed speech.

Given that the tendency for mothers to speak in an exaggerated way to their infants is consistent across languages (Fernald et al., 1989; Fernald & Morikawa, 1993), it may be that the infant-directedness of speech is a key factor in infants' language learning. While this point is debatable (and is, in fact, vigorously debated), it does seem that infants develop their preference for maternal infant-directed speech postnatally, and are thus not biologically predisposed to exhibit such a preference. They do, however, enter the world with a bias to listen to the mother's voice, a significant factor underlying the development of mother–infant communication.

Infant-Directed Speech or Happy Speech?

While the acoustical properties of infant-directed speech appear to underlie its effectiveness in attracting infants' attention, the particular components that drive infants' extended preference are less clear. There is evidence that the preference for affective speech begins very early in infancy. Infants are able to discriminate between positive and negative emotions when they are born (Mastropieri & Turkewitz, 1999), and respond differently to positive and negative emotions as conveyed by tone of voice (Fernald, 1992; Papousek et al., 1990). It is unsurprising then that the positive effect in infant-directed speech predicts a positive attitude and thus captures infants' attention more than neutral or negative speech. Positive effect in any form of speech encourages infants to pay attention to the person producing it, particularly familiar individuals (e.g., caregivers), whereas negative speech may pose a threat and motivate an infant to withdraw from the speaker in whatever way possible. Therefore, the influence of the affective quality of infant-directed speech has been the focus of much recent research.

In an important initial study on this issue, Kitamura and Burnham (1998) found that infants did not show a preference for infant-directed relative to adult-directed speech when speakers' pitch characteristics varied but their effect remained constant. Conversely, if speakers' pitch characteristics were held constant but their effect varied, then infants did demonstrate a preference for the infant-directed speech. This experiment provided a clear demonstration of the importance of the affective component of infant-directed speech—as distinguishable from pitch alone—in the preference that infants convey for it. Of course, people are generally happy when they address infants, so the issues of pitch and effect are tightly intertwined. Singh, Morgan, and Best (2002) replicated and extended Kitamura and Burnham's study by constructing stimuli in which effect and pitch were manipulated independently. They likewise found no preference for infant-directed over adult-directed speech given a constant (positive) effect. They noticed, however, that when adult-directed speech contained more positive effect than the infant-directed speech, infants preferred it. This shows that the higher and more variable pitch characteristics of infant-directed speech are not sufficient to determine infants' speech preferences. Rather, the (positive) affective properties of speech directed to infants interact with the tendency to exaggerate pitch contours, driving infants' preference for and attention to it.

Since "happy talk" draws infants' attention in a positive way, caregivers (and doting others) are more inclined to manipulate their vocal acoustics to elicit this response (Singh et al., 2002). Indeed, and perhaps unsurprisingly, adults rate infants' facial responses to infant-directed speech as more "attractive" than their facial responses to adult-directed speech (Werker & McLeod, 1989). Infants' preference for positive emotion, along with adults' inclination to produce happy talk when speaking to them, is thus an important contributor to their preference for infant-directed speech.

All of this may seem fairly obvious, but clear documentation of the forces driving infant preference matter at least in part because the positivity underlying this form of speech has been shown to affect infant development as well. In recent years, advances in infant-friendly neurophysiological techniques have allowed researchers to link previously established behavioral preferences to underlying neural processes. For example, maternally produced infant-directed speech has been shown to increase activity in infants' frontal cortex, a region important to the development of emotion processing capabilities into adulthood (Naoi et al., 2011). Frontal lobe development is related to positive emotions and positive interactions between mothers and infants (Davidson & Fox, 1982; Dawson et al., 1999), and it may contribute to the strength of the emotional bond between mother and infant (Purhonen et al., 2004). Indeed, when neonates' cortical activity was assessed while they listened to stories read by their mothers in either infant- or adult-directed speech, there was greater frontal lobe activity during the infant-directed speech readings (Saito et al., 2007). In short, the emotional properties of infant-directed speech contribute to positive interactions with caregivers, which in turn may serve as the basis for social learning by providing infants with the opportunity to interpret emotional signals from others and to react to them (Naoi et al., 2011).

The Beginning of Communication

Maternally produced infant-directed speech not only has strong influences on infants' processing of emotions, but also on establishment of the communication process itself. In an ERP study comparing infants' responses to words pronounced by their mother and by an unfamiliar woman, researchers found that early auditory components were accelerated in response to the mother's voice, and that infants were better able to learn words from their mothers (Dehaene-Lambertz et al., 2010). Maternal vocalizations elicit neural activity in the left hemisphere, particularly in the posterior temporal lobe (Dehaene-Lambertz et al., 2010; Purhonen et al., 2004), a network of cortical regions that will eventually emerge as the hub supporting language processing in the developing brain.

Maternal infant-directed speech affects early development of this language network in a variety of ways. First, infants strengthen emotional bonds by allocating attentional resources to their own mother's voice (Purhonen et al., 2004). Attending to the mother's speech can be highly rewarding for infants, providing additional motivation for infants to devote their attention to and selectively prefer their mothers' speech over the speech of others (Barker & Newman, 2004; Cooper et al., 1997). By securing infants' attention, maternal infant-directed speech allows infants to gain experience with the linguistic structure of their native language, while making language-related events more salient to the infant (Naoi et al., 2011). Infants can then begin segmenting the speech stream and learning the myriad object-label associations in their world (Graf Estes et al., 2007), a difficult process that is the foundation of subsequent language development.

Effect of Depressed Mothers on Child Language

The findings reviewed thus far serve to clarify the relationship between infants' speech preferences and processing biases. Clearly, maternal infant-directed speech is a critical component in infants' early language learning. The earliest infant preferences tend toward the perceptually salient, language-general (even nonlinguistic) aspects of an auditory scene, including infant-directed speech and positive effect (Mastropieri & Turkewitz, 1999; Singh et al., 2002) as reviewed here. Generally, infants can rely on their caregivers to produce speech full of such characteristics, and language development proceeds normally. But what happens to an infant's language when these aspects of the speech signal are compromised, as is the case in the speech of depressed mothers?

Positive speech greatly affects infants' social and linguistic development and, not surprisingly, there is growing evidence that an abundance of negative or neutral speech can have a detrimental effect on early development. For example, Weinberg and Tronick (1998) found that infants as young as three months are sensitive to their mothers' depression. Indeed, depressed mothers differ from nondepressed mothers in their effect and in the style of interaction they display with their infants. Depressed mothers express less positive effect, are less responsive, and tend to be emotionally withdrawn from their infants (Bigatti et al., 2001). In turn, infants of depressed mothers show impairment on a number of typical functions, including social, emotional, and cognitive ones (Weinberg & Tronick, 1998). While much research has been devoted to the negative effects of maternal depression on infant developmental outcomes in general, it has been more difficult to determine whether these effects directly relate to changes in the expression of emotion in the maternal speech itself.

Given that the affective quality of mothers' speech plays a role in language learning, it stands to reason that the lack of positive effect in depressed mothers' speech should affect this process. Indeed, Breznitz and Sherman (1987) found that depressed mothers vocalize less often and do not respond as quickly to the cessation of their children's speech as nondepressed mothers do. Since these depressed mothers do not reinforce communication, their children learn to keep interaction to a minimum and speak less in general. Similarly, Bigatti and colleagues (2001) observed that depressed mothers engage in fewer literacy-enhancing behaviors with their children than nondepressed mothers. When four years old, the children of depressed mothers scored lower on measures of language ability; by age five, maternal depression affected the children's performance in school (Bigatti et al., 2001). Additionally, depressed mothers were found to be less likely to use complex language with their children (e.g., questions, explanations, suggestions), which in turn affected the children's language abilities (Bigatti et al., 2001). These are just a handful of the results showing that negative maternal effect, both specific to speech and conveyed more generally, contributes to poor developmental outcomes, including language outcomes, in the children exposed to it.

While the general affective difference in speech produced by depressed mothers relative to nondepressed mothers is a factor in early language development, the quantity and complexity of language used by these mothers also appears to play a role. Many of the studies reviewed here focused on effects of maternal depression on language in children well past infancy. But research on the relationship between the sheer volume of language exposure during early infancy and subsequent language learning highlights another avenue by which maternal depression can influence the learning process, even in the first year of a child's life. In the next section, we review findings on the contribution of quantity of exposure to language development.

Structure in the Signal: Quality and Quantity Matter

From the inception of formal study of infant- and child-directed speech, researchers have noted the high frequency of exact and periphrastic repetitions of phrases and sentences

(Ferguson, 1964; Snow, 1972); the individual words contained in these phrases and sentences necessarily are repeated as well. In addition to speech quality, quantity of exposure has emerged as a key factor in the language learning process. Interestingly, quantity is something that was long taken for granted as a relative constant. In a seminal study, however, Hart and Risley (1995) demonstrated that the raw number of words children hear varies enormously as a function of a family's socioeconomic status, with average income families producing up to double the number of words as is produced by lower income families. These researchers made the (then provocative) suggestion that such differences in frequency of exposure might underlie the reliable differences in literacy outcomes observed as children from these families enter and proceed through formal education.

A wealth of research conducted since Hart and Risley's (1995) study has shown that the amount of language that infants and young children are exposed to before the age of three is, indeed, positively correlated with ensuing language production skills and cognitive development more generally (e.g., Arterberry et al., 2007; Bornstein & Haynes, 1998; Huttenlocher, 1991, Huttenlocher, 1998; Pan et al., 2005; Shonkoff & Phillips, 2000). This is often mediated by socioeconomic status (Hoff, 2003). It stands to reason then that the amount of language infants experience—even during the earliest stages of postnatal life—should affect the acquisition process. To understand how this may be, it helps to understand that particular aspects of language structure are consistent across languages. In recent years researchers have demonstrated that infants are highly sensitive to such structure, particularly when they have ample language around them from which to extract structural regularities.

Earlier, we reviewed findings on the influence of prosody (particularly that employed in infant-directed speech) on how infants attend to speech. We observed that, while prosodic form varies across languages, the infant-directedness of mothers' speech to infants does not. This prosodic structure helps infants separate continuous speech into smaller chunks of speech. Young learners can then use a variety of distributional strategies to pull words out of the chunks themselves. The simplest example of this is that *a priori* knowledge of certain high frequency words (e.g., the infant's own name) (Bortfeld et al., 2005) can help further delineate where other words begin and end. In other words, while prosodic organization of speech provides initial edges in otherwise continuous speech, continued exposure to the regular patterns within the smaller "chunks" of speech those edges create, allows infants to break them down further. This does, in fact, appear to be the case, as a wealth of recent evidence has highlighted different forms of structural information in the speech signal.

As demonstrated by Saffran and colleagues (Saffran, Aslin, & Newport, 1996), infants deal with the speech segmentation problem at least in part by taking advantage of distributions inherent in speech. In this study, infants were exposed to artificial languages that were synthesized so that there were no acoustic cues to word boundaries and no silences between syllables. The languages consisted of concatenated strings of trisyllabic nonsense words. Despite having no acoustic cues to guide the segmentation process, infants were able to distinguish between the languages' words (consistent trisyllabic strings) and "part words" (in this case, trisyllables created by pairing the syllable from the end of one word with the first two syllables of another) when these subsequently were presented to them in isolation. The researchers argued that the only way infants could distinguish words from partwords in these experiments was on the basis of the statistical coherence between syllables of words as compared to the lack of statistical coherence between partword syllables. Although words occurred more frequently than part words in the original experiment, these researchers subsequently demonstrated that infants' ability was not simply a function of frequency. Rather, infants discriminated words from part words on the basis of differences in their transitional probabilities (that is, the odds that one syllable would follow another) because the transitional probabilities are higher between syllables that are part of the same word and thus consistently occur together relative to those between partword syllables (Aslin et al., 1998).

The original research on this matter employed speech stimuli with nothing but statistical form, a design feature that was necessary to establish that infants can segment speech on the basis of statistical cues alone. Subsequent research has demonstrated that statistical structure interacts with a variety of other cues to structure, such as the prosodic contours inherent in infant-directed speech (Bortfeld & Morgan, 2010; Hay et al., 2011). While a review of the details of this more recent research is beyond the scope of this chapter, suffice it to say that if infants are learning about language based on the interaction of word frequency, the structural distributions within and between those words, and the acoustic cues that highlight which words go together, then the more speech an infant hears, the more likely he or she will be able to use all these cues as a guide to learning language. Consistent with Hart and Risley's (1995) original argument, there is now plenty of evidence that early differences in the amount of speech children are exposed to influences language ability in subsequent years of life. Indeed, researchers have returned to the rather obvious conclusion that language begins with simple exposure (and lots of it), inspiring a new generation of "talk-to-your-children" public service announcements. Indeed, if structure is inherent in the signal, then exposure to more of that signal will better allow a child to learn the structure.

The Importance of Adult–Infant "Conversations"

But if exposure matters, does it matter where the exposure is coming from? The push to get kids listening to more language—any language—has, in fact, raised as many questions about language learning as the research it was based on answered. For example, is overheard speech (e.g., speech between other speakers) as helpful as speech directed to the child him or herself? Does speech from electronic media count towards the total exposure tally? Does it matter if the speech is infant-directed, or will adult-directed speech serve the same purpose? These are just a sampling of the questions that the push for more exposure has raised. Of course, things are rarely as simple as they seem, and recent research suggests that mere exposure to adult speech is not sufficient for the development of language. Rather, an emerging view is that the most critical aspect of adults' speech to infants is that it fosters attempts on the infants' part to actually speak. Therefore, speech that does not foster a child's own speech, such as electronic television programs, may actually be counterproductive in helping children learn language.

Data support this view. In a recent study, Zimmerman and colleagues (2009) observed that the frequency of adult–child conversations was associated with robust language development. Conversely, after controlling specifically for interactive speech, no correlation was found between exposure to speech from television and other media and a child's subsequent language development. Rather, it appears that heavy media exposure during the early childhood years has a deleterious effect on language learning outcomes. Just a handful of these negative effects are: delays in language development, poor overall language development, poor reading skills, poor math skills, and problems with attention (Zimmerman & Christakis, 2005; Zimmerman et al., 2007; Zimmerman et al., 2009). One way that media can produce these negative outcomes is simply by reducing a child's opportunities for verbal interactions with his or her caregivers. Adding support to this argument are data showing that the number of conversational turns that adult caregivers and their children share is positively correlated with scores on a well-validated measure of language development (Zimmerman et al., 2009). Clearly, two-sided conversations are extremely important for language learning to proceed. Therefore, parents should not only be encouraged to provide their children with language input by speaking and reading to them, but they should try to get their young children speaking as much as possible too.

Two-Sided Conversation Provides Structured Input and Structured Feedback

Language is embedded in a social context and language learning takes place in the context of responsive social exchanges between caregivers and children. Of course, caregivers can elicit speech from their infants and young children in a variety of ways, particularly by being sensitive to their language abilities and responding to their efforts to speak in a supportive and contingent manner. Adults are most efficient at promoting language development when they calibrate their own speech to be just challenging enough for their child; neither so simplistic that the child learns nothing from the model, nor so sophisticated that the child is confused. Because maintaining adult speech in this range depends on a caregiver being in touch with his or her child's rapidly changing abilities, a caregiver's own frequent exposure to the child's language (e.g., through active conversation) will help guide appropriate tuning to the child's specific developmental level (Zimmerman et al., 2009).

But how do conversations between caregivers and infants proceed, given their inherent one-sidedness? Recent research on this topic has demonstrated that optimum occasions for language learning occur when adult speech is focused on and relevant to an infant's own attentional focus. Caregivers who are responsive to the foci of their infants' attention may specifically support advances in language development by providing labels for objects and events when they are receiving joint attention, thereby easing the challenge to infants of matching linguistic symbols to their referents and reinforcing the social-communicative function of language itself. When caregivers are particularly sensitive to their infants' interests and abilities, they will often match the semantic and syntactic content of their utterances to the children's level of understanding. For example, maternal speech that systematically matches infants' own speech on a variety of features strongly predicts children's linguistic abilities (Tamis-LeMonda et al., 2001). Mothers who respond to their children's communicative attempts during exploratory bouts key into the same topics of interest as their infants. The children "signal" choices about communication and mothers react to those signals in a sensitive manner. In this way, mothers provide infants with semantically relevant and interpretable speech because they follow up on topics introduced by the child him- or herself.

Aside from simply providing appropriate language structure at the appropriate time, direct, contingent interaction allows parents to provide error correction, whether explicitly or implicitly. Poverty-of-the-stimulus arguments (Chomsky, 1980) notwithstanding, early language development has been shown to benefit from active correction of errors by adult speakers. More conversations mean more opportunities for mistakes and corrections to be made, not to mention an increase in opportunities for children to use and consolidate newly acquired language. Finally, more conversation is a sign of greater adult responsiveness to a child's communication (Zimmerman et al., 2009), and thus the quality of the child's model for how to coordinate his or her attention with that of the social partner. A child's coordination skills have been shown to influence development of representational abilities in subsequent activities, such as in the language used during play (Adamson et al., 2004; Carpenter et al., 1998; Delgado et al., 2002; McCune 1995; Morales et al., 2005). The prevalence of "two-sided conversations" between caregivers and infants relate to the subsequent achievement of several language milestones (Nicely et al., 1999; Rollins, 2003; Tamis-LeMonda et al., 2001).

Contingent Learning: From Caregivers to Infants (and Back Again)

Beginning at the earliest stages of communication, infants' noncry vocalizations serve as salient social signals, and caregivers (socially and emotionally) reinforce these vocalizations. Indeed, contingent vocal responses to prelinguistic vocalizations are a typical characteristic of caregivers' reinforcing behavior. For example, caregivers spontaneously responded to 30–50 percent of noncry sounds in spontaneous interactions with their infants (Goldstein & West, 1999), and this responsiveness facilitated subsequent development of phonology and speech (Goldstein & Schwade, 2008; Goldstein et al., 2003; Gros-Louis et al., 2006). Several factors have been identified in this process.

First, maternal feedback to prelinguistic vocalizations influences the production of more developmentally advanced vocalizations, suggesting that effects of maternal responsiveness on vocal development start during the prelinguistic phase. In an analysis of unstructured play sessions between mothers and infants, mothers responded contingently to prelinguistic vocalizations over 70 percent of the time, and with more vocal responses than any other kind of response (e.g., gazes, smiling, physical contact) (Gros-Louis et al., 2006). Therefore, the form of behavioral responses from infants' social partners can encourage infants' own production of particular vocalizations, infants' vocal development (through the introduction of new sounds), and infants' efforts to improvise approximating speech sounds.

Second, adults' sensitivity to differences in prelinguistic vocalizations suggests that they may respond differently to different sounds, serving as a scaffold for language development. For example, mothers not only provided contingent responses to their infants' vocalizations, but those responses were specific to particular vocalization types (Gros-Louis et al., 2006). Mothers provided distinct verbal feedback to vowel-like and consonant–vowel vocalizations, giving interactive-vocal responses significantly more to consonant–vowel clusters than vowel-like sounds. These, in turn, resulted in an increase in the production of more developmentally advanced vocalizations on the part of the infants (Gros-Louis et al., 2006). Thus, co-occuring responses by mothers, in addition to their contingent responses, provide information to infants about the effectiveness of their vocal production. In this way, mothers encourage the use of particular sounds, giving them meaning, and frame interactions with infants through them (Papousek & Papousek, 1989).

But much of this research is correlational. To examine the role of caretaker–child interaction in vocal development in a more controlled way (i.e., beyond observations of natural, spontaneous interaction scenarios), researchers instructed mothers precisely *when* to respond to infant vocalizations (Goldstein, King, & West, 2003). Half of the infant–mother pairs tested were trained to respond contingently to infant's vocalizations with nonvocal social responses like smiling and touching, while the other half were instructed to respond based on the response schedules of the mothers in the contingent group, but to do so noncontingently. Infants who received social feedback contingent on their vocalizations produced more developmentally advanced vocalizations during the manipulation, as well as after maternal responding was no longer being manipulated, compared to those infants who received feedback independent of when they vocalized. Similar results have been observed in studies of unstructured mother–infant interactions (e.g., Hsu & Fogel, 2003).

In yet another study, when caregivers responded contingently to infants' vocalizations with speech, infants structured their own sounds to match the phonological patterns they heard (Goldstein & Schwade, 2008). For example, when infants were given vowel sounds as feedback, they produced more vowel sounds, but when they were given words as feedback, they produced more consonant–vowel combinations. This demonstrates that infant vocalizations can themselves be operantly conditioned with appropriate social reinforcement. In fact, changes in vocalizing in response to high levels of social reinforcement are a key characteristic of infant–caregiver dyadic interaction, and infants who learn the contingency between their own vocalizations and the responses of their caregivers have thus learned to influence the behavior of social partners; an important step forward in early communicative development.

In short, caregivers' contingent and positive responses to infants' vocalizations influence and advance these prelinguistic productions. Infants learn that their own vocalizations elicit responses, marking the beginning of their use of vocalizations as bids for social interaction. In this way, infants learn to guide the structure of interactions and to predict the outcome of ensuing interactions (i.e., to communicate). Thus, a functional perspective has emerged whereby infants' sounds can be understood not only in terms of their acoustic properties but also in terms of their ability to regulate and be regulated by social interactions with receivers of the sounds. This is infant communication.

Conclusion

Communication is inherently social. At the earliest stages of development, infants are being influenced by the sounds around them. Subsequently, caregivers' biases to communicate in particular ways help infants focus their attention specifically on speech sounds. The inherent structure of the speech signal together with the contingent structure of the infant–caregiver interaction serve to highlight regularities in speech and in interactive form; infants respond to this, as reflected in their subsequent productions of new vocal forms. Particular maternal responses, such as imitations and expansions, correlate positively with language development. Through these responses, infants learn the association between the production of certain sounds and their outcomes. Finally, caregivers' input during social interactions and early "conversations" scaffold language learning by providing information about activities and objects that are the focus of infants' attention in the first place. In sum, socially guided communication is fundamental to infants' initial vocal development, laying the foundation for subsequent advances in language learning.

References

Adamson, L. B., Bakeman, R., & Deckner, D. F. (2004). The development of symbol-infused joint engagement. *Child Development*, 75, 1171–87.

Arterberry, M. E., Midgett, C., Putnick, D. L., & Bornstein, M. H. (2007). Early attention and literacy experiences predict adaptive communication. *First Language*, 27, 175–89.

Aslin, R. N., Saffran, J. R., & Newport, E. L. (1998). Computation of conditional probability statistics by human infants. *Psychological Science*, 9, 321–24.

Barker, B. A., & Newman, R. S. (2004). Listen to your mother! The role of talker familiarity in infant streaming. *Cognition, 94*, B45–B53.

Bertoncini, J., & Mehler, J. (1981). Syllables as units in infant perception. *Infant Behavior and Development, 4*, 271–84.

Bigatti, S. M., Cronan, T. A., & Anaya, A. (2001). The effects of maternal depression on the efficacy of a literacy intervention program. *Child Psychiatry and Human Development, 32*, 147–62.

Bornstein, M. H., & Haynes, O. M. (1998). Vocabulary competence in early childhood: measurement, latent construct, and predictive validity. *Child Development, 69*, 654–71.

Bortfeld, H. & Morgan, J. (2010). Is early word-form processing stress-full? How natural variability supports recognition. *Cognitive Psychology, 60*, 241–66.

Bortfeld, H., Morgan, J., Golinkoff, R., & Rathbun, K. (2005). Mommy and me: familiar names help launch babies into speech stream segmentation. *Psychological Science, 16*, 298–304.

Breznitz, Z., & Sherman, T. (1987). Speech patterning of natural discourse of well and depressed mothers and their young children. *Child Development, 58*, 395–400.

Carpenter, M., Nagell, K., & Tomasello, M. (1998). Social cognition, joint attention, and communicative competence from 9 to 15 months of age. *Monographs of the Society for Research in Child Development, 63*(4), 1–174.

Chomsky, N. (1980). *Rules and representations.* Oxford: Basil Blackwell.

Christophe, A., & Dupoux, E. (1996). Bootstrapping lexical acquisition: the role of prosodic structure. *The Linguistic Review, 13*, 383–412.

Christophe, A., Dupoux, E., Bertoncini, J., & Mehler, J. (1994). Do infants perceive word boundaries? An empirical study of the bootstrapping of lexical acquisition. *Journal of the Acoustical Society of America, 95*, 1570–80.

Cooper, R. P. and Aslin, R. N. (1994). Developmental differences in infant attention to the spectral properties of infant-directed speech. *Child Development, 65*, 1663–77.

Cooper, R., Abraham, J., Berman, S., & Staska, M. (1997). The development of infants' preference for motherese. *Infant Behavior & Development, 20*, 477–88.

Cutler, A., Dahan, D. & van Donselaar, W. (1997). Prosody in the comprehension of spoken language: A literature review. *Language and Speech, 40*, 141–201.

Davidson, R. J., & Fox, N. A. (1982). Asymmetrical brain activity discriminates between positive and negative affective stimuli in human infants. *Science, 218*, 1235–37.

Dawson, G., Frey, K., Panagiotides, H., Yamada, E., Hessl, D., & Osterling, J. (1999). Infants of depressed mothers exhibit atypical frontal electrical brain activity during interactions with mother and with a familiar, nondepressed adult. *Child Development, 70*, 1058–66.

DeCasper, A. J., & Fifer, W. P. (1980). Of human bonding: Newborns prefer their mothers' voices. *Science, 208*, 1174–76.

DeCasper, A. J., Lecanuet, J., Busnel, M., & Granier-Deferre, C. (1994). Fetal reactions to recurrent maternal speech. *Infant Behavior & Development, 17*, 159–64.

DeCasper, A. J., & Prescott, P. A. (1984). Human newborns' perception of male voices: Preference, discrimination, and reinforcing value. *Developmental Psychobiology, 17*, 481–91.

DeCasper, A. J., & Spence, M. J. (1986). Prenatal maternal speech influences newborns' perception of speech sounds. *Infant Behavior and Development, 9*, 133–50.

Dehaene-Lambertz, G. G., Montavont, A. A., Jobert, A. A., Allirol, L. L., Dubois, J. J., Hertz-Pannier, L. L., & Dehaene, S. S. (2010). Language or music, mother or Mozart? Structural and environmental influences on infants' language networks. *Brain and Language, 114*, 53–65.

Delgado, C. E., Mundy, P., Crowson, M., Markus, J., Yale, M., & Schwartz, H. (2002). Responding to joint attention and language development: A comparison of target locations. *Journal of Speech, Language, and Hearing Research, 45*, 715–19.

Ferguson, C. A. (1964). Baby talk in six languages. *American Anthropologist, 66*, 103–14.

Fernald, A. (1992). Human maternal vocalizations to infants as biologically relevant signals: An evolutionary perspective. In J. H. Barkow, L. Cosmides, & J. Toobey (Eds.), *The adapted mind: Evolutionary psychology and the generation of culture* (pp. 391–428). Oxford: Oxford University Press.

Fernald, A., & Morikawa, H. (1993). Common themes and cultural variations in Japanese and American mothers' speech to infants. *Phonetica, 57*, 242–54.

Fernald, A., & Simon, T. (1984). Expanded intonation contours in mothers' speech to newborns. *Developmental Psychology, 20*, 104–13.

Fernald, A., Taeschner, T., Dunn, J., Papousek, M., Boysson-Bardies, B., & Fukui, I. (1989). A cross-language study of prosodic modifications in mothers' and fathers' speech to preverbal infants. *Journal of Child Language, 16*, 477–501.

Goldstein, M. H., King, A. P., & West, M. J. (2003). Social interaction shapes babbling: Testing parallels between birdsong and speech. *Proceedings of the National Academy of Sciences, 100*, 8030–35.

Goldstein, M. H., & Schwade, J. A. (2008). Social feedback to infants' babbling facilitates rapid phonological learning. *Psychological Science, 19*, 515–22.

Goldstein, M. H., & West, M. J. (1999). Consistent responses of human mothers to prelinguistic infants: The effect of prelinguistic repertoire size. *Journal of Comparative Psychology, 113*, 52–58.

Graf Estes, K., Evans, J. L., Alibali, M. W., & Saffran, J. R. (2007). Can infant map meaning to newly segmented words? Statistical segmentation and word learning. *Psychological Science, 18*, 254–60.

Gros-Louis, J., West, M. J., Goldstein, M. H., & King, A. P. (2006). Mothers provide differential feedback to infants' prelinguistic sounds. *International Journal of Behavioral Development, 30*, 509–16.

Hart, B. & Risley, T. R. (1995). *Meaningful Differences in the Everyday Experience of Young American Children*. Baltimore, MD: P. H. Brookes.

Hay, J. F., Pelucchi, B., Graf Estes, K., & Saffran, J. R. (2011). Linking sounds to meanings: Infant statistical learning in a natural language. *Cognitive Psychology, 63*, 93–106.

Hepper, P. G., & Shahidullah, S. B. (1994). Development of fetal hearing. *Archives of Disease in Childhoold Fetal Neonatal Edition, 71*, F81–F87.

Hoff, E. (2003). The specificity of environmental influence: socioeconomic status affects early vocabulary development via maternal speech. *Child Development, 74*, 1368–78.

Hsu, H. C., & Fogel, A. (2003). Social regulatory effects of infant nondistress vocalizations on maternal behavior. *Developmental Psychology, 39*, 976–91.

Huttenlocher, J. (1991). Early vocabulary growth: relation to language input and gender. *Developmental Psychology, 27*, 236–48.

——(1998). Language input and language growth. *Preventive Medicine, 27*, 195–99.

Jusczyk, P. W. (1997). *The Discovery of Spoken Language*. Cambridge, MA: MIT Press.

Kisilevsky, B. S., Hains, S. M. J., Jacquet, A. Y., Granier-Deferre, C., & Lecanuet, J. P. (2004). Maturation of fetal responses to music. *Developmental Science, 7*, 550–59.

Kisilevsky, B. S., Hains, S. J., Lee, K., Xie, X., Huang, H., Ye, H., Zhang, K., & Wang, Z. (2003). Effects of experience on fetal voice recognition. *Psychological Science, 14*, 220–24.

Kitamura, C., & Burnham, D. (1998). The infant's response to maternal vocal affect. In C. Rovee-Collier, L. Lipsitt, & H. Hayne (Eds.), *Advances in infancy research* (vol. XII, pp. 221–36). Stamford, CT: Ablex.

Mastropieri, D., & Turkewitz, G. (1999). Prenatal experience and neonatal responsiveness to vocal expressions of emotion. *Developmental Psychobiology, 35*, 204–14.

McCune, L. (1995). A normative study of representational play in the transition to language. *Developmental Psychology, 31*, 198–206.

Mehler, J., Bertoncini, J., Barrière, M., & Jassik-Gerschenfeld, D. (1978). Infant recognition of mother's voice. *Perception, 7*, 491–97.

Mehler, J., Jusczyk, P., Lambertz, G., Halsted, N., Bertoncini, J., & Amiel-Tison, C. (1988). A precursor of language acquisition in young infants, *Cognition, 29*, 143–78.

Moon, C., Panneton-Cooper, R., & Fifer, W. P. (1993). Two-day-olds prefer their native language. *Infant Behavior and Development, 16*, 495–500.

Morales, M., Mundy, P., Crowson, M. M., Neal, A. R., & Delgado, C. E. F. (2005). Individual differences in infant attention skills, joint attention, and emotion regulation behavior. *International Journal of Behavioral Development, 29*, 259–63.

Morgan, J., & Demuth, K. (Eds.) (1996). *Signal to syntax: bootstrapping from speech to grammar in early acquisition*. Mahwah, NJ: Lawrence Erlbaum Associates.

Morokuma, S., Fukushima, K., Kawai, N., Tomonaga, M., Satoh, S., & Nakano, H. (2004). Fetal habituation correlates with functional brain development. *Behavioural Brain Research, 153*, 459–63.

Naoi, N., Minagawa-Kawai, Y., Kobayashi, A., Takeuchi, K., Nakamura, K., Yamamoto, J., & Kojima, S. (2011). Cerebral responses to infant-directed speech and the effect of talker familiarity. *Neuroimage, 59*, 1735–44.

Nazzi, T., Bertoncini, J., & Mehler, J. (1998). Language discrimination by newborns. Towards an understanding of the role of rhythm. *Journal of Experimental Psychology: Human Perception and Performance, 24,* 1–11.

Newport, E. L. (1975). Motherese: the speech of mothers to young children. Ph.D. dissertation, University of Pennsylvania.

Nicely, P., Tamis-LeMonda, C. S., & Bornstein, M. H. (1999). Mother's attuned milestones. *Infant Behavior and Development, 22,* 557–68.

Ockleford, E. M., Vince, M. A., Layton, C., & Reader, M. R. (1988). Responses of neonates to parents' and others' voices. *Early Human Development, 18,* 27–36.

Pan, B. A., Rowe, M. L., Singer, J. D., & Snow, C. E. (2005). Maternal correlates of growth in toddler vocabulary production in low-income families. *Child Development, 76,* 763–82.

Papousek, M., Bornstein, M. H., Nuzzo, C., Papousek, H., & Symmes, D. (1990). Infant responses to prototypical melodic contours in parental speech. *Infant Behavior and Development, 13,* 539–45.

Papousek, M., & Papousek, H. (1989). Forms and functions of vocal matching in interactions between mothers and their precanonical infants. *First Language, 9,* 137–58.

Purhonen, M., Kilpeläinen-Lees, R., Valkonen-Korhonen, M., Karhu, J., & Lehtonen, J. (2004). Cerebral processing of mother's voice compared to unfamiliar voice in 4-month-old infants. *International Journal of Psychophysiology, 52,* 257–66.

Ramus, F., Hauser, M. D., Miller, C., Morris, D., & Mehler, J. (2000). Language discrimination by human newborns and by cotton-top tamarin monkeys. *Science, 288,* 349–51.

Rollins, P. R. (2003). Caregivers' contingent comments to 9-month-old infants: relationships with later language. *Applied Psycholinguistics, 24,* 221–34.

Saffran, J. R., Aslin, R. N., Newport, E. L. (1996). Statistical learning by 8-month-old infants. *Science, 274,* 1926–28.

Saito, Y., Aoyama, S., Kondo, T., Fukumoto, R., Konishi, N., Nakamura, K., Kobayashi, M., & Toshima, T. (2007). Frontal cerebral blood flow change associated with infant-directed speech. *Archives of Disease in Childhood Fetal Neonatal Edition, 92,* F113–16.

Shi, R., Werker, J. F., & Morgan, J. L. (1999). Newborn infants' sensitivity to perceptual cues to lexical and grammatical words. *Cognition, 72,* B11–B21.

Shonkoff, J. P., & Phillips D. (2000). *From neurons to neighborhoods: The science of early childhood development.* Washington, DC: National Academy Press.

Singh, L., Morgan, J. L., & Best, C. T. (2002). Infants' listening preferences: baby talk or happy talk? *Infancy, 3,* 365–94.

Snow, C. E. (1972). Mothers' speech to children learning language. *Child Development, 43,* 549–65.

Tamis-LeMonda, C. S., Bornstein, M. G., Kahana-Kalman, R., Baumwell, L., & Cyphers, L. (1998). Predicting variation in the timing of language milestones in the second year: an events history approach. *Journal of Child Language, 25,* 675–700.

Tamis-LeMonda, C. S., Bornstein, M. H., & Baumwell, L. (2001). Maternal responsiveness and children's achievement of language milestones. *Child Development, 72,* 748–67.

Ward, C. D., & Cooper, R. (1999). A lack of evidence in 4-month-old human infants for paternal voice preference. *Developmental Psychobiology, 35,* 49–59.

Weinberg, M. K., & Tronick, E. Z. (1998). Emotional characteristics of infants associated with maternal depression and anxiety. *Pediatrics, 102,* 1298–304.

Werker, J. F., & McLeod, P. J. (1989). Infant preference for both male and female infant-directed talk: a developmental study of attentional and affective responsiveness. *Canadian Journal of Psychology, 43,* 230–46.

Zimmerman, F. J., & Christakis, D. A. (2005). Children's television viewing and cognitive outcomes: a longitudinal analysis of national data. *Archives of Pediatric & Adolescent Medicine, 159,* 619–25.

Zimmerman, F. J., Christakis, D. A., & Meltzoff, A. N. (2007). Associations between media viewing and language development in children under age 2 years. *Journal of Pediatrics, 151,* 364–68.

Zimmerman, F. J., Gilkerson, J., Richards, J. A., Christakis, D. A., Xu, D., Gray, S., & Yapanel, U. (2009). Teaching by listening: the importance of adult-child conversations to language development. *Pediatrics, 124,* 342–49.

16

Parent and Sibling Interactions During Middle Childhood

Laura Stafford

Only recently has middle childhood garnered serious research attention, as children's early experiences were once thought to be the driving, and even immutable, force behind adult development and behavior. An emphasis on the influence of early childhood left little room for interest in family interaction beyond the first few years (Goodnow, 2006). Over the past few decades this view has been substantively challenged. In 1984, a landmark report concluded that the experiences of middle childhood played a more critical predictive role in later adolescence and adulthood than did those of early childhood (Collins, 1984). In summarizing a more recent longitudinal series of studies Huston and Ripke (2006) reached a similar conclusion: "Although the preschool years establish the base for future development, experiences in middle childhood can sustain, magnify, or reverse the advantages or disadvantages that children acquire in the preschool years" (p. 2).

It is now accepted that middle childhood experiences are of consequence. One type of such middle childhood experience, interaction with parents and siblings, is the focus here. Attention is given to the role parenting, coparenting, parental differential treatment to siblings, and to the role sibling relationships appear to play in school age children's immediate assets (i.e., social competencies) and engagement in risky behaviors. Social competencies are of concern due to their associations with peer competencies and hence appropriate socialization. Risky behaviors are deemed significant for the immediate health and well-being of the child.

Middle childhood, often referred to as "school age," is generally considered as approximately five to 12 years of age. The beginning is marked by the entry into formal education, around age five in most Western societies. Thirteen is considered to be the entry point into adolescence and thus the end of middle childhood. The ultimate goal during this period is the appropriate socialization of the child into adolescence and adulthood. Though family structures and forms vary greatly, when children are involved the family is charged with the function of socialization (Lerner & Spainer, 1978). Once considered the task of the mother, increasingly socialization is recognized as occurring within a family system (Bowen, 1978). Attention has turned to parenting by both parents, the interaction between parents, and the influence of siblings.

Of course, what counts as appropriate socialization varies considerably by culture and time (Goode & Jones, 2008). Even within the U.S.A., during the past century cultural emphasis has shifted away from compliance and obedience of the school age child (Smith, 1999) to social competencies (Peterson & Hann, 1999). These social skills should manifest in peer proficiency and academic achievement (Sroufe, Egeland, Carlson, & Collins, 2005). It is during middle childhood that children must demonstrate the ability to navigate school achievement and peer relationships in order to successfully transition into adolescence and adulthood (DeFries, Plomin, & Fulker, 1994). The domains generally prioritized as the tasks of middle childhood, not surprisingly, mirror those prioritized by current Western society as appropriate adult socialization: relational and occupational success.

Though both academic and peer success are considered developmental tasks of this age, greater attention to peer success is granted here. Even so, it should be noted that peer relationships and academic achievement are inter-related and both are associated with immediate health and well-being of the child. Children who fare well in school have fewer behavioral problems in the short run and higher life satisfaction and more successful relationships in the long run (Durlak, 2001).

Social Competencies

"Peer competence ... refers to the ability of children to maintain positive relationships with others over time and successfully achieve personal goals in different social situations" (Wong, Diener, & Isabella, 2008, p. 176). Early research concentrated on rejection by peers and the association between rejection by peers and later adulthood problems is well documented (Bagwell, Schmidt, Newcomb, & Bukowski, 2001).

Recently, multiple longitudinal studies (some over 40 years) emphasize the value of peer acceptance. Harmonious peer relationships are predictive of higher rates of retention and advancement at work, more satisfying romantic relationships, and a lower incidence of relational violence (Collins & van Dulmen, 2006). Peer competencies are also coupled with adult occupational success (Masten, Desjardins, McCormick, Kuo, & Long, 2010). In addition to long-term correlates, peer acceptance or rejection is related to a host of more proximal correlates such as emotional and behavioral problems, school drop out, and substance abuse (Goodnow, 2006).

Neither peer competence nor academic success can be achieved without underlying social or communicative competencies. However, such competencies were not of concern in early work. Hopper (1971) noted that considerable research had been devoted to language development, but scarce attention had been given to the development of communication competencies or to the ways children learn to interact in social situations. The Speech Communication Association (now known as the National Communication Association) came to share this view issuing a report on the development of children's communication skills (Allen & Brown, 1976). Though work on language development continues to overshadow that on communication development, a sizable body of research on child communication competencies has been generated. Three global categories of communication competencies seem to be particularly relevant to peer relationships. These include the provision of emotional support, the management of conflict, and the use of display rules.

"The capacity to provide emotional support is a central component of the child's social competence" (Burleson & Kunkel, 2002, p. 81). Indeed growing evidence reveals that children who skillfully provide emotional support and comfort are better liked and accepted (Clark, MacGeorge, & Robinson, 2008) and fare better academically (Burleson

& Kunkel, 2002) than those less skilled. The provision of emotional support includes comforting, expressing sympathy, advising, helping, and sharing (Clark et al., 2008).

Similarly, children who are able to engage in amicable conflict resolution are more likely to be accepted by others (Kupersmidt & Dodge, 2004) and to achieve academic success (Westby, 1998). Alternatively, aggression and coercion as conflict strategies are associated with rejection and peer difficulties (Rubin, Bukowski, & Parker, 1998). Despite such findings, it is probable that no one specific strategy is uniformly better or worse. Rather, social competence may entail the use of the appropriate strategy for a particular conflict with a particular person (Joshi, 2008). The socially skilled child knows when "anti-social" strategies might be effectively employed.

Finally, display rules have been defined as "socially appropriate emotional responses to a given situation" (McDowell & Parke, 2000, p. 415). These involve proper emotional expression and management of aggression. Both physical and social aggression and the inappropriate use of display rules in middle childhood have been linked to low school achievement and difficulty with peer relationships (Underwood, Beron, & Rosen, 2009).

Of course social competencies, peer acceptance, and the engagement in deviant or risky behaviors cannot be separated. Acceptance by all peers is not necessarily positive. Clearly, inclusion in the wrong peer group (e.g., gangs) can hold sway on engagement in risky behaviors. Also, involvement in gangs in early adolescence is potentially precipitated through the exclusion or rejection by other perhaps more socially acceptable peers during middle childhood (Dishion, Nelson, & Yasui, 2005) and this exclusion may well be traced back to a dearth of social competencies.

Though most attention has been given to the accomplishments of peer acceptance and it's requisite social competencies, and to some extent academic achievement, growing attention is being paid to the function family interaction serves in the immediate health and well-being of the child, such as the engagement in high risk behaviors such as drug abuse, early sexual activity, smoking, or criminal activity.

Parenting

The general principle that parents influence the socialization of children is virtually universally accepted (Cummings, Davies, & Campbell, 2000; Maccoby, 1992). Despite the growing and diverse number of theories of family interaction (see Caughlin, Koerner, Schrodt, & Fitzpatrick, 2011) across disciplines, scholars have largely agreed on two major dimensions of parenting associated with socialization: control and warmth. In addition, given concern with risky behaviors such as smoking, drug use and the like, research has begun to accumulate on parental targeted talk to children about such behaviors.

Parenting as warmth is the demonstration of acceptance, emotional availability, and sensitivity. Parenting as control is the management of a child's behaviors (Cummings et al., 2000). Positive parenting as control includes clearly setting rules, consistent enforcement of those rules, monitoring and supervision, consideration of the child's viewpoint, and discipline through induction and reasoning.

The two dimensions of warmth and control form the basis of Baumrind's (1971) well-known parenting styles wherein the authoritative style (appropriate levels of expression of parental warmth or acceptance, clear boundaries, expressions of support, and appropriate exertion of control) is considered optimal (Hillaker, Brophy-Herb, Villarruel, & Haas, 2008). Indeed, inappropriate or inconsistent control or warmth has been linked not only to deficits in social communication competencies and the ability to form successful peer relationships but also with child delinquency, externalizing behaviors, eating disorders, and self-esteem issues (Kjobli & Hagen, 2009; Segrin, 2006; Underwood et al., 2009).

Though not always labeled as such, much family communication can be subsumed under the global categories of control and warmth going back at least until Symonds (1939). Further, many prominent approaches to the study of family interaction are akin to or extensions of these fundamental concepts. For example, Fitzpatrick and colleagues' (e.g., Fitzpatrick & Ritchie, 1994; Koerner & Fitzpatrick, 2006) work on family communication patterns directly builds on these ideas. In discussing the school age child's environment they note: "Family communication environments vary in their levels of restrictiveness and permissiveness as well as in their levels of warmth and openness" (Fitzpatrick & Marshall, 1996, p. 380). Within this program of study, interactions are conceptualized as involving conformity orientations (the degree of use of parental power in guiding conversations) and conversation orientations (the degree of warmth encouragement of the child to be expressive and contributive) and are built around the ideas of control and warmth or demandingness and responsiveness.

The notions of warmth and control are also evident in Olson's much investigated circumplex model (e.g., Olson, Russell, & Sprenkle, 1989). The two primary dimensions of this model are flexibility and cohesion. Flexibility involves the control in terms of the adaptation of rules, roles, and power structures. Cohesion refers to the emotional bonding or closeness of the family members and thus is akin to warmth. A third dimension of the circumplex model is communication. Optimal communication in this model involves attentiveness and empathy which can also be related to warmth.

Parents facilitate (or inhibit) social competencies not only through their direct interaction with their children. Parents also are consequential for the development of competencies through the provision of opportunities for children. Children whose parents provide appropriate opportunities seem to be more accepted by their peers (McDowell & Parke, 2009). For example, school age children who participate in organized activities outside of school (e.g., sports teams or school clubs) have been found to have higher social skills than those who do not. Of course children who participate may initially have higher social skills (Howie, Lukacs, Pastor, Reuben, & Mendola, 2010). Provision of appropriate opportunities brings with it the risk of exposure to undesired ones. As part and parcel of socialization, parents serve as gate-keepers and monitors of children's use of unstructured time.

An interaction opportunity warranting parental gate-keeping even within the home is the school age child's use of communication technologies such as the Internet and mobile phone. ICTs are now simply inherent in the larger role of parenting (Shepherd, Arnold, & Gibbs, 2006). Receiving a mobile phone is a rite of passage and the age at which a child receives a mobile phone continues to decline (Nurullah, 2009). Access to such technologies can provide opportunities for the development of social competencies as peer relationships are increasingly conducted online and via mobile phone.

Some investigations connect child engagement in emailing, chatting, and messaging to less loneliness and high quality friendships. Alternatively, intensive playing of online games or simply surfing has been connected to lower social competencies. Of course cause and effect are not known; those with good peer skills may more easily engage in online communicative activities with peers and those without such skills might be more inclined to engage in individual gaming and surfing (Punamäki, Wallenius, Hölttö, Nygård, & Rimpelä, 2009).

Parents are differentially knowledgeable or skilled in providing guidance in their children's use of multiple technologies (Berson, Wang, Jaruszewicz, Hartle, & Rosen, 2010). Yet even those with knowledge are differentially involved in setting boundaries. Parental warmth and control are related to the way in which children use the Internet (Valcke, Bonte, Wever, & Rots, 2010). Permissive parenting can increase exposure to risks (e.g., cyber-bulling or exploitation). Authoritarian parenting can squelch a child's use of technology for both peer and educational functions. (See Jennings and Wartella, Chapter 27, this volume, for a discussion of communication technology and the family).

Parental warmth and control during middle childhood are relevant to the immediate health and well-being of the child. When it comes to the engagement in risky and unhealthy behaviors, peers are often thought to have more authority in the middle school years, but some propose that parental input has been underestimated. At least in some domains, such as substance abuse, parents are likely to be more powerful than peers during middle childhood (Kelly, Comello, & Edwards, 2004). Harsh parenting in terms of verbal attacks, physical discipline, and especially physical and sexual abuse increase the likelihood of substance abuse, whereas discipline through discussion and reasoning seems to act in a preventative manner (Dodge, Malone, Lansford, Miller-Johnson, Pettit, & Bates, 2006).

In addition to examining global parental styles and unhealthy behaviors, talking directly about such behaviors merits attention. Most examinations are concerned simply with frequency of talk or whether or not parents are open or willing to talk with children. Mere frequency or openness may not be an effective disincentive (Miller-Day & Kam, 2010). Rather, the enactment of targeted communication is advocated. Targeted communication includes warnings, providing advice in regard to peer pressure, setting rules, and even relaying personal stories with the direct intent of deterrence. An effect for parental target talk on predicting intentions of both drug use and alcohol use, as well as delaying the onset of sexual activity have been found (Miller-Day, 2008; Miller-Day & Kam, 2010; O'Donnell, Wilson-Simmons, Dash, Jeanbaptiste, Myint, Moss, & Stueve, 2007).

Despite a cultural emphasis on talking to children about such issues, and parental beliefs that they should, many parents do not (Wilson, Dalberth, Koo, & Gard, 2010). The likelihood of engaging in targeted talk seems to be somewhat contingent on the family environment and warm relationships between parents and children (Miller-Day, 2008; Wilson et al., 2010). Other factors predictive of targeted talk often include the parent's own comfort level, experience or knowledge of the topic, perceptions that children are too young, or doubts about the efficacy of such talk (Deblinger, Thakkar-Kolar, Berry, & Schroeder, 2010; Wilson et al., 2010).

Coparenting

Interactions between some family members impact (or spill over) to the relationships between other family members (Belsky, 1984). In theory, the quality of parental interaction affects the child as this interaction is argued to influence individual parenting practices and therefore child behavior. Coparenting, in particular, has received significant attention. (See Beaton, Doherty, & Wenger, Chapter 14, this volume).

Coparenting was first considered as occurring between divorced individuals who attempted to continue joint parenting (see Ahrons, 1981). Such joint effort between ex-spouses was considered dysfunctional and clearly not in the best interest of the child by most family therapists well into the 1980s (Ahrons, 2007). However, since that time, it has been recognized that positive coparenting relationships between caregivers regardless of marital or residential status is important for children. Coparenting can be thought of as interactions that occur between the child's caregivers in regard to parenting regardless of marital status. Coparenting consists of many aspects including division of child care, engagement in day-to-day lives of children, as well as the degree to which parents endorse or undermine each other's parenting practices. This concept has also been applied in the context of step-parent–parent relationships. Conceivably, the concept of coparenting could extend to other caregiver relationships (e.g., when a grandparent and parent share primary child care responsibilities).

With a school age child, spillover effects of coparenting might emerge either in positive domains such as collaboration and cooperation, or negative ones such as hostility and conflict (Kjobli & Hagen, 2009). More research has examined negative aspects than positive. There is abundant evidence that difficult parental interactions are related to problematic parenting practices, and resultant problematic child outcomes. This seems to be especially the case in regard to overt and negative conflict. Parental conflict may be physically and mentally exhausting, generating negative emotions (e.g., anger) in a parent (Kjobli & Hagen, 2009) which in turn elicits harsh, unsupportive, and inconsistent parenting. It is also plausible that poor coparenting may decrease relational satisfaction or increase conflict, which both reciprocally feed back into problematic parenting practices and in turn increases the possibility of problematic child behavior resulting in strained parenting practices (Morrill, Hines, Mahmood, & Cordova, 2010).

Less study has considered whether collaborative positive parenting acts in the same manner (Segrin, 2006). However, evidence is beginning to accumulate in support of the idea that positive coparental interaction promotes positive parent–child interactions (Doohan, Carrere, Siler, & Beardslee, 2009). The same reciprocal effects may be found; parents who are collaborative tend to use more effective parenting resulting in cooperative children and consequently do not engage in a negative bidirectional cycle between child behavior and coparenting but rather a positive one.

Parental Differential Treatment

The majority of investigations of parenting only considers one child. Parenting often occurs simultaneously with two or more children. Though in the U.S.A., strong cultural norms have long existed against demonstrating a preference for one offspring or another (McHale, Updegraff, Jackson-Newsom, Tucker, & Crouter, 2000; Parsons, 1974), such a sentiment, its enactment by parents and perceptions of parental preferential treatment by children are not uncommon. It should be noted however, that differential treatment is not necessarily preferential treatment, though some research considers the two synonymously and have assumed that differential treatment is almost inherently preferential, or at least perceived by children as such.

Like other research on parenting, study of parental differential treatment has focused on the two global areas of control and parental responsiveness or warmth. Numerous studies have offered some support to the premise that preferential treatment is associated with poorer individual adjustment as well as poor relationships between siblings (Atzaba-Poria & Pike, 2008; McHale et al., 2000). The least favored child is more likely to exhibit lower feelings of self-worth and self-esteem, more depression, higher levels of aggression, and problematic externalization behaviors (Suitor, Sechrist, Plikuhn, Pardo, & Pillemer, 2008). Evidence is less conclusive about the effects of being the favored child. However, the bulk of the evidence suggests that parental preferential treatment is a problematic issue for all siblings. The most consistent set of findings is that inequitable treatment is negatively associated with the quality of siblings' relationships with each other (Suitor et al., 2008).

Children's perceptions of differing parenting are not always negative. Siblings might recognize parental differences, yet see such treatment as fair and reasonable rather than preferential. School age children's perceptions of the fairness of differential treatment between themselves and their adolescent siblings is more predictive of their own adjustment and their relationship with their siblings than the perception of mere differential treatment per se (McHale et al., 2000). Differential parenting can and often is appropriate parenting when parents are responsive to individual differences in children, and siblings may be aware of this (Kowal & Kramer, 1997). It is preferential treatment, or children's perception of such, that is of concern.

Some scholars examine potential causes of parental differential and preferential treatment rather than the outcomes of such treatment. Much speculation is offered that different parenting towards different children is largely determined by the children. Perhaps parents respond to genetic differences, differences in children's personalities and actions, or the child's health (Suitor et al., 2008). Differential treatment of siblings may also occur based on the age of child, the age gap between children, and differing relationships among siblings (Suitor et al., 2008; Turkheimer & Waldron, 2000).

Differential parenting practices may be predicted by factors other than the child as well. Levels of marital satisfaction appear to be associated with differential treatment of siblings (Atzaba-Poria & Pike, 2008). Favoritism has often been found to be more prevalent when parents are having marital problems or when they are experiencing more stress (Suitor et al., 2008). Less uniform parenting is also more likely in chaotic households (Kretschmer & Pike, 2009).

Siblings

Though parents are charged with socialization, siblings' relationships also play a substantial role in this socialization (Jenkins & Dunn, 2009). During middle childhood, children generally spend more time with their siblings than with their parents. Children often develop bonds with siblings prior to other peers, and sibling relationships are formed well before romantic ones. Siblings sometimes reside together in the absence of one or both parents, and siblings typically outlive their parents. As a consequence, a sibling relationship is often one's longest lasting relationship throughout life.

Siblings may be warm, affectionate, and collaborative, or quarrelsome, jealous, and aggressive, or experience conflicted feelings about each other. The sibling relationship is complex and varies tremendously across sibling pairs even in the same household (Jenkins & Dunn, 2009). For example, when they are younger, a greater power and knowledge difference is often evident, yielding an asymmetrical relationship in some ways similar to a parent–child relationship. A school age child may care for younger siblings and provide guidance in instrumental tasks. The same child might turn to older siblings as confidants, resources, or mediators with parents. As children become older, they move closer and closer to peer-like relationships of relatively equal power.

Sibling relationships are connected to children's adjustment (Brody, 1998). Like parental relationships, more attention has been given to sibling conflict or hostility and potential problematic behavior than to the potential for sibling relationships to be associated with prosocial behavior. Sibling conflict during middle childhood has been related to depression, anxiety, and delinquency even after controlling for individual parent–child relationships and quality of marital relationships (Stocker, Burwell, & Briggs 2002). Sibling conflict can give rise to behavioral issues and social skills deficits (Kim, McHale, Crouter, & Osgood, 2007). Yet, some associations between sibling conflict and child problems have been shown to be quite small, indicating that conflict among siblings may be normative.

A certain amount of sibling rivalry and conflict might not only be normative, but might be promotive of social competencies. School age children with one or more siblings have been found to have better social skills than only children (Downey & Condron, 2004). Only children have been found to be less liked by peers and more likely to be victimized by peers in middle childhood, indicating that siblings provide opportunities to develop social skills as well as experience in conflict management (Kitzman, Cohen, & Lockwood, 2002).

Though less research on warm sibling relationships has been conducted than on con-flictual ones, and some investigations suggest the possibility the mere presence of a sibling tends to promote social competencies, some work specifically addresses positive relation-ships. Warm relationships among siblings appear to be more predictive of individual outcomes and positive adjustment than difficult ones (Pike, Coldwell, & Dunn, 2005). Further, cooperative and friendly play among siblings seems to be associated with social skills in peer interactions (Downey & Condron, 2004). Siblings can also provide social support for one another as well as model and reinforce desired social behaviors (Kim et al., 2007).

The relationship between siblings appears to be related to the effectiveness of parental conflict intervention. When school age siblings have a warm relationship and parents have modeled positive conflict management in triadic play with school age children, children are likely to invoke those same techniques in dyadic play. However, when siblings have less warm relationships, they are less likely to invoke those positive techniques in the parent's absence (Recchia & Howe, 2009).

Though a warm relationship between siblings is generally desirable, in some circum-stances, warmth might have its drawbacks. Sibling deviant behavior coupled with a warm sibling relationship has been connected to substance abuse (Stormshak, Comeau, & Shepard, 2004). Siblings, especially those with warm relationships, can provide support and reinforcement of deviant behavior for each other (Kim et al. 2007). Though most research on substance abuse focuses on peer pressure, siblings may be a stronger force than peers for two reasons. First, in middle childhood siblings are likely to spend more time with each other than with peers. Second, sibling relationships are more likely to be continuous whereas sets of peers can change with changes in schools, family moves, or changes in parenting arrangements (Stormshak et al. 2004).

Family Systems and Beyond

Numerous theories have been applied to family interaction. Arguably, most theories of family interaction can be subsumed within family systems theory and extensions or modifications thereof. Systems theories have been applied specifically to families with school age children going back at least to Minuchin (1974). Though general systems theory can be traced to von Bertalanffy (1968), the systems framework most often applied to families is Bronfenbrenner's (1986) ecological perspective.

Though family systems ostensibly are concerned with the multi-directional influences of individuals and relationships on other individuals and relationships, even within a systems perspective family interaction during middle childhood ultimately centers on child outcomes. Though not denying multi-directional interactions with macroscopic cultural forces or microscopic genetic ones, systems theorists maintain that the relationships between the individuals within the family are of most consequence for the child (Belsky, 1984; Hinde & Stevenson-Hinde, 1987).

Family systems include boundaries, fluidity and change, interdependence, multi-directional and circular causality, and openness (Stafford & Dainton, 1995). Systems are conceived of as recursive spirals moving through time (Kouros, Cummings, & Davies, 2010).

Family boundaries can be manifested as structures and they are simply too diverse to pronounce one form as typical (Caughlin et al., 2011). Parents might or might not cohabitate, might or might not be married, might be homosexual or heterosexual. Parents might be biological, step, foster or adoptive. Primary caregivers might be cross-residential or cross-generational. Siblings can be biological, adoptive, step, half, functional, foster or fictive. Biological siblings can live in different households. Regardless of the plethora of family structures, socialization largely occurs during middle childhood. And this socialization is the responsibility of the family, and communication is central to this task (Caughlin, Petronio, & Middleton, this volume). Aside from a few limited domains (e.g., divorced families), research is sparse beyond the "traditional" family structure. This is especially the case in regard to various sibling configurations such as the relationships among siblings across households. What little research that does exist, seldom focuses on the school age child.

Family structures are not only diverse, they are fluid; family boundaries are not permanent. Families may go through several structural transitions (e.g., divorce, remarriage) (Kouros et al., 2010). Parents, other caregivers, or siblings can move in and out of the home due to divorce, (re)marriage, employment, incarceration or deployment. Children who have experienced numerous transitions have lower general well-being than those who have experienced only one or no transitions.

Scholarship is more likely to be focused on structures than on fluidity or family interactions accompanying transitions. Transitions early in elementary school have been correlated with later friendship difficulties and loneliness in later grade school (Cavanagh & Huston, 2008). Such changes can threaten a child's sense of security and connection and generate stress in caregivers who in turn may offer poorer or less consistent parenting.

Family interactions during transitional periods can also function protectively. For example, "optimistic communication" about family transitions during middle childhood appears to help children maintain a sense of security during such changes (Winter, Davies, & Cummings, 2010). However, this seems most likely to occur when levels of disruption are low. The same buffering effect is not as pronounced among children with high levels of family instability. Siblings have sometimes been found to be a source of support for school age children during stressful transitions as well (Gass, Jenkins, & Dunn, 2007).

Change is inherent in open systems and, due to interdependence among family members, modifications in the relationships between some family members affect other family members. For instance, marital conflict is associated with childhood problems but the nature of marital interactions is not consistent. One study found that a decrease in parental conflict over a three-year period of early middle childhood was more predictive of child problems than was initial marital conflict (Kouros et al., 2010). Similarly, increases in sibling conflict from middle childhood through adolescence are linked to increases in depressive symptoms during that time frame, whereas increases in sibling intimacy are linked to decreases in depressive symptoms and increases in peer competencies (Kim et al., 2007). Further, among siblings, as perceptions of parental differential treatment lessen across middle childhood and adolescence, so do symptoms of depression (Shanahan, McHale, Crouter, & Osgood, 2008).

Family systems consider not only parental or sibling influences on children, but also bi- and multi-directional influences and circular causality. As noted, family systems theorists often center attention on child development. However, children are also causal agents within the family system. For example, though parents are typically thought to socialize the children, children also socialize parents, often through the introduction to new experiences and domains, such as school clubs and sporting events, especially during the school age years (Ambert, 2001). One example is in the realm of communication technologies. It is acknowledged that by the time children are tweens, if not before, they often know more about computer use than parents. Children often serve as the socializing agent of the parents into the world online. Further, children who have warm relationships with their parents are more likely to actively teach their parents about the Internet than those who do not (Grossbart, Hughes, Pryor, & Yost 2002).

Influence with the system can be circular. For example, school age children's time online has been associated with poorer parent–child relationships. This could be the child choosing to spend more time online due to problematic parent–child relationships or the increased online time might cause poor parent–child relationships. Perhaps each circularly reinforces the other. Or possibly this finding reflects the typical development of moving from parents to peers during later middle childhood (Punamäki et al., 2008).

Systems are not only comprised of multiple sub-systems, they are also open systems with neighborhoods, communities and cultures. Scholars have tended to emphasize either the family or the community on the child's engagement in deviant behaviors. Criminologists have placed more emphasis on neighborhood, and developmentalists more on family (Goodnow, 2006). A typical way to accommodate both views is to consider the family as allowing the development of susceptibility to certain types of behavior, and the neighborhood the opportunity for engagement (Goodnow, 2006). Cultures or communities have often been thought by developmental scholars as playing an indirect role in child outcomes through influences on parenting practices. A more systemic approach is to consider the complex and mutual direct and indirect contributions of the community to the family interactions and to the child (Goodnow, 2005).

Systems affect changes within systems over time (Masten & Chicchetti, 2010). As systems morph, questions arise about the potential cumulative effects and about the unique or immutable contributions of middle childhood interactions and environments. Systemic life-span development perspectives recognize that multiple systems through multiple domains interact and affect each other across time and that multi-directional interactions within one system at one point in time affect and are affected by other interactions at other points in time.

Conclusions

As should be clear, most research on families with a school age child remains unidirectional in nature, concentrating on the parental (or sibling) effects on the child's development. Increased attention should be given to children as active agents and the ways in which they might influence their families. Even though primary focus continues on a child's socialization as the outcome, our knowledge remains limited. To date we can offer global conclusions that appropriate levels of parental warmth and control, positive (or at least nonconflicted) interactions between coparents, perceived equitable treatment of siblings, and positive sibling relationships, appear to facilitate the school age child's short term social and academic competencies as well as long-term adolescent and adult socialization. Moreover, paths of association may be direct and indirect. For example, the manner in which parents interact with children influences cognitive components that aid the child in social information processing which in turn guides their interactions and hence their peer acceptance (Rah & Parke, 2008).

It must not be forgotten that a child's course of development is constantly changing as family structures, interactions, relationships and communities change. Maturation is a series of nonsummative recursive loops. That is, the whole of one's experiences are not uniquely defined by any one interaction, nor are interactions merely summative. Further interdependence and circular causality yield directionality of influence on children almost impossible to definitively discern. As a consequence, it is difficult to ascertain if family interaction during middle childhood is indeed truly a unique contributor to long-term socialization. Nevertheless, research in the past few decades suggests that this time period, and family interactions within this time period, may well be especially critical, much more so than previous generations had assumed. In addition, it is unequivocal that interactions between school age children and their families is of great consequence to children's immediate health and well-being.

Though certainly of importance, it is unlikely that early experiences, even those within the formative period of middle childhood, are immutable. Also, more than one course or trajectory is possible, as from different places, through different means, individuals may reach the same end. No one way to parent, no one type of family structure, no one type of sibling relationship serves all children equally well. Despite such complexities, or perhaps because of them, family communication scholars should continue to strive to understand the types of interactions that appear to serve families well and to act as advocates for the translation of research into best family practices. Nonetheless, even in the "best" family environments some children falter. In turn, though particular types of family interactions may seem to be maladaptive, considerable evidence points to children's resilience and their propensity to develop into healthy adults despite the communication practices within their families.

References

Ahrons, C. R. (2007). Introduction to the special issue on divorce and its aftermath. *Family Process*, 46, 3–6.

——(1981). The continuing coparental relationship between divorced spouses. *American Journal of Orthopsychiatry*, 51, 415–28.

Allen, R. R., & Brown, K. L. (Eds.) (1976). *Developing communication competence in children: A report of the Speech Communication Association's national project of speech communication competencies*. Falls Church, VA: Speech Communication Association.

Ambert, A. M. (2001). *The effects of children on parents*, 2nd edn). Binghampton, NY: Hawthorne Press.

Atzaba-Poria, N., & Pike, A. L. (2008). Correlates of parental differential treatment: Parental and contextual factors during middle childhood. *Child Development*, 79, 217–32.

Bagwell, C. L., Schmidt, M. E., Newcomb, A. F., & Bukowski, W. M. (2001). Friendship and peer rejection as predictors of adult adjustment. In D. W. Nangle & C. A. Erdley (Eds.), *New directions for child and adolescent development: The role of friendship in psychological adjustment*, Vol. XCI (pp. 25–49). San Francisco, CA: Jossey Bass.

Baumrind, D. (1971). Current patterns of parental authority. *Developmental Psychology*, 4, 1–103.

Belsky, J. (1984). The determinants of parenting: A process model. *Child Development*, 55, 83–96.

Berson, I., Wang, X., Jaruszewicz, C., Hartle, L. & Rosen, D. (2010). Young children's technology experiences in multiple contexts: Bronfenbrenner's ecological theory reconsidered. In I. R. Berson & M. J. Berson (Eds.), *High tech tots: Childhood in a digital world* (pp. 23–47). Greenwich, CT: Information Age.

Bowen, M. (1978). *Family therapy in clinical practice*. New York: Jason Aronson.

Brody, G. H. (1998). Sibling relationship quality: Its causes and consequences. *Annual Review of Psychology*, 49, 1–24.

Bronfenbrenner, U. (1986). Ecology of the family as a context for human development: Research perspectives. *Developmental Psychology*, 22, 723–42.

Burleson, B. R., & Kunkel, A. (2002). Parental and peer contributions to the emotional support skills of the child: From whom do children learn to express support? *The Journal of Family Communication*, 2, 79–97.

Caughlin, J. P., Koerner, A. F., Schrodt, P., & Fitzpatrick, M. A. (2011). Interpersonal communication in family relationships. In M. L. Knapp & J. A. Daly (Eds.), *The Sage Handbook of interpersonal communication*, 4th edn (pp. 679–714). Thousand Oaks, CA: Sage.

Cavanagh, S. E., & Huston, A. C. (2008). The timing of family instability and children's social development. *Journal of Marriage & Family*, 70, 1258–70.

Clark, R. A., MacGeorge, E. L., & Robinson, L. (2008). Evaluation of peer comforting strategies by children and adolescents. *Human Communication Research*, 34, 319–45.

Collins, W. A. (Ed.) (1984). *Development during middle childhood: The years from six to twelve*. Washington, DC: National Academy Press.

Collins, W. A., & van Dulmen, M. (2006). The significance of middle childhood peer competence for work and relationships in early adulthood. In A. C. Huston & M. N. Ripke (Eds.), *Developmental contexts in middle childhood: Bridges to adolescence and adulthood* (pp. 24–40). Cambridge: Cambridge University Press.

Cummings, E. M., Davies, P. T., & Campbell, S. B. (2000). *Developmental psychopathology and family process: Theory, research, and clinical implications*. New York: Guilford Press.

Deblinger, E., Thakkar-Kolar, R. R., Berry, E. J., & Schroeder, C. M. (2010). Caregivers' efforts to educate their children about child sexual abuse. *Child Maltreatment*, 15, 91–100.

DeFries, J. C., Plomin, R., & Fulker, D. W. (1994). Nature and nurture in middle childhood. In J. C. DeFries, R. Plomin, & D. W. Fulker (Eds.), *Nature and nurture during middle childhood* (pp. 1–8). Cambridge, MA: Blackwell.

Dishion, T. J., Nelson, S. E., & Yasui, M. (2005). Predicting early adolescent gang involvement from middle school adaptation. *Journal of Clinical Child & Adolescent Psychology*, 34, 62–73.

Dodge, K. A., Malone, P. S., Lansford, J. E., Miller-Johnson, S., Pettit, G. S., & Bates, J. E. (2006) Toward a dynamic developmental model of the role of parents and peers in early onset substance use. In A. Clarke-Stewart & J. Dunn (Eds.), *Families count: Effects on child and adolescent development* (pp. 104–34). Cambridge: Cambridge University Press.

Doohan, E. M., Carrere, S., Siler, C., & Beardslee, C. (2009). The link between the marital bond and future triadic family interactions. *Journal of Marriage and Family*, 71, 892–904.

Downey, D. B., & Condron, D. J. (2004). Playing well with others in kindergarten: the benefit of siblings at home. *Journal of Marriage and Family*, 66, 333–50.

Durlak, J. A. (2001). School problems of children. In C. Walker & M. C. Roberts (Eds.), *Handbook of clinical and child psychology*, 3rd edn (pp. 561–75). New York: Wiley.

Fitzpatrick, M., & Marshall, L. J. (1996). The effect of family communication environments on children's social behavior during middle childhood. *Communication Research*, 23, 379–407.

Fitzpatrick, M. A., & Ritchie, L. D. (1994). Communication schemata within the family: Multiple perspectives on family interaction. *Human Communication Research*, 20, 275–301.

Gass, K., Jenkins, J., & Dunn, J. (2007). Are sibling relationships protective? A longitudinal study. *Journal of Child Psychology & Psychiatry*, 48, 167–75.

Goode, T. D., & Jones, W. A. (2008). Cultural influences on child development: The middle years. In T. P. Gullotta & G. M. Blau (Eds.), *Family influences on childhood behavior and development* (pp. 63–95). New York: Routledge.

Goodnow, J. J. (2005). Contexts, diversity, pathway: Advances and next steps. In C. R. Cooper, C. T. García Coll, W. T. Barktko, H. Davis & C. Chatman (Eds.), *Developmental pathways through middle childhood* (pp. 295–312). Mahwah, NJ: Lawrence Erlbaum Associates.

——(2006). Second looks at views of development, families, and communications, and at translations into practice. In A. Clarke-Stewart & J. Dunn (Eds.), *Families count: Effects on child and adolescent development* (pp. 337–60). Cambridge: Cambridge University Press.

Grossbart, S., Hughes, S. M., Pryor, S., & Yost, A. (2002). Socialization aspects of parents, children, and the Internet. In S. M. Broniarczyk & K. Nakamoto (Eds.), *Advances in consumer research*, Vol. XXIX (pp. 66–70). Valdosta, GA: Association for Consumer Research.

Hillaker, B., Brophy-Herb, H. E., Villaruel, F., & Haas, B. (2008). The contributions of parenting to social competencies and positive values in middle school youth: positive family communication, maintaining standards, and supportive family relationships. *Family Relations*, 57, 591–601.

Howie, L. D., Lukacs, S. L., Pastor, P. N., Reuben, C. A., & Mendola, P. (2010). Participation in activities outside of school hours in relation to problem behavior and social skills in middle childhood. *Journal of School Health*, 80(3), 119–25.

Hinde, R. S. & Stevenson-Hinde, J. (1987). Interpersonal relationships and child development. *Developmental Review*, 7, 1–21.

Hopper, R. (1971). Communication development and children's responses to questions. *Speech Monographs*, 38, 1–9.

Huston, A. C., & Ripke, M. N. (2006). Middle childhood: Contexts of development. In A. C. Huston & M. N. Ripke (Eds.), *Developmental contexts in middle childhood: Bridges to adolescence and adulthood* (pp. 1–22). Cambridge: Cambridge University Press.

Jenkins, J., & Dunn, J. (2009). Siblings within families: Levels of analysis and patterns of influence. In L. Kramer & K. J. Conger (Eds.), *Siblings as agents of socialization: New directions for child and adolescent development*, Vol. CXXVI (pp. 79–93). San Francisco, CA: Jossey-Bass.

Joshi, A. (2008). Conflict resolution between friends during middle childhood. *Journal of Genetic Psychology*, 169, 133–48.

Kelly, K. J., Comello, M. G., & Edwards, R. W. (2004). Attitudes of rural middle-school youth toward alcohol, tobacco, drugs, and violence. *Rural Educator*, 25, 19–24.

Kim, J. Y., McHale, S. M., Crouter, A. C., & Osgood, D. (2007). Longitudinal linkages between sibling relationships and adjustment from middle childhood through adolescence. *Developmental Psychology*, 43, 960–73.

Kitzman, K., Cohen, R., & Lockwood, R. (2002). Are only children missing out? Comparison of the peer-related social competence of only children and siblings. *Journal of Social and Personal Relationships*, 19, 299–317.

Kjobli, J., & Hagen, K. (2009). A mediation model of interparental collaboration, parenting practices, and child externalizing behavior in a clinical sample. *Family Relations*, 58, 275–88.

Koerner, A. F., & Fitzpatrick, M. A. (2006). Family conflict communication. In J. Oeztel & S. Ting-Toomey (Eds.), *The Sage handbook of conflict communication* (pp. 159–83). Thousand Oaks, CA: Sage.

Kouros, C. D., Cummings, E. M., & Davies, P. T. (2010). Early trajectories of interparental conflict and externalizing problems as predictors of social competence in preadolescence. *Development and Psychopathology*, 20, 527–37.

Kowal, A., & Kramer, L. (1997). Children's understanding of parental differential treatment. *Child Development*, 68, 113–26.

Kretschmer, T., & Pike, A. (2009). Young children's sibling relationship quality: distal and proximal correlates. *Journal of Child Psychology & Psychiatry*, 50, 581–89.

Kupersmidt, J. B., & Dodge, K. A. (Eds.) (2004). *Children's peer relations: From development to intervention.* Washington, DC: American Psychological Association.

Lerner, R. M., & Spainer, G. B. (1978). *Child influences on marital interaction: A life-span perspective.* New York: Academic Press.

Maccoby, E. E. (1992). The role of parents in the socialization of children: An historical overview. *Developmental Psychology*, 28, 1006–17.

Masten, A. S., Desjardins, C., McCormick, C. M., Kuo, S. I., & Long, J. D. (2010). The significance of childhood competence and problems for adult success in work: A developmental cascade analysis. *Development and Psychopathology*, 22, 679–94.

Masten, A. S., & Chicchetti, C. (2010). Developmental cascades. *Development and Psychopathology*, 22, 491–95.

McDowell, D. J., & Parke, R. D. (2000). Differential knowledge of display rules for positive and negative emotions: Influences from parents, influences on peers. *Social Development*, 9, 415–32.

——(2009). Parental correlates of children's peer relations: An empirical test of a tripartite model. *Developmental Psychology, 45*, 224–35.

McHale, S. M., Updegraff, K. A., Jackson-Newsom, J., Tucker, C. J., & Crouter, A. C. (2000). When does parents' differential treatment have negative implications for siblings? *Social Development, 9*, 149–72.

Miller-Day, M. (2008). Talking to youth about drugs: What do youth say about parental strategies? *Family Relations, 57*, 1–2.

Miller-Day, M., & Kam, J. (2010). More than just openness: Developing and validating a measure of targeted parent–child communication about alcohol. *Health Communication, 25*, 293–302.

Minuchin, S. (1974). *Families and family therapy.* Cambridge, MA: Harvard University Press.

Morrill, M. I., Hines, D. A., Mahmood, S., & Cordova, J. V. (2010). Pathways between marriage and parenting for wives and husbands: The role of coparenting. *Family Process, 49*, 59–73.

Nurullah, A. S. (2009). The cell phone as an agent of social change. *Rocky Mountain Communication Review, 6*, 19–25.

O'Donnell, L., Wilson-Simmons, R., Dash, K., Jeanbaptiste, V., Myint, U. A., Moss, J., & Stueve, A. (2007). Saving sex for later: Developing a parent–child communication intervention to delay sexual initiation among young adolescents. *Sex Education, 7*, 107–25.

Olson, D., Russell, C. S., & Sprenkle, D. J. (Eds.) (1989). *Circumplex model: Systematic assessment and treatment of families.* Binghamton: Hawthorne Press.

Parsons, T. (1974). Age and sex in social structure. In R. L. Coser (Ed.), *The family: Its structures and functions* (pp. 243–55). New York: St. Martins. (Reprinted from *American Sociological Review, 7*, 604–16 [1942].)

Peterson, G. S., & Hann, D. (1999). Socialization children and parents in families. In M. B. Sussman, S. K. Steinmetz, & G. W. Peterson (Eds.), *Handbook of marriage and the family*, 2nd edn (pp. 237–370). New York: Plenum Press.

Pike, A., Coldwell, J., & Dunn, J. F. (2005). Sibling relationships in early/middle childhood: links with individual adjustment. *Journal of Family Psychology, 19*, 523–32.

Punamäki, R. L., Wallenius, M., Hölttö, H., Nygård, C. H., & Rimpelä, A. (2008). The associations between information and communication technology (ICT) and peer and parent relations in early adolescence. *International Journal of Behavioral Development, 33*, 556–64.

Rah, Y., & Parke, R. D. (2008). Pathways between parent–child interactions and peer acceptance: The role of children's social information processing. *Social Development, 17*, 341–57.

Recchia, H. E., & Howe, N. (2009). Associations between social understanding, sibling relationship quality, and siblings' conflict strategies and outcomes. *Child Development, 80*, 1564–78.

Rubin, K. H., Bukowski, W., & Parker, J. G. (1998). Peer interactions, relationships and groups. In W. Damon (Series Ed.) & N. Eisenberg (Vol. Ed.), *Handbook of child psychology.* Vol. III: *Social, emotional and personality development*, 5th edn (pp. 619–700). New York: Wiley.

Segrin, C. (2006). Family interactions and well-being: Integrative perspectives. *The Journal of Family Communication, 6*, 3–21.

Shanahan, L., McHale, S. M., Crouter, A. C., & Osgood, D. (2008). Linkages between parents' differential treatment, youth depressive symptoms, and sibling relationships. *Journal of Marriage & Family, 70*, 480–94.

Shepherd, C., Arnold, M., & Gibbs, M. (2006). Parenting in the connected home. *Journal of Family Studies, 12*, 203–22.

Smith, T. W. (1999). *The emerging 21st century American family.* University of Chicago, National Opinion Research Center.

Sroufe, L., Egeland, B., Carlson, E. A., & Collins, W. A. (2005). *The development of the person: The Minnesota study of risk and adaptation from birth to adulthood.* New York: Guildford Press.

Stafford, L., & Dainton, M. (1995). Parent–child interaction within the family system. In T. J. Socha & G. Stamp (Eds.), *Parents, children, and communication: Frontiers of theory and research* (pp. 3–21). Hillsdale, NJ: Lawrence Erlbaum Associates.

Stocker, C. M., Burwell, R. A., & Briggs, M. L. (2002). Sibling conflict in middle childhood predicts children's adjustment in early adolescence. *Journal of Family Psychology, 16*, 50–57.

Stormshak, E. A., Comeau, C. A., & Shepard, S. A. (2004). The relative contribution of sibling deviance and peer deviance in the prediction of substance use across middle childhood. *Journal of Abnormal Child Psychology, 32*, 635–49.

Suitor, J. J., Sechrist, J., Plikuhn, M., Pardo, S. T., & Pillemer, K. (2008). Within-family differences in parent–child relations across the life course. *Current Directions in Psychological Science, 17,* 334–38.

Symonds, P. (1939). *The psychology of parent–child relationships.* New York: Appleton-Century Crofts.

Turkheimer, E., & Waldron, M. (2000). Nonshared environment: A theoretical, methodological, and quantitative review. *Psychological Bulletin, 126,* 78–108.

Underwood, M. K., Beron, K. J., & Rosen, L. H. (2009). Continuity and change in social and physical aggression from middle childhood through early adolescence. *Aggressive Behavior, 35,* 357–75.

Valcke, M., Bonte, S., Wever, & Rots, I. (2010). Internet parenting styles and the impact on internet use of primary children. *Computers & Education, 55,* 454–64.

von Bertalanffy, K. L. (1968). *General system theory: Foundations, development, applications,* New York: George Braziller.

Westby, C. E. (1998). Communication refinement in school age and adolescence. In W. O. Haynes & B. B. Shulman (Eds.), *Communication development* (pp. 311–60). Baltimore, MD: New Waverly Press.

Wilson, E. K., Dalberth, B. T., Koo, H. P., & Gard, J. C. (2010). Parents' perspectives on talking to preteenage children about sex. *Perspectives on Sexual & Reproductive Health, 42,* 56–63.

Winter, M. A., Davies, P. T., & Cummings, E. (2010). Children's security in the context of family instability and maternal communications. *Merrill-Palmer Quarterly, 56,* 131–42.

Wong, M. S., Diener, M. L., & Isabella, R. A. (2008). Parents' emotion related beliefs and behaviors and child grade: Associations with children's perceptions of peer competence. *Journal of Applied Developmental Psychology, 29,* 175–86.

17

Parent–Child Communication During Adolescence

Susan Branje, Brett Laursen, and W. Andrew Collins

Conventional wisdom regards parent–adolescent communication as an oxymoron. As is often the case with adolescence, however, conventional wisdom can be misleading. Although communication during the adolescent years certainly is a challenge for parents and children, this challenge stems primarily from the changing nature of the relationship, not from an inherent inability of adolescents and parents to engage in meaningful conversation (for recent reviews, see Laursen & Collins, 2009; Smetana, Campione-Barr, & Metzger, 2006). As families navigate the transition from childhood into adulthood, the frequency and content of their interactions change. Increasing adolescent autonomy inevitably alters patterns of self-disclosure, shared experiences, and perceptions of privacy and responsibilities. Yet even in the face of these significant alterations, familial emotional bonds are noteworthy for their resilience and continuity.

To the extent that there is a generation gap, it is as much a product of incongruent perceptions and expectations as it is of inadequate or insufficient conversation (Steinberg, 2001). Parents and adolescents do not necessarily share the same view of the relationship and their ability to communicate, nor are their perspectives typically congruent with those of observers outside the relationship. Parents and adolescents pursue different implicit goals and timetables regarding the adolescent's autonomy, which may give rise to communication difficulties (Collins & Laursen, 2004). But families differ widely in the extent to which autonomy has a corrosive effect on parent–child communication. For some it is a difficult passage, but most families are well equipped to navigate the developmental challenges of adolescence.

This chapter will describe how patterns of parent–child communication are transformed across adolescence years in terms of changes in the nature and functions of relationships. We will focus on salient aspects of parent–adolescent relationships that best illustrate alterations in patterns of communication. The chapter is divided into five sections. The first section provides an overview of theoretical accounts of parent–child relationships during adolescence. Most models of development assume perturbations in family relationships during the adolescent years, although there is less agreement as to the implications for family communication. The second section describes continuity and change in manifestations of parent–adolescent closeness. For most families, closeness and interdependence decline across adolescence, but the fall-off in intimate communication appears to be especially pronounced for those in troubled relationships. The third section describes continuity and change in manifestations of parent–adolescent conflict. Expressions of anger and coercion may increase during the transition from childhood to adolescence, particularly among families with prior communication difficulties, but strife is not a normative feature of this age period. The fourth section describes continuity and change in manifestations of parent–adolescent monitoring and information management. Parental control of adolescents' unsupervised activities may increasingly threaten adolescents' growing needs for autonomy, and parents need to provide an emotional climate in which adolescents voluntarily disclose information about their activities and whereabouts. The concluding remarks place changing patterns of parent–adolescent communication in the larger context of relationship transformations from childhood to adulthood.

Theoretical Accounts of Continuity and Change in Parent–Adolescent Relationships

Conceptual models of developmental changes in parent–adolescent relationships vary in whether their primary focus is on the adolescent or on the relationship. Those that focus on the adolescent emphasize that changes in the parent–adolescent relationship result from the child's biological or cognitive maturation. For decades, the prevalent theoretical perspective was that the manner in which family relationships are transformed and the ensuing consequences for family communication depend on the nature and processes of individual maturation. In contrast, models that focus on the relationship tend to emphasize continuity and the enduring nature of parent–child bonds. These models hold that because the relationship is inherently stable, functional properties of family communication remain constant despite adolescent development and alterations in the content and form of interactions.

Models of Individual Change and Their Implications for Parent–Adolescent Communication

Psychoanalytic theorists assumed that hormonal changes at puberty give rise to unwelcome oedipal urges that foster impulse control problems and anxiety, as well as rebelliousness and distance from the family (Freud, 1958). More recent psychoanalytic formulations (Blos, 1979; Erikson, 1968) presume that puberty is the driving force toward individuation from parents through a process that emphasizes adolescent autonomy striving and ego identity development rather than impulse control. These models agree that parental deidealization and psychic emancipation drive a wedge between parents and children that is exacerbated by inner turmoil produced by adolescent hormonal fluctuations. Heightened conflict and diminished closeness following pubertal maturation result in deteriorated family communication. Although conflict should abate and efforts may be undertaken to re-establish closeness once pubertal maturation and individuation are complete, the end result is permanent changes in the parent–child relationship that permit the adolescent to participate in family communication as an adult.

Evolutionary views also emphasize the role of puberty in transforming relationships and communication (Hill, 1988; Steinberg, 1989). According to these views, the origins of this process lie with evolutionary pressures on the child to move away from the family to find a sexual partner. Physical and cognitive advances foster autonomy striving and individuation, which heighten conflict with, and diminish closeness to, parents. In turn, increased autonomy and individuation may help to promote pubertal development by creating distance between adolescents and parents and encouraging children to look elsewhere for mates. Increased conflict and diminished closeness are presumed to be an integral part of the move toward adolescent independence and inevitably impede family communication. Nevertheless, a prior history of responsive parenting, which is thought to provide a foundation of warmth and respect, as well as grandparental investment in offspring once children make the transition to parenthood, may enable parents and children to transcend the difficulties of adolescence in young adulthood (Crosnoe & Elder, 2002; Gray & Steinberg, 1999).

A related group of maturational models hold that change in parent–adolescent relationships results from cognitive development. These models start from the premise that global advances in adolescent abstract reasoning foster a nuanced appreciation of interpersonal distinctions and an increasingly reciprocal and egalitarian view of parent–child relationships (Youniss & Smollar, 1985). Cognitive advances may also prompt adolescents to perceive as personal decisions issues that were previously considered to be under parental jurisdiction (Smetana & Asquith, 1994). Parental reluctance to conform to these views by transforming their vertical affiliation into a horizontal one and by granting more autonomy creates conflict and curtails closeness. Once relationship roles and expectations are renegotiated in a mutually satisfactory way and parents have reduced their control, conflict should subside and parents and adolescents may re-establish closeness.

These models of individual change imply that because parents and adolescents necessarily go through a period in which they experience the same interactions differently, communication between parents and adolescents may be impaired as a consequence of relationship change. After relationship roles have been successfully realigned, parents and children may develop a more sophisticated framework for constructive communication (Collins & Laursen, 2000). Given that perceptions mediate relationship experiences, reports of change in parent–adolescent communication are expected to vary across participants and one or both of these insider perspectives are likely to be at odds with independent outsider perspectives.

Models of Relationship Change and their Implications for Parent–Adolescent Communication

Alternative models of parent–adolescent relationships focus on forces for stability within the dyad, rather than on the impact of individual change on the dyad. Attachment theory is the most common relational perspective, and argues that the quality of the parent–child relationship is inherently stable over time. According to this perspective, one person's behavior with another is guided by a set of relatively stable cognitive representations derived from a history of interactions in attachment relationships (Bowlby, 1969). As a mutually regulated system, parents and children jointly work to maintain the relationship in a manner consistent with their cognitive representations. Specific interactions may vary from one age to the next, depending on the developmental challenges of the period, but the functional significance of interactions and the role of parents as a secure base for exploration are expected to vary little over time (Ainsworth, 1989). Although maturational changes in the adolescent stimulate greater autonomy-striving that transforms patterns of communication with parents, perceptions of the quality of the relationship should remain fairly stable. Separation and individuation may precipitate conflict and diminished feelings of closeness for a time and may make parental control less desirable, but the magnitude of these changes and their impact on the relationship should reflect the prior history of the relationship (Allen & Manning, 2007). Adolescents and parents with a history of sensitive, responsive interactions and strong emotional bonds may experience only temporary communication difficulties, whereas those in poorer quality relationships are more likely to sustain disruption and unresolved issues.

Social relations or interdependence models also emphasize the inherent stability of parent–child relationships (Laursen & Collins, 2009). In an interdependent relationship, partners engage in mutually influential exchanges and share the perception that their connections are reciprocal and enduring (Reis, Collins, & Berscheid, 2000). Interdependence is a hallmark of all close relationships and is manifested in frequent, strong, and diverse interconnections maintained over an extended time (Kelley et al., 1983). These enduring interconnections are internalized by participants and organized into mental schemas that shape expectations concerning future interactions. The obligatory nature of parent–child relationships fosters expectations of interdependence, and participants come to expect behaviors of each other that maintain the connections between them. Patterns of communication established during childhood are likely to be carried forward into adolescence, but cognitive advances make adolescents realize that the rules of reciprocity and social exchange that govern interactions with friends are not similarly applied to interactions with parents (Youniss & Smollar, 1985). Greater autonomy offers adolescents the opportunity to revise interconnections with parents so that they better reflect relationship costs and benefits (Laursen & Bukowski, 1997). The amount of change should vary depending on the degree to which the relationship is perceived to be inequitable. Poor quality relationships may experience difficulty with adjustment of parental control, an upsurge in conflict, and a concomitant decline in closeness as adolescents express a growing dissatisfaction with unequal treatment and unfavorable outcomes. High quality relationships, however, may change little, or even may improve, as participants build on mutually beneficent patterns of exchange and attempt to adjust for past inequities.

Both the individual and the relational perspectives on parent–adolescent relationships emphasize three key features of communication: closeness, which functions as a potential attractor that helps to maintain connections between family members despite changes in the individuals; conflict, which functions as a potential repellent that creates psychological and physical distance between family members; and parental monitoring, which is closely related to adolescent information management. These features of communication are the features of relationship change most salient to parents (Shearer, Crouter, & McHale, 2005). The remaining sections of our chapter focus on these three relationship features, with particular attention to their implications for communication in the family.

Continuity and Change in Parent–Adolescent Closeness

Closeness refers to the degree to which individuals affect and are affected by each other. Commonly invoked indicators of closeness include affection, cohesion, companionship, interdependence, intimacy, and trust. There is considerable continuity between positive features of relationships during adolescence and those earlier in life, despite the altered patterns of interaction, emotion, and cognition. Around the world, parents and adolescents perceive relationships with one another as warm and supportive (Collins & Repinski, 2001).

Developmental Trends

Continuities in parent–child relationships co-exist with significant changes in the amount, content, and perceived meaning of interactions, in expressions of positive and negative effect, and in interpersonal perceptions of participants (Collins & Laursen, 2000). Closeness and intimacy during adolescence are manifest in different forms than in earlier life. Cuddling and extensive joint interactions decline as children mature, but conversations in which information is conveyed and feelings are expressed increase. These adaptations are appropriate responses to the maturity level and changing needs of the adolescent.

Age-related differences in absolute levels of parent–child closeness are well documented. Subjective rankings of closeness and objective measures of interdependence similarly decrease across the adolescent years. The amount of time parents and adolescents spend together declines in a linear fashion from preadolescence to late adolescence (Larson, Richards, Moneta, Holmbeck, & Duckett, 1996). Relative to preadolescents, adolescents perceive less companionship and intimacy with parents and report lower feelings of acceptance by parents and satisfaction with family life (Hill, 1988). Although perceptions of relationships remain generally warm and supportive, perceived parental support decreases from early to middle adolescence but tends to increase again from mid to late adolescence (De Goede, Branje, & Meeus, 2009). Similar developmental trajectories in warmth and closeness have been found in ethnic minority youth, with some variations in the timing of when closeness declines (Fuligni, 1998).

The quality of relationships at the outset of adolescence is indicative of changes that take place in relationships across adolescents. Mothers and children who report low levels of negativity in early adolescence enjoy sustained high levels of support across adolescence. But for those with initially high levels of negativity, perceived support starts low and drops precipitously (Laursen, DeLay, & Adams, 2010). In a German study, three developmental trajectories of mother–adolescent and father–adolescent relationships were found (Seiffge-Krenke, Overbeek, & Vermulst, 2010). The majority of adolescents showed high and slightly decreasing levels of closeness and stable low levels of conflict, but about one-third of the adolescents reported increasingly negative relationships with parents, and about 10 percent of the adolescents were characterized by low and decreasing closeness and negative effect.

Reports of age-related diminished closeness may overstate the significance of changes in parent–adolescent relationships because they focus exclusively on change at the level of the group without considering change at the level of the family. When closeness is examined in terms of the rank order of a single family on a particular dimension relative to other families on the same dimension, a picture of relationship cohesion emerges. For instance, longitudinal data from the Pittsburgh Youth Study revealed moderate to high levels of stability in parent and child reports of positive and negative relationship qualities (Loeber et al., 2000). Indeed, across childhood and adolescence the relative ordering of families on various dimensions of closeness remained fairly constant from one year to the next, even though the mean level of each variable fell. Yet for most youth, parents remain the most influential of all adolescent relationships, shaping most of the important decisions confronting children, even as their authority over mundane details such as attire wanes (Collins, Maccoby, Steinberg, Hetherington, & Bornstein, 2000). These findings suggest a complex dynamic of relationship continuity and change that disprove the conventional view of an abrupt descent into distance and alienation.

Reporter Perspectives

Parent and adolescent views of the family are notable for their divergence, particularly during early adolescence. There is more overlap between maternal and paternal reports of their own relationship with an adolescent child and in adolescents' perception of the mother–child and father–child relationships than in the reports of parent and child (Cook & Goldstein, 1993). Whereas parents seem to give greater weight to the distinctiveness of their relationships with children, adolescents' perceptions of parents are more driven by their general view of the family (Branje, van Aken, & van Lieshout, 2002). Parents, especially mothers, tend to hold a more optimistic view of the parent–child relationship than adolescents. Mothers routinely report more warmth and affection among family members than do children, which may be an attempt to ward off the decline in maternal life satisfaction that accompanies adolescent detachment (Silverberg & Steinberg, 1990). Mismatches and developmental expectations are highest at the outset of adolescence, and adolescent and parent discrepant views of positive and negative features of their relationship gradually grow more convergent over time (Collins & Laursen, 2004). It is important not to overstate the significance of perceptual differences. The variance that reporters share, not the variance that is unique to one or another member of the relationship, accounts for associations between parent and adolescent reports of relationship quality and adolescent well-being (Laursen, Furman, & Mooney, 2006).

Individual Differences

Closeness varies from one adolescent to another and from one parent–adolescent pair to another. Adolescents spend more time and are more apt to share feelings with their mothers (Steinberg & Silk, 2002). In contrast, adolescents view fathers as somewhat distant authority figures to be consulted primarily for information and material support. Three possible explanations for these absolute differences are that (a) the predominant paternal role of playmate may become irrelevant and even embarrassing for adolescents, (b) in many cultures men are associated with disciplinary functions, and (c) fathers tend to interact less sensitively with children than mothers (Lewis & Lamb, 2003). Compared to daughters, sons have similarly warm relationships with mothers, but are typically closer to fathers. These trends tend to accelerate across the adolescent years, yet gender differences also have roots in earlier phases of the relationship. One longitudinal study showed that although father involvement during childhood predicted father–adolescent closeness for sons and daughters, these links were stronger for girls than for boys (Flouri & Buchanan, 2002).

Variation in closeness in the parent–adolescent relationship tends to be associated with family structure. Interparental conflict, divorce, and single-parenthood appear to be related to lower warmth and intimacy (Hetherington & Stanley-Hagan, 2002; Krishna-kumar & Buehler, 2000; Loeber et al., 2000). These findings suggest problems in the marital system to spillover into the parenting system and thus to affect the parent–child system. Birth order of the adolescent may also affect developmental changes in parent–adolescent closeness. Although both firstborns' and second-borns' reports of parental warmth declined from early to mid adolescence, paternal warmth declined less for second-borns than for firstborns, suggesting that fathers learn from their experience with the firstborn child (Shanahan, McHale, Crouter, & Osgood, 2007).

Moreover, higher parent–adolescent closeness is associated with fewer adjustment problems for adolescents. Accumulating evidence suggests that child adjustment problems predict changes in relationship support rather than the other way around (Branje, Hale, & Meeus, 2008; Hafen & Laursen, 2009). Interindividual differences in relationship warmth tend to increase with age, primarily because of increases in the magnitude of genetic effects. These findings suggest that developmental changes in closeness are interpreted as reflecting genotype–environment correlation processes whereby adolescents increasingly influence the parent–child relationship (McGue, Elkins, Walden, & Iacono, 2005).

Implications for Family Communication

Communication is a core element both of interdependence between family members and their subjective feelings of closeness. Disruptions of established patterns of interaction inevitably mean that parent–adolescent communication will differ in frequency, content, and tenor from that of earlier age periods (Collins & Laursen, 2000). Families differ in the degree to which they are affected by individual and relationship changes. Most are able to capitalize on greater adolescent maturity by fostering patterns of sustained communications that promote a psychological closeness that is less dependent on frequent interactions. They do so by adapting prior interconnections to meet new demands for adolescent autonomy (Steinberg & Silk, 2002). Families with a history of communication problems, however, are missing the adaptive interconnections that form the foundation for new forms of closeness during this period of detachment and, thus, may be unable to surmount the barriers to effective communication that arise during adolescence.

Continuity and Change in Parent–Adolescent Conflict

Conflict, defined in terms of disagreement and overt behavioral opposition, is ubiquitous in all close relationships, but it is especially prominent between family members. Surveys of adolescents indicate that disagreements are most common with mothers, followed by siblings, friends, and romantic partners, then fathers. Angry disputes arise more frequently with family members than with close peers (Laursen & Collins, 1994). Most parent–adolescent disagreements concern mundane topics, famously tagged by Hill (1988) as "garbage and galoshes" disputes. Parent–adolescent conflicts usually adhere to a coercive script: Relative to those with friends, disagreements with parents more often involve a combination of power assertive resolutions, neutral or angry effect, and win–lose outcomes (Adams & Laursen, 2001). Reflecting the asymmetry in power, the majority of disagreements between parents and adolescents end through compromise or win-loss resolutions; standoff is relatively rare (Recchia, Ross, & Vickar, 2010).

Developmental Trends

Until recently conflict with parents was thought to follow an inverted-U shaped function that peaked during mid adolescence, but meta-analytic methods revealed that this presumed trend was an artifact of the failure to distinguish quantity from affective tenor (Laursen, Coy, & Collins, 1998). The evidence indicates a decline in the frequency of conflict with parents from early adolescence to late adolescence. However, anger in these conflicts increases from early adolescence to mid adolescence, with little change thereafter. Longitudinal studies suggest an inverted U-shaped development of conflict intensity (De Goede et al., 2009).

No reliable age differences have been found in topics or outcomes of parent–adolescent conflict, but there is some indication that resolutions may change across the adolescent years, with rates of submission declining and rates of disengagement increasing (Smetana, Daddis, & Chuang, 2003). Conflict management in the parent–adolescent relationship changes in favor of a more horizontal relationship. From early to middle adolescence, adolescents increasingly use positive problem solving and withdrawal, although their use of negative conflict management with mothers temporarily increases as well. Parents use less negative conflict management over time, and fathers increasingly use positive problem solving and withdrawal (van Doorn, Branje, & Meeus, 2011). The goals of conflicts change with age as well: older adolescents report more dominance and emotional support goals and less instrumental goals than younger adolescents. This possibly reflects their stronger metacognitive abilities and their increasing infuriation with maternal restraints in a relationship that is expected to become more egalitarian (Lundell, Grusec, McShane, & Davidov, 2008).

Reporter Perspectives

Parents and adolescents are known to experience their relationships in dramatically different terms. Adolescents appear to have a more accurate (or more honest) view than parents of unpleasant aspects of the relationship. When it comes to describing family conflict, reports from independent observers frequently match those of adolescent children, but neither observer nor adolescent reports accord with parent reports of the same events (Gonzales, Caucé, & Mason, 1996). Particularly mothers tend to underestimate the incidence of parent–adolescent conflict, but at the same time they overestimate its severity (Steinberg, 2001). Not coincidentally, mothers also report the most negative repercussions from conflict with adolescent children (Silverberg & Steinberg, 1990). Chief explanations for these findings are that (a) mothers experience conflict as a personal failure, because it is an indictment of their ability to serve as family conciliators and peacemakers (Vuchinich, 1987), and (b) conflict is the primary vehicle through which adolescents renegotiate their role in the family, which inevitably diminishes maternal (but not necessarily paternal) authority (Steinberg, 1989). The fact that parent and child reports of conflict appear to converge during late adolescence suggests that disagreements, however unpleasant they may be, play an important role in aligning expectations and facilitating communication among family members (Collins, Laursen, Mortensen, Luebker, & Ferreira, 1997).

Individual Differences

Parent–child conflict behavior and patterns of developmental change may be moderated by characteristics of individual participants, such as gender and puberty, and characteristics of the family, such as family structure and climate. Accumulating evidence shows that conflict and negative effect are higher in mother–daughter relationships than in other parent–child relationships (Laursen & Collins, 1994). A meta-analysis revealed that conflict rates decline more across adolescence in mother–child relationships than in father–child relationships (Laursen et al., 1998), but gender does not moderate developmental trends in conflict effect. Conflict resolutions vary as a function of parent and adolescent gender. Compromise is more common with mothers than with fathers, and disengagement and giving in are more typical of conflict with sons than of conflict with daughters (Smetana et al., 2003; Vuchinich, 1987). Again, there is no reliable evidence that gender moderates patterns of developmental change.

Variation attributed to puberty may be parsed into two sources: pubertal status and pubertal timing. Pubertal status refers to the child's absolute level of physical maturation.

Meta-analytic comparisons yield a small positive linear association between pubertal status and parent–adolescent conflict effect such that greater maturity is linked to greater negative effect (Laursen et al., 1998). Conflict frequency was not related to pubertal status. Pubertal timing refers to the child's relative level of physical maturation. Early maturing sons and daughters appear to experience more frequent and more intense parent–child conflict than adolescents maturing on-time (Steinberg, 1989). Several explanations for these findings have been offered, most suggesting that parents do not agree with children that physical precocity is a sufficient basis for enhanced autonomy. In general, the effects of pubertal timing on parent–adolescent conflict are larger and more robust than those for pubertal status (Laursen & Collins, 1994).

Furthermore, conflict behavior may be moderated by characteristics of the family. Although on average parent–child conflicts may be more frequent in adolescence than in other periods of life, only a small portion of parent–adolescent dyads have frequent and angry disagreements (Branje, van Doorn, van der Valk, & Meeus, 2009) and the most conflictual parent–adolescent dyads had more problematic relationships in childhood as well (Smetana, 2008). Whether and how conflicts are resolved may be more important than the occurrence of conflicts. Most conflicts between parents and children do not have a long-term negative impact on the relationship (van Doorn, Branje, Hox, & Meeus, 2009), but chronic fighting with negative conflict management strategies has been linked to adolescent maladjustment (Branje et al., 2009). One important study illustrates how the impact of conflict varies across parent–adolescent relationships. High levels of conflict predicted poor outcomes regardless of relationships quality, but moderate amounts of conflict may be beneficial for those whose relationships are good (Adams & Laursen, 2007). When adolescents reporting no conflicts with mothers and fathers are compared to those reporting an average number of conflicts, the latter had higher school grades if they were in better but not poorer quality relationships and reported more withdrawal if they were in poorer but not better quality relationships.

As with closeness, birth order is another moderating factor in developmental changes in parent–adolescent conflict. In line with a spillover model, changes in relationships between firstborn children and parents dictate the timing of changes in relationships between later born children and parents, so that elevation in parent–adolescent conflict frequency is timed to firstborns' transition to adolescence for both first- and secondborns (Shanahan, McHale, Osgood, & Crouter, 2007). These findings may be explained by sibling modeling and imitation, a general increase in family conflict during firstborns' transition to adolescence, or a parental desire to avoid differential treatment.

Implications for Family Communication

Almost 40 years ago, Bandura (1964) argued against the impression that adolescence brought about a precipitous upsurge in parent–child conflict. Instead, difficulties in parent–adolescent relationships are lawfully related to, and consistent with, difficulties in preadolescent relationships. Although many families experience a modest uptick in conflict at the outset of adolescence, conflict during adolescence may actually strengthen the parent–child relationship by providing a much-needed vehicle for communication (Laursen & Collins, 1994). Disagreements offer parents and adolescents a forum for revising expectations and renegotiating roles and responsibilities in a manner commensurate with the autonomy typically accorded to youth in a particular culture (Collins et al., 1997). Most families successfully meet this challenge because they are able to draw on healthy patterns of communication established in response to the challenges of earlier age periods. However, families who do not learn to communicate effectively when children are young are at risk for dysfunctional discord during adolescence because these families may be incapable of constructively addressing the developmental challenges of autonomy and the transformations in parent–child relationships that accompany it.

Continuity and Change in Parental Monitoring and Adolescent Information Management

Adolescents spend most of their daily leisure time in activities with peers that go unsupervised by adults. Monitoring of adolescents' leisure activities, such as structuring the child's environment and tracking the child's behavior, has long been considered as an important way for parents to remain informed about adolescents' activities and whereabouts (Dishion & McMahon, 1998). Recent studies that operationalized control as behavioral control instead of parental knowledge suggested, however, that parental knowledge results from adolescent spontaneous disclosure of information more than from parental active soliciting for information or behavioral control (Keijsers, Frijns, Branje, & Meeus, 2009; Stattin & Kerr, 2000). Thus, disclosure of information by the adolescent seems to enable parental supervision. These mixed findings are comprehensible when one considers that parental control is incompatible with one of the major developmental tasks in adolescence: to become an autonomous and independent individual (Blos, 1979). In this chapter, we will distinguish parental solicitation for information, parental control, and adolescent disclosure as information management activities that allow parents to keep track of, and acquire knowledge about, adolescents' lives and activities.

Developmental Trends

The stage-environment fit perspective (Eccles et al., 1991) emphasizes that levels of parental control and regulation should match adolescents' developmental needs. Parents need to find an optimal balance between parental control and support for autonomy. As adolescents get older, they experience an increasing need for privacy, independence, and autonomy and consider it less legitimate for parents to exert control over things they consider their personal jurisdiction (Smetana & Asquith, 1994). Parents gradually relax their control as adolescents get older (Keijsers et al., 2009), although parents' soliciting for information, which is a less intrusive way of being involved in adolescents' lives, tends to remain stable. Most parents thus respect the growing need for autonomy of their child and use less intrusive ways to acquire knowledge about the whereabouts and activities of their aging child, resulting in a lower level of parental knowledge as adolescents get older (Loeber et al., 2000).

Adolescents are also active agents in claiming autonomy by strategically withholding information from parents about their activities and whereabouts. By not disclosing to their parents, adolescents have the power to undermine parental control and create a more egalitarian distribution of power in the relationship. Adolescents increasingly consider information as private or personal and legitimate to withhold from their parents (Smetana, Metzger, Gettman, & Campione-Barr, 2006). With age, they disclose less to their parents and increasingly have secrets from their parents (Keijsers et al., 2009; Keijsers, Branje, Frijns, Finkenauer, & Meeus, 2010). This type of information management plays a facilitating role in gaining autonomy, but also may damage mutual trust and understanding in the parent–child relationship (Finkenauer, Engels, & Kubacka, 2008). Adolescents thus have to optimize their information management towards parents to reach a balance between independence and connectedness to parents.

Reporter Perspectives

Adolescents and their parents are known to have discrepant expectations regarding the timing of transitions in authority, autonomy, and responsibilities. Adolescents would like their autonomy to increase more rapidly than parents wish (Collins et al., 1997), and parents think adolescents are more obligated to disclose to them than adolescents themselves think (Smetana, Metzger, et al., 2006). These different expectations are reflected in divergent perceptions: Adolescents report lower levels of disclosure to parents and a stronger decline in disclosure than parents do, and strikingly, they also report lower levels of parental control and parental solicitation for information than parents do (Keijsers et al., 2009). Possible explanations for these findings are (a) the generational stake, or the tendency for adolescents to emphasize autonomy and for parents to emphasize continuity in relationships (Bengtson, Schaie, & Burton, 1995) and (b) adolescents become increasingly proficient in managing personal information, making it increasingly difficult for parents to recognize what they don't know.

In addition to the divergent reports of adolescents versus parents, accumulating evidence shows that mothers report higher levels of adolescent disclosure and parental solicitation and control than fathers do (Keijsers et al., 2009). Although adolescents also report more disclosure to mothers than to fathers, mothers tend to overestimate adolescents' disclosure to a greater extent than fathers do (Smetana, Metzger, et al., 2006). These findings may reflect the greater involvement of mothers in parenting of adolescent children compared to fathers (Lewis & Lamb, 2003). A study that showed that fathers have more knowledge about their children when mothers work longer hours (Crouter, Helms-Erikson, Updegraff, & McHale, 1999) suggests that when fathers increase their involvement, adolescent disclosure and paternal control may also increase.

Individual Differences

Developmental changes in parental monitoring and adolescent information management may depend on characteristics of individual participants, such as gender of the adolescent. Accumulating evidence suggests gender differences in the development of absolute levels of monitoring, disclosure, and secrecy, with stronger decreases in monitoring knowledge and stronger increases in secrecy for boys (Keijsers et al., 2010; Laird, Pettit, Bates, & Dodge, 2003). The effects on relationship quality tend to differ for boys and girls as well. For example, secrecy and relationship quality were longitudinally and bidirectionally related in girls but not in boys (Keijsers et al., 2010). These findings underscore that connectedness, intimacy, and reciprocity in the parent–child relationship are more central in the development of girls than in the development of boys (Youniss & Smollar, 1985). Compared to boys, girls may experience higher relational costs of secrecy that do not outweigh the benefits of secrecy in the form of higher autonomy, and girls may therefore more often choose to reveal personal information.

Monitoring behavior and disclosure may also be moderated by characteristics of the parent–child dyad and by family structure. Especially in families with a positive family climate in which children feel supported by their parents, adolescents are more likely to understand high parental control as privacy invasive or excessively controlling (Hawk, Hale, Raaijmakers, & Meeus, 2008; Stattin & Kerr, 2000). Adolescents from authoritative homes are also more likely to disclose and less likely to lie (Darling, Cumsille, Caldwell, & Dowdy, 2006). This differential effect of parental control under different emotional family climates suggest that the merits of parental control have been overestimated, and that excessive levels can be interpreted as developmentally inappropriate parenting. Regarding family structure, single-parent families report lower monitoring knowledge and less monitoring than families with two biological parents present in the household (Laird, Pettit, Dodge, & Bates, 2003; Loeber et al., 2000).

Implications for Family Communication

Adolescents have an increasing need for autonomy and parent–child communication needs to change to meet these changing needs. Driven by the increasing need for autonomy and independence, adolescents establish boundaries around information they consider personal and want to keep secret (Finkenauer et al., 2008), and as they get older they disclose less to parents about their whereabouts and activities. Parents tend to gradually relax control during adolescence, suggesting that parents generally acknowledge their child's increasing need for autonomy and collaborate in creating a more egalitarian relationship (Laursen & Bukowski, 1997). By establishing a positive family climate, parents can create an environment in which adolescents are willing to disclose information about their personal lives, thereby enabling parents to guide and support their adolescent and to stimulate adolescent well-being. Parents who use intrusive levels of control will likely elicit adolescent secrecy and inhibit healthy autonomy development and individuation.

Conclusions

This brief, selective review underscores several principles of parent–child communication during adolescence and points the way to areas of inquiry requiring greater attention. Relationships do not operate in a vacuum. Youth who have better quality relationships with parents also tend to have better quality relationships with friends (De Goede, Branje, Delsing, & Meeus, 2009), and youth who receive similarly high levels of support from friends and parents are better adjusted than those with differing levels of relationship support (e.g., Laursen, Furman, & Mooney, 2006). Findings such as these suggest that greater attention must be given to adolescent relationship networks. Parent–adolescent relationships are known to differ as a function of characteristics of the family and the environment, including culture and ethnicity, household structure, and socioeconomic status (see Laursen & Collins, 2009, for review). Some contextual variables, such as differences in family communication related to parental divorce and remarriage, are beginning to come into focus (Hetherington & Stanley-Hagan, 2002), but other critical variables, such as ethnic group (García Coll & Pachter, 2002) and social class differences (Hoff, Laursen, & Tardiff, 2002), remain poorly understood. A better understanding of these differences is essential because differences resulting from circumstances of economic disadvantage and experiences as members of minority groups almost certainly affect responses to the changes of adolescence. Greater attention to contextual processes is imperative because it may very well be the case that normative adolescent development encompasses several different pathways of parent–child relationship transformation that vary as a function of environmental demands (Collins et al., 2000). We anticipate this research will reveal differences across settings in typical patterns of communication and control but similarities in pathways of influence such that families emphasizing mutuality, respect for the child's opinions, and training for maturity will be most effective in helping adolescents develop attitudes and behaviors appropriate to their society.

Three principles of family communication stand out from our review. First, the vagaries of communication are deeply embedded in qualities of the parent–adolescent relationship. Some differences between communication during adolescence and communication during childhood reflect physical and cognitive development, as well as normative psychosocial changes in autonomy striving. Other differences, however, reflect the ability of the family to cope with the developmental demands of adolescence. As families adapt long-standing expectations and interaction patterns to maturational changes in the child, communication typically falters for a time and then recovers much of its accustomed fluency, albeit in more adult forms. Second, despite significant changes in communication during the adolescent years, most families experience a reassuring continuity in their emotional bonds. Relative to families with a history of communication difficulties, those families that enter adolescence with a history of positive, responsive communication appear to experience fewer disruptions in communication and cope more constructively with those disruptions. In this manner, families that build upon prior successful developmental transitions handle the demands of adolescence by revising communication patterns in a manner appropriate for incipiently adult offspring. Third, parent–adolescent conflict is normative, and fosters communication that is integral to necessary realignments of relationship roles. This constructive process is most likely to occur when conflicts are neither extreme nor persistent and when they arise in a warm and close relationship. The successful ability of most parent–adolescent dyads to balance conflict, closeness, and information management during this period of relationship transformation reaffirms the integral role of communication in human functioning.

References

Adams, R., & Laursen, B. (2001). The organization and dynamics of adolescent conflict with parents and friends. *Journal of Marriage and Family, 63,* 97–110.

——(2007). The correlates of conflict: Disagreement is not necessarily detrimental. *Journal of Family Psychology, 21,* 445–58.

Ainsworth, M. D. S. (1989). Attachments beyond infancy. *American Psychologist, 44,* 709–16.

Allen, J. P., & Manning, N. (2007). From safety to affect regulation: Attachment from the vantage point of adolescence. In M. Scharf & O. Mayseless (Eds.), *Attachment in adolescence: Reflections and new angles—New directions for child and adolescent development* (No. 117, pp. 23–39). San Francisco, CA: Jossey-Bass.

Bandura, A. (1964). The stormy decade: Fact or fiction? *Psychology in the Schools, 1,* 224–31.

Bengtson, V. C., Schaie, K. W., & Burton, L. M. (Eds.) (1995). *Adult intergenerational relations: Effects of societal change.* New York: Springer.

Blos, P. (1979). *The adolescent passage.* New York: International Universities Press.

Bowlby, J. (1969). *Attachment and loss. Vol. I: Attachment.* New York: Basic Books.

Branje, S. J. T., van Doorn, M. D., van der Valk, I. E., & Meeus, W. H. J. (2009). Parent–adolescent conflict, conflict resolution, and adolescent adjustment. *Journal of Applied Developmental Psychology, 30,* 195–204.

Branje, S. J. T., Hale, W. W. III, & Meeus, W. H. J. (2008). Reciprocal development of parent–adolescent support and adolescent problem behaviors. In M. Kerr, H. Stattin, & R. Engels (Eds.), *What can parents do? New insights into the role of parents in adolescent problem behaviour* (pp. 135–62). Chichester: Wiley.

Branje, S. J. T., van Aken, M. A. G., & van Lieshout, C. F. M. (2002). Relational support in families with adolescents. *Journal of Family Psychology, 16,* 351–62.

Collins, W. A., & Laursen, B. (2000). Adolescent relationships: The art of fugue. In C. Hendrick & S. S. Hendrick (Eds.), *Close relationships: A sourcebook* (pp. 59–69). Thousand Oaks, CA: Sage.

Collins W. A., & Laursen B. (2004). Parent–adolescent relationships and influences. In R. M. Lerner & L. Steinberg (Eds.), *Handbook of adolescent psychology*, 2nd edn (pp. 331–61). Hoboken, NJ: Wiley.

Collins, W. A., Laursen, B., Mortensen, N., Luebker, C., & Ferreira, M. (1997). Conflict processes and transitions in parent and peer relationships: Implications for autonomy and regulation. *Journal of Adolescence, 12*, 178–98.

Collins, W. A., Maccoby, E., Steinberg, L., Hetherington, E. M., & Bornstein, M. (2000). Contemporary research on parenting: The case for nature and nurture. *American Psychologist, 55*, 218–32.

Collins, W. A. & Repinski, D. J. (2001). Parents and adolescents as transformers of relationships: Dyadic adaptations to developmental change. In J. R. M. Gerris (Ed.), *Dynamics of parenting: International perspectives on nature and sources of parenting* (pp. 429–43). Leuven: Garant.

Cook, W. L., & Goldstein, M. J. (1993). Multiple perspectives on family relationships: A latent variables model. *Child Development, 64*, 1377–88.

Crosnoe, R. A. & Elder, E. H., Jr. (2002). Life course transitions, the generational stake, and grandparent–grandchild relationships. *Journal of Marriage and Family, 64*, 1089–96.

Crouter, A. C., Helms-Erikson, H., Updegraff, K., & McHale, S. M. (1999). Conditions underlying parents' knowledge about children's daily lives in middle childhood: Between- and within-family comparisons. *Child Development, 70*, 246–59.

Darling, N., Cumsille, P., Caldwell, L. L., & Dowdy, B. (2006). Predictors of adolescents' disclosure to parents and perceived parental knowledge: Between- and within-person differences. *Journal of Youth and Adolescence, 35*, 667–78.

De Goede, I., Branje, S., & Meeus, W. (2009). Developmental changes in adolescents' perceptions of relationships with their parents. *Journal of Youth and Adolescence, 38*, 75–88.

De Goede, I. H. A., Branje, S. J. T., Delsing, M. J. M. H., & Meeus, W. H. J. (2009). Linkages over time between adolescents' relationships with parents and friends. *Journal of Youth and Adolescence, 38*, 1304–15.

Dishion, T. J., & McMahon, R. J. (1998). Parental monitoring and the prevention of child and adolescent problem behavior: A conceptual and empirical formulation. *Clinical Child and Family Psychology Review, 1*, 61–75.

Doorn, M. D. van, Branje, S. J. T., Hox, J. J., & Meeus, W. H. J. (2009). Intraindividual variability in adolescents' perceived relationship satisfaction: The role of daily conflict. *Journal of Youth and Adolescence, 38*, 790–803.

Doorn, M. D. van, Branje, S. J. T., & Meeus, W. H. J. (2011). Developmental changes in conflict resolution styles in parent–adolescent relationships: A four-wave longitudinal study. *Journal of Youth and Adolescence, 40*, 97–107.

Eccles, J. S., Buchanan, C. M., Flanagan, C., Fuligni, A., Midgley, C., & Yee, D. (1991). Control versus autonomy during early adolescence. *Journal of Social Issues, 47*, 53–68.

Erikson, E. H. (1968). *Identity: Youth and crisis*. New York: Norton.

Finkenauer, C., Engels, R., & Kubacka, K. (2008). Relational implications of secrecy and concealment in parent–adolescent relationships. In M. Kerr, H. Stattin, & R. Engels (Eds.), *What can parents do? New insights into the role of parents in adolescent problem behavior* (pp. 43–61). New York: John Wiley & Sons.

Flouri, E., & Buchanan, A. (2002). What predicts good relationships with parents in adolescence and partners in adult life: Findings from the 1958 British birth cohort. *Journal of Family Psychology, 16*, 186–98.

Freud, A. (1958). Adolescence. *Psychoanalytic Study of the Child, 13*, 255–78.

Fuligni, A. J. (1998). The adjustment of children from immigrant families. *Current Directions in Psychological Science, 7*, 99–103.

García Coll, C., & Pachter, L. M. (2002). Ethnic and minority parenting. In M. Bornstein (Ed.), *Handbook of parenting* (Vol. IV, pp. 1–20). Mahwah, NJ: Lawrence Erlbaum Associates.

Gonzales, N. A., Caucé, A. M., & Mason, C. A. (1996). Interobserver agreement in the assessment of parental behavior and parent–adolescent conflict: African American mothers, daughters, and independent observers. *Child Development, 67*, 1483–98.

Gray, M., & Steinberg, L. (1999). Unpacking authoritative parenting: Reassessing a multidimensional construct. *Journal of Marriage and Family, 61*, 574–87.

Hafen, C. A., & Laursen, B. (2009). More problems and less support: early adolescent adjustment forecasts changes in perceived support from parents. *Journal of Family Psychology*, 23, 193–202.

Hawk, S. T., Hale, W. W., Raaijmakers, Q. A. W., & Meeus, W. (2008). Adolescents' perceptions of privacy invasion in reaction to parental solicitation and control. *Journal of Early Adolescence*, 28, 583–608.

Hetherington, E. M., & Stanley-Hagan, M. (2002). Parenting in divorced and remarried families. In M. Bornstein (Ed.), *Handbook of parenting* (Vol. III, pp. 287–315). Mahwah, NJ: Lawrence Erlbaum Associates.

Hill, J. P. (1988). Adapting to menarche: Familial control and conflict. In M. R. Gunnar & W. A. Collins (Eds.), *The Minnesota Symposia on Child Psychology*, Vol. XXI: *Development during the transition to adolescence* (pp. 43–77). Hillsdale, NJ: Lawrence Erlbaum Associates.

Hoff, E., Laursen, B., & Tardiff, T. (2002). Socioeconomic status and parenting. In M. Bornstein (Ed.), *Handbook of parenting* (Vol. II, pp. 231–52). Mahwah, NJ: Lawrence Erlbaum Associates.

Keijsers, L., Branje, S., Frijns, T., Finkenauer, C., & Meeus, W. (2010). Gender differences in keeping secrets from parents in adolescence. *Developmental Psychology*, 46, 293–98.

Keijsers, L., Frijns, T., Branje, S. J. T., & Meeus, W. (2009). Developmental links of adolescent disclosure parental solicitation and control with delinquency: Moderation by parental support. *Developmental Psychology*, 45, 1314–27.

Kelley, H. H., Berscheid, E., Christiansen, A., Harvey, J. H., Huston, T. L., Levinger, G., McClintock, E., Peplau, L. A., & Peterson, D. R. (1983). *Close relationships*. New York: Freeman.

Krishnakumar, A. & Buehler, C. (2000). Interparental conflict and parenting behaviors: A meta-analytic review. *Family Relations*, 49, 25–44.

Laird, R. D., Pettit, G. S., Bates, J. E. & Dodge, K. A. (2003). Parents' monitoring-relevant knowledge and adolescents' delinquent behavior: Evidence of correlated developmental changes and reciprocal influences. *Child Development*, 74, 752–68.

Laird, R. D., Pettit, G. S., Dodge, K. A., & Bates, J. E. (2003). Change in parents' monitoring knowledge: Links with parenting, relationship quality, adolescent beliefs, and antisocial behavior. *Social Development*, 12, 401–19.

Larson, R. W., Richards, M. H., Moneta, G., Holmbeck, G., & Duckett, E. (1996). Changes in adolescents' daily interactions with their families from ages 10 to 18: Disengagement and transformation. *Developmental Psychology*, 32, 744–54.

Laursen, B., & Bukowski, W. M. (1997). A developmental guide to the organisation of close relationships. *International Journal of Behavioral Development*, 21, 747–70.

Laursen, B., & Collins, W. A. (1994). Interpersonal conflict during adolescence. *Psychological Bulletin*, 115, 197–209.

Laursen, B., & Collins, A. W. (2009). Parent–adolescent relationships during adolescence. In R. M. Lerner & L. Steinberg (Eds.), *Handbook of adolescent psychology*, 3rd edn (Vol. II, pp. 3–42). Hoboken, NJ: Wiley.

Laursen, B., Coy, K. C., & Collins, W. A. (1998). Reconsidering changes in parent–child conflict across adolescence: A meta-analysis. *Child Development*, 69, 817–32.

Laursen, B., DeLay, D., & Adams, R. E. (2010). Trajectories of perceived support in mother-adolescent relationships: The poor (quality) get poorer. *Developmental Psychology*, 46, 1792–98.

Laursen, B., Furman, W., & Mooney, K. S. (2006). Predicting interpersonal competence and self-worth from adolescent relationships and relationship networks: Variable-centered and person-centered perspectives. *Merrill-Palmer Quarterly*, 52, 572–600.

Lewis, C., & Lamb, M. E. (2003). Fathers' influences on children's development: the evidence from two-parent families. *European Journal of Psychology of Education*, 18, 211–28.

Loeber, R., Drinkwater, M., Yin, Y., Anderson, S. J., Schmidt, L. C., & Crawford, A. (2000). Stability of family interaction from ages 6 to 18. *Journal of Abnormal Child Psychology*, 28, 353–69.

Lundell, L. J., Grusec, J. E., McShane, K. E., & Davidov, M. (2008). Mother–adolescent conflict: Adolescent goals, maternal perspective-taking, and conflict intensity. *Journal of Research on Adolescence*, 18, 555–71.

McGue, M., Elkins, I., Walden, B., & Iacono, W. G. (2005). Perceptions of the parent–adolescent relationship: A longitudinal investigation. *Developmental Psychology*, 41, 971–84.

Recchia, H. E., Ross, H. S., & Vickar, M. (2010). Power and conflict resolution in sibling, parent–child, and spousal negotiations. *Journal of Family Psychology*, 24, 605–15.

Reis, H. T., Collins, W. A., & Berscheid, E. (2000). The relationship context of human behavior and development. *Psychological Bulletin, 126*, 844–72.

Seiffge-Krenke, I., Overbeek, G., & Vermulst, A. (2010). Parent–child relationship trajectories during adolescence: Longitudinal associations with romantic outcomes in emerging adulthood. *Journal of Adolescence, 33*, 159–71.

Silverberg, S. B., & Steinberg, L. (1990). Psychological well-being of parents with early adolescent children. *Developmental Psychology, 26*, 658–66.

Shanahan, L., McHale, S. M., Osgood, D. W., & Crouter, A. C. (2007). Conflict frequency with mothers and fathers from middle childhood to late adolescence: Within- and between-families comparisons. *Developmental Psychology, 43*, 539–50.

Shanahan, L., McHale, S. M., Crouter, A. C., & Osgood, D. W. (2007). Warmth with mothers and fathers from middle childhood to late adolescence: within- and between-families comparisons. *Developmental Psychology, 43*, 551–63.

Shearer, C. L., Crouter, A. C., & McHale, S. M. (2005). Parents' perceptions of changes in mother–child and father–child relationships during adolescence. *Journal of Adolescent Research, 20*, 662–84.

Smetana, J. G. (2008). Conflicting views of conflict. *Monographs of the Society for Research in Child Development, 73*, 161–68.

Smetana, J. G., & Asquith, P. (1994). Adolescents' and parents' conceptions of parental authority and personal autonomy. *Child Development, 65*, 1147–62.

Smetana, J. G., Campione-Barr, N., & Metzger, A. (2006). Adolescent development in interpersonal and societal contexts. *Annual Review of Psychology, 57*, 255–84.

Smetana, J. G., Daddis, C., & Chuang, S. S. (2003). "Clean your room!" A longitudinal investigation of adolescent–parent conflict and conflict resolution in middle-class African American families. *Journal of Adolescent Research, 18*, 631–50.

Smetana, J. G., Metzger, A., Gettman, D. C., & Campione-Barr, N. (2006). Disclosure and secrecy in adolescent–parent relationships. *Child Development, 77*, 201–17.

Stattin, H., & Kerr, M. (2000). Parental monitoring: A reinterpretation. *Child Development, 71*, 1072–85.

Steinberg, L. (1989). Pubertal maturation and parent–adolescent distance: An evolutionary perspective. In G. Adams, R. Montemayor, & T. Gullota (Eds.), *Biology of adolescent behavior and development* (pp. 82–114). Newbury Park, CA: Sage.

——(2001). We know some things: Adolescent–parent relationships in retrospect and prospect. *Journal of Research on Adolescence, 11*, 1–19.

Steinberg, L., & Silk, J. S. (2002). Parenting adolescents. In M. H. Bornstein (Ed.), *Handbook of parenting.* Mahwah, NJ: Lawrence Erlbaum Associates.

Vuchinich, S. (1987). Starting and stopping spontaneous family conflicts. *Journal of Marriage and the Family, 49*, 591–601.

Youniss, J., & Smollar, J. (1985). *Adolescent relations with mothers, fathers, and friends.* Chicago, IL: University of Chicago Press.

18

Communication During Emerging Adulthood

Brian J. Willoughby and Jeffrey J. Arnett

Young adulthood has always held a prominent place in the study of families and family communication. Young adulthood has traditionally been seen as a period of individual transition and union formation that was accompanied by vast changes in family dynamics and communication patterns. Arnett (2000, 2007) has suggested that the phase of life from 18 to 25 represents a new developmental stage for most young adults, a stage he designated as emerging adulthood. Emerging adulthood represents a unique moment in the life course, unique in terms of the content, quality and mediums of communication with family, friends, and romantic partners.

In this chapter, we seek to place emerging adulthood in the context of family communication. Since Arnett (2000) formally proposed emerging adulthood as a distinct, developmental period more than a decade ago, scholars have eagerly sought to understand how emerging adulthood and the changes associated with this time period are linked to communication trends with parents, peers, and romantic partners. We first introduce and summarize the scholarship which has outlined how and why emerging adults are a unique developmental population. We then discuss and summarize relevant research on communication patterns during emerging adulthood with three vital systems: parents, friends, and romantic partners. We then overview the unique place technology has on the communication that takes place during emerging adulthood. We then turn our attention to priorities and avenues for future work on emerging adulthood and family communication. We first discuss how two social science theories, social learning theory and family life course theory, might be particularly useful in conceptualizing communication patterns during emerging adulthood across multiple systems. Finally, we highlight several major limitations of current scholarship in this area and suggest directions for future research on communication during emerging adulthood. We note that our discussion (and the research in general) largely centers on communication among emerging adults in Western, industrialized countries and refer the reader to the excellent chapter by Gaines and colleagues (this volume) for an in-depth discussion of ethnic and multicultural issues and differences in relation to family communication.

Overview of Emerging Adulthood

The Historical Context of Emerging Adulthood

The theory of emerging adulthood proposes that a new life stage has arisen between adolescence and young adulthood over the past half century in industrialized countries. Fifty years ago, most young people in these countries had entered stable adult roles in love and work by their late teens or early twenties. Relatively few people pursued education or training beyond secondary school, and consequently most young men were full-time workers by the end of their teens. Relatively few women worked in occupations outside the home, and the median age of marriage in 1960 was around 20 years old for women in the U.S.A. and most other industrialized countries (Arnett & Taber, 1994). The median marriage age for men was around 22, and married couples usually had their first child about one year after their wedding day. All told, for most young people half a century ago, their teenage adolescence led quickly and directly to stable adult roles in love and work by their late teens or early twenties.

Now all that has changed. A higher proportion of young people than ever before—nearly 70 percent in the U.S.—pursue education and training beyond secondary school (National Center for Education Statistics, 2009). For most, the early twenties are not a time of entering stable adult work but a time of immense job instability; the average number of job changes from age 20 to 29 in the U.S.A. is seven. The median age of entering marriage in the U.S.A. is now 26 for women and 28 for men (U.S. Bureau of the Census, 2010). In Europe, median ages of entering marriage are even higher, usually 28–32 (Douglass, 2007). Consequently, a new period of the life course, emerging adulthood, has been created, lasting from the late teens through the mid twenties.

The Social and Cultural Context of Emerging Adulthood

One of the fascinating aspects of the rise of emerging adulthood over the past half century is how the same demographic changes have taken place across the industrialized world: longer and more widespread education, lower birth rates, and later ages of marriage and parenthood (Arnett, 2011a). These changes have occurred in the English-speaking countries of the U.S.A., Canada, the U.K., Australia, and New Zealand; all over Europe; and in the Asian industrialized countries of Japan and South Korea. Similar demographic changes have also taken place in developing countries around the world, although at present post-secondary education is less common in these countries than OECD countries and ages of entering marriage and parenthood are not yet as high.

Within industrialized countries, social class has a substantial influence on the path through emerging adulthood, especially as it influences education (Hamilton & Hamilton, 2006). Although participation in post-secondary education has expanded greatly over the past half century, across industrialized countries 5–50 percent do not continue education beyond secondary school (UNdata, 2010). Also, it is well established that educational attainment is the strongest predictor of future earnings throughout adult life (Day & Newburger, 2002). However, we know much less about possible social class differences during emerging adulthood in family relations, romantic relationships, friendships, and plans for the future, among many other areas (Arnett, Kloep, Hendry, & Tanner, 2011).

The Developmental Context of Emerging Adulthood

Emerging adulthood is not merely an "extended adolescence," because unlike adolescents, emerging adults are not in secondary school, are not going through puberty, and are not legally dependent on their parents (Arnett, 2004). Nor is emerging adulthood merely part of a "young adulthood" stretching from age 18 to 39, because the years 18–25 tend to be far less stable and structured than the period from the late twenties through the thirties (Arnett, 2011b).

Arnett has proposed five features that distinguish emerging adulthood from the adolescence that precedes it or the young adulthood that follows it (Arnett, 2004). Emerging adulthood is the *age of identity explorations*, that is, the period of life when people are moving toward making crucial choices in love and work, based on their judgment of their interests and preferences and how these fit into the possibilities available to them. It is the *age of instability*, because in the course of pursuing their identity explorations emerging adults frequently change love partners, jobs, educational directions, and living arrangements. It is the *self-focused age*, because it is the period of life when people have the fewest daily role obligations and thus the greatest scope for independent decision-making. It is the *age of feeling in-between*, because emerging adulthood is when people are most likely to feel they are neither adolescents nor adults but somewhere in-between, on the way to adulthood but not there yet. Finally, it is the *age of possibilities*, because no matter what their lives are like now, nearly everyone believes in emerging adulthood that eventually life will smile on them and they will achieve the adult life they envision. These features distinguish emerging adulthood from adolescence or young adulthood but are not unique to it. All of them begin in adolescence and continue into young adulthood, but emerging adulthood is when they reach their peak.

Systems of Communication During Emerging Adulthood

Within this historical, cultural, and development context of emerging adulthood, communication plays a vital role in the day-to-day lives of emerging adults. As emerging adults seek to establish their autonomy from parents and begin to take on adult roles, their communication shifts at multiple points of interaction. Three of the most vital systems of interactions during emerging adults are those with parents, with friends, and with romantic partners. In this section, we review the current research findings regarding communication with each of these systems during emerging adulthood.

Communication with the Parental System

Communication patterns with immediate family members often serve as the basis for communication patterns with others. Although emerging adults are often going through many individual changes regarding work, education, and residential location and have often moved away from their parent's home, communication with parents and other family members still plays an important role in their lives (MacMillan & Copher, 2005; Thornton, Orbuch, & Axinn, 1995). For example, despite the many changes that occur during emerging adulthood, research has suggested that parent–child interactions remain somewhat stable during this period (Thornton, Orbuch, & Axinn, 1995) and most emerging adults report that their relationship quality with their parents improved during emerging adulthood (Aquilino, 1997; Arnett, 2004; Lefkowitz, 2005; Thornton, Orbuch,

& Axinn, 1995). Despite reporting less contact with parents, many emerging adults report that communication with parents also became more open and of better quality during emerging adulthood (Lefkowitz, 2005).

Research has also found that parents and emerging adults have reciprocal effects on the well-being of each other (Knoester, 2003). Specifically, Knoester found in a national sample of emerging adults that changes in emerging adults' psychological well-being were associated with similar changes in parents' psychological well-being. Additionally, in families where parents have high levels of marital discord and distress, parental disclosure of family and marital issues increases mental health symptoms among emerging adults (Schrodt & Afifi, 2007). Despite the potential for decreased communication with parents during emerging adulthood, scholarship has consistently found that this relationship is still an important component of emerging adult development and well-being.

One key to understanding parent–child communication during emerging adulthood is to understand that communication patterns during this time period in the life course are strongly affected by previous interactions and patterns. As is the case with many developmental areas, interactional patterns established in childhood and adolescence influence interactions during emerging adulthood. While communication with parents does change during emerging adulthood, those changes are better viewed as variations of communication patterns established during adolescence than completely new ways of interacting. For example, issues of autonomy have been found to continue to dominate communication between emerging adults and their parents. Jensen and colleagues (2004) found that emerging adults frequently cited lying to parents as a means of asserting autonomy, although the overall frequency of lying decreased from adolescence to emerging adulthood. Although communication with parents is linked to previous interaction, some research suggests important communication shifts do occur during emerging adulthood. Aquilino (1997) found that less than 10 percent of the variance in parent–child relations during emerging adulthood was explained by interactional patterns during childhood, suggesting that communication does alter during the transition to adulthood. Using a national dataset, Aquilino found that most changes during emerging adulthood centered on emerging adults becoming more open and close with their parents as they took on more adult roles like long-term union formation and employment.

If communication with parents continues to be important during emerging adulthood, what are parenting and emerging adults communicating about? One of the goals of parent–child communication during emerging adulthood continues to be the transmission of values, attitudes, and behaviors from parents to their children (Miller & Glass, 1989). As parents are able to implicitly and explicitly communicate their feelings and values, they hope their children will adapt similar values, thus promoting intergenerational solidarity (Bengtson & Roberts, 1991) and promoting relationship quality. Evidence suggests that congruence between parents and children on many values and attitudes remains strong during emerging adulthood (Bucx, Raaijmakers, & Van Wel, 2010; Willoughby, Carroll, Vitas, & Hill, 2011). Although most of this intergenerational transmission likely takes place during childhood and adolescence, scholars have suggested that attitudes and values are still malleable during adulthood (Vollebergh, Iedema, & Raaijmakers, 2001) and communication with parents and other family members likely continues to facilitate this transmission.

Another key content area of parent–child communication centers on sex and dating. Emerging adults tend to increase the amount of conversations with parents that center on sex and dating as they enter emerging adulthood (Jensen et al., 2004; Morgan, Thorne,

& Zurbriggen, 2010). Some of this sexual communication seems to be moderated by the gender of both the parent and the emerging adult. Mothers are more likely to convey sexual information to their children than fathers (Downie & Coates, 1999) and emerging adult women are more likely to receive restrictive sex messages from their parents, whereas young men are more likely to receive permissive sex messages from parents (Morgan et al. 2010).

Communication with the Friendship System

Like interactions with parents, communication with friends and peers during emerging adulthood is also an extension of the trends established during adolescence. Many emerging adults feel more comfortable communicating with peers than parents on certain topics, sex being perhaps the most widely researched example (Dilorio et al., 1999; Lefkowitz, Boone, & Shearer, 2004). Communication with friends is typically centered on strengthening peer support networks and providing an outlet for emerging adults to express concerns, emotions, and successes. Having friends in which emerging adults can confide is an important resource for many emerging adults. This openness enhances the friendship itself, as emerging adults who have higher levels of disclosure to their friends often find those friendship relationships strengthened (Valkenburg & Peter, 2009). This closeness and intimacy with friends typically becomes more important during emerging adulthood for most individuals (Montgomery, 2005).

Communication content with peers is also different than with other systems during emerging adulthood. For example, emerging adults report that peers are the most reliable source of information on sex related topics (Kallen et al., 1983) and much of the communication during emerging adulthood among peers is centered on social activities. One of the primary context areas of peer group communication is to coordinate social events such as parties and sporting activities. These shared events are one of the most cited reasons for emerging adult peer interaction (Davis, 2010).

Also like parental communication, gender plays a key role in the content of communication among peers during emerging adulthood. For instance, and possibly counter to conventional wisdom, males tend to discuss sex and dating with their peers less frequently than females (Dilorio et al., 1999; Lefkowitz, Boone, & Shearer, 2004) and female same-sex friendships are often closer than male same-sex friendships (Johnson, 2004). Korobov and Thorne (2006) suggested that discussing intimacy and relationship matters may be viewed as non-normative for most emerging adult men. Scholars have noted that same-sex friendships are characterized by different types of interactions compared to cross-sex friendships (Afifi & Burgoon, 1998) and emerging adults tend to be closer and more committed in general to same-sex friends (Johnson, 2004). Scholars also noted that emerging adults tend to avoid certain topics with cross-sex friends (Baxter & Wilmot, 1985) such as previous relationships with members of the opposite sex and discussing the current state of the friendship.

Communication Within Romantic Partnership Systems

While exploring individual identity and transitioning into educational and vocational settings, emerging adulthood is also a time of developing and changing dating and romantic relationship behavior. Emerging adults are typically exploring and experimenting with relationships and love in ways that are different than relationships during adolescence

(Reifman, 2010). Romantic partners during emerging adulthood often serve as interactional partners that set the foundation for communication patterns in future relational interactions in marriage and other long-term unions.

Emerging adults often utilize communication with romantic partners to evaluate, define, and clarify relationships (Clark & Beck, 2010). As emerging adulthood is typically a time period of multiple romantic partners, emerging adults utilize communication with current and potential partners to evaluate their suitability as long-term partners. This is perhaps best illustrated by first date scripts. First dates represent an important evaluation period for most individuals as they seek to both determine if their date is worthy of a new relationship and seek to be desired by their date as well (Laner & Ventrone, 2000). Communication during first dates is largely evaluative as both partners seek to learn more about their date as they make decisions about behavior on this date and beyond. Emerging adults tend to follow strict scripts in such interactions (Laner & Ventrone, 1998, 2000) and are typically guarded about the type of information they convey in early dating relationships (Clark & Beck, 2010). Early dates with close friends are also marked by more intimate conversations than dates with new acquaintances (Morr & Mongeau, 2004). Being able to have quality conversations with a romantic partner is viewed by many emerging adults as a key marker of good relationship chemistry (Peretti & Abplanalp, 2004). As emerging adulthood is perhaps the time period in the life course associated with more formal dating than any other period, these communication scripts are important for reducing anxiety and helping direct interactions between romantic partners.

Another important component of communication between romantic partners during emerging adulthood centers on the negotiation of sexual and intimate behaviors. In an environment of heightened sexual awareness and behavior, romantic partners must send and decode messages regarding desired and acceptable intimate acts. Research has suggested that much of this communication during emerging adulthood is non-verbal (Henningsen, 2004) and emerging adult women tend to favor this type of indirect communication regarding sexual behaviors (Lindgren et al., 2009). Given this heavy reliance on indirect and non-verbal communication, there is a high likelihood of misinterpretations between romantic partners (Farris, Treat, Viken, & McFall, 2008). In an interview study with college students, Lindgren et al. (2009) found that men were likely to perceive higher sexual intentions than women were trying to convey. These findings have been suggested to be primarily due to emerging adult men's inability to interpret and accurately perceive women's non-verbal cues in a romantic setting (Farris et al., 2008). Men are also more likely to interpret flirting behavior as a sexual invitation compared to women (Henningsen, 2004). The ability of emerging adult couples to openly negotiate sexual intimacy becomes a key factor in determining relational outcomes and even potentially dangerous outcomes such as sexual coercion (Farris et al., 2008).

Communication Across Multiple Systems

Although emerging adult communication and interactions with parents, friends, and romantic partners may each be unique and different, it is important to keep in mind that these interactions operate in tandem and simultaneously on a day-to-day basis. For instance, as emerging adults deepen a commitment to a romantic partner, the frequency of contact with other systems such as parents and peers may change. Recent findings have suggested that emerging adults who transition to long-term unions having less contact with parents (Bucx, Van Wel, Knijn, & Hagendoorn, 2008). Bucx and colleagues also found that the transition to parenthood during emerging adulthood may likewise shift communication with other systems. Emerging adults who transition to parenthood and begin raising their own children tend to have more frequent contact with both their father and mother (Bucx et al., 2008). Interactions across one system can also influence and predict communication trajectories in other areas of communication. For example, parent–child relationships have been shown to influence relationship quality in young adulthood (Conger, Cui, & Lorenz, 2010). These interactions across multiple systems create complexity and depth to communication structures during emerging adulthood that need to be accounted for in order to understand how communication influences emerging adult development across numerous areas.

Technology: A Facilitator and Hindrance to Emerging Adult Communication

Any discussion of communication during emerging adulthood would be incomplete without an overview of the role that technology plays among this age cohort. Some scholars have suggested that emerging adulthood may be a time period of unique technology use (Axelsson, 2010; Jones, 2002) with emerging adults utilizing technology in their communication more so than any other age group. In a study of Swedish emerging adults, Axelsson (2010) found that 77 percent of emerging adults sent at least one text message a day, with almost 20 percent sending ten or more per day. Eighty-six percent of emerging adults also made at least one cell phone call per day. These usage rates were higher than both younger adolescents and older adults in the sample. American emerging adults use social networking sites, use instant messaging, read blogs and play online games more than older generations (Zickuhr, 2010). Online social communication and blogging has likewise increased exponentially in recent years and over half of all bloggers are under the age of 30 (Lenhart & Fox, 2006).

Technology could have two possible effects on individual and family communication during emerging adulthood (Mikami, Szwedo, Allen, Evans, & Hare, 2010). On one hand, technology has the potential to enhance communication by making such communication easier, more frequent and removing communication barriers such as distance and cost (Howard, Rainie, & Jones, 2001). However, some scholars have pointed out that technology may have negative effects on communication during emerging adulthood. For example, excessive use of technology has been linked to negative outcomes on the individual level and less overall communication with family and friends (Kraut et al., 1998). Odaci and Kalkan (2010) also found that high usage of the Internet was linked to loneness and communication anxiety among emerging adults. These results highlight that most technology has the potential for both positive and negative effects. Here we highlight some of the recent research on how technology may facilitate or hinder healthy communication during emerging adulthood.

As emerging adults move away from adolescent friends and family members, technology can make frequent communication possible despite the possibility of emerging adults being separated from family by long distances. Research suggests that technology may be particularly important in terms of maintaining contact with immediate family members after emerging adults leave home. For example, cell phones are the most common mechanisms for contacting immediate family members during emerging adulthood (Axelsson, 2010).

More recent technology, such as social networking sites, has also become a key resource for maintaining and building friendships during emerging adulthood (Ellison,

Steinfield, & Lampe, 2007). Ellison and colleagues found that college students who utilized Facebook were able to maintain and build peer networks. Valkenburg and Peter (2007) likewise found that frequent instant messaging (IMs) between friends improve relationship quality. In an interview study of emerging adult women, Davis (2010) found that friendship communication was identified as the central purpose of blogging for the women interviewed. Other research, however, has suggested that communication through technology alone does not support strong peer relationships. Online friendships rarely become as close as face-to-face friendships (Mesch & Talmud, 2007; Parks & Roberts, 1998) and some studies have suggested that Internet use may hinder face-to-face relationship quality (Papacharissi & Rubin, 2000).

Despite these potential downfalls, many emerging adults may prefer online communication to face-to-face interaction, believing that online communication is easier. Caplan (2007) argued that socially anxious young adults may prefer technology based communication to face-to-face interaction because it allowed them to exercise more control over social interactions. Caplan found support for this hypothesis after surveying undergraduate students and finding that social anxiety was significantly related to a higher preference for online social interaction. Likewise, two separate studies found that the social and personal benefits of social networking for emerging adults were stronger for emerging adults with low self-esteem and low life satisfaction (Ellison et al., 2007). Some forms of technology can also open up new communication avenues for emerging adults. For example, personal blogs now allow individuals to share their views, opinions and lives with a large audience (Davis, 2010; Huffaker & Calvert, 2005). Often, emerging adults use blogs and personal websites to communicate with others about themselves (Davis, 2010), perhaps facilitating identity exploration and development. Davis (2010) also found that many emerging adult bloggers begin to utilize blog posts to communicate about their opinions of things outside of personal experiences such as political viewpoints. This allows emerging adults to express their new and developing view about the world around them.

Communication via technology can also connect emerging adults with unfamiliar peers or potential romantic partners. A recent study suggested that about 10 percent of college students have attempted to find a romantic partner online (Donn & Sherman, 2002). Limited research has suggested that emerging adults who utilized online communication with unfamiliar persons tended to report having higher self-esteem and lower anxiety (Gross, 2009). Despite this, easy and plentiful connections to new people and existing peer groups may facilitate negative experiences for emerging adults such as increased exposure to sexual predators and a higher likelihood of cyber-bulling.

Beyond influencing existing and new relationships, technology may also help emerging adults achieve better overall communication. Communication facilitated by technology may help emerging adults perceive fewer social cues to limit self-disclosure which may translate to increased open expressions of feelings and thoughts. College students have reported that they feel less shy when communicating online (Knox, Daniels, Sturdivant, & Zusman, 2001) and levels of reported shyness decrease in online interactions compared to face-to-face interactions (Yuen & Lavin, 2004). Conversely, online communication lacks the verbal and other face-to-face cues essential to proper communication and accurate interpretation of communication messages (Antheunis et al., 2010). This leaves open the possibility that interactions online or through other technological media may be interpreted incorrectly and have led some scholars to label online communication media as "impoverished communicative environments" (Whalen, Pexman, & Gill, 2009).

Although much more research is needed to truly understand how technology influences emerging adult communication, we recognize it likely plays a crucial role. While the effect of technology may be positive or negative depending on the context in which it is utilized, scholars should consider the role of technology as an important component of emerging adult communication.

Moving Forward

Applying Theory to Emerging Adult Communication

A prominent role and goal of social science theory is to provide useful frameworks and terminology in order to understand, analyze, and explain the social world around us. It is helpful then to turn to social science theory in order to frame any discussion of family communication during emerging adulthood. Due to the unique social, cultural, and familial environments encountered by many emerging adults previously discussed, we believe that both a family life course perspective (MacMillan & Copher, 2005) and social learning theories (Bandura, 1977) may be particularly useful frameworks through which to analyze and interpret communication during emerging adulthood. After outlining why the precepts and hypotheses proposed by each theory may be particularly useful in the study of emerging adulthood, we offer a series of foci that each theory would suggest for emerging adult communication scholars in the future.

Family Life Course Perspective

A family life course perspective (Elder, 1994; MacMillan & Copher, 2005) suggests that we can only understand the family system by understanding the interconnected life trajectories and transitions of those within the family. One of the key aspects of a life course perspective on development is that individuals and families undergo key transitions that impact their behavior, dynamics, and structure. Transitions during the life course help give individuals and families meaning and help them structure and interpret their lives (Elder, 1994). During these key moments of the life course, individuals change and shift their roles, behaviors and relationships and although they may be short in duration, these transitions can often have long-term and long-standing effects on the individuals involved.

Family life course theory may be particularly useful in understanding emerging adult communication due to this focus on transitions, pathways and change. Emerging adulthood is a time period marked by many and varied transitions (Arnett, 2000, 2004) and a family life course perspective argues that these changes that occur to both emerging adults and those they interact with will influence future interactions and communication (Bucx et al., 2008). Family communication roles are altering as emerging adults move out of their parent's home, attend secondary education, or enter the work force. Research has suggested that these transitions are key moments of interactional change. For example, as emerging adults make the transition to marriage, communication with parents becomes less frequent (Bucx et al., 2008). The transition to a university setting has also been linked, many changes in the parent–child relationship such as feelings of closeness, feelings of respect for parents with and feelings of more independence from parents (Lefkowitz, 2005).

Another important notion from family life course theory is the concept of linked lives (Elder, 1994), or the idea that human lives are interdependent and the interactions between individuals across the life course is central to understanding human behavior. As emerging adults go through the transitions associated with emerging adulthood, their peers, parents, and romantic partners are likewise undergoing normative and non-normative transitions that will influence the context, structure, and content of their communication. There is certainly evidence that emerging adults are influenced by the social relationships around them. As previously discussed, emerging adult development is closely linked to their relationships with parents (Knoester, 2003) and peers (Montgomery, 2005).

These concepts of family life course theory can be used to create scholarly focal points as research on emerging adult communication continues to push forward. A family life course perspective offers several priorities for emerging adult communication scholars. We offer three key areas of potential future scholarly work based on this perspective:

1 Investigating how major transitions such as transitions to college, employment, and long-term relationships during emerging adulthood create focal points for understanding communication patterns.
2 Investigating if the different family, peer, and romantic roles emerging adults enter or leave influence communication patterns.
3 Investigating if communication between emerging adults and those they have close social relationships with influences their individual behavior and developmental trajectories.

Social Learning Theories

Although social learning theory is often attributed to the work of Bandura (1977), scholars have suggested that a social learning perspective really encompasses a range of theories which have similar underlying premises (Curran, White, & Hansell, 1997). The central premise of most social learning theories is that individuals learn behavior, values, and tendencies by observing both the behaviors and consequences for those behaviors of those around them.

Although social learning perspectives have not been used widely in communication research, other areas of emerging adult scholarship have drawn heavily from their ideas. For example, social learning theories have been used to understand emerging adult binge drinking behavior (Curran et al., 1997) and delinquency (Boeringer, Shehan, & Akers, 1991). This research has focused primarily on how risk behaviors commonly seen during emerging adulthood may be based on previously learned tendencies from important role models such as parents and peers.

Less work has been done linking social learning to family communication. However, the tenets of social learning theories suggest some important ramifications for emerging adult communication. First, we would expect to find strong and consistent links between the communication styles of parents and those of their children. As a primary source of social learning, emerging adults likely model communication styles and patterns from their parents as they observed them growing up.

Second, social learning theories may be particularly useful in the study of emerging adulthood by focusing on how social interactions may influence the specific behaviors of emerging adults. Much attention has been placed on certain behaviors of emerging adults such as risk-taking (Dworkin, 2005) and educational attainment (Lefkowitz, 2005). Social learning theory suggests that communication with others may serve as an important motivator, driving emerging adults toward certain types of behaviors. Utilizing ideas from social learning theories can help scholars focus on what types of interactions may be the most influential in directing emerging adult behavior and trajectories.

Like family life course theory, social learning theories offer important priorities for future work on emerging adult communication. We offer two additional areas of future study based on the precepts of social learning theories:

1 Investigating how communication styles are transmitted and learned during emerging adulthood.
2 Investigating how communication changes based on social environment and interaction with others.

Limitations of Current Scholarship and Future Directions

Despite the growing body of scholarship on emerging adult communication, several limitations continue to hamper our understanding of this developmental period. One of the key limitations to this area of scholarship is that emerging adult scholarship is still largely defined by two distinct and separate areas of scholarship. One body of scholarship involves adolescent and developmental scholars who have approached emerging adulthood by extending research lines from adolescent development to emerging adulthood development. These scholars tend to focus on issues of transition, individual behavior and identity formation and tend to ignore or omit emerging adults who make early adult transitions into marriage and parenthood.

On the other hand, a body of research exists, largely from the sociology and family fields, which focuses on family transitions such as parenting and marriage during emerging adulthood. This body of research often lacks any developmental focus. There remains a need to merge the perspectives of both of these lines of research in the future to truly understand emerging adulthood and the interactions that place during this time period. For example, no research currently exists that focuses on communication during the transition to parenthood during emerging adulthood that considers the unique developmental context of this period. Scholars should investigate how developmental trends and trajectories during emerging adulthood work together with family and role transitions to develop a complete conceptual model for the lives of emerging adults. As suggested in this chapter, utilizing both family life course and social learning perspectives can aid in developing some of these questions.

Another ongoing limitation of research on emerging adulthood is its reliance on college student populations, often emerging adults from middle to upper-class families. Most of the research cited and discussed in this chapter relies on college samples and populations. Although most authors are quick to point to this as a limitation of their individual studies, scholars still need to reach out and sample non-college emerging adults. As noted by some of the prominent national studies of emerging adults who do not attend college, emerging adults who live in low income situations or who enter the work force likely differ in important ways compared to college-bound emerging adults (Arnett, Kloep, Hendry, & Tanner, 2011).

Finally, research on emerging adult communication should also branch out and extend the range of communication content areas focused on. Currently, most of the research on emerging adult communication content focuses on sexual or relational behavior and parent–child communication. Although this is likely an artifact of many adolescent scholars interested in sexual and relational behavior moving their lines of scholarship into emerging adulthood, research is needed in other content areas of emerging adult communication such as interactions centered on employment, education, and recreation. Although a large body of research exists and is growing around parent–child communication during emerging adulthood, a particularly striking gap in our current understanding of emerging adult communication is on sibling interactions (for a recent exception see Conger & Little, 2010). Research has suggested that sibling relationships are an important aspect of an individual's well-being and behavior (Scharf, Shulman, & Avigad-Spitz, 2005). More research is needed to understand communication between siblings as one or more enter and exit emerging adulthood. Research on communication with other family members, such as grandparents and extended family members is also limited.

As the study of emerging adulthood continues to grow, it will become increasingly important to understand the interactional and communication patterns of emerging adults and how those interactions influence the important development that takes place during emerging adulthood. During the past decade, the scholarship focused on emerging adulthood has boomed, and the next decade surely holds many important innovations and discoveries into the interactions emerging adults have during this important stage in the life course.

References

Afifi, W. A., & Burgoon, J. K. (1998). "We never talk about that": A comparison of cross-sex friendships and dating relationships on uncertainty and topic avoidance. *Personal Relationships*, 5, 255–72.

Antheunis, M. L., Valkenburg, P. M., & Peter, J. (2010). Getting acquainted through social network sites: Testing a model of online uncertainty reduction and social attraction. *Computers in Human Behavior*, 26, 100–9.

Aquilino, W. S. (1997). From adolescent to young adult: A prospective study of parent–child relations during the transition to adulthood. *Journal of Marriage and Family*, 59, 670–86.

Arnett, J. J. (2000). Emerging adulthood: A theory of development from the late teens through the twenties. *American Psychologist*, 55, 469–80.

——(2004). *Emerging adulthood: The winding road from the late teens through the twenties.* Oxford: Oxford University Press.

——(2007). Suffering, selfish, slackers? Myths and reality about emerging adults. *Journal of Youth and Adolescence*, 36, 23–29.

——(2011a). Emerging adulthood(s): The cultural psychology of a new life stage. In L. A. Jensen (Ed.), *Bridging cultural and developmental psychology: New syntheses in theory, research, and policy* (pp. 255–75). Oxford: Oxford University Press.

——(2011b). New horizons in emerging and young adulthood. In A. Booth & N. Crouter (Eds.), *Early adulthood in a family context* (pp. 231–44). New York: Springer.

Arnett, J. J., Kloep, M., Hendry, L. A., & Tanner, J. L. (2011). *Debating emerging adulthood: Stage or process?* Oxford: Oxford University Press.

Arnett, J. J., & Taber, S. (1994). Adolescence terminable and interminable: When does adolescence end? *Journal of Youth and Adolescence*, 23, 517–37.

Axelsson, A. (2010). Perpetual and personal: Swedish young adults and their use of mobile phones. *New Media Society*, 12, 35–54.

Bandura, A. (1977). *A social learning theory.* Englewood Cliffs, NJ: Prentice-Hall.

Baxter, L. A., & Wilmot, W. W. (1985). Taboo topics in close relationships. *Journal of Social and Personal Relationships*, 2, 253–69.

Bengtson, V. L., & Roberts, R. E. L. (1991). Intergenerational solidarity in aging families: An example of formal theory construction. *Journal of Marriage and Family*, 53, 856–70.

Boeringer, S. B., Shehan, C. L., & Akers, R. L. (1991). Social contexts and social learning in sexual coercion and aggression: Assessing the contribution of fraternity membership. *Family Relations*, 40, 58–64.

Bucx, F., Raaijmakers, Q., & Van Wel, F. (2010). Life course stage in young adulthood and intergenerational congruence in family attitudes. *Journal of Marriage and Family, 72*, 117–34.

Bucx, F., Van Wel, F., Knijn, T., & Hagendoorn, L. (2008). Intergenerational contact and the life course status of young adult children. *Journal of Marriage and Family, 70*, 144–56.

Caplan, S. E. (2007). Relations among loneliness, social anxiety, and problematic internet use. *Cyberpsychology & Behavior, 10*, 234–42.

Clark, M. S., & Beck, L. A. (2010). Initiating and evaluating close relationships: A task central to emerging adults. In F. D. Fincham & M. Cui (Eds.), *Romantic relationships in emerging adulthood* (pp. 190–212). Cambridge: Cambridge University Press.

Conger, K. J., & Little, W. M. (2010). Sibling relationships during the transition to adulthood. *Child Development Perspectives, 4*, 87–94.

Conger, R. D., Cui, M., & Lorenz, F. O. (2010). Intergenerational continuities in economic pressure and couple conflict in romantic relationships. In F. D. Fincham & M. Cui (Eds.), *Romantic relationships in emerging adulthood* (pp. 101–22). Cambridge: Cambridge University Press.

Curran, G. M., White, H. R., & Hansell, S. (1997). Predicting problem drinking: A test of an interactive social learning model. *Alcoholism: Clinical and Experimental Research, 21*, 1379–90.

Davis, K. (2010). Coming of age online: The developmental underpinnings of girls' blogs. *Journal of Adolescent Research, 25*, 145–71.

Day, J. C., & Newburger, E. C. (2002). *The big payoff: Educational attainment and synthetic estimates of work-life earnings*. Washington, DC: U.S. Department of Commerce.

Dilorio, C., Kelley, M., & Hockenberry-Eaton, M. (1999). Communication about sexual issues: Mothers, fathers, and friends. *Journal of Adolescent Health, 24*, 181–89.

Donn, J. E., & Sherman, R. C. (2002). Attitudes and practices regarding the formation of romantic relationships on the Internet. *Cyberpsychology & Behavior, 5*, 107–23.

Douglass, C. B. (2007). From duty to desire: Emerging adulthood in Europe and its consequences. *Child Development Perspectives, 1*, 101–8.

Downie, J., & Coates, R. (1999). The impact of gender on parent–child sexuality communication: Has anything changed? *Sexual & Marital Therapy, 14*, 109–21.

Dworkin, J. (2005). Risk taking as developmentally appropriate experimentation for college students. *Journal of Adolescent Research, 20*, 219–41.

Elder, G. H. (1994). Time, human agency, and social change: Perspectives on the life course. *Social Psychology Quarterly, 57*, 4–15.

Ellison, N. B., Steinfield, C., & Lampe, C. (2007). The benefits of Facebook "friends": Social capital and college students' use of online social network sites. *Journal of Computer-mediated Communication, 12*, 1143–68.

Farris, C., Treat, T. A., Viken, R. J., & McFall, R. M. (2008). Sexual coercion and the misperception of sexual intent. *Clinical Psychology Review, 28*, 48–66.

Gross, E. F. (2009). Logging on, bouncing back: An experimental investigation of online communication following social exclusion. *Developmental Psychology, 45*, 1787–93.

Hamilton, S., & Hamilton, M. A. (2006). School, work, and emerging adulthood. In J. J. Arnett & J. L. Tanner (Eds.), *Emerging adults in America: Coming of age in the 21st century* (pp. 257–77). Washington, DC: APA Books.

Henningsen, D. D. (2004). Flirting with meaning: An examination of miscommunication in flirting interactions. *Sex Roles, 50*, 481–89.

Howard, P., Rainie, L., & Jones, S. (2001). Days and nights on the Internet. *American Behavioral Science, 45*, 383–404.

Huffaker, D. A., & Calvert, C. L. (2005). Gender, identity, and language use in teenage blogs. *Journal of Computer-mediated Communication, 10*, Article 1. Retrieved January 3, 2011, from http://jcmc.indiana.edu/vol10/issue2/huffaker.html.

Jensen, L. A., Arnett, J. J., Feldman, S. S., & Cauffman, E. (2004). The right to do wrong: Lying to parents among adolescents and emerging adults. *Journal of Youth and Adolescence, 33*, 101–12.

Johnson, H. D. (2004). Gender, grade, and relationship differences in emotional closeness within adolescent friendships. *Adolescence, 39*, 243–55.

Jones, S. (2002). The Internet goes to college: How students are living in the future with today's technology. *Pew Internet and American Life Project*. Retrieved from http://www.pewinternet.org/Reports/2002/The-Internet-Goes-to-College.aspx.

Kallen, D. J., Stephenson, J. J., & Doughty, A. (1983). The need to know: Recalled adolescent sources of sexual and contraceptive information and sexual behavior. *Journal of Sex Research, 19,* 137–59.

Knoester, C. (2003). Transitions in young adulthood and the relationship between parent and offspring well-being. *Social Forces, 81,* 1431–58.

Knox, D., Daniels, V., Sturdivant, L., & Zusman, M. E. (2001). College student use of the Internet for mate selection. *College Student Journal, 35,* 158–61.

Korobov, N., & Thorne, A. (2006). Intimacy and distancing: Young men's conversations about romantic relationships. *Journal of Adolescent Research, 21,* 27–55.

Kraut, R., Patterson, M., Lundmark, V., Kiesler, S., Mukopadhyay, T., & Scherlis, W. (1998). Internet paradox: A social technology that reduces social involvement and psychology well-being? *American Psychologist, 53,* 1017–31.

Laner, M. R., & Ventrone, N. A. (1998). Egalitarian daters/traditionalist dates. *Journal of Family Issues, 19,* 468–77.

——(2000). Dating scripts revisited. *Journal of Family Issues, 21,* 488–500.

Lefkowitz, E. S. (2005). "Things have gotten better": Developmental changes among emerging adults after the transition to university. *Journal of Adolescent Research, 20,* 40–63.

Lefkowitz, E. S., Boone, T. L., & Shearer, C. L. (2004). Communication with best friends about sex-related topics during emerging adulthood. *Journal of Youth and Adolescence, 33,* 339–51.

Lenhart, A., & Fox, S. (2006). Bloggers: A portrait of the internet's new storytellers. Pew Internet & American Life Project. Retrieved from http://www. pewinternet.org/Reports/2006/Bloggers.aspx.

Lindgren, K. P., Schacht, R. L., Pantalone, D. W., Blayney, J. A., & George, W. H. (2009). Sexual communication, sexual goals, and students' transition to college: Implications for sexual assault, decision-making, and risky behavior. *Journal of College Student Development, 50,* 491–503.

MacMillan, R., & Copher, R. (2005). Families in the life course: Interdependency of roles, role configurations, and pathways. *Journal of Marriage and Family, 67,* 858–79.

Mesch, G. S., & Talmud, I. (2007). Similarity and the quality of online and offline social relationships among adolescents in Israel. *Journal of Research on Adolescence, 17,* 455–66.

Mikami, A. Y., Szwedo, D. E., Allen, J. P., Evans, M. A., & Hare, A. L. (2010). Adolescent peer relationships and behavior problems predict young adults' communication on social networking websites. *Developmental Psychology, 46,* 46–56.

Miller, R. B., & Glass, J. (1989). Parent–child attitude similarity across the life course. *Journal of Marriage and the Family, 51,* 991–97.

Montgomery, M. J. (2005). Psychosocial intimacy and identity: From early adolescence to emerging adulthood. *Journal of Adolescent Research, 20,* 346–74.

Morgan, E. M., Thorne, A., & Zurbriggen, E. L. (2010). A longitudinal study of conversations with parents about sex and dating during college. *Developmental Psychology, 45,* 139–50.

Morr, M. C., & Mongeau, P. A. (2004). First-date expectations: The impact of sex of initiator, alcohol consumption, and relationship type. *Communication Research, 31,* 3–35.

Papacharissi, Z., & Rubin, A. M. (2000). Predictors of internet use. *Journal of Broadcasting & Electronic Media, 44,* 175–96.

Parks, M. R., & Roberts, L. D. (1998). Making moosic: The development of personal relationships on line and a comparison to their off-line counterparts. *Journal of Social and Personal Relationships, 15,* 517–37.

Peretti, P. O., & Abplanalp, R. R. (2004). Chemistry in the college dating process: Structure and function. *Social Behavior and Personality, 32,* 147–54.

Odaci, H., & Kalkan, M. (2010). Problematic internet use, loneliness and dating anxiety among young adult university students. *Computers & Education, 55,* 1091–97.

Reifman, A. (2010). Romantic relationships in emerging adulthood: Conceptual foundations. In F. D. Fincham & M. Cui (Eds.), *Romantic relationships in emerging adulthood* (pp. 15–25). Cambridge: Cambridge University Press.

Scharf, M., Shulman, S., & Avigad-Spitz, L. (2005). Sibling relationships in emerging adulthood and in adolescence. *Journal of Adolescent Research, 20,* 64–90.

Schrodt, P., & Afifi, T. D. (2007). Communication patterns that predict young adults' feelings of being caught and their associations with mental health and family satisfaction. *Communication Monographs, 74,* 200–28.

Thornton, A., Orbuch, T. L., & Axinn, W. G. (1995). Parent–child relationships during the transition to adulthood. *Journal of Family Issues, 16*, 538–64.

UNdata (2010). Gross enrollment ratio in tertiary education. United Nations Statistics Division. Retrieved November 5, 2010, from http://data.un.org/Data.aspx?d=GenderStat&f=inID%3A68.

U.S. Bureau of the Census (2010). *Statistical abstract of the United States*. Washington, DC: U.S. Bureau of the Census.

Valkenburg, P. M., & Peter, J. (2007). Who visits online dating sites? Exploring some characteristics of online daters. *Cyberpsychology & Behavior, 10*, 849–52.

——(2009). Social consequences of the Internet for adolescents: A decade of research. *Current Directions in Psychological Science, 18*, 1–5.

Vollebergh, W. A. M., Iedema, J., & Raaijmakers, Q. A. W. (2001). Intergenerational transmission and the formation of cultural orientations in adolescence and young adulthood. *Journal of Marriage and Family, 63*, 1185–98.

Whalen, J. M., Pexman, P. M., & Gill, A. J. (2009). "Should be fun not!": Incidence and marking of nonliteral language in e-mail. *Journal of Language and Social Psychology, 28*, 263–80.

Willoughby, B. J., Carroll, J. S., Vitas, J., & Hill, L. (2011). When are you getting married? The intergenerational transmission about attitudes regarding marital timing and marital importance. *Journal of Family Issues, 33*, 223–45.

Yuen, C. N., & Lavin, M. J. (2004). Internet dependence in the collegiate population: The role of shyness. *Cyberpsychology & Behavior, 7*, 379–83.

Zickuhr, K. (2010). Generations 2010. Retrieved December 30, 2010, from http://pewinternet.org/Reports/2010/Generations-2010.aspx.

19

Widening Circles

Interactive Connections Between Immediate Family and Larger Social Networks

Maria Schmeeckle and Susan Sprecher

Introduction

Individuals, couples, and immediate families exist within wider interactive worlds. These wider circles of social networks and extended families have always been around, but in every era they take on their own forms and nuances. This chapter takes up the challenge of synthesizing the latest interdisciplinary research on the interactive connections between the wider circles of social networks and immediate family dynamics at the small group level.

We begin the chapter by defining *social networks*, *extended families*, and the *primary partnerships* which are embedded in and influenced by social networks and extended families. Second, we highlight recent themes in the literature on social networks and extended families that are related to communication. Next, we explore how social networks (including extended families) affect primary partnerships, as well as parenting and child outcomes. Turning our attention in the opposite direction, we then explore how transitions in primary partnerships and immediate families affect social networks and extended families. We end the chapter with suggestions for future directions in these areas of research.

Definitions and Concepts

Social Networks

In one approach to the study of social networks, groups of people are asked about their relationships with each other, for the purpose of mapping their patterns of interaction. This approach began with Moreno's (1951) sociometric studies of naturally occurring groups and is exemplified more recently by Wellman's studies of personal communities (e.g., Hampton & Wellman, 1999). (An example of such a network study conducted with extended families can be found in Widmer and LaFarga [2000] and Widmer [2006]). Network data from all or most people in a group are difficult to obtain and analyze.

The second and more common approach to studying social networks is to identify the relationships that individuals have with others, but from the individuals' perspective only. These networks have been referred to as "ego-centered" or "personal" (Allan, 2006). Who are included in an individual's network will depend on the researcher's definition of network and the related criteria used to identify network members. For example, individuals can be asked who is important to them, with whom they interact, to whom they feel close, or from whom they receive support or would call on for assistance. The criteria can also be combined (e.g., "Name your close others with whom you communicate on a weekly basis"). The most expansive definition of a social network are others *known* by the person, which has been referred to as a person's *global network* (Milardo, 1992). Practically, though, enumerating the network of all known others for a particular ego would be difficult if not impossible. Most often, social network researchers ask individuals about specific networks, and present a finite space for responses.

A major distinction in the literature is between the *psychological network*, which consists of people defined to be important or significant, and the *interactive network*, which consists of people with whom one interacts on a frequent basis (Milardo, 1992; Surra & Milardo, 1991). Milardo (1989) found that when individuals were asked to generate both types of networks, the overlap between the two networks was only 25 percent. As noted by Parks (2007), however, the interactive network in Milardo's study was limited to individuals with whom there was communication in the past 24 hours. Parks argued that the psychological network and the interactive network may be better conceptualized as different sectors of the same overall network.

Social networks or sectors of networks, regardless of the specific criteria used to generate them, can vary on several properties. One network property is *size*, which refers to the number of people in the particular network or network sector. *Composition* refers to the type of individuals or relationships within the network. One common way to characterize the composition is the proportion of kin to nonkin, but a social network can be divided by any number of dimensions, including the proportion of those similar on some demographic trait (e.g., sex, age, race) versus those who are different. A third characteristic of networks is *density*. This refers to the degree that the network members themselves are interconnected. Other examples of network concepts include strength of network ties (e.g., strong versus weak) and the existence of cliques (cohesive subgroups). For ego-centered networks, these network properties would be assessed from the individual's perspective. For further discussion of network properties, see Felmlee (2003), Parks (2007), and Schmeeckle and Sprecher (2004).

Regardless of whether the social network for an individual is psychological or interactive, small or large, dense or loosely connected, there are certain types of "Others" likely to be included in it. Most people would include their immediate family members (e.g., spouses, children) and at least some of their extended family when asked to indicate who is in their social network. In fact, it is possible to view the extended family as a special type of network or network sector (see discussion below). Most studies on kin networks have not been conducted by network analysts or personal relationship researchers, but by family scholars. In the next section, we discuss how extended families have been defined in the family literature.

Extended Families

An important component of social networks that is studied on its own is the extended family. Extended families are often studied without an explicit definition of what is meant by this term. In this chapter we highlight four ways of conceptualizing extended family membership. The first three align with a cross-cultural study of kinship conducted by Murphy (2008): *close primary kin* consist of adult children and their parents and siblings; *secondary kin who are blood relatives* include aunts, uncles, cousins, nephews, and nieces; and *secondary affinal kin* are those related through marriage, and include parents-in-law and brothers- and sisters-in-law. Stepparents, stepsiblings, and other steprelatives might be included in this category as well. To these three types we add a fourth, *voluntary kin*, following Braithwaite et al. (2010). *Voluntary kin* are individuals who are not related by blood or law but who are considered to be kin or relatives. Examples include "other-mothers" who help to raise the children of friends or neighbors (Collins, 1990), godparents, former steprelatives and in-laws (Schmeeckle, Giarrusso, Feng, & Bengtson, 2006), and the "rainbow kinship" networks of gay men in Los Angeles (Stacey, 2004).

Just as there are various ways that social network members have been identified in actual research, extended family members have also been enumerated in various ways. One way is to ask people to list all known genetic and affinal kin, as was done in a recent study by Roberts and Dunbar (2011). Another approach is to identify different types of relatives and gather information about people in each of the types (Murphy, 2008).

Primary Partnerships Within Social Networks and Extended Families

Networks and extended families can be reduced to a constellation of pairs or dyads; in fact, the social dyad can be considered to be the simplest form of a network (Smith & Christakis, 2008). Arguably, the most important identifiable dyad for an individual is the romantic pair, which can be in the form of a marital, cohabiting, or dating relationship. We will refer to this dyad, regardless of its specific form, as the *primary partnership*. Not all adults, at any given time, are in such a partnership. Furthermore, of those who are, some would view their membership in another social dyad (e.g., with their child, with their best friend) to be more important. Nonetheless, society places importance on the primary partnership. Relationship researchers have examined how larger social networks influence primary partnerships, as well as how primary partnerships impact the larger network. Much less research examines how other pairs—friends, siblings, parent–child, or grandparent–grandchild—are impacted by larger social networks.

Current Research About Social Networks and Extended Families

Changing Communication Processes

People have more ways than ever before to communicate with others, including with distant social network members and extended families. Traditional means of communication, which include face-to-face interaction, landline phones, and letter writing, of course, still exist. Although landline phones and letter writing may be decreasing, face-to-face interactions have not been replaced, but rather have been supplemented by new forms of communication technologies, which include cell phones (voice, text, photos, videos) and Internet (e.g., email, instant messaging, web-based Internet calls, blogs, Twitter, multiplayer videogames, and social networks such as Facebook). Despite the worry expressed by some (e.g., Nie, 2001) that new forms of communication technology have reduced face-to-face interactions with neighbors, extended family members, and even with one's immediate family and intimate others, this appears not to be the case. Recent evidence indicates that people do not have less face-to-face interaction with others, as compared to years ago, and there is even some evidence to indicate that overall communication with others has increased, especially by those who frequently use cell phones and the Internet (e.g., Boase, Horrigan, Wellman, & Rainie, 2006; Kennedy, Smith, Wells, & Wellman, 2008; Wang & Wellman, 2010). Wang and Wellman (2010) argue: "We believe that the growing number of friends in America is linked in part to the proliferation, popularity, and penetration of social media; increasingly diversified Intenet users; and ubiquitous mobile connections" (p. 1163).

Growing evidence indicates that people use social networking sites such as Facebook to not only stay in touch with the inner core of their network but also to re-connect with peripheral members, including long distance relatives and friends (e.g., Ellison, Steinfield, & Lampe, 2007; Subrahmanyam, Reich, Waechter, & Espinoza, 2008). Facebook began in 2004 to connect university students, but then expanded to include high school students and then adults of all ages. Profile information and public wall posts are visible to network members identified or confirmed as "friends," and therefore people with whom one does not typically have much face-to-face contact (because of geographical distance or busy lives) can still have knowledge of one's life.

Some studies have asked adults of diverse ages about their perceptions of how new communication technologies have affected their interactions with others. In a nationally representative phone survey of 2,252 adults in 2007–9 (e.g., Kennedy et al., 2008), most of the households represented in the study used the Internet and cell phones. About 90 percent of the participants reported that the Internet had no impact on the time they spent with family members, friends, or at social events. In addition, respondents reported that the Internet and cell phones had either increased the quality of communication with family members who did not live with them (53 percent) or made no difference (44 percent); only 2 percent believed that they had decreased it. A similar pattern of results was found for the effect of communication technology on the quality of communication with members of their household and with friends. About 25 percent believed that the Internet and cell phones made it possible for their family to be closer than was the case when their family was growing up; only 11 percent believed that it made their family less close (60 percent believed that it did not make a difference).

A second, recent large-scale study that focused on asking people their views of the effect of communication technologies on their interactions with others was conducted with a representative sample of Canadians in August of 2009 (reported in Wellman, Garofalo, & Garofalo, 2009). Only 7 percent of the respondents believed that communication technology made them less connected to their family; 35 percent said that the technology made them feel closer and more connected to each other. Women, as "kin-keepers" and facilitators of social connections were found to use the Internet to do such network and kin bonding activities as sending electronic family newsletters, photos, and social invitations (Wellman et al., 2009).

Other research has examined whether people who are heavy users of communication technologies differ from those who are light users or nonusers in aspects of their social and extended family networks. This research has shown that people who are heavy users of the Internet generally have more (not less) friends, social contact, confidants, and interaction opportunities than those who are light users or nonusers (e.g., Hampton, Sessions, Her, & Rainie, 2009).

Although communication technologies can increase people's ability to stay in touch with their network members in beneficial ways, there is also an interesting shift in long-distance communication that can have more mixed implications for kin and networks.

Landline phones connect households, but cell phones and the Internet connect individuals, which has been referred to as "networked individualism" (Wellman et al., 2009). Thus, the increasing use of cell phones may lead to the reduced likelihood of interacting with others in the household beyond the one being called.

Social Networks

In this section, we discuss two interesting lines of sociological research about social networks, both of which have links to the topic of family communication.

Are Americans' Discussion Networks Shrinking?

In 2006, headlines appeared in the popular media, such as "The lonely American just got a bit lonelier" (*New York Times*) and "Study: 25% of Americans have no one to confide in" (from *USA Today*). The media flurry about lonely and isolated Americans arose from a publication by a team of respected sociologists who presented data from the General Social Survey (GSS) on changes in Americans' discussion networks from 1985 to 2004 (McPherson, Smith-Lovin, & Brashears, 2006). GSS participants surveyed in the different years were asked: "Looking back over the last six months—who are the people with whom you discussed matters important to you?" Participants were also asked other questions, including the relationship they had with each person. Results indicated that from 1985 to 2004, the number of discussion partners decreased from 2.94 to 2.08, the percentage who reported four or five others decreased from 33 percent to 15.3 percent, and the percentage of participants who reported discussing important matters with no one increased from 10 percent to almost 25 percent. Although the researchers found that both family and nonfamily confidants decreased, the decrease was greater for nonfamily connections. They concluded that Americans' social contacts can be described as a "densely connected, close, homogeneous set of ties slowly closing in on itself, becoming smaller, more tightly interconnected, more focused on the very strong bonds of the nuclear family" (p. 371). The researchers speculated that the decrease could be due to more hours spent at work, the growing influence of Internet communication, and the subsequent reduction in time spent in traditional social settings and public spaces. These speculations were consistent with earlier observations of Putnam (2000), who had written in *Bowling Alone* that there was a decrease from the 1960s through 2000 in various activities and forms of social engagement.

The findings published in 2006 (McPherson et al.) claiming a decrease in Americans' discussion networks created an academic debate. For example, Fischer (2009) questioned some of the original claims, obtained NORC's assistance in finding a coding error for 41 cases, and re-analyzed the data. Although the decrease in discussion networks was attenuated slightly after the correction, it was still found. To further bolster his argument that the original finding of increased social isolation was an anomaly, Fischer analyzed other, relevant items in the GSS, and found that responses to the other items did not show a decrease in Americans' social networks over the same period of time. For example, there was not a change found in how often the participants reported spending a social evening with relatives, neighbors, or friends outside the neighborhood or in the reported number of friends and relatives with whom the participants kept in touch at least once a year (the average was about 15).

Other recent data also suggest that Americans' discussion networks have not decreased over this recent period of time, and may have even increased. Wang and Wellman (2010) selected from a national study conducted by the Center for Digital Future, the 2002 and 2007 American samples of adults aged 24 to 74, and compared them on their number of friends. Only about 5 percent of the participants in 2002 reported not having any friends whom they see or speak to at least once a week, and this percentage did not change for the 2007 sample. The average number of friends the participants met with or spoke to at least weekly in both years was approximately 10. In addition, they found that heavy Internet users actually had more "offline" friends in 2007 than in 2002.

Another recent study that examined trends over time in the size of Americans' social networks was conducted by the Pew Internet and American Life Project, with a phone survey with 2,512 Americans in summer of 2008 (Hampton et al., 2009). Similar to the procedure in the GSS, the Pew participants were asked to indicate with whom they had discussed important matters in the past six months. The researchers reported that Americans are not as isolated as was believed to be the case based on the GSS trend data; they found that only 5.8 percent reported "no one" to either question. However, they did report that the average size of Americans' core discussion groups had declined since 1985, by approximately one confidant (they compared their responses to those of the GSS data from 1985). Participants in 2008 had an average of three core network members.

Social Networks and Social Contagions

A second recent line of research has examined social contagion through social networks—for example, how behaviors spread from person to person through a social network (e.g., Christakis & Fowler, 2009). More specifically, this research has considered how health behaviors (e.g., obesity, smoking, smoking cessation, consumption of alcohol, exercise) and affective states (happiness, optimism, depression, loneliness) can ripple through a social network. This work is based primarily on a longitudinal cohort study that began in 1948 with an original cohort of 5,209 residents from the town of Framingham (Massachusetts) and which has continued not only with the original cohort but also with their children and spouses (N = 5,124) and grandchildren who entered the study in 2002 (N = 4,095). A frequently cited finding from this research is that the likelihood that individuals became obese over time is associated with the likelihood that their social contacts, including friends of friends, became obese (Christakis & Fowler, 2007). Another well-publicized finding is about the spread of happiness: clusters of happy people and clusters of unhappy people can be identified in larger social networks, with happiness spreading through a social network to a greater degree than unhappiness (Fowler & Christakis, 2008).

The researchers argued that there are various mechanisms by which behaviors can be transmitted through a network (e.g., Christakis & Fowler, 2009). First, people may copy other people's specific behaviors (e.g., eating habits) if they have direct interaction with them or share an environment. The second mechanism, and the one they argued is probably most responsible for social contagion, is the spread of norms. Likely, norms, such as changing expectations or standards, can spread with minimal contact and through Internet communication. The most recent finding from this line of research is that divorce can also spread through a network, a topic that we discuss more later.

Extended Families

The literature on extended families tends to be fragmented, with many studies focused on specific types of relationships rather than the kinship group as a whole (Silverstein & Giarrusso, 2010). Adult children's relationships with parents, and grandparent–grand-child relationships have received significantly more attention than other types of extended family members (Milardo, 2010). Here we will discuss a recent line of research that has attempted to address the lack of attention to aunts, uncles, nieces and nephews.

These secondary kin, when studied, become visible as important contributing members of families. Strong-Boag's (2009) historical look at aunts in Canada demonstrates their vital role as alternative caregivers to nieces and nephews when parents could not fulfill their duties. Richardson's (2009) study of inner city African American boys and their single mothers revealed the serendipitous finding of vital surrogate father roles performed by the mothers' brothers (the boys' uncles), leading Richardson to consider these uncles as a "second line of defense" for single mothers, after the grandmothers. Milardo (2010), in a groundbreaking book, *The Forgotten Kin: Aunts and Uncles*, draws upon 104 interviews with aunts, uncles, nieces, and nephews. His findings reveal that aunts and uncles serve as adjuncts to parents, as surrogate parents, and as "third parties with unique perspectives." They exchange gifts, provide encouragement, and share their skills and knowledge with nieces and nephews. They help to mediate relationships in the extended family by passing on family stories and traditions. Taken together, these studies demonstrate the importance of secondary kin, and the ways these extended family members supplement and substitute for care and communication in immediate families.

Social Networks' and Extended Families' Influences on Primary Partnerships

Just as individuals are connected with others, so is every dyad connected with other individuals and relationships. Furthermore, social networks and extended families exert influence on primary partnerships—their initiation, development, maintenance, and whether they end and how.

Communication Processes Involved in Social Network Influences

There are various ways that social networks and extended families may influence primary partnerships, and most involve communicative processes that directly or indirectly facilitate or hinder a targeted relationship. Many years ago, Leslie, Huston, and Johnson (1986) asked college students to identify the specific types of activities that their parents directed to their romantic relationship. Common approving behaviors included asking about the partner, being pleasant to the partner, and inviting the two as a couple to events or activities. Disapproving behaviors including talking about others they could date, encouraging them to wait until they were older to become involved, and not communicating with the partner. More recently, Sprecher (2011) has shown that network members recognize that they engage in negative behaviors directed toward disapproved relationships and positive behaviors directed toward approved relationships. Today, network members likely provide their social reactions to a targeted relationship not only face-to-face, but also through email messages and Facebook posts. Although the network may not always give interfering or negative statements, the omission of positive and inclusive messages can be also interpreted as negative reactions and can have the same consequences as outright rejection (Buckley, Winkel, & Leary, 2004).

According to a symbolic interactionist perspective, positive reactions from the social network can enhance the partners' identity as a couple (Lewis, 1973). In addition, positive social network reactions can facilitate an increase in interdependence between the two partners (Milardo, 1982). Omission of positive reactions or actual interfering and negative statements can have the opposite effects, a decrease in dyadic identity and in interdependence. Another process by which social networks influence primary partnerships is through *information*. This information can be either positive (e.g., learning about desirable traits of a partner manifested in other contexts that are witnessed by mutual friends) or negative (e.g., learning about a partner's sexual infidelity from a friend). Information can serve to reduce uncertainty about the partner, which can enhance the likelihood that the relationship develops (e.g., Berger, 1988).

The network can also be responsible, directly or indirectly, for two people meeting in the first place, and this process likely involves communication processes (Christakis & Fowler, 2009; Sprecher, Felmlee, Orbuch, & Willetts, 2002). Passive social proximity effects occur when two people have a greater chance of meeting because of having friends or other network members in common even though the friends may not intentionally bring them together (Parks, 2007). More direct influences on the initiation process occur when the social network members try to influence the likelihood that two people meet and like each other.

Network Influences on Primary Partnerships

Network influences on dyads continue once relationships have developed. There is evidence to indicate that when network support for a relationship is forthcoming (at least as perceived by the members of the couple), dating partners experience greater satisfaction, more love and commitment for each other, and a greater likelihood of remaining together over time (e.g., Parks, Stan, & Eggert, 1983; Sprecher & Felmlee, 1992; 2000). Similar positive associations between network support and relationship quality have been found in marital relationships (e.g., Bryant & Conger, 1999). In an exception, however, an early classic study found that greater parental interference in the relationship increased the intensity of the love over time, perhaps due to a reactance effect (Driscoll, Davis, & Lipetz, 1972). (For more review of these studies, see earlier reviews by Schmeeckle & Sprecher, 2004; Sprecher et al, 2002; and Sprecher, Felmlee, Schmeeckle, & Shu, 2006).

An increasing number of studies has examined actual network members' assessments of a relationship (e.g., Agnew, Loving, & Drigotas, 2001; Etcheverry, Le, & Charania, 2008; Loving, 2006). The general finding from these studies is that friends, particularly female friends, have accurate perceptions of the quality and outcome of the targeted relationship. The studies have also found that network members have a less optimistic view of the relationship than do members of the couples. One explanation for this is that network members, unlike romantic partners, do not have positive illusions about the relationship (e.g., Murray & Holmes, 1997), which are views that are more positive than warranted. In addition, network members may engage in behaviors toward the relationship which ultimately create a self-fulfilling prophecy. Indirect evidence of this network influence was found by Felmlee (2001), who found that a friend's approval of a dating relationship was associated with the decreased likelihood of the couple breaking up. As an extension of this research, Sprecher (2011), examined how network members believed that their communications intended to either facilitate or hinder a relationship had an effect on the targeted relationship, from their perspective. About two-thirds of the participants believed that their reactions had an effect on the relationship, generally a slight effect.

Social Networks' and Extended Families' Influences on Parenting and Child Outcomes

Social networks influence not only primary adult partnerships in families but also parent–child relationships and children's development. In particular, the parents' integration within a larger social network can influence their success at raising children who are academically and socially well-adjusted and who are launched successfully into adulthood.

A distinction can be made between direct and indirect influences of parents' networks on the development of children (Cochran, 1990; Cochran & Brassard, 1979). Parent(s)' social networks can provide direct influences on children by providing other sources of interactions, experiences, and resources for them in addition to those provided by the parent(s). For example, parent(s)' adult friends and relatives may provide childcare, alternative role models, gifts, and additional social stimulation and opportunities. Social networks influence the development of children indirectly by affecting the ability of the parents to perform parental roles. Social networks can provide parents with support and advice about parenting behaviors, role models for parenting behavior, and emotional and instrumental support (e.g., Cochran, 1990; Helms-Erikson & Proulx, 2001). The influence of social networks and extended family may not always be positive for child outcomes, however. For example, network members can place demands upon parents, which can reduce the amount of time they have for the child. In addition, some network members may be poor role models, give bad parenting advice, and provide harmful experiences for others' children.

Of all network members, grandparents (parents' parents) are most often identified as assistants in the raising of children. Bengtson (2001) and others (e.g., Szinovacz, 1998) have argued that because of demographic changes, including decreased mortality rates and high divorce rates, grandparents are becoming more important than ever as sources of nurturance, socialization, economic assistance, role modeling, and other types of support for children raised in various family forms. Indeed, some grandparents take on the parenting role, either part-time or full-time.

As mentioned earlier, other relatives such as aunts and uncles (Milardo, 2010) also play important roles in the development of children. Close adult friends are significant as well. Research (as summarized by Cochran, 1990; and e.g., Romano, Hubbard, McAuliffe, & Morrow, 2009; Uhlendorff, 2000) has found that the number of close and reliable friends is associated with positive outcomes for the parenting process, including mother's satisfaction with parenting, mother's responsiveness to the child, positive mother–child interaction, and the social and academic adjustment of the child.

Working parents of minor-age children establish "networks of interdependence" around themselves to help them in raising their children (Hansen, 2005). Hansen examined these networks of care surrounding European American families across the social class spectrum. Networks of interdependence included friends and extended family members as mentioned above, but also paid caregivers, neighbors, and institutional care providers. More affluent parents relied to a greater degree on friends than they did on extended family members. Hansen elucidated how parents identify, screen, engage and mobilize potential caregivers. Children themselves serve as links to potential caregivers through their friendships and connections in neighborhoods.

Large, diverse, and loosely knit social networks that consist of a large proportion of nonkin may be especially useful at the time a family is launching an adolescent. This is because having a range of diverse social ties increases the likelihood that there will be social ties (called "weak ties" by Granovetter, 1982) that can connect the family to other persons previously unknown to them but who might be able to provide educational or work opportunities, as well as romantic opportunities.

Primary Partnership Influences on Social Networks and Extended Families

We have already focused on how social networks and extended families influence primary partnerships. In this section, we consider the opposite direction of influence, how primary partnerships affect social networks and extended families. Major life course transitions are often accompanied by changes to social lives that affect family interaction and communication. Here we consider transitions related to partnership, parenthood, partnership dissolution, remarriage, and widowhood.

A dominant theme in the research on how moving into partnership affects social networks is a focus on social network contraction. Many years ago, the hypothesis of *dyadic withdrawal* was proposed (e.g., Johnson & Leslie, 1982), predicting that as couples progressed toward marriage, they would withdraw their involvement in their respective social networks. Although not always referred to using this label, past and current research about the effects of marriage and cohabitation on social networks shows evidence for this dyadic withdrawal, especially from friends (Bidart & Lavenu, 2005; Milardo, Johnson, & Huston, 1983). Contact and emotional care with parents have also been found to be less intense for married individuals than those who are unmarried or divorced, leading some researchers to refer to marriage as a "greedy institution" (Sarkisian & Gerstel, 2008).

Another theme in the social network literature regarding the transition to primary partnership focuses on the blending of partners' social networks. Partners develop mutual friends and incorporate each other's relatives and prior friends into their networks. Therefore, network overlap typically increases during this transition (e.g., Milardo, 1982; Milardo et al., 1983). Parks et al. (1983) refer to this process as *dyadic realignment*.

Research on the transition to parenthood also identifies ways that social networks contract and get restructured after the birth of a child. Numerous studies note a reduction in sociability for parents as they adjust to parenthood (e.g., Bidart & Lavenu, 2005; Bost, Cox, Burchinal, & Payne, 2002; Knoester & Eggebeen, 2006). Interactive networks tend to become smaller, although parents may intensify their reliance on subsets of their social networks, such as close primary extended family members and friends who are also parents (Bost et al., 2002; Knoester & Eggebeen, 2006).

The dissolution of primary partnerships also tends to bring about contractions and restructuring in social networks. Individuals often sharply reduce interaction with their partner's relatives, friends and associates (Milardo, 1987), although temporary declines in contact with network members after a separation may be followed by reinvestments later (Terhell, van Groenou & van Tilburg, 2007). Another common form of social network restructuring after a relationship breakup is that the composition of social networks is also likely to change, including an increase in the proportion of unmarried friends to married friends in the post-divorce network (e.g., Milardo, 1987; Terhell et al., 2007).

A somewhat different approach to the restructuring of social networks following divorce has to do with "social contagion," which was discussed earlier. One couple's relationship dissolution can lead to a ripple effect, in that other couples in the network can become more susceptible to divorce or dissolution. This likely occurs in part because having a friend or relative experience a divorce or relationship dissolution makes it seem more acceptable to an individual, already considering divorce, to also take this step; i.e., it reduces social barriers to divorce (e.g., Berscheid & Campbell, 1981). In fact, the "contagion of divorce" can spread as far as friends two degrees removed from a couple (McDermott, Fowler, & Christakis, 2009). With more divorces, two additional people become potentially available as relationship partners to others, potentially increasing the contagion effect even more.

Remarriages or subsequent partnerships bring new opportunities and complexities to immediate families and social networks. With remarriage and repartnership, a complex collection of new immediate and extended stepfamily relationships can be considered. Children of divorce may live part-time in the households of both biological parents, creating what has been called the *binuclear family* (Ahrons, 1994) The divorces and remarriages of multiple parents and stepparents can create very complicated inter-connected households, expand social networks, and necessitate complex decisions about inclusion and exclusion related to extended family gatherings (Johnson, 2000). Former secondary affinal kin may be retained as voluntary kin.

With all this complexity, change and choice become key factors in remarriage-extended family networks. Kinship systems may become larger and more complex over time (Johnson, 2000), or they may weaken with subsequent divorces or partnership dissolutions (Lambert, 2007). Inclusive or exclusive behaviors can occur from all sides—there may not be consensus about who is in the extended family system. Children too, make inclusion decisions after remarriage. Multiple factors such as co-residence and relationship stability affect the extent to which children consider stepparents to be members of their families, and the probability of ties with a whole new branch of secondary affinal kin (Schmeeckle et al., 2006).

Research on widowhood shows that the restructuring of social networks and intensification of already-formed relationships is common. The loss of a spouse can weaken certain relationships in the social network, such as those with in-laws and couple-oriented friendships (Lamme, Dykstra, & Brose Van Groenou, 1996). Yet the time period after being widowed can also be a time of very strong ties with friends and extended family. Widowed individuals in later life tend to have smaller social networks but a greater volume of interaction, closeness, and network density within their social circles (Cornwell, Laumann, & Schumm, 2008).

Future Research Directions and Conclusions

It is clear from the studies discussed here that social networks and extended families affect and are affected by family communication at the individual and small group level. Past research, however, has not adequately recognized the significant influence of social networks and extended families on immediate family relationship dynamics, and vice versa. The literatures about social networks and extended families are rich with insights and concepts that can be usefully applied to the study of family communication.

Despite this useful potential, more could be done to integrate ideas across research on social networks and extended families. In particular, those doing research on extended families might use more network concepts. A recent example of this cross-pollination was Widmer's (2006) study of family-based social capital. Using the "Family Network Method," Widmer identified seven types of family configurations, which reflected different levels of network density. Widmer also used a free listing technique in identifying family members, thus avoiding the tendency in the extended family literature of focusing on only one relationship type at a time.

Another noticeable outcome of our review is how new technologies are expanding the modes of communication that people are using and the prevalence of contact across social networks. It appears that new technologies have enhanced communication in myriad ways. While alarmist concerns seem overblown, changing norms have brought concerns and will probably continue to do so. A recent cover story in the news illustrates what we mean. At the end of 2010, USA Today ran the headline, "The Year We Stopped Talking" (Jayson, 2010). The article emphasized that while Americans were "more connected than ever, just not in person" they were experiencing high levels of divided attention. New books such as Turkle's (2011) *Alone Together: Why We Expect More from Technology and Less from Each Other* and Fischer's (2011) *Still Connected: Family and Friends in America Since 1970* are grappling with how the latest communication revolutions are affecting the quality of connections. This will be a fascinating topic to explore as even more modes of communication are created and a higher proportion of people use them.

Thinking spatially as well, we are curious how communication technologies will affect social networks and extended families at a more global level. The Internet has made it possible to maintain connections across much larger geographic regions than in the past (Christakis & Fowler, 2009), and we expect to see more research focused on communication across large geographic areas. In addition, research using data from multiple countries reveals the impact of factors affecting extended family communication at more macro levels than have usually been considered. Murphy's (2008) research on kinship across 27 countries demonstrates that kinship interaction varies across countries and is affected by such factors as religious attendance and north–south geographic differences (within Europe).

Issues of power and inequality, advantage and disadvantage shape connections between social networks and immediate families. It was beyond our focus to discuss this at length in this chapter, but we wish to acknowledge the importance of differences across race, citizenship status, and social class. Relative deprivation seems to be associated with a greater reliance upon extended families, affecting migration, co-residence, socializing, and support (Bashi, 2007; Hansen, 2005; Sarkisian, Gerena, & Gerstel, 2006). This is an important dimension in the literature, reminding us that communication opportunities and necessities are shaped by people's access to resources and location within societies.

A final dimension we consider important to explore in the future is the potential for social network disruptions in contemporary social life. Factors such as divorce, cohabitation, relationship fluctuation, and childbearing outside of marriage can lead to unclear boundaries in families (Cherlin, 2010), and sudden "truncation" of social networks (Widmer, 2006). Interventions designed to help children, such as placement into foster care, can lead to a drastic loss in established ties to extended family members and friends (Perry, 2006). Exploring disruption in communication for social networks and extended family members among those in more fragile family situations, and the ways that networks serve as safety nets may provide practical guidelines for the stability of relationships.

313

In conclusion, the studies we have reviewed here demonstrate the powerful impact of social networks and extended families on immediate family experiences. We encourage researchers to avoid studying primary partnerships and parents and children in isolation. We live in a world of widening circles, that appear to grow even wider with advances in technology and the shrinking significance of geographic space.

References

Agnew, C. R., Loving, T. J., & Drigotas, S. M. (2001). Substituting the forest for the trees: Social networks and the prediction of romantic relationship state and fate. *Journal of Personality and Social Psychology, 81*,1042–57.

Ahrons, C. R. (1994). *The good divorce.* New York: HarperCollins.

Allan, G. (2006). Social networks and personal communities. In A. L. Vangelisti & D. Perlman (Eds.), *The Cambridge handbook of personal relationships* (pp. 657–71). Cambridge: Cambridge University Press.

Bashi, V. F. (2007). *Survival of the knitted: Immigrant social networks in a stratified world.* Palo Alto, CA: Stanford University Press.

Bengtson, V. L. (2001). Beyond the nuclear family: The increasing importance of multigenerational bonds. *Journal of Marriage and Family, 63,* 1–16.

Berger, C. R. (1988). Uncertainty and information exchange in developing relationships. In S. Duck (Ed.), *Handbook of personal relationships: Theory, research, and interventions* (pp. 239–56). Chichester: Wiley & Sons.

Berscheid, E., & Campbell, B. (1981). The changing longevity of heterosexual close relationships: A commentary and forecast. In M. J. Lerner & S. C. Lerner (Eds.), *The justice motive in social behavior* (pp. 209–34). New York: Plenum.

Bidart, C. & Lavenu, D. (2005). Evolutions of personal networks and life events. *Social Networks, 27,* 359–76.

Boase, J., Horrigan, J. B., Wellman, B., & Rainie, L. (2006). The strength of internet ties. *Pew Internet and American Life Project.* Retrieved November 1, 2010, from http://www.pewinternet.org/pdfs/PIP_Internet/ties.pdf.

Bost, K. K., Cox, M. J., Burchinal, M, R., & Payne, C. (2002). Structural and supportive changes in couple's family and friendship networks across the transition to parenthood. *Journal of Marriage and Family, 64,* 517–31.

Braithwaite, D. O., Bach, B. W., Baxter, L. A., DiVerniero, R., Hammonds, J. R., Hosek, A. M., Willer, E. K., & Wolf, B. M. (2010). Constructing family: A typology of voluntary kin. *Journal of Social and Personal Relationships, 27,* 388–407.

Bryant, C. M., & Conger, R. D. (1999). Marital success and domains of social support in long-term relationships: Does the influence of network members ever end? *Journal of Marriage and the Family, 61,* 437–50.

Buckley, K. E., Winkel, R. E., & Leary, M. R. (2004). Reactions to acceptance and rejection: Effects of level and sequence of relational evaluation. *Journal of Experimental Social Psychology, 40,* 14–28.

Cherlin, A. J. (2010). Demographic trends in the United States: A review of research in the 2000s. *Journal of Marriage and Family, 72*(3), 403–19.

Christakis, N. A., & Fowler, J. H. (2007). The spread of obesity in a large social network over 32 years. *New England Journal of Medicine, 357,* 370–79.

——(2009). *Connected: The surprising power of our social networks and how they shape our lives.* New York: Little Brown.

Cochran, M. (1990). Personal networks in the ecology of human development. In M. Cochran, M. Larner, D. Riley, L. Gunnarsson, & C. R. Henderson, Jr. (Eds.), *Extending families:The social networks of parents and children* (pp. 3–33). Cambridge: Cambridge University Press.

Cochran, M. M., & Brassard, J. A. (1979). Child development and personal social networks. *Child Development, 50,* 601–16.

Collins, P. H. (1990). *Black feminist thought: Knowledge, consciousness, and the politics of empowerment.* New York: Routledge.

Cornwell, B., Laumann, E. O., & Schumm, L. P. (2008). The social connectedness of older adults: A national profile. *American Sociological Review, 73*, 185–203.

Driscoll, R., Davis, K. E., & Lipetz, M. E. (1972). Parental interference and romantic love: The Romeo and Juliet effect. *Journal of Personality and Social Psychology, 24*, 1–10.

Ellison, N. B., Steinfield, C., & Lampe, C. (2007). The benefits of Facebook "friends:" Social capital and college students' use of online social network sites. *Journal of Computer-Mediating Communication, 12*, 1143–68.

Etcheverry, P. E., Le, B., & Charania, M. R. (2008). Perceived versus reported social referent approval and romantic relationship commitment and persistence. *Personal Relationships, 15*, 281–95.

Felmlee, D. H. (2001). No couple is an island: A social network perspective on dyadic stability. *Social Forces, 4*, 1259–87.

——(2003). Interaction in social networks. In J. DeLamater (Ed.), *Handbook of social psychology* (pp. 389–409). New York: Kluwer-Plenum.

Fischer, C. (2009). The 2004 GSS finding of shrunken social networks: An artifact? *American Sociological Review, 74*, 657–69.

——(2011). *Still connected: Family and friends in America since 1970.* New York: Russell Sage Foundation.

Fowler, J. H., & Christakis, N. A. (2008). Dynamic spread of happiness in a large social network: Longitudinal analysis over 20 years in the Framingham Heart study. *British Medical Journal, 337*, a2338.

Granovetter, M. (1982). The strength of weak ties: A network theory revisited. In P. V. Marsden & N. Lin (Eds.), *Social structure and network analysis* (pp. 105–30). London: Sage.

Hampton, K., Sessions, L., Her, E. J., & Rainie, L. (2009). *Social isolation and new technology: How the Internet and mobile phones impact Americans' social networks.* Washington, DC: Pew Internet & American Life Project, November.

Hampton, K., & Wellman, B. (1999). Netville online and offline: Observing and surveying a wired suburb. *American Behavioral Scientist, 43*, 475–92.

Hansen, K. V. (2005). *Not-so-nuclear families: Class, gender, and networks of care.* New Brunswick, NJ: Rutgers University Press.

Helms-Erikson, H., & Proulx, C. M. (2001). *What's a mother to do? Mothers' reliance on close friends as sources of parenting support.* Poster presented at the annual meeting of the National Council on Family Relations, Rochester, NY.

Jayson, S. (2010). The year we stopped talking. *USA Today*, December 30, pp. A1, A2.

Johnson, C. L. (2000). Perspectives on American kinship in the later 1990s. *Journal of Marriage and the Family, 62*, 623–39.

Johnson, M. P., & Leslie, L. (1982). Couple involvement and network structure: A test of the dyadic withdrawal hypothesis. *Social Psychology Quarterly, 45*, 34–43.

Kennedy, T. L. M., Smith, A., Wells, A. T., & Wellman, B. (2008). *Networked families.* Washington, DC: Pew Internet & American Life Project, October. Retrieved November 1, 2010, from http://www/pewinternet.org/pdfs/PIP_Networked_Family.pdf.

Knoester, C. & Eggebeen, D. J. (2006). The effects of the transition to parenthood and subsequent children on men's well-being and social participation. *Journal of Family Issues, 27*, 1532–60.

Lambert, A. N. (2007). Perceptions of divorce advantages and disadvantages: A comparison of adult children experiencing one parental divorce versus multiple parental divorces. *Journal of Divorce and Remarriage, 48*, 55–77.

Lamme, S., Dykstra, P. A., & Broese Van Groenou, M. I. (1996) Rebuilding the network: New relationships in widowhood. *Personal Relationships, 3*, 337–49.

Leslie, L. A., Huston, T. L., & Johnson, M. P. (1986). Parental reactions to dating relationships: Do they make a difference? *Journal of Marriage and the Family, 48*, 57–66.

Lewis, R. A. (1973). Social reactions and the formation of dyads: An interactionist approach to mate selection. *Sociometry, 36*, 409–18.

Loving, T. J. (2006). Predicting dating relationship fate with insiders' and outsiders' perspective: Who and what is asked matters. *Personal Relationships, 13*, 349–62.

McDermott, R., Fowler, J. H., & Christakis, N. A. (2009). Breaking up is hard to do, unless everyone else is doing it too: social network effects on divorce in a longitudinal sample followed for 32 years, October 18. Available at SSRN: http://ssrn.com/abstract=1490708.

McPherson, M., Smith-Lovin, L., & Brashears, M. (2006). Social isolation in America. *American Sociological Review, 71*, 353–75.

Milardo, R. M. (1982). Friendship networks in developing relationships: Converging and diverging social environments. *Social Psychology Quarterly, 45,* 162–72.

——(1987). Changes in social networks of men and women following divorce. *Journal of Family Issues, 8,* 78–96.

——(1989). Theoretical and methodological issues in identifying the social networks of spouses. *Journal of Marriage and the Family, 51,* 165–74.

——(1992). Comparative methods for delineating social networks. *Journal of Social and Personal Relationships, 9,* 447–61.

——(2010). *The forgotten kin: aunts and uncles.* Cambridge: Cambridge University Press.

Milardo, R. M., Johnson, M. P., & Huston, T. L. (1983). Developing close relationship: Changing patterns of interactions between pair members and social networks. *Journal of Personality and Social Psychology, 44,* 964–76.

Moreno, J. L. (1951). *Sociometry, experimental method and the science of society: An approach to a new political orientation.* Beacon, NY: Beacon House.

Murphy, M. (2008). Variations in kinship networks across geographic and social space. *Population and Development Review, 34,* 19–49.

Murray, S. L., & Holmes, J. G. (1997). A leap of faith? Positive illusions in romantic relationships. *Personality and Social Psychology Bulletin, 23,* 586–604.

Nie., N. H. (2001). Sociability, interpersonal relationships, and the Internet. *American Behavioral Scientist, 45,* 420–35.

Parks, M. R. (2007). *Personal relationships, personal networks.* Mahwah, NJ: Lawrence Erlbaum Associates.

Parks, M. R., Stan, C. M., & Eggert, L. L. (1983). Romantic involvement and social network involvement. *Social Psychology Quarterly, 46,* 116–31.

Perry, B. L. (2006). Understanding social network disruption: The case of youth in foster care. *Social Problems, 53*(3), 371–91.

Putnam, R. (2000). *Bowling alone: The collapse and revival of American community.* New York: Simon & Schuster.

Richardson, J. B. Jr. (2009). Men do matter: Ethnographic insights on the socially supportive role of the African American uncle in the lives of inner-city African American male youth. *Journal of Family Issues, 30,* 1041–69.

Roberts, S. G. B., & Dunbar, R. I. M. (2011). Communication in social networks: Effects of kinship, network size, and emotional closeness. *Personal Relationships, 18,* 439–52.

Romano, L. J., Hubbard, J. A., McAuliffe, M. D., & Morrow, M. T. (2009). Connections between parents' friendships and children's peer relationships. *Journal of Social and Personal Relationships, 26,* 315–25.

Sarkisian, N., & Gerstel, N. (2008). Till marriage do us part: Adult children's relationships with their parents. *Journal of Marriage and Family, 70,* 360–76.

Sarkisian, N., Gerena, M., & Gerstel, N. (2006). Extended family ties among Mexicans, Puerto Ricans, and Whites: Superintegration or disintegration? *Family Relations, 55,* 331–44.

Schmeeckle, M., Giarrusso, R., Feng, D., & Bengtson, V. L. (2006) What makes someone family? Adult children's perceptions of current and former stepparents. *Journal of Marriage and Family, 68,* 595–610.

Schmeeckle, M., & Sprecher, S. (2004). Extended family and social networks. In A. Vangelisti (Ed.), *Handbook of family communication* (pp. 349–75). Mahwah, NJ: Lawrence Erlbaum Associates.

Silverstein, M. & Giarrusso, R. (2010). Aging and family life: A decade review. *Journal of Marriage and Family, 72*(5), 1039–58.

Smith, K. P., & Christakis, N. A. (2008). Social networks and health. *Annual Review of Sociology, 34,* 405–29.

Sprecher, S. (2011). The influence of social networks on romantic relationships: Through the lens of the social network. *Personal Relationships, 18,* 630–44.

Sprecher, S., & Felmlee, D. (1992). The influence of parents and friends on the quality and stability of romantic relationships: A three-wave longitudinal investigation. *Journal of Marriage and the Family, 54,* 888–900.

——(2000). Romantic partners' perceptions of social network attributes with the passage of time and relationship transitions. *Personal Relationships, 7,* 325–40.

Sprecher, S., Felmlee, D., Orbuch, D. L., & Willetts, M. C. (2002). Social networks and change in personal relationships. In A. Vangelisti, H. Reis, & M. A. Fitzpatrick (Eds.), *Stability and change in relationships* (pp. 257–84). Cambridge: Cambridge University Press.

Sprecher, S., Felmlee, D., Schmeeckle, M., & Shu, X. (2006). No breakup occurs on an island: Social networks and relationship dissolution. In M. Fine & J. Harvey (Eds.), *Handbook of divorce and relationship dissolution* (pp. 457–78). Mahwah, NJ: Lawrence Erlbaum Associates.

Stacey, J. (2004) Cruising to familyland: Gay hypergamy and rainbow kinship. *Current Sociology*, 52(2), 181–97.

Strong-Boag, V. (2009). Sisters doing for themselves, or not: Aunts and caregiving in Canada. *Journal of Comparative Family Studies*, 40, 791–807.

Subrahmanyam, K., Reich, S. M., Waechter, N., & Espinoza, G. (2008). Online and offline social networks: Use of social networking sites by emerging adults. *Journal of Applied Developmental Psychology*, 29, 420–33.

Surra, C., & Milardo, R. (1991). The social psychological context of developing relationships: Psychological and interactive networks. In D. Perlman & W. Jones (Eds.), *Advances in personal relationships* (Vol. III, pp. 1–36). London: Jessica Kingsley.

Szinovacz, M. (1998). *Handbook on grandparenthood*. Westport, CT: Greenwood Press.

Terhell, E. L., Broese van Groenou, M. I., & van Tilburg, T. (2007). Network contact changes in early and later postseparation years. *Social Networks*, 29, 11–24.

Turkle, S. (2011) *Alone together: Why we expect more from technology and less from each other*. New York: Basic Books.

Uhlendorff, H. (2000). Parents' and children's friendship networks. *Journal of Family Issues*, 21, 191–204.

Wang, H., & Wellman, B. (2010). Social connectivity in America: Changes in adult friendship network size from 2002 to 2007. *American Behavioral Scientist*, 53, 1148–69.

Wellman, B., Garofalo, A., & Garofalo, U. (2009). The Internet, technology, and connectedness. *Transition*, 39, 5–7.

Widmer, E. D. (2006). Who are my family members? Bridging and binding social capital in family configurations. *Journal of Social and Personal Relationships*, 23, 979–98.

Widmer, E. D., & LaFarga, L. (2000). Family networks: A sociometric method to study relationships in families. *Field Methods*, 12, 108–28.

Part V
Family Communication Processes

20

When Families Manage
Private Information

John P. Caughlin, Sandra Petronio,
and Ashley V. Middleton

Popular advice admonishes people about the dangers of family members keeping "dark secrets" (Bradshaw, 1995, p. 27) or "the emotional fallout that often occurs when families keep secrets" (Webster, 1991, p. xi). Indeed, many families conspire to keep dangerous secrets like violence or child abuse (e.g., Petronio, Reeder, Hecht, & Mont' Ros-Mendoza, 1996; Smith, 1992). However, family members also conceal private information for prosocial reasons. For example, a wife may protect her husband from embarrassment by refraining from mentioning that he secretly wears a toupee. When family members collaborate to keep information private, it can contribute to their sense of bonding and trust with each other, protecting family privacy boundaries from outsiders (Afifi & Steuber, 2009; Petronio, 2002; Vangelisti, 1994). In contrast, revealing private information about another family member can be viewed as a betrayal if the family established rules prohibiting the disclosure (Morr Serewicz & Canary, 2008).

Such examples may suggest that deciding whether to reveal or conceal private information about the family is easy; for example, one might have a simple rule forbidding disclosures that are harmful to family members. However, privacy issues are more complicated for three reasons. First, revealing and concealing are both necessary for family functioning (Petronio, 2002). Family members need to be connected to each other through shared confidences, but they also need to keep some information from others to negotiate or maintain their own distinct identities. Second, because both revealing and concealing are beneficial (Frijns & Finkenauer, 2009), families must manage the way they make choices about disclosing and retaining their privacy. Although some choices may be easy, many are not. For example, in some cases of domestic violence, family members feel two simultaneous needs: to protect the solidarity of the family by limiting disclosure, and to alleviate harmful effects of violence by disclosing to outsiders (Fitzpatrick, 2002). Third, many family privacy issues involve information that some members keep from others within the same family. In such instances, bonding with one member by sharing private information may simultaneously betray another family member (Petronio, 2002). In short, the privacy issues among and between members are myriad and have important implications for the success of the family and its members.

The current chapter examines such issues by selectively reviewing research on family privacy, secrecy, topic avoidance, and disclosure. Our intention is to illustrate main foci of the literature rather than offer a comprehensive summary. The chapter is framed by Petronio's (2002, 2010) communication privacy management (CPM) theory, which uses a boundary metaphor to illustrate the way people manage their privacy. The theory argues that people believe they have the right to control their private information because they feel they own it and they believe controlling this information protects them from vulnerabilities. For CPM, control is achieved through the use of privacy rules that individuals develop to make decisions about how to regulate boundary permeability (i.e., degree of access to private information), linkages (i.e., connections allowing others into a privacy boundary), and ownership (i.e., the belief that one has responsibility for controlling information). In families, people typically own both personally private information and co-own information with other family members. When family members co-own private information, they are expected to coordinate privacy rules for third-party disclosures with original owners. Using the theoretical structure of CPM, the chapter is divided into three main sections:

1 how families manage private information;
2 consequences of changes in privacy rules for family privacy boundaries;
3 suggestions for future research on privacy within families.

How Families Manage Private Information

To understand how families manage private information, two main concepts from CPM are helpful to give the big picture: family privacy boundaries and privacy rules that are used to coordinate these boundaries.

Family Privacy Boundaries

CPM theory posits that family members create and manage privacy boundaries to protect or grant access to private information.[1] Privacy boundaries also mark borders of ownership and levels of control (thick and thin boundaries), as well as illustrate the management process. According to CPM theory, people own information they consider belonging to them and are co-owners of, or stakeholders in, private information that is shared by others (Petronio, 2002). Co-ownership is particularly important in families given their collective nature. CPM argues that there are two types of family privacy boundaries: external and internal cells (Petronio, 2002, 2010). The external privacy boundary protects whole family information (Vangelisti, 1994). For example, some people might say, "in my family, we never tell outsiders about family finances." Because all members co-own such information, they typically coordinate regulation of this information in a unified manner often establishing a "family privacy orientation" (Petronio, 2010). Co-ownership within internal family privacy cells includes only certain members. For example, siblings sharing knowledge of one parent's extramarital affair may cooperate to keep their knowledge from both parents (Thorson, 2009). Controlling access creates a privacy boundary cell separating the siblings from the parents.

Linkages

Linkages into privacy boundaries (internal and external) occur both when one family member (or one group of family members) gives permission to know private information and when one discloses personal or collectively held private information to others. The formation of such linkages depends on privacy rules that people use to make judgments about who should be privy to the information (Petronio, 2002, 2010). One common "linkage rule" children use within families is evident in the tendency of children to tell their mother more private information than they tell their father (e.g., Denholm-Carey & Chabassol, 1987).

Permeability

Privacy boundaries vary in permeability, meaning there are gradations in the accessibility to private information (Petronio, 2002, 2010). For example, as evidenced by reports that almost all families keep some secrets from outsiders (Vangelisti & Caughlin, 1997), the existence of a privacy boundary around family members is likely ubiquitous, yet the level of privacy control typically varies depending on a host of issues including motivations. Family members, as a consequence, regulate permeability in a number of ways. For example, family members can limit the degree of accessibility to private information by keeping a secret, which involves intentionally concealing information from others (Bok, 1983). Another way family members decrease the permeability of privacy boundaries is by avoiding topics (Caughlin & Afifi, 2004; Dailey & Palomares, 2004). Finally, family members can increase the permeability of a privacy boundary by granting greater access to private information across personal and collective boundaries (Waterman, 1979).[2]

Co-ownership

Although disclosing, avoiding topics, and keeping secrets may seem to be actions individuals engage in alone, Petronio (2002, 2010) argues that collective boundaries can be constructed through the linkages that are created when individuals divulge private information or otherwise give permission for others to know it. Once information is shared, it is considered co-owned because individuals can no longer unilaterally control how the information is (or is not) disseminated. Co-owners of private information are stakeholders in the information; therefore they must collectively negotiate decisions about granting or denying access to others. There are a number of possible collective privacy boundaries with families, including ones involving dyads, larger groups, or even the whole family.

The extant literature contains numerous examples of how ownership or co-ownership of information is associated with various privacy boundaries within or around families. For example, siblings often cooperate to keep secrets from their parents (Caughlin et al., 2000). Also, most families keep at least one secret that family members co-own, which forms a privacy boundary around that information and those members (Vangelisti, 1994; Vangelisti & Caughlin, 1997). Family members can also co-own private information with somebody outside the family and keep it from others in their family, such as when family members confide information pertinent to their family to a therapist but not to other family members (Brendel & Nelson, 1999).

Although privacy boundaries within a family must be negotiated, coordination can be difficult. CPM refers to such cases as privacy turbulence (Petronio, 2002, 2010). For example, one family member may attempt to appropriate control as in the case of parents who are perceived as invading their child's privacy (Ledbetter et al., 2010; Petronio, 1994) or in cases when one family member's standards for disclosures differs greatly from another family member's (Caughlin, 2003). Likewise, family privacy dilemmas cause turbulence as does confidants receiving unwanted disclosures that obligate them to provide support (Petronio, 2010).

Developing Privacy Rules to Coordinate Family Privacy Boundaries

Although numerous privacy rules are used to manage privacy boundaries, Petronio (2002) argues that there are two basic modes of privacy rules, protection rules and accessibility rules that are derived from five criteria: culture, gender, motivations, context, and perceived risk–benefit ratio. These criteria interact to shape specific decisions about whether to reveal private information, which confidant(s) should receive the information, when it should be divulged, and how it should be framed to manage impressions (Bute & Vik, 2010; Durham, 2008; Thorson, 2009). Considering the impact these criteria have on rule development and enactment helps to discern when members engage in protection or allow access (Petronio, 2010). Although all criteria have been found to predict the choices of privacy rules, three (culture, gender, and motivations) have been selected in this chapter to illustrate their utility for understanding privacy in families.

Privacy Protection Rules

There are many ways in which each criterion impacts protection rules for families and their members. Although we explore them individually, often these criteria work in conjunction with each other.

Culture

Given that privacy is often a cultural value, families from one culture regulate privacy boundaries to be more or less protective than families in other cultures. Families may import those cultural values as the basis for their family privacy orientation, teaching protection rules to preserve family integrity or guard secrets (Morr Serewicz & Canary, 2008; Petronio, 2010). Parents, for example, may teach their children culturally based privacy protection rules to learn when self-expression is considered inappropriate (Kim & Sherman, 2007). Cultural-based privacy rules explain why there are distinctions in how family members from different cultures protect information, such as the differences in secretive behavior between African American and Hmong adolescents (Bakken & Brown, 2010). The influence of culture can be subtle and complex. In Western cultures, there is a high value placed on openness, but this does not mean that families do not develop privacy protection rules. Consistent with the general cultural values, many families claim to be completely open, but they nevertheless carefully avoid talking about issues like sex (Kirkman, Rosenthal, & Feldman, 2005). That is, due to a cultural preference toward openness, many families do not recognize or will not admit the privacy protection rules that are implicit in their actions.

Gender

Meta-analyses have shown that differences between men and women in communicative behaviors like disclosures tend to be smaller than is often assumed (e.g., Dindia & Allen, 1992). Nevertheless, the differences that do exist are meaningful, and privacy protection rules in families are influenced by gender and sex. Certain types of private information, such as abortion or premarital pregnancy, may be more sensitive for women than men (and therefore need more protection). Research suggests that adolescent boys tend to be more secretive with their parents than are girls (Keijsers, Branje, Frijns, Finkenauer, & Meeus, 2010). Additionally, adolescents and young adults avoid topics more with fathers than they do with mothers (Golish & Caughlin, 2002). Withholding information also can have different implications based on gender: Young adults' concealment from mothers is more likely to be associated with problem behaviors than is concealment from fathers (Smetana, Villalobos, Rogge, & Tasopoulos-Chan, 2010).

Motivations

Individuals have many motivations for protecting privacy boundaries in families. Vangelisti (1994; Vangelisti & Caughlin, 1997) conducted a series of studies in which respondents reported reasons they kept secrets from other members of their family and from outsiders. Although Vangelisti labeled these reasons "functions," they likewise can be thought of as motivations for keeping secrets. For example, bonding was a reason that involves keeping a secret because it promotes cohesiveness and identification among the family members who keep the secret. Family members also keep secrets to avoid negative evaluation (Vangelisti, 1994), as in cases when family members see a secret as a source of shame (Mason, 1993). Even when unjustified, family members may believe that they will be blamed or rejected by others if they reveal a secret such as sexual abuse (Petronio et al., 1996).

Family members also may be motivated to keep secrets for maintenance reasons, such as preventing disruptions to family closeness and stress to family members (Vangelisti, 1994). For example, parents with HIV may not disclose this to a child who is thought to be too young to understand or too likely to suffer from excessive worrying (Schrimshaw & Siegel, 2002). Some individuals also report keeping family secrets simply because they do not believe the information is other people's business (Vangelisti, 1994). Another motivation for keeping secrets is to put up a defense against the possibility that others may use the information against them. Finally, sometimes people keep secrets because they believe they do not know how to effectively disclose private information to others (Afifi & Steuber, 2009; Caughlin, Afifi, Carpenter-Theune, & Miller, 2005).

Privacy Accessibility Rules

Culture

Although privacy accessibility rules are distinct from privacy protection rules, they are based on similar criteria (Petronio, 2002, 2010). Culture influences individuals' rules for revealing information, as demonstrated by Americans' tendency to value open disclosure in intimate relationships (Derlega, Metts, Petronio, & Margulis, 1993). Sometimes there are both similarities and differences between cultures; for example, safer-sex disclosure among sub-Saharan couples is, in some ways, comparable to that among U.S. couples, but disclosure in this context is also unique because of cultural norms that sanction the involvement of family members in couple communication (Miller, Golding, & Ngula, 2009).

Gender

Privacy access rules are also influenced by gender (Petronio, Martin, & Littlefield, 1984). There is a tendency for women to disclose more to their spouses and to their parents than do men (Dindia & Allen, 1992), suggesting different rules for revelation depending on gender. As with the other privacy rule criteria, gender is salient for some disclosure decisions but not others. Serovich and Greene (1993), for instance, found that married women were more likely than married men to think it is appropriate to disclose HIV testing information to members of their nuclear and extended families; nevertheless, Serovich and Greene found no gender differences regarding disclosures to nuclear and extended families among dating individuals.

Motivations

There are a number of motivations for revealing private information in families. Vangelisti, Caughlin, and Timmerman (2001) identified nine criteria individuals commonly use when deciding whether to reveal a family secret to outsiders. Consistent with the CPM notion that individuals engage in a complex calculus when determining whether to reveal private information, the nine criteria interacted in theoretically interesting ways. For example, one criterion was relational security (i.e., feelings of closeness and trust with the potential confidant). Although people reported that they would generally need to feel close to somebody to reveal their secret, such relational security by itself was not enough to make someone reveal (Vangelisti et al., 2001).

Individuals' tendency to reveal a family secret also may depend on whether they have an *urgent need* to talk to somebody about private information to relieve a burden (Helft & Petronio, 2007; Vangelisti et al., 2001). According to Stiles' (1987) fever model, individuals' need to talk with someone can be so great that they experience psychological distress. Decisions to reveal private information also are influenced by beliefs about whether the confidant will *accept* a family member if the private information is revealed (Durham, 2008; Johnson, Kass, & Natowicz, 2005; Vangelisti et al., 2001). For instance, gay sons and lesbian daughters are more likely to come out to a parent if they believe the parent will be accepting rather than rejecting (Ben-Ari, 1995).

Along similar lines, some family members wait for implicit or explicit *permission* before revealing private information. Permission can involve tacit permission from the confidant that revealing the information is acceptable (Petronio et al., 1996), or it can involve wanting to receive consent from other family members before revealing collectively owned private information to somebody outside the family (Vangelisti et al., 2001). From a CPM perspective, permission is an example of how decisions to reveal private information often are complicated by co-ownership of information. In some cases, the mutual responsibility implied by co-ownership is so salient that individual family members report that they would not reveal certain private information unless the potential confidant became a member of the family (Morr Serewicz & Canary, 2008; Vangelisti et al., 2001).

Finally, there may be times when specific criteria outweigh other factors in decisions about revealing family secrets. When individuals believe another person has an *important reason* to know the information (e.g., that person was having a crisis related to the secret), they may tell the person even if the other criteria would tend to impel them to continue concealing the secret (Vangelisti et al., 2001).

Consequences of Changes in Privacy Rules

CPM argues that there are ramifications for the decisions people make about revealing or concealing private information (Petronio, 2002, 2010). Most notably, CPM theoretically incorporated the fact that privacy management can and does become turbulent. Decisions to reveal or conceal have consequences that can lead to privacy management breakdowns for families and anyone else regulating private information (Petronio, 2002). This section examines the consequences for families of both concealing private information and revealing it because CPM argues that each can be better understood when both are considered.

Consequences of Families Concealing Private Information

A number of outcomes can occur when family members conceal information within interior and exterior family privacy boundaries. The synchronized boundary coordination of privacy rules involved in concealment may indicate that a family is functioning well; however, rule coordination can also have negative consequences for the family and its members. Three types of consequences for concealing private information mentioned frequently in the family privacy literature are bonding, creating and maintaining boundaries, and experiencing stress from keeping secrets.

Bonding

Perhaps the most often cited potential benefit of concealing private information is bonding among those who are linked within a collective privacy boundary. Individuals who share private information can feel marked as insiders, leading to a sense of loyalty and cohesiveness (Bok, 1983). Sharing a bond can also motivate individual family members to keep the family's secrets (Vangelisti & Caughlin, 1997). Although bonding typically may be considered prosocial, there are potential risks. Sometimes, family members feel so connected and loyal they will not reveal a family secret, even when the costs of keeping the secret are personally very high, such as refraining from revealing when a child develops symptoms of a psychotic disorder (Saffer, Sansone, & Gentry, 1979).

Creating and Maintaining Privacy Boundaries

Privacy boundaries can help families with the task of creating and maintaining functional interconnections among their members. When internal privacy cells are created and sanctioned by the members, the boundaries that create these cells can be beneficial because they allow dyadic or triadic autonomy and individual autonomy, thereby respecting the rights to link only certain members while controlling others' access to particular information. When daughters, for example, disclose concerns about gynecological issues to only their mothers, there usually are no hard feelings if the exclusion is discovered by other members. In fact, when families allow for these kinds of internal privacy rules they create a more flexible, comfortable, and supportive environment (Petronio, 2010).

Even in families that have internal privacy rules that work well for them, there are life-cycle experiences that challenge the status-quo of privacy rules for families. For instance, when children reach adolescence, they often decrease the amount of permeability between themselves and their parents by concealing more information than they had previously (Hawk, Hale, Raaijmakers, & Meeus, 2008; Petronio, 1994). Failure to respect the emergence of individual privacy rights between generations can be associated with negative outcomes for family members; for example, anorexia in daughters is sometimes linked with a parent engaging in overly zealous information-seeking regarding the daughter, which may impede the daughter's ability to establish individual autonomy within the family (Dalzell, 2000). On the other hand, consequences of changing privacy rules and new boundary formations can be more functional than dysfunctional. As blended families form, for example, keeping some private information from new stepfamily members can sometimes help individuals adjust to their new family configuration (Braithwaite, Toller, Daas, Durham, & Jones, 2008). Given that many children and adolescents brought into blended families feel pressure to immediately form close bonds (Bray & Kelly, 1999), keeping some information within a protected privacy boundary and not telling the new stepfamily members may allow the children to feel they own something apart from the newcomers. Concealing some private information may ease the pressure to establish "meaningful" relationships with strangers that are defined as "family" (Schrodt, 2007).

Although managing collectively defined privacy boundaries is important in families, the CPM theory suggests that privacy boundaries can become too impermeable (Petronio, 2002, 2010). For example, if a family is very successful at negotiating extremely restrictive privacy boundaries, the relatively impermeable boundary that results may have negative consequences for the family or its members. Indeed, family members' perceptions of whether and to what extent secrets are kept are associated with dissatisfaction with their family (Finkenauer, Frijns, Engels, & Kerkhof, 2005; Finkenauer, Kerkhof, Righetti, & Branje, 2009; Vangelisti & Caughlin, 1997). Similarly, young adult children's satisfaction is inversely associated with the extent to which they are allowed to conceal topics from their parents (Frijns & Finkenauer, 2009; Frijns, Keijsers, Branje, & Meeus, 2010), and parents' satisfaction is inversely associated with the extent to which they perceive their child avoids topics (Caughlin & Golish, 2002).

Experiencing Stress

There are many reasons why keeping a secret may cause tension or anxiety. The consequence of drawing thick privacy boundaries around personally private information can impact not only the secret keeper but also other members of a family. Parents who decide to keep an extramarital affair secret to protect the children, for example, would likely exhibit residual tension, even after the affair had ended and the couple decided to stay together. Secrets also can harm those who keep them. Keeping secrets is associated with individuals' level of tension, loneliness, behavioral impulsiveness, and even stress related physical health problems (Kelly, 2002; Frijns & Finkenauer, 2009). Thus, when access is not an option for other family members, the impermeability of a member's privacy boundaries becomes a burden because members expect to have some access. When the boundary lines are so restrictive, the outcome can be difficult for all family members.

Consequences of Families Revealing Private Information

One benefit of revealing personal information is to avoid problems associated with the potential burden of keeping information private. That is, some of the consequences of revealing private information are in juxtaposition to the consequences of concealing private information. There are other effects of revealing, however, that cannot be easily deduced from knowing the effects of concealing information.

Revealing Private Information and Family Members' Well-Being

There is abundant evidence that disclosing secrets or traumatic experiences can have both mental and physical health benefits (for reviews, see Kelly, 2002; Smyth & Pennebaker,

2001). Although this benefit provides a strong reason for verbalizing revelations, it is important to keep in mind this does not necessarily mean that people need to tell their secrets to the target of the secrecy to get the benefits of disclosure. The research suggests that the act of disclosing enhances well-being primarily because it helps individuals better understand the circumstances surrounding whatever information they disclose (Kelly, Klusas, von Weiss, & Kenny, 2001; Shim, Cappella, & Han, 2011). This implies that a person keeping a secret from one family member can benefit by talking about the secret with some other person (e.g., another family member, a counselor, or a trusted friend) or even by writing about the secret (Pennebaker, 1997).

Revealing Private Information and Social Support

Despite the risk that family members might not be supportive when another family member divulges private information, disclosing private information is a primary way to solicit social support from family members (Derlega et al., 1993). Parents living with AIDS, for example, may find it necessary to discuss their symptoms and prognosis with extended family members to secure instrumental assistance in caring for their children (Gewirtz & Gossart-Walker, 2000). Also, disclosing one's HIV status to members of one's family of origin is positively associated with perceptions of receiving social support from the family (Kadushin, 2000).

Consequences for Confidants

It is important to keep in mind that decisions about revealing information do not only affect the person disclosing the information; the target of such disclosures is also affected (Petronio & Reierson, 2009). Telling a family member certain kinds of information may be hurtful to that family member, and sometimes other family members do not want to be told everything (Petronio & Gaff, 2010). Moreover, the effects on the confidant then have consequences for the discloser that need to be considered; for example, individuals vary considerably in how supportively they react to learning stigmatized information about a family member (e.g., Caughlin et al., 2009).

Considering Consequences of Revealing and Concealing Together

As the preceding discussion illustrates, both revealing and concealing private information in families have a number of possible positive and negative outcomes. The impact of revealing or concealing likely depends on numerous factors such as culture, gender, motivations, and context. For example, although perceiving other family members as avoiding topics is generally associated with dissatisfaction, this association is moderated by perceived motivations, such as whether one is viewed as trying to protect oneself or relationships (Afifi, Olson, & Armstrong, 2005; Caughlin & Afifi, 2004; Donovan-Kicken & Caughlin, 2009). Consequently, recent research emphasizes the importance of considering the motivations when examining associations between concealing information and relationship quality (Afifi, McManus, Hutchinson, & Baker, 2007; Afifi et al., 2005; Caughlin & Afifi, 2004; Donovan-Kicken & Caughlin, 2009). That is, it is too simplistic to simply list the consequences of revealing and concealing because the particular consequences are contingent on the particular circumstances.

Future Directions in Family Privacy Research

The review in this chapter hints at the richness of the literature on family privacy management. Despite the richness of this literature, there are many issues that have not been fully explored. Below we describe four areas of research that have received some attention in the literature (especially recently) but also warrant considerable focus in future research.

Managing Multiple Privacy Boundaries Within Families

The CPM theory emphasizes how family members coordinate to maintain collective privacy boundaries (Petronio, 2010). As joint stakeholders or co-owners of jointly held information, family members must negotiate rules for regulating access to their private information. Although CPM gives the needed apparatus to explore multiple relationships, many studies concentrate on the relationship between individuals and the larger whole of the family (Afifi et al., 2007). However, more information is needed about how families deal with privacy management collectively. Addressing this gap in our understanding involves numerous interrelated questions. For example, when a family forms an exterior privacy boundary around private information, how do all the family members know that the information is supposed to be protected? How do members become socialized and learn expected privacy behavior?

Presumably, there are many specific means for negotiating rules regulating when, how, and if private information is revealed or concealed. Some families may reach an agreement about protecting private information through easy and implicit negotiations. The privacy rules for boundary management in these cases likely are derived from family members' previous experiences with similar situations or similar types of private information. They also may rely on relatively concrete privacy orientations that have developed over time (Petronio, 2002). In other cases, members may need to explicitly negotiate privacy rules because the privacy needs are new or different than those families have experienced before (Durham, 2008).

The complexity of families means that the joint negotiation of privacy rules and regulation of privacy boundaries may not always happen smoothly. Boundary turbulence erupts when family members are unable to reach agreement about how to handle the information, when someone makes a mistake, or intentionally violates these rules (Petronio, 2002, 2010). For example, spouses' disagreements about disclosures of infertility can cause relational challenges and privacy disruptions (Steuber & Solomon, 2010).

Considering the Recipient

In the past several years, there has been a notable increase in research on the role confidants play in the family (e.g., Petronio, 2010; Petronio & Reierson, 2009). Still, compared to the enormous literature on people who reveal or conceal private information, we know much less about recipients of private information. Family members who act as confidants often are challenged to maintain a relationship with the discloser, even if they are not prepared to cope with the information that was revealed (Petronio, Sargent, Andea, Reganis, & Cichocki, 2004). For example, the majority of mothers with HIV tell their children (Kirshenbaum & Nevid, 2002), even if some of these children are not ready to deal with such an important disclosure.

Considering the confidant underscores the need to recognize that disclosure, privacy, confidentiality, and secrecy involve both a person who reveals or conceals, and a potential recipient (Petronio, 2010). This point is particularly evident in families because families are systemic, which implies that each individual's actions can influence the other family members. Although it is difficult to study family members functioning as a group, such group level analyses are important for understanding and investigating privacy boundary coordination and turbulence within families (Petronio, Jones, & Morr, 2003). Thus, at a minimum, considering recipients in conjunction with those revealing and concealing is the first step in coming to a more complete understanding of family privacy (Caughlin et al., 2009).

Communication Technology and Family Privacy

The communication technologies available to family members have changed rapidly. Even with the most recent past generation, communication technologies like email have gone from unknown to passé (Ojalvo, 2010). Given the ready accessibility of personal information and the growing popularity of social networking sites, the question of ownership rights to this information is a challenge for families (Child & Petronio, 2011). Children using the Internet may reveal information about family income or the household's telephone numbers. Obviously, these actions may compromise parents' privacy, yet may be seen by the children as innocent actions (Branscomb, 1994). Conversely, older family members may be more apt to share personal information on social networking sites than are adolescents; for example some parents make childhood pictures of their (now) adolescent children available to others (e.g., Child & Petronio, 2011). Parents may believe they own the rights to share their family information, whereas their children may view such dissemination as a violation of their privacy.

Although parents' ability to divulge embarrassing information clearly predates the Internet, the potential speed, range, and permanence of this dissemination is heightened by such communication technologies. Computer technology is now essential to many families' everyday existence, but the implications of these technologies are far from clear. New technologies have multiple effects; for example, the expanding use of cell phones and personal computers may enable family members to communicate with one another more frequently, but increased usage of these technologies can also blur individual privacy boundaries (Ledbetter et al., 2010).

In addition to considering multiple effects of technology, family communication scholars should focus on how the *way* family members communicate with technologies matters. Understanding the privacy implications of a particular communication technology will likely depend on how families use them. For example, in some cases an adolescent may use a smartphone primarily to connect to peers or other people outside their family, which would create greater autonomy from the family. In other cases, spouses may use the same smartphone (and its embedded GPS) to monitor their partner's messages and location at all times (Gupta, 2010). Clearly, such behaviors would have very different family privacy implications.

Family Health and Privacy

As with advances in technology, the changing landscape of family health has significant implications for privacy management, providing ample ground for future research. One challenge concerns the fact that family members and physicians often have different privacy rules about medical information; for example, parents of children in sudden medical crises commonly believe that they have the right to know all medical information and observations, but physicians are more apt to conceive of specific results and observations as something that they own and can conceal until they are ready to divulge diagnoses and proposed treatments (Duggan & Petronio, 2009). Clearly, such circumstances can lead to turbulence for privacy boundary management between families and physicians, complicating the purely medical aspects of the crisis.

In addition to causing turbulence between families and physicians, medical encounters can also lead to privacy management disruptions among family members (Petronio & Lewis, 2010). Given our aging population, it is becoming more common for a family member to accompany older adults when they visit their physician to serve as an advocate and to help interpret medical diagnoses and instructions. Yet having another family member present may complicate the management of private information. Patients and other family members may assume different privacy rules during clinical visits, which can lead to turbulence in different ways. For example, family members may reveal to physicians that patients continue to smoke, even when the patient did not wish to divulge this (Petronio et al., 2004), and families with a terminally ill member can become frustrated when some members of the family want to discuss the details of the prognosis with the physician while other family members want to maintain hope and optimism by avoiding those same details (e.g., Caughlin, Mikucki-Enyart, Middleton, Stone, & Brown, 2011).

Another potential catalyst for boundary turbulence among family members is the increased availability of genetic information and testing (Petronio & Gaff, 2010). With some conditions, parents may feel guilt about being carriers or may not even understand the nature of the disease (Fanos & Johnson, 1995). Such attitudes and beliefs about genetic diagnoses can lead family members to conceal information about diseases; for instance, some grandparents purposely conceal the presence of Huntington's Disease in the family from subsequent generations (Sobel & Cowan, 2000), and parents may hide their own or their spouse's genetic test results from their children out of fear that potential partners or in-laws may reject their child if the potential for a genetic illness is known (Petronio & Gaff, 2010).

Although such intrafamily secrets may seem extreme, disclosing such information can entail large risks to family members. Sobel and Cowan (2000) reported a case when a husband divorced his wife after he learned she tested positive for the gene causing Huntington's Disease. Given the high stakes, hiding the family history of genetic predispositions could be perceived as protecting a family member from the risks involved with testing. Equally probable, some family members may not want to know genetic testing results of a family member. If the person who was tested wants to tell other family members, but some family members do not want to know the information, this could easily create privacy boundary turbulence within families. Conversely, parents may feel compelled to disclose their adult child's illness to others in the family, despite the adult child's wishes to keep the information private (Johnson, Kass, & Natowicz, 2005).

Along with genetic testing, scientific advances in infertility treatments have implications for health and privacy in families (Bute & Vik, 2010). As advanced infertility treatments have become more well known, people in a couple's social network may feel it is appropriate to ask personal questions about those treatments. Doing so can cause dilemmas for couples both because discussing treatments can lead to further undesired disclosures about infertility challenges and because engaging in these treatments is often stressful (Bute & Vik, 2010). Further, although treatments have advanced, the stigma associated with infertility remains and can impact the level of comfort in making disclosures about decisions to seeking treatment. Overall, infertility-related stigma appears to inter-act with gender such that husbands' experiences of stigma tend to suppress disclosures to friends whereas wives' experiences of stigma tend to increase disclosures (Steuber & Solomon, 2010).

Conclusion

There were two main goals for this chapter: selectively reviewing the existing research on privacy in families and suggesting areas for future research. By using the CPM theory to frame the chapter, we discussed how family members collectively manage privacy boundaries. Family privacy issues are often complex; for instance, unlike most traditional self-disclosure scholarship, much of what is considered private information in families is co-owned among members. This has numerous implications, including the need for family members to negotiate with each other when creating and maintaining collective rules for coordinating family privacy boundaries. Although we discussed the existing literature on how family members develop privacy rules, we also advocate continued work to better understand how such rules are negotiated among family members.

This chapter also summarized a number of consequences for revealing or concealing private information pertaining to families. One theme that runs through this discussion is that consequences are often simultaneously positive and negative. When a family collaborates to keep a secret, for example, it may lead the family members to bond in a satisfying way. That same bonding, however, may make it difficult for a family member to break those family privacy rules when the member feels it is more advantageous to do so. In short, the consequences of revealing or concealing private information are typically complex, which makes simple prescriptions about telling or not telling private information unproductive.

Finally, based on the existing literature and trends in society, we suggested four cor-ridors for future research on family privacy. From a theoretical standpoint, CPM theory points to a greater need for scholars to examine how family members simultaneously manage multiple privacy boundaries. There is also a need to balance the voluminous research on individuals who reveal or conceal information with more investigations into the potential confidants of that information. From a practical standpoint, innovative communication technologies and the intersection between healthcare and families provide important and interesting questions for scholars interested in family privacy.

Notes

1 It is important to recognize that the CPM focus on private information excludes some issues that can be described as privacy issues within families. For example, the term "privacy" sometimes refers to family members' rights to make decisions without being influenced by the larger community or government. A pregnant woman's decision regarding whether she should have an abortion, for instance, can be discussed as a type of privacy issue. Such "decisional privacy" issues are beyond the scope of the current chapter.

2 Although disclosing private information typically is a means of creating a relatively permeable boundary (and keeping secrets or avoiding topics are typically means of creating relatively impermeable boundaries), it is important to recognize that such associations are not absolute. As Cooper (1994) pointed out in her study of a Soviet spy, disclosing private information about oneself can be done selectively to create a false impression, even if the disclosures are true. For example, one can create the impression of being an open person by disclosing about one's attitudes or personal life. In the case of the Soviet spy, the openness about some issues

functioned to prevent other individuals from questioning whether the spy might be hiding something; thus, disclosing information actually helped the spy create a very impermeable boundary with respect to some private information.

References

Afifi, T. D., McManus, T., Hutchinson, S., & Baker, B. (2007). Inappropriate parental divorce disclosures, the factors that prompt them, and their impact on parents' and adolescents' well-being. *Communication Monographs, 74,* 78–102.

Afifi, T. D., Olson, L. D., & Armstrong, C. (2005). The chilling effect and family secrets: Examining the role of self protection, other protection, and efficacy. *Human Communication Research, 31,* 564–98.

Afifi, T. D., & Steuber, K. (2009). The Revelation Risk Model (RRM): Factors that predict the revelation of secrets and the strategies used to reveal them. *Communication Monographs, 76,* 144–76.

Bakken, J. P., & Brown, B. B. (2010). Adolescent secretive behavior: African American and Hmong adolescents' strategies and justifications for managing parents' knowledge about peers. *Journal of Research on Adolescence, 20,* 359–88.

Ben-Ari, A. (1995). Coming out: A dialectic of intimacy and privacy. *Families in Society, 76,* 306–14.

Bok, S. (1983). *Secrets: On the ethics of concealment and revelation.* New York: Vintage Books.

Bradshaw, J. (1995). *Family secrets: What you don't know can hurt you.* New York: Bantam Books.

Braithwaite, D. O., Toller, P. W., Daas, K. L., Durham, W. T., & Jones, A. C. (2008). "Centered but not caught in the middle": Stepchildren's perceptions of dialectical contradictions in the communication of their co-parents. *Journal of Applied Communication Research, 36,* 33–55.

Branscomb, A. W. (1994). *Who owns information? From privacy to public access.* New York: Basic Books.

Bray, J. H., & Kelly, J. (1999). *Stepfamilies: Love, marriage, and parenting in the first decade.* New York: Broadway Books.

Brendel, J. M., & Nelson, K. W. (1999). The stream of family secrets: Navigating the islands of confidentiality and triangulation involving family therapists. *Family Journal: Counseling & Therapy for Couples & Families, 7,* 112–17.

Bute, J. J., & Vik, T. A. (2010). Privacy management as unfinished business: Shifting boundaries in the context of infertility. *Communication Studies, 61,* 1–20.

Caughlin, J. P. (2003). Family communication standards: What counts as excellent family communication and how are such standards associated with family satisfaction? *Human Communication Research, 29,* 5–41.

Caughlin, J. P., & Afifi, T. D. (2004). When is topic avoidance unsatisfying? Examining moderators of the association between avoidance and dissatisfaction. *Human Communication Research, 30,* 479–513.

Caughlin, J. P., Afifi, W. A., Carpenter-Theune, K., & Miller, L. E. (2005). Reasons for, and consequences of, revealing secrets in close relationships: A longitudinal study. *Personal Relationships, 12,* 43–59.

Caughlin, J. P., Brashers, D. E., Ramey, M. E., Kosenko, K. A., Donovan-Kicken, E., & Bute, J. J. (2009). The message design logics of responses to HIV disclosures. *Communication Monographs, 34,* 655–84.

Caughlin, J. P., & Golish, T. D. (2002). An analysis of the association between topic avoidance and dissatisfaction: Comparing perceptual and interpersonal explanations. *Communication Monographs, 69,* 275–95.

Caughlin, J. P., Golish, T. D., Olson, L. N., Sargent, J. E., Cook, J. S., & Petronio, S. (2000). Intrafamily secrets in various family configurations: A communication boundary management perspective. *Communication Studies, 51,* 116–34.

Caughlin, J. P., Mikucki-Enyart, S. L., Middleton, A. V., Stone, A. M., & Brown, L. E. (2011). Being open without talking about it: A rhetorical/normative approach to understanding topic avoidance in families after a lung cancer diagnosis. *Communication Monographs, 78,* 409–36.

Child, J. T., & Petronio, S. (2011). Unpacking the paradoxes in CMC relationships: The challenges of blogging and relational communication on the Internet. In K. B. Wright & L. M. Webb (Eds.), *Computer mediated communication in personal relationships* (pp. 21–40). New York: Lang.

Cooper, V. W. (1994). The disguise of self-disclosure: The relationship ruse of a Soviet spy. *Journal of Applied Communication Research, 22,* 338–47.

Dailey, R. M., & Palomares, N. A. (2004). Strategic topic avoidance: An investigation of topic avoidance frequency, strategies used, and relational correlates. *Communication Monographs, 71,* 471–96.

Dalzell, H. J. (2000). Whispers: The role of family secrets in eating disorders. *Eating Disorders, 8,* 43–61.

Denholm-Carey, J. & Chabassol, D. J. (1987). Adolescents' self-disclosure of potentially embarrassing events. *Psychological Reports, 60,* 45–46.

Derlega, V. J., Metts, S., Petronio, S., & Margulis, S. T. (1993). *Self-disclosure.* Newbury Park, CA: Sage.

Dindia, K., & Allen, M. (1992). Sex differences in self-disclosure: A meta-analysis. *Psychological Bulletin, 112,* 106–24.

Donovan-Kicken, E., & Caughlin, J. P. (2009). A multiple goals perspective on topic avoidance and relationship satisfaction in the context of breast cancer. *Communication Monographs, 77,* 231–56.

Duggan, A. P., & Petronio, S. (2009). When your child is in crisis: Navigating medical needs with issues of privacy management. In T. Socha & G. Stamp (Eds.), *Interfacing outside of home: Parents and children communicating with society* (pp. 117–32). New York: Routledge.

Durham, W. T. (2008). The rules-based process of revealing/concealing family planning decisions of voluntarily child-free couples: A privacy management perspective. *Communication Studies, 59,* 132–47.

Fanos, J. H., & Johnson, J. P. (1995). Barriers to carrier testing for adult cystic fibrosis sibs: The importance of not knowing. *American Journal of Medical Genetics, 59,* 85–91.

Fitzpatrick, M. A. (2002). Policing family violence. In H. Giles (Ed.), *Law enforcement, communication and community* (pp. 129–53). Amsterdam: Benjamins.

Finkenauer, C., Frijns, T. Engels, R. C. M. E., & Kerkhof, P. (2005). Perceiving concealment in relationships between parents and adolescents: Links with parental behavior. *Personal Relationships, 12,* 387–406.

Finkenauer, C., Kerkhof, P., Righetti, F., & Branje, S. (2009). Living together apart: Perceived concealment as a signal of exclusion in marital relationships. *Personality and Social Psychology Bulletin, 35,* 1410–22.

Frijns, T., & Finkenauer, C. (2009). Longitudinal associations between keeping a secret and psychosocial adjustment in adolescence. *International Journal of Behavioral Development, 33,* 145–54.

Frijns, T., Keijsers, L., Branje, S., Meeus, W. (2010). What parents don't know and how it may affect their children: Qualifying the disclosure-adjustment link. *Journal of Adolescence, 33,* 261–70.

Gewirtz, A., & Gossart-Walker, S. (2000). Home-based treatment for children and families affected by HIV and AIDS: Dealing with stigma, secrecy, disclosure, and loss. *Child and Adolescent Psychiatric Clinics of North America, 9,* 313–30.

Golish, T. D., & Caughlin, J. P. (2002). "I'd rather not talk about it." Adolescents' and young adults' use of topic avoidance in stepfamilies. *Journal of Applied Communication Research, 30,* 78–106.

Gupta, D. (2010). SpouseSpy cell phone software hits the market to expose cheating spouses. December 8. Retrieved from http://www.prnewswire.com.

Hawk, S. T., Hale, W. W., Raaijmakers, Q. A. W., & Meeus, W. (2008). Adolescents' perceptions of privacy invasion in reaction to parental solicitation and control. *The Journal of Early Adolescence, 28,* 583–608.

Helft, P. R., & Petronio, S. (2007). Communication pitfalls with cancer patients: "Hit-and-run" deliveries of bad news. *Journal of the American College of Surgeons, 205,* 807–11.

Johnson, S., Kass, N. E., & Natowicz, M. (2005). Disclosure of personal medical information: Differences among parents and affected adults for genetic and nongenetic conditions. *Genetic Testing, 9,* 269–80.

Kadushin, G. (2000). Family secrets: Disclosure of HIV status among gay men with HIV/AIDS to the family of origin. *Social Work in Health Care, 30*(3), 1–17.

Keijsers, L., Branje, S. J. T., Frijns, T., Finkenauer, C., & Meeus, W. (2010). Gender differences in keeping secrets from parents in adolescence. *Developmental Psychology, 46,* 293–98.

Kelly, A. E. (2002). *The psychology of secrets.* New York: Kluwer Academic/Plenum.

Kelly, A. E., Klusas, J. A., von Weiss, R. T., & Kenny, C. (2001). What is it about revealing secrets that is beneficial? *Personality & Social Psychology Bulletin, 27,* 651–65.

Kim, H. S., & Sherman, D. K. (2007). "Express yourself:" Culture and the effect of self-expression on choice. *Journal of Personality and Social Psychology, 92,* 1–11.

Kirkman, M., Rosenthal, D. A., & Feldman, S. S. (2005). Being open with your mouth shut: The meaning of "openness" in family communication about sexuality. *Sex Education, 5,* 49–66.

Kirshenbaum, S. B. & Nevid, J. S. (2002). The specificity of maternal disclosure of HIV/AIDS in relationship to children's adjustment. *AIDS Education & Prevention*, 14, 1–16.

Ledbetter, A. M., Heiss, S., Sibal, K., Lev, E., Battle-Fisher, M., Shubert, N. (2010). Parental invasive and children's defensive behaviors at home and away at college: Mediated communication and privacy boundary management. *Communication Studies*, 61, 184–204.

Mason, M. (1993). Shame: Reservoir for family secrets. In E. Imber-Black (Ed.), *Secrets in families and family therapy* (pp. 29–43). New York: Norton.

Miller, A. N., Golding, L., & Ngula, K. W. (2009). Couples' communication on sexual and relational issues among Akamba in Kenya. *AJAR: African Journal of Aids Research*, 8, 51–60.

Morr Serewicz, M. C., & Canary, D. J. (2008). Assessments of disclosure from the in-laws: Links along disclosure topics, family privacy orientations, and relational quality. *Journal of Social and Personal Relationships*, 25, 333–57.

Ojalvo, H. E. (2010). Do you use email? *The New York Times*, December 21. Retrieved from http://www.nytimes.com.

Pennebaker, J. W. (1997). *Opening up: The healing power of expressing emotions* (rev. edn). New York: Guilford Press.

Petronio, S. (1994). Privacy binds in family interactions: The case of parental privacy invasion. In W. R. Cupach & B. H. Spitzberg (Eds.), *The dark side of interpersonal communication* (pp. 241–57). Mahwah, NJ: Lawrence Erlbaum Associates.

——(2002). *Boundaries of privacy: Dialectics of disclosure*. Albany, NY: SUNY Press.

——(2010). Communication privacy management of families: What do we know? *Journal of Family Theory and Review*, 2, 175–96.

Petronio, S. & Gaff, C. (2010). Managing privacy ownership and disclosure. In C. Gaff & C. Bylund (Eds.), *Family communication about genetics: Theory and practice*. London: Oxford Press.

Petronio, S., Jones, S., & Morr, M. C. (2003). Family privacy dilemmas: Managing communication boundaries within family groups. In L. Frey (Ed.), *Group communication in context: Studies of bona fide groups* (pp. 23–56). Mahwah, NJ: Lawrence Erlbaum Associates.

Petronio, S. & Lewis, S. (2010). Medical disclosure in oncology: Families, patients, and providers. In M. Miller-Day (Ed.), *"Going through this together:" Family communication, connection, and health transitions*. New York: Peter Lang.

Petronio, S., Martin, J., & Littlefield, R. (1984). Prerequisite conditions for self-disclosing: A gender issue. *Communication Monographs*, 51, 268–73.

Petronio, S., Reeder, H. M., Hecht, M. L., & Mon't Ros-Mendoza, T. (1996). Disclosure of sexual abuse by children and adolescents. *Journal of Applied Communication Research*, 24, 181–99.

Petronio, S. & Reierson, J. (2009). Regulating the privacy of confidentiality: Grasping the complexities through communication privacy management theory. In T. Afifi, & W. Afifi (Eds.), *Uncertainty, information management and disclosure decisions: Theories and applications* (pp. 365–83). New York: Routledge.

Petronio, S., Sargent, J., Andea, L., Reganis, P., & Cichocki, D. (2004). Family and friends as healthcare advocates: Dilemmas of confidentiality and privacy. *Journal of Social and Personal Relationships*, 21, 33–52.

Saffer, J. B., Sansone, P., & Gentry, J. (1979). The awesome burden upon the child who must keep a family secret. *Child Psychiatry and Human Development*, 10, 35–40.

Schrimshaw, E. W., & Siegel, K. (2002). HIV-infected mothers' disclosure to their uninfected children: Rates, reasons, and reactions. *Journal of Social and Personal Relationships*, 19, 19–43.

Schrodt, P. (2007). Development and validation of the Stepfamily Life Index. *Journal of Social and Personal Relationships*, 23, 427–44.

Serovich, J. M., & Greene, K. (1993). Perceptions of family boundaries: The case of disclosure of HIV testing information. *Family Relations*, 42, 193–97.

Shim, M., Cappella, J. N., & Han, J. Y. (2011). How does insightful and emotional disclosure bring potential health benefits? Study based on online support groups for women with breast cancer. *Journal of Communication*, 61, 432–54.

Smetana, J. G., Villalobos, M., Rogge, R. D., & Tasopoulos-Chan, M. (2010). Keeping secrets from parents: Daily variations among poor, urban adolescents. *Journal of Adolescence*, 33, 321–31.

Smith, G. (1992). The unbearable traumatic past: Child sexual abuse. In V. P. Varma (Ed.), *The secret life of vulnerable children* (pp. 130–56). New York: Routledge.

Smyth, J. M., & Pennebaker, J. W. (2001). What are the health effects of disclosure? In A. Baum, T. A. Revenson, & J. E. Singer (Eds.), *Handbook of health psychology* (pp. 339–48). Mahwah, NJ: Lawrence Erlbaum Associates.

Sobel, S. K., & Cowan, D. B. (2000). Impact of genetic testing for Huntington disease on the family system. *American Journal of Medical Genetics, 90*, 49–59.

Steuber, K. R., & Solomon, D. H. (2010). *Factors that predict married partners' disclosures about infertility to social network members.* Presentation at the annual convention of the National Communication Association, San Francisco, CA, November.

Stiles, W. B. (1987). "I have to talk to somebody:" A fever model of disclosure. In V. Derlega & J. Berg (Eds.), *Self-disclosure: Theory, research, and therapy* (pp. 257–82). New York: Plenum Press.

Thorson, A. R. (2009). Adult children's experiences of their parents' infidelity: Communicative protection and access rules in the absence of divorce. *Communication Studies, 60*, 32–48.

Vangelisti, A. L. (1994). Family secrets: Forms, functions, and correlates. *Journal of Social and Personal Relationships, 11*, 113–35.

Vangelisti, A. L., & Caughlin J. P. (1997). Revealing family secrets: The influence of topic, function, and relationships. *Journal of Social and Personal Relationships, 14*, 679–705.

Vangelisti, A. L., Caughlin, J. P., & Timmerman, L. M. (2001). Criteria for revealing family secrets. *Communication Monographs, 68*, 1–27.

Waterman, J. (1979). Family patterns of self-disclosure. In G. J. Chelune and Associates (Eds.), *Self-disclosure: Origins, patterns, and implications of openness in interpersonal relationships* (pp. 225–42). San Francisco, CA: Jossey-Bass.

Webster, H. (1991). *Family secrets: How telling and not telling affects our children, our relationships, and our lives.* Reading, MA: Addison-Wesley.

21

Conflict and Relational Quality in Families

Alan L. Sillars and Daniel J. Canary

Conflict is one of the most studied aspects of family relationships (Bradbury, Rogge, & Lawrence, 2001), with the dominant concern being relational quality (i.e., satisfaction, stability, adaptability, nurturance). Although the amount or severity of conflict is one marker of relational quality, many authors foreground the response to conflict (Canary, Cupach, & Messman, 1995). Charny (1980) exemplifies this spirit by declaring that: "what really becomes important in family life is not the ability to stay out of trouble but to get out of trouble, that is, the ability to process conflicts and dilemmas and unfairness constructively" (p. 43). Such a perspective highlights communication processes; communication being the principal means by which conflicts are managed to the benefit or detriment of families.

While undoubtedly central, the role of communication in family conflict is complex. As this review illustrates, a number of factors influence how communication is used, what it signifies, and how family members respond. Thus, family conflict communication should not be reduced to a dichotomy between constructive and destructive forms. The impacts of communication on family well-being do not rest so much on messages or message patterns in isolation but on the interplay of messages, relational contexts, and interpretive frameworks.

In the first section of the chapter, we examine communicative acts and patterns and summarize research on relational impacts of communication. Next, we highlight contextual factors that shape communication and moderate associations with relational quality. Last, the review considers interpretive processes that affect the meaning and outcomes of communication.

Conceptualizing Conflict Communication

Typology of Communicative Acts

Communication during family conflict can be described at the level of broad styles (e.g., to compete or compromise) or specific acts and patterns (e.g., criticism or negative reciprocity). Two dimensions identified by van de Vliert and Euwema (1994)—activeness and agreeableness—can organize both general styles and most communicative acts identified by family researchers. We re-conceptualize these dimensions as qualities of messages, namely: (1) directness (i.e., engagement versus avoidance), and (2) valence (i.e., positive/negative, or face-attacking versus face-honoring moves; Ting-Toomey & Kurogi, 1998). By crossing the two dimensions, van de Vliert and Euwema (1994) derived four overarching conflict strategies: negotiation, nonconfrontation, direct fighting, and indirect fighting. Using the same categories, Table 21.1 synthesizes communicative codes from several observational coding schemes for couple conflict.

Table 21.1 Communication Codes in Observational Marital Research

---

Negotiation: Direct and Face Honoring

Accept Responsibility (Weiss, 1993)
  (statement that "I" or "we" are responsible for the problem)
Approve (Weiss, 1993)
  Statement that favors couple's or partner's attributions, actions, or statement
Analytic Remarks (Sillars, 1986)
  Descriptive Statements; Disclosive Statements; Qualifying Statements; Soliciting Disclosure; Soliciting Criticism
Cognitive Acts (Raush et al., 1974)
  Opening the issue/probe; Seeking information; Giving information; Suggesting course of action; Giving reasons; Exploring consequences
Conciliatory Remarks (Sillars, 1986)
  Supportive remarks; Concessions; Acceptance of responsibility
Mindreading/Positive (Gottman, 1979)
  Beliefs about the partner's internal states, said with positive or neutral effect
Problem Description (Weiss, 1993)
Problem-solving/Information Exchange (Gottman, 1979)
Propose Change (Weiss, 1993)
  Compromise; Negative Solution (proposal for termination or decrease of behavior);
  Positive Solution (proposal for initiation or increase of behavior)
Reconciling Acts (Raush et al., 1974)
  Accepting blame or responsibility; Showing concern for other's feelings; Seeking reassurance; Attempting to make-up; Offering help or reassurance
Resolving Acts (Raush et al., 1974)
  Accepting the other's plans, ideas, feelings; Introduce compromise; Offer to collaborate in planning
Summarizing Self/Summarizing Other (Gottman, 1979)

Direct Fighting: Direct and Face Attacking

Blame (Weiss, 1993)
  Criticize; Mindread Negative (statement assuming a negative mindset or motivation of the partner); Put Down; Threat; Hostile or Negative Voice Tone
Coercive Acts/Personal Attacks (Raush et al., 1974)
  Using external power; Commanding; Demanding compensation; Inducing guilt or attacking other's motives; Disparaging the other; Threatening the other
Confrontative Remarks (Sillars, 1986)
  Personal Criticism; Rejection; Hostile Imperatives; Presumptive Remarks
Denying validity of other's arguments (Raush et al., 1974)
Interrupt (Weiss, 1993)
Mindreading/Negative (Gottman, 1979)
  Beliefs about the partner's internal states, said with negative effect
Rejecting Acts (Raush et al., 1974)
  Recognizing other's motive as a strategy or calling the other's bluff; Rejection

Alan L. Sillars and Daniel J. Canary

Table 21.1 (continued)

Nonconfrontation: Indirect and Face Honoring

Changing the Subject (Raush et al., 1974)
Denial and Equivocation (Sillars, 1986)
    Direct or Implicit Denial (that a conflict exists); Evasive Remarks (failure to acknowledge or deny the presence of a conflict following a prompt)
Disengage (Weiss, 1993)
    Expressing the desire not to talk about an issue
Off Topic (Weiss, 1993)
Topic Management (Sillars, 1986)
    Topic Shifts (terminating discussion before it has reached natural completion)
    Topic Avoidance (statements that explicitly avoid or limit discussion)

Indirect Fighting: Indirect and Face Attacking

Avoiding Blame or Responsibility (Raush et al., 1974)
Denial of Responsibility (Sillars, 1986)
Dysphoric Affect (Weiss, 1993)
    Affect communicating depression, sadness, self-complaint, or whiny voice
Excuse (Weiss, 1993)
Giving up or Leaving the Field (Rausch et al., 1974)
Hostile Jokes and Questions (Sillars, 1986)
Turn Off (Weiss, 1993)
Withdrawal (Weiss, 1993)

Polysemous: Variable Meanings

Agreement/Disagreement (Gottman, 1979; Rausch et al., 1974; Weiss, 1993)
Appealing Acts (Raush et al., 1974)
    Appeals to fairness; Appeals to other's motives; Offering something else to win one's goal; Appealing to other's love; Pleading or coaxing
Communication Talk (Gottman, 1979)
    Communication about communication
Compliance/Non-compliance (Gottman, 1979; Weiss, 1993)
Expressing Feelings about a Problem (Gottman, 1979)
Facilitation (Weiss, 1993)
    Assent (listener states "yeah," nods head); Humor (lighthearted, not sarcasm); Metacommunication (statements that direct the flow of conversation); Question; Paraphrase/Reflection
Friendly Joking (Sillars, 1986)
Noncommittal Remarks (Sillars, 1986)
    Noncommittal Statements; Noncommittal Questions; Abstract Remarks; Procedural Remarks

---

In the first edition of this anthology, all codes were subsumed under van de Vliert and Euwema's four categories. However, some acts, referred to here as *polysemous*, have variable meaning and may fit multiple categories. For example, verbal metacommunication (talk about communication) can serve negotiation by clarifying ground rules and areas of misunderstanding. Yet, preoccupation with metacommunication may indicate relationship trouble (Watzlawick, Beavin, & Jackson, 1967). In Gottman's (1979) research, distressed married couples became mired in extended chains of negative metacommunication, in contrast to the brief and intermittent metacommunicative exchanges of nondistressed couples. Similarly, joking can act as nonconfrontation that deflects attention from an issue, a form of indirect fighting, or a way to build consensus and reduce negative effect (Alberts, 1990).

Conflict Patterns

People do not simply choose one type of message over others; instead, they construct messages in situ while reacting to others. Most research in this regard involves the sequential structure of conflict—how one message elicits an immediate response.

An over-riding tendency is to respond in kind; for example, when one person speaks in a confrontational fashion, odds increase of the next speaker doing likewise (Sillars & Wilmot, 1994). When responses are highly predictable, the interaction contains a "static" quality with recurring arguments or escalating denial (Raush, Barry, Hertel, & Swain, 1974). This is reflected, for example, in negative reciprocity; a pattern characteristic of distressed couples (see Caughlin, Vangelisti, & Mikucki-Enyart, in press). Negative reciprocity may occur symmetrically, as in "cross-complaining" (complaint/counter-complaint; Gottman, 1979) and "squabbling" (disagreement followed by disagreement; Schaap, Buunk, & Kerkstra, 1988), or asymmetrically, as in attack–defend. In interactional systems characterized by high negative reciprocity, conversations may begin positively but become progressively more negative after the first provocation, reflected in extended chains of reciprocal negative messages. That is, negativity represents an "absorbing state" (Gottman, 1994). In contrast, family systems characterized by greater variety control escalation by counterbalancing confrontation with questions, jokes, or brief avoidance before re-engaging an issue (Sillars & Wilmot, 1994).

A common nonreciprocal pattern is the "demand–withdraw" pattern, whereby one person attempts to discuss an issue and the other person avoids (see Eldridge & Christensen, 2002). Demand–withdraw patterns predict marital dissatisfaction beyond overall negativity in the home, although this association weakens when partners show affection (Caughlin & Huston, 2002).

In marriage, wife–demand/husband–withdraw is more common than the reverse, one explanation being inequity in housework and child care; that is, women have greater reason to seek change and men to maintain the status quo (e.g., Heavey, Layne, & Christensen, 1993). Other interpretations concern biological differences in reactivity to stress (i.e., males withdraw to contain emotional flooding; Gottman, 1994) and gender socialization; for instance, girls often engage in interactive forms of play where relational talk is formulated; thus, better preparing them to address conflict in adult relationships (Gottman & Carrere, 1994). However, sex differences in demand–withdraw roles often reverse, especially when discussion involves husbands' complaints (Eldridge & Christensen, 2002).

Caughlin and Ramey (2005) examined demand–withdraw in parent–adolescent relationships, finding parallels to marital research. Although parent–demand/adolescent–withdraw was more common than the reverse, there was again a shift in roles depending on whose complaint was discussed. Caughlin and Malis (2004) found lower adolescent satisfaction when adolescents demanded and parents withdrew; whereas parental dissatisfaction related to both adolescent and parent demand–withdraw patterns. These findings held true even after controlling for the total amount of conflict.

Serial Arguments

Roloff and Johnson (2002) note that many disputes end without resolution—people leave the scene, refuse to discuss an issue further, or simply stop arguing. Thus, the same issue may become the basis for *serial arguments*. Serial arguments consist of clusters of episodes, with clusters dispersed over longer periods. Serial arguments are kept alive and episodes linked through rumination (Roloff & Johnson, 2002), including imagined dialogue in which individuals replay past arguments and rehearse future ones (Honeycutt, 2010). Thus, previous arguments may resume with little apparent interruption, despite the time elapsed between episodes.

Relational quality relates to the frequency of argumentative episodes; however, the more crucial factor seems to be whether individuals perceive progress in resolving issues (Miller, Roloff, & Malis, 2007). Partners in intimate relationships become pessimistic about resolvability when confrontations involve cross-complaining and demand–withdraw, the sequence is highly predictable, they dwell on what was said, and they cope by avoiding one another later (Johnson & Roloff, 1998). Conversely, when individuals perceive constructive communication during episodes, they retain optimism that issues can be resolved (Bevan, Finan, & Kaminsky, 2008; Johnson & Roloff, 1998). At the same time, Miller et al. (2007) note that some conflicts are not resolvable and, in such cases, optimism about resolution can simply lock partners into prolonged conflict.

Relational Impacts of Family Conflict Communication

Directness of Communication

Classic conflict theorists emphasize its positive functions, for example, in preventing stagnation, releasing tension, and airing and solving problems (Coser, 1956; Deutsch, 1973). Conversely, in social systems that suppress conflict, hostilities accumulate and become more threatening to the system (Coser, 1956). When applied to families, this suggests the importance of establishing a communication environment that tolerates expression of conflict and encourages direct negotiation of grievances. At the same time, the need to provide an outlet for expression is balanced by need for discretion. Direct speech acts compound the face-threats associated with conflict and risk retaliatory attacks on speaker identity (Ting-Toomey & Kurogi, 1998). The style of speaking labeled *negotiation* anticipates this problem through direct but face-honoring communication. Yet, identity issues are so salient in conflict that even overtly self-effacing comments are sometimes construed as indirect criticism (see the later section on communicative attributions/ frames). Further, as noted above, recurring negotiation of irresolvable issues can evolve into ritualized serial argument. Thus, some conflicts might be better managed by conciliation or acceptance (Miller et al., 2007).

Studies generally find negative associations between conflict avoidance and couple or family satisfaction (Caughlin et al., in press). However, most studies use self-report measures of conflict style. It is not clear how accurately individuals can report avoidance; although Roberts (2000) found only a weak correlation between reported and observed avoidance for wives and a null association for husbands. We suspect that people disengage from conflict in numerous routine ways with only partial awareness. As such, reported avoidance may be especially affected by implicit relationship theories (e.g., happy couples do not avoid).

Observational studies of avoidance are inconsistent but generally do not support a strong link between avoidance and concurrent or prospective relationship satisfaction (see Roberts, 2000). Moreover, some research suggests that avoidance can take different forms with different relational meanings. Raush et al. (1974), for example, noted that spouses who avoided confrontation often colluded by supporting one another's denial and externalization of conflict. Moreover, this collusion had different consequences depending on the purpose of avoidance:

> The conjoint defensive contract usually fails when avoidance is used for coping with an existent conflict. That is, when each partner denies any interpersonal implications of his own or his partner's behavior, yet by his actions implies fault in the other, the interpersonal tension mounts. And since the underlying interpersonal issue is avoided, there can be no genuine mutually satisfactory resolution.
>
> *(pp. 79–80)*

On the other hand, when avoidance occurred in a context of clearly differentiated roles, a mutual bond of affection, and congruous intra-psychic styles (e.g., a de-emphasis of feeling and introspection), then avoidance seemed to promote compatibility. Similarly, Gottman (1994) identified one type of happily married couple, called "conflict minimizers," who downplayed the importance of disagreements, engaged in little verbal give and take, and combined avoidance with positive affection.

One way to view these observations is that avoidance has different relational consequences when used to maintain positive and affectionate relationships than when it represents sullen withdrawal or refusal to address complaints. Smith, Vivian, and O'Leary (1990) found that disengagement during problem-solving was associated with decreased satisfaction over a 30-month period, except when disengagement was coupled with positivity, in which case disengagement predicted increased satisfaction. Similarly, Roberts (2000) found that reported avoidance and angry withdrawal correlated with concurrent and prospective satisfaction of both husbands and wives, but most of these associations were nonsignificant after controlling for hostility. Thus, much of the apparent impact of conflict avoidance may reflect message valence, not directness.

The meaning and impact of conflict avoidance also rest on the nature of the conflict issue. People sometimes use avoidance as a response to problems considered unimportant; at other times they cordon off issues that are irresolvable or too costly to confront (Roloff & Ifert, 2000). In yet other cases, avoidance may represent self-defense (e.g., a "chilling effect") where partners withhold information because the other person is seen as more powerful and/or potentially aggressive (Solomon, Knobloch, & Fitzpatrick, 2004).

Several other factors moderate relational impacts of avoidance (see Roloff & Ifert, 2000). Caughlin and Afifi (2004) considered how boundaries of privacy alter the effects of avoidance. They found that desire for privacy, reasons for avoidance (e. g., protection of the relationship), and assessments of partner communication competence moderated links between avoidance and satisfaction in relationships of parents and adult children. Afifi, McManus, Steuber, and Coho (2009) found that sex differences interacted with avoidance to affect relational satisfaction. For example, men's satisfaction was not linked to their partner's avoidance, whereas women's satisfaction was negatively affected by partner avoidance.

Message Valence

Numerous studies confirm the ubiquitous presence of negative communication in maladjusted couples/families and greater incidence of supportive messages in well-adjusted relationships (see Caughlin et al., in press; Cummings & Patrick, 2010; Fincham & Beach,

1999; Gottman, 1994). The research includes a number of longitudinal studies, some reporting that negative communication in premarital and newlywed phases predicts divorce and marital distress over a decade later (Birditt, Brown, Orbuch, & Mcilvane, 2010, Clements, Stanley, & Markman, 2004). Negativity is a stronger predictor of marital satisfaction and stability than positivity (Caughlin et al., in press; Gottman, 1994). However, positivity acts as a buffer to moderate impacts of negative conflict on satisfaction over time (Huston & Chorost, 1994; M. D. Johnson et al., 2005). Thus, couples who have intense, negative arguments may still have satisfying marriages if they are otherwise affectionate, as in the case of Gottman's (1994) "volatile" couples.

Although many studies support a link between message valence and relational quality, certain caveats apply. First, ostensibly "positive" communication can serve negative functions and vice versa, as when positive messages reproduce maladaptive accommodation or negative confrontation brings needed attention to problems. Arguing from a dialectical perspective, Erbert and Duck (1997) critique the tendency to search for ideal patterns of communication defined by their association with satisfaction. Fluctuating cycles involving negative/positive communication and satisfaction/dissatisfaction constitute normal adaptation to relational polarities and contradictions, such as the simultaneous need for connection/autonomy and stability/change (Ebert & Duck, 1997).

Longitudinal studies illustrate the potential for negative messages to have paradoxical effects. Most research supports the expected connection between negativity early in marriage and later dissatisfaction and divorce; however, several other studies report "reversal" effects, whereby negativity is associated with initial dissatisfaction but stable or improved satisfaction over time (see Fincham & Beach, 1999; McNulty & Russell, 2010). Some authors express skepticism about the interpretation of reversal effects (Caughlin et al., in press; Fincham & Beach, 1999); others suggest that negative confrontation motivates partners to make constructive changes (Gottman, 1994; McNulty & Russell, 2010). Adding further complexity, McNulty and Russell (2010) found evidence that reversal effects depend on the severity of couple problems. When couples had only minor problems initially, then negative messages (e.g., blame, rejection) were associated with decreased satisfaction later, suggesting that negative communication made minor problems worse. However, the same negative messages were associated with increased satisfaction in relationships facing more serious problems. Thus, McNulty and Russell argue that "behaviors that feel bad temporarily may demonstrate long-term benefits to the relationship if they help couples resolve important problems" (p. 588).

Second, the causal framework typically employed in family research assumes that negative communication causes dissatisfaction and instability; yet the research cannot rule out the possibility that existing incompatibilities cause negativity rather than the reverse (Bradbury, et al., 2001; Caughlin et. al., in press). Likewise, recollections of conflict in positive terms can reflect a satisfying relational environment. Most likely, communication and satisfaction are mutually causal. Noller, Feeney, Bonnell, and Callan (1994) found that communication predicted satisfaction during the initial years of marriage; however, initial satisfaction also predicted later communication. Spouses high in satisfaction after two years were less likely to manipulate the partner, avoid dealing with conflict, behave coercively, or enact demand–withdraw patterns.

Third, it is not yet apparent that specific forms of negative/positive communication have unique effects as some authors claim. Gottman (1994, p. 45) acknowledges hearing criticism that the general connection between negativity and marital dissatisfaction is obvious and uninteresting. In response, Gottman (pp. 64–65) argues that the results are not trivial when one examines specific codes and code sequences associated with dissatisfaction. However, this assumes that the same key predictors will emerge consistently across independent samples, which has not been the case. Gottman, Coan, Carrere, and Swanson (1998) replicated some elements of Gottman's (1994) "Four Horsemen of the Apocalypse"—the observation that specific negative acts (complaint/criticism, defensiveness, contempt, and stonewalling) contribute to a process cascade that portends declining satisfaction and eventual marital break-up. However, Gottman et al. (1998) based their analysis on a revised set of "horsemen" (defensiveness, contempt, and belligerence) and milder forms of negativity also predicted divorce in this study (among wives). Negative reciprocity and anger, which predicted marital outcomes in other studies (see Bradbury et al., 2001; Caughlin et al., in press; Gottman et al., 1998), were not related to satisfaction or stability in Gottman et al. (1998).

Thus, *some* forms of negativity generally predict relational outcomes in a given study; intense and prolonged negativity being more problematic than occasional negativity balanced by positive interactions (Gottman, 1994). However, there is no compelling evidence that certain ways of being negative are uniquely toxic. Moreover, it can be misleading to speak of the effects of messages (either their valence or directness) independent of relational context that contributes to the meaning of communication.

The Relational Context of Family Conflict

Relational context affects conflict in a number of ways (Bradbury & Fincham, 1991). Along with the contextual moderators noted above (e.g., reasons for avoidance, resolvability of issues, overall affection), we highlight three factors featured in communication research: relational standards, cultural differences, and family stages.

Relational Standards

Relational standards reference expected and preferred patterns of relating; for example, how much spouses believe that they should maintain personal boundaries or share decisions (Gordon, Baucom, Epstein, Burnett, & Rankin, 1999) and the extent to which family members believe in showing politeness or addressing problems openly (Caughlin, 2003). Relational standards are a source of conflict and dissatisfaction when individually held ideals do not match perceived reality (Caughlin, 2003) or are not shared (Acitelli, Kenny, & Weiner, 2001). It follows that individuals with extreme ideals are primed for disappointment and conflict. "Unrealistic" expectations for intimate relationships (e.g., disagreements are inherently destructive, mindreading is expected) are linked to instability, dissatisfaction, and negative communication in married and cohabiting, same sex couples (Eidelson & Epstein, 1982; Kurdek, 1991).

In addition to being a potential source of conflict, relational standards shape the response to conflict. For example, parents, adolescents, and young adults from families who prioritize frequent and open communication (i.e., *conversation oriented* families) report direct conflict styles, especially when high conversation orientation is combined with low conformity (i.e., the *pluralistic* family type). Individuals report more avoidance and accommodation in conformity oriented families (Koerner & Fitzpatrick, 1997; Shearman & Dumlao, 2008; Zhang, 2007). Similarly, couple conflict is influenced by implicit relationship models (Fitzpatrick, 1988). *Traditional* couples interact in a manner that reflects their emphasis on openness balanced with social restraint; for example, they discuss relationship

345

expectations and enact "validation" and "contract" sequences (e.g., husband offers information, wife agrees) (Fitzpatrick, 1988). Traditional couples endorse conflict rules more than other couples (e.g., "listen to partner," "don't get angry"), reflecting strong norms for what is permissible and appropriate (Honeycutt, Woods, & Fontenot, 1993). *Independents* stress verbal negotiation and thus, confront one another and share information. Wanting to remain autonomous, *separates* typically use indirect messages and withhold complaints (Solomon et al., 2004) but confront one another once complaints are introduced (Fitzpatrick, 1988).

Some research indicates that relational standards moderate connections between communication and relationship satisfaction. Gordon et al. (1999) found stronger correlations between communication and adjustment among wives who prioritized intimate and equitable communication. Caughlin (2003) found a positive correlation between "maintenance communication" (e.g., disclosure, discussion of problems) and family satisfaction among young adults who endorsed relationship-focused family standards (e.g., openness); however, the correlation reversed directions among those who did not endorse such standards. Sillars, Pike, Jones, and Redmon (1983) found that satisfied *independent* couples discussed conflicts directly; however, satisfied *separates* were avoidant and restrained in their communication.

The above studies suggest that family members communicate about conflict more directly when relational standards prioritize open communication; moreover, satisfaction reflects the congruence of perceived or actual communication with preferred patterns of relating. The same observations apply when relational standards are culturally based.

Culture

U.S. based family research typically operates from an "open-affectionate" relationship ideal that prioritizes directness (Matsunaga & Imahori 2009). In contrast, many Japanese young adults endorse a "high-context" cluster of family standards (e.g., mindreading, avoidance, child obedience), which relates to their use of avoidance and conciliation in family conflicts (Matsunaga & Imahori 2009). As Matsunaga and Imahori observe, some high context family standards (e.g., mindreading) are among the beliefs characterized as unrealistic and dysfunctional in U.S. samples (Eidelson & Epstein, 1982).

Much of the culturally based family conflict research distinguishes individualist and collectivist patterns of conflict. Although a useful heuristic for organizing broad differences, this distinction masks complexity for a number of reasons, some of which we note below. Generally speaking, individualists are expected to express family conflict more openly than collectivists due to greater emphasis on expressing and defending self versus maintaining harmonious relations and honoring the face concerns of others (Ting-Toomey & Kurogi, 1998). In collectivist, high power distance cultures (i.e., *vertical collectivism*), there are especially strong pressures to avoid face-threatening communication (Oetzel, Ting-Toomey, Chew-Sanchez, Harris, Wilcox, & Stumpf, 2003). However, these norms seem to regulate parent–child communication to a greater extent than couple communication. In fact, belief in vertical collectivism was associated with greater serial arguing among Malagasy couples (Radanielina-Hita, 2010). Radanielina-Hita reasons that, in marriage, collectivist concerns for preserving face may be overridden by the need to talk things out, given the constant presence of the other.

Additionally, collectivist norms for parent–child conflict may be evolving as a function of globalization/modernization. In traditional Chinese culture, parents expect children to perform filial piety (respect for parents and elders) and to obey and conform without question (Zhang, 2007). Yet, young Chinese adults report more conversation-oriented than conformity-oriented family communication patterns and more collaborating and accommodating during conflicts with parents than avoiding (Zhang, 2007). Zhang suggests that, while Chinese children continue to avoid direct confrontation with parents, there has been a cultural shift toward equality and independence, such that younger Chinese see a problem-solving approach as ideal.

The above findings suggest that it can be misleading to characterize family conflict patterns based on traditional values alone, given cultural change and within-culture diversity. The importance of within-culture diversity is illustrated by Oetzel et al. (2003). Overall, young adults from individualist, small power distance cultures (Germany, U.S.A.) reported more dominating and integrating facework strategies in conflicts with parents and siblings, and less avoiding facework, than young adults from collectivist, large power distance cultures (Japan, Mexico). However, individual self-construal styles (independent versus interdependent) had much stronger effects on facework than national culture.

Although certain culturally based relational standards (e.g., authority, restraint, harmony) reduce conflict expression, the same norms have the paradoxical effect of increasing the significance of conflict that does surface. In a diary study, Asian American adolescents reported less inter-parental conflict than European American adolescents, but Asian youth also felt more distressed when parental arguments occurred (Chung, Flook, & Fuligni, 2009). Another study found that Latina and African American girls showed more respect to mothers while discussing conflicts than European American girls. However, African American and Latina mothers reported more intense conflicts when expression of respect was low (Dixon, Graber, & Brooks-Gunn, 2008). Conversely, cultural groups who express conflict freely seem to acquire tolerance for negative communication. Some studies have observed weaker associations between negativity and marital dissatisfaction in cultural groups who are less restrained in expressing negativity (Halford, Hahlweg, & Dunne, 1990; Krokoff, Gottman, & Roy, 1988; Winkler & Doherty, 1983). This suggests that negativity does not mean the same thing to groups with different norms for confrontation and emotional expression. Instead, negativity likely has a greater impact on family and individual adjustment to the extent that it violates cultural norms.

Family Stages and Transitions

Most studies suggest that conflict increases over the early years of marriage, reflecting adjustment to spousal and parenting roles (see Simpson, Rholes, Campbell, Wilson, & Tran, 2002), followed by decreased conflict and more stable pattern of adjustment at some point thereafter (Birditt et al., 2010; Silverstein & Giarrusso, 2010). Longer married couples have fewer disagreements (McGonagle, Kessler, & Schilling, 1992) and engage in less explicit negotiation of conflicts, less negativity, and more avoidance by comparison to young couples (Carstensen, Gottman, & Levenson, 1995; Zietlow & Sillars, 1988). These aggregate differences mask diversity, as some research identifies a conflicted subgroup among long married couples (Dickson, 1995; Zietlow & Sillars, 1988). Nonetheless, nondistressed couples married at least 40 years reported difficulty thinking of recent conflict and showed a tendency to de-emphasize, deflect, and make light of it (Dickson, Hughes, Manning, Walker, Bollis-Pecci, & Gratson, 2002). By contrast, the couples recalled intense disagreements over individual differences, parenting, and other issues within the early years of marriage.

Aggregate trends in conflict experienced at different family stages are partly attributable to relationship re-negotiation that takes place during transitions. Life transitions (e.g., onset to marriage and parenthood, relocation, career changes) tend be compacted in early marriage, so this can be a period of intense negotiation that places a premium on conflict management (Sillars & Wilmot, 1989). The same may be said for the onset to adolescence in parent–child relations, which typically brings an increase in petty conflicts (Branje, Laursen, & Collins, Chapter 17, this volume; Steinberg & Morris, 2001), followed by decreased conflict once more equal and adult-like relationships are established (Steinberg & Morris, 2001). The transition to retirement also seems to increase marital conflicts initially, especially when one spouse continues to work, although these conflicts typically subside after a few years (Moen, Kim, & Hofmeister, 2001).

In sum, research suggests that conflict tends to peak at transition points in family relationships and further, communication patterns are often more direct and confrontational reflecting the pressures associated with transitional phases. This picture is consistent with the *relational turbulence* model, which suggests that people are emotionally and behaviorally reactive during relationship transitions, due to heightened uncertainty and disruption of everyday goals (Knobloch & Theiss, 2010; Solomon, Weber, & Steuber, 2010). Thus, conversations are more challenging and irritations more severe (Solomon et al., 2010). Problem-solving communication might be expected to have the greatest impact on relational quality during such periods of relationship renegotiation (Fincham & Beach, 1999; Solomon et al., 2010). Conversely, the significance of conflict management may recede during stable periods, as other facets of relationships assume greater importance than expressive communication and problem solving (e.g., satisfaction derived from companionship and "survivorship" in later marriage; see Sillars & Wilmot, 1989).

The research reviewed above suggests that communication patterns have variable meaning depending on relational context. In the next section we examine meaning from a different standpoint, focusing on individual attributions and interpretive frames for communication. Several lines of research suggest that difficult conflicts are characterized by lack of coordination over the meaning of messages and nature of conflict issues.

Communicative Attributions and Frames

Information Versus Bias

Intuitively, we expect people to understand one another better if they discuss conflicts directly instead of speaking evasively or withdrawing. Yet, several studies found little connection between how directly couples or families discussed conflicts and whether individuals could accurately describe the perspectives of other family members (see Sillars, 2011).

The weak connection between communicative directness and inter-subjective understanding might be explained, in part, by the cognitive environment of intimate conflict, which tends to reinforce perspective-driven processing of messages. Given the intense familiarity of family members and repetitiveness of many conflicts, individuals may view potential sources of information selectively, fail to monitor for new information, make new inferences conform to existing relationship theories, and attach a high degree of certainty to inferences about others, regardless of their actual diagnostic value (Sillars, 2011; Thomas & Fletcher, 1997). Further, cognitive demands during communication, particularly angry, stressful interactions, can increase selective attention to information that serves persuasive and defensive goals; thereby limiting understanding of alternative perspectives (Sillars, 2011). Mood states and the emotional climate of relationships also affect selective attention to and interpretation of messages. For example, unhappy spouses are more cognitively and behaviorally reactive to partner negativity than happy spouses because the residue of negative thoughts and feelings from past conflicts affects processing of ongoing interactions (Bradbury & Fincham, 1991).

Thus, perspective-driven biases can affect message reception during family conflict, leading to incongruent perception of the stream of communication. As noted below, incongruent perception of communication seems especially characteristic of more intense conflicts and unhappy relationships.

Encoding–Decoding of Emotional/Relational Communication

The interactional consequences of incongruent perception are discussed by Watzlawick, et al. (1967) in their landmark work on relational communication. These authors suggest that repetitive conflicts are perpetuated by an "inability to metacommunicate," a condition characterized by incongruent relational meanings (e.g., a husband believes he is being helpful, his wife sees his statement as condescending). This condition is "binding" in that efforts to talk about conflict rely on the same patterns of communication and interpretation that are the source of difficulty. Thus, talking about the problem can exacerbate it (e.g., the husband's self-explanations are taken as further condescension).

The "inability to metacommunicate" phenomenon is parallel to misunderstanding of emotional communication found among distressed married couples. Several studies used a task in which one spouse expressed messages meant to convey positive, neutral, or negative meaning, while the other spouse decoded the messages. The verbal content was scripted and ambiguous (e.g., "What are you doing?" "You really surprised me this time!"), so meaning was entirely based on vocal and other nonverbal cues. High adjustment couples had greater encoding–decoding accuracy than low adjustment couples in this research (Gottman & Porterfield, 1981; Kahn, 1970; Koerner & Fitzpatrick, 2002; Noller, 1980) and in analogous studies using the "talk table" procedure (Notarius, Benson, Sloane, Vanzetti, and Hornyak, 1989), suggesting that incongruent encoding–decoding contributes to conflict in unhappy couples (e.g., the listener assigns negative meaning to messages intended as neutral or positive). Notarius et al. (1989) found evidence of both "negative sentiment override" among distressed spouses (i.e., attributing negative meaning to outwardly neutral messages) and "positive sentiment override" among nondistressed spouses (attributing neutral or positive meaning to negative messages). Some research points to husbands in low adjustment couples as the primary source of encoding–decoding difficulty (Gottman & Porterfield, 1981; Noller, 1980) but this is not confirmed in other studies (e.g., Koerner & Fitzpatrick, 2002; Noller & Venardos, 1986).

Attributing Communicative Intent

In two studies that supported the thrust of encoding–decoding studies, Noller and colleagues (Guthrie & Noller, 1988; Noller & Ruzzene, 1991) had spouses discuss a problem, then separately watch a videotape of the discussion and report on communicative intent. The intent of messages, as reported by the sender and inferred by receiver, was less similar in low versus high adjustment couples, as was the perceived message valence associated with intentions. Distressed spouses also made more negative inferences about partner intent (Noller & Ruzzene, 1991), which is a trend borne out in other studies (e.g., Sillars, Roberts, Leonard, & Dun, 2000; Vangelisti, Corbin, Lucchetti, & Sprague, 1999).

Attributions about speaker intent help determine relational impacts of messages, as illustrated by research on *hurtful* communication in families and close relationships. When asked to identify hurtful messages or events from past experiences, individuals commonly reference direct, face-attacking messages, such as accusations and negative evaluations in adult relationships (Vangelisti, 1994) or disrespect, teasing, and criticism in mother–child relationships (Mills & Piotrowski, 2009). However, the sense of emotional injury that defines hurtful communication is a function of cognitive appraisal, not the message alone (Fitness & Warburton, 2009). Perceived intentionality has a strong effect on appraisal of messages as hurtful (Vangelisti & Young, 2000), as do receiver characteristics that create heightened vigilance toward hurtful intent, such as low self-esteem, rejection sensitivity, and anxious–ambivalent attachment style (see Fitness and Warburton, 2009). Thus, the same message might be construed as hurtful in one family context but not another (Mills & Piotrowski, 2009).

Aside from influencing the emotional response to communication (e.g., whether criticism is appraised as hurtful), attributions about speaker intent underlie interpretation of the message itself, including its pragmatic meaning (e.g., whether a statement represents criticism versus something else). Inferences about pragmatic intent are made continuously during communication and, although not routinely problematic (Jacobs, 2002), these inferences reflect distinct perspective biases during conflicts. Sillars et al. (2000) examined spontaneous thoughts about communication that spouses reported during video recall of conflict discussions; finding that spouses subjectively "coded" interaction in self-serving terms. That is, spouses attributed neutral and direct communication much more to self, and acts of avoidance and confrontation more to the partner. A similar study of parent–adolescent conflict using video recall identified generational biases in spontaneous inferences about communication (Sillars, Smith, & Koerner, 2010). Parents attributed negative emotions (e.g., feeling frustrated), confrontational intent (e.g., being deliberately manipulative), and avoidance thoughts (e.g., not wanting to talk) to children more than children reported having such thoughts. Conversely, adolescents over-attributed controlling thoughts to parents.

Extreme biases in attributions for communication may be a precipitating factor in marital violence (see Robillard & Noller, 2011). Schweinle, Ickes and Bernstein (2002) suggest that aggressive men are hyper-vigilant toward signs of rejection and therefore, attribute criticism to outwardly neutral messages. In support, the authors found that physically aggressive husbands over-attributed criticism and rejection to women they had not met. Using an adaptation of the encoding–decoding task, Robillard and Noller (2011), found that physically aggressive men, especially those high in rejection sensitivity, had a tendency to construe wives' positive or neutral messages as negative and moreover, to see these messages as critical and rejecting. Nonviolent men, by contrast, showed a positive decoding bias. Sillars, Leonard, Roberts, and Dun (2002) also identified strong biases in the attributions that aggressive husbands made about their own and their wives' communication during video recall of interactions.

Naturally, attributions for communication reflect both accuracy and bias (Segrin, Hanzal, & Domschke, 2009). Separate reports of conflict by husbands versus wives and parents versus adolescents tend to show moderate agreement (Noller & Callan, 1988; Rhoades & Stocker, 2006; Segrin et al., 2009). Further, summary self-reports of constructive versus negative communication in marriage correlate with observational measures of the same (Hahlweg, Kaiser, Christensen, Fehm-Wolfsdorf, & Groth, 2000). However, a few studies indicate that perceptions of the spouse's conflict style relate more consistently to observer coding of marital interactions than self-perceived conflict styles (Rhoades & Stocker, 2006; Sanford, 2010; Sillars et al., 2000), suggesting that self-perceptions may be subject to greater bias relative to observer-defined codes.

Family Conflict Frames

Conflict frames represent distinct ways of defining what a particular conflict is about; such as a substantive disagreement, clash of values, or power struggle (see Drake & Donohue, 1996; Rogan, 2006). A key insight from literature on conflict frames is that conflicts involve implicit negotiation to define the issues underlying conflict, not just direct clash over those issues. In Drake and Donohue's (1996) approach, language choice frames a topic by highlighting certain qualities; in divorce mediation, a wife's framing of child support in terms of fairness serves as a proposal to discuss value aspects of the settlement. When partners converge on a particular way of talking about conflict (i.e., as hinging on facts, interests, values, or relationships), this represents a form of cooperation that allows negotiation to progress. Thus, the number of interim agreements forged by spouses during mediation relates to their convergence on common frames (Drake & Donohue, 1996).

A seemingly commonplace example of divergent frames is where one party applies a "content" frame; that is, interpreting conflict as a negotiation of overt, instrumental issues; whereas the other party applies a frame highlighting relational issues. Sillars et al. (2000) observed a tendency whereby one spouse (typically the husband) tracked communication primarily in terms of the ostensible topic of discussion (money, housework, etc.), whereas the partner focused on the process of interaction and implicit relationship messages contained therein (e.g., a husband reported thinking that his band could only practice on Tuesdays and Fridays, while his wife reported thinking that he does not listen to her). In such cases, one spouse often assigned poignant relational meaning to messages that the more literal spouse did not recognize.

A related phenomenon is that disputants may conceptualize issues at different levels of generality; for example, as isolated behavior (not listening) or as a broader pattern or personality problem (e.g., not listening relates to general insensitivity; Roloff & Johnson, 2002). Framing issues as personality problems escalates conflict and may contribute to relationship distress; for example, Alberts (1988) found that poorly adjusted married couples were apt to direct complaints at broad personal characteristics of the partner. Conflict is more easily discussed and managed when framed as a disagreement over specific behaviors or decisions versus abstract relational, identity, and value issues (Deutsch, 1973). Further, when these frames are invoked unevenly—one party frames a disagreement in concrete terms; the other regards it as symbolic of a general relational pattern—issue negotiation may be especially difficult to coordinate.

Research on interpretive frames and attributions for communication suggests that, in difficult cases of family conflict, individuals come to view communication in an incongruous manner, thus making verbal negotiation unreliable and potentially self-defeating. On the other hand, *transformative* psychological processes (e.g., forgiveness, commitment, sacrifice) can moderate reactivity to negative communication, thereby allowing conflicts to be aired with greater chance of constructive outcomes (Fincham, Stanley, & Beach, 2007).

This suggests that self-reflective reframing of conflict can promote flexibility and control over reactive impulses that might otherwise follow from negative attributions and frames (see, e.g., Canary & Lakey, 2006).

Conclusion

The central idea anchoring this review is that relational quality reflects the interplay of messages, relational contexts, and interpretive frameworks. We began by examining communicative acts and patterns, noting the dominance of two dimensions—message directness and valence. In addition, *polysemous* messages represent communicative acts that may be interpreted in variable ways with alternative outcomes. To be clear, the distinction is relative—all messages are polysemous to an extent (e.g., Jacobs, 2002). For example, a single message (e.g., "That's not going to work.") could be criticism, stonewalling, or problem-solving depending on presumed speaker intent. Thus, the communication codes used in family conflict research, commonly referred to as "communication behavior," are not behavior in a literal sense (i.e., mere sounds and gestures) but speech acts whose meaning is contextual, interpretive, and subject to negotiation. These codes—as with other social behaviors—evade strictly objective measurement and require the assumption that coders are at best inter-subjective agents who have a roughly equivalent take on the functions of messages.

The situation faced by coders is analogous to that of family members; however, meanings assigned by family members are shaped by relationship-specific theories, emotional investment, and participation in conflict communication. Thus, messages are less likely to be taken at "face value" by family members than neutral observers. Moreover, for family members, coordination of meaning is a delicate affair with important consequences. The research reviewed here identifies several perspective biases in the meanings assigned and inferences derived from couple and family communication. In some cases, these biases complicate conflict management by making communication unreliable and creating vigilance toward, and reactivity to, negative messages. Such dynamics seem especially significant in conflicts that prove difficult to manage, where talking directly fails to improve the situation or makes things worse.

An overriding goal of family conflict research has been to isolate patterns that contribute to relational quality, mainly through the strategy of contrasting communication characteristics of well-adjusted and distressed relationships. The research yields a few well-replicated results (i.e., high negativity, negative reciprocity, and demand–withdraw in distressed relationships), along with a number of provocative, if less robust, patterns of a more specific nature (e.g., the "four horsemen"). These findings help to inform clinical interventions; however, they represent extremes and disregard variation in relationships that hang around the mean. If we drop out cases of severe or chronic negativity, it is more difficult to say what patterns of communication are constructive or destructive to relationships in any absolute way. Rather, connections between communication and relational quality vary by relational context, including the overall affective climate of relationships, personally and culturally preferred patterns of relating, transitional pressures, and situational needs for accommodation or confrontation. In this sense, "constructive communication" is not a behavioral script but a process of adaptation that can assume multiple forms. Thus, readers must judiciously apply research on conflict patterns in a probabilistic and contingent manner to allow for situations that are modified by culture and context.

References

Acitelli, L. K., Kenny, D. A., & Weiner, D. (2001). The importance of similarity and understanding of partners' marital ideals to relationship satisfaction. *Personal Relationships, 8,* 167–85.

Afifi, T. D., McManus, T., Steuber, K., & Coho, A. (2009). Verbal avoidance in intimate conflict situations. *Human Communication Research, 35,* 357–83.

Alberts, J. K. (1988). An analysis of couples' conversational complaints. *Communication Monographs, 55,* 184–97.

——(1990). The use of humor in managing couples' conflict interactions. In D. D. Cahn (Ed.), *Intimates in conflict: A communication perspective* (pp. 105–20). Hillsdale, NJ: Lawrence Erlbaum Associates.

Bevan, J. L., Finan, A., & Kaminsky, A. (2008). Modeling serial arguments in close relationships: The serial argument process model. *Human Communication Research, 34,* 600–24.

Birditt, K. S., Brown, E., Orbuch, T. L., & Mcilvane, J. M. (2010). Marital conflict behaviors and implications for divorce over 16 years. *Journal of Marriage and Family, 72,* 1188–204.

Bradbury, T. N., & Fincham, F. D. (1991). A contextual model for advancing the study of marriage. In G. J. O. Fletcher & F. D. Fincham (Eds.), *Cognition in close relationships* (pp. 127–47). Hillsdale, NJ: Lawrence Erlbaum Associates.

Bradbury, T., Rogge, R., & Lawrence, E. (2001). Reconsidering the role of conflict in marriage. In A. Booth, A. C. Crouter, & M. Clements (Eds.), *Couples in conflict* (pp. 59–81). Hillsdale, NJ: Lawrence Erlbaum Associates.

Canary, D. J., Cupach, W. R., & Messman, S. J. (1995). *Relationship conflict.* Thousand Oaks, CA: Sage.

Canary, D. J., & Lakey, S. G. (2006). Managing conflict in a competent manner: A mindful look at events that matter. In J. G. Oetzel & S. Ting-Toomey (Eds.), *The Sage handbook of conflict communication: Integrating theory, research, and practice* (pp. 185–210). Thousand Oaks, CA.: Sage.

Carstensen, L. L., Gottman, J. M., & Levenson, R. W. (1995). Emotional behavior in long-term marriage. *Psychology and Aging, 10,* 140–49.

Caughlin, J. P. (2003). Family communication standards: What counts as excellent family communication and how are such standards associated with family satisfaction? *Human Communication Research, 29,* 5–40.

Caughlin, J. P. & Afifi, T. D. (2004). When is a topic avoidance unsatisfying? Examining moderators of the association between avoidance and dissatisfaction. *Human Communication Research, 30,* 479–513.

Caughlin, J. P., & Huston, T. L. (2002). A contextual analysis of the association between demand/withdraw and marital satisfaction. *Personal Relationships, 9,* 95–119.

Caughlin, J. P., & Malis, R. S. (2004). Demand/withdraw between parents and adolescents as a correlate of relational satisfaction. *Communication Reports, 17,* 59–71.

Caughlin, J. P., & Ramey, M. E. (2005). The demand/withdraw pattern of communication in parent–adolescent dyads. *Personal Relationships, 12,* 337–55.

Caughlin, J. P., Vangelisti, A. L., & Mikucki-Enyart, S. (in press). Conflict in dating and marital relationships. In J. G. Oetzel & S. Ting-Toomey (Eds.), *The Sage handbook of conflict communication: Integrating theory, research, and practice,* 2nd edn. Thousand Oaks, CA: Sage.

Charny, I. W. (1980). Why are so many (if not really all) people and families disturbed? *Journal of Marital and Family Therapy, 6,* 37–45.

Chung, G. H., Flook, L., & Fuligni, A. J. (2009). Daily family conflict and emotional distress among adolescents from Latin American, Asian, and European backgrounds. *Developmental Psychology, 45,* 1406–15.

Clements, M. L., Stanley, S. M., Markman, H. J. (2004). Before they said "I do": Discriminating among marital outcomes over 13 years. *Journal of Marriage and the Family, 66,* 613–26.

Coser, L. (1956). *The functions of social conflict.* New York: The Free Press.

Cummings, M. E., & Patrick, D. (2010). *Marital conflict and children: An emotional security perspective.* New York: Guilford Press.

Deutsch, M. (1973). *The resolution of conflict: Constructive and destructive processes.* New Haven, CT: Yale University Press.

Dickson, F. C. (1995). The best is yet to be: Research on long-lasting relationships. In J. T. Wood & S. Duck (Eds.), *Understanding relationship processes: Off the beaten track* (pp. 22–50). Beverly Hills, CA: Sage.

Dickson, F. C., Hughes, P. C., Manning, L. D., Walker, K. L., Bollis-Pecci, T., & Gratson, S. (2002). Conflict in later-life, long-term marriages. *Southern Communication Journal*, 67, 110–21.

Dixon, S. V., Graber, J. A., & Brooks-Gunn, J. (2008). The roles of respect for parental authority and parenting practices in parent–child conflict among African American, Latino, and European American families. *Journal of Family Psychology*, 22, 1–11.

Drake, L. E., & Donohue, W. A. (1996). Communicative framing theory in conflict resolution, *Communication Research*, 23, 297–322.

Eidelson, R. J., & Epstein, N. (1982). Cognition and relationship maladjustment: Development of a measure of dysfunctional relationship beliefs. *Journal of Consulting and Clinical Psychology*, 50, 715–20.

Eldridge, K. A., & Christensen, A. (2002). Demand-withdraw communication during couple communication: A review and analysis. In P. Noller & J. A. Feeney (Eds.), *Understanding marriage: Developments in the study of couple interaction* (pp. 289–322). Cambridge: Cambridge University Press.

Erbert, L. A. & Duck, S. W. (1997). Rethinking satisfaction in personal relationships from a dialectical perspective. In R. J. Sternberg & M. Hojjat (Eds.), *Satisfaction in close relationships* (pp. 190–216). New York: Guilford Press.

Fincham, F. D., & Beach, S. R. H. (1999). Conflict in marriage: Implications for working with couples. *Annual Review of Psychology*, 50, 47–77.

Fincham, F. D., Stanley, S. M., & Beach, S. R. H. (2007). Transformative processes in marriage: An analysis of emerging trends. *Journal of Marriage and Family*, 69, 275–92.

Fitness, J., & Warburton, W. (2009). Thinking the unthinkable: Cognitive appraisals and hurt feelings. In A. L. Vangelisti (Ed.), *Feeling hurt in close relationships* (pp. 35–49). Cambridge: Cambridge University Press.

Fitzpatrick, M. A. (1988). *Between husbands and wives: Communication in marriage*. Newbury Park, CA: Sage.

Gordon, K. C., Baucom, D. H., Epstein, N., Burnett, C. K., & Rankin, L. A. (1999). The interaction between marital standards and communication patterns: How does it contribute to marital adjustment? *Journal of Marital and Family Therapy*, 25, 211–23.

Gottman, J. M. (1979). *Marital interactions: Experimental investigations*. New York: Academic Press.

——(1994). *What predicts divorce? The relationship between marital processes and marital outcomes*. Hillsdale, NJ: Lawrence Erlbaum Associates.

Gottman, J. M. & Carrere, S. (1994). Why can't men and women get along? In D. J. Canary & L. Stafford (Eds.), *Communication and relational maintenance* (pp. 61–90). San Diego, CA: Academic Press.

Gottman, J. M., Coan, J., Carrere, S., & Swanson, C. (1998). Predicting marital happiness and stability from newlywed interactions. *Journal of Marriage and the Family*, 60, 5–22.

Gottman, J. M., & Porterfield, A. L. (1981). Communicative competence in the nonverbal behavior of married couples. *Journal of Marriage and the Family*, 4, 817–24.

Guthrie, D. M., & Noller, P. (1988). Married couples' perceptions of one another in emotional situations. In P. Noller & M. A. Fitzpatrick (Eds.), *Perspectives on marital interaction* (pp. 153–81). Philadelphia, PA: Multilingual Matters.

Hahlweg, K., Kaiser, A., Christensen, A., Fehm-Wolfsdorf, G., & Groth, T. (2000). Self-report and observational assessment of couples' conflict: The concordance between the Communication Patterns Questionnaire and the KPI observation system. *Journal of Marriage and the Family*, 62, 61–67.

Halford, W. K., Hahlweg, K., & Dunne, M. (1990). The cross-cultural consistency of marital communication associated with marital distress. *Journal of Marriage and the Family*, 52, 487–500.

Heavey, C. L., Layne, C., & Christensen, A. (1993). Gender and conflict structure in marital interaction: A replication and extension. *Journal of Consulting and Clinical Psychology*, 61, 16–27.

Honeycutt, J. M. (2010). Forgive but don't forget: Correlates of rumination about conflict. In J. M. Honeycutt (Ed.), *Imagine that: Studies in imagined interactions*. Cresskill, NJ: Hampton.

Honeycutt, J. M., Woods, B. L., & Fontenot, K. (1993). The endorsement of communication conflict rules as a function of engagement, marriage and marital ideology. *Journal of Social and Personal Relationships*, 10, 285–304.

Huston, T. L., & Chorost, A. (1994). Behavioral buffers on the effect of negativity on marital satisfaction: A longitudinal study. *Personal Relationships*, 1, 223–39.

Jacobs, S. (2002). Language and interpersonal communication. In M. L. Knapp & J. A. Daly (Eds.), *Handbook of interpersonal communication* (pp. 213–39). Thousand Oaks, CA: Sage.

Johnson, K. L., & Roloff, M. E. (1998). Serial arguing and relational quality: Determinants and consequences of perceived resolvability. *Communication Research*, 25, 327–43.

Johnson, M. D., Cohan, C. L., Davila, J., Lawrence, E., Rogge, R. D., Karney, B. R., Sullivan, K. T., & Bradbury, T. N. (2005). Problem-solving skills and affective expressions as predictors of change in marital satisfaction. *Journal of Consulting and Clinical Psychology*, 73, 15–27.

Kahn, M. (1970). Nonverbal communication and marital satisfaction. *Family Process*, 9, 449–56.

Knobloch, L. K., & Theiss, J. A. (2010). An actor-partner interdependence model of relational turbulence: Cognitions and emotions. *Journal of Social and Personal Relationships*, 27, 595–619.

Koerner, A. F. & Fitzpatrick, M. A. (1997). Family type and conflict: The impact of conversation orientation and conformity orientation on conflict in the family. *Communication Studies*, 48, 59–75.

——(2002) Nonverbal communication and marital adjustment and satisfaction: The role of decoding relationship relevant and relationship irrelevant affect. *Communication Monographs*, 69, 33–51.

Krokoff, L. J., Gottman, J. M., & Roy, A. K. (1988). Blue-collar and white-collar marital interaction and communication orientation. *Journal of Social and Personal Relationships*, 5, 201–21.

Kurdek, L. A. (1991). Correlates of relationship satisfaction in cohabiting gay and lesbian couples: Integration of contextual, investment, and problem-solving models. *Journal of Personality and Social Psychology*, 61, 910–22.

Matsunaga, M., & Imahori, T. T. (2009). Profiling family communication standards: A U.S.–Japan comparison. *Communication Research*, 36, 3–31.

McGonagle, K. A., Kessler, R. C., and Schilling, E. A. (1992). The frequency and determinants of marital disagreements in a community sample. *Journal of Social and Personal Relationships*, 9, 507–24.

McNulty, J. K., & Russell, V. M. (2010). When "negative" behaviors are positive: A contextual analysis of the long-term effects of problem-solving behaviors on changes in relationship satisfaction. *Journal of Personality and Social Psychology*, 98, 587–604.

Miller, C. W., Roloff, M. E., & Malis, R. S. (2007). Understanding interpersonal conflicts that are difficult to resolve: A review of literature and presentation of an integrated model. In C. S. Beck (Ed.), *Communication Yearbook 31* (pp. 118–71). New York: Lawrence Erlbaum Associates.

Mills, R. S. L., & Piotrowski, C. C. (2009). Haven in a heartless world? Hurt feelings in the family. In A. L. Vangelisti (Ed.), *Feeling hurt in close relationships* (pp. 260–87). Cambridge: Cambridge University Press.

Moen, P., Kim, J. E., & Hofmeister, H. (2001). Couples' work/retirement transitions, gender, and marital quality. *Social Psychology Quarterly*, 64, 55–71.

Noller, P. (1980). Misunderstandings in marital communication: A study of couples' nonverbal communication. *Journal of Personality and Social Psychology*, 39, 1135–48.

Noller, P., & Callan, V. J. (1988). Understanding parent–adolescent interactions: Perceptions of family members and outsiders. *Developmental Psychology*, 24, 707–14.

Noller, P., Feeney, J. A., Bonnell, D., & Callan, V. (1994). A longitudinal study of conflict in early marriage. *Journal of Social and Personal Relationships*, 11, 233–52.

Noller, P., & Ruzzene, M. (1991). Communication in marriage: The influence of affect and cognition. In G. J. O. Fletcher & F. Fincham (Eds.), *Cognition in close relationships* (pp. 203–33). Hillsdale, NJ: Lawrence Erlbaum Associates.

Noller, P., & Venardos, C. (1986). Communication awareness in married couples. *Journal of Social and Personal Relationships*, 3, 31–42.

Notarius, C. I., Benson, P. R., Sloane, D., Vanzetti, N. A., & Hornyak, L. M. (1989). Exploring the interface between perception and behavior: An analysis of marital interactions in distressed and nondistressed couples. *Behavioral Assessment*, 11, 39–64.

Oetzel, J., Ting-Toomey, S., Chew-Sanchez, M. I., Harris, R., Wilcox, R., & Stumpf, S. (2003). Face and facework in conflicts with parents and siblings: A cross-cultural comparison of Germans, Japanese, Mexicans, and U.S. Americans. *Journal of Family Communication*, 3, 67–93.

Radanielina-Hita, M. L. (2010). Let's make peace! A cross-cultural analysis of the effects of serial arguing behaviors in romantic relationships: The case of Malagasy romantic partners. *Journal of Intercultural Communication Research*, 39, 81–103.

Raush, H. L., Barry, W. A., Hertel, R. K., & Swain, M. A. (1974). *Communication, conflict, and marriage*. San Francisco, CA: Jossey-Bass.

Rhoades G. K., & Stocker, C. M. (2006). Can spouses provide knowledge of each other's communication patterns? A study of self-reports, spouses' reports, and observational coding. *Family Process*, 45, 499–511.

Roberts, L. J. (2000). Fire and ice in marital communication: Hostile and distancing behaviors as predictors of marital distress. *Journal of Marriage and the Family, 62,* 693–707.

Robillard, L., & Noller, P. (2011). Rejection sensitivity, violence, and decoding deficits in married men. In J. L. Smith, W. Ickes, J. Hall, & S. Hodges (Eds.), *Managing interpersonal sensitivity: Knowing when—and when not—to understand others* (pp. 143–67). Hauppauge, NY: Nova Science.

Rogan, R. G. (2006). Conflict framing categories revisited. *Communication Quarterly, 54,* 157–73.

Roloff, M. E., & Ifert, D. E. (2000). Conflict management through avoidance: Withholding complaints, suppressing arguments, and declaring topics taboo. In S. Petronio (Ed.), *Balancing the secrets of private disclosures* (pp. 151–63). Mahwah, NJ: Lawrence Erlbaum Associates.

Roloff, M. E., & Johnson, K. L. (2002). Serial arguing over the relational life course: Antecedents and consequences. In A. L. Vangelisti, H. T. Reis, & M. A. Fitzpatrick (Eds.), *Stability and change in relationships* (pp. 107–28). Cambridge: Cambridge University Press.

Sanford, K. (2010). Assessing conflict communication in couples: Comparing the validity of self-report, partner-report, and observer ratings. *Journal of Family Psychology, 24,* 165–74.

Schaap, C., Buunk, B., & Kerkstra, A. (1988). Marital conflict resolution. In P. Noller, & M. A. Fitzpatrick (Eds.), *Perspectives on marital interaction* (pp. 203–44). Clevedon: Multilingual Matters.

Schweinle, W., Ickes, W., & Bernstein, I. (2002). Empathic inaccuracy in husband to wife aggression: The overattribution bias. *Personal Relationships, 9,* 141–58.

Segrin, C., Hanzal, A., & Domschke, T. J. (2009). Accuracy and bias in newlywed couples' perceptions of conflict styles and the association with marital satisfaction. *Communication Monographs, 76,* 207–33.

Shearman, S., & Dumlao, R. (2008). A cross-cultural comparison of family communication patterns and conflict between young adults and parents. *Journal of Family Communication, 8,* 186–211.

Sillars, A. L. (1986). *Procedures for coding interpersonal conflict.* Unpublished coding manual.

Sillars, A. (2011). Motivated misunderstanding in family conflict discussions. In J. L. Smith, W. Ickes, J. Hall, & S. Hodges (Eds.), *Managing interpersonal sensitivity: Knowing when—and when not—to understand others* (pp. 193–213). Hauppauge, NY: Nova Science.

Sillars, A. L., Pike, G. R., Jones, T. S. & Redmon, K. (1983). Communication and conflict in marriage. In R. Bostrom (Ed.), *Communication yearbook 7* (pp. 414–29). Beverly Hills, CA: Sage.

Sillars, A., Leonard, K. E., Roberts, L. J., & Dun, T. (2002). Cognition and communication during marital conflict: How alcohol affects subjective coding of interaction in aggressive and nonaggressive couples. In P. Noller & J. A. Feeney (Eds.), *Understanding marriage: Developments in the study of couple interaction* (pp. 85–112). Cambridge: Cambridge University Press.

Sillars, A., Roberts, L. J., Leonard, K. E., & Dun, T. (2000). Cognition during marital conflict: The relationship of thought and talk. *Journal of Social and Personal Relationships, 17,* 479–502.

Sillars, A., Smith, T., & Koerner, A. (2010). Misattributions contributing to empathic (in)accuracy during parent–adolescent conflict discussions. *Journal of Social and Personal Relationships, 27,* 727–47.

Sillars, A. L. & Wilmot, W. W. (1989). Marital communication across the life span. In J. F. Nussbaum (Ed.), *Life-span communication: Normative issues* (pp. 225–53). Hillsdale, NJ: Lawrence Erlbaum Associates.

——(1994). Communication strategies in conflict and mediation. In J. Wiemann & J. A. Daly (Eds.), *Communicating strategically: Strategies in interpersonal communication* (pp. 163–90). Hillsdale, NJ: Lawrence Erlbaum Associates.

Silverstein, M. & Giarrusso, R. (2010). Aging and family life: A decade review. *Journal of Marriage and Family, 72,* 1039–58.

Simpson, J. A., Rholes, W. S., Campbell, L., Wilson, C., & Tran, S. (2002). Adult attachment, the transition to parenthood, and marital well-being. In P. Noller & J. Feeney (Eds.), *Understanding marriage: Developments in the study of couple interaction* (pp. 385–410). Cambridge: Cambridge University Press.

Smith, D. A., Vivian, D., & O'Leary, D. (1990). Longitudinal prediction of marital discord from premarital expressions of affect. *Journal of Consulting and Clinical Psychology, 58,* 790–98.

Solomon, D. H., Knobloch, L. K., & Fitzpatrick, M. A. (2004). Relational power, marital schema, and decisions to withhold complaints: An investigation of the chilling effect on confrontation in marriage. *Communication Studies, 55,* 146–67.

Solomon, D. H., Weber, K. M., Steuber, K. (2010). Turbulence in relational transitions. In S. W. Smith and S. R. Wilson (Eds.) *New directions in interpersonal communication* (pp. 115–34). Thousand Oaks, CA: Sage.

Steinberg, L., & Morris, A. S. (2001). Adolescent development. *Annual Review of Psychology*, 52, 83–110.

Thomas, G. & Fletcher, G. J. O. (1997). Empathic accuracy in close relationships. In W. Ickes (Ed.), *Empathic accuracy* (pp. 194–217). New York: Guilford Press.

Ting-Toomey, S., & Kurogi, A. (1998). Facework competence in intercultural conflict: An updated face-negotiation theory. *International Journal of Intercultural Relations*, 22, 187–225.

van de Vliert, E., & Euwema, M. C. (1994). Agreeableness and activeness as components of conflict behaviors. *Journal of Personality and Social Psychology*, 66, 674–87.

Vangelisti, A. L. (1994). Messages that hurt. In W. R. Cupach & B. H. Spitzberg (Eds.), *The dark side of interpersonal communication* (pp. 53–82). Hillsdale, NJ: Lawrence Erlbaum Associates.

Vangelisti, A. L., Corbin, S. D., Lucchetti, A. E., & Sprague, R. J. (1999). Couples' concurrent cognitions: The influence of relational satisfaction on the thoughts couples have as they converse. *Human Communication Research*, 25, 370–98.

Vangelisti, A. L., & Young, S. L. (2000). When words hurt: The effects of perceived intentionality on interpersonal relationships. *Journal of Social and Personal Relationships*, 17, 393–424.

Watzlawick, P., Beavin, J., & Jackson, D. D. (1967). *Pragmatics of human communication: A study of interactional patterns, pathologies, and paradoxes*. New York: Norton.

Weiss, R. L. (1993). *Marital Interaction Coding System-IV (MICS-IV)*. Unpublished coding manual.

Winkler, I., & Doherty, W. J. (1983). Communication style and marital satisfaction in Israeli and American couples. *Family Process*, 22, 221–28.

Zhang, Q. (2007). Family communication patterns and conflict styles in Chinese parent–child relationships. *Communication Quarterly*, 55, 113–28.

Zietlow, P. H. & Sillars, A. L. (1988). Life stage differences in communication during marital conflicts. *Journal of Social and Personal Relationships*, 5, 223–45.

22

Persuasion and Families

Steven R. Wilson, Lisa M. Guntzviller,
and Elizabeth A. Munz

The persuasion literature has deep roots including a rhetorical tradition dating to the ancient Greeks (Leff & Procario, 1985) and an attitude change tradition dating to the mid 1900s (Dillard & Pfau, 2002). Both traditions typically focus on persuasion in public and mass communication contexts, such as within social movements or health communication campaigns.

Given this focus, finding a chapter on the topic in the *Handbook of Family Communication* may seem surprising. Yet two studies illustrate how common persuasive attempts are within families. In the first, 60 college students recorded over 3,000 diary entries describing people they tried to influence over a 12-week period (Cody, Canary, & Smith, 1994). Parents were the third most frequent target for the college students' persuasive attempts even though many students no longer lived in their parents' household. Common reasons for attempting to persuade a parent included seeking assistance, advocating a shared activity, and offering the parent advice.

Earlier in the lifespan, Oldershaw, Walters, & Hall (1989) analyzed persuasive episodes as 43 mothers and their pre-school children engaged in mealtime, free-play, and clean-up activities. Mothers on average made 75 requests of their children per hour, or more than one request per minute. Children did not comply with 35 percent of these requests—a rate of child noncompliance typical for nonclinical samples at this age (Chamberlain & Patterson, 1996). Mothers used a variety of strategies when attempting to persuade their child such as explaining consequences of the child's actions, expressing disapproval of perceived misbehavior, modeling desired behavior, and offering positive consequences if the child complied.

As these studies illustrate, persuasion involves an intentional attempt by a speaker, via reason giving, to influence the attitudes, beliefs, and behaviors of others who have some measure of choice about how to respond (O'Keefe, 2002). Attempts to persuade are intentional in that a speaker wants to shape, strengthen, or modify another person's beliefs or behaviors (Miller, 1980), but speakers may not consciously plan how to pursue their goals (Kellermann, 1992). The reasons speakers provide when trying to persuade may include appeals to core values, linkages with important social groups, or explanations of tangible benefits (Kelman, 1958). The boundary between persuasion and coercion can be fuzzy, such as when parents give reasons while also implying that their child ultimately must comply (Wilson, Whipple, & Grau, 1996).

In this chapter, we clarify how persuasion has been conceptualized in both parent–child and marital relationships, review what currently is known regarding a limited number of questions about persuasion and families, and suggest avenues for integrating theory and research on persuasion, parenting, and marriage. Throughout the chapter, we highlight multiple goals that both motivate and constrain family members during persuasive episodes, the relational meanings family members attribute to persuasive messages, and the interactional nature of persuasion. Keeping these objectives in mind, we turn to persuasion in parent–child relationships.

Persuasion in Parent–Child Relationships

Conceptualizing Persuasive Messages and Interactions

Defining Parental Discipline and Parenting Styles

Parents' persuasive attempts have been studied under the labels of "parental discipline" and "parenting style." Discipline refers to "the methods parents use to discourage inappropriate behavior and gain compliance from children" (Locke & Prinz, 2002, p. 897). Discipline encompasses a broad range of behaviors that parents use to shape and regulate their children's behavior (e.g., reasoning, modeling, warning). In the context of discipline, parents may be motivated and constrained by a variety of short- and longer-term goals such as ceasing irritating child behavior, keeping a child safe, inculcating family and community values, maintaining a positive parent–child relationship, and fostering a child's autonomy, assertiveness, and potential (Grusec, Goodnow, & Kuczynski, 2000; Socha, 2006).

Scholars also distinguish parenting styles and practices. Hart, Newell, and Olsen (2003) define parenting styles as "aggregates or constellations of behaviors that describe parent–child interactions over a wide range of situations that are presumed to create a pervasive interactional climate" (p. 762). In contrast, Darling & Steinberg (1993) describe parenting practices as "behaviors defined by specific content and socialization goals" (p. 492); thus, actions such as spanking or attending parent–teacher conferences are parenting practices. Parenting styles provide a context in which particular practices occur, and the meaning and impact of particular practices may differ when they are performed by parents who typically enact different styles.

Among numerous conceptions of parenting style, two of the most influential are Hoffman's (1980) typology of discipline and Baumrind's (1973) taxonomy of parenting styles.

Hoffman's Discipline Types

Hoffman (1980) explores the effects on parental discipline on children's internalization of values. Discipline episodes often arise when children face conflicts between their own desires and prevailing moral standards. According to Hoffman, parents who repeatedly use particular forms of discipline help their child develop the inner resources (e.g., empathy) needed to behave morally. Hoffman distinguishes three forms of discipline that parents use in response to perceived child misbehavior:

1 power assertion, or the use or threat of physical force, control over the child's material resources, or other punitive sanctions;

2 love withdrawal, or the use of direct but nonphysical expressions of anger or disapproval of the child, such as ignoring the child, isolating the child, or threatening to leave the child;

3 induction, or providing reasons why the child must behave differently such as by appealing to the child's pride, desire to be grown up, or concern for others.

Inductive discipline, defined broadly, includes any appeal in which parents offer reasons why their child needs to change his or her behavior. "Reasoning," however, has been treated as a catch-all category that may include messages ranging from "normative statements, discussion of consequences, discussion of the feelings of others ... to noninformative and superfluous verbalizations" (Grusec & Goodnow, 1994, p. 7). Within this broad category, Hoffman (1980) argues that other-oriented induction, in which parents point out implications of their child's actions for others, is especially important in promoting the internalization of values.

Many studies of parental control or regulation are organized loosely around Hoffman's forms of discipline (e.g., Applegate, Burke, Burleson, Delia, & Kline, 1985; Oldershaw, Walters, & Hall, 1986). Oldershaw et al. analyzed maternal control strategies during videotaped free-play and clean-up activities. A control sequence began each time that a mother issued a request or command, and continued until her child complied or she gave up seeking compliance. For each sequence, the authors assessed whether the mother's initial and follow-up commands were accompanied by control strategies. Oldershaw et al. label strategies such as reasoning, bargaining, and approval as "positively oriented" because they "mainly involve dealing with the child on an intellectual level and engaging in rational discussion that excludes any implied or real threat of punishment" (p. 725). Positively oriented strategies correspond with Hoffman's broad usage of inductive discipline. In contrast, Oldershaw et al.'s "power-assertive" control strategies, such as threats to punish or humiliation, "reflect the [authoritarian] role a parent assumes over a child" (p. 725). These strategies correspond with Hoffman's power-assertive discipline, though some (e.g., humiliation) also could entail love withdrawal.

Baumrind's Parenting Styles

Baumrind's (1973) taxonomy of parenting styles also has been employed to describe parents' use of persuasion. Baumrind initially identified three groups of children rated as:

1 high in vitality, self-reliance, approach tendency, and self-control (Pattern I);
2 low in peer affiliation and vitality as well as approach tendency (Pattern II);
3 low in self-reliance, self-control, and approach tendency (Pattern III).

Based on videotaped mother–child interactions as well as home observations, Baumrind then compared parents of these three groups along four dimensions:

1 *control*, or a parent's attempts to modify their child's behavior;
2 *maturity demands*, or parental pressure for the child to perform up to his/her ability intellectually and socially;
3 *clarity of parent–child communication*, or the extent to which parents use overt rather than manipulative control strategies and give reasons to obtain child compliance;
4 *nurturance*, or parental acts that express warmth and involvement.

Baumrind labeled parents of Pattern I children *authoritative* because they displayed high levels of control and maturity demands combined with high levels of nurturance, relied more on positive than negative sanctions, encouraged their child to express him/herself when the child disagreed, and persisted until their child complied using power assertion if necessary. Parents of Pattern II children are called *authoritarian* in that they displayed high levels of control along with low levels of clarity and nurturance, relying on power-assertive forms of discipline and expressed less child approval than the other two groups. Parents of Pattern III children are labeled *permissive* because they displayed low levels of control and maturity demands combined with higher levels of nurturance; these parents were less likely than authoritative parents to enforce rules or structure their child's activities, but used love withdrawal (e.g., ridicule) more often when seeking their child's compliance.

Baumrind (1996) argues parenting styles vary along two dimensions. *Responsiveness* "refers to the extent to which parents initially foster individuality and self-assertion by being attuned, supportive, and acquiescent to the child's needs and demands" (p. 410). *Demandingness* "refers to the claims that parents make on children to become integrated into the family and community by their maturity expressions, supervision, disciplinary efforts, and willingness to confront a disputative child" (p. 411). Authoritative parents are responsive and demanding, whereas the other styles involve either low responsiveness (authoritarian) or demandingness (permissive). Many researchers have analyzed parental styles using Baumrind's taxonomy (e.g., Bayer & Cegala, 1992; Stephenson, Quick, & Hirsch, 2010).

Mixing and Sequencing Persuasion and Other Forms of Discipline

A simplified reading of Hoffman or Baumrind's work might suggest that parents can be neatly divided into groups such as "parents who reason with their children" versus "parents who are power assertive." Yet Hoffman maintains that most disciplinary responses, including those involving induction, also include elements of power assertion and love withdrawal (1980, p. 320). Baumrind's authoritative style also depicts parents who mix induction with power assertion (1996, p. 412).

Consistent with such thinking, parents of pre-school children often mix forms of discipline both within and across conversational turns from the same control episode (Wilson, Cameron, & Whipple, 1997). In addition, parents use different types and combinations of induction and power assertion depending on how their child has misbehaved (Wilson et al., 1996). When parents with adolescents set rules regarding risky health choices, they also mix induction (communicating expectations clearly, providing reasons) and power assertion (monitoring the child's actions, using threats of negative sanctions) (Baxter, Bylund, Imes, & Routsong, 2009). Studies suggest that the effects of induction depend on how a parent mixes and sequences it with other forms of discipline as well as whether the parent's reasoning fits the nature of the misdeed and their child's age (Grusec & Goodnow, 1994). Rather than focusing only the use of induction, Grusec et al. (2000) call for work that shows "more explicit interest in the agency of parents and children, that is, in the meanings they construct of each other's behavior, in their capacity for strategic action, and in their ability to act 'as if' the other also is an agent" (p. 205).

Children's Responses to Parents' Persuasive Attempts

Children, from infancy onward, are active participants during persuasive episodes, and their behavior affects parental responses at the same time at which it is influenced by them

(Wilson et al., 1997). The most common way young children's reactions to their parents' requests have been assessed is with measures of child compliance, which occurs when "the child obeyed immediately after a parental request or after a short delay" (Chamberlain & Patterson, 1996, p. 206). Rates of child compliance typically are defined as the number of instances of compliance divided by the total number of child responses (compliance plus noncompliance). Aside from assessing compliance/noncompliance as a dichotomy, a smaller number of studies investigate how children comply with parental requests.

Kochanska & Aksan (1995) distinguish two forms of child compliance with parental requests. Children at times display *committed compliance* when they comply wholeheartedly, "fully endorsing and 'embracing' the maternal agenda as their own" (p. 237). At other times children display *situational compliance* when they are "essentially cooperative with the parent and nonoppositional [but] at the same time lack sincere commitment. Such compliance would appear to be mostly ... maintained by the parent's sustained control" (p. 237). For both toddlers and preschoolers, children's rates of committed compliance are inversely associated with their rates of situational compliance (Chen et al., 2003; Kochanska and Aksan, 1995). Rates of committed compliance, but not situational compliance, are positively associated with (a) displays of mutual positive effect between the mother and child, and (b) mothers' use of induction as opposed to power assertion (Kochanska & Aksan, 1995). In a longitudinal study (Kochanska, Coy, & Murray, 2001), children's rates of committed compliance with "don't" commands (e.g., telling children not to touch attractive objects) increased substantially from toddlerhood to preschool but then leveled off, whereas rates of committed compliance with "do" commands (telling children to put away toys after playing), increased more slowly but steadily across both developmental periods. Children who displayed committed compliance when their mothers were present also were more likely to continue complying when their mother left the room. In sum, committed compliance reflects "an early form of the internationalization of rules for behavior" as well as "the first step in the progress toward internal control" (Kochanska et al., 2001 p. 1108).

Aside from developing increased self-regulation, children also display increasing sophistication in their abilities to resist control as they mature. McQuillen, Higginbotham, & Cummings (1984) assessed developmental changes in how first-, fourth-, and tenth-graders would refuse a request from their mother, a friend, and a younger sibling. Children's responses to each request were coded into one of four categories adapted from McLaughlin, Cody, and Robey's (1980) typology of compliance–resistance strategies. Over half of the responses from first-graders across situations were nonnegotiation, whereas only one-third of the responses from tenth-graders fell into this category. Fourth- and tenth-graders were more likely than first-graders to vary their own compliance-resisting strategies depending on the source of the request (e.g., mother versus younger sibling) and the persuasive strategy included with the request.

Representative Findings

Having clarified how persuasion has been conceptualized in parent–child relationships, we now turn to what is known about two specific questions about persuasion and parenting.

Control Dynamics associated with Parental Physical and Verbal Aggression.

Child maltreatment is an immense, persistent social problem (Wilson, 2012). Although the etiology of child maltreatment is complex, reflecting the interplay of individual, family, community, and cultural factors (Belsky, 1993), parent–child interactions are the immediate antecedent to most episodes of child abuse, and physically abusive parents often seek their child's compliance in ways that heighten the risk of child maltreatment (Wilson, in press). This section focuses on control dynamics in families where parents are physically or verbally aggressive.

A growing body of research compares interactions between physically abusive parents and their children versus interactions between nonmaltreating parents and children from socio-demographically similar families (see Wilson, Norris, Shi, & Rack, 2010; Wilson, Rack, Shi, & Norris, 2008). For example, Oldershaw et al. (1986) compared the control strategies used by 10 physically abusive mothers and 10 nonmaltreating mothers matched on education and income as they interacted with one of their pre-school children. Abusive mothers:

a   issued a larger number of initial commands;
b   issued more initial commands in an effectively neutral rather than positive tone of voice;
c   issued more initial commands with no accompanying control strategy;
d   used every power-assertive strategy more often and several positively oriented strategies less often when they did use a control strategy.

Rates of child noncompliance with initial commands were much higher for abused (53 percent) than for nonmaltreated children (22 percent).

Following child noncompliance, abusive mothers differed from comparison mothers in that the former group issued more repeat commands with no accompanying control strategy or with a power-assertive strategy, and more repeat commands in a negative or neutral rather than positive tone. When their child did comply, abusive mothers: (a) were equally likely to criticize as praise their child in the conversational turn immediately following compliance, and (b) were more likely than comparison mothers to continue seeking compliance after their child complied because they did not notice their child had complied. By failing to notice or consistently praise child compliance, abusive mothers inadvertently may encourage future noncompliance.

Based on findings such as these, several scholars have proposed social-interaction models of child abuse (see Wilson, 2012). For example, Reid (1986) argues that the probability of child abuse is a function of (a) the number of discipline confrontations parents have with children and (b) the degree to which parents can resolve such confrontations quickly, without the parent resorting to physical aggression (p. 239). In a meta-analysis of observational studies comparing parent–child interactions in families with and without a documented history of child physical abuse, Wilson, Shi, Tirmenstein, Norris, & Rack (2006) found that abused children scored nearly one-half of a pooled standard deviation higher than nonmaltreated children in rates of noncompliance (mean-weighted $d = .45$, $CI_{95d} = .26$ to $.65$ based on 13 effects, $N = 743$ children). This finding may reflect that physically abusive parents, more than nonmaltreating parents, react inconsistently to aversive child behavior such as noncompliance, being more like to demand that the child comply but then to withdraw after additional child resistance to avoid further conflict (Cerezo & D'Ocon, 1999). Such a pattern results in escalating cycles of parental demands and child resistance over time, which leaves physically abusive parents simultaneously feeling angry and powerless (Bugental et al., 1989). Parents and children thus co-create patterns that put children at risk for abuse.

Similar control dynamics distinguish families in which parents are high versus low in trait verbal aggression. Trait VA refers to "the tendency to attack the self-concepts of

Steven R. Wilson, Lisa M. Guntzviller, and Elizabeth A. Munz

individuals instead of, or in addition to, their position on topics of communication" (Infante, 1987, p. 164). Parents high in trait VA tend to enact an authoritarian parenting style (Bayer & Cegala, 1992), use corporal punishment with adolescent children (Roberto, Carlyle, & Goodhall, 2007), and endorse beliefs and perceptions that put parents at risk for child abuse (Wilson, Hayes, Bylund, Rack, & Herman, 2006). Interestingly, mothers high in trait VA also display different control dynamics than low trait VA mothers even during free-play, being more likely to use commands and suggestions as well as negative physical touch to control the activities and pace at which they and their child play (Roberts, Wilson, Delaney, & Rack, 2009; Wilson, Roberts, Rack, & Delaney, 2008). Although frequent exposure to verbally aggressive messages itself is not healthy for children (Morgan & Wilson, 2005), these findings suggest that parents who are high in trait VA enact control dynamics with their children reminiscent of those displayed by physically abusive parents even when situational stimuli (e.g., child misbehavior) that might elicit verbally aggressive behavior are not present.

Comparisons of Corporal Punishment Across Race, Ethnicity, and Culture

Corporal punishment has been defined as "the use of physical force with the intention of causing a child to experience pain but not injury for the purposes of correction or control of the child's behavior" (Straus, 1994, p. 4). There are mixed findings regarding whether the relationship between parenting practices such as corporal punishment and child outcomes differ for families of varying races and ethnicities. Several investigators have concluded that physical discipline as practiced by African American mothers does not result in the same types of negative child outcomes as when practiced by European American mothers (Baumrind, 1972; Lansford, Deater-Deckard, Dodge, Bates, & Pettit, 2004; McLeod, Kruttschnitt, & Dornfeld, 1994). There also is some evidence, however, to suggest similarities in associations between corporal punishment and child outcomes for diverse families. Amato & Fowler (2002) used longitudinal data from the National Survey of Families and Households to determine that harsh punishment (i.e., how often a parent reporting slapping or spanking a child or yelling at a child) was negatively associated with child adjustment variables for families of varying race, ethnicity, family structure, and socioeconomic status. Other studies also report more similarities than differences for Caucasian and African American boys' outcomes associated with their parents' physical discipline (Pardini, Fite, & Burke, 2008; Whiteside-Mansell, Bradley, Owen, Randolph & Cauce, 2003).

Another finding common across racial groups is that the effects of corporal punishment depend on the quality of the parent–child relationship in which such practices are embedded. McLloyd and Smith (2002) assessed 401 Hispanic, 550 African American, and 1,039 European American children and their mothers over a six-year period. For all three groups, spanking and maternal emotional support interacted in their effects on changes in rates of child behavior problems over time. For mothers who provided only low levels of emotional support, overall rates of spanking were positively associated with increased rates of reported child behavior problems over the six-year period. Spanking was not associated with increases in child behavior problems in the context of high maternal emotional support.

There are a number of possible explanations for mixed findings regarding the impact of corporal punishment in families of different races and ethnicities, including differences across studies in measurement procedures (self-report, teacher report, other parent report, or observational measures) used to assess parenting practices and child outcomes (Berlin et al., 2009; Nelson, Hart, Yang, Olsen & Jin, 2006), Researchers also need to disentangle racial or ethnic background from socioeconomic status (SES) when explaining possible differences.

Researchers are beginning to address a need to understand the meaning of parenting styles and physical discipline in different cultural contexts outside of the U.S. with some studies suggesting differences between U.S. findings and findings in other countries, and other findings suggesting similarities across countries as contexts. Regarding differences between countries, Chao (1994) reports a positive association between authoritarian Chinese parenting styles and children's school achievement which runs contrary to the outcomes of authoritarian parenting styles for many U.S. samples. Similarities between U.S. samples and other samples are found in Alyahri and Goodman's (2008) report of correlations between corporal punishment and children's school performance and psychopathology in Yeman.

These findings from other countries highlight the importance of attending to the meanings or messages conveyed by power-assertive forms of discipline for parents and children (McLoyd & Smith, 2002). For parents, corporal punishment may be perceived to be instrumental in achieving parenting goals (e.g., teaching children right from wrong) (Taylor, Hamvas, & Paris, 2011). Parents may also view spanking as an adaptive response to risky environments. For children, the meanings conveyed by corporal punishment influence its ultimate outcomes (Gershoff, 2002). Research conducted in China, India, the Philippines, Thailand and Jamaica suggests that children's perceptions of maternal hostility mediate the relationship between corporal punishment and children's adjustment. When children perceive corporal punishment as a sign that their mothers are hostile, they are more likely to be anxious or aggressive; when children view corporal punishment as normative, they may not assign rejection or lack of love to this parenting practice and are less likely to experience the same outcomes (Lansford et al., 2010; Smith, Springer & Barrett, 2011).

There are several steps which can enhance our understanding of parents' discipline practices in a culturally informed manner. Researchers can attend to diversity within groups, rely on multiple methodologies to gain a range of participants' perspectives, and ground the measurement of parenting practices within the experiences of a given culture or co-culture (Tamis-LeMonda, Briggs, McClowry, & Snow, 2008). In other words, the ways in which parents view the parenting role and family relationships will shape their discipline strategies.

Persuasion in Marital Relationships

Conceptualizing Persuasive Messages and Interactions

Persuasion in marriage has been studied under the rubric of power strategies and tactics. Although power has been theorized in many ways, two assumptions underlie most views. First, power is reflected in the ability of those who wield it to impact others' behaviors, beliefs, and emotions. Second, power is relational in that it is a function of a target's dependence on the source for achieving desired outcomes (Stafford, 2008). To analyze power relationally, we must explore how spouses react to their partner's attempts to assert control (Millar & Rogers, 1987).

Scholars have turned attention to how power is expressed in marriage. Similar to parent–child relationships, spouses may be motivated and constrained by a variety of short- and longer-term goals when they attempt to influence each other, such as wanting their partner to act differently, maintaining a satisfying marital relationship, respecting their spouse's and maintaining their own autonomy, and communicating caring (Caughlin & Scott, 2010; Goldsmith, Lindholm-Gumminger, & Bute, 2006). Among the many typologies of power or influence strategies in marriage, we review those developed by Falbo & Peplau (1980) and Overall, Fletcher, Simpson, & Silbey (2009). The former is one of the best-known typologies, whereas the latter has been applied to observational data of couple interactions.

Falbo and Peplau's (1980) Power Strategies

To develop a typology, Falbo and Peplau initially asked 50 college-age lesbians, 50 gay men, 50 heterosexual women, and 50 heterosexual men to write an open-ended essay on "how I get (my romantic partner) to do what I want" (p. 620). Based on themes in the data, the authors identified 13 power strategies. During phase two, nine experts rated the similarity of these strategies, and multidimensional scaling was used to interpret their ratings. Two dimensions captured experts' ratings. *Directness* refers to the degree to which speakers say what they want and overtly attempt to alter their partner's behavior. Asking, telling, stating the importance, talking, and reasoning anchor the "direct" end of this dimension, whereas suggesting (hinting), withdrawal, positive effect (putting the target in a good mood) and negative effect (guilt) anchor the "indirect" end. *Bilaterality* refers to the degree to which speakers engage their partner in a discussion about how to proceed. Persuasion, bargaining, reasoning, talking and positive effect anchor the "bilateral" end of this dimension; laissez-faire, withdrawal, telling, asking and negative effect anchor the "unilateral" end.

Researchers using Falbo and Peplau's typology to study influence in marriage usually create composite scores assessing the degree to which spouses rely on direct, indirect, bilateral, and unilateral strategies, and then explore associations between self-reported scores and gender (wives versus husbands), culture, perceived distribution of relational power, and marital satisfaction. Although marital satisfaction has been positively associated with the use of direct rather than indirect strategies in some studies with U.S. couples (Aida & Falbo, 1991; Weigel, Bennett, & Ballard-Reisch, 2006, but not Butterfield & Lewis, 2002), some evidence suggests this finding may not generalize across cultures (Belk et al., 1988; Kim & Wilson, 1994).

Overall et al.'s (2009) Regulative Strategies

Overall and colleagues created a typology of strategies individuals in intimate relationships use to regulate each other's behaviors. The authors conceptualize regulative strategies as varying along two dimensions labeled *directness* and *valence*. Direct strategies are explicit and overt in seeking change, whereas indirect strategies use passive or covert means of inducing change. Negative strategies include hostile, critical, or demanding behaviors whereas positive strategies express positive effect or demonstrate understanding of the partner's perspective. A partner's response to a regulative attempt also can vary along these same dimensions. Overall et al. initially propose a typology of six strategies that are direct/negative (coercion and autocracy), indirect/negative (manipulation and supplication), direct/positive (reasoning), and indirect/positive (soft positive).

Overall et al. (2009) had couples discuss one issue where the female desired change in her male partner and a second where the male desired change in his female partner. Coders rated the degree to which both partners (the "agent" and "target" of change) used the six strategies. When multidimensional scaling was used to analyze these ratings, a two-dimensional solution emerged where autonomy and coercion fell into one quadrant, manipulation and supplication into a second, reasoning into a third, and soft/positive into a fourth. Ratings were collapsed to create overall scores for direct/negative, indirect/negative, direct/positive, and indirect positive strategies. Immediately afterward, both parties perceived that the discussion had been more successful when agents used more indirect/positive strategies, but less successful when agents used more direct/negative or direct/positive strategies. Yet agents who used more direct/negative and direct/positive strategies during the initial discussion subsequently perceived that their partner changed more over the 12-month period, whereas those using indirect strategies did not perceive that their partner changed. Direct strategies made the target aware of the agent's concern and in some cases motivated the target to attempt to change. Direct/negative strategies, however, also risk reciprocal spirals of negative spousal behavior that could undermine relational satisfaction. Whether this would occur may depend on the target's openness to change; indeed, targets who used more indirect/positive and fewer direct/negative strategies during the initial discussion (i.e., who were more receptive when their partner asked for change) perceived that they changed more over time.

Representative Findings

Health-Related Social Control

Rooted in sociology, the concept of social control has been used to help explain the health benefits of close relationships (Umberson, 1992). Strong interpersonal ties such as marriage are thought to reduce an individual's propensity for engaging in risky behavior and encourage health-promoting behaviors through two mechanisms. Individuals in close relationships may feel an obligation or responsibility to protect their health because others depend on them, a process referred to as indirect social control. Direct social control "involves requests, reminders, threats, or rewards from significant others that encourage engagement in a healthier lifestyle" (Tucker, 2002, p. 387). A growing literature explores the conditions under which social control attempts by spouses encourage or impede the partner's adherence to recommended lifestyle changes (e.g., diet, exercise) and subsequent health.

In an early longitudinal study, Umberson (1992) asked a nationally representative sample of adults "how often does anyone tell or remind you to do anything to protect your health?" (p. 909). Results revealed that:

1 Married individuals identified their spouse as the person most likely to engage in health social control attempts with them.
2 Husbands were more likely than wives to report being targets of health social control.
3 For husbands and wives, frequency of social control was associated with a reduction in some health risk behaviors (e.g., smoking) though not all (e.g., alcohol consumption) three years later.

Researchers have explored what individuals actually say or do when attempting to exert health-related social control (Goldsmith et al., 2006; Lewis, Butterfield, Darbes, & Johnston-Brooks, 2004; Tucker & Mueller, 2000). Although spouses use tactics from Falbo and Peplau's (1980) typology when trying to influence their partner's health behavior (e.g., exercising), these newer studies show that spouses rely on other tactics as well. For example, spouses may change household routines or the couple's use of time to make it easier for their partner to perform the desired behavior (e.g., cooking meals at home rather than eating fast food). According to Lewis et al., such tactics "reflect social control as accommodation and adjustment rather than the simple exercise of power or influence" (p. 678).

As this newer research illustrates, health-related social control can be conceptualized in various ways, and the outcomes differ depending on its conceptualization. Franks, Stephens, Rook, Franklin, Keteyian, & Artinian (2006) distinguish between health-related support and control. The authors define health-related support as "spouses' … affirmation of patients' own efforts to initiate or sustain prescribed health behavior changes" (p. 313); thus it involves behaviors such as listening to a spouse's [patient's] concerns, assisting a spouse in making the change, and encouraging a spouse to make healthy choices. In contrast, they define health-related control as "spouses' efforts to induce patients to initiate or sustain prescribed health behavior changes when [patients] have been unable or unwilling to do so on their own" (p. 313), through behaviors such as reminding a spouse to perform healthy behaviors, trying to influence a spouse's choices about how to care for his/her health, and trying to stop a spouse from performing unhealthy behaviors. When defined exclusively in terms of tactics that are intrusive or designed to cause guilt, health-related control may not result in desirable outcomes. In a longitudinal study of 94 couples, one of whom (the patient) was undergoing cardiac rehabilitation, Franks et al. show that spouse reports of support predicted better patient mental health six months later, whereas spouse reports of social control predicted reduced patient health behaviors and mental health over time.

Although these results highlight the potential for health-related control to backfire, Frank et al.'s (2006) conception of health-related support actually falls within our definition of persuasion. Following Miller (1980), we view persuasion as encompassing not only attempts to change undesired behaviors but also to reinforce desired behaviors by partners. It may be too simple to treat some behaviors as "support" but others as "control" since the same behavior (e.g., encouraging a partner to make healthy choices) may be interpreted as communicating support (e.g., caring) in one context but control (e.g., a desire to dominate) in a different context (Dillard, Solomon, & Palmer, 1999; Goldsmith et al., 2006).

A partner's reactions to a spouse's health-related social control thus may differ depending on the nature of their marital relationship (Dillard & Fitzpatrick, 1985). Several studies have found statistical interaction effects consistent with such thinking. For example, Tucker (2002) found that for older adults (65–80 years), when relationship satisfaction with spouses or adult children was low, more frequent direct social control by family members was associated with greater negative effect (e.g., resentment, irritation) and more instances of hiding the unhealthy behavior. When relationship satisfaction was high, however, increased direct social control did not elicit these negative reactions. Rook, August, Stephens, & Franks (2011) likewise concluded that "Among patients who do not expect spouses to be involved in their disease management, social control may have the unwelcome, and potentially offensive, connotation that patients are unable to manage their condition successfully" (p. 14), whereas such unwelcome connotations are less likely to occur among patients who expect greater spousal involvement.

Demand–Withdraw Communication

Viewing power as a relational concept implies that studies of persuasion need to explore the dynamics of how couples seek *and* resist compliance. Research on demand–withdraw in marriage explores a specific pattern "during which one partner attempts to engage the other in discussing an issue by criticizing, complaining, or suggesting change while the other partner attempts to end the discussion or avoid the topic by changing the subject, remaining silent, or even leaving the room" (Klinetob & Smith, 1996, p. 946).

When assessed cross-sectionally, using both self-report and observational measures, numerous studies have found that demand–withdraw is associated with relationship dissatisfaction (Baucom, McFarland, & Christensen, 2010; Christensen, Eldridge, Catta-Preta, Lim, & Santagata, 2006; Reham & Holtzworth-Munroe, 2006); this finding has been replicated across several national cultures as well as with same-sex and cross-sex couples. In marriage and dating relationships, demand–withdraw is associated with anger, stress, intrusive thoughts, hyperarousal, direct/negative influence tactics, perceived irresolvability of the problem, and physical aggression (Malis & Roloff, 2006; McGinn, McFarland, & Christensen, 2009; Papp, Kouros, & Cummings, 2009; Sagrestano, Heavey, & Christensen, 1999). Demand–withdraw also is inversely associated with feeling understood by one's spouse, and such feelings partially mediate the impact of the pattern on marital dissatisfaction (Weger, 2005).

The picture is more complicated, however, when demand–withdraw communication and satisfaction are assessed over time and/or within a larger relational context. Prospective research indicates that current dissatisfaction appears to predict future demand–withdraw as much as the opposite (Noller, Feeney, Bonnell, & Callan, 1994). The negative effects of demand–withdraw on marital satisfaction are mitigated when couples also engage in high levels of affectionate expression (Caughlin & Huston, 2002). In addition, Heavey et al. (1993) found that wife-demand/husband-withdraw predicted a decline in wives' marital satisfaction from one year to the next, but husband-demand/wife-withdraw actually predicted an *increase* in wives' marital satisfaction over the same time period. Heavey et al. speculate that wives may interpret demanding behavior by their husbands as a sign of the man's commitment to their marriage, which may lead to more positive outcomes over time. Similar to our discussions of parental discipline as well as health social control, these findings highlight the importance of attending to the meanings that women and men ascribe to both demand and withdraw behaviors over time and within the larger context of their marriage.

Aside from investigating associations with marital satisfaction, researchers have posited explanations for why couples engage in demand–withdraw. Three theoretical explanations are the gender/individual difference perspective, social-structure perspective, and conflict-structure perspective. The gender/individual differences explanation asserts that women in general have greater needs for connection whereas men have greater needs for autonomy and/or are more reactive to physiological stress; thus, men withdraw more frequently in the face of persuasive attempts (Caughlin & Vangelisti, 2000). The social-structural explanation suggests that power dynamics favor husbands, thus the wife demands in the attempt to gain power and the husband withdraws, attempting to avoid power changes (Klinetob & Smith, 1996; Sagrestano et al., 1999). The conflict structure hypothesis asserts that topic importance determines which spouse demands and which withdraws (McGinn et al., 2009; Heavey et al., 1993). If a topic is relevant to one spouse but not the other, than the latter spouse will withdraw while the former demands.

Although each of these perspectives can explain some aspects of demand–withdraw, none completely accounts for the entire body of findings (Caughlin & Scott, 2010).

Recently, Caughlin & Scott (2010) have re-conceptualized demand–withdraw from a multiple goals framework, arguing that these seemingly contrasting explanations can be encompassed within such a perspective. An individual may have a primary goal or main purpose for an interaction, but also may be constrained by secondary goals relevant to the situation, such as maintaining the relationship or presenting oneself in a certain way (Dillard, Segrin, & Harden, 1989; Wilson, 2002). Thus, individuals may pursue multiple goals simultaneously in an interaction, approach or avoid discussions differently depending on their secondary goals, and change their goals over the course of an interaction (Caughlin & Scott, 2010). Because of the ability of a multiple goals perspective to examine differences within *and* between dyads, Caughlin and Scott argue that their perspective can explain more than which spouse is likely to occupy the roles of demanding and withdrawing. They also suggest that different constellations of goals will result in different forms of demand–withdraw, which in turn might be associated with different relational outcomes.

Future Directions

Our chapter assesses how persuasion has been conceptualized in the family, focusing on parent–child and marital relationships. Although scholars working in these two contexts rarely cite each other's research, our review reveals many similarities. Several dimensions of persuasive appeals appear salient in both relationships. When attempting to exert influence, parents (Baumrind, 1973) and spouses (Overall et al., 2009) vary the degree to which they do so directly or indirectly. Parents (Hoffman, 1980) and spouses (Falbo & Peplau, 1980) often provide reasons when seeking behavior change, though simple requests without explicit reasoning are common in both relationships (Oldershaw et al., 1986; Tucker & Mueller, 2000). Parents (Applegate et al., 1985) and spouses (Franks et al., 2006) also differ in whether they tend to stress the positive consequences of a proposed action versus punitive sanctions, though the mixing of persuasion and coercion occurs in both contexts. Scholars have investigated resistance to persuasion in both relationships in the form of child noncompliance with parental requests (Chamberlain & Patterson, 1996), reactance to spousal health-related social control (Franks et al., 2006) and demand–withdraw patterns (Caughlin & Scott, 2010).

Scholars in both contexts have recognized that power and intimacy shape family members' choices, interpretations, and responses to persuasive strategies. Family members who feel powerless at times employ aggressive forms of influence in an attempt to regain power, whether they are physically abusive parents (Bugental et al., 1989) or spouses embroiled in demand–withdraw patterns (Sagrestano et al., 1999). Affection shapes family members' interpretations of what others might perceive as aggressive communication, such that the effect of parental power-assertion on child misbehavior is mitigated by parental emotional support (McLoyd & Smith, 2002), just as the effect of spousal social control on negative emotions is tempered by relational satisfaction (Tucker, 2002).

We see a need for theories that can account for regularities across parent–child and marital relationships. Although reactance theory (Burgoon, Alvaro, Grandpre, & Voulodakis, 2002) or relational framing theory (Dillard et al., 1999), might be useful in this regard, Brown and Levinson's (1987) politeness theory is promising because politeness reflects *and* defines relational power and intimacy. Briefly, the theory assumes that speakers in all cultures desire to maintain face, which is subdivided into *positive face* or the desire to have one's attributes and actions approved by significant others, and *negative face* or the desire to be free from unnecessary constraint. Although relational interdependence creates motives for family members to support each others' face, many speech acts threaten face. Attempts to persuade constrain the target's negative face, and by implicitly projecting presumed identities also may threaten both parties' positive face (Wilson, 2002).

Although persuasive appeals threaten face, not all do so equally. Brown & Levinson (1987) argue that in any culture, power and intimacy influence the "weightiness" of a face-threatening act (FTA), such that the same act is more face threatening as a target's power relative to a speaker increases, or the social distance between a speaker and target increases. To manage face threats, speakers often use two forms of politeness or language that attends to the target's face. *Indirectness* occurs when a speaker says something that given the circumstances implies a different or additional meaning. *Mitigation* includes redressive actions such as apologies, reasoning, or compliments. As the weightiness of an FTA increases, speakers are more likely to pursue change indirectly and to include redressive actions in their persuasive appeals.

Politeness theory offers one explanation for many similarities in persuasion in parent–child and marital relationships. Whether family members make requests indirectly, provide reasons, or avoid coercive pressure, all impact the perceived politeness of persuasive appeals. Family members may interpret resistance to their requests as a sign that their spouse or child views their desires as unimportant or lacks respect for their authority, and thus use aggressive forms of influence to regain face. Relational closeness reduces the degree of face threat communicated by demands or power assertion, and hence parental warmth or spousal affection can alter interpretations of persuasive attempts. Families who enact high levels of psychological interdependence, and hence expect more mutual involvement in health decisions, may be less reactive to social control attempts by spouses or adult children because members view such actions as less face threatening than in families with lower levels of interdependence.

It might seem ironic that politeness theory offers a useful framework for studying persuasion in families, since a good deal of the research we review indicates that family members often are not very polite to each other. Politeness theory, however, does not assume that family members always will be polite, but rather that they vary the degree to which they are polite or impolite depending on the amount of perceived threat to the target's face. "Face" also might seem less relevant in family relationships, since we might expect that individuals could "be themselves" with their families. As Cupach & Metts (1994) have argued, however:

> the complexity of managing face is increased for partners in close relationships ... part of the reason a couple defines itself as intimate is that the need to "perform" ... is considered unnecessary; yet in this very act of dropping pretense arises the probability of threatening each other's face and, ultimately, sense of social competence.
>
> *(p. 2)*

Thus, the way that a parent influences his/her child allows the child to have more or less "face" within their relationship, in the sense of validating the child's competence, worth, and autonomy. The same holds true in terms of whether spouses are responsive to each other's influence.

Applications of politeness theory need to be integrated with detailed analyses of family forms and structures (Wilson, 2002). Relevant questions include: What attributes do husbands and wives, gay or lesbian partners, mothers and fathers, sons and daughters, stepparents and stepchildren, grandmothers and grandfathers, and so forth, desire to be seen as possessing in the eyes of other family members? What rights and obligations do these roles entail in various cultures? How do family members negotiate levels of power and distance in their family, and in what ways does persuasion reinforce or challenge existing levels? Future research inspired by frameworks that transcend specific family relationships, such as politeness theory, may lead to a more integrated understanding of persuasion and families.

References

Aida, Y., & Falbo, T. (1991). Relationships between marital satisfaction, resources, and power strategies. *Sex Roles, 24*, 43–56.

Alyahri, A., & Goodman, R. (2008). Harsh corporal punishment of Yemeni children: Occurrence, type and associations. *Child Abuse & Neglect, 32*, 766–73.

Amato, P. R. & Fowler, F. (2002). Parenting practices, child adjustment, and family diversity. *Journal of Marriage and Family, 64*, 703–16.

Applegate, J. L., Burke, J. A., Burleson, B. R., Delia, J. G., & Kline, S. L. (1985). Reflection-enhancing parental communication. In I. E. Sigel (Ed.), *Parental belief systems: The psychological consequences for children* (pp. 107–42). Hillsdale, NJ: Lawrence Erlbaum Associates.

Baucom, B. R., McFarland, P., & Christensen, A. (2010). Gender, topic, and time in observed demand/withdraw interaction in cross-sex and same-sex couples. *Journal of Family Psychology, 24*, 233–42.

Baumrind, D. (1972). An exploratory study of the socialization effects on Black children: Some Black-White comparisons. *Child Development, 43*, 261–67.

——(1973). The development of instrumental competence through socialization. In A. D. Pick (Ed.), *Minnesota symposium on child psychology* (Vol. VII, pp. 3–46). Minneapolis, MN: University of Minnesota Press.

——(1996). The discipline controversy revisited. *Family Relations, 45*, 405–11.

Baxter, L. A., Bylund, C. L., Imes, R., & Routsong, T. (2009). Parent–child perceptions of parental behavioral control through rule-setting for risky health choices during adolescence. *Journal of Family Communication, 9*, 251–71.

Bayer, C. L., & Cegala, D. (1992). Trait verbal aggressiveness and argumentativeness: Relations with parenting style. *Western Journal of Communication, 56*, 301–10.

Belk, S. S., Snell, W. E., Garcia-Falconi, R., Hernandez-Sanchez, J. E., Hargrove, L., & Holtzman, W. H. (1988). Power strategy use in the intimate relationships of women and men from Mexico and the United States. *Personality and Social Psychology Bulletin, 14*, 439–47.

Belsky, J. (1993). Etiology of child maltreatment: A developmental-ecological analysis. *Psychological Bulletin, 114*, 413–34.

Berlin, L. J., Malone, P. S., Ayoub, C., Ispa, J. M., Fine, M. A., Brooks-Gunn, J.,& Bai, Y. (2009). Correlates and consequences of spanking and verbal punishment for low-income White, African American, and Mexican American toddlers. *Child Development, 80*, 1403–20.

Brown, P., & Levinson, S. C. (1987). *Politeness: Some universals in language usage*. Cambridge: Cambridge University Press.

Bugental, D. B., Blue, J., Cruzcosa, M. (1989). Perceived control over caregiving outcomes: Implications for child abuse. *Developmental Psychology, 25*, 532–39.

Burgoon, M. E., Alvaro, E., Grandpre, J., & Voulodakis, M. (2002). Revisiting the theory of psychological reactance: Communicating threats to attitudinal freedom. In J. P. Dillard & M. Pfau (Eds.), *The persuasion handbook: Developments in theory and practice* (pp. 213–32). Thousand Oaks, CA: Sage.

Butterfield, R. M., & Lewis, M. A. (2002). Health-related social influence: A social ecological perspective on tactic use. *Journal of Social and Personal Relationships, 19*, 505–26.

Caughlin, J. P., & Huston, T. L. (2002). A contextual analysis of the association between demand/withdraw and marital satisfaction. *Personal Relationships, 9*, 95–119.

Caughlin, J. P., & Scott, A. M. (2010). Towards a communication theory of the demand/withdraw pattern of interaction in interpersonal relationships. In S. W. Smith & S. R. Wilson (Eds.), *New directions in interpersonal communication research* (pp. 180–200). Thousand Oaks, CA: Sage.

Caughlin, J. P., & Vangelisti, A. L. (2000). An individual difference explanation of why married couples engage in the demand/withdraw pattern of conflict. *Journal of Social and Personal Relationships, 17*, 523–51.

Cerezo, M. A., & D'Ocon, A. (1999). Sequential analyses in coercive mother–child interactions: The predictability hypothesis in abusive versus nonabusive dyads. *Child Abuse & Neglect, 20*, 573–87.

Chamberlain, P., & Patterson, G. R. (1996). Discipline and child compliance in parenting. In M. Bornstein (Ed.), *Handbook of parenting. Vol. IV: Applied and practical parenting* (pp. 205–25). Mahwah, NJ: Lawrence Erlbaum Associates.

Chao, R. K. (1994). Beyond parental control and authoritarian parenting style: Understanding Chinese parenting through the cultural notion of training. *Child Development, 65*, 1111–19.

Chen, X., Rubin, H. R., Liu, M., Chen, H., Wang, L., Li, D. et al. (2003). Compliance in Chinese and Canadian toddlers: A cross-cultural study. *International Journal of Behavioral Development, 27*, 428–36.

Christensen, A., Eldridge, K., Catta-Preta, A. B., Lim, V. R., & Santagata, R. (2006). Cross-cultural consistency of the demand/withdraw interaction pattern in couples. *Journal of Marriage and the Family, 68*, 1029–44.

Cody, M. J., Canary, D. J., & Smith, S. W. (1994). Compliance-gaining goals: An inductive analysis of actor's goal types, strategies, and successes. In J. A. Daly and J. Wiemann (Eds.), *Communicating strategically* (pp. 33–90). Hillsdale, NJ: Lawrence Erlbaum Associates.

Cupach, W. R., & Metts, S. (1994). *Facework*. Thousand Oaks, CA: Sage.

Darling, N, & Steinberg, L. (1993). Parenting style as context: An integrative model. *Psychological Bulletin, 113*, 487–96.

Dillard, J. P., & Fitzpatrick, M. A. (1985). Compliance-gaining in marital interaction. *Personality and Social Psychology Bulletin, 11*, 419–33.

Dillard, J. P., & Pfau, M. (Eds.) (2002). *The persuasion handbook: Developments in theory and practice.* Thousand Oaks, CA: Sage.

Dillard, J. P, Segrin, C., & Harden, J. M. (1989). Primary and secondary goals in the production of interpersonal influence messages. *Communication Monographs, 56*, 19–38.

Dillard, J. P., Solomon, D. H., & Palmer, M. T. (1999). Structuring the concept of relational communication. *Communication Monographs, 23*, 703–23.

Falbo, T., & Peplau, L. A. (1980). Power strategies in intimate relationships. *Journal of Personality and Social Psychology, 38*, 618–28.

Franks, M. M., Stephens, M. A. P., Rook, K. S., Franklin, B. A., Keteyian, S. J., & Artinian, N. T. (2006). Spouses' provision of health-related support and control to patients participating in cardiac rehabilitation. *Journal of Family Psychology, 20*, 311–18.

Gershoff, E. T. (2002). Corporal punishment by parents and associated child behaviors and experiences: A meta-analytic and theoretical review. *Psychological Bulletin, 128*, 539–79.

Goldsmith, D. J., Lindholm-Gumminger, K., & Bute, J. J. (2006). Communication about lifestyle change between cardiac patients and their spouses. In R. M. Dailey & B. A. LePoire (Eds.), *Applied interpersonal communication matters: Family, health, and community relations* (pp. 95–117). New York: Peter Lang.

Grusec, J. E., & Goodnow, J. J. (1994). Impact of parental discipline methods on the child's internalization of values: A reconceptualization of current points of view. *Developmental Psychology, 30*, 4–19.

Grusec, J. E., Goodnow, J. J., & Kuczynski, L. (2000). New directions in analyses of parenting contributions to children's acquisition of values. *Child Development, 71*, 205–11.

Hart, C. H., Newell, L., & Olsen, S. F. (2003). Parenting skills and social/communicative competence in childhood. In J. O. Greene & B. R. Burleson (Eds.), *Handbook of communication and social interaction skills* (pp. 753–97). Mahwah, NJ: Lawrence Erlbaum Associates.

Heavey, C. L., Layne, C., & Christensen, A. (1993). Gender and conflict structure in marital interaction: A replication and extension. *Journal of Consulting and Clinical Psychology, 61*, 16–27.

Hoffman, M. L. (1980). Moral development in adolescence. In J. Adleson (Ed.), *Handbook of adolescent psychology* (pp. 295–343). New York: Wiley.

Infante, D. A. (1987). Aggressiveness. In J. C. McCroskey & J. A. Daly (Eds.), *Personality and interpersonal communication* (pp. 157–94). Newbury Park, CA: Sage.

Kellermann, K. (1992). Communication: Inherently strategic and primarily automatic. *Communication Monographs, 59*, 288–300.

Kelman, H. C. (1958). Compliance, identification, and internalization: Three processes of attitude change. *Journal of Conflict Resolution, 2*, 51–60.

Kim, M. S., & Wilson, S. R. (1994). A cross-cultural comparison of implicit theories of requesting. *Communication Monographs, 61*, 210–35.

Klinetob, N. A., & Smith, D. A. (1996). Demand–withdraw communication in marital interaction: Tests of interspousal contingency and gender role hypotheses. *Journal of Marriage and the Family, 58*, 945–57.

Kochanska, G., & Aksan, N. (1995). Mother–child mutually positive affect, the quality of child compliance to requests and prohibitions, and maternal control as correlates of early internalization. *Child Development, 66*, 236–54.

Kochanska, G., Coy, K. C., & Murray, K. T. (2001). The development of self-regulation in the first four years of life. *Child Development, 72*, 1091–111.

Lansford, J. E., Deater-Deckard, K., Dodge, K. A., Bates, J. E., & Pettit, G. S. (2004). Ethnic differences in the link between physical discipline and later adolescent externalizing behaviors. *Journal of Child Psychology and Psychiatry, 45*, 801–12.

Lansford, J. E., Malone, P. S., Dodge, K. A., Chang, L., Chaudhary, N., Tapanya, S., & Deater-Deckard, K. (2010). Children's perceptions of maternal hostility as a mediator of the link between discipline and children's adjustment in four countries. *International Journal of Behavioral Development, 34*, 452–61.

Leff, M. C., & Procario, M. O. (1985). Rhetorical theory in speech communication. In T. W. Benson (Ed.), *Speech communication in the 20th Century* (pp. 3–27). Carbondale, IL: Southern Illinois University Press.

Lewis, M. A., Butterfield, R. M., Darbes, L. A., & Johnston-Brooks, C. (2004). The conceptualization and assessment of health-related social control. *Journal of Social and Personal Relationships, 21*, 669–87.

Locke, L. M., & Prinz, R. J. (2002). Measurement of parental discipline and nurturance. *Clinical Psychology Review, 22*, 895–929.

Malis, R. S., & Roloff, M. E. (2006). Demand/withdraw patterns in serial arguments: Implications for well-being. *Human Communication Research, 32*, 198–216.

McGinn, M. M., McFarland, P. T., & Christensen, A. (2009). Antecedents and consequences of demand/withdraw. *Journal of Family Psychology, 23*, 749–57.

McLaughlin, M. L., Cody, M. J., & Robey, C. S. (1980). Situational influences on the selection of strategies to resist compliance-gaining attempts. *Human Communication Research, 7*, 14–36.

McLeod, J., Kruttschnitt, C., & Dornfeld, M. (1994). Does parenting explain the effects of structural conditions on children's antisocial behavior? A comparison of Blacks and Whites. *Social Forces, 73*, 575–604.

McLoyd, V. C., & Smith, J. (2002). Physical discipline and behavior problems in African American, European American, and Hispanic children: Emotional support as a moderator. *Journal of Marriage and the Family, 64*, 40–53.

McQuillen, J. S., Higginbotham, D. C., & Cummings, M. C. (1984). Compliance-resisting behaviors: The effects of age, agent, and types of request. In R. N. Bostrom (Ed.), *Communication yearbook 8* (pp. 747–62). Beverly Hills, CA: Sage.

Millar, F. E., & Rogers, L. E. (1987). Relational dimensions of interpersonal dynamics. In M. E. Roloff & G. R. Miller (Eds.), *Interpersonal processes: New directions in communication research* (pp. 117–38). Newbury Park, CA: Sage.

Miller, G. R. (1980). On being persuaded: Some basic distinctions. In M. E. Roloff & G. R. Miller (Eds.), *Persuasion: New directions in theory and research* (pp. 105–22). Beverly Hills, CA: Sage.

Morgan, W. M., & Wilson, S. R. (2005). Nonphysical child abuse: A review of the literature and challenge to communication scholars. In P. J. Kalbfleisch (Ed.), *Communication yearbook 29* (pp. 1–34). Mahwah, NJ: Lawrence Erlbaum Associates.

Nelson, D. A., Hart, C. H., Yang, C., Olsen, J. A., & Jin, S. (2006). Aversive parenting in China: Associations with child physical and relational aggression. *Child Development, 77*, 554–72.

Noller, P., Feeney, J. A., Bonnell, D., & Callan, V. J. (1994). A longitudinal study of conflict in early marriage. *Journal of Social and Personal Relationship, 11,* 233–52.

O'Keefe, D. J. (2002). *Persuasion: Theory and research,* 2nd edn. Thousand Oaks, CA: Sage.

Oldershaw, L., Walters, G. C. & Hall, D. K. (1986). Control strategies and noncompliance in abusive mother–child dyads: An observational study. *Child Development, 57,* 722–32.

Oldershaw, L., Walters, G. C., & Hall, D. K. (1989). A behavioral approach to the classification of different types of physically abusive mother–child dyads. *Merrill-Palmer Quarterly, 35,* 255–79.

Overall, N. C., Fletcher, G. J. O., Simpson, J. A., & Sibley, C. G. (2009). Regulating partners in intimate relationships: The costs and benefits of different communication strategies. *Journal of Personality and Social Psychology, 96,* 620–39.

Papp, L. M., Kouros, C. D., & Cummings, E. M. (2009). Demand–withdraw patterns in marital conflict in the home. *Personal Relationships, 16,* 285–300.

Pardini, D. A., Fite, P. J., & Burke, J. D. (2008). Bidirectional associations between parenting practices and conduct problems in boys from childhood to adolescence: The moderating effect of age and African-American ethnicity. *Journal of Abnormal Child Psychology, 36,* 647–62.

Reid, J. B. (1986). Social-interactional patterns in families of abused and nonabused children. In C. Zahn-Waxler, E. M Cummings, & R. Iannotti (Eds.), *Altruism and aggression: Biological and social origins* (pp. 238–55). Cambridge: Cambridge University Press.

Reham, U. S., & Holtzworth-Munroe, A. (2006). A cross-cultural analysis of the demand–withdraw marital interaction: Observing couples from a developing country. *Journal of Consulting and Clinical Psychology, 74,* 755–66.

Roberto, A. J., Carlyle, K. E., & Goodhall, C. E. (2007). Communication and corporal punishment: The relationship between self-report parent verbal and physical aggression. *Communication Research Reports, 24,* 103–11.

Roberts, F., Wilson, S. R., Delaney, J., & Rack, J. J. (2009). Distinguishing communication behaviors of mothers high and low in trait verbal aggression: A qualitative analysis of mother–child playtime interactions. In D. D. Cahn (Ed.), *Family violence: Communication processes* (pp. 155–78). Albany, NY: SUNY Press.

Rook, K. S., August, K. J., Stephens, M. A. P., & Franks, M. M. (2011). When does spousal social control provoke negative reactions in the context of chronic illness? The pivotal role of patients' expectations. *Journal of Social and Personal Relationships, 28,* 772–89.

Sagrestano, L. M., Heavey, C. L., & Christensen, A. (1999). Perceived power and physical violence in marital conflict. *Journal of Social Issues, 55,* 65–79.

Smith, D. E., Springer, C. M., & Barrett, S. (2011). Physical discipline and socioemotional adjustment among Jamaican adolescents. *Journal of Family Violence, 26,* 51–61.

Socha, T. J. (2006). Orchestrating and directing domestic potential through communication: Toward a positive reframing of "discipline." In L. H. Turner & R. West (Eds.), *The family communication sourcebook* (pp. 219–36). Thousand Oaks, CA: Sage.

Stafford, L. (2008). Social exchange theories. In L. Baxter & D. O. Braithwaite (Eds.), *Engaging theories in interpersonal communication: Multiple perspectives* (pp. 377–90). Thousand Oaks, CA: Sage.

Stephenson, M. T., Quick, B. L., & Hirsch, H. A. (2010). Evidence in support of a strategy to target authoritarian and permissive parents in antidrug media campaigns. *Communication Research, 37,* 73–104.

Straus, M. A. (1994). *Beating the devil out of them: Corporal punishment in American families.* New York: Lexington Books.

Tamis-LeMonda, C. S., Briggs, R. D., McClowry, S. G., & Snow, D. L. (2008). Challenges to the study of African American parenting: Conceptualization, sampling, research, approaches, measurement, and design. *Parenting: Science and Practice, 8,* 319–58.

Taylor, C. A., Hamvas, L., & Paris, R. (2011). Perceived instrumentality and normativeness of corporal punishment use among black mothers. *Family Relations, 60,* 60–72.

Tucker, J. S. (2002). Health-related social control within older adults' relationships. *Journal of Gerontology, 57B,* 387–95.

Tucker, J. S., & Mueller, J. S. (2000). Spouses' social control of health behaviors: Use and effectiveness of specific strategies. *Personality and Social Psychology Bulletin, 26,* 1120–30.

Umberson, D. (1992). Gender, marital status, and the social control of health behavior. *Social Science & Medicine, 34,* 907–17.

Weger, H. (2005). Disconfirming communication and self-verification in marriage: Associations among the demand/withdraw interaction, feeling understood, and marital satisfaction. *Journal of Social and Personal Relationships, 22*, 19–31.

Weigel, D. J., Bennett, K. K., & Ballard-Reisch, D. S. (2006). Influence strategies in marriage: Self and partner links between equity, strategy use, and marital satisfaction and commitment. *Journal of Family Communication, 6*, 77–95.

Whiteside-Mansell, L., Bradley, R. H., Owen, M. T., Randolph, S. M, & Cauce, A. M. (2003). Parenting and children's behavior at 36 months: Equivalence between African American and European American mother–child dyads. *Parenting: Science and Practice, 3*, 197–234.

Wilson, S. R. (2002). *Seeking and resisting compliance: Why people say what they do when trying to influence others.* Thousand Oaks, CA: Sage.

——(2012). Social-interactional perspectives on child maltreatment: How can they contribute to relationship science? In O. Gillath, G. Adams, & A. D. Kunkel (Eds.), *Relationship science: Integrating evolutionary, neuroscience, and sociocultural approaches* (pp. 113–33). Washington, DC: American Psychological Association.

Wilson, S. R., Cameron, K. A., & Whipple, E. E. (1997). Regulative communication strategies within mother–child interactions: Implications for the study of reflection-enhancing parental communication. *Research on Language and Social Interaction, 30*, 73–92.

Wilson, S. R., Hayes, J., Bylund, C. E., Rack, J. J., & Herman, A. P. (2006). Mothers' trait verbal aggressiveness and child abuse potential. *Journal of Family Communication, 6*, 279–96.

Wilson, S. R., Norris, A., M. Shi, X., & Rack, J. J. (2010). Comparing physically abused, neglected, and non-maltreated children during interactions with their parents: A meta-analysis of observational studies. *Communication Monographs, 77*, 543–78.

Wilson, S. R., Rack, J. J., Shi, X., & Norris, A. M. (2008). Comparing physically abusive, neglectful, and non-maltreating parents during interactions with their children: A meta-analysis of observational studies. *Child Abuse & Neglect, 32*, 897–911.

Wilson, S. R., Roberts, F., Rack, J. J., & Delaney, J. E. (2008). Mothers' trait verbal aggressiveness as a predictor of maternal and child behaviors during playtime interactions. *Human Communication Research, 34*, 392–422.

Wilson, S. R., Shi, X., Tirmenstein, L., Norris, A., & Rack, J. J. (2006). Parental physical negative touch and child noncompliance in abusive, neglectful, and comparison families: A meta-analysis of observational studies. In L. H. Turner & R. West (Eds.), *The family communication sourcebook* (pp. 237–58). Thousand Oaks, CA: Sage.

Wilson, S. R., Whipple, E. E., & Grau, J. (1996). Reflection-enhancing regulative communication: How do parents vary across misbehavior types and child resistance? *Journal of Social and Personal Relationships, 13*, 553–69.

23

The Communication of Emotion in Families

Julie Fitness

Introduction

The family is the fundamental social group to which humans belong from birth, and it plays a critical role in shaping who we are and how we live, and love, throughout the course of our lives. If we are fortunate, our family provides emotional sustenance and support, a "haven in a heartless world." For those less fortunate, the family may be a crucible of painful emotions that drive family members to suicide, homicide, or at least, permanent estrangement from one another. For most of us, family life is constituted by a rich and complex array of feelings and emotions, including love, pride, anger, and even at times, hate; it can be the source of our greatest joys and sorrows. Every family member is a potentially powerful source of emotion for every other family member, and every family member's expression of emotion has a more or less powerful impact on other family members. Emotions, then, are the currency of family relationships, imbuing them with meaning and importance.

In the years since the first edition of this *Handbook* was published, research on emotion has flourished, though much of it has focused on emotion in a rather abstract, rather than relational, sense. This is starting to change, with scholars from a variety of disciplines now recognizing the fundamentally social nature of emotions and their functions (e.g., see Niedenthal & Brauer, 2012). In particular, there is a growing emphasis on the informational and communicative aspects of emotions and on the ways in which they motivate potentially adaptive behaviors in ourselves and in those closest to us, in the interests of our shared survival. Even so, there are still large gaps in our understanding of the functions of emotions within particular relationship contexts, including the family. My aim in this chapter is to provide an overview of some of the most recent and interesting research on emotion, with a particular focus on the nature and function of emotion communication within families. Following a brief account of the functionalist approach to emotion, I will discuss recent emotion communication research in marital and parent–child relationships, focusing on the nature of emotion socialization within the familial context. I will then discuss the emotional lives of siblings and the dynamics of emotion communication within families, including the creation and transmission of emotion climates. The chapter will close with a discussion of adaptive emotion functioning in families, and suggest some avenues for future research in this fascinating and important aspect of human relationships.

A Functionalist Approach to Emotion Communication in Marriage

The functionalist approach to emotion argues that humans are born with a number of evolved, "hard-wired" emotion systems that serve critical informational and motivational functions (see Fitness, Fletcher & Overall, 2007). The experience of anger, for example, signals that our goals are being thwarted and energizes us for battle, while the experience of fear alerts us to danger and urges us to freeze or flee, depending on the context. More positively, feelings of romantic love inform (or misinform) us that our beloved has the capacity to fulfill our desires and goals, and motivate us to bond with and commit to them (Gonzaga, Keltner, Londahl, & Smith, 2001). However, the informational function of emotions goes much further than this. Specifically, emotions also function to send information to others about the state of our needs and goals, and this is critical for our welfare and survival. Babies, for example, express happiness, sadness, and anger within the first few days of life, and caregivers respond appropriately to these signals (Scharfe, 2000). Similarly, throughout life, expressions of anger communicate goal-frustration and a desire for others to put things right; expressions of fear communicate danger and a desire for protection; expressions of joy communicate that we have resources (including positive feelings) to share, which in turn make us a valued social partner.

Nowhere is the profound functionality of human emotions so much in evidence as within that hothouse of feeling, the human family. Families are prototypically communal contexts, characterized by complex interdependencies and shared responsibilities for members' welfare (see Clark, Fitness, & Brissette, 2001, for a review). Consequently, the expression of emotions is an integral feature of family life, signaling members' survival and welfare needs to those who, theoretically at least, are most willing to meet those needs (Clark & Finkel, 2005). Given this, it is not surprising that researchers have found positive associations between marital happiness and spouses' abilities to both clearly express their own emotions, and accurately identify their partners' emotions (e.g., Gottman, 1994; Noller & Ruzzene, 1991). Further, and in line with the functionalist perspective, proponents of an increasingly popular form of marital therapy that focuses explicitly on emotion communication (emotion-focused therapy) argue that spouses' emotional attunement, deriving from their abilities to accurately mirror and validate each other's emotions, is a critical component of happy and successful marital relationships (e.g., see Greenberg & Goldman, 2008).

It is important to note here that, although emotional expressiveness is in itself an adaptive feature of successful relationships, not every emotional expression plays an adaptive role in day-to-day family functioning. One of the most welcome recent research developments in this field, then, is the increasing emphasis on specific emotions (in the marital context, at least) and the signals communicated via different kinds of emotional expressions about partners' underlying needs and motivations. These expressions may, in turn, have positive or negative consequences for relationship functioning. For example, Sanford and Grace (2011) reported the findings of a series of factor analytic studies drawing from data collected with more than 3,500 married individuals. On the basis of these data they identified two, basic dimensions of interpersonal distress associated with relationship conflict, with each dimension reflecting a particular underlying concern: perceived status threat, reflecting power and control-related concerns, and perceived neglect,

Communicating Emotion in Families

reflecting lack of love and/or belonging concerns. Sanford and Grace argue that each of these concerns is, in turn, associated with one of three types of emotions: hard (e.g., anger and other assertion-related emotions), soft (e.g., sadness and other vulnerability-related emotions), and so-called "flat" emotions, conveying boredom, disengagement and lack of interest. A spouse's perception that her relationship partner is expressing hard emotion tends to elicit a defensive, reciprocal response, whereas perceptions that a partner is expressing soft emotion are more likely to elicit an empathic, caring response (see also Clark, Pataki & Carver, 1996). In their own research, Sanford and Grace (2011) found evidence supporting their model; further, they found that individuals who observed an increase in their partner's flat emotion, or disengagement, perceived this to indicate partner neglect, or lack of love. This is reminiscent of earlier research describing the corrosive effects of "stone-walling" in marital interactions (e.g., Gottman, 1994), and underscores research on spouses' use of "the silent treatment" to punish one another; a behavior which some spouses have argued is worse than being physically beaten (Zadro, Arriaga & Williams, 2008).

Of course, spouses' perceptions of each other's emotions may not be accurate; e.g., a stone-walling spouse may be highly aroused physiologically (Gottman & Levenson, 2002). Further, researchers have demonstrated that spouses' perceptions of how accurately they communicate their emotions may be misguided (Koerner & Fitzpatrick, 2002; Thomas, Fletcher, & Lange, 1997). For example, a spouse may believe she is communicating soft emotion (anxiety and a need for reassurance) to her partner, but her facial expression, tone of voice and gestures may actually be sending an angry, rather than anxious, message. Further, her partner is likely to respond to what appears to be an expression of "hard" emotion with anger, rather than empathy. Or a spouse may do a good job, objectively speaking, of communicating soft emotion, but her partner may be a poor reader of emotion signals and again, respond with anger. In both cases the most likely outcome is an escalating spiral of reciprocated hurt and hostility, and increasing marital distress (Gottman, 1994).

An interesting question, then, is why some partners appear to be more skilled than others in accurately sending and interpreting emotion signals. Several factors that affect emotional communication processes and outcomes in marriage have been identified, including transient moods and chronic emotional dispositions (Bradbury & Fincham, 1987; Fitness, 1996). For example, in a recent study of marital conflict, Papp, Kouros, and Cummings (2010) asked 267 couples to participate in laboratory-based conflict discussions, after which they rated both their own and their spouses' perceived positivity, anger, sadness, and fear. Compared to nondepressed spouses, depressed spouses assumed greater similarity between themselves and their partners with respect to negative emotions, suggesting they were more likely to perceive negative signals from their partners than had actually been sent. Ironically, such negative perceptions may elicit the kinds of defensive partner responses that confirm a depressed spouse's pessimistic outlook (Segrin, 1998).

Another important factor that affects emotion communication in marriage derives from spouses' relationship histories, and in particular, their early attachment relationships with caregivers. As noted by attachment theorists (e.g., Shaver, Collins, & Clark, 1996), individuals develop schemas about what to expect from adult intimate relationships, based on the security or otherwise of their attachment relationships in childhood. Within adult romantic relationships, individuals' attachment schemas influence both their own emotion communication styles and their responses to their partners' needs and expressions of emotion. Individuals with secure attachment styles, for example, are comfortable with the expression of a range of emotions, and are appropriately responsive to their part-ners' emotional expressions (Feeney, 1999). Attachment-avoidant individuals, however, tend to discount their partners' needs or react to them with anger; they also tend to distance themselves from their partners when experiencing stress themselves (Simpson, Rholes, & Nelligan, 1992). Anxiously attached individuals respond inconsistently to their partners' needs, and are vigilant for signs of rejection. They also express negative emotions such as anger and jealousy more intensely and more often than secure individuals (Shaver et al., 1996).

With respect to gender differences in marital emotion communication, research con-ducted some 20 years ago found that women were generally better than men at both accurately encoding and decoding emotional expressions, and that women tended to express "soft" emotions more frequently than men, who tended to express "hard" emotions more frequently than women (see Brody, 1999, for a review). However, such findings are highly dependent on context and it cannot be taken for granted that they hold over time (or across cultures). In particular, as men's and women's roles both in the family and the wider community have changed within Western culture, it may be that men are considerably more willing to express vulnerable emotions within the family than in earlier times (see Rohner & Veneziano, 2001); however, much of the evidence in support of this proposition is anecdotal and derives from the popular press. This in turn underscores the necessity for social scientists to be ever willing to re-examine research questions for which the data—and answers—may well have changed over time.

In summary, spouses' accuracy in sending and interpreting emotion messages is an important predictor of their marital happiness. Such emotional attunement enables spouses to respond sensitively to each other's needs and strengthens their perceptions that they are truly cared for. However, different emotions send different messages about spouses' needs and desires, and not every kind of emotional expression has positive outcomes for the marital relationship. Further, families typically comprise many more interdependent relationships than the marital one, adding further complexity to familial emotion dynamics. Indeed, it may be within the parent–child relationship, rather than the marital relationship, that some of our most intense emotions are experienced and expressed on a daily basis. In the next section of this chapter I will discuss what we know about emotional communication between parents and their children, and consider how children learn to become emotionally competent (or incompetent) within the family context, as a function of what psychologists refer to as emotion socialization.

Socializing Emotion: Learning Emotion Rules in the Family

As noted previously, human infants are born with the ability to express a number of emotions that serve to alert caregivers to their needs, and ensure those needs are met. Researchers have documented how in the earliest months of an infant's life, parents are oriented toward protecting and comforting their infants, and they respond to infants' emotional signals with support and encouragement (Barry & Kochanska, 2010). However, as children grow older, parents become more control and discipline-oriented, and increasingly concerned with socializing their children into the emotion norms of the family and wider community. This means teaching children, both directly and indirectly, how to regulate negative emotions such as anger, fear, and sadness, such that they acquire the kind of emotional competence that creates socially competent adults. Further, Fredrickson (1998) noted that effective socialization also involves emotion *cultivation*, whereby parents strive to cultivate or encourage positive emotions in their children via such techniques as arranging social activities with other children, creating stimulating environments and learning opportunities for their children, and encouraging their children to reflect on their positive experiences. Fredrickson (1998) describes several benefits for children deriving from parental cultivation of their positive emotions, including enhanced feelings of well-being and broadened capacities for learning and creativity. Further, the ability to generate positive emotions can serve as a useful tool for regulating the experience and expression of negative emotions, while happy children also tend to build strong social networks and resources by virtue of their desirability as social partners. Each of these outcomes contributes to children's social competence.

Of course, parents must draw upon their own emotional competence (or lack thereof) when attempting to socialize their children's emotions. Two general approaches to parental socialization practices have been identified (Gottman, Katz, & Hooven, 1996). The supportive "emotion coaching" approach derives from an emotion philosophy that endorses family members' feelings as valid and important. Parents holding this philosophy actively teach children about the causes, features, and consequences of emotions, and help them to regulate and deal constructively with difficult emotions such as anger, fear, and sadness. In contrast, the dismissing approach to emotion socialization is associated with a philosophy that regards emotions as dangerous and/or unimportant, to be dismissed, changed or even punished by parents as quickly as possible. This latter orientation is associated with emotional suppression and minimization, which, in Western cultures at least (see discussion below) is associated with children's lower social competence and higher externalizing problems (Eisenberg, Cumberland & Spinrad, 1998).

There are many factors that influence parental emotion socialization orientations and practices. For example, in a longitudinal study examining the effects of maternal depression and attachment security on children's understanding of emotion at the ages of two and three, Raikes and Thompson (2006) found a significant, negative effect of mothers' depression over time on their children's emotion understanding. These researchers also found that more securely attached mother–child pairs made more references to emotion in conversation, which, in turn, promoted children's emotion understanding. As several researchers have noted, children in a secure attachment relationship learn that expressing their emotions elicits parental attention to their needs. Thus, securely attached children tend to be emotionally expressive and are able to both understand and regulate their own and others' emotions (Scharfe, 2000). Conversely, parents with insecure attachment styles tend to endorse emotion socialization practices in line with their own experiences and expectations of attachment relationships. For example, Magai (1999) found that parents with fearful attachment styles were more likely than nonfearful parents to physically punish and shame their children for expressing their needs, just as they were themselves shamed as children. Parents with an avoidant style, on the other hand, may discourage or dismiss children's emotional expressions altogether.

Of course, emotion socialization is a reciprocal process. Thus, while some children have calm, agreeable temperaments and may be easily coached, others may have more difficult temperaments; they may be shy, anxious, irritable, or emotionally labile (Lytton, 1990). These children may pose difficulties for parents who have different temperaments and who cannot understand, appreciate, or meet their children's emotional needs. For example, in a recent study, Rasbash, Jenkins, O'Connor, Tackett and Reiss (2011) investigated individual (including genetic) and relationship influences on expressions of negativity and positivity in 687 families. They found that overall, family members are much more consistent in the negativity that they direct toward others than in the negativity they elicit from others, and that there are genetic contributions to family members' negativity that play a unique role in shaping their emotional lives and interactions. Further, there are structural features of family life that can create conflict around emotion socialization practices. For example, Rasbash et al. (2011) found that children showed higher mean levels of negativity and lower mean levels of positivity as actors than did parents, no doubt reflecting the inevitable power imbalance in the parent–child relationship and the frustrations experienced by low power individuals.

Finally, it is important to consider the wider cultural context when exploring emotion socialization practices. Much of the research discussed here has been conducted with middle-class American families. However, different cultures have different emotion rules depending on the relative importance they place on the self versus the group (e.g., see Planalp & Fitness, 1999). For example, in so-called collectivist cultures (e.g., Japan, China, and Korea) family harmony is prized and individual needs may be subordinated to the needs of others. Accordingly, the open expression of anger is discouraged because it disrupts social relationships and puts individual needs ahead of group needs. Conversely, in individualist cultures (e.g., North America), independence and individual achievement are prized and the expression, rather than suppression, of emotions such as anger is encouraged in the pursuit of individual needs and goals.

These cultural differences were demonstrated in a study that found U.S. children showed much more anger and aggression in symbolic play than Japanese children (Zahn-Waxler et al., 1996). In addition, U.S. mothers encouraged their children's open expression of emotions, whereas Japanese mothers fostered sensitivity to other children's emotional needs (see also Eisenberg, Liew, & Pidada's study [2001] of emotional expressiveness in Indonesian families, and Yang & Rosenblatt's analysis [2001] of the role of shame in Korean families). In a further, more recent example of the ways in which different cultures socialize children to regulate their emotions in ways that fit with cultural norms and values, Soto et al. (2011) found that, as expected, suppressing the expression of emotions was associated with adverse psychological functioning for European Americans; however, this was not the case for Chinese participants. Similarly, in a laboratory experiment, Ng, Pomerantz and Lam (2007) found that when children succeeded on a test, American mothers were more likely than Chinese mothers to provide positive comments (i.e., cultivating positive emotions) whereas Chinese mothers were more likely than American mothers to make neutral or task-relevant statements than overtly positive ones. The function of this emotion dampening is to discourage "too much" happiness in preference to what Soto et al. (2011) refer to as the "middle way," characterized by efforts to achieve a balance between positive and negative emotions and not favoring one kind over the other (see also Tao, Zhou, & Wang, 2010).

In summary, some parents actively coach their children about emotions and help them develop sophisticated understandings of their own and others' emotional lives, while other parents discourage or even punish the expression of emotions. Clearly, there is still much to learn about other styles and philosophies of emotion within the family, and importantly, about the content and function of emotion rules according to cultural differences in emotion-related values and norms. However, it is also important to note that parents are not the only familial agents of emotional socialization. Sibling relationships are also profoundly emotional, with brothers and sisters both competing with one another for resources and providing mutual support, sometimes throughout their lives. In the next section of this chapter I will discuss some of the causes and outcomes of emotions in sibling relationships with a particular focus on jealousy and envy (since these have attracted the most research attention). I will also point the way to further research in this important, but understudied, familial context.

Emotions in Sibling Relationships

Sibling relationships have been described as quintessentially emotional (Bedford & Avioli, 1996). Of all the emotions experienced by siblings toward one another, however, jealousy and envy tend to be regarded as prototypical (Volling, McElwain, & Miller, 2002); indeed, in one interview study with 5th and 6th graders, Thompson and Halberstadt (2008) found sibling jealousy was reported in 98 percent of families, occurring on average once a month.

The most frequently cited reasons for sibling jealousy include the loss of exclusivity and diversion of parental attention once there is more than one child in the family, and perceived parental favoritism (see also Fitness, 2005; Rauer & Volling, 2007). However, there are other important causes of sibling jealousy. For example, Volling et al. (2002) found a positive association between parents' marital unhappiness and sibling jealousy, suggesting that parental conflict may heighten the experience and expression of negative emotions in the family. Part of this effect may be accounted for by children modeling their parents' angry and aggressive behaviors (Boyum & Parke, 1995); however, this heightened negativity may also be a function of so-called emotion contagion, whereby individuals unconsciously "catch" emotions like anxiety, anger, and depression from one another (Hatfield, Cacioppo, & Rapson, 1993). Further, some children are more sensitive to perceived frustration than others and are prone to frequent displays of anger; such children also tend to display more jealousy than less chronically angry children (Volling et al., 2002).

Interestingly, parental reactions to displays of sibling jealousy tend to be more positive than negative. In studies of children's anger tantrums, for example, Hart (2010) noted that parents provided more warmth and reassurance if the perceived cause of the tantrum was rivalry-related, than if it were frustration. One possible reason for this is that parents in Western cultures, at least, have been exposed to a considerable amount of information in the popular press about "sibling rivalry" and may believe that children's expressions of jealousy and envy are normal and natural. Parents may also feel some guilt if they perceive that they have, indeed, treated their children differently. Further, just as jealousy expressions may be interpreted as a signal of love in romantic relationships (see Fitness, 1996), so too parents may perceive sibling rivalry as somewhat flattering (after all, the children are fighting for the parent's attention and love). As Hart notes, however, this perception also presents parents with a dilemma: if a child's jealous displays are interpreted as signals of love, then how can a parent discipline a child for expressing such feelings?

It is also important to emphasize that siblings are allies as well as competitors, and sibling relationships may be a source of emotional support throughout life and into old age (Gold, 1989). Researchers have found, for example, that when exposed to marital conflict, some older siblings increase protective, care-giving behaviors toward younger siblings (Cummings & Smith, 1989). Warm sibling relationships have also been identified as powerful contexts for the development of trust, self-disclosure skills, and socioemotional understanding (Howe, Aquan-Assee, Bukowski, Lehoux, & Rinaldi, 2001). There is still much to learn, however, about how and when different emotions are experienced and

383

expressed within sibling relationships, and there is a need to consider a much wider array of sibling emotions than jealousy and envy (see Brody, 2004). In particular, we still know relatively little about the origins and functions of sibling love and hate throughout the lifespan, and the emotions that keep siblings "stuck like glue" or forever estranged. We also know little about how emotions and emotional expressions might differ depending on the age, birth order, and gender composition of the sibling (and frequently today, step-sibling) relationship, and about the ways in which emotional experiences with siblings in childhood may shape adults' understandings and experiences of emotion in later life (and in particular, with their own children).

In summary, sibling relationships are characterized, in part, by the expression of negative emotions such as jealousy and envy as a function of their intrinsically competitive nature. However, siblings may also form strong attachment bonds and experience highly positive emotions toward one another. There is no doubt that sibling relationships play a powerful role in shaping our ongoing emotional lives with others, though their role may be unrecognized. In the next section of the chapter I will move from a consideration of individual types of family relationships to a more holistic view of the family as an emotional system in its own right. In particular, I will review both the dynamics of emotion communication within the family and the creation of emotional family climates.

The Dynamics of Emotion Communication Within the Family

Families are dynamic systems comprising complex patterns of interdependencies and expectations. Every family member is affected by what happens to every other member, with important implications for the experience and expression of emotions. For example, and as noted previously, emotions within highly communal relationships may be contagious, with both positive and negative outcomes. In a study exploring the effects of positive affectivity on marital functioning, Gordon and Baucom (2009) found that individuals who are typically very happy, and individuals who perceive their spouses to be very happy, have more satisfying marriages. "Catching" another family member's happiness and excitement creates shared feelings of warmth and closeness, and may strengthen the relationship.

However, emotion sharing is not always a positive experience. For example, when one spouse is depressed, the degree to which the couple is emotionally close is a risk factor for the other spouse also becoming depressed (Tower & Kasl, 1995). The powerfully contagious nature of negative emotions was also demonstrated by Thompson and Bolger (1999), who found that depression in one partner reduces happiness in the other, rather than the other way around. Emotions, then, may cascade through families and create emotional atmospheres, or climates, that affect the day-to-day feelings and functioning of family members. Belsky, Youngblade, Rovine, and Volling (1991), for example, reported that as men became more dissatisfied with their marriages, they expressed more negative emotions to their children. Their children, in turn, reciprocated their fathers' negative emotions which increased their fathers' dissatisfaction with parenting and the marital relationship. Fathers then retreated further from the family, increasing their wives' and children's distress. Given that siblings may react to a general climate of negativity by fighting with one another, further upsetting their parents (Brody, 1998), it is easy to see how a whole family may become immersed in hostility and distress as a function of spousal unhappiness. Further, Rasbash et al. (2011) have noted how individuals may feel quite comfortable within the family context to "ignore the social niceties that require the reciprocation of positive effect and the inhibition of negative effect" (p. 486) and to express the kinds of irritable and ill-mannered behaviors that would not be acceptable in the wider community. Indeed, this can be observed in any number of Western television shows focusing on family life in which insults, verbal abuse, and mutual shaming appear to be normative.

So what constitutes adaptive emotion functioning in the family? According to Blechman (1990), the key characteristics include the open communication of feelings and emotions, the frequent expression of positive emotions, and the ability to monitor and regulate emotional expression (e.g., keeping anger and bad temper in check). In line with these recommendations is a growing body of research on the benefits of expressing explicitly positive emotions in close relationships. For example, Gable, Reis, Impett, and Asher (2004) found that so-called capitalization, or communicating with others about personal positive events, was positively associated with the experience of positive emotions and enhanced well-being on a daily basis, above and beyond the impact of the positive events themselves. Further, when others were perceived to respond positively to the sharing of positive events, the beneficial effects were even greater.

There is also evidence for the benefits of positive emotion expression in research focusing on the family. For example, Barry and Kochanska (2010) found that healthy marriages are associated with more positive emotion expression between parents and their children, with mothers' marital happiness associated with more expressions of joy and fathers' happiness associated with more displays of affection. These findings underscore how important it is in close relationship contexts, not simply to reduce or avoid the expression of negative emotions, but to actively generate and express positive emotions. Carstensen, Gottman, and Levenson (1995), for example, found that spouses in long-term, happy marriages express conflict-related emotions much less frequently than they express affection and good humor. They note the importance of expressing positive emotions for building cultures in which family members treat one another with fondness and respect, accept and respond to the emotional expression of one another's needs, and cultivate warmth, and emotional connectedness with one another.

An important question, then, concerns how to generate the kinds of positive emotions that are clearly so beneficial for relationships. Here, some of the most pertinent recommendations come from Berscheid's seminal work on emotion in relationships (e.g., see Berscheid & Ammazzalorso, 2001). According to the Emotion-in-Relationships model, generating positive emotions in relationships requires partners to make active efforts to surprise and delight each other; to work together in pursuit of shared goals and dreams; and to actively care for and support each other in times of illness and/or stress. Generating emotions such as interest and excitement is also important, with shared participation in novel and exciting activities creating feelings of cohesion and mutual pleasure, and strengthening social bonds (Aron et al., 2000; Gonzaga et al., 2001). In this sense, families that play together may well stay together.

In summary, adaptive family functioning involves the open exchange of emotions, the frequent generation and expression of positive emotions, and the ability to effectively regulate and manage emotions. Further, the emphasis on the role of open, positive emotion expression and emotion regulation in adaptive family functioning is echoed in the growing literatures on emotional competence (e.g., Eisenberg, Cumberland, & Spinrad, 1998; Saarni, 2001) and emotional intelligence (e.g., Fitness, 2006). Typical definitions of these closely related constructs include such features as the ability to accurately encode and decode emotions, the ability to understand the meanings of emotions and to be able to respond appropriately to them, and the ability to effectively manage and regulate both one's own and others' emotions. Emotionally intelligent families, then, may be those in which family members feel validated and embraced within a culture of mutual regard. There is still much to be learned, however, about how to achieve such adaptive outcomes, and the roles of different emotions in generating and maintaining them. In the final section of the chapter, I will suggest some avenues for further research on emotion communication in families, and draw some conclusions about our current understanding of this important topic.

Agenda for Future Research

As noted in the introduction, the study of emotion communication in families has been relatively sparse. There are still gaps in our understanding of how different kinds of emotions are communicated and miscommunicated in families, for what purposes, and with what outcomes. In addition, and as noted in the first edition of this Handbook, much of the research that has been conducted to date has focused on dyads (i.e., spouses, or parents and children, or siblings), rather than on the family system as a whole. Again, in researchers' defense, it should be noted that although the "family as a system" metaphor is a powerful one (Reis, Collins, & Berscheid, 2000), the scientific study of such complex patterns of interdependent relationships poses some extraordinary methodological and ethical challenges. It is important to acknowledge, though, that the emotional functioning of the family overall is not a simple function of the sum of its parts.

As noted at the beginning of this chapter, an important recent development in the study of emotions has been the increasing emphasis on understanding their causes, functions, and outcomes. This emphasis has provided a strong theoretical framework for studying the dynamic features of emotions within the family context. However, there is still much to learn, especially in relation to positive emotions. For example, Goetz, Keltner and Simon-Thomas (2010) have argued that compassion is a distinct emotion that arises in response to a perception of another's suffering, and that is associated with subjective feelings of concern and behaviors that aim to alleviate that suffering (including physical soothing). Clearly, there are many opportunities for both eliciting and receiving compassion within parent–child, sibling, and spousal relationships (especially in times of illness and stress); however, little is known about how and when compassion is given and received between family members. Similarly, Lishner, Batson and Huss (2011) have discussed the features and functions of so-called "other-oriented" emotions such as tenderness and sympathy, emotions that may be particularly salient within the familial context. For example, they describe tenderness as an expansive, "warm and fuzzy" feeling that derives from the perceived vulnerability of another and the perception that he or she is in need of protection (e.g., observing a loved child, asleep in bed). The experience and expression of such positive feelings have not been the focus of study within family relationships, yet may play a major role in their maintenance. In particular, feelings of tenderness may play an important role in ameliorating the experience and expression of "harder" emotions, such as anger or contempt.

Gratitude, too, is a positive emotion that may play an important role in adaptive family functioning, especially in response to expressions of love and tenderness from others. As Algoe, Haidt and Gable (2008) have argued, feelings of gratitude help us to "find, remind, and bind ourselves to attentive others" (p. 429). In this way, gratitude builds positive relationships with the people who care about us (see also Kubacka, Finkenauer, Rusbult, & Keijsers, 2011). It is interesting, then, to speculate about the outcomes of feeling underappreciated in family relationships ("how sharper than a serpent's tooth than to have a thankless child," as Shakespeare's King Lear noted). Too little gratitude for benefits bestowed by others may generate both "hard" (anger) and "soft" (hurt, sad) emotions with potentially negative outcomes, not only for parent–child relationships, but for family relationships more generally.

Of course, while it is relatively easy to identify interesting and unexplored research topics in this field, choosing appropriate methodologies is more difficult and requires considerable ingenuity and resourcefulness. As noted by Rasbash et al. (2011), the use of observational data is "the gold standard in family research" (p. 485). However, such research is expensive and challenging to run. No doubt, laboratory-based observational studies will continue to be important, as will more naturalistic observations in different kinds of familial contexts (see Teti & Cole, 2011, for an excellent review of useful methodologies). The most important point, however, is that the choice of method is theoretically driven so that with each piece of the puzzle we uncover, we obtain a richer, more coherent, and more integrated picture of emotion communication processes and functions within family life.

Conclusions

Families are profoundly emotional contexts. When we express our emotions within the family, we expose our deepest needs and vulnerabilities. In turn, the response of family members to the expression of our emotions colors our perceptions and beliefs about ourselves and others, and helps form the template from which we, in turn, respond to others' needs. Throughout this chapter, I have stressed the potentially adaptive nature of emotions and the functions they serve in informing ourselves and others about our needs. Certainly, emotions can motivate dysfunctional or destructive behaviours, but they always tell us something important about who we are and what we care about, and nowhere is this informational function more important than in the context of the family. It is my hope that within another 10 years, there will be an opportunity to write a fresh chapter on this fascinating topic that demonstrates significant advances in our knowledge and understanding of emotion communication in family relationships.

References

Algoe, S. B., Haidt, J., & Gable, S. L. (2008). Beyond reciprocity: Gratitude and relationships in everyday life. *Emotion, 8*, 425–29.

Aron, A., Norman, C., Aron, E., McKenna, C., & Heyman R. (2000). Couples' shared participation in novel and arousing activities and experienced relationship quality. *Journal of Personality and Social Psychology, 78*, 273–84.

Barry, R. A., & Kochanska, G. (2010). A longitudinal investigation of the affective environment in families with young children: From infancy to early school age. *Emotion, 10*, 237–49.

Bedford, V. H., & Avioli, P. S. (1996). Affect and sibling relationships in adulthood. In C. Magai & S. McFadden (Eds.), *Handbook of emotion, adult development, and aging* (pp. 207–25). New York: Academic Press.

Belsky, J., Youngblade, L., Rovine, M., & Volling, B. (1991). Patterns of marital change and parent–child interaction. *Journal of Marriage and the Family, 53*, 487–98.

Berscheid, E. & Ammazzalorso, H. (2001). Emotional experience in close relationships. In G. J. O. Fletcher & M. S. Clark (Eds.), *Blackwell handbook of social psychology: Interpersonal processes* (pp. 308–30). Malden, MA: Blackwell.

Blechman, E. A. (1990). A new look at emotions and the family: A model of effective family communication. In E. Blechman (Ed.), *Emotions and the family* (pp. 201–24). Hillsdale, NJ: Lawrence Erlbaum Associates.

Boyum, L. A., & Parke, R. D. (1995). The role of family emotional expressiveness in the development of children's social competence. *Journal of Marriage and the Family, 57,* 593–608.

Bradbury, T. N., & Fincham, F. D. (1987). Affect and cognition in close relationships: Toward an integrative model. *Cognition and Emotion, 1,* 59–87.

Brody, G. H. (1998). Sibling relationship quality: Its causes and consequences. *Annual Review of Psychology, 49,* 1–24.

——(2004). Siblings' direct and indirect contribution to child development. *Current Directions in Psychological Science, 3,* 124–26.

Brody, L. (1999). *Gender, emotion, and the family.* Cambridge, MA: Harvard University Press.

Carstensen, L. L., Gottman, J. M., & Levenson, R. W. (1995). Emotional behavior in long-term marriage. *Psychology and Aging, 10,* 140–49.

Clark, M. S., & Finkel, E. J. (2005). Willingness to express emotion: The impact of relationship type, communal orientation, and their interaction. *Personal Relationships, 12,* 169–80.

Clark, M. S., Fitness, J., & Brissette, I. (2001). Understanding people's perceptions of relationships is crucial to understanding their emotional lives. In G. J. O. Fletcher & M. S. Clark (Eds.), *Blackwell handbook of social psychology: Interpersonal processes* (pp. 253–78). Malden, MA: Blackwell.

Clark, M. S., Pataki, S. P., & Carver, V. H. (1996). Some thoughts and findings on self-presentation of emotions in relationships. In G. J. O. Fletcher & J. Fitness (Eds.), *Knowledge structures in close relationships: A social psychological approach* (pp. 247–74). Mahwah, NJ: Lawrence Erlbaum Associates.

Cummings, E. M., & Smith, D. (1989). The impact of anger between adults on siblings' emotions and social behavior. *Journal of Child Psychology and Psychiatry, 25,* 63–74.

Eisenberg, N., Cumberland, A., & Spinrad, T. (1998). Parental socialization of emotions. *Psychological Inquiry, 9,* 241–73.

Eisenberg, N., Liew, J., & Pidada, S. (2001). The relations of parental emotional expressivity with quality of Indonesian children's social functioning. *Emotion, 1,* 116–36.

Feeney, J. (1999). Adult attachment, emotional control, and marital satisfaction. *Personal Relationships, 6,* 169–85.

Fitness, J. (1996). Emotion knowledge structures in close relationships. In G. J. O. Fletcher & J. Fitness (Eds.), *Knowledge structures in close relationships: A social psychological approach* (pp. 195–217). Mahwah, NJ: Lawrence Erlbaum Associates.

——(2005). Bye bye, black sheep: The causes and consequences of rejection in family relationships. In K. Williams, J. Forgas & W. von Hippel (Eds.), *The social outcast: Ostracism, social exclusion, rejection, and bullying* (pp. 445–68). Hove: Psychology Press.

——(2006). The emotionally intelligent marriage. In J. Ciarrochi, J. Forgas, & J. Mayer (Eds.), *Emotional intelligence in everyday life: A scientific inquiry,* 2nd edn (pp. 129–39). New York: Psychology Press.

Fitness, J., Fletcher, G. J. O., & Overall, N. (2007). Attraction and intimate relationships. In J. Cooper & M. Hogg (Eds.), *Sage handbook of social psychology: Concise Student Edition* (pp. 219–40). Thousand Oaks, CA: Sage.

Fredrickson, B. (1998). Cultivated emotions: Parental socialization of positive emotions and self-conscious emotions. *Psychological Inquiry, 9,* 279–81.

Gable, S. L., Reis, H. T., Impett, E. A., & Asher, E. R. (2004). What do you do when things go right? The intrapersonal and interpersonal benefits of sharing positive events. *Journal of Personality & Social Psychology, 87,* 228–45.

Goetz, J. L., Keltner, D., & Simon-Thomas, E. (2010). Compassion: An evolutionary analysis and empirical review. *Psychological Bulletin, 136,* 351–74.

Gold, D. T. (1989). Sibling relationships in old age: A typology. *International Journal of Aging and Human Development, 28,* 37–51.

Gonzaga, G. C., Keltner, D., Londahl, E. A., & Smith, M. D. (2001). Love and the commitment problem in romantic relations and friendship. *Journal of Personality and Social Psychology, 81,* 247–62.

Gordon, C. L., & Baucom, D. H. (2009). Examining the individual within marriage: Personal strengths and relationship satisfaction. *Personal Relationships, 16,* 421–35.

Gottman, J. M. (1994). *What predicts divorce? The relationship between marital processes and marital outcomes.* Hillsdale, NJ: Lawrence Erlbaum Associates.

Gottman, J. M., & Levenson, R. W. (2002). A two-factor model for predicting when a couple will divorce: Exploratory analyses using 14-year longitudinal data. *Family Process, 41*, 83–110.

Gottman, J. M., Katz, L. F., & Hooven, C. (1996). Parental meta-emotion philosophy and the emotional life of families: Theoretical models and preliminary data. *Journal of Family Psychology, 10*, 243–68.

Greenberg, L. S., & Goldman, R. N. (2008). *Emotion-focused couples therapy: The dynamics of emotion, love, and power*. Washington, DC: American Psychological Association.

Hart, S. L. (2010). The socialization of sibling rivalry. In S. L. Hart & M. Legerstee (Eds.), *Handbook of jealousy: Theory, research, and multidisciplinary approaches* (pp. 418–42). Oxford: Wiley-Blackwell.

Hatfield E, Cacioppo J. T., & Rapson, R. L. (1993). Emotional contagion. *Current Directions in Psychological Science, 2*, 96–99.

Howe, N., Aquan-Assee, J., Bukowski, W., Lehoux, P., & Rinaldi, C. (2001). Siblings as confidants: Emotional understanding, relationship warmth, and sibling self-disclosure. *Social Development, 10*, 439–54.

Koerner, A., & Fitzpatrick, M. (2002). Nonverbal communication and marital adjustment and satisfaction: The role of decoding relationship-relevant and relationship-irrelevant affect. *Communication Monographs, 69*, 33–51.

Kubacka, K., Finkenauer, C., Rusbult, C. E., & Keijsers, L. (2011). Maintaining close relationships: Gratitude as a motivator and a detector of maintenance behaviour. *Personality & Social Psychology Bulletin, 37*, 1362–75.

Lishner, D. A., Batson, C. D., & Huss, E. (2011). Tenderness and sympathy: Distinct empathic emotions elicited by different forms of need. *Personality & Social Psychology Bulletin, 37*, 614–25.

Lytton, H. (1990). Child and parent effects in boys' conduct disorder: A reinterpretation. *Developmental Psychology, 26*, 683–704.

Magai, C. (1999). Affect, imagery, and attachment: Working models of interpersonal affect and the socialization of emotion. In J. Cassidy & P. R. Shaver (Eds.), *Handbook of attachment* (pp. 787–802). New York: Guilford Press.

Ng., F., Pomerantz, E., & Lam, S. (2007). European American and Chinese parents' responses to children's success and failure: Implications for children's responses. *Developmental Psychology, 43*, 1239–55.

Niedenthal, P. M., & Brauer, M. (2012). Social functionality of human emotion. *Annual Review of Psychology, 63*, 259–85.

Noller, P., & Ruzzene, M. (1991). The effects of cognition and affect on marital communication. In G. J. O. Fletcher & F. D. Fincham (Eds.), *Cognition in close relationships* (pp. 203–33). Hillsdale, NJ: Lawrence Erlbaum Associates.

Papp, L. M., Kouros, C. D., & Cummings, E. M. (2010). Emotions in marital conflict interactions: Empathic accuracy, assumed similarity, and the moderating context of depressive symptoms. *Journal of Social and Personal Relationships, 27*, 367–87.

Planalp, S., & Fitness, J. (1999). Thinking/feeling about social and personal relationships. *Journal of Social and Personal Relationships, 16*, 731–50.

Raikes, H. A., & Thompson, R. A. (2006). Family emotional climate, attachment security and young children's emotion knowledge in a high risk sample. *British Journal of Developmental Psychology, 24*, 89–104.

Rasbash, J., Jenkins, J., O'Connor, T. G., Tackett, J., & Reiss, D. (2011). A social relations model of observed family negativity and positivity using a genetically informative sample. *Journal of Personality and Social Psychology, 100*, 474–91.

Rauer, A. J., & Volling, B. L. (2007). Differential parenting and sibling jealousy: Developmental correlates of self-esteem, attachment, and jealousy in young adults' romantic relationships. *Personal Relationships, 14*, 495–511.

Reis, H. T., Collins, W. A., & Berscheid, E. (2000). The relationship context of human behavior and development. *Psychological Bulletin, 126*, 844–72.

Rohner, R., & Veneziano, R. (2001). The importance of father love: History and contemporary evidence. *Review of General Psychology, 5*, 382–405.

Saarni, C. (2001). Epilogue: Emotion communication and relationship context. *International Journal of Behavioral Development, 25*, 354–56.

Sanford, K., & Grace, A. J. (2011). Emotion and underlying concerns during couples' conflict: An investigation of within-person change. *Personal Relationships, 18,* 96–109.

Scharfe, E. (2000). Development of emotional expression, understanding, and regulation in infants and young children. In R. Bar-On & D. Parker (Eds.), *Handbook of emotional intelligence* (pp. 244–62). San Francisco, CA: Jossey-Bass.

Segrin, C. (1998). Interpersonal communication problems associated with depression and loneliness. In P. Andersen & L. Guerrero (Eds.), *Handbook of communication and emotion* (pp. 215–42). New York: Academic Press.

Shaver, P. R., Collins, N., & Clark, C. (1996). Attachment styles and internal working models of self and relationship partners. In G. J. O. Fletcher & J. Fitness (Eds.), *Knowledge structures in close relationships: A social psychological approach* (pp. 25–61). Mahwah, NJ: Lawrence Erlbaum Associates.

Simpson, J. A., Rholes, W. S., & Nelligan, J. S. (1992). Support-seeking and support-giving within couples in an anxiety-provoking situation: The role of attachment styles. *Journal of Personality and Social Psychology, 62,* 434–46.

Soto, J. A., Perez, C. R., Kim, Y.-H., Lee, E. A., & Minnick, M. (2011). Is expressive suppression always associated with poorer psychological functioning? A cross-cultural comparison between European Americans and Hong Kong Chinese. *Emotion, 11,* 1450–55.

Tao, A., Zhou, Q., & Wang, Y. (2010). Parental reactions to children's negative emotions: Prospective relations to Chinese children's psychological adjustment. *Journal of Family Psychology, 24,* 135–44.

Teti, D. M., & Cole, P. M. (2011). Parenting at risk: New perspectives, new approaches. *Journal of Family Psychology, 25,* 625–34.

Thomas, G., Fletcher, G. J. O., & Lange, C. (1997). On-line empathic accuracy in marital interaction. *Journal of Personality and Social Psychology, 76,* 72–89.

Thompson, A., & Bolger, N. (1999). Emotional transmission in couples under stress. *Journal of Marriage and the Family, 61,* 38–48.

Thompson, J. A., & Halberstadt, A. G. (2008). Children's accounts of sibling jealousy and their implicit theories about relationships. *Social Development, 17,* 488–511.

Tower, R. B., & Kasl, S. V. (1995). Depressive symptoms across older spouses and the moderating effect of marital closeness. *Psychology and Aging, 10,* 625–38.

Volling, B., McElwain, N. L., & Miller, A. (2002). Emotion regulation in context: The jealousy complex between young siblings and its relations with child and family characteristics. *Child Development, 73,* 581–600.

Yang, S., & Rosenblatt, P. (2001). Shame in Korean families. *Journal of Comparative Family Studies, 32,* 361–75.

Zadro, L., Arriaga, X. B., & Williams, K. D. (2008). Relational ostracism. In J. P. Forgas & J. Fitness (Eds.), *Social relationships: Cognitive, affective, and motivational processes* (pp. 305–20). New York: Psychology Press.

Zahn-Waxler, C., Friedman, R. J., Cole, P. M., Mizuta, I., & Hiruma, N. (1996). Japanese and U.S. preschool children's responses to conflict and distress. *Child Development, 67,* 2462–77.

24

Family Stories and Storytelling

Windows into the Family Soul

Jody Koenig Kellas and April R. Trees

Stories are ubiquitous, taken-for-granted threads in the fabric of our linguistic, cognitive, and relational lives. Humans make sense of life through narrative without even knowing it (Bruner, 1990; Fisher, 1987). Although often everyday, mundane, and repetitive, stories also serve as unique, informative units of discourse and/or modes of thought, sense-making, identity construction, and constitutive talk. Family stories draw people in, teach them lessons, and stay with them long after they've been told. They are at once entertaining and horrifying, sad and hopeful, everyday and far-reaching. They are passed down from generation to generation and pepper the daily or weekly conversations between family members. Family stories help us make sense of, celebrate, and cope with happy and difficult lived experiences. In short, stories are in many ways at the center of daily, communicated family life.

Just as "stories are data with a soul" (Brown, 2010), families are stories with souls. Stories affect and reflect what really matters to a family (Stone, 2004) and telling them constitutes the bright and dark sides of family culture and meaning (Koenig Kellas, 2005; Koenig Kellas, Willer, & Kranstuber, 2010). According to Fiese and Winter (2009), "family stories are verbal accounts of personal experiences that are important to the family, depict rules of interaction, reflect beliefs about the trustworthiness of relationships, and impart values connected to larger social institutions" (p. 626). Family stories provide a *window* into family culture (e.g., Koenig Kellas, 2005), typically through an analysis of the content, coherence, and communicative processes of the story and storytelling interaction (Fiese & Winter, 2009).

The research on family stories is embedded within an extensive body of research on narrative that spans disciplinary and paradigmatic lines. Narrative is at once known as a paradigm (Fisher, 1987), the center of a paradigmatic shift (i.e., the narrative turn, see Bochner, 2002), a method (Riessman, 2008), a genre (Ochs, 1997), and a discourse unit (Labov & Waletsky, 1967). It is also the focus of theoretical insight into the ways in which humans both make sense of, and create, identity (for a review, see Koenig Kellas, 2008).

In the current chapter, we offer a glimpse into the family soul by showing what narratives *say* and *do* in the realm of family life. We review literature on the functions of family stories in and beyond the family system, including *creating, socializing,* and *coping.* In addition, we issue a call for future research on family stories and storytelling that is empirically tested, theoretically driven, applied, and socially significant.

The Functions of Stories and Storytelling in Families

Researchers have identified several functions relevant to stories and storytelling within the family (e.g., Bylund, 2003; Galvin, 2003). In the section that follows, we describe the overarching themes that lend intelligibility to narrative functions specific to stories and storytelling in the family, including creating, socializing, and coping.

Creating: Constructing Individual and Family Identity

Perhaps the most noted and central function of family stories is the creation and maintenance of individual and family identities (Koenig Kellas, 2005; Stone, 2004). We are born into family stories. Although they provide a window into family culture to those outside the family (Koenig Kellas, 2005; Vangelisti et al., 1999), they also are told within the family in ways that build the identity of the family as a whole and its individual members. In her foundational work on family stories, Stone (2004) argues that family stories shape us. These stories are passed down from generation to generation, creating multigenerational threads of meaning in both family and individual identity. Of course, these narrative constructions also are situated against the backdrop of cultural master narratives about family that shape and reflect our narrative practices (Langellier & Peterson, 2004).

Constructing Family Identity

Stories told within the family are powerful means by which a family comes to construct a group identity. Family definition stories (Stone, 2004), family identity stories (Koenig Kellas, 2005), and family legacies (Stone, 2004; Thompson, Koenig Kellas, Soliz, Thompson, Epp, & Schrodt, 2009) all refer to stories that family members tell when they try to articulate who the family is. For example, stories that last across generations and teach simple, straightforward themes about family identity become *family legacies*—stories used to evaluate the overall sense of who a family is and how an individual can evaluate him or herself in relation to the family. In a study on family legacies, Thompson et al. (2009) identified three themes of positive family legacies including hard-working, caring for others, and family cohesion. In addition, Thompson et al. found that participants tended to reject negative family stories as family legacies. This is consistent with Stone (2004), who claims that family members adopt primarily positive legacies that promote their preferred image of the family. Generally, even when negative, "humdrum," or "unattractive" characteristics emerge in family stories, they are combined with positive family qualities to "demonstrate that the family is indeed 'special' and in some way superior to all other families" (Stone, 2004, p. 35). Thus, family stories make the family unique, and families embrace, tell, and retell the stories that knit together that special family identity.

The themes of such family stories serve an evaluative function, providing insight into what makes people happy or unhappy in their families and offering telling information about family culture. Vangelisti et al. (1999), for example, found that individuals who told family stories containing themes such as togetherness, care, humor, reconstruction, or adaptability were more satisfied with their families, whereas people whose stories contained themes of hostility, divergent values, chaos, personality attributes, or hostility were more dissatisfied. Similarly, families whose identity stories were told around the theme of stress were much less satisfied than those whose story themes revolved around accomplishment (Koenig Kellas, 2005).

Storytelling *interaction* may tell us just as much about a family's culture as the thematic content of the narrative. For example, the interactional behaviors that characterize family storytelling also predict elements of family culture such as cohesion, adaptability, and satisfaction (Koenig Kellas, 2005; Trees & Koenig Kellas, 2009). In a study of jointly told family identity stories, Koenig Kellas (2005) found that families who identified as a story-telling family (i.e., told stories together and often), families who engaged in high levels of perspective-taking during the joint storytelling episodes, and families who produced more statements about who members are in relation to the family as a whole, also reported higher levels of family functioning. Thus, storytelling creates multigenerational possibilities for perpetuating and/or (re)framing family identity through content and process.

Langellier and Peterson's (2006) narrative performance theory focuses on the performative, discursive production of family through family storytelling. As a discursive means by which people "do" family, storytelling is both a performance in the family (i.e., something the family performs) and is performative (i.e., a way of constructing family identity). Narrative performance theory focuses on the meanings relevant to family story content (content-ordering), the labor and process of family storytelling such as *who* tells *what when* (task-ordering), and the ways in which the content and process of stories are innovated and interpreted within particular sociohistorical conditions across generations (group-ordering). In their research, Langellier and Peterson (1993; 2004) demonstrate the ways in which storytelling performs family as small group culture, including attempts to tell good stories, produce good families, and potentially sanction, control, and critique family members.

In sum, families are systems in which the interaction processes, patterns, legacies, and themes of family stories all have implications for reflecting and affecting family culture. Family identity stories are living, breathing, negotiated stories transactionally constructed among family members. These processes matter to understanding how we narratively inherit (Goodall, 2005) and pass on individual and family identities.

Constructing Individual Identity

Just as families inherit stories that construct a sense of family identity, family stories also help individuals to understand, articulate, and construct their own sense of individual identity (Stone, 2004). According to Stone (2004), "We are shaped by our families' notions of our identities … and among the primary vehicles families use to mirror us to ourselves are the family stories we hear about ourselves" (p. 167).

In his theory of narrative identity, McAdams (1993) positions identity as narratively constructed. We make sense of who we are through the multiple images, characters, and stories that impact us across our lives. The relationship between infants and their parents sets the stage for the lasting tone of their personal myth. In the pre-school years, images of important characters, such as parents, may become enduring images that affect the adult life story. Adolescents become independent myth-makers, and young adults focus on developing a solid sense of their own life story character(s). In older adulthood, individuals think more about the generativity of their personal myths. McAdams further explains, "The stories we create influence the stories of other people, those stories give rise to still others, and soon we find meaning and connection within a web of storymaking and story living" (p. 37). Family members and the stories they tell are intimately woven into the web of our individual narrative identity.

Although many of the stories we hear and tell about ourselves reflect unique parts of our individual life stories (McAdams, 1993), much research has focused on *creation stories* (Galvin, 2003)—birth narratives, adoption narratives, and marital origin stories. These canonical stories help construct a sense of individual and couple identity.

Birth Stories

According to Galvin (2003), "a child's birth or 'entrance' story defines who the child is, narrates the process by which he or she was born into the family, and contributes to the family. It contains messages of desire, emotion, significance, and expectations" (p. 241). Parents share these stories with their children, and children weave them into their personal myths.

Birth stories are at once representations of women as (emergent) mothers and representations of children and how they can understand themselves in relation to the family. Reese (1996) claims that birth stories serve as the first chapter in individuals' overall life stories and therefore provide children with their first story from which to evaluate self. Over time these stories become part of the fabric of individuals' life stories (McAdams, 1993) and have implications for children's self-esteem and well-being (Friedlander, 1999). Hayden, Singer, and Chrisler (2006), for example, found that the more often daughters reported having heard their birth story, the more descriptive it was, and the more positive it was, the higher daughters reported their self-esteem and mother–daughter attachment to be.

Non-traditional Family "Birth" Stories

Not all families fit the master narrative of heterosexual romantic love, marriage, and the procreation of biological children. Instead, increasingly "non-traditional," discourse-dependent (Galvin, 2006) families rely on narratives and storytelling to help family members (and outsiders) make sense of how they came to be (see also Koenig Kellas, Willer et al., 2010). Adoptive, foster, same-sex, and stepfamilies often must do extra "narrative work" in order to help children come to terms with the family form and their place in it. For example, Becker-Weidman and Shell (2010) suggest that helping children with trauma-attachment problems (e.g., foster children, children adopted from orphanages, children who were adopted out of abusive situations) restory their personal myths can have significant healing benefits. They recommend that parents consistently tell "claiming stories," or stories about how the child entered into the family, as a method of helping the child become socialized to the family and restory a preferred individual life story or personal identity.

Research on narratively creating identity in adoptive families also focuses on these claiming stories (also known as entrance stories, Krusiewicz & Wood, 2001, or creation stories, Galvin, 2003). Perhaps not surprisingly, adoptive parents identify positive motivations and functions for telling adoption stories to their children, whereas adoptees list both positive and negative elements of hearing and interpreting stories about adoption. For example, in describing the stories they tell their adopted children, parents reported emphasizing themes such as destiny, compelling connection, rescue, legitimacy

(Krusiewicz & Wood, 2001), providing a complete history, and positively reinforcing the child and his or her place in the family (Harrigan, 2010). Parents demonstrate a thoughtful and concerted effort to portray birth parents in a positive light while at the same time reassuring the child that they were wanted, special, and that the parents and the family will be a permanent "forever family" (Harrigan, 2010, p. 33; Krusiewicz & Wood, 2001). Adolescent and adult adoptees, on the other hand, include a balance of both positive and negative themes in their versions of entrance stories, such as openness, being chosen, fate, and rescue, but also deception, an uncomfortable sense of difference, and anxiety about reconnecting with birthparents (Kranstuber & Koenig Kellas, 2011). It is possible that not all parents devote careful attention to helping adoptees craft their entrance narratives or it may be the parent and adoptee stories differ because of factors such as their role in the family and identity formation.

Although far less researched and far less told, stepfamilies and same-sex parented families also make sense of their beginnings through narrative mechanisms. Koenig Kellas et al. (2009), for example, found five frames through which stepfamilies narratively reconstructed their stepfamily beginnings, including sudden (rushed, secretive), dark-sided (scandalous, complicated), ambivalent (a mix of highs and lows), idealized (easy transition to feeling like a family), and incremental (organized, clear, and open communication). Participants who told idealized family beginning stories were more satisfied than those who told dark-sided or sudden stories. Although these results are not particularly surprising, they do point to the importance of story framing. Members of discourse dependent families, such as stepfamilies or same-sex headed families, can craft stories that counter the predominant master narratives that privilege biological nuclear families (e.g., Jones, 2003).

Marital Origin Stories

Whereas birth and entrance narratives focus primarily on the identity of one family member, marital origin stories set the tone for a foundational family relationship. Research on couples' stories about how they met, fell in love, and got married demonstrates that "how a couple views its past predicts its future" (Buehlman, Gottman, & Katz, 1992, p. 295) and helps to explain its current marital functioning (see Holmberg, Orbuch, & Veroff, 2004).

Using the oral history interview (OHI), for example, Buehlman and her colleagues (1992) found that both content and process variables, including low levels of fondness toward the spouse, glorifying the struggle, and we-ness, and high levels of negativity, chaos, and disappointment in the marriage predicted divorce. *Marital bond*, "a score ascertained from marital storytelling behaviors and representing positive perceptions of one's spouse and relationship," has been negatively related to loneliness, depression, and feeling flooded, and positively related to marital satisfaction (Doohan, Carrère, & Riggs, 2010, p. 57).

Holmberg, Orbuch, and Veroff (2004) and colleagues also have examined the thematic and process-oriented nature of couples telling their origin story. Their research shows that couples negotiate joint narratives through varying degrees of conflict, continuation, collaboration, confirmation, and nonresponsive interactional behaviors and that similarity in storytelling behavior predicts well-being. Moreover, they found that spouses' happiness "was closely connected to the kinds of stories they told, the feelings they attributed to their discussion, the issues and problems that became the foci of their concerns, and even how 'good' a story they told" (Holmberg et al., 2004, p. 101). Both the content and process of marital origin stories matters for the health and well-being of the couple. Telling canonical stories, such as birth, adoption, or marriage stories, often becomes ritualized interaction, which further contributes to the creation of family culture and identity.

Ritualizing Family Identity Through Storytelling

Rituals are jointly enacted relational practices that are repeated and have symbolic meaning for relational members (see Bruess & Pearson, 1997, for a review). Both rituals and stories create family identity and meaning (Jorgenson & Bochner, 2004) such that "storytelling ritually and routinely enacts a family and enhances its stories of experience" (Langellier & Peterson, 2004, p. 34).

This happens in a number of ways. First, the telling of (certain) family stories may become ritualistic in the family. For example, parents might tell their child his or her birth story every year on his or her birthday or spouses may relive the story of the wedding day each year on their anniversary. Second, the family's way of telling the story may become ritualistic. For instance, several parents of internationally adopted children in Harrigan's (2010) research often used the same artifacts (e.g., videos, photos) each time they told their child the adoption entrance narrative. The same words, gestures, pauses for dramatic effect, punchlines, and story morals might be delivered in a manner that become just as meaningful as the story itself.

Third, family stories are often told during the practice of other family rituals. Fiese and Marjinsky (1999), for example, observed that, "The repetitive nature of patterned routines, such as dinnertime, often leads to the creation of distinct images of how family members interact with each other" (p. 53). Blum-Kulka (1993) found cultural differences in the storytelling rituals at dinnertime such that American family stories focused more on the present and happenings outside the home, whereas Israeli families tended to emphasize more the past, happenings within the home, and the whole family as the protagonist.

Finally, we tell stories *about* family rituals (e.g., Christmas traditions, yearly vacations). Telling the story about a family ritual can help create a sense of family identity by reminding members of the practices they hold dear.

Summary

Stories are told and retold ritualistically in the family. Family storytelling affects and reflects an overall sense of family identity, perpetuates family legacies across generations, and helps shape individual identities by helping children make sense of who they are in relation to the family. In understanding the construction of individual and family identity through family stories, both content and process matter.

Socializing: Teaching Lessons Through Storytelling

In addition to the construction of identity, telling family stories also functions to socialize family members to the rules and norms of family life. Reminiscing about a family's past entertains but also teaches. The stories that parents and grandparents tell about their childhood (e.g., Fiese & Bickham, 2004), stories that parents tell about their children (e.g., Miller,

Sandel, Liang, & Fung, 2001), and stories told within the family about shared experiences (Stone, 2004) socialize children into cultural and familial expectations for what to value and how to behave. Parents' interaction with children as they reminisce together also helps children develop narrative skills and contributes to children's emotional, cognitive, and social development (e.g., Bohanek, Marin, & Fivush, 2008; Haden, Haine, & Fivush, 1997).

Lessons to be Learned in Family Stories

Family stories teach lessons about values (Fiese & Bickham, 2004), appropriate behavior (Miller et al., 2001), and how to enact roles in the family (Fiese & Bickham, 2004; Gallo, 2009). These family socialization stories reflect cultural as well as familial values (Miller et al., 2001). They can be multigenerational, told by or with grandparents (Nussbaum & Bettini, 1994) and/or parents (Fiese & Bickham, 2004; Fiese, Hooker, Kotary, Schwagler, & Rimmer, 1995). Family socialization stories include narratives about childhood experiences, transgressions, and health legacies.

Childhood Stories Across Generations

Both parents and grandparents tell stories about their own childhoods in order to communicate moral values in addition to developing family histories and sustaining connections across generations (Fiese & Bickham, 2004). Fiese and Bickham (2004) examined parents' stories about childhood and found that affiliation was the most common theme in parents' stories, emphasizing the value and importance parents place on family and connections. Parents also taught lessons through stories about family roles and routines, valuing hard work, and avoiding trouble by not following the parents' example (Fiese & Bickham).

Narrative socialization is a gendered process in the family. For example, fathers tend to tell more stories of achievement and independence than do mothers, particularly when children are preschool age and male (Fiese & Bickham, 2004; Fiese & Skillman, 2000, Fiese et al., 1995). Moreover, fathers tell, and sons hear, stories with stronger themes of autonomy than the stories mothers tell and daughters hear (Fiese & Skillman, 2000). Similarly, Nussbaum and Bettini (1994) found that grandmothers told grandchildren stories focused on family development when talking about what is important in life more frequently than grandfathers did. These sex differences reinforce the practices of gender socialization that seem to pervade the process of family storytelling. Family stories have been referred to as the woman's sphere (Stone, 2004), and Reese (1996) claims that women place more importance on autobiography and life history than men. Thus, males and females seem to be socialized to, and through, family narratives differently.

Transgression Narratives

Stories about getting into trouble or bad behavior also appear in research on narrative contributions to children's moral development. These include stories parents tell about their own childhood, but also co-narrated stories about the child's rule violations. Miller and colleagues (e.g., Miller, Fung, & Mintz, 1996; Miller et al., 2001), for example, studied variations in how stories of children's cultural code violations were told in Taiwanese and Euro-American families. Taiwanese parents were more likely to tell the story of their child's transgressions than their own, be directly critical of the child, make the rule violation the central point of the transgression story, and end the story with an explicit statement about what should be learned from it (Miller et al., 1996; Miller, Wiley, Fung, & Liang, 1997). Euro-American parents, however, tended to minimize transgression narratives and, when they were told, focus on the humorous aspects as well as positive assessments of the child (Miller et al., 1996; Miller et al., 2001). Additionally, Euro-American parents were much more likely than Taiwanese parents to tell stories of their own transgressions in childhood as a way to teach a lesson to their child about how to behave and assure children of the possibility of redemption in the future. These narrative differences reflect cultural understandings of the self, the parent–child relationship, and the use of narrative socialization practices.

Health Legacies

Family storytelling communicates general messages about values, but stories in the family construct meanings for how to understand family health experiences more specifically as well (Gallo, 2009; Manoogian, Harter, & Denham, 2010). Stone (2004) shows that clusters or collections of family stories paint a picture of the family's overall orientation toward illness (e.g., as the only way to get attention; as prohibited; as blameworthy). Additionally, narratives about illness set up family expectations for the roles family members take in coping with health problems (Gallo, 2009). For example, Alemán and Helfrich (2010) co-constructed mother–daughter stories with themes such as loss, denial, anxiety, and care, as ways of coping with what it means to be a member of a family with a narrative inheritance (Goodall, 2005) of matriarchal dementia.

Finally, stories "instruct us about what to notice and how to judge actions and outcomes" (Manoogian et al., 2010, p. 41). Manoogian et al.'s research on the health legacies of families with Type 2 diabetes observed both the power of family stories and the possibilities of renegotiating family understandings through narrative. Intergenerational lynchpins, for example, shared stories about family members' experience with diabetes as lessons about how to manage the disease differently from the past, whereas intergenerational buffers tried to silence family stories about illness. As a part of socialization, family stories reveal and influence health practices.

Reminiscing and Child Development

Parents not only tell stories, they also teach children how to become (good) storytellers. How parents interact with children as they reminisce about past events contributes to children's narrative skill development and other developmental outcomes (e.g., emotional development, Oppenheim, Nir, Warren, & Emde, 1997; perceptions of the self, Bohanek, Marin, Fivush, & Duke, 2006; autobiographical memory, Nelson & Fivush, 2004). For very young children who do not yet have narrative skills, parental reminiscing about the past helps to teach children what goes into a good story (e.g., context information; evaluative material). Additionally, as parents collaborate with children to tell their stories, they create a scaffold for children to practice the skills necessary to create a culturally appropriate, coherent, complete story.

A central focus in this research has been on parental elaboration, or the degree to which parents include detail, ask questions, provide and seek information, and comment on children's contributions (Fivush, 2006; Fivush, Haden, & Reese, 2006). Less elaborative parents tend to ask repetitive questions and provide minimal detail when telling stories themselves (Fivush, 2006; Haden et al., 1997). Elaboration encourages children to provide more information or detail in the stories that they are telling (Fivush, 2006; Peterson & McCabe, 2004). For example, children with more elaborative mothers learn to create more coherent and detailed stories with greater inclusion of their own perspective when they begin telling their own stories independently (Peterson & McCabe, 2004).

Moreover, the content of parents' narratives also contributes to narrative skill development. Haden et al. (1997), for example, found that mothers' use of evaluations (e.g., feelings and other types of sense-making) when reminiscing with children predicted young children's incorporation of evaluation into their independent narratives a year and a half later. Research also suggests sex (see Fivush, 2006, for a review) and cultural (see Wang, 2004, for a review) differences in these narrative processes. Overall, the research on parent–child reminiscing demonstrates that the content and process of parental storytelling with children affects outcomes important to child development, including emotional development and narrative skill.

Summary

Both stories and storytelling in the family teach children important cultural and familial lessons about what good behavior is as well as what a good story looks like. Additionally, developing narrative skill through co-constructing narratives together has important consequences for children's emotional and cognitive development. Thus, socialization through family narratives is important to developing morals, values, lessons, and communication competence relevant both within and outside the family.

Coping: Making Sense of Stressors

In addition to creating and communicating family culture and identity and teaching children lessons, stories also function to facilitate coping in the family. Family members facing a stressor (e.g., illness, divorce) tell interdependent or shared (Koenig Kellas & Trees, 2006) stories about their experiences, and these narratives can help family members to make sense of difficult life events. In addition, the content of family stories sends "potent messages concerning admired behaviors and preferred solutions in times of crisis and transitions" (Gallo, 2009, p. 4). Two major areas of research on family storytelling in times of stress or crisis include research on family sense-making in jointly told stories and research on family narrative therapy.

Family Sense-Making

Previous research shows that putting one's experience into words through narrative writing may create coherent meaning for the experience, help one develop a sense of control over the problem, encourage the processing of feelings, or mitigate the negative effects of suppressing feelings and thoughts (Sloan & Marx, 2004). Although much research on expressive writing has focused on the benefits of putting individual trauma into story form, several researchers have extended the focus on narrating difficulty to consider how the family makes sense of its world together through shared stories (e.g., Koenig Kellas & Trees, 2006; Koenig Kellas, Trees et al., 2010; Trees & Koenig Kellas, 2009) and stories that children tell with the help of their parents (e.g., Bohanek et al., 2008; Sales & Fivush, 2005).

Families vary in the degree to which they develop shared meaning in their stories of stress (Bohanek et al., 2006; Koenig Kellas & Trees, 2006). Some families collaboratively construct a shared understanding, coming to a family-level evaluation of stressful events and what they mean (Koenig Kellas & Trees, 2006). In other families, stories reflect individual meaning-making, with each family member offering his or her particular understanding of what the experience means. Finally, telling a story does not automatically ensure sense-making, and Koenig Kellas and Trees (2006) observed some families with incomplete sense-making whose narratives contained no conclusions for either the family or the individual. They found that interactional sense-making behaviors during joint storytelling, including engagement, turn-taking, perspective-taking, and coherence, facilitate collaborative sense-making processes. Similarly, Kiser, Baumgardner, and Dorado (2010) suggested a coordinated perspective emerges in family stories by developing a storyline with relevant parts of family members' experiences included, appreciating multiple points of view, creating space for multiple family members to contribute, and constructing a shared frame.

Creating a coherent, complete narrative that hangs together can create order out of complex, messy, confusing events (Fivush, Hazzard, Sales, Sarfati, & Brown, 2003; Koenig Kellas, 2008). More coherent stories about coping with pediatric asthma and its effects on family life, for example, related to better problem-solving and family functioning (Fiese & Wamboldt, 2003). Additionally, coherence in couples' jointly told stories of marital stress predicted husbands' better mental health (Koenig Kellas, Trees et al., 2010).

Family members also need to be attentive to issues of power and control in family stories (Kiser et al., 2010), providing space for multiple family members to contribute their perspective. Not everyone in the family necessarily experiences a stressor in the same way. Given this, joint family storytelling creates opportunities to recognize and learn from the perspectives of others in the family (Koenig Kellas & Trees, 2006). This can contribute to well-being also. For example, couples' balanced and dynamic turn-taking predicted fewer mental health symptoms for husbands, and wives' perspective-taking predicted less perceived stress for husbands (Koenig Kellas, Trees et al., 2010).

Finally, affective communication (e.g., labeling emotions) and cognitive processing words (e.g., causal explanations) appear to be important elements in joint narrative sense-making between parents and children (Kiser et al., 2010; Sales & Fivush, 2005). Using more emotion words in narratives about emotional experiences, for example, can facilitate emotion regulation and adjustment (Bohanek et al., 2008; Oppenheim et al., 1997), particularly positive emotion words (Ramirez-Esparza & Pennebaker, 2006). Emotion words, however, do not always predict positive coping outcomes. Sales and Fivush (2005), for example, found that emotion words were helpful in conjunction with causal explanations for experiences but detrimental when they occurred without causal sense-making. In sum, a growing body of research shows that jointly telling family stories about difficulties can help family members create meaning out of complexity, develop hope, and cope with family difficulty, stress, and trauma.

Family Narrative Therapy

Hope plays a significant role in family narrative therapy, a second major line of research on narrative coping in the family. Family trauma can disrupt family stories and storytelling skills (Kiser et al., 2010), and narrative therapy (Monk, 1997; White, 2007) helps families take problematic narratives and reframe them, creating more generative stories for the family. Creating a new story, in part, gives families new language to talk about their problem and recasts family members as active agents in the story rather than helpless participants without control (Gallo, 2009; White, 2007).

Narrative therapy encourages families to rethink what they include in the story they tell about themselves and reframe the storyline, changing the language they use to talk about the problem. Often families' stories about stressful experiences are problem-saturated, focusing on the difficulties, problems, and barriers to solutions that families may face and placing blame on specific characters in the story. Because of this, externalizing the problem becomes one key part of narrative therapy (Kiser et al., 2010; Ramey, Tarulli, Frijters, & Fisher, 2009; White, 2007). Externalizing uses the language of the story to separate family members from the problem (e.g., by giving the problem a label) and to identify other possibilities in the experience of the problem or contradictory stories (e.g., times when the family successfully overcame the problem or exceptions to their typical experience with it) (Ramey et al., 2009). Externalizing the problem in their stories aids family members in gaining control over the problem instead of being the problem. This process also helps family members identify "sparkling moments," or exemplary times when good things happened, that are helpful in constructing an alternative narrative (Monk, 1997; White, 2007).

Ultimately, then, narrative therapy assists families in re-storying their experience, creating new narratives that construct a different life story in relationship to the stressors faced by the family. Rather than problem-saturated narratives that focus blame on an individual, alternative stories construct family members as separate from, and working together against, the problem (Monk, 1997; White, 2007). Positive experiences or past moments of triumph over the problem that otherwise have been overlooked become the building blocks of these new stories (Monk, 1997). Creating alternative narratives helps families develop new strategies for coping with life stressors, improving their problem-solving skills when faced with setbacks. The value of re-storying rests on the belief that families "change their lives by changing their stories" (Gallo, 2009, p. 10).

Summary

As a sense-making process, family storytelling constructs an understanding of family stressors and what they mean both for individuals and for the family as a whole. Narrating difficulty in the family offers the possibility of organizing, making sense of, and creating coherence out of chaos. Families facing trauma or difficulty can, through narrative therapy processes, restory their experience to develop a different understanding of the problem faced and the family's ability to respond to and cope with that problem.

Foreshadowing: Directions for Future Research

Given the significance of narrative in our relational lives, research on family stories and story telling offers a significant avenue for understanding family identity and sense-making processes. Although the literature on family stories across disciplines is already substantial, we believe there are a number of empirical, theoretical, and applied directions for future research that would add to our understanding of family stories and storytelling.

Empirical Directions

Although we have outlined many characteristics, processes, practices, and functions associated with family stories, research has just begun to scratch the surface of these often taken for granted constructions. First, we need additional research from family communication scholars on stories that emerge in everyday family talk. Several scholars have debated the utility and worth of big stories (e.g., canonical, life stories, Freeman, 2006) versus small stories (e.g., everyday stories, Bamberg, 2006), and research has examined small stories in specific contexts on a relatively small scale (e.g., dinnertime, Blum-Kulka, 1993). We also need to understand how the content and process of everyday storytelling in families is patterned, functional, and related to family culture. With video and diary methods we may be able to gage even better the ways in which stories act as interactions that build a vision of the family and help family members share each other's worlds.

This also means focusing more attention on the context within which family stories occur. Much of the research on family narratives focuses on the content or process of the stories themselves (Fiese & Winter, 2009), but we know less about the situational and interactional contexts in which they take place. What are the interaction sequences within which narratives occur (what elicits them, how are they responded to); who tells stories to whom about what in what settings following what norms? For example, stories can be used as a tool for giving advice (e.g., Manoogian et al., 2010). Understanding the circumstances under which these types of narratives emerge (effectively and ineffectively) in the family would provide insight into this process of support. Moreover, understanding how socialization narratives surface in conversations between parents and children (e.g., about the use of drugs or alcohol) in combination with their longitudinal effects would give parents and practitioners information about effective socialization practices.

Finally, researchers, practitioners, and family members would benefit from better empirical evidence about the benefits and risks of storytelling in families. Koenig Kellas (2005) found modest empirical support for the idea that "a family who tells stories together, stays together" (i.e., storytelling families reported higher levels of satisfaction and functioning). Yet we also know that storytelling in families can have undesirable outcomes such as discrepancy and control (see Koenig Kellas, Willer et al., 2010). Intervention studies that compare families who are encouraged to tell stories together with control groups might better illuminate the possible benefits (e.g., increased cohesion) and possible risks (e.g., increased conflict) of encouraging the practice of family storytelling.

Theoretical Directions

Narrative research has been somewhat atheoretical (Koenig Kellas, 2008). Although we do have some well-established theories and bodies of literature, the narrative paradigm (Fisher, 1987) is more closely tied to rhetorical than family analyses. Moreover, Langellier and Peterson's (2006) narrative performance theory is an important contribution to understanding the performing and performative nature of family identity. At the same time, its roots in semiotic phenomenology and performance allow certain investigations and preclude others. Well-established bodies of research in other fields are informative (e.g., the expressive writing paradigm, Pennebaker, 1997; the life story approach, McAdams, 1993), but these often overlook an analysis of the communication of stories. Thus, communication theories aimed at understanding family storytelling are currently lacking and sorely needed.

Applied Directions

Perhaps the most exciting potential for family narrative scholarship lies in its applied potential. How, for example, can the ideas of narrative therapy (e.g., reframing) be adapted and used by families not in therapy? How can we teach families to elicit, listen to, collaborate in, and/or respond to stories that might help family members cope with difficulty? Based on the principles of narrative therapy, for example, Willer (2009) conducted a narrative metaphor intervention in which adolescent girls told stories and drew metaphors about a time another girl was mean to them and found links between the intervention and girls' mental health over time. Willer designed the intervention specifically so it would be accessible to nonexperts, such as teachers, counselors, and parents. More research needs to take an interdisciplinary and applied focus and seek out ways to help families narratively help themselves.

Our research on interactional sense-making (e.g., Koenig Kellas, Trees et al., 2010; Trees & Koenig Kellas, 2009) suggests that perspective-taking may be an aspect of joint storytelling particularly suited to helping families. When families use narratives to make sense of identity and stressors, the ability to attend to and confirm another's perspective is consistently predictive of family and individual health. Thus, we might design interventions and training sessions for couples and families on how to better take one another's narrative perspective.

Research on narrative medicine has already begun to make these connections. Charon (2006), for example, outlines the ways in which she helps her patients comply, cope with illness, and make sense of diagnoses by listening to, writing down, and sharing with the patient the story he or she tells during the office visit. Similarly, Trees, Koenig Kellas, and Roche (2010) explored ways in which family genetic counselors might use family narrative to help families author their stories about genetic disorders. Stories are powerful relational, sense-making, identity-building tools that may help families better connect and cope. Family communication researchers need to empirically and theoretically test their power.

Conclusion

Families are stories with souls. The research on family stories supports the notion that stories are at the center of a myriad family functions. Although sometimes overlooked, stories play a powerful role in families and storytelling processes affect and reflect family culture. Future research is needed to build upon the foundations outlined in this chapter and harness the interdisciplinary, empirical, theoretical, and applied possibilities of family narratives and storytelling.

References

Aleman, M. W., & Helfrich, K. W. (2010). Inheriting the narratives of dementia: A collaborative tale of a mother and daughter. *Journal of Family Communication, 10*, 7–23.

Bamberg, M. (2006). Stories big or small: Why do we care? *Narrative Inquiry, 16*, 139–47.

Becker-Weidman, A., & Shell, D. (2010). Storytelling: How to use stories to help your children. In A. Becker-Weidman & D. Shell (Eds.), *Attachment parenting: Developing connections and healing children* (pp. 159–71). Lanham, MD: Jason Aronson.

Blum-Kulka, S. (1993). "You gotta know how to tell a story": Telling, tales, and tellers in American and Israeli narrative events at dinner. *Language in Society, 22*, 361–402.

Bochner, A. P. (2002). Perspectives on inquiry III: The moral of stories. In M. L. Knapp, & J. A. Daly (Eds.) *Handbook of interpersonal communication*, 3rd edn (pp. 73–101). Thousand Oaks, CA: Sage.

Bohanek, J. G., Marin, K. A., & Fivush, R. (2008). Family narratives, self, and gender in early adolescence. *Journal of Early Adolescence, 28*, 153–76.

Bohanek, J. G., Marin, K. A., Fivush, R., & Duke, M. (2006). Family narrative interaction and children's sense of self. *Family Process, 45*, 39–54.

Brown, B. (2010, June). Expanding your perception. Video podcast retrieved from http://www. wimp.com/expandingperception.

Bruess, C. J. S., & Pearson, J.C. (1997). Interpersonal rituals in marriage and adult friendship. *Communication Monographs*, 64, 25–46.

Bruner, J. (1990). *Acts of meaning*. Cambridge, MA: Harvard University Press.

Buehlman, K. T., Gottman, J. M., & Katz, L. F. (1992). How a couple views their past predicts their future: Predicting divorce from an oral history interview. *Journal of Family Psychology*, 5, 295–318.

Bylund, C. (2003). Ethnic diversity and family stories. *Journal of Family Communication*, 3, 215–36.

Charon, R. (2006). The self-telling body. *Narrative Inquiry*, 16, 191–200.

Doohan, E. M., Carrère, S., & Riggs, M. L. (2010). Using relational stories to predict the trajectory toward marital dissolution: The oral history interview and spousal feelings of flooding, loneliness, and depression. *Journal of Family Communication*, 10, 57–77.

Fiese, B. H., & Bickham, N. L. (2004). Pin-curling grandpa's hair in the comfy chair: Parents' stories of growing up and potential links to socialization in the preschool years. In M. W. Pratt & B. H. Fiese (Eds.), *Family stories and the life course: Across time and generations* (pp. 259–77). Mahwah, NJ: Lawrence Erlbaum Associates.

Fiese, B. H., Hooker, K. A., Kotary, L., Schwagler, J., & Rimmer, M. (1995). Family stories in the early stages of parenthood. *Journal of Marriage and the Family*, 57, 763–70.

Fiese, B. H., & Marjinsky, K. A. T. (1999). Dinnertime stories: Connecting family practices with relationship beliefs and child adjustment. *Monographs for the Society for Research in Child Development*, 64, 52–68.

Fiese, B. H., & Skillman, G. (2000). Gender differences in family stories: Moderating influence of parent gender role and child gender. *Sex Roles*, 43, 267–84.

Fiese, B. H., & Wamboldt, F. S. (2003). Coherent accounts of coping with a chronic illness: Convergences and divergences in family measurement using narrative analysis. *Family Process*, 42, 439–51.

Fiese, B. H., & Winter, M. A. (2009). Family stories and rituals. In J. Bray & M. Stanton (Eds.), *The Wiley-Blackwell handbook of family psychology* (pp. 625–36). Malden, MA: Wiley-Blackwell.

Fisher, W. R. (1987). *Human communication as narration: Toward a philosophy of reason, value, and action*. Columbia, SC: University of South Carolina Press.

Fivush, R. (2006). Maternal reminiscing style and children's developing understanding of self and emotion. *Clinical Social Work Journal*, 35, 37–46.

Fivush, R., Haden, C. A., & Reese, E. (2006). Elaborating on elaborations: Role of maternal reminiscing style in cognitive and socioemotional development. *Child Development*, 77, 1568–88.

Fivush, R., Hazzard, A., Sales, J. M., Sarfati, D., & Brown, T. (2003). Creating coherence out of chaos? Children's narratives of emotionally positive and negative events. *Applied Cognitive Psychology*, 17, 1–19.

Freeman, M. (2006). Life "on holiday"? In defense of big stories. *Narrative Inquiry*, 16, 131–38.

Friedlander, M. L. (1999). Ethnic identity development of internationally adopted children and adolescents: Implications for family therapists. *Journal of Marital and Family Therapy*, 25, 43–60.

Gallo, C. (2009). The stories of chronic illness: Narrative roles and family therapy. In J. D. Atwood & C. Gallo (Eds.), *Family therapy and chronic illness* (pp. 1–16). New Brunswick, NJ: Transaction.

Galvin, K. (2006). Diversity's impact on defining the family: Discourse-dependence and identity. In L. H. Turner, & R. West (Eds.), *The family communication sourcebook* (pp. 3–19). Thousand Oaks, CA: Sage.

Galvin, K. (2003). International and transracial adoption: A communication research agenda. *Journal of Family Communication*, 3, 237–53.

Goodall, H. L., Jr. (2005). Narrative inheritance: A nuclear family with toxic secrets. *Qualitative Inquiry*, 11, 492–513.

Haden, C. A., Haine, R. A., & Fivush, R. (1997). Developing narrative structure in parent–child reminiscing across the preschool years. *Developmental Psychology*, 33, 295–307.

Harrigan, M. M. (2010). Exploring the narrative process: An analysis of the adoption stories mothers tell their internationally adopted children. *Journal of Family Communication*, 10, 24–39.

Hayden, J. M., Singer, J. A., & Chrisler, J. C. (2006). The transmission of birth stories from mother to daughter: Self-esteem and mother-daughter attachment. *Sex Roles*, 55, 373–83.

Holmberg, D., Orbuch, T. L., & Veroff, J. (2004). *Thrice told tales: Married couples tell their stories.* Mahwah, NJ: Lawrence Erlbaum Associates.

Jones, A. C. (2003). Reconstructing the stepfamily: Old myths, new stories. *Social Work, 48,* 228–36.

Jorgenson, J., & Bochner, A. P. (2004). Imagining families through stories and rituals. In A. L. Vangelisti (Ed.) *Handbook of family communication* (pp. 513–38). Mahwah, NJ: Lawrence Erlbaum Associates.

Kiser, L. J., Baumgardner, B., & Dorado, J. (2010). Who are we, but for the stories we tell: Family stories and healing. *Psychological Trauma: Theory, Research, Practice, and Policy, 2,* 243–49.

Koenig Kellas, J. (2008). Narrative theories: Making sense of interpersonal communication. In L. A. Baxter & D. O. Braithwaite (Eds.), *Engaging theories in interpersonal communication: Multiple perspectives* (pp. 241–54). Thousand Oaks, CA: Sage.

Koenig Kellas, J. (2005). Family ties: Communicating identity through jointly told family stories. *Communication Monographs, 72,* 365–89.

Koenig Kellas, J., & Trees, A. R. (2006). Finding meaning in difficult family experiences: Sense-making and interaction processes during joint family storytelling. *Journal of Family Communication, 6,* 49–76.

Koenig Kellas, J., LeClair-Underberg, C., Baxter, L. A., Braithwaite, D. O., Thatcher, M. S., Routsong, T. R., & Lamb Normand, E. (2009). Narratively (re)framing stepfamily beginnings: The relationship between adult stepchildren's stepfamily origin stories and their perceptions of the family. Paper presented to the Central States Communication Association, St. Louis, MO.

Koenig Kellas, J., Trees, A. R., Schrodt, P., LeClaire-Underberg, C., & Willer, E. K. (2010). Exploring links between well-being and interactional sense-making in married couples' jointly told stories of stress. *Journal of Family Communication, 10,* 174–93.

Koenig Kellas, J., Willer, E., & Kranstuber, H. (2010). Fairytales and tragedies: Narratively making sense of (and the dark side of making sense) of personal relationships. In B. H. Spitzberg & W. R. Cupach (Eds.), *The dark side of close relationships,* 2nd edn (pp. 63–93). Mahwah, NJ: Lawrence Erlbaum Associates.

Kranstuber, H., & Koenig Kellas, J. (2011). Instead of growing under her heart, I grew in it: The relationship between adoption entrance narratives and adoptees' self-concept. *Communication Quarterly, 59,* 179–99.

Krusiewicz, E. S., & Wood, J. T. (2001). He was our child from the moment we walked in that room: Entrance stories of adoptive parents. *Journal of Social and Personal Relationships, 18,* 785–803.

Labov, W., & Waletsky, J. (1967). Narrative analysis: Oral versions of personal experience. In J. Helm (Ed.), *Personal essays on the verbal and visual arts: Proceedings of the 1966 annual spring meeting of the American Ethnological Society* (pp. 12–44). Seattle, WA: University of Washington Press.

Langellier, K. M., & Peterson, E. E. (1993). Family storytelling as a strategy of social control. In D. K. Mumby (Ed.), *Narrative and social control: Critical perspectives.* Newbury Park, CA: Sage.

Langellier, K. M., & Peterson, E. E. (2004). *Storytelling in daily life: Performing narrative.* Philadelphia, PA: Temple University Press.

Langellier, K. M., & Peterson, E. E. (2006). Narrative performance theory: Telling stories, doing family. In D. O. Braithwaite & L. A. Baxter (Eds.), *Engaging theories in family communication* (pp. 99–114). Thousand Oaks, CA: Sage.

Manoogian, M. M., Harter, L. M., & Denham, S. A. (2010). The storied nature of health legacies in familial experience of Type 2 Diabetes. *Journal of Family Communication, 10,* 40–56.

McAdams, D. P. (1993). *The stories we live by: Personal myths and the making of the self.* New York: Guilford Press.

Miller, P. J., Fung, H., & Mintz, J. (1996). Self-construction through narrative practices: A Chinese and American comparison of early socialization. *Ethos, 24,* 237–80.

Miller, P. J., Wiley, A. R., Fung, H., & Liang, C. (1997). Personal storytelling as a medium of socialization in Chinese and American families. *Child Development, 68,* 557–68.

Miller, P. J., Sandel, T. L., Liang, C., & Fung, H. (2001). Narrating transgressions in Longwood: The discourses, meanings, and paradoxes of an American socialization practice. *Ethos, 29,* 159–86.

Monk, G. (1997). How narrative therapy works. In G. Monk, J. Winslade, K. Crocket, & D. Epston (Eds.), *Narrative therapy in practice: The archaeology of hope* (pp. 3–31). San Francisco, CA: Jossey-Bass.

Nelson, K., & Fivush, R. (2004). The emergence of autobiographical memory: A social cultural developmental theory. *Psychological Review, 111,* 486–511.

Nussbaum, J. F., & Bettini, L. (1994). Shared stories of the grandparent–grandchild relationship. *International Journal of Aging and Human Development, 39*, 67–80.

Ochs, E. (1997). Narrative. In T. A. van Dijk (Ed.) *Discourse as structure and process: Discourse studies—A multidisciplinary introduction* (pp. 185–207). Thousand Oaks, CA: Sage.

Oppenheim, D., Nir, A., Warren, S., & Emde, R. N. (1997). Emotion regulation in mother–child narrative co-construction: Associations with children's narratives and adaptation. *Developmental Psychology, 33*, 284–94.

Pennebaker, J. W. (1997). *Opening up: The healing power of emotional expression.* New York: Guilford Press.

Peterson, C., & McCabe, A. (2004). Echoing our parents: Parental influences on children's narration. In M. W. Pratt & B. H. Fiese (Eds.), *Family stories and the life course: Across time and generations* (pp. 258–77). Mahwah, NJ: Lawrence Erlbaum Associates.

Ramey, H. L., Tarulli, D., Frijters, J. C., & Fisher, L. (2009). A sequential analysis of externalizing in narrative therapy with children. *Contemporary Family Therapy, 31*, 262–79.

Ramirez-Esparza, N., & Pennebaker, J. W. (2006). Do good stories produce good health? Exploring words, language, and culture. *Narrative Inquiry, 16*, 211–19.

Reese, E. (1996). Conceptions of self in mother–child birth stories. *Journal of Narrative and Life History, 6*, 23–38.

Riessman, C. K. (2008). *Narrative methods for the human sciences.* Los Angeles, CA: Sage.

Sales, J. M., & Fivush, R. (2005). Social and emotional functions of mother–child reminiscing about stressful events. *Social Cognition, 23*, 70–90.

Sloan, D. M., & Marx, B. P. (2004). Taking pen to hand: Evaluating theories underlying the written disclosure paradigm. *Clinical Psychology: Science and Practice, 11*, 121–37.

Stone, E. (2004). *Black sheep and kissing cousins: How our family stories shape us.* New Brunswick, NJ: Transaction.

Thompson, B., Koenig Kellas, J., Soliz, J., Thompson, J., Epp, A., & Schrodt, P. (2009). Family legacies: Constructing individual and family identity through intergenerational storytelling. *Narrative Inquiry, 19*, 106–34.

Trees, A. R., & Koenig Kellas, J. (2009). Telling tales: Enacting family relationships in joint storytelling about difficult family experiences. *Western Journal of Communication, 31*, 91–111.

Trees, A. R., Koenig Kellas, J., & Roche, M. (2010). Family narratives. In C. Gaff & C. Bylund (Eds.), *Family communication about genetics: Theory and practice* (pp. 68–86). Oxford: Oxford University Press.

Vangelisti, A. L., Crumley, L. P., & Baker, J. L. (1999). Family portraits: Stories as standards for family relationships. *Journal of Social and Personal Relationships, 16*, 335–68.

Wang, Q. (2004). The cultural context of parent–child reminiscing: A functional analysis. In M. W. Pratt & B. H. Fiese (Eds.), *Family stories and the life course: Across time and generations* (pp. 279–301). Mahwah, NJ: Lawrence Erlbaum Associates.

White, M. (2007). *Maps of narrative practice.* New York: W. W. Norton & Co.

Willer, E. K. (2009). Experimentally testing a narrative sense-making metaphor intervention: Facilitating communicative coping about social aggression with adolescent girls. Unpublished doctoral dissertation. University of Nebraska-Lincoln.

Part VI
Communication and Contemporary Family Issues

25

After the Workday Ends

How Jobs Impact Family Relationships

Shu-wen Wang and Rena L. Repetti

"The family is a haven in a heartless world."

Attributed to Christopher Lasch, historian and
author of Haven in a heartless world: The family besieged (1977)

"If you had a stressful day at work, it gets stressful when you get home, it gets stressful when you get to the kids or your husband. You know, things don't work out right the whole evening. And then you're not feeling well, then you have a headache and uh, you're not eating, you're not sleeping."

Mother from Family 2, UCLA Center on Everyday Lives of Families (2002)

After the Workday Ends: How Jobs Impact the Family

There are probably no two other aspects of everyday life that come together with such regularity, yet complexity, as work and family. Dual income families with children are currently the predominant household composition in the U.S.A. (Bianchi & Raley, 2005), replacing the family structure of decades past in which husbands worked outside the home and wives worked inside the home. The traditional family structure, primarily the result of changes in American society following World War II, contributed to the notion of home as a haven, where working husbands retired from the stresses of the workday to the restorative domestic sphere nurtured by their wives. Demographic shifts to the typical American household are due primarily to women entering the paid workforce en masse, with the workforce today comprised of about 49 percent women and 51 percent men (Bond, Thompson, Galinsky, & Prottas, 2003). The labor force participation rate of all women ages 25–54 has hovered around 75 percent since the 1990s (Pew Research Center, 2007), and 2007 statistics show that 71 percent of mothers with children under 18 worked outside the home, compared to just 47 percent in 1975 (Galinsky, Aumann, & Bond, 2008). As women's roles have changed dramatically over the past several decades, men have also experienced an evolution in the family realm, with married and employed fathers increasing the time they spend on household labor and childcare from 100 to 150 minutes per day, between 1965 and 2003 (Hook, 2006). Clearly, most individuals in contemporary American society will grapple first hand with the challenges involved with employment outside the home, maintaining a household, and attending to relationships with spouse, children, and extended family. Indeed, the intersection of work and home is a key issue for today's families.

Compounding the challenges of balancing employment and family is the fact that most workers feel burdened, pressured, and generally stressed by their jobs. Studies have shown that a large proportion of employed individuals report some stress at work, with 29 percent reporting feeling "quite a bit or extremely stressed at work" (Barsade, Wiesenfeld, & The Marlin Company, 1997). In fact, three-quarters of employees believe that workers today experience more job stress than a generation ago (Princeton Survey Research Associates, 1997). Feelings of pressure and burden from occupations may be attributed, in part, to the fact that people are simply working more hours; the combined weekly work hours of dual-earner couples with children under the age of 18 has increased from 81 to 91 hours since the 1970s (Bond, Thompson, Galinsky, & Prottas, 2003). It is little wonder that jobs and families have been characterized as competing "greedy institutions" demanding commitment and resources (Coser, 1974) from individuals who have finite quantities of both. While the home was once popularly depicted as a safe haven to which working individuals could retreat and recuperate from job stress (Baruch, Biener, & Barnett, 1987), this conceptualization of the separate natures of occupational and home domains is no longer applicable to the experiences of today's families. As illustrated by the Mother from Family 2 at the start of this chapter, wellness in the workplace and wellness in the home are intertwined, and experiences on the job may impact the interpersonal dynamics of the family.

We focus this chapter on how characteristics of occupations and subjective experiences at work *spillover* and impact family interactions, relationships, and routines.[1] According to the spillover model, jobs are thought to impact the worker's cognitions, mood, and physiology, and carry over into the home by shaping the worker's subsequent interactions with family members. Research has documented that employment can influence individual health and well-being in multiple ways, and that job stress in particular can have a negative effect on health (e.g., cardiovascular outcomes [Schnall, Schwartz, Landsbergis, Warren, & Pickering, 1998], depression and anxiety [Melchior, et al., 2007]). This chapter focuses on occupational influences on *interpersonal* well-being in the context of the family. First, we address how the characteristics and requirements of positions, such as work schedule or level of job autonomy, impact the family. Next, we look at how subjective experiences and perceptions in the workplace, particularly job stress, influence family relationships, and highlight how different aspects of the family relational climate act as contextual moderators in shaping how work permeates the family. Last, we describe some key contemporary issues that the work–family field is grappling with and propose an agenda for future research.

Influence of Job Characteristics on Family Relationships

Jobs can differ in myriad ways—the income that they provide, the time they require, the schedules they impose, and the activities and tasks they involve all vary tremendously. Such occupational characteristics are related to important qualities of family relationships, such as the employee's marital stability and satisfaction, the routines followed at home, and the harshness as well as the closeness and warmth of family relationships. Jobs represent an investment of an individual's time and energy in return for resources, such as income and status, which enhance family life. The evidence for how much family relationships benefit from occupational positions and the income they bring is seen in the negative repercussions of job loss and unemployment. Long-term unemployment can be associated with devastating outcomes for families. The data show increased risks of divorce and child abuse, with economic hardship acting as the primary mediator of the effects of unemployment on families (Christoffersen, 2000; Strom, 2003).

Of course one of the major trade-offs for the resources that jobs provide is a draining of some of the time that a spouse or parent can directly devote to the family. However, even though longer work hours are associated with greater family scheduling difficulties and perceptions of more work–family strain, there is no evidence for a linear association between more time at work and greater marital and family difficulties (Barnett, 2006). In a prospective longitudinal study of dual-earner families, the amount of time that both spouses devoted to paid positions was linked to their perceptions of marital quality, but the direction of effects depended on whether the individual worked more or fewer than the average number of hours. Among those working fewer hours than average, declines in work hours were associated with improvements in marital quality, whereas for those working more hours than average, increases in work hours were linked to marital improvements. The authors interpreted this pattern as indicating that marital relationships benefit when couples maximize whatever strategy suits them best for balancing occupations and family; as the work time "fit" improves, so does the marriage (Barnett, Gareis, & Brennan, 2009). The complexity of associations between time devoted to jobs and perceptions of family life was illustrated in survey data from a large representative sample of employed adults in the U.S.A. Those working longer hours were more likely to feel that their family life was enhanced by their occupational experiences, as well as being more likely to report that their jobs detracted from their involvement at home (Grzywacz, Almeida, & McDonald, 2002). The scheduling of work time over the day appears to be much more important than the absolute number of hours devoted to a job, particularly for families with children living at home. Night, evening, and rotating shifts interfere with the time that couples and families spend together and disrupt family routines (Barnett, 2006). For instance, one of the most common family rituals, the family dinner, may be a rare event when a parent works a nonday shift (Presser, 2005). Unsurprisingly, marital dissatisfaction and disruption are higher when one member of a couple works at night (Barnett, 2006).

Many people willingly choose more time on the job in return for higher wages (Ruhm, 2005), and more work hours—even nonday shifts—can have benefits for families. In addition to financial rewards, research shows that mothers' increased work hours are linked with greater father involvement in, and knowledge about, their children's daily lives (Crouter, Bumpus, Maguire, & McHale, 1999; Crouter & McHale, 1993). One reason mothers and fathers choose a nonstandard work schedule is because by "tag teaming" hours at their jobs, they maximize the amount of time that one parent is with the children (Bianchi & Raley, 2005). In fact, evidence indicates that when mothers work nonday shifts, fathers spend more time with their children and are more aware of their children's activities (Barnett & Gareis, 2007; Staines & Pleck, 1983). A critical variable in understanding this work–family linkage is the degree of control that an individual can exert over the amount and scheduling of their work time; shift schedules are much less likely to have negative effects on family relationships when they are voluntarily chosen (Barnett, 2006; Staines & Pleck, 1983). Individual differences in control over scheduling extra hours at work may explain why the research literature has not found longer hours linked in a uniformly positive or negative direction with marital and family relationship outcomes (Perry-Jenkins, 2005).

Another characteristic of jobs with relevance for family dynamics is the level of autonomy they afford, which is reflected in the amount of control the employee exerts over not only "when," but also "where" and "how" work is accomplished. Job autonomy is tied up with other characteristics of an occupation, such as the degree of cognitive complexity involved in the tasks that are performed. Employees who see their positions as allowing autonomy and requiring a high level of skill report the belief that what they do at work contributes in a beneficial way to their behavior and activities at home. Those associations are not restricted to self-reported job characteristics; beliefs about the benefits of work experiences for family life are more likely to be reported by people employed in occupations that are objectively categorized as requiring greater intellectual capability and social skills (Grzywacz & Butler, 2005). According to Kohn and Schooler (1982), a parent's child-rearing values and behavior are shaped by the level of self-direction he or she experiences at work (which is correlated with job autonomy and complexity). This idea has been supported by research showing that parents whose jobs involve greater autonomy and complexity impose less restrictive control (Mason, Cauce, Gonzales, Hiraga & Grove, 1994) and use more inductive reasoning with their children (Whitbeck et al., 1997). Their parenting is less authoritarian and harsh, and more warm and responsive (Greenberger et al., 1994; Grimm-Thomas & Perry-Jenkins, 1994; Whitbeck et al., 1997), and their home environments are characterized by more emotional support and intellectual stimulation (Cooksey, Menaghan, & Jekielek, 1997; Menaghan & Parcel, 1991; Parcel & Menaghan, 1994).

The research discussed here suggests that occupations influence family relationships by enlarging some resources (e.g., financial), constricting others (e.g., time), and perhaps by socializing values and ways of relating to others. Of course jobs are not randomly distributed in society; the characteristics of a spouse's or parent's work life are inextricably tied to his or her level of education, skills, motivation, and numerous other personal qualities that impact family relationships, such as child rearing practices. In other words, the factors that select individuals into particular occupations can act as "third variables" that contribute to linkages between the characteristics of work and family. In short, the interplay between job characteristics and interpersonal processes in families is dynamic and complex.

Influence of Job Experiences and Perceptions on Family Relationships

The characteristics of jobs and the tasks and requirements they entail are usually beyond the influence of workers. However, what research has shown is that the *subjective* experience of the workplace and the perceptions employees have of their jobs can have just as much—if not more—of an impact on the employee, and subsequently, the family. After all, aspects of a position that frustrate one worker may be perfectly satisfactory to another, and day-to-day fluctuations in workplace experiences of the same individual can have short-term effects on the family environment. Here, we turn our attention to the subjective experiences and perceptions that individuals have on the job, and review how the "felt" qualities of work influence family relationships.

While most of this research has looked at the effects of job stress on the health and well-being of employees and their families, there is also a literature on *positive spillover*, where positive experiences in the workplace (e.g., satisfaction, support, and self-efficacy) shape experiences in the home. For example, in one study, reports of more job satisfaction in the afternoon at work were associated with higher levels of marital satisfaction later that evening, an association that was mediated jointly by positive and negative effect (Heller & Watson, 2005). Models that include positive in addition to negative work–family spillover have been found to have added utility in depicting the associations between occupations and domestic life (Kinnunen, Feldt, Geurts, & Pulkkinen, 2006), and a growing body of research on work–family facilitation has shown that various forms of facilitation (i.e., energy-based, time-based, economic, and psychological) have favorable effects for home performance, satisfaction, and commitment (van Steenbergen, Ellemers, & Mooijaart, 2007). Thus, positive experiences in the occupational domain can have desirable effects on home life and family relationships.

This chapter focuses on the much more extensive literature on the effects that *job stressors* have on family interactions and relationships. However, we note that some of the research reviewed here infers an experience of stress at work from measures that could also be interpreted in the opposite direction. For example, if perceptions of a work environment as being unsupportive are correlated with more negative interactions with one's spouse, the same correlation could be interpreted to indicate that a more supportive environment is associated with fewer negative marital interactions. Thus, these job stress findings may also speak to how employment experiences can positively impact family life.

There is a large body of research investigating work–family conflict (also termed work–family interference) that looks generally at perceptions of interrole conflict between the two domains of work and family. A meta-analysis of work–family satisfaction and conflict (Ford, Heinen, & Langkamer, 2007) determined that job stress made the greatest unique contribution to the perception that employment interferes with family, above and beyond the effects of work hours and the level of involvement in one's position. As noted at the start of this chapter, most workers report some job stress and a significant amount report extreme job stress and burn-out. When asking how subjective experiences and perceptions of the workplace as stressful impact the family, it is important to distinguish between chronic job stress (i.e., perceiving one's job as highly demanding every day) and short-term daily job stressors (i.e., experiencing fluctuations in day-to-day job stress). We review research findings about both the chronic and the short-term effects of occupational stressors on the family.

Decrease in Engagement and Time Spent with Family

One of the main ways in which working a stressful job influences families is through its draining effect on an employee's energy and cognitive resources (Doumas, Margolin, & John, 2008). Studies have found that when workers regularly feel depleted by their jobs, they may be less likely to participate actively in family life. This decreased involvement in the family can take the form of simply knowing less about the activities of family members. In one study, both parents were less knowledgeable about their children's experiences, activities, and whereabouts when fathers were employed in more demanding jobs (i.e., long work hours, high role overload, and high job pressure) (Bumpus, Crouter, & McHale, 1999), and another study found that fathers were less knowledgeable about their young adolescent children when fathers described greater negative spillover from work in their home life (Bumpus, Crouter, & McHale, 2006). The importance of adequate parental knowledge of children's experiences for effective monitoring has been widely documented by studies demonstrating low levels of parental knowledge to be linked with negative child and adolescent outcomes (e.g., substance use and delinquency; Fletcher, Steinberg, & Williams-Wheeler, 2004). Across studies, the effect of job stress on parental knowledge was observed among fathers, but job stress was not associated with mothers' knowledge about their children (e.g., Bumpus et al., 1999; Bumpus et al., 2006; Crouter, et al., 1999). This difference may be due to the scripted nature of men and women's roles in the household, with the negative effects of occupational stress less likely to impact wives who are typically primarily responsible for childcare and maintaining the domestic sphere (Almeida, Wethington, & Chandler, 1999).

Another form of decreased involvement linked with chronic job stress is spending less time with family members. Fathers reporting more work-to-family negative spillover were found to be less centrally involved in their children's experiences as measured by the percentage of children's time across all activities spent with fathers (Bumpus et al., 2006). And more time pressure on the job has been associated with less time allocated to parenting in a sample of employed mothers and fathers of five- to seven-year-olds (Greenberger, O'Neil, & Nagel, 1994). Likewise, greater work pressure has been linked with difficulties performing family roles such as spending time with spouse and completing household chores (Hughes, Galinsky, & Morris, 1992). In sum, these findings suggest that occupations experienced as highly demanding detract from a worker's ability to be fully engaged with and knowledgeable about family members. This stands in contrast with the literature reviewed earlier that indicated no across-the-board effects of the amount of time spent at work on family relationships, and highlights the importance of subjective employment experiences for relationship dynamics in the home.

When taking a close-up view of how *daily* job stressors impact families in the short-run, researchers have identified a *social withdrawal* response that seems consonant with the decreased knowledge and engagement described above for chronic job stress. For example, university employees were less likely to engage in social activities with their families on days they described experiencing high work-to-family conflict, even after controlling for the amount of time the employees spent at home (Ilies, Schwind, Wagner, Johnson, DeRue, & Ilgen, 2007). In a sample of male air traffic controllers, a short-term increase in behavioral (i.e., distraction, unresponsiveness, and disinterest in social interaction) and emotional withdrawal (i.e., fewer expressions of anger and aggression) from spouse (Repetti, 1989) and children (Repetti, 1994) was detected on workdays characterized by greater subjective and objective workload (i.e., lower visibility and more air traffic volume). Results from another sample of dual-earner couples corroborated these findings; both husbands and wives reported greater behavioral withdrawal from spouses following socially stressful workdays, and wives also withdrew from their husbands on days of heavy workload (Story & Repetti, 2006). Less angry and more withdrawn behavior was also detected among husbands (but not among wives) in another daily diary study of dual-earner couples (Schulz et al., 2004). These daily report findings are consistent with naturalistic observations of working mothers' daily reunions at daycare with their preschool children over five consecutive weekdays; mothers were observed to be less talkative and affectionate with their children following days marked by greater workload or interpersonal stress (Repetti & Wood, 1997a). In sum, these accounts of daily social withdrawal in response to job stress may foreshadow the diminished knowledge and involvement in the family that is linked with chronic job stress.

Increase in Conflict and Tension in Family Relationships

On the flip side of a decrease in family engagement and time spent with family is an increase in social behavior that is more involved, angry, and conflictive. Working in a highly demanding job, marked by fast pace or a heavy workload, or being employed in a hostile or unsupportive work environment, can lead to feelings of irritability and anger that carry over from the workplace into the home. One effect of this negative mood spillover process is an increase in relationship conflict. For example, long work hours and high role overload were associated with more conflictive and less positive marital and parent–adolescent relationships (Crouter, Bumpus, Head, & McHale, 2001). Furthermore, findings from two studies suggest that parent–adolescent conflict links high job demands with negative youth outcomes. In one study, work pressure and feelings of work overload were associated with more conflict in the parent–adolescent relationship, which in turn predicted less well-being among offspring (Crouter et al., 1999). Another sample of dual-earner couples and their adolescent children found that greater father-adolescent conflict mediated the link between fathers' workload and adolescent problem behaviors (Galambos, Sears, Almeida, & Kolaric, 1995).

Evidence also suggests that working in an environment that is cold, unsupportive, or hostile can shape the quality of family interactions. For instance, in the air traffic controller study mentioned above, being part of a conflictive or unsupportive work team, as reported by the air traffic controllers and corroborated by their coworkers, was associated with more negative emotion (i.e., hostility, anger, and tension), and less positive emotion (i.e., closeness and warmth) during interactions with school-age children in the home (Repetti, 1994). In another study, both mothers' and fathers' interactions with their 12-month-old infants were rated as more negative and intrusive, and less positive (i.e., less responsive, stimulating, and reciprocal) if mothers reported a less cohesive and committed social climate at work three months prior (Costigan, Cox, & Cauce, 2003). In addition, the combination of a demanding job and low supervisor support has been associated with more frequent marital arguments (Hughes et al., 1992).

Negative mood spillover has also been detected on a short-term daily basis, whereby fluctuations in daily job stress covary with the quality of family interactions later that day. Negative emotions, such as anger and anxiety, have been found to carry over from work to home among employed parents (Judge & Ilies, 2004; Matjasko & Feldman, 2006). An increase in negative emotions following stressful and negatively arousing days on the job may be one of the mechanisms by which experiences at work impact dynamics in the home. For example, an early daily diary study observed an increased probability of spouse arguments on days in which husbands had an argument at work (Bolger, DeLongis, Kessler, & Wethington, 1989). Additionally, Story and Repetti (2006) directly tested and found support for negative mood as a mediator of a linkage between workload and marital anger among the wives in a sample of dual-earner couples. Negative mood spillover has also been observed in parent interactions with children. Air traffic controllers reported expressing more anger and using more discipline with children on days of greater interpersonal stress at work (Repetti, 1994), and mothers who endorsed more depressive symptoms reported more aversive or impatient interactions with their preschool children following stressful workdays (Repetti & Wood, 1997a).

Individual Differences in Responses to Job Stress

It is interesting that research has uncovered two such different effects of job stress on family dynamics. Wouldn't a withdrawal from social interaction preclude opportunities for negative engagement with family members? Likewise, workers who are angry and irritable in their exchanges with spouse and children could hardly be viewed as withdrawing from interactions. Some research points to individual differences in responses to job stress that moderate the effects of job stress on family interactions (Repetti & Saxbe, 2009). For example, in a study of dual-earner families conducted by the UCLA Center on Everyday Lives of Families (CELF), we observed withdrawal and negative spillover responses in different groups of fathers. Families with school-age children were filmed as they went about their daily routines over the course of a week, and we selected 30 second clips at 10 minute intervals on the weeknights of observation in order to examine the social and emotional behavior of working parents. By focusing on the first hour that an employed parent spent with spouse and children after returning home from work, we were able to examine the immediate effects of job stress on family dynamics. Participants also completed a measure of trait neuroticism (that is, a dispositional tendency towards emotional instability; items measured proneness to feeling "anxious," "helpless," and "worthless") and reported on job stressors on each day of observation. Results showed that job stress was correlated with social withdrawal (i.e., less behavioral involvement, less negative emotions) only among fathers who were *low* on trait neuroticism, whereas job stress was linked with negative engagement (i.e., more behavioral involvement, more negative emotions) among fathers who were *high* on trait neuroticism (Wang, Repetti, & Campos, 2011). These findings suggest that responses to job stress are patterned and multiply-determined, and that emotional well-being may be a critical factor in conditioning the effect of job stress on family relationships.

Implications of Daily Responses to Job Stress for the Family

Daily studies provide a window into how occupational experiences lead to subtle day-to-day adjustments in a worker's social behavior with spouse and children that can accumulate over time to affect the overall quality of family relationships and functioning. An employee in a generally low-stress job may come home and respond irritably to, or withdraw from, her husband and children a few days a month on stressful workdays, without causing damage to her relationships; after all, families have been generally observed to be resilient in the face of significant life events and daily challenges (Patterson, 2002). However, an employee who is affected by a chronically stressful job may find that the subtle changes to her mood and behavior snowball over time to create a family context prone to conflict and low in feelings of cohesion and warmth. For instance, the effects of daily withdrawal may accumulate over time and damage family relationships (Repetti & Wood, 1997b), perhaps through decreasing time spent with, and knowledge about, spouse and child. Indeed, a longitudinal study of dual-earner couples caring for children and elderly parents found that social withdrawal predicted more depression and work–family conflict one year later (Neal & Hammer, 2009). Additionally, because job stress doesn't only increase negative emotion behavior but also decreases positive emotion behavior, it appears that potentially protective or reparative processes may be removed from the family environment on a daily basis. Thus, daily withdrawal from family members or the daily carry over of negative moods on the job into the home can damage family relationships and impede family functioning over the long haul.

It may seem logical, then, to conclude that daily withdrawal and negative mood spillover have across-the-board negative implications for family well-being. However, social withdrawal on a short-term daily basis can be an adaptive short-term response to job stress, facilitating recovery from high levels of arousal while also shielding workers from family interactions that may aggravate an already highly reactive state (Repetti, 1992). For example, in a sample of families with single working mothers, spending time alone was found to buffer the transmission of daily negative emotions from the mothers to their children (Larson & Gillman, 1999). In sum, research that zooms in for a closer look at daily work–family processes has identified daily responses to job stress that can have long-term implications for family relationships and well-being. In particular, while daily withdrawal responses may be adaptive in the short-term, they can also accumulate over time and negatively impact cohesion and closeness in the family.

The Role of the Family in Shaping the Impact of Job Stress on Family Relationships

Thus far, we have treated the effects of job stress on the family as being due to the experiences, behavior, and well-being of the worker. However, other members of a family also contribute to relationship dynamics and therefore, either directly (e.g., through their own behavior) or indirectly (e.g., through their contribution to the relationship climate), influence work–family spillover processes. Some studies have examined how the reactions of family members and the quality of family relationships shape the way that stress from work is carried over into the home. For example, preschool children were observed to display more positive behaviors in their reunion interactions with their mothers on days when their mothers spoke less or expressed less affection (Repetti & Wood, 1997a). Perhaps on those occasions, the children increased their efforts to engage their mothers (for example, by asking more questions). In a sample of dual-earner couples, individuals who reported higher levels of conflict at home were more reactive to daily job stress, showing more expressions of marital anger and more withdrawal behaviors (Story & Repetti, 2006). This finding suggests that an existing conflictive environment can exacerbate the effects of occupational stress.

The CELF observational study mentioned above offers some insight into the family context to which parents return after work. Campos and colleagues (2009) focused on the moment of reunion between working parents and family members who were already at home. Mothers, who typically returned home earlier than fathers, were often met with positive behaviors (e.g., affectionate actions or speech) and reports of information. Fathers also received positive behaviors; however, they were more likely than mothers to be ignored by family members already engaged in activities. Although this analysis did not look specifically at job stress, it does underscore that re-entry into home life after a day on the job does not take place in a vacuum. Perhaps a withdrawal response to a stressful day at work is facilitated by distracted and nonattentive family members.

Aspects of the marital relationship also appear to be relevant for modulating the effects of job experiences on family dynamics. For example, in one study, husbands who reported higher levels of marital satisfaction showed decreases in marital anger, whereas more maritally satisfied wives showed increases in marital anger, following days of high job stress (Schulz et al., 2004). It may be that these sex patterns are due to differences in how spouses support one another's recovery after a stressful workday. For instance, the decrease in anger expressions observed among the men in happy marriages may reflect a process of social withdrawal that was facilitated by their wives. Indeed, higher levels of emotional support from wives seemed to promote behavioral and emotional withdrawal in male air traffic controllers following stressful workdays (Repetti, 1989), and in another study, wives were much more likely than husbands to increase their housework efforts on days their spouses reported greater job stress (Bolger et al., 1989). These instances of emotional and instrumental support by wives appear to provide husbands with the time, space, and empathic understanding that allow husbands the freedom to disengage from family interactions and responsibilities. It is interesting to note that in the Bolger et al. study, husbands were less likely than wives to complete additional household chores on days their spouses were stressed by work. It may be, then, that when employed wives returned home after a stressful workday, the demands of the household and the lack of support from husbands prevented a period of rest and recuperation, and instead con- tributed to increases in angry or irritable behavior. In the same vein, Schulz and colleagues suggested that perhaps it is this dynamic—high job stress coupled with unrelenting home demands and lack of spousal support—that makes more happily married wives (who may expect support from their husbands) more prone to anger expressions compared to less happily married wives (who may not expect support from their husbands).

An extensive body of research has examined the interdependencies and behavioral patterns that broadly characterize marital interactions, concluding that behavior in the marital relationship does not exist in a vacuum and instead is shaped by multiple factors, including the partner's experiences, expectations, and behavior (Bradbury, Fincham, & Beach, 2000). Scholars have proposed that coping in couples is largely a dyadic process and have demonstrated that examining how couples cope together, in addition to studying individual coping, has great relevance for understanding relationship functioning and stability (Bodenmann, 2005). Aspects of an interaction or relationship are best con- ceptualized as resulting from the interactive and transactional effects of both partners' experiences, cognitions, and behavior. In particular, studies on marital support have shown that individuals are more likely to provide support to their spouses on days in which they themselves received support, and that individuals reporting greater relationship satisfaction are more likely to provide support on a daily basis (e.g., Iida, Seidman, Shrout, Fujita, & Bolger, 2008). Research on marital stress generation has also provided evidence regarding the transactional nature of support exchanges that are shaped by *how* support is solicited, provided, and received; for example, depressed wives were found to engage in negative support behavior with their husbands that contributed to greater marital stress (Davila, Bradbury, Cohan, & Tochluk, 1997). Perhaps the conflictive ways in which they initiated or responded to support prompted a mutual negative response from husbands. Indeed, marital research has identified a process of negative effect reciprocity in marital interactions, whereby negative behavior is returned with negative behavior (Kim, Capaldi, & Crosby, 2007).

The transactional nature of marital behavior applies when looking at the influence of job stress on marital relationships as well. Individuals may be influenced by job stress, both in their *provision* of support to a spouse, as well as the *receipt* of support from a spouse. For instance, an employed wife who has, herself, completed a highly demanding work- day may be dealing with the residual effects of job stress in the form of negative mood or energy depletion, and may be ill equipped to respond to, and support the needs of, a spouse. Similarly, it may also be that some types of responses to job stress are more easily supported than others, impacting the likelihood that support will be received. For example, a worker who expresses irritability, anger, or impatience with a spouse may find himself less likely to elicit a supportive response compared to a worker who retreats and "needs space." In sum, a supportive interaction between spouses is a multi-determined process that may be linked with job stress in different ways—both as a resource and mitigating factor in an employed person's recovery from job stress, as well as an outcome that is shaped by the job stress experiences of both partners. The interactive effects of job stress on relationships, and in particular the role played by marital support processes, is a rich area for further investigation.

Contemporary Issues and Research Agenda

The conceptual and methodological challenges of research on the effects of occupations on the family continue to change with the shifting landscape of contemporary workers' jobs and family lives. In an age of virtual offices, flexible work schedules, long hours and overwork, and round-the-clock communication via the Internet and wireless communication, is it even possible to agree on the boundaries of a job? The notion of the workday taking place in a brick-and-mortar setting peopled by supervisors and coworkers, and contained between the hours of 8am and 5pm, may soon become a relic of the past.

Compounding this issue is the fact that there are myriad outcomes in the family domain that are relevant in the work–family field. Repetti (2005) has described the impact of jobs on health and well-being as reflecting a "cascade" of effects, with multiple intermediary steps linking job qualities and experiences with health and well-being endpoints. Selecting which outcomes are of interest in that "cascade" drastically changes the aspect or segment of work–family process that is studied, the scope of the question, and the time frame of the investigation. For example, examining how job stress impacts parent–child relationship closeness involves the selection of a distal outcome (i.e., relationship closeness) that lies farther downstream in the cascade of work–family effects. To study this question, the researcher must adjust the scope of the investigation to look at variables, such as parental well-being or parental monitoring, that lie *en route* to the relationship outcome, in order to understand how job stress ultimately detracts from parent–child relationship closeness. This type of investigation calls for a longitudinal design that takes place over months or years in order to measure these variables. On the other hand, a research study that looks at provision of social support following stressful days on the job entails a more proximal outcome (i.e., daily support provision) that requires an up-close investigation of intermediary processes such as short-term changes in mood or energy depletion. Daily diary or experience sampling methods would be more suitable for this scenario.

These conceptual issues point to the importance of appropriate measurement and methodology. The majority of the studies reviewed in this chapter rely on cross-sectional self-report methods that are influenced by reporter recall and social desirability biases. Furthermore, cross-sectional self-reports provide a single snapshot of complex and dynamic phenomena from which researchers sometimes try to derive an understanding of underlying processes. Daily diary studies, experience sampling methodology, and other approaches that take repeated measurements permit a more direct examination of process by analyzing change over time (Bolger, Davis, & Rafaeli, 2003). In addition, very few of the studies reviewed here employ observational methods. Observations in naturalistic contexts (Repetti & Wood, 1997a; Wang et al., 2011) provide ecologically valid data on actual behavior and experiences, adding rich description to work–family research. We recommend that future work make use of integrated methods that incorporate naturalistic observation, diary reports, and traditional self-reports to permit a multidimensional and close-up view of work–family processes. Such an integrated approach holds promise in helping illuminate the mechanisms that bring about the differences detected at the "surface" via cross-sectional self-report methods.

Moreover, there is a great need for further study of the work–family experiences representative of the diverse range of families that comprise contemporary American society. The vast majority of published studies focus on the experiences of educated, middle-class, Caucasian couples who work standard schedules. We know much less about the experiences of single-parent, low-income, ethnic minority, and gay and lesbian families, or the experiences of families where parents are employed in jobs with non-standard schedules or shifts. Additionally, we need better data on the developmental trajectory of work–family processes as families progress through different life phases. For example, jobs are likely to impact couples with young children differently than couples with adolescent children or "empty-nesters" whose grown children have moved out of the home. In particular, the work–family experiences of older adults have become increasingly relevant given the aging of the American population and the fact that more individuals are delaying retirement and remaining in the paid labor force.

Last, we recognize that there is an incredible body of work on work–family associations and processes, but fear that these findings are not translated in ways that effectively enhance public understanding of work–family issues. The successful application of work–family research for public consumption is necessary to help support evidence-based initiatives for optimal workplace practices and healthy family functioning. We urge researchers to venture beyond academic circles in disseminating and discussing research findings, making use of accessible online resources such as the Sloan Work and Family Research Network, and engaging in dialogue with nonresearch professionals in the field.

Acknowledgment

The authors are grateful to Elinor Ochs and the other members of the UCLA Center on Everyday Lives of Families, and to the Alfred P. Sloan Foundation. Shu-wen Wang's work on this paper was supported by a Dissertation Year Fellowship and the Dr. Ursula Mandel Scholarship, both awarded by the UCLA Graduate Division.

Note

1 We do not review research on how experiences in the family affect work life because the majority of studies in this area focus on work-to-family influences and an emphasis on family relationship outcomes is consistent with the theme of this volume.

References

Almeida, D. M., Wethington, E., & Chandler, A. L. (1999). Daily transmission of tensions between marital dyads and parent–child dyads. *Journal of Marriage and the Family, 61*, 49–61.

Barnett, R. C. (2006). The relationship of the number and distribution of work hours to health and quality-of-life (QOL) outcomes. In P. L. Perrewé & D. C. Ganster (Eds.), *Research in Occupational Stress and Well Being: Vol. 5. Employee Health and Coping Methodology*. Bingley: Emerald Group.

Barnett, R. C., Gareis, K. C., & Brennan, R. T. (2009). Reconsidering work time: A Multivariate longitudinal within-couple analysis. *Community, Work and Family, 12*, 105–33.

Barnett, R. C., & Gareis, K. C. (2007). Shift work, parenting behaviors, and children's socioemotional well-being. *Journal of Family Issues, 28*, 727–48.

Barsade, S., Wiesenfeld, B., & The Marlin Company (1997). *Attitudes in the American workplace III*. New Haven, CT: Yale University School of Management.

Baruch, G. K., Biener, L., & Barnett, R. C. (1987). Women and gender in research on work and family stress. *The American Psychologist, 4*, 130–36.

Bianchi, S. M., & Raley, S. B. (2005). Time allocation in families. In S. M. Bianchi, L. M. Casper, & R. B. King (Eds.), *Work, family, health, and well-being* (pp. 21–42). Mahwah, NJ: Lawrence Erlbaum Associates.

Bodenmann, G. (2005). Dyadic coping and its significance for marital functioning. In T. Revenson, K. Kayser, & G. Bodenmann (Eds.), *Couples coping with stress: Emerging perspectives on dyadic coping* (pp. 33–50). Washington, DC: American Psychological Association.

Bolger, N., Davis, A., & Rafaeli, E. (2003). Diary methods: Capturing life as it is lived. *Annual Review of Psychology, 54*, 579–616.

Bolger, N., DeLongis, A., Kessler, R. C., & Wethington, E. (1989). The contagion of stress across multiple roles. *Journal of Marriage and the Family, 51*, 75–183.

Bond, J. T., Thompson, C., Galinsky, E., & Prottas, D. (2003). *Highlights of the 2002 National Study of the Changing Workforce*. New York: Families and Work Institute.

Bradbury, T. N., Fincham, F. D., & Beach, S. R. H. (2000). Research on the nature and determinants of marital satisfaction: A decade in review. *Journal of Marriage and the Family, 62*, 964–80.

Bumpus, M. F., Crouter, A. C., & McHale, S. M. (1999). Work demands of dual-earner couples: Implications for parents' knowledge about children's daily lives in middle childhood. *Journal of Marriage and the Family, 61*, 465–75.

——(2006). Linkages between negative work-to-family spillover and mothers' and fathers' knowledge of their young adolescents' daily lives. *Journal of Early Adolescence, 26*, 36–59.

Campos, B., Graesch, A. P., Repetti, R. L., Bradbury, T. N., & Ochs, E. (2009). Opportunity for interaction? A naturalistic observation study of dual-earner families after work and school. *Journal of Family Psychology, 23*, 798–807.

Christoffersen, M. N. (2000). Growing up with unemployment: A study of parental unemployment and children's risk of abuse and neglect based on national longitudinal 1973 birth cohorts in Denmark. *Childhood, 7*, 421–38.

Cooksey, E. C., Menaghan, E. G., & Jekielek, S. M. (1997). Life-course effects of work and family circumstances on children. *Social Forces, 77*, 637–67.

Coser, L. A. (1974). *Greedy institutions: Patterns of undivided commitment*. New York: Free Press.

Costigan, C. L., Cox, M. J., & Cauce, A. M. (2003). Work-parenting linkages among dual-earner couples at the transition to parenthood. *Journal of Family Psychology, 17*, 397–408.

Crouter, A. C., Bumpus, M. F., Maguire, M. C., & McHale, S. M. (1999). Linking parents' work pressure and adolescents' well-being: Insights into dynamics in dual-earner families. *Developmental Psychology, 35*, 1453–61.

Crouter, A. C., & McHale, S. M. (1993). Temporal rhythms in family life: Seasonal variation in the relation between parental work and family processes. *Developmental Psychology, 29*, 198–205.

Crouter, A. C., Bumpus, M. F., Head, M. R., & McHale, S. M. (2001). Implications of overwork and overload for the quality of men's family relationships. *Journal of Marriage and the Family, 63*, 404–16.

Davila, J., Bradbury, T. N., Cohan, C. L., & Tochluk, S. (1997). Marital functioning and depressive symptoms: Evidence for a stress generation model. *Journal of Personality and Social Psychology, 73*, 849–61.

Doumas, D. M., Margolin, G., John, R. S. (2008). Spillover patterns in single-earner couples: Work, self-care, and the marital relationship. *Journal of Family Economic Issues, 29*, 55–73.

Fletcher, A. C., Steinberg, L., & Williams-Wheeler, M. (2004). Parental influences on adolescent problem behavior: Revisiting Stattin and Kerr. *Child Development, 75*, 781–96.

Ford, M. T., Heinen, B. A., & Langkamer, K. L. (2007). Work and family satisfaction and conflict: A meta-analysis of cross-domain relations. *Journal of Applied Psychology, 92*, 57–80.

Galambos, N. L., Sears, H. A., Almeida, D. M., & Kolaric, G. C. (1995). Parents' work overload and problem behavior in young adolescents. *Journal of Research on Adolescence, 5*, 201–23.

Galinsky, E., Aumann, K., & Bond, J. T. (2008). *2008 National study of the changing workforce: Times are changing—Gender and generation at work and home*. New York: Families and Work Institute. Retrieved from http://familiesandwork.org/site/research/reports/Times_Are_Changing.pdf.

Greenberger, E., O'Neil, R., & Nagel, S. K. (1994). Linking workplace and homeplace: Relations between the nature of adults' work and their parenting behaviors. *Developmental Psychology, 30*, 990–1002.

Grimm-Thomas, K., & Perry-Jenkins, M. (1994). All in a day's work: Job experiences, self-esteem, and fathering in working-class families. *Family Relations, 43*, 174–81.

Grzywacz, J. G., & Butler, A. B. (2005). The impact of job characteristics on work-to-family facilitation: Testing a theory and distinguishing a construct. *Journal of Occupational Health Psychology, 10*, 97–109.

Grzywacz, J. G., Almeida, D. M., & McDonald, D. A. (2002). Work–family spillover and daily reports of work and family stress in the adult labor force. *Family Relations, 51,* 28–36.

Heller, D., & Watson, D. (2005). The dynamic spillover of satisfaction between work and marriage: The role of time and mood. *Journal of Applied Psychology, 90,* 1273–79.

Hook, J. L. (2006). Care in context: Men's unpaid work in 20 countries, 1965–2003. *American Sociological Review, 71,* 639–60.

Hughes, D., Galinsky, E. & Morris, A. (1992). Job characteristics and marital quality: Specifying linking mechanisms. *Journal of Marriage and the Family, 54,* 31–41.

Iida, M., Seidman, G., Shrout, P. E., Fujita, K., & Bolger, N. (2008). Modeling support provision in intimate relationships. *Journal of Personality and Social Psychology, 94,* 460–78.

Ilies, R., Schwind, K. M., Wagner, D. T., Johnson, M. D., DeRue, D. S., & Ilgen, D. R. (2007). *Journal of Applied Psychology, 92,* 1368–79.

Judge, T. A., & Ilies, R. (2004). Affect and job satisfaction: A study of their relationship at work and at home. *Journal of Applied Psychology, 89,* 661–73.

Kim, H. K., Capaldi, D. M., & Crosby, L. (2007). Generalizability of Gottman and colleagues' affective process models of couples' relationship outcomes. *Journal of Marriage and Family, 69,* 55–72.

Kinnunen, U., Feldt, T., Geurts, S., & Pulkkinen, L. (2006). Types of work–family interface: well-being correlates of negative and positive spillover between work and family. *Scandinavian Journal of Psychology, 47,* 149–62.

Kohn, M. L., & Schooler, C. (1982). Job conditions and personality: A longitudinal assessment of their reciprocal effects. *American Journal of Sociology, 87,* 1257–86.

Larson, R. W., & Gillman, S. (1999). Transmission of emotions in the daily interactions of single-mother families. *Journal of Marriage and the Family, 61,* 21–37.

Mason, C. A., Cauce, A. M., Gonzales, N., Hiraga, Y., & Grove, K. (1994). An ecological model of externalizing behaviors in African-American adolescents: No family is an island. *Journal of Research on Adolescence, 4,* 639–55.

Matjasko, J. L., & Feldman, A. F. (2006). Bringing work home: The emotional experiences of mothers and fathers. *Journal of Family Psychology, 20,* 47–55.

Melchior, M., Caspi, A., Milne, B. J., Danese, A., Poulton, R., & Moffitt, T. E. (2007). Work stress precipitates depression and anxiety in young, working women and men. *Psychological Medicine, 37,* 1119–30.

Menaghan, E. G., & Parcel, T. L. (1991). Determining children's home environments: The impact of maternal characteristics and current occupational and family conditions. *Journal of Marriage and the Family, 53,* 417–31.

Neal, M. B., & Hammer, L. B. (2009). Dual-earner couples in the sandwiched generation: Effects of coping strategies over time. *The Psychologist-Manager Journal, 12,* 205–34.

Parcel, T. L., & Menaghan, E. G. (1994). Early parental work, family social capital, and early childhood outcomes. *The American Journal of Sociology, 99,* 972–1009.

Patterson, J. M. (2002). Integrating Family Resilience and Family Stress Theory. *Journal of Marriage and Family, 64,* 2, 349–60.

Perry-Jenkins, M. (2005) Work in the working class: Challenges facing families. In S. M. Bianchi, L. M. Casper, & R. B. King (Eds.), *Work, family, health, and well-being* (pp. 453–72). Mahwah, NJ: Lawrence Erlbaum Associates.

Pew Research Center (2007). *From 1997 to 2007: Fewer mothers prefer full-time work.* Washington, DC: Pew Research Center. Retrieved from http://pewresearch.org/assets/social/pdf/WomenWorking.pdf.

Presser, H. B. (2005). Embracing complexity: Work schedules and family life in a 24/7 economy. In S. M. Bianchi, L. M. Casper, & R. B. King (Eds.), *Work, family, health, and well-being* (pp. 43–48). Mahwah, NJ: Lawrence Erlbaum Associates.

Princeton Survey Research Associates (1997). *Labor day survey: State of workers.* Princeton, NJ: Princeton Survey Research Associates.

Repetti, R. L. (1989). Effects of daily workload on subsequent behavior during marital interaction: The roles of social withdrawal and spouse support. *Journal of Personality and Social Psychology, 57,* 651–59.

——(1992). Social withdrawal as a short-term coping response to daily stressors. In H. S. Friedman (Ed.), *Hostility, coping, and health* (pp. 151–65). Washington, DC: American Psychological Association.

——(1994). Short-term and long-term processes linking job stressors to father–child interaction. *Social Development, 3,* 1–15.

——(2005). A psychological perspective on the health and well-being consequences of parental employment. In S. M. Bianchi, L. M. Casper, & R. B. King (Eds.), *Work, family, health and well-being* (pp. 245–58). Mahwah, NJ: Lawrence Erlbaum Associates.

Repetti, R. & Saxbe, D. (2009). The effects of job stress on the family: One size does not fit all. In R. Crane and E. J. Hill (Eds.), *Handbook of families and work: Interdisciplinary perspectives* (pp. 62–78). Lanham, MD: University Press of America.

Repetti, R. L., & Wood, J. (1997a). Effects of daily stress at work on mothers' interactions with preschoolers. *Journal of Family Psychology, 11,* 90–108.

——(1997b). Families accommodating to chronic stress: Unintended and unnoticed processes. In B. H. Gottlieb (Ed.), *Coping with chronic stress* (pp. 191–220). New York: Plenum.

Ruhm, C. J. (2005). How well do government and employer policies support working parents? In S. M. Bianchi, L. M. Casper, & R. B. King (Eds.), *Work, family, health, and well-being* (pp. 313–25). Mahwah, NJ: Lawrence Erlbaum Associates.

Schnall, P. L., Schwartz, J. E., Landsbergis, P. A., Warren, K., & Pickering, T. G. (1998). A longitudinal study of job strain and ambulatory blood pressure: Results from a three year follow-up. *Psychosomatic Medicine, 60,* 697–706.

Schulz, M. S., Cowan, P. A., Cowan, C. P., & Brennan, R. T. (2004). Coming home upset: Gender, marital satisfaction and the daily spillover of workday experience into couple interactions. *Journal of Family Psychology, 18,* 250–63.

Staines, G. L., & Pleck, J. H. (1983). *The impact of work schedules on the family.* Ann Arbor, MI: Institute for Social Research, University of Michigan, Survey Research Center.

Story, L. B., & Repetti, R. (2006). Daily occupational stressors and marital behavior. *Journal of Family Psychology, 20,* 690–700.

Strom, S. (2003). Unemployment and families: A review of research. *Social Service Review, 77,* 399–430.

van Steenbergen, E. F., Ellemers, N., & Mooijaart, A. (2007). How work and family can facilitate each other: Distinct types of work–family facilitation and outcomes for women and men. *Journal of Occupational Health Psychology, 12,* 279–300.

Wang, S., Repetti, R. L., & Campos, B. (2011). Job stress and family social behavior: The moderating role of neuroticism. *Journal of Occupational Health Psychology, 16*(4), 441–56.

Whitbeck, L. B., Simons, R. L., Conger, R. D., Wickrama, K. A. S., Ackley, K. A., & Elder, G. H., Jr. (1997). The effects of parents' working conditions and family economic hardship on parenting behaviors and children's self-efficacy. *Social Psychology Quarterly, 60,* 291–303.

26

The Media and Family Communication

Barbara J. Wilson and Kristin L. Drogos

Communication technologies permeate the homes of American families today. The average child lives in a household with four television sets, two radios, three DVD or VCR players, two CD players, two video game consoles, and two computers (Rideout, Foehr, & Roberts, 2010). Moreover, children spend over seven and a half hours each day using these media (Rideout et al., 2010). In many American homes, the television occupies a central space in the main gathering area, often accompanied by a surround-sound system and other technologies to heighten the quality and realism of the viewing experience.

Given their prominence, the media are clearly an integral part of the daily routines of family life. Families eat meals around the television set, parents read the newspaper comics to young children, and siblings gather together to watch a rented movie on a DVD player. But the media can be used to avoid family interactions as well. The purpose of this chapter is to explore the relationship between media technologies and family communication. To illustrate how multi-faceted this relationship is, consider the following example of a six-year-old girl entering her parents' bedroom one morning before school.

"Mom, what happened to his face?" the girl asked, looking at a close-up on the television screen of a young man being interviewed on *The Today Show*.

"He got burned, honey. He got too close to fire and it burned his body. That's why we always tell you to be careful because fire is dangerous," her mother replied.

"But Mom, why is he crying?"

"Well, he's sad because he is hurt pretty badly but he's also happy because he survived. Now, that's enough, this is the news and it's not really a kid's show," her mother said as she turned the TV off.

At dinner that evening, the 6-year-old returned to the topic even though the TV was not on at the time: "Mom, Dad, I know what you're supposed to do if you are ever in a fire. You're supposed to STOP, DROP, and ROLL," she proclaimed as she fell on the floor, demonstrating the moves. "Right?"

Obviously, the media triggered this parent–child interaction, which evolved into a larger discussion of fire safety, emotional responses to tragedy, and even coping. Yet the example also illustrates how families influence individual media experiences. In this case, the mother curtailed her child's exposure to the story by turning the TV off and by holding back the fact that the injured man had been involved in a terrorist attack in Pakistan. The mother also used this instance to establish control over the medium and to help define news as a particular genre of programming. The fact that the conversation continued later that day illustrates the widespread influence of the media beyond particular moments of exposure.

This chapter will explore how the media are intricately connected to the family, serving as a stimulant, backdrop, and negotiated space for the dynamics of daily interaction. To set the stage, the first section of the chapter will describe how families use the media. Families differ in how much time they spend with different technologies and where media are placed within the household. The second section will explore the impact of the media on family life and, in particular, family communication. In addition to shaping our expectations about family roles and relationships, the media can directly stimulate family interaction, as in the example above. Alternatively, the media can hinder interaction and cause conflict.

The third section of the chapter will turn the relationship around and explore the ways in which family communication can moderate and influence media experiences. Families differ in their communication styles, which can affect media habits. In addition, some parents actively engage in mediation strategies to enhance children's learning from the media and to prevent harmful effects of exposure to certain types of content. The chapter concludes with a brief discussion of the role of the media within the family system and with suggestions for future research.

A point about scope is in order. Chapter 27 of this volume deals with the use of digital media in the family, so the present chapter will concentrate mostly on traditional media, such as television, film, radio, and print. However, we do overview emerging research on newer media in the relevant sections on family communication. Admittedly, distinctions between traditional and new media are somewhat artificial as many of these technologies are converging. Instead of going to a theater, families can now order a movie on demand using their home digital cable system. Alternatively, they can watch movies and even TV programs online. The development of digital media is producing a high degree of interactivity and integration across different forms of media.

Family Use of Mass Media

Ownership

Nearly all households (98 percent) in the U.S.A. have a television set and a large majority (88 percent) have a DVD player (Nielsen Media Research, 2009). Cable television is also commonplace, with 84 percent of households with children subscribing to some type of extra service (Rideout et al., 2010). In fact, almost half (46 percent) of American families own four technologies that are described as "media staples" in the home: a television set, a recording device, video game equipment, and a computer (Woodard & Gridina, 2000).

Though most children grow up today in multimedia households, ownership of certain technologies varies by family income and parental education. For instance, higher income families are more likely to have Internet access in the home (Rideout et al., 2010). In addition, children whose parents are college-educated are more likely to have home access to the Internet than are children whose parents do not have a college degree (Rideout et al., 2010).

One consequence of the proliferation of newer technologies is the migration of older equipment to children's bedrooms. Indeed, almost three-quarters (71 percent) of American children between the ages of 8 and 18 have a television set in their bedroom and over half (57 percent) have a VCR or DVD player (Rideout et al., 2010). In addition, almost half (49 percent) of children have cable access in their rooms. Such personal availability increases with age, such that 71 percent of children over the age of eight have a TV set in their room. Somewhat surprisingly, income does not necessarily provide children with greater private access to the media. In fact, children in higher income homes are *less* likely to have a TV in their room than are children in lower income families (Roberts et al., 1999). Parental education is also negatively related to placing a TV in a child's bedroom (Gentile & Walsh, 2002).

Children not only have media in their bedroom, but they also increasingly have access to mobile media that allow them to be in front of a screen at any time and in any place. In a recent national survey, 76 percent of American children between the ages 8 and 18 reported having their own iPod or MP3 player (Rideout et al., 2010). Furthermore, two-thirds (66 percent) had their own cell phone and nearly a third (29 percent) had their own laptop. Ownership of technology increases with age; in 2009, 75 percent of American teens had a cell phone compared to only 30 percent of 8- to 10-year-olds (Lenhart, Ling, Campbell, & Purcell, 2010).

Obviously, children who have their own media devices, whether portable or in the bedroom, are less likely to be supervised by their parents. In addition, as children spend time alone watching movies, listening to music, and in many cases surfing the Internet, they have fewer opportunities to engage in social interaction and family activities. This issue will be discussed below in the section on TV centrality.

Time Spent with Media

Given all this technology, how much actual time do families devote to the media? The average American child (8 to 18 years of age) spends over seven hours each day with some form of mediated communication (Rideout et al., 2010). Nearly four and a half hours of this time is devoted to watching television, which continues to monopolize children's media profiles. But children are not the only members of the family who watch a lot of TV. Televisions are turned on for at least eight hours a day in the typical U.S. household (Nielsen Media Research, 2007). It is not surprising, then, that television has been referred to as another member of the family (Gunter & Svennevig, 1987).

Even very young children spend a fair amount of time with television. According to recent national statistics, nearly half (43 percent) of babies between the ages of 6 months and 23 months watch television daily (Rideout & Hamel, 2006). Moreover, despite the fact that the American Academy of Pediatrics (AAP) discourages media exposure for children under the age of two (AAP, 2011), American babies in this age range watch an average of one to two hours of TV per day (Rideout & Hamel, 2006). Even more surprising, over one-third (36 percent) of children under six years have a TV set in their bedroom (Rideout & Hamel, 2006).

In contrast to television, children and teens spend an hour and a half each day with computers (Rideout et al., 2010). This figure undoubtedly will rise as young people increasingly acquire laptops and other portable devices with Internet access and as more television content moves online. Nevertheless, despite all the newer technologies, television still dominates most families' media experiences (Robinson, Kestnbaum, & Kohut, 2000). In accord, much of the research on media and families has focused on television over other technologies, as we shall see throughout this chapter. The next two sections explore how central television is in some homes and what families do while watching TV.

TV Centrality in the Household

When television was first introduced in the 1950s, families organized their homes around this new medium (Andreasen, 2001). The television set was considered a decorative piece of furniture that occupied a regal space in the living room. In the 1960s and 1970s, television moved to the family room but was still considered the center of household activity. As the technology improved, families purchased additional sets so that today, 83 percent of American households own multiple TV sets (Nielsen Media Research, 2009). The growing number of private viewing spaces now found in bedrooms and basements means that children often watch television alone or with siblings and friends (Roberts et al., 1999).

However, the trend toward privatization has been curtailed somewhat by recent architectural changes in the home. Beginning in the 1990s, new housing has tended to feature more open floor plans with cathedral ceilings and a "great room" for joint activities. The advent of the home theater system allows families to recreate the "electronic hearth" (Andreasen, 2001), this time with large-screen TVs, high-definition resolution, DVD equipment, and surround sound systems.

Nevertheless, not all families orient themselves around the media. Comstock and Paik (1991) coined the term "household centrality" to refer to how central or pervasive television is in the home. According to these scholars, high centrality refers to families that watch a great deal of television and have very few rules governing the use of TV by children. In a recent national study of over 3,000 children, 45 percent reported that the TV is turned on "most of the time" in their house, even if no one is watching it (Rideout et al., 2010). Moreover, 64 percent said television is usually on during mealtimes. Thus, for many families television is a constant backdrop to most activities.

As it turns out, centrality of television is related to socioeconomic status. Parents with less income and less education are more likely themselves to watch TV, less likely to have rules about television, and more likely to allow children to have a TV in their bedroom (Rideout et al., 2010). Television is also more central in African American families than in Caucasian families, even when controlling for socioeconomic status (Rideout et al., 2010). For example, African American children live in households with more TV sets, spend more time watching TV, are more likely to have a television set in their bedroom, and are more likely to eat meals with the TV on.

Centrality of television also varies by family composition. Compared to two-parent families, children in single-parent homes spend more time watching TV, are more likely to eat meals with the TV on, are more likely to have a TV in the bedroom, and are less likely to have rules regarding television use (Woodard & Gridina, 2000). These patterns suggest that in homes with less parental assistance, television gets used more for babysitting and for companionship.

Media and Other Activities

Children as well as adults rarely pay full attention to the television when it is on (Schmitt, Anderson, & Collins, 1999). Viewers get distracted, engage in conversation, and multi-task.

In one national survey, four in ten (40 percent) children reported doing "something else" while watching TV, including using other media (Roberts et al., 2005). In another study, video cameras were installed in the homes of 106 families to observe viewing behaviors over a ten-day period (Schmitt, Woolf, & Anderson, 2003). The researchers found that 46 percent of all viewing time was spent engaged in some additional activity. Social interaction was the most common concurrent activity for all ages, dispelling the myth that television prevents families from having conversation. Children most often talked with siblings, though when they conversed with an adult it was more often the mother than the father. Among children, playing and eating were the next most common activities. For adults, reading and doing chores were the next most common, with women more likely than men to do household duties while viewing. The researchers also observed a fair amount of cuddling while viewing, especially between parents and young children.

Nevertheless, TV can hamper interaction, especially during meals. Martini (1996) video-taped 59 Japanese American and Caucasian families while they ate dinner. Nearly half of the Japanese American families regularly had the TV set turned on during the evening meal. When the TV was on, family members often sat facing the set rather than each other, and they also moved about the room quite often during the meal. Furthermore, these families generally conversed less often than did Caucasian families, most of whom did not have the TV on during dinner. The nature of the talk differed too. Japanese American families talked more about television and about activities they were doing while they ate, whereas Caucasian families talked more about events that had occurred during the day, emotions they were experiencing, and abstract topics involving the physical and social world.

Having the television on during meal times not only constrains talk, but also has health implications. Children are less likely to consume healthy foods and more likely to consume snacks while watching television compared to doing other activities (Matheson, Killen, Wang, Varady, & Robinson, 2004). These patterns are exacerbated when families watch television during mealtimes (Coon, Goldberg, Rogers, & Tucker, 2001). Moreover, a longitudinal study found that children who watched more TV during kindergarten and first grade and who ate fewer meals with their family were significantly more likely to be overweight in the third grade, even after controlling for sex, race, and family socioeconomic status (Gable, Chang, & Krull, 2007).

Clearly, American families today spend a great deal of time with the media, especially television. Adults and children negotiate how central television is in daily life, where to locate the technology in the home, and how to integrate television and other media with household activities like eating meals. Terms such as "electronic hearth" and "electronic babysitter" reveal just how pivotal television is in family life. The next section explores the impact of the media on family life.

The Impact of the Media on Family Communication

The sheer amount of time families spend with television means that the medium itself shapes and defines the context in which family interaction often occurs. Based on his ethnographic research in homes, Lull (1988) argued that, "Television viewing and talk about television are extensions of nearly all forms of interpersonal communication that take place between family members" (p. 246). This section will explore how the media contextualize and impact family interaction as well as power within the family system.

Expectations About Family Life

Family members certainly learn about families from their own experiences, but they also can develop ideas from the media, particularly television. According to cultivation theory (Gerbner, Gross, Morgan, & Signorielli, 1994), television is a centralized cultural story-teller that conveys a consistent set of images and representations of the world. These ritualized messages steadily and repeatedly shower viewers with a socially constructed view of reality (Gerbner, et al., 1994). In support of the theory, a great deal of evidence indicates that compared to light viewers, heavy viewers believe there is more violence in the world and are more frightened of being victims of that violence (see Morgan & Shanahan, 1996).

Television presents a fairly formulaic view of families too. For example, TV families featured in prime time are frequently headed by two parents (Robinson & Skill, 2001), with only the father employed outside the home (Heintz-Knowles, 2001). Even programs targeted to children underrepresent the proportion of single-parent homes compared to U.S. population statistics (Callister, Robinson, & Clark, 2007). Television also provides a fairly limited view of families of color. African American families are featured more often now than in the early days of television, but they are still relatively rare (Robinson & Skill, 2001). Furthermore, Latino, Asian American, and Native American families are almost nonexistent on television (Douglas, 2003).

Perhaps more important than the form of TV families is what they do when on the screen. Television parents exhibit fairly traditional gender roles. For instance, mothers are more likely to be expressive and nurturing with children, whereas fathers are more likely to be directive and decisive (Douglas, 2003). In addition, family interactions on TV are characterized primarily by mutual affection and cooperation (Callister & Robinson, 2010) and problems get solved easily (Weiss & Wilson, 1996). One study found that very few episodes of family programming depicted instances of conflict between work and family, and rarely was this conflict the central story line (Heintz-Knowles, 2001). This pattern contrasts markedly with real life, where dual-earner families are on the rise and report experiencing great stress in trying to balance work with home (Jacobs & Gerson, 2001).

Such images can cultivate ideas about family life. For instance, in one study of over 600 fourth, sixth, and eight graders, children who frequently viewed family shows were more likely to believe that real-life families are supportive and compliant than were those who seldom watched such programs (Buerkel-Rothfuss, Greenberg, Atkin, & Neuendorf, 1982). These relationships held up even after controlling for grade level, sex, race, socioeconomic status, number of siblings, and total amount of TV viewing. Moreover, the relationships were strongest among children who perceived television as realistic and who reported that they learned about families from TV. Notably, exposure to family shows was not related to beliefs about how much real-life families ignore or yell at each other, which is consistent with the overall affiliative nature of such content.

In another study, Heintz (1992) surveyed 381 children between the ages of 7 and 13 about television and about their views of families. Roughly 50 percent of the children reported learning "most of the things I know" about how kids interact with parents, as well as how siblings act toward each other, from TV. Indeed, young children's personal experiences with families are often limited to their own household and a few neighbors and friends. Consistent with this social learning from television, Heintz (1992) found a high degree of similarity between children's descriptions of real-life families and their descriptions of TV families. Most families were characterized as happy, helpful, nice, and cohesive, though TV families were seen as funnier than real-life families. Heintz (1992) also found that children from single-parent homes gave more negative descriptions of both real and TV fathers than did children from two-parent homes. This finding supports the idea that people form generalized mental impressions or schemas that are derived from exemplars in real life as well as in the media (Shrum, 2009). According to principles of heuristic processing, heavy television viewers are prone to rely on mental shortcuts derived from TV when making judgments about the world (Shrum, 2009).

The correlational patterns described above are bolstered by one experimental study of children's reactions to family sitcoms. Weiss and Wilson (1998) exposed elementary schoolers to an episode of *Full House* in which a child character experienced a negative emotional event in the family (e.g., a bicycle accident with an uncle). Among children who perceived the sitcom as realistic, exposure to the episode altered their perceptions of comparable emotional events in real life. In other words, a single family show had an impact on children's judgments about family events in the real world.

Adolescents also show evidence of cultivation from media exposure. In a national survey of over 3,000 high schoolers, heavy viewers of TV were more likely than light viewers to say that they wanted to get married, that they would stay married to the same person for life, and that they would have children (Signorielli, 1991). In another study, teens who frequently watched soap operas expressed fairly unrealistic views about single mothers (Larson, 1996). Compared to nonviewers, viewers were more likely to believe that single mothers have good jobs and are well-educated, do not live in poverty, and have babies who are as healthy as most babies. Young people who frequently view soap operas also are more likely to believe that marriages are fragile, that a greater proportion of people are divorced, and that a higher proportion of married people have illegitimate children and extramarital affairs (Buerkel-Rothfuss & Mayes 1981). In contrast to soap operas, other media content may foster traditional views of family life. For example, teens who are frequent viewers of family-centered TV programs are more likely than light viewers to believe that mothers should be devoted to caring for children and in charge of the household (Ex, Janssens, & Korzilius, 2002).

Overall, then, there is consistent evidence that heavy exposure to the media is associated with particular and often unrealistic views of marriage and family. Yet despite the use of multiple controls, most evidence to date is correlational so it is difficult to assert causality. The most likely scenario is that particularly for youth, the media together with personal experiences contribute to the development of schemas about the family. Once established, those schemas affect how individuals interpret and respond to subsequent encounters with fictional families in the media (Heintz, 1992). These schemas also are likely to affect how individuals respond to their own families in real life. As an example, several married adults in one focus group study reported paying close attention to relationships on television and comparing those fictional examples to their own marriages (Gantz, 2001). They also reported having tried conflict resolution strategies they had seen on television in their own relationships. Such findings support the idea that television is a major source of socialization about the family.

Media and Family Interaction

Most of the research on the impact of media on family interaction has centered on television, which is more likely to be a shared activity than is reading a book or surfing the Internet. Yet families differ greatly as to how much TV they actually watch together (Lull, 1980a). Obviously, individuals are less likely to view programs together when there are multiple TV sets in the home. In addition, studies indicate that younger children are more likely to watch TV with parents than are older children (Roberts et al., 1999), children generally watch more often with siblings than with parents (Lawrence & Wozniak, 1989), and children are more likely to coview with a parent when they watch adult-oriented programs than when they watch child-oriented programs (St. Peters, Fitch, Huston, Wright, & Eakins, 1991).

When coviewing does occur, television has the potential to enhance family interaction in several ways. At a minimum, it brings families together into a shared social space and can foster a feeling of togetherness (Lull, 1990). In one survey, 59 percent of married adults reported that television provided an opportunity to spend time with their spouses (Gantz, 1985). Research also indicates that youth who are frequent viewers of TV spend more overall time with families (Rideout et al., 2010) and report more positive effect for family members (Larson & Kubey, 1983) than do light viewers.

Television also provides stories, topics, and jokes to stimulate conversation in families (Lull, 1990). In some cases, certain types of programs can provide a reference point for parents to use in discussing sensitive or complex topics with children (Kaiser Family Foundation and Children Now, 1996). In other cases, children themselves can use television to stimulate talk. In one observational study, Reid and Frazer (1980) found that children used commercials to initiate conversation with parents about ambiguous advertising techniques as well as about topics unrelated to advertising. A recent experiment found that certain infant-directed videos actually can promote parent–child talk. In the study, parents who watched *Sesame Beginnings*, which models parent–child interaction, for two weeks at home with their infants spent significantly more time talking and singing with their infant during a free-play session in the lab than did parents who watched non-instructional videos or no videos at all (Pempek, Demers, Hanson, Kirkorian & Anderson, 2011). Even married couples can find television to be a conversational stimulant. Fallis, Fitzpatrick, and Friestad (1985) found that among adults who were classified as emotionally distant from their spouses, TV viewing was positively associated with a greater tendency to discuss relational and family issues in the marriage.

Also on the positive side, television can enrich nonverbal interaction in families. In one study, Brody, Stoneman, and Sanders (1980) observed preschoolers for 20 minutes with their parents, half the time while watching TV and half the time during family play. The researchers found a dramatic increase in physical contact between parents and the child while watching TV as compared to playing. However, fathers in particular were less likely to look at their child when the TV set was on rather than off. Other studies have documented that family members often sit close together (Schmitt, Woolf, & Anderson, 2003) and even physically comfort each other while watching television (Wilson & Weiss, 1993).

Despite these potential positive effects, there is no doubt that television can hinder talk too. The same study by Brody et al. (1980) that found an increase in touching when the TV was turned on also found a decrease in verbal interaction between parents and preschoolers. Even parental talk with babies is affected by television. One study found that when parents watched television or DVDs with their infants, they talked less to their offspring than when the television was turned off (Pempek et al., 2011). A recent experiment showed that even background television can reduce the communication between parents and infants (Kirkorian et al., 2009).

Indirectly, television can have broader effects on very young children's language development. In a recent longitudinal study, Christakis and his colleagues (2009) had a sample of over 300 babies (2–48 months) wear a digital recorder on random days for a two-year period. The researchers found that television exposure was associated with reductions over time in child vocalizations and conversational turns as well in the number of words that the child heard from an adult. In a similar study by the same researchers, the number of conversational turns that young children had with an adult caretaker predicted increased language development six months later (Zimmerman et al., 2009). Furthermore, having the television on in a room reduced the number of conversation turns.

Even when television programming is designed to be "educational," infants seem to learn better from face-to-face-communication. In one recent study, 12- to 18-month olds watched popular baby videos for four weeks at home, either with or without parental interaction during the programming (DeLoache et al., 2010). Afterward, they were tested on 25 vocabulary words featured in the videos. Compared to a no-video control group, neither of the video conditions improved vocabulary. Moreover, a fourth condition involving just parental instruction on the 25 words outperformed both video groups. Other research confirms that infants learn to imitate simple behaviors more easily from live interaction than from watching a model on the screen (Hayne et al., 2003). All in all, having a television turned on for long periods of time in households with very young children may be detrimental to infant development.

Irrespective of age, reduction in human interaction will occur any time attention is drawn to the screen and away from other people in the room. Therefore, scholars need to take an expansive view of verbal interaction, looking at talk that occurs not only during a program but also during commercial breaks and once a program is over. In some cases, television may have its greatest impact on interaction outside the viewing context altogether (Alexander, 2001), where it may be used to establish common ground, initiate conversations, and even debate popular culture.

Rather than increasing or decreasing conversation, television may be used in some families to avoid talk altogether. Rosenblatt and Cunningham (1976) found that television viewing was positively related to family tension, even after controlling for socio-economic status, number of people in the household, and whether the family was headed by one or two parents. The researchers also found that TV viewing was higher in homes with greater population density (persons per room), suggesting that the media may provide a way to head off stress associated with overcrowding. Television can be used to cope with other family tensions as well. One study found that children with alcoholic fathers watched more television than did children whose fathers drank moderately or not at all (Brooks, Gaines, Mueller, & Jenkins, 1998). Other studies have documented that children in high stress environments are likely to be heavy viewers of television (Henggeler, Cohen, Edwards, Summerville, & Ray, 1991).

Clearly, television has mixed effects on family interaction. What about newer technologies such as cell phones and the Internet? A national survey of over 2,000 adults reveals that the picture is mixed here too (Kennedy, Smith, Wells, & Wellman, 2008). Married couples who both owned cell phones reported that they contacted their spouse on a daily basis to chat and to coordinate schedules more often than did couples with no cell phones. In addition, parents reported more daily contact with their child if they owned a cell phone compared to a landline. Furthermore, one in four (25 percent) respondents felt that their family today was closer than their childhood family because of the Internet and cell phones. Still, most respondents (60 percent) reported no impact of these technologies on the closeness of their families. On the negative side, families with high levels of technology were less likely to eat dinner together and more likely to feel dissatisfied with the amount of time they spent together. It is difficult to draw causal conclusions here, especially given that technology ownership also was associated with longer work hours.

Other studies confirm these mixed patterns. In an in-depth study of Dutch families, Christensen (2009) found that cell phones helped busy, spatially dispersed families feel a "connected presence" through the use of frequent calls and text messages. The Internet may be different, however. Nie, Hillygus, and Erbring (2002) found that adults who spent more time with the Internet, particularly at home and on the weekends, spent less time in face-to-face interaction with family members. Supporting this idea, a survey of over 200 fourth through sixth grade Korean children found that greater use of the Internet was related to a perceived decline in family time (Lee & Chae, 2007). Moreover, time spent playing games online was correlated with a perceived decline in both family time and family talk.

To summarize, media serve a variety of social functions in the family. They can help bring families together or they can keep them apart. Likewise, media can facilitate the expression of ideas and be used as the basis for talk or they can be used to avoid conversation. Future studies need to move beyond descriptive data and begin to delineate the conditions under which television and newer media serve these very different purposes. Do crises such as divorce or substance abuse alter the role of media in family interactions? Do family life cycles impact how media are used? For example, is television used differently when a child is born or when a family member retires? Addressing such questions will guide us toward a more integrated understanding of the social impact of media use on the family.

Conflict Over the Media

Family conflict occurs over a variety of issues, including the media. For example, two family members simultaneously may want to use a piece of technology that is designed for individual use. Even when media technology can be shared, family members may disagree on what to listen to or watch. Buying additional equipment and moving older technologies to children's bedrooms is one way to reduce family conflict over access to the media. Yet even in homes with multiple televisions, families still can have preferences for certain sets because of location or advanced capabilities (Lull, 1978).

How often do the media cause conflict in families? Several scholars have looked at marital conflict in particular as it relates to the media. In one study, Gantz (2001) conducted a series of focus groups, intensive interviews, and a survey to further explore marital conflict over television. In the survey portion, 145 adults were asked how often several potentially problematic behaviors regarding TV had occurred in their household. The vast majority acknowledged that in the past year television had interfered with a shared marital activity, prevented someone from doing household chores, and interfered with a conversation one spouse was trying to have with the other spouse. Women reported being more bothered than men by these disruptions, yet the overall ratings were low, suggesting that TV was not perceived as much of a problem in these marriages. The focus groups and interviews further revealed that couples did sometimes disagree on what to watch and on the volume level of television, but that none of these conflicts were considered serious and that they were easily resolved by using separate TV sets or by leaving the room to pursue other activities. Although Gantz (2001) found a great deal of partner accommodation and flexibility regarding media habits, he acknowledged that such adaptation may be less common in seriously troubled marriages and in crowded households with limited technology.

One way families can make adjustments is to establish informal or formal rules about control of the media. For example, fathers consistently are perceived by other family members as having the most influence in selecting TV programs to watch (Lull, 1978). Adult males in families also typically dominate the remote control device (Gantz, 2001). Even among gay couples, there is typically a dominant remote control user, although lesbian couples are more likely to share the device (Walker, 1996).

Patterns of control can be challenged, however. Gantz (2001) has documented that marital battles do occur over the remote control device. In particular, women complain that men engage in too much grazing (i.e., flipping from channel to channel) and often change the channel during inopportune times in a program. Yet in the end, women seldom take charge of the remote control; instead they are more likely to move to another TV set if remote control behaviors become too annoying (Walker, 1996).

Power and control are seldom equal in parent–child relationships either. Children are far less influential than their parents in determining what families view on TV (Lull, 1978). In accord with this, children report being less satisfied than parents with the way their families make decisions about television (Lull, 1982). Even teens struggle with control issues. In one study, 37 percent of adolescents reported that they argue with their parents over TV at least once in awhile (Morgan, Alexander, Shanahan, & Harris, 1990).

Children also can disagree with each other over the media. In the study by Morgan and his colleagues (1990) mentioned above, a substantially higher proportion of teens reported arguing about television with siblings (60 percent) than with parents (37 percent). It stands to reason that sibling conflict may be greater given that children are more likely to watch TV with a brother or sister than a parent (Roberts et al., 1999). But even here, there is a "pecking order"; older siblings typically dominate over younger siblings in disagreements about program selections (Zahn & Baran, 1984).

Not only does program selection cause difficulties, but particular types of messages in the media can instigate family conflict as well. For example, research indicates that exposure to TV advertising can result in parent–child friction (e.g., Buijzen & Valkenburg, 2003). In one study, preschoolers who were randomly assigned to view a cartoon containing six food commercials engaged in significantly more attempts to get a parent to purchase products during a subsequent grocery store visit than did preschoolers who had seen the same cartoon without ads in it (Stoneman & Brody, 1981). Furthermore, mothers of the preschoolers who had seen the ads engaged in substantially more control strategies during the shopping trip, such as telling the child "no" and encouraging the child to put items back on the shelf.

Newer technologies, such as cell phones, also can trigger family disputes. Lenhart and her colleagues (2010) found that teens' attachment to their phones is a source of conflict and regulation for parents. Indeed, a majority of parents surveyed by the researchers reported that they attempt to regulate their teen's cell phone use by either checking the content of the phone (64 percent), limiting the times of day a child can use the cell (52 percent), or even taking the phone away from the teen as a form of punishment (62 percent). Although most teens agreed that the cell phone kept them linked to family, some reported feeling suffocated by the constant connectivity to their parents. Computer and Internet use also can be a point of contention within modern families. Much like cell phone use, many parents try to monitor their children's computer activities. One national survey of 800 parent and teen dyads found that a majority of adolescents (60 percent) reported having rules about the Internet, which many felt were an impingement on their growing need for autonomy (Mesch, 2006). These rules were related to family conflict about Internet use, which occurred among 40 percent of those surveyed. Furthermore, conflict about adolescents' use of the Internet occurred more frequently in families where the child was perceived as the computer expert.

Based on research reviewed here, it is clear that television and other media can instigate conflict among family members. In most families, disagreements over how to use the media are perceived as fairly manageable and even predictable. In general, the same power differentials that exist in other family routines get played out in front of the television screen. Some of this conflict can be alleviated by having additional TV sets and private media spaces in the home. But future research should examine how families with fewer resources as well as those with high degrees of conflict cope with the media. In addition, studies need to explore how disagreements about content and equipment get resolved, especially as media technologies become increasingly personal and interactive.

The Impact of the Family on Media Experiences

Up to this point, we have considered ways in which the media influence, transform, and provide a context for family communication. But the family itself also impacts people's media experiences. Families have different values and communication styles, which in turn affect how children use the media. In addition, parents differ greatly as to how often and in what ways they help their children deal with media. Each of these topics will be considered below.

Family Communication Patterns

Early work by Chaffee and McLeod revealed that parents have different values regarding communication that they teach and reinforce during child rearing (McLeod, Atkin, & Chaffee, 1972). Some parents are socio-oriented in that they emphasize harmony, conformity, and getting along with others. Other parents are concept-oriented because they encourage expression of ideas, critical thinking, and open debate of opinions. Chaffee and McLeod devised the Family Communication Patterns (FCP) typology whereby families could fit into one of four quadrants based on whether they score low or high on these two orientations.

The typology has spawned a great deal of research, much of which indicates that the norms of communication in a family can predict a great deal about media habits. For example, socio-oriented families watch more television overall but consume less news in the media than do concept-oriented families (Lull, 1980b). Socio-oriented individuals are more likely to use TV for social purposes like family solidarity, companionship, and having conversation (Lull, 1980b). Consistent with these social motives, adolescents from socio-oriented families tend to share viewing patterns with their parents more so than do teens in families where this orientation is weak (Chaffee & Tims, 1976). In contrast, concept-oriented families perceive television as a way to instill values and facilitate arguments, reflecting their overall emphasis on ideas rather than people (Lull, 1980b). As might be expected, concept orientation is positively associated with adolescents' interest in politics, discussion about political issues, and attention to political campaigns (Chaffee & Tims, 1976).

The dimensions also are predictive of what parents do *while* viewing television with children. Fujikola and Austin (2002) surveyed over 200 parents of third, sixth, and ninth graders and found that concept-oriented parents were more likely to critique TV messages and talk about television content with their children than were socio-oriented parents. In contrast, socio-oriented parents were more likely to coview or watch TV with their children. Recent research suggests that family communication styles may even buffer some of the negative effects of the media. In a survey of 360 parent–child dyads, Buijzen and Valkenburg (2005) assessed children's television viewing habits, their consumer behaviors, and family communication. The researchers found that concept-oriented communication moderated (and weakened) the relationship between exposure to advertising and children's purchase requests and materialism as well as parent–child conflict. Socio-communication had no such moderating effect. The researchers argued that parents who discuss consumer decision making and encourage independent thinking help arm their children against persuasive advertising compared to parents who encourage conformity.

Although the FCP dimensions have been used widely in media research, they have not been immune to critique. Ritchie and Fitzpatrick (1990) challenged the assumption that norms of communication are widely shared within a family. They found considerable within-family variation when surveying each parent separately as well as the children, suggesting a more complex model of family norms and patterns of interaction. In addition, the longstanding interpretation of the two dimensions has been questioned. Ritchie (1991), for example, found evidence that socio-orientation is actually associated with parental assertion of power and control, which often produces congruency rather than harmony, whereas concept-orientation is associated with supportive and open communication. This revised interpretation coalesces with research indicating that families high in concept orientation, not socio-orientation, exhibit more warmth and affection (Krcmar, 1996). The revised dimensions also parallel a large body of research in child development that characterizes parenting styles in terms of both affection and control (Demo & Cox, 2000).

To summarize, family communication patterns clearly affect the amount of time spent with the media as well as preferences for certain types of content. The FCP model has dominated the research in this area for the past 25 years, but has been challenged on both conceptual and methodological grounds. Future studies should look more closely at the extent to which family members agree on communication norms and values, and also the extent to which these particular dimensions are valid across families that differ by race and ethnicity, composition, income, and even size.

Family Mediation

There is little doubt that extensive exposure to the media, particularly television, can result in harmful effects on children such as increasing aggression, causing fear reactions, and teaching stereotypes (see Strasburger, Wilson, & Jordan, 2009). Given that TV is difficult to avoid, considerable interest has been given to ways in which adults can "mediate" or alter a child's viewing experiences. The goal of mediation typically is to prevent antisocial outcomes from media exposure, but mediation also can be used to enhance positive effects such as learning from educational programming (e.g., Corder-Bolz, 1980). Over the past few decades, researchers have used the term "mediation" to refer to a host of different activities, resulting in conceptual confusion in the literature (Nathanson, 2001a). Today, most researchers agree that there are three major forms of mediation: instructive mediation, restrictive mediation, and coviewing (e.g., Borzekowski & Robinson, 2007).

Instructive mediation refers to discussions that parents or other adults have with children about television and other media. The goal typically is to explain content or evaluate it in some way. Restrictive mediation refers to rules that parents set about how much time and what types of content children are permitted to experience with TV and in other media. Coviewing is the most elusive form of mediation to define. At a minimum, coviewing refers to those occasions in which parents watch television with their child. However, conversation can occur during this coviewing which, if it pertains to TV, also entails elements of instructive mediation. Still, coviewing can occur without talk, and instructive mediation can occur outside of coviewing. Thus, researchers argue that the two forms of mediation should be kept conceptually and methodologically distinct (e.g., Nathanson, 2001a).

Frequency of Mediation

The amount of mediation that occurs in families is typically measured through self-report data. Not surprisingly, parents' reports of how often they engage in mediation often differ from those of children. For example, 62 percent of American parents report having rules that govern their children's television viewing (Stanger & Gridina, 1999), yet in a national survey of children themselves, only 46 percent report that there are rules about what they can watch on TV, and that figure drops to 26 percent among children over the age of 14 (Rideout et al., 2010). Such discrepancies emerge even when parents and children from the same families are queried (Vittrup, 2009). Part of the discrepancy presumably is due to social desirability on the part of parents. Yet it is also the case that children may be unaware of certain mediation efforts, like rules, unless they are explicitly stated by parents. In addition, discussions about the media that occur outside the context of exposure may go unnoticed by children and even by parents themselves. Clearly, researchers need to make efforts to validate self-reports of mediation through the use of observational techniques in the home and even alternative self-report measures such as diaries.

Despite differing views on the frequency of mediation, both parents and children seem to recognize that the Internet is different than more traditional media. In a recent national survey, children between the ages of 8 and 18 more often reported that they have rules about what they are allowed to do on the computer than about what they can watch on TV, what music they can listen to, or what videogames they can play (Rideout et al., 2010). Indeed, a majority of parents say that they mediate their children's use of the Internet in some way (Livingstone & Helsper, 2008). This parental intervention is certainly fueled by concerns over children talking with strangers (Peter et al., 2006) and revealing personal information (Lenhart, Madden, & Hitlin, 2005) online.

The logistics of such mediation are complicated by the fact that youth are often more adept at using the Internet than their parents are (Livingstone & Helsper, 2008). Nevertheless, parents have devised several methods for helping children navigate the Internet and often these tactics are adaptations from TV mediation (Warren & Bluma, 2002). One common approach is to use some form of restrictive mediation (Eastin, Greenberg, & Hofschire, 2006), which typically involves setting rules about when and for how long children can go online. Other strategies include purchasing blocking software that prevents children from visiting particular websites and setting computers up in public spaces in the home to monitor what children are doing online (Cottrell et al., 2007). Despite a plethora of popular software products, technological restriction is the least utilized tactic among parents (Cottrell, et al., 2007).

Although less prevalent than restrictive mediation, parents also report that they "co-use" or "co-surf" the Internet with their children (Livingstone & Helsper, 2008). Much like coviewing television, co-use of the Internet does not necessarily mean that parents talk to their children about the websites. However, research suggests that some parents do engage in instructive mediation by discussing particular websites with children, providing both positive and negative evaluations of the content (Livingstone & Helsper, 2008). Even here, though, parents and children differ in their perception of how often this type of mediation occurs. In one study, slightly over half of parents (52 percent) reported that they have conversations with their teenager about inappropriate websites whereas only 20 percent of their adolescents reported having such discussions (Cottrell et al., 2007).

Parents apply the same three types of mediation to video game play as they do to TV viewing and Internet use (Nikken & Jansz, 2006). A study of 500 Dutch parent–child dyads found that parents most often employ restrictive mediation by specifying which games can be played and which are forbidden, and by monitoring gaming behavior (Nikken & Jansz, 2006). The second most used strategy is active mediation, which entails telling children that games are just fantasy, pointing out good and bad things about the game, and explaining what happens in a game. Parents are least likely to use co-play, or playing the video game with their child, as a form of mediation.

Predictors of Mediation

Some parents mediate a great deal, whereas others do very little to intervene in their children's media habits (Austin et al., 1999). Several factors consistently emerge as predictors of parental mediation. One is the age of the child. Parents are far more likely to prohibit the viewing of certain TV programs, control the overall amount of viewing, and discuss television with younger than with older children (Warren et al., 2002). Research indicates that younger children are more susceptible to the harmful effects of television (Paik & Comstock, 1994), so it is encouraging that parents are exercising greater intervention with younger viewers. Coviewing, on the other hand, does not seem to be consistently related to age (Dorr, Kovaric, & Doubleday, 1989; Nathanson, 2001b). Age of the child not only predicts television mediation but also Internet monitoring. Several recent studies indicate that parents mediate the Internet more often with younger children than with older children or teens (Livingstone & Helsper, 2008; Wang, Bianchi & Raley, 2005).

Another predictor of mediation is parental attitudes toward the media. Studies show that parents who are concerned about the harmful effects of television, particularly of violent and frightening content, engage in more restrictive as well as instructive mediation with their children (e.g., Warren et al., 2002). Moreover, parents who are less trusting of TV advertising report more often discussing the unreal nature of commercials and of television in general with their children (Austin et al., 1999). Likewise, parents who perceive that videogames have a negative effect on children are more inclined to use restrictive and active mediation (Nikken & Jansz, 2006). On the other hand, parents who believe that television can teach positive lessons about the world are more likely to coview or simply watch TV with their children than are parents who do not hold this view (Nathanson, 2001b). Similarly, parents who perceive that videogames can have a positive effect on children's social and emotional well-being are more likely to co-play with their offspring than are other parents (Nikken & Jansz, 2006).

Parental demographics are less useful in predicting mediation, in part because of inconsistencies in the findings. For example, some studies have found that mothers more often engage in mediation with television (Valkenburg et al., 1998) and with video games (Nikken & Jansz, 2006) than fathers do. Yet others have found that sex of the parent does not predict mediation (Warren et al., 2002). Still others, particularly those that focus on the Internet, have found that mediation occurs more often with fathers than with mothers (e.g., Wang et al., 2005). Employment outside the home seems to curtail mediation (Warren, 2005), which may partly account for divergent findings by parent sex across studies. Also, some studies suggest that parents who are highly educated are more likely to set rules about television and to discuss TV with their children (e.g., Borzekowski & Robinson, 2007), whereas others find no relationship between parent education and such mediation efforts (e.g., Warren et al., 2002). Looking beyond demographics, Warren and his colleagues examined level of parental involvement as a predictor of mediation (Warren et al., 2002). They found that parents who share domestic activities like schoolwork and household projects with their children are more likely to engage in all three forms of mediation (instructive, restrictive, and coviewing). In fact, shared activities were better predictors of mediation than was the sheer amount of time parents spent with children in the home.

Parenting style also seems to predict mediation approaches. Eastin and his colleagues (2006) surveyed 520 mothers about Internet monitoring of their teens. They found that mothers who used an authoritative parenting style (i.e., assertive but supportive) were more likely to engage in both instructive and restrictive Internet mediation than were those who used authoritarian (i.e., demanding but not supportive) or neglectful (neither demanding nor supportive) styles. Even co-use or coviewing of websites with teens occurred more often with authoritative mothers.

Finally, the extent of technology in the home seems to affect mediation. For example, as the number of television sets increase, there is less parental control over what children watch and when (van der Voort et al., 1992). Parental sophistication with technology also matters (Livingstone & Helsper, 2008). One study of 749 parent–teen dyads found that Internet-experienced parents were more likely to install monitoring software as well as check the websites their children visited than were other parents (Wang et al., 2005).

Impact of Mediation

Most research on the impact of mediation has concentrated on instructive strategies that involve talking with a child about media content. For example, laboratory studies indicate that watching with an adult who asks questions and provides information can increase preschoolers' learning from educational programs such as *Sesame Street* (Corder-Bolz, 1980). Experiments suggest that adult commentary about television can also help children to better recall and understand program content (Valkenburg et al., 1998; Watkins, Calvert, Huston-Stein, & Wright, 1980). Most of these studies involve single interventions with adult mediators who are not the children's parents. However, several correlational studies have looked at the impact of ongoing efforts by parents themselves. In one study, parental conversation about TV was related to a better understanding of how unrealistic television is among children (Messaris & Kerr, 1983). Another study tracked kindergartners and first graders and found that early parental discussion of TV predicted higher comprehension of content and greater ability to discriminate reality from fantasy one year later (Singer, Singer, Desmond, Hirsch, & Nicol, 1988).

Clearly, parental discussion can boost children's learning from television. It may also impact learning from computers. One study of 200 Korean fourth through sixth graders found that parental discussion and endorsement of good websites as well as co-use of the Internet predicted an increase in children's self-reported use of the Internet for educational purposes (Lee & Chae, 2007).

Instructive mediation also can prevent harmful effects from occurring. Watching with an adult who comments on the unrealistic nature of TV can reduce children's fear reactions to scary programming (Cantor, Sparks, & Hoffner, 1988; Wilson & Weiss, 1991). Moreover, hearing a parent or an adult make negative evaluations about TV violence can reduce children's approval of interpersonal aggression (Corder-Bolz, 1980) and decrease their tendency to act aggressively after viewing such material (Nathanson, 1999). An adult who simply encourages a child to think about the victim of violence can encourage more critical attitudes toward TV content and even decrease the tendency to engage in aggression afterward (Nathanson & Cantor, 2000). Moreover, parents who discuss and evaluate advertising can help children resist persuasive appeals in commercials (Buijzen & Valkenburg, 2005). Finally, adult commentary about gender stereotypes on television can encourage children to be more critical of such content and even reduce stereotyped attitudes in some cases (Nathanson, 2010).

Less research has been conducted on the impact of restrictive mediation. In general, children who watch excessive amounts of television are at greater risk for a variety of harmful outcomes (see Strasburger, Wilson, & Jordan, 2009), so that any effort to monitor and control children's viewing is likely to offset these patterns. In fact, Robinson and his colleagues found that a six-month classroom intervention to reduce television and videogame use among third and fourth graders significantly decreased their aggressive behavior (Robinson, Wilde, Navracruz, Haydel, & Varady, 2001), requests for toys (Robinson, Saphir, Kraemer, Varady, & Haydel, 2001), and even body fat levels (Robinson, 1999). Beyond school, parental regulation can produce similar beneficial outcomes (Nathanson, 1999).

Parental rules can be effective in managing the Internet too. Livingstone and Helsper (2008) surveyed over 800 U.K. teens and their parents about Internet mediation in the home. Overall, parental rules about the Internet were associated with a lower likelihood that adolescents engaged in a variety of potentially risky activities online, such as visiting chat rooms and downloading software. These patterns held up regardless of whether rulemaking was measured using the parents' or the children's reports. However, having rules about the Internet had no impact on teens' self-reported exposure to risky content (e.g., violent, pornographic, stranger interaction) on the Internet. A similar study found that parental monitoring of the Internet was associated with teens engaging in less disapproved behavior online, but only when the youth were aware of their parents' mediation efforts (Cottrell et al., 2007). All in all, restrictive mediation seems to work best with youth when it is not so prohibitive that it creates a "forbidden fruit" type of effect (Bushman & Cantor, 2003; Livingstone & Helsper, 2008) and when the restrictions are presented in the context of open and supportive parent–child communication (Cottrell et al., 2007).

The third form of mediation, coviewing or co-using, is more difficult to ascertain because it sometimes includes discussion of the content as well. Those studies that isolate mere viewing from instructive mediation suggest that coviewing by itself does not necessarily help children become more sophisticated viewers (Dorr et al., 1989) nor does it prevent children from learning aggressive attitudes and behaviors from TV (Nathanson, 1999). In fact, coviewing a violent program with a parent can be interpreted by the child as an endorsement of such content (Nathanson, 2001b). Likewise, a recent study found that co-playing *age-inappropriate* videogames with a parent was associated with increased depression and anxiety among adolescent girls (Coyne, Padilla-Walker, Stockdale, & Day, 2011). On the other hand, playing age-appropriate games with a parent predicted positive outcomes such as decreased aggression and increased prosocial behavior in girls. Yet these patterns were based on correlational data and none were observed among teen boys. Clearly, more work on the co-use of newer media is needed.

There is one arena in which coviewing can actually have a beneficial or therapeutic effect. Several studies suggest that watching with a parent can help a child feel less frightened during a scary program (see Cantor, 1998a). Notably, children who watch television with siblings instead of parents can also profit from coviewing. In one study, Wilson and Weiss (1993) found that watching with an older sibling reduced preschoolers' fear responses to a suspenseful movie scene. The sibling pairs often sought physical comfort from each other during the program, and the older sibling also verbally reassured the preschooler. However, watching with an older sibling actually reduced preschoolers' comprehension of the program, suggesting that coviewers sometimes can be distracting.

To summarize, families play a critical role in how children respond to media content. Parents who actively discuss and evaluate media messages with their children can increase the prosocial effects and also ameliorate some of the harmful effects of exposure. Setting limits and rules about exposure also can be beneficial, especially if such restrictions foster a more critical orientation to the media (Desmond, Singer & Singer, 1990). However, there is some evidence that extreme levels of restrictive mediation can backfire (Nathanson, 1999), which actually can result in heightened attraction to objectionable content (Cantor, 1998b). Merely watching programs, playing videogames, or surfing the Internet with children and not discussing the content seems like a missed opportunity for parents, particularly if these co-use experiences are perceived by children as an endorsement of the messages. Still, much of this research is based on what parents *say* they do. Future studies need to incorporate observational measures of ongoing interactions as families experience media together. Studies that have done this suggest that topics of conversation are rich and diverse, talk differs greatly as a function of the type of content involved, and both verbal and nonverbal interaction occurs in front of the screen (Brody et al., 1980; Schmitt et al., 2003; Wilson & Weiss, 1993).

Conclusions

The relationship between the media and family communication is complex and interdependent (Andreasen, 2001). Family life is organized and defined in part by media technologies, particularly television. From a family systems perspective, the media provide a useful framework for studying how families define themselves and create a socially constructed set of roles, values, and norms (Alexander, 2001). In turn, the family exercises influence over the media experiences of its members both inside and outside the home. Hence, there is a complicated set of pathways that connect these two institutions.

Several conclusions can be drawn from this chapter. First, the media strongly shape the rhythms of family life (Jordan, 1992). In many families, the architecture of the house, evening meals, and even conversations are structured around large-screen TV sets with accompanying audio-visual technology. But even in homes where television is less central, the newspaper and radio are often integral to adult routines, and books, DVDs, and even videogames are frequently part of children's bedtime rituals. As families structure their activities around the media, the technologies themselves become part of how family members negotiate their social reality. To capture these systemic relationships, researchers need to move beyond self-report data and observe families as they grapple with the media. Recording family interactions in the home, engaging in participant observation, and even using media diaries over time are all methods that have been under-utilized but that represent rich opportunities to address these issues.

Second, the media play an important role in shaping our beliefs and expectations about family life. Our views of the family come from a variety of sources of information, including personal experience. According to theorizing by Koerner and Fitzpatrick (2002), cognitive representations of the family include information about intimacy, affection, power, and even values regarding communication. These relational schemas are built over time and influence how people interpret and interact with members of their family. A child who spends a great deal of time alone in her bedroom watching television is likely to develop schemas about families that are fairly idealized. Is that child prone to disappointment and frustration when her own family life differs from these television ideals? Future research needs to consider the impact of both idealized and dysfunctional media images of the family on relational beliefs. Studies also need to explore the extent to which media in bedrooms can isolate children from other socializing forces, making parasocial relationships with media characters a potential substitute for the family itself.

Third, the nature of the family is undergoing rapid institutional change that is not often reflected in research. At present, we know a great deal about how middle-class, Caucasian families interact with the media. But we know very little about media experiences in families of color, single-parent families, gay and lesbian families, blended families, grandparent-headed families, dual-career families, and even adoptive families. The fact that African American families watch more television (Rideout et al., 2010) and that working-class families use television less ritualistically (Jordan, 1992) are signals that we need to be more sensitive to diversity among families when we study media habits and family communication.

The media too are undergoing change. Traditional forms of media are converging and interactive technologies are rapidly becoming the norm. Furthermore, digital technologies are making mediated experiences seem ever more realistic and life-like. It is clear too that family communication is being transformed as it is mediated increasingly by computers, cell phones, and other devices. What impact are these mobile technologies having on family closeness, conflict, and well-being? And as media use becomes increasingly personal and portable, how will parents monitor and mediate their children's exposure?

Finally, the vast majority of the studies to date are cross-sectional and often correlational. It is difficult to draw firm conclusions from such research about the factors that are responsible for variations in family communication and media use. Longitudinal studies of families are urgently needed in this arena. Such research can address how the media influence family communication over time as well as how changes in the structure of the family affect media habits and experiences. Longitudinal studies also can explore the impact of crises and different life cycles in the family on communication patterns and media use. In general, we need more sophisticated theories and methods to capture the complexities of how families of the 21st century are dealing with rapidly changing media technologies and content.

References

Alexander, A. (2001). The meaning of television in the American family. In J. Bryant & J. A. Bryant (Eds.), *Television and the American family*, 2nd edn (pp. 273–87). Mahwah, NJ: Lawrence Erlbaum Associates.

American Academy of Pediatrics (2011). Media use by children younger than 2 years. *Peadiatrics*, 128, 1040–45.

Andreasen, M. (2001). Evolution in the family's use of television: An overview. In J. Bryant & J. A. Bryant (Eds.), *Television and the American family*, 2nd edn (pp. 3–30). Mahwah, NJ: Lawrence Erlbaum Associates.

Austin, E. W., Bolls, P., Fujioka, Y., & Engelbertson, J. (1999). How and why parents take on the tube. *Journal of Broadcasting and Electronic Media*, 43, 175–92.

Borzekowski, D. L., & Robinson, T. N. (2007). Conversations, control, and couch-time: The assessment and stability of parental mediation styles and children's TV and video viewing. *Journal of Children and Media*, 1, 162–76.

Brody, G. H., Stoneman, Z., & Sanders, A. K. (1980). Effects of television viewing on family interactions: An observational study. *Family Relations*, 29, 216–20.

Brooks, P. H., Gaines, L. S., Mueller, R., & Jenkins, S. (1998). Children's television watching and their fathers' drinking practices. *Addiction Research*, 6, 27–34.

Buerkel-Rothfuss, N. L., & Mayes, S. (1981). Soap opera viewing: The cultivation effect. *Journal of Communication*, 31, 108–15.

Buerkel-Rothfuss, N. L., Greenberg, B. S., Atkin, C. K., & Neuendorf, K. (1982). Learning about the family from television. *Journal of Communication*, 32, 190–201.

Buijzen, M., & Valkenburg, P. M. (2003). The unintended effects of television advertising: A parent–child survey. *Communication Research*, 30, 483–503.

——(2005). Parental mediation of undesired advertising effects. *Journal of Broadcasting & Electronic Media*, 49, 153–65.

Bushman, B. J., & Cantor, J. (2003). Media ratings for violence and sex: Implications for policy makers and parents. *American Psychologist*, 58, 130–41.

Callister, M. A., & Robinson, T. (2010). Content analysis of physical affection within television families during the 2006–7 season of U.S. children's programming. *Journal of Children and Media*, 4, 155–73.

Callister, M. A., Robinson, T., & Clark, B. R. (2007). Media portrayals of the family in children's television programming during the 2005–6 season in the U.S. *Journal of Children and Media*, 1, 142–61.

Cantor, J. (1998a). *"Mommy, I'm scared": How TV and movies frighten children and what we can do to protect them*. New York: Harcourt Brace.

——(1998b). Ratings for program content: The role of research findings. In K. Jamieson (Ed.), *The Annals of the American Academy of Political and Social Science*, 557, 54–69.

Cantor, J., Sparks, G. G., & Hoffner, C. (1988). Calming children's television fears: Mr. Rogers vs. The Incredible Hulk. *Journal of Broadcasting and Electronic Media*, 32, 271–88.

Chaffee, S. H., & Tims, A. R. (1976). Interpersonal factors in adolescent television use. *Journal of Social Issues*, 32, 98–115.

Christakis, D. A., Gilkerson, J., Richards, J. A., Zimmerman, F. J., Garrison, M. M., Xu, D., Gray, S., & Yapanel, U. (2009). Audible television and decreased words, infant vocalizations, and conversational turns. *Archives of Pediatrics & Adolescent Medicine*, 162, 554–58.

Christensen, T. H. (2009). "Connected presence" in distributed family life. *New Media Society*, 11, 433–51.

Comstock, G., & Paik, H. (1991). *Television and the American child*. San Diego, CA: Academic Press.

Coon, K. A., Goldberg, J., Rogers, B. L., & Tucker, K. L. (2001). Relationships between use of television during meals and children's food consumption patterns. *Pediatrics*, 107, 167.

Corder-Bolz, C. R. (1980). Mediation: The role of significant others. *Journal of Communication*, 30, 106–18.

Cottrell, L., Branstetter, S., Cottrell, S., Rishel, C., & Stanton, B. F. (2007). Comparing adolescent and parent perceptions of current and future disapproved internet use. *Journal of Children and Media, 1*, 210–26.

Coyne, S. M., Padilla-Walker, L. M., Stockdale, L., & Day, R. D. (2011). Game on: Coplaying video games during adolescence. *Journal of Adolescent Health, 49*, 160–65.

DeLoache, J. S., Chiong, C., Sherman, K., Islam, N., Vanderborght, M., Troseth, G. L., Strouse, G. A., O'Doherty, K. (2010). Do babies learn from baby media? *Psychological Science, 21*, 1570–74.

Demo, D. H., & Cox, M. J. (2000). Families with young children: A review of research in the 1990s. *Journal of Marriage and the Family, 62*, 876–95.

Desmond, R. J., Singer, J. L., & Singer, D. G. (1990). Family mediation: Parental communication patterns and the influences of television on children. In J. Bryant (Ed.), *Television and the American family* (pp. 293–309). Hillsdale, NJ: Lawrence Erlbaum Associates.

Dorr, A., Kovaric, P., & Doubleday, C. (1989). Parent–child coviewing of television. *Journal of Broadcasting and Electronic Media, 33*, 35–51.

Douglas, W. (2003). *Television families: Is something wrong in suburbia?* Mahwah, NJ: Lawrence Erlbaum Associates.

Eastin, M. S., Greenberg, B. S., & Hofschire, L. (2006). Parenting the Internet. *Journal of Communication, 56*, 486–504.

Ex, C.T., Janssens, J, M., & Korzilius, H. P. (2002). Young females' images of motherhood in relation to television viewing. *Journal of Communication, 52*, 952–71.

Fallis, S. F., Fitzpatrick, M. A., & Friestad, M. S. (1985). Spouses' discussion of television portrayals of close relationships. *Communication Research, 12*, 59–81.

Fujikola, Y., & Austin, E. A. (2002). The relationship of family communication patterns to parental mediation styles. *Communication Research, 29*, 642–65.

Gable, S., Chang, Y., & Krull, J. L. (2007). Television watching and frequency of family meals are predictive of overweight onset and persistence in a national sample of school-aged children. *Journal of the American Dietetic Association, 107*(1), 53–61.

Gantz, W. (1985). Exploring the role of television in married life. *Journal of Broadcasting and Electronic Media, 29*, 65–78.

——(2001). Conflicts and resolution strategies associated with television in marital life. In J. Bryant & J. A. Bryant (Eds.), *Television and the American family*, 2nd edn (pp. 289–316). Mahwah, NJ: Lawrence Erlbaum Associates.

Gentile, D. A., & Walsh, D. A. (2002). A normative study of family media habits. *Applied and Developmental Psychology, 23*, 157–78.

Gerbner, G., Gross, L., Morgan, M., & Signorielli, N. (1994). Growing up with television: The cultivation perspective. In J. Bryant & D. Zillmann (Eds.), *Media effects: Advances in theory and research* (pp. 17–41). Hillsdale, NJ: Lawrence Erlbaum Associates.

Gunter, B., & Svennevig, M. (1987). *Behind and in front of the screen: Television's involvement with family life.* London: Libbey & Company.

Hayne, H., Herbert, J., & Simcock, G. (2003). Imitation from television by 24- and 30-month-olds. *Developmental Science, 6*, 254–61.

Heintz, K. E. (1992). Children's favorite television families: A descriptive analysis of role interactions. *Journal of Broadcasting and Electronic Media, 36*, 443–51.

Heintz-Knowles, K. E. (2001). Balancing acts: Work-family issues on prime-time TV. In J. Bryant & J. A. Bryant (Eds.), *Television and the American family*, 2nd edn (pp. 177–206). Mahwah, NJ: Lawrence Erlbaum Associates.

Henggeler, S. W., Cohen, R., Edwards, J. J., Summerville, M. B., & Ray, G. E. (1991). Family stress as a link in the association between television viewing and achievement. *Child Study Journal, 21*, 1–10.

Jacobs, J. A., & Gerson, K. (2001). Overworked individuals or overworked families? Explaining trends in work, leisure, and family time. *Work and Occupations, 28*, 40–63.

Jordan, A. B. (1992). Social class, temporal orientation, and mass media use within the family system. *Critical Studies in Mass Communication, 9*, 374–86.

Kaiser Family Foundation and Children Now (1996). *The family hour focus groups: Children's responses to sexual content on TV and their parents' reaction.* Oakland, CA: Author.

Kennedy, T. L. M., Smith, A., Wells, A. T., & Wellman, B. (2008). *Networked Families*, October 18. Retrieved from http://www.pewinternet.org/Reports/2008/Networked-Families.aspx.

Kirkorian, H. L., Pempek, T. A., Murphy, L. A., Schmidt, M. E., & Anderson, D. R. (2009). The impact of background television on parent–child interaction. *Child Development, 80*, 1350–59.

Koerner, A. F., & Fitzpatrick, M. A. (2002). Toward a theory of family communication. *Communication Theory, 12*, 70–91.

Krcmar, M. (1996). Family communication patterns, discourse behavior, and child television viewing. *Human Communication Research, 23*, 251–77.

Larson, M. S. (1996). Sex roles and soap operas: What adolescents learn about single motherhood. *Sex Roles, 35*(1–2), 97–110.

Larson, R., & Kubey, R. (1983). Television and music: Contrasting media in adolescent life. *Youth & Society, 15*, 13–31.

Lawrence, F. C., & Wozniak, P. H. (1989). Children's television viewing with family members. *Psychological Reports, 65*, 395–400.

Lee, S., & Chae, Y. (2007). Children's internet use in a family context: Influence on family relationships and parental mediation. *CyberPsychology & Behavior, 10*, 640–44.

Lenhart, A., Ling, R., Campbell, S., & Purcell, K. (2010). Teens and mobile phones, April 20. Retrieved from http://pewinternet.org/Reports/2010/Teens-and-Mobile-Phones.aspx.

Lenhart, A., Madden, M., & Hitlin, P. (2005). Teens and technology. Retrieved from http://www.pewinternet.org/~/media//Files/Reports/2005/PIP_Teens_Tech_July2005web.pdf.

Livingstone, S., & Helsper, E. J. (2008). Parental mediation of children's internet use. *Journal of Broadcasting & Electronic Media, 52*, 581–99.

Lull, J. (1978). Choosing television programs by family vote. *Communication Quarterly, 26*, 53–57.

——(1980a). The social uses of television. *Human Communication Research, 6*, 197–209.

——(1980b). Family communication patterns and the social uses of television. *Communication Research, 7*, 319–34.

——(1982). How families select television programs: A mass-observational study. *Journal of Broadcasting, 26*, 801–11.

——(1988). *World families watch television.* Beverly Hills, CA: Sage.

——(1990). *Inside family viewing: Ethnographic research on television's audience.* New York: Routledge.

Martini, M. (1996). "What's new?" at the dinner table: Family dynamics during mealtimes in two cultural groups in Hawaii. *Early Development and Parenting, 5*, 23–34.

Matheson, D. M., Killen, J. D., Wang, Y., Varady, A., & Robinson, T. N. (2004). Children's food consumption during television viewing. *American Journal of Clinical Nutrition, 79*, 1088–94.

McLeod, J. M., Atkin, C. K., & Chaffee, S. H. (1972). Adolescents, parents and television use: Adolescent self-report measures from Maryland and Wisconsin samples. In G. A. Comstock, E. A. Rubinstein, & J. P. Murray (Eds.), *Television and social behavior* (Vol. III, pp. 173–239). Washington, DC: U.S. Government Printing Office.

Mesch, G. S. (2006). Family characteristics and intergenerational conflicts over the Internet. *Information, Communication & Society, 9*, 473–95.

Messaris, P., & Kerr, D. (1983). Mothers' comments about TV: Relation to family communication patterns. *Communication Research, 10*, 175–94.

Morgan, M., & Shanahan, J. (1996). Two decades of cultivation analysis: An appraisal and a meta-analysis. In B. Burleson (Ed.), *Communication yearbook* (Vol. XX, pp. 115–51). Thousand Oaks, CA: Sage.

Morgan, M., Alexander, A., Shanahan, J., & Harris, C. (1990). Adolescents, VCRs, and the family environment. *Communication Research, 17*, 83–106.

Nathanson, A. I. (1999). Identifying and explaining the relationship between parental mediation and children's aggression. *Communication Research, 26*, 124–43.

——(2001a). Mediation of children's television viewing: Working toward conceptual clarity and common understanding. In W. B. Gudykunst (Ed.), *Communication yearbook* (Vol. XXV, pp. 115–51). Mahwah, NJ: Lawrence Erlbaum Associates.

——(2001b). Parent and child perspectives on the presence and meaning of parental television mediation. *Journal of Broadcasting and Electronic Media, 45*, 201–20.

——(2010). Using television mediation to stimulate nontraditional gender roles among Caucasian and African American children in the U.S. *Journal of Children and Media, 4*, 174–90.

Nathanson, A. I., & Cantor, J. (2000). Reducing the aggression-promoting effect of violent cartoons by increasing children's fictional involvement with the victim: A study of active mediation. *Journal of Broadcasting & Electronic Media, 44*, 125–42.

Nie, N. H., Hillygus, D. J., & Erbing, L. (2002). Internet use, interpersonal relations, and sociability: A time diary study. In B. Wellman & C. Haythornthwaite (Eds.), *The Internet in everyday life* (pp. 215–43). Oxford: Blackwell.

Nielsen Media Research (2007). *Nielsen reports television tuning remains at record levels*, October 17. Retrieved from http://www.nielsen.com/us/en/insights/press-room/2007/Nielsen_Reports_Television_Tuning_Remains_at_Record_Levels.html.

——(2009). *More than half the homes in the U.S. have three or more TVs*, July 20. Retrieved from http://blog.nielsen.com/nielsenwire/media_entertainment/more-than-half-the-homes-in-us-have-three-or-more-tvs.

Nikken, P., & Jansz, J. (2006). Parental mediation of children's videogame playing: A comparison of the reports by parents and children. *Learning, Media and Technology, 31*, 181–202.

Paik, H., & Comstock, G. (1994). The effects of television violence on antisocial behavior: A meta-analysis. *Communication Research, 21*, 516–46.

Pempek, T. A., Demers, L. B., Hanson, K., Kirkorian, H. L., & Anderson, D. R. (2011). The impact of baby videos on parent–child interaction. *Journal of Applied Developmental Psychology, 32*, 10–19.

Peter, J., Valkenburg, P. M., & Schouten, A. P. (2006). Characteristics and motives of adolescents talking with strangers on the Internet. *Cyber Psychology & Behavior, 9*, 526–30.

Reid, L. N., & Frazer, C. F. (1980). Children's use of television commercials to initiate social interaction in family viewing situations. *Journal of Broadcasting, 24*, 149–58.

Rideout, V. J., Foehr, U. G., & Roberts, D. F. (2010). *Generation M²: Media in the lives of 8-to 18-year olds*. Menlo Park, CA: Kaiser Family Foundation.

Rideout, V. J., & Hamel, E. (2006). *The media family: Electronic media in the lives of infants, toddlers, preschoolers and their parents*. Menlo Park, CA: Kaiser Family Foundation.

Ritchie, L. D. (1991). Another turn of the information revolution: Relevance, technology, and the information society. *Communication Research, 18*, 412–27.

Ritchie, L. D., & Fitzpatrick, M. A. (1990). Family communication patterns: Measuring intrapersonal perceptions of interpersonal relationships. *Communication Research, 17*, 523–44.

Roberts, D. F., Foehr, U. G., Rideout, V. J., & Brodie, M. (1999). *Kids & media @ the new millennium*. Menlo Park, CA: Kaiser Family Foundation.

Roberts, D. F., Foehr, U. G., & Rideout, V. J. (2005). *Generation M: Media in the lives of 8–18 year-olds*. Menlo Park, CA: Kaiser Family Foundation.

Robinson, J. D., & Skill, T. (2001). Five decades of families on television: From the 1950s through the 1990s. In J. Bryant & J. A. Bryant (Eds.), *Television and the American family*, 2nd edn (pp. 139–62). Mahwah, NJ: Lawrence Erlbaum Associates.

Robinson, J. P., Kestnbaum, M., & Kohut, A. (2000). Personal computers, mass media, and other uses of free time. In G. D. Garson (Ed.), *Social dimensions of information technology: Issues for the new millennium*. Hershey, PA: Idea.

Robinson, T. N. (1999). Reducing children's television viewing to prevent obesity: a randomized controlled trial. *Journal of American Medical Association, 282*(16), 1561–67.

Robinson, T. N., Saphir, M. N., Kraemer, H. C., Varady, A., & Haydel, K. F. (2001). Effects of reducing television viewing on children's requests for toys: A randomized controlled trial. *Journal of Developmental and Behavioral Pediatrics, 22*, 179–84.

Robinson, T. N., Wilde, M. L., Navracruz, L. C., Haydel, K. F., & Varady, A. (2001). Effects of reducing children's television and video game use on aggressive behavior: A randomized controlled trial. *Archives of Pediatrics & Adolescent Medicine, 155*, 17–23.

Rosenblatt, P. C., & Cunningham, M. R. (1976). Television watching and family tensions. *Journal of Marriage and the Family, 38*, 105–11.

Schmitt, K. L., Anderson, D. R., & Collins, P. A. (1999). Form and content: Looking at visual features of television. *Developmental Psychology, 35*, 1156–67.

Schmitt, K. L., Woolf, K. D. & Anderson, D. R. (2003). Viewing the viewers: Viewing behaviors by children and adults during television programs and commercials. *Journal of Communication, 53*, 265–81.

Shrum, L. J. (2009). Media consumption and perceptions of social reality: Effects and underlying processes. In J. Bryant & M. Oliver (Eds.), *Media Effects: Advances in Theory and Research*, 3rd edn (pp. 34–49). New York: Routledge.

Signorielli, N. (1991). Adolescents and ambivalence toward marriage: A cultivation analysis. *Youth and Society, 23*, 121–49.

Singer, J. L., Singer, D. G., Desmond, R., Hirsch, B., & Nicol, A. (1988). Family mediation and children's cognition, aggression, and comprehension of television: A longitudinal study. *Journal of Applied Developmental Psychology*, 9, 329–47.

St. Peters, M., Fitch, M., Huston, A. C., Wright, J. C., & Eakins, D. J. (1991). Television and families: What do young children watch with their parents? *Child Development*, 62, 1409–23.

Stanger, J. D., & Gridina, N. (1999). *Media in the home 1999: The fourth annual survey of parents and children.* Washington, DC: The Annenberg Public Policy Center.

Stoneman, Z., & Brody, G. H. (1981). Peers as mediators of television food advertisements aimed at children. *Developmental Psychology*, 17, 853–58.

Strasburger, V. C., Wilson, B. J., & Jordan, A. B. (2009). *Children, adolescents, and the media*, 2nd edn. Thousand Oaks, CA: Sage.

Valkenburg, P. M., Krcmar, M., & de Roos, S. (1998). The impact of a cultural children's program and adult mediation on children's knowledge of and attitudes towards opera. *Journal of Broadcasting and Electronic Media*, 42, 315–26.

van der Voort, T. H., Nikken, P., & van Lil, J. E. (1992). Determinants of parental guidance of children's television viewing: A Dutch replication study. *Journal of Broadcasting and Electronic Media*, 36, 61–74.

Vittrup, B. (2009). What U.S. parents don't know about their children's television use: Discrepancies between parents' and children's reports. *Journal of Children and Media*, 3, 51–67.

Walker, A. J. (1996). Couples watching television: Gender, power, and the remote control. *Journal of Marriage and the Family*, 58, 813–23.

Wang, R., Bianchi, S. M., & Raley, S. B. (2005). Teenagers' internet use and family rules: A research note. *Journal of Marriage and Family*, 67, 1249–58.

Warren, R., & Bluma, A. (2002). Parental mediation of children's internet use: The influence of established media. *Communication Research Reports*, 19, 8–17.

Warren, R. (2005). Parental mediation of children's television viewing in low-income families. *Journal of Communication*, 55, 847–63.

Warren, R., Gerke, P., Kelly, M. A. (2002). Is there enough time on the clock? Parental involvement and mediation of children's television viewing. *Journal of Broadcasting and Electronic Media*, 46, 87–111.

Watkins, B., Calvert, S., Huston-Stein, A., & Wright, J. C. (1980). Children's recall of television material: Effects of presentation mode and adult labeling. *Developmental Psychology*, 16, 672–74.

Weiss, A. J., & Wilson, B. J. (1996) Emotional portrayals in family television series that are popular among children. *Journal of Broadcasting and Electronic Media*, 40, 1–29.

——(1998). Children's cognitive and emotional responses to the portrayal of negative emotions in family-formatted situation comedies. *Human Communication Research*, 24, 584–609.

Wilson, B. J., & Weiss, A. J. (1991). The effects of two reality explanations on children's reactions to a frightening movie scene. *Communication Monographs*, 58, 307–26.

——(1993). The effects of sibling coviewing on preschoolers' reactions to a suspenseful movie scene. *Communication Research*, 20, 214–48.

Woodard, E. H., & Gridina, N. (2000). *Media in the home 2000: The fifth annual survey of parents and children.* Philadelphia, PA: Annenberg Public Policy Center.

Zahn, S. B., & Baran, S. J. (1984). It's all in the family: Siblings and program choice conflict. *Journalism Quarterly*, 61, 847–52.

Zimmerman, F. J., Gilkerson, J., Richards, J. A., Christakis, D. A., Xu, D., Gray, S., & Yapanel, U. (2009). Teaching by listening: The importance of adult–child conversations to language development. *Pediatrics*, 124, 342–49.

27

Digital Technology and Families

Nancy A. Jennings and Ellen A. Wartella

Over the years, many of the triumphs and struggles of families have remained the same. Generation after generation, babies are still attached to their mothers, and teens still yearn for their independence. While some things remain the same, changes in society place new constraints on the family process. Within the past three decades, we have seen an incredibly rapid growth in digital technologies in forms of mechanical advances in computers and cell phones and in the development of mechanisms for communication through social networking and entertainment through smartphone Apps. Although we are learning more about what role these digital technologies have in the lives of children and adults, we also must learn how these technologies are affecting family relationships and family life.

This chapter will discuss the research on digital media technology on families. We will explore family systems through the life course and encounter how different technologies impact family life at different stages from infanthood to adolescence. We will find general conclusions regarding the impact of digital technologies on family life and provide suggestions for further research in the field of media and family studies.

Technology in the Home

Media continue to saturate family households. For young children between the ages of eight months and eight years, 2.97 televisions, 1.61 computers, 1.99 videogames and 3.89 DVD/video players reside in the average American home (Lapierre, Piotrowski, & Linebarger, 2010). Homes for older children between the ages of eight and 18 years contain on average 3.8 TVs, 2.8 DVD or VCR players, one digital video recorder, 2.2 CD players, 2.5 radios, two computers, and 2.3 console videogame players (Rideout et al., 2010). Over the past ten years, there has been a steady increase in accessibility of media platforms for young people between the ages of eight and 18 years. The explosion in mobile media contributes dramatically to this phenomenon. In the past five years, the percentage of eight- to 18-year-olds who own a laptop has grown from 12 percent to 26 percent; cell phone ownership has leaped from 39 percent to 66 percent, and iPod or MP3 player ownership has soared from 18 percent to 76 percent (Rideout et al., 2010). Along with media ownership, access to the Internet has reached new heights. For families with children between the ages of eight months and eight years, 84.1 percent of parents indicate they have home Internet access, and 74.8 percent claim that they have high-speed Internet access (Lapierre et al., 2010). Similarly with older children between the ages of eight and 18 years, 84 percent of families have Internet access and 59 percent indicate they have high-speed or wireless access to the Internet (Rideout et al., 2010).

While digital technologies have blanketed family life from infancy, the use of these technologies seems to change during the life course of growing children. For preschoolers between the ages of two and five years, television viewing has reached an eight-year high, climbing to more than 3.5 hours (213 minutes) on an average day (Gutnick, Robb, Takeuchi, & Kotler, 2011). However, as children grow, their media habits change. Between the ages of seven and nine years, children expand their media habits from primarily television viewing into use of digital technologies such as the Internet and videogames (Gutnick et al., 2011). Internet use changes with 30 percent of three- to five-year-olds accessing the Internet on a typical day, whereas 50 percent of six- to nine-year-olds go online on a typical day (Gutnick et al., 2011). Similar changes are noted with videogame use. Less than half of six-year-olds play videogames on an average day compared to over 70 percent of eight-year-olds (Gutnick et al., 2011). As children's dexterity with small gadgets increases with their developing fine-motor skills, their increased ability to focus on activities for longer periods, to think logically, and to read opens new opportunities for engagement with digital technologies. Similarly, teen use of mobile devices provides a second shift in the media habits of contemporary youth. As children mature from eight- to ten-year-olds to 15- to 18-year-olds, ownership of hand-held videogame players decreases while ownership of cell phones, laptops, and iPod/MP3 players increases (Rideout et al., 2010).

Taken in a larger societal context, these changes in media preferences may also be the result of rapid changes in technological forms and uses. Since 1990, advances in digital technologies have been dramatic and abundant. Four significant events occurred in the early 1990s which have had an unforeseen impact on computer and Internet use. First, in May 1990, Microsoft Window 3.0 was first released. This version of Windows laid the foundation for the look and feel of future generations of this operating system complete with color graphics and icons (Windows, 2011), making it competitive with the graphical interface offered by Apple with the Mac. Second, Intel released the Pentium processor (Intel Museum, n.d.) in 1993, shattering previous records on processing speed and setting a new standard for processing capabilities. Third, the National Science Foundation lifted all restrictions to commercial content on the Internet (Common Standards, n.d.). Finally, Mosaic, a graphical web browser, was released to the public in 1993 (About NCSA Mosaic, 2011). This was a significant step forward for widespread Internet use by offering an attractive interface with icons and pictures, "software easy to use and appealing to 'non-geeks'" (About NCSA Mosaic, 2011). These events profoundly changed the nature of the digital experience, particularly for children born during this time and beyond. With these changes to the digital environment, children grew up with lightning fast computer processors, icons and graphics to help lead them to content even before they could read, and a seamless merger between commercial and noncommercial content online. Prensky (2001) refers to the rapid growth in digital technology as a "'singularity'—an event which changes things so fundamentally that there is absolutely no going back" (p. 1). As such, children enter this world as digital natives (Prensky, 2001), fluent in the "language of computers, video games, and the Internet" (p. 1), living among digital immigrants who "always retain, to some degree, their 'accent,' that is, their foot in the past" (p. 3). Within the family context, digital natives and immigrants live together, forging new ground as they adopt and adapt new technologies in the home.

Therefore, we must consider the implications of these changes on family structures within the larger societal environment that includes these rapid technological advancements.

Life Course Paradigm

A small amount of attention has been given to theory development of families' use of technology in the home. Jordan (2003) suggests that a family structures framework provides a mechanism by which to assess how media use (and in this case uses of technology) "'fit' with the norms, values, and beliefs that define the family system." (p. 143). As such, scholars have used this paradigm to distinguish the impact of digital technologies on structural components of the family system such as family boundaries and family cohesion. The family structures literature provides a framework to pull apart the subsystems and dynamics of the family process (Jennings & Wartella, 2004). However, given the vast and rapid changes in digital technologies within the past three decades, this framework is limited in its applicability to the contextual changes in society. Therefore, theoretical approaches that incorporate changes in time and historical context provide a better frame for exploring the rapid changes in technology use within family structures.

Two theoretical approaches to the study of family include family development theory and life course theory. Watt and White (1999) utilize family development theory to focus on the role of technology on different family stages and the sequencing and timing of transitions between stages. As such, they suggest that technological innovations influence family roles and specializations which then have influence on subsequent family stages and transitions. In their discussion of seven stages of family development (mate selection, early marriages, preschool children, elementary school children, adolescents, post-parenting, and retirement families), technological innovations influence the ways in which family members communicate, work, and recreate.

Not only are families progressing and changing, but the technologies available for use are changing as well. Therefore, as a complement to the family structures framework and family development theory, the life course paradigm embeds these structures and stages within social institutions and historical context. As such, the life course paradigm emphasizes the social pathways of human development in and across historical time incorporating macro level structures and social institutions with micro level individual experiences (Elder, 2003). Five principles guide the life course paradigm. First, the principle of life-span development posits that human development and aging are a lifelong process (Elder, 2003). This principle was first articulated by Elder in 2003 but was inherent in his previous explanations of the life course paradigm. As such, Elder contends that human development does not stop at the age of 18 years, and that adults can and do experience fundamental change and growth. This coincides with the seven stages of family development which begins at an adult level when a family is first formed through mate selection (Watt & White, 1999). Second, the principle of agency states that "individuals construct their own life course through the choices and actions they take within the opportunities and constraints of history and social circumstance" (Elder, 2003, p. 11). This favors a constructionist position in the process of development and makes individuals active participants in their own life pathways. Third, the principle of time and place involves the contextualization of life course within historical times and places (Elder, 2003). Individual life courses reflect different historical effects, often in the form of cohort effects. Elder (1994) cites the growth of mass media as one of the most influential historical changes for American children in the 20th century. Similarly, the continuous and quick growth of digital technologies has made a substantial impact on the lives of children growing up as digital natives. Fourth, the principle of timing gives merit to the impact of life transitions, events, and behavioral patterns on their timing in a person's life (Elder, 2003). The personal impact of any change will be dependent upon when this change occurred in someone's life. Finally, the fifth principle of linked lives contends that "lives are lived interdependently and socio-historical influences are expressed through this network of shared relationships" (Elder, 2003, p. 13). These shared relationships include those expressed in the family as well as those outside of the family structure including friends and coworkers. This last principle is the cornerstone of one of the most influential changes in digital technologies, online social networking.

Family Structures Within Socio-historical Changes

Technological changes have a profound effect on the family. Yet, as Watt and White (1999) suggest, the influence of these changes varies depending on the family stage that is experienced at the time of the change. For example, while Mesch (2006) contends that Internet use in families with adolescents tends to blur family boundaries, he points to other research (Hughes & Hans, 2001) that suggests Internet use for empty-nest families is associated with high family cohesion with the Internet functioning as a tool of communication between parents and grown children living at a distance. Moreover, uses of technology change as children develop, and as a result, parental concerns and rules regarding media use change (Jennings & Wartella, 2004). Therefore, this next section examines the impact of technological change on family relationships at different stages of family development.

Parents, Media, and Babies

Baby media have exploded in the past decade, and children younger than two are showing increased use of these baby media. In 1997, the first Baby Einstein video, called *Baby Einstein*, was released. This video and its successors gave rise to an explosion of screen media targeted at infants, including television shows like *Teletubbies* and *Classical Baby*, an array of video/DVD products (*Brainy Baby*, *Baby Mozart*), the cable channel BabyFirstTV, and computer software for laptops as well as portable devices like cell phones. As noted in some of the earliest research into young children's attention to and imitation of screen models, children younger than two likely do not attend to (and by implication learn from) screen models when the material is inappropriate or of low interest (McCall et al., 1977). While the videos were initially marketed as a line of instructional videos to teach babies about the humanities (including music and art), the Baby Einstein Comp clarified this intention, indicating the videos are designed to promote parent–child interaction by providing a "digital board book" allowing a parent to have two free hands while enjoying and experiencing the video with their little one—leaving their hands free to clap, point to objects and interact with their baby. Across all of these infant media outlets, the program content is intended (either implicitly or explicitly) to provide children with educational or informational programming in an entertaining presentational style that elicits the children's attention and demonstrates to the parents that their infants are learning. For instance, the Baby Einstein series of DVDs focuses on educational themes such as language, numbers, shapes, colors, seasons, art, classical music, and nature. And over the past several years, academic researchers have begun to study various aspects of infants' media exposure, including whether infants learn from such screen media, how screen media changes parent–child interactions, and the potential effects of media exposure on cognitive development.

There is evidence from two major national studies conducted in the past eight years by the Kaiser Family Foundation suggesting that screen media are enormously popular with young children. Children from birth to two years of age watch about an hour and 15 minutes a day of television and video/DVDs (Kaiser Family Foundation, 2003, 2006; Vandewater et al., 2007), and much of what children watch is produced specifically for them (Garrison & Christakis, 2005; Vandewater, Bickham, & Lee, 2006; Vandewater et al., 2007). There are various estimates of the proliferation of baby videos. According to the *New York Times*, in 2003, 32 percent of all new babies born in the U.S.A. had watched the *Baby Einstein* video (Lewin, 2003).

There have been very few studies of parental attitudes about infant media. The Kaiser Family Foundation (2003, 2006) has found that parents generally believed in the positive role infant media could play in their children's development. In the 2003 Kaiser Family Foundation report, parents of children from birth to six years of age were asked their opinions about the potential of television in learning. Forty-two percent of parents believed that television mostly helped children's learning, compared to 27 percent who felt it mostly hurt learning and 21 percent who felt it did not affect learning either way. The same study found that 58 percent of parents believed that educational television was very important for children's intellectual development, with 49 percent feeling the same about educational videos and DVDs. It should be noted that this survey did not ask specifically about infant DVDs and included older children.

In a nationally representative survey of 1,051 parents of children aged between six months and six years, 42 percent of parents believed that television was "a lot" or "somewhat" helpful in teaching young children to get along with others (Kaiser Family Foundation, 2006). Another 52 percent of parents felt that television was "a lot" or "somewhat" important in helping their children to be ready to learn in school. When asked specifically about baby videos, 48 percent of parents believed that baby videos had a positive effect on early childhood development. Of these parents, 41 percent based their impressions on their own experiences. Vandewater et al. (2005) reanalyzed the Kaiser Family Foundation's (2003) data to examine parental attitudes toward screen media by parents in heavy television use households. For children under the age of two, parents in constant television households (where television is on "always" or "most of the time," even if no one is watching) were twice as likely as other parents to view educational television as a very important contributor to healthy development (Vandewater et al., 2005). These data suggest that some parents may feel that baby videos are an acceptable way to occupy their children, because they are presumed safe and potentially educational.

The rise of baby media over the past decade has been the result of multiple factors, not the least of which is more positive parental views of the educational potential of educational media for preschool children. Academic research on the impact of such media is just starting to accumulate, and the popularization of such research is relatively meager. What research exists suggests that baby videos as currently constructed are less efficient mechanisms for teaching babies words, for instance, than is adult child interaction (Wartella, Richert, & Robb, 2010). However, the trends suggest that baby media will be a part of American children's lives for the time to come.

Preschoolers and Their Families

As toddlers mature into preschoolers, digital technologies become more widely used. Preschoolers increasingly use computers, Internet, and videogames, but much less often than television (Gutnick et al., 2011). Moreover, access and use of digital media are not equally distributed and changes with age. For example, at age three, only about a quarter of children go online daily, but by age five, nearly half go online daily (Kotler, 2010 as reported in Gutnick et al., 2011). Similar results are seen with handheld videogames. According to the NPD Group (2010), only about 20 percent of four- and five-year-olds use handheld video-games while almost half (46 percent) of seven-year-olds use them (as cited in Gutnick et al., 2011). While preschoolers don't personally own smartphones, many young children are using them. Known as the pass-back effect, parents or other adults are allowing their child to use their mobile device, usually for short sessions, with the understanding that the child will pass back the device to the parent or adult (Chiong & Shuler, 2010). This phenomenon was first noted in 2009 and in a recent study of four- to seven-year-olds, nearly two-thirds of the children reported that they have used an iPhone (Chiong & Shuler, 2010).

The limited research on families with preschoolers and new technologies provides meaningful insight concerning digital media within the family structure. From observations of family interactions, Plowman, McPake, and Stephen (2010) conclude that pre-school children were "discriminating users of technology" (p. 68), expressing individual preferences and different dispositions that guided the integration of technology in their family lives, thus giving the preschooler a great deal of agency. Even though some children lived in homes with a high degree of accessibility to technology, children were not necessarily drawn to those resources, despite the invitations extended by their parents (Plowman et al., 2010). Indeed, preschoolers in all households that they observed engaged in a range of nontechnological activities, although at times, the technology seemed to blend with the child's play. Plowman and her colleagues offer an example of a preschool boy who liked to download and print pictures of characters from a website, attach them to cardboard and play with the cut-out images with their other toys. These experiences, however, must be placed within the values of the parents concerning new technologies. Some parents were very enthusiastic and encouraged their preschooler's engagement with digital media. In these families, parents spoke of their child's developing technological skills with pride. In other households, parents valued traditional activities such as dressing up and outdoor play more than technological play. As such, these parents encouraged traditional activities, expressing that they would rather wait until their child was older to engage with technologies (Plowman et al., 2010). Moreover, parents were the most commonly mentioned source of support for learning digital technologies by preschoolers (Stephen, McPake, Plowman, & Berch-Heyman, 2008). As preschoolers seek advice, they find a way to enter into family interactions and shared family practices.

Siblings of preschoolers also seem to play a role in the socialization of digital technology for young children. Through discussions with three-, four-, and five-year-olds, Stephen and her colleagues (2008) discovered that preschoolers perceive that they share digital media with their older siblings. For example, one preschool girl indicated that her brother showed her how to use a game on the computer, and a boy preschooler reported that he was able to share his sister's videogame system (Playstation) with her. Moreover, Stephen and her colleagues suggest that children perceive of digital technology as "resources to be grown into and out of like toys or clothes" (p. 109). Indeed younger children seem to reject pretend mobile phones for phones that look more realistic, or even for their parent's phone. However, this should not be surprising given the number of Applications available on smartphones for preschoolers. In June, 2009, almost half (47 percent) of the top 100 top-selling paid Apps in the education section of the iTunes App store were targeted towards preschoolers or elementary-aged children, and 60 percent of the top 25 targeted toddlers/preschoolers (Shuler, 2009). As such, then, digital technologies are no longer just meant for adults, giving validation to the preschooler's viewpoint while still raising concerns over their use with these young digital natives.

Middle Childhood, Technology, and Families

For children in middle childhood, videogame play is particularly important. Over half of eight- to ten-year-olds (59 percent) and 11- to 14-year-olds (57 percent) use videogames on any given day compared to only a little over a third (39 percent) of 15- to 18-year-olds (Roberts, Foehr, & Rideout, 2005). As expected, then, far more eight- to ten-year-olds (66 percent) and 11- to 14-year-olds (60 percent) own a handheld videogame player than 15- to 18-year-olds (41 percent), and these children in middle childhood are also far more likely to have a videogame console in their bedroom than older adolescents (Roberts et al., 2005). Moreover, there has been a significant increase in videogame play since 2004, particularly for handheld video gaming. Recent data suggest that console videogame play peaks for 11- to 14-year-olds at a daily average of 43 minutes while younger children spend more time with handheld games than older adolescents (Rideout et al., 2010).

While video gaming plays an important role for children in middle childhood, computer and Internet use occupies less time during middle childhood. Even though children's overall recreational computer time increased from 1999 to 2004, eight- to ten-year-olds spent the least amount of average daily time using a computer (37 minutes) compared to 11- to 14-year-olds who spent on average about an hour (1 hour 2 minutes) on a computer daily and 15- to 18-year-olds who spent nearly an hour and a half (1 hour 22 minutes) daily in 2004 (Roberts et al., 2005). More recent data suggest that trend continues. In 2009, eight- to ten-year-olds spent more time on computers daily (46 minutes) than in 2004, but children in this age group were still using computers far less than older children (1 hour 46 minutes) and adolescents (1 hour 39 minutes) (Rideout et al., 2010).

Families with children in middle childhood seem to cope with these changing interests in digital technologies with various mediation strategies. Interestingly, Nikken and Jansz (2006) conclude that parents employ similar mediation strategies to videogames as they do to television viewing: (a) restrictive mediation (limiting videogame play or the type of videogame played), (b) active mediation (expressed approval or disapproval of videogames and discussing videogame play within the family), and (c) co-playing (playing videogames together). Mothers applied more restrictive and active mediation strategies for videogame play than fathers, but interestingly, co-playing was done equally among mothers and fathers (Nikken & Jansz, 2006). This is quite unlike early research on videogames which indicated that fathers are more likely to play videogames and work with the computer with their children than mothers (Bird, Goss, & Bird, 1990; Mitchell, 1985; Tinnell, 1985). This may be related to the increase in game play among women as a reflection of societal changes as well. Today, 40 percent of videogame players are women, and 48 percent of parents indicate they play videogames with their child at least weekly (Entertainment Software Association, 2010). Parents indicate the primary reasons they co-play videogames are (a) because it's fun for the entire family; (b) because the parent is asked to play; (c) parents use videogame co-play as a way to socialize with their children; and (d) parents can monitor game content when they co-play (Entertainment Software Association, 2010). Research suggests that parents who play videogames tend to be more positive about the effects of videogames and apply all forms of mediation strategies more often than nonvideogame players (Nikken, Jansz, & Schouwstra, 2007).

Restrictive mediation strategies have been of primary focus in the research literature. Interestingly, age differences seem to appear particularly for the youngest of children in middle childhood, coinciding with their increased videogame use. In the U.S.A., eight- to 14-year-olds report that their parents have more rules regulating time spent with videogames than 15- to 18-year-olds. This trend continues and becomes more apparent with the increased videogame usage reported by children in this age group in 2009. Almost half (45 percent) of eight- to ten-year-olds reported that their parents had rules about how much time they could spend with videogames. Similarly, almost a third (31 percent) of children between the ages of 11 and 14 years reported parental rules on time spent with videogames compared to only 18 percent of 15- to 18-year-olds (see Table 27.1). Parents of younger children in middle childhood are also more likely to have rules about what type of videogames the child can play, both in 2004, and 2009 (see Table 27.1). Similar results have been found abroad as well, indicating that parents of younger children in middle childhood and children who were more enthusiastic about videogame play were more likely to utilize restrictive mediation strategies than for older children or those less excited about videogames (Nikken & Jansz, 2006).

While videogame play was the primary digital media use for children in early middle childhood, computer use soars for children as they age into the pre-teen and teenage years. Children who are eight- to ten-years-old spend the least amount of time with computers, averaging 46 minutes per day. By contrast, 11- to 14-year-olds spend an hour more on average (1 hour 46 minutes) per day and 15- to 18-year-olds spend 1 hour 39 minutes per day with computers (Rideout et al., 2010). Similar trends were observed in 2005, such that the youngest members of the group (eight- to ten-year-olds) were using computers the least (only 37 minutes per day on average). However, daily computer use increased for each age group peaking at almost an hour and a half (1 hour 22 minutes) for 15- to 18-year-olds (Roberts et al., 2005).

Interestingly, parental rules about computer use have increased dramatically between 2004 and 2009. In 2004, children expressed that their parents had rules about how long they could be on the computer (28 percent), what they could do on the computer (32 percent), and that their parents usually knew which websites they were visiting (30 percent) (Roberts et al., 2005). By 2009, the rules had changed. Over half of the children (52 percent)

Table 27.1 Parental Rules about Video Games

	Rules about which video games child can play		Rules about how long child can play video games	
	2004[a]	2009[b]	2004[a]	2009[b]
8- to 10-year-olds	32%	54%	34%	45%
11- to 14-year-olds	25%	33%	27%	31%
15- to 18-year-olds	5%	12%	11%	18%

Source:
[a] (Roberts et al., 2005)
[b] (Rideout et al., 2010)

indicated their parents had rules regarding what they are allowed to do on the computer, and a little over a third (36 percent) had rules about how long they could be on the computer (Rideout et al., 2010). Moreover, age plays a key role in the presence of computer rules. By the time a child leaves middle childhood, fewer children indicate their parents have computer rules. In 2004, significantly more eight- to ten-year-olds (44 percent) and 11- to 14-year-olds (34 percent) indicated they had rules on what they were allowed to do on the computer than 15- to 18-year-olds (18 percent) (Roberts et al., 2005). This continued in 2009, although at a much higher rate. Significantly more eight- to ten-year-olds (64 percent) and 11- to 14-year-olds (60 percent) had rules governing what they did on the computer compared to only 36 percent of 15- to 18-year-olds (Rideout et al., 2010).

These rules are particularly critical in terms of children's use of digital technologies, particularly for Internet use. Among fourth-, fifth-, and sixth-grade Korean children, Lee and Chae (2007) discovered a relationship between the child's perception of parental mediation of the Internet and the types of activities done online. Children who reported that their parents recommend good websites to them were more likely to use the Internet for educational purposes. Similarly, children who reported that they used the Internet together with their parents (co-using) were also more likely to use the Internet for educational purposes. Co-using was also related to Internet use for communication such that the more co-using, the more the children were involved with online communication (Lee & Chae, 2007). Interesting, restrictive mediation, that is limiting which websites the child can visit, was not related to any type of children's online activities. However, Internet supervision at home did have an impact on children's practice of unsafe behaviors (Valcke, Schellens, Van Keer, & Gerarts, 2007). Specifically, children who reported having at least some level of control of their Internet use by parents at home were less likely to pass personal information and pictures to unknown chat contacts than those without parental supervision. This has implications for the restrictive mediation strategy so readily employed in the U.S.A. The restrictive mediation strategy may not be effective in the types of activities children choose online, but it does seem to have an impact on some safe online behaviors for children in this age group.

Children's online activities also seem to be related to their time spent together as a family and on their family communication. The amount of time children spent online was positively related to perceived declines in family time but was not related to perceived decline in family communication (Lee & Chae, 2007). As such, Lee and Chae suggest that Internet use may displace passive family time rather than active family time, such as family communication. However, the types of online activities were important factors in children's perceptions of family time and family communication. The frequency of online gaming was a significant factor in both perceived decline in family time and perceived decline in family communication (Lee & Chae, 2007). Educational online activities were not related to perceived declines in family time or in family communication. Lee and Chae conclude that while online gaming may be detrimental to family time and family communication, educational online activities do not threaten family relationships. However, online communication activities were marginally related to perceived declines in family communication, but no relationship with perceived family time (Lee & Chae, 2007). This may be a result of children's interest in using digital technologies to keep in touch with their friends more so than with their family. Qualitative interviews with Norwegian children between the ages of ten and 12 years suggest that communication technologies, particularly mobile phones, weaken family ties while strengthening peer bonds (Kaare, Brandtzæg, Heim, & Endestad, 2007). Within the child's lifespan, however, peers become increasingly important. Therefore, it would seem a natural transition for children on the verge of adolescence to shift their communication habits.

Adolescence, Teenagers, and Their Families

As children get older, families experience a complex dance of balancing the child's growing independence with the parent's need to protect and support the child. Digital technologies such as cell phones and laptops offer tools that fulfill both the needs of the child and the parent although the struggle to maintain a balance remains within the family structure. Research on the impact of new technologies on parent–teen relationships is mixed. Richards and her colleagues (2010) found that for 14- and 15-year-olds, more time spent playing on the computer (not for homework) was associated with poor attachment to parents. Mesch (2003) also found that the type of Internet use was related to teen's relationships with their parents. He found that for Israeli adolescents using the Internet for educational purposes was positively related to perceived closeness of adolescents to their parents. However, Durkin and Barber (2002) discovered that teens who played computer games reported greater family cohesion than teens who did not play computer games. Interestingly, each of these studies involved data collection at different time periods, although with teens of similar age. Of these three studies, Durkin and Barber's teens were collected in 1988, Mesch in 2000, and Richards and her colleagues in 2004. Therefore, changes in computer and Internet use over this time frame may account for the differences observed.

Parenting rules and attitudes about computer and Internet use have also changed with time. While fewer parents of 15- to 18-year-olds have rules about what their child can do on the computer than parents of children between the ages of eight to 14 years, twice as many parents of older teens had these rules in 2009 than in 2004. Indeed, rules about what a child is permitted to do on the computer increased dramatically for children of all ages within those five years (see Table 27.2). Interestingly, even though the majority of parents of online teens believe the Internet is beneficial for their teens, significantly fewer parents of online teens reported that the Internet was a good thing for their teen in 2006 (59 percent) than in 2004 (67 percent) (Macgill, 2007). Parents who were more highly educated and parents who had more wireless devices such as PDAs or laptops are more likely to think the Internet is a good thing for teens than less educated parents and parents without wireless technology (Macgill, 2007). This may be a reflection of historical changes in the types of technologies available. Between 2004 and 2009, social networking sites such as MySpace and Facebook came of age. Indeed, Lenhart (2007a) refers to 2005–6 as "the year of myspace" noting that more than 100 million accounts had been

Table 27.2 Parental Rules about Computer Use

	Rules about what child can do on the computer	
	2004[a]	2009[b]
8- to 10-year-olds	44%	64%
11- to 14-year-olds	34%	60%
15- to 18-year-olds	18%	36%

Source:
[a] (Roberts et al., 2005)
[b] (Rideout et al., 2010)

created on MySpace and that it was the third most popular website in the U.S.A. Facebook, another social networking site, was growing quickly and surpassed MySpace, becoming the most popular social networking site in January 2009 (Thornton, 2009). Accompanying this growth in social networking sites were reports of a new form of bullying carried out online referred to as cyber-bulling. Between 1999 and 2005, teens reporting online harassment increased by 50 percent (Wolak, Mitchell, & Finkelhor, 2006). In 2006, almost a third (32 percent) of online teens indicate they have been a victim of a range of cyber-bulling activities including reposting or forwarding a private email, spreading rumors online, receiving threatening emails or IMs, or having an embarrassing picture posted (Lenhart, 2007b).

Parents employ different types of mediation strategies with various outcomes. Eastin (2006) and his colleagues found associations between parenting style and Internet mediation techniques employed in homes with teenagers. Specifically, authoritative parents (those parents characterized by high levels of demand accompanied by warmth) use evaluative and restrictive mediation strategies much more frequently than authoritarian (high demand but low warmth) or neglectful (low demand and low warmth) parents. Moreover, authoritative parents use technological blocking as a restrictive mediation tool more frequently than parents using other parenting styles. Interestingly, Mesch (2009) reports a relationship between parental mediation strategies and online victimization of teens. Of the different mediation techniques examined, Mesch (2009) reports that evaluative techniques seem to decrease the risk of exposure to online bullying. Specifically, teens of parents who have rules on which websites their teens were allowed to visit were statistically less likely to be a victim of online cyber-bulling than teens without these rules. Computer location, restrictions on the amount of time teens spent online, and rules about information sharing online did not influence the risk of cyber-bulling for teens. Mesch (2009) concludes that parents who discuss online safety with their teens create awareness of the potential dangers online.

Not only are teens using computers and the Internet, but they are increasingly using mobile phones as well. In 2009, 75 percent of teens between the ages of 12 and 17 years owned a cell phone, compared to 45 percent in 2004 (Lenhart, Ling, Campbell, & Purcell, 2010). Moreover, teens who use landline phones has decreased from 39 percent in 2006 to 30 percent in 2009 while teens who use text messaging has increased from 27 percent to 54 percent over the same time period (Lenhart et al., 2010). Compared to adults, teens are far more likely to text than adults, but teens and adults are similar in their use of cell phones for voice calling (Lenhart, 2010). Teens will use the asynchronous communication of texting to broach difficult subjects with their parents (Devitt & Roker, 2009). For example, one 15-year-old girl said, "Well, I think mobiles can be really good if you've got something you don't wanna tell straight away, like texting my mum that I was getting bullied. You might not wanna say that to her straight out, like" (Devitt & Roker, 2009, p. 192).

Interestingly, when teens use voice calling on their cell phones, they are most likely calling their parents (Lenhart et al., 2010). The direction of the call has particular implications for parent–teen relationships. Teens who receive calls from their parents are often annoyed with their surveillance (Ribak, 2009). One 17-year-old reports, "A call from my parents is annoying if it has no purpose. It's not the time, it's just annoying—control conversations are very annoying: 'Where are you?' 'When will you be back?' these conversations are very annoying as a means for control" (Ribak, 2009, p. 190). This ethnographic research is supported in recent survey research of teens. Adolescents reported greater parent conflict when parents called their cell phones for monitoring, tracking schoolwork, or when upset, than when the teen initiated the call. However, adolescents who initiate cell phone calls with their parents were more likely to report better relationships with their parents than those who did not call their parents (Weisskirch, 2010).

These effects may be a result of the sense of independence that cell phones provide for teens. Ribak (2009) suggests that cell phones operate as a transitional object, allowing for intergenerational distance while maintaining intimacy when needed. Parents can feel reassured of the safety and well-being of their teen when they hear their voice, while teens express appreciation of the independence that this "lifeline" can provide (Devitt & Roker, 2009). Cell phone ownership is a "symbolic step away from the home" (Ling, 2000, p. 110) for teens while providing a sense that their parents are "absent-though-ever-present" (Ribak, 2009, p. 191). In the words of a 17-year-old girl, "The mobile reinforces the sense of independence because you can allow yourself to be where you want and everything, and you know that at worst, you have your mobile with you ... you can simply call your parents. It sort of guards you ... it's like you're never alone." (Ribak, 2009, p. 191).

Conclusion and Discussion

Digital technologies play different roles for families at different stages in the life course. For children of all ages, television screens are important, as viewing television content makes up the lion's share of their time spent with media. However, as children age, different forms of digital technologies become increasingly important. For families in early stages with babies, far less emphasis is placed on new digital technologies. While preschoolers do not own digital technologies such as a laptop or cell phone, they are using these devices and passing personal devices back and forth with their parents. Children in middle childhood co-play videogames with siblings and parents. Through adolescence, teenagers move away from videogame play and put more value on cell phones than videogames. To that extent, we do see a progression of the importance of different technologies as different stages for contemporary youth.

Not only does the value of different technologies change, but the associations and use of technologies within the family structure also changes through the life course of the family. Preschoolers see technologies as a way to participate in the family process and share experiences with parents and siblings. For children in middle childhood, the digital technology becomes a larger platform for families to engage in shared activities, thus building family relationships. With the passage into adolescence, digital technologies take on a new role and act as tools of independence for the teen and a means to stay connected to the distant teen at a moment's notice. Teens also use the technology for security as they explore the world, having contact with parents when needed.

As technologies change, family practices accommodate to the new influences in family life. The use of digital technologies in the family seems to embody the established relationships within the family, making the process of family relations and family communication more visible. Teen–parent interactions are able to be tracked by text message trails and cell phone call records. The amount of time spent playing on videogame systems like the Wii is recorded by the device itself with a full report available within a few button clicks. Email trails, comments on social networking sites, shared photos online, and family members recreated in avatar and profile form on videogame systems provide documentation of lived family experiences. The technology itself highlights the relationships within the family and tells the tale of how the digital natives and digital immigrants integrate their lives together.

While we are beginning to get a better picture of family life with digital technologies, research needs to continue and expand, particularly as technologies continue to expand and evolve. Soon, these digital natives will begin their own families. Research suggests that the more familiar people are with technology, the more they trust it. Much of the digital natives' experiences have been with digital immigrants who are trying to keep up with changes in technology and who may question the use of digital technology within their family. How will the experiences of digital natives growing up with digital immigrants influence their own parenting? What will the next generation of technological advances bring that will influence family relationships and interactions? Furthermore, there needs to be a greater attempt to apply theory to practice. Use of digital media technology in the family setting continues to be undertheorized. Very little work has been applied to families and digital technologies beyond the use of mediation strategies in the home.

There is much speculation regarding the impact of the digital technologies on family life, yet so little research to substantiate these claims. What we do know is that much like earlier media technologies, the digital technologies are being quickly adopted by families with children, but differently across the life course. We also know that the pace of technological development has not slowed and that as children embrace these technologies, families do as well. Different technologies have more importance at different stages of family development, and these technologies serve different roles either as a relationship builder for preschoolers and children in middle childhood or as a tool for emancipation for teenagers and adolescents. Truly, this line of research requires an interdisciplinary approach. Scholars from family studies, child development, and communication need to work together to create an integrated understanding of digital natives, digital immigrants and their digital lives.

References

About NCSA Mosaic (2011). Retrieved from http://www.ncsa.illinois.edu/Projects/mosaic.html.

Bird, G. A., Goss, R. C., & Bird, G. W. (1990). Effects of home computer use on fathers' lives. *Family Relations, 39*, 438–42.

Chiong, C., & Shuler, C. (2010). *Learning: Is there an app for that? Investigations of young children's usage and learning with mobile devices and apps.* New York: The Joan Ganz Cooney Center at Sesame Workshop.

Common Standards (n.d.). Retrieved from http://www.fcc.gov/omd/history/internet/making-connections.html.

Devitt, K., & Roker, D. (2009). The role of mobile phones in family communication. *Children & Society, 23*, 189–202.

Durkin, K., & Barber, B. (2002). Not so doomed: computer game play and positive adolescent development. *Applied Developmental Psychology, 23*, 373–92.

Eastin, M., S., Greenberg, B. S., & Hofschire, L. (2006). Parenting the Internet. *Journal of Communication, 56*, 486–504.

Elder, G. H. (2003). The emergence and development of life course theory. In J. T. Mortimer & M. J. Shanahan (Eds.), *Handbook of the life course* (pp. 3–19). New York: Kluwer Academic/Plenum.

——(1994). Time, human agency, and social change: Perspectives on the life course. *Social Psychology Quarterly, 57*, 4–15.

Entertainment Software Association (2010). 2010 Sales, demographics, and usage data: Essential facts about the computer and video game industry. Retrieved from http://www.theesa.com/facts/pdfs/ESA_Essential_Facts_2010.pdf.

Garrison, M., & Christakis, D. A. (2005). *A teacher in the living room? Educational media for babies, toddlers, and preschoolers.* Menlo Park, CA: Kaiser Family Foundation.

Gutnick, A. V., Robb, M., Takeuchi, L., & Kotler, J. (2011). *Always connected: The new digital media habits of young children.* New York: The Joan Ganz Cooney Center at Sesame Workshop. Retrieved from http://www.joanganzcooneycenter.org/upload_kits/jgcc_alwaysconnected.pdf.

Hughes, R., & Hans, J. (2001). Computers, the Internet, and families. *Journal of Family Issues, 22,* 776–90.

Intel Museum (n.d.). Retrieved from http://www.intel.com/about/companyinfo/museum/archives/timeline.htm.

Jennings, N., & Wartella, E. (2004). Technology and the family. In A. L. Vangelisti (Ed.), *The handbook of family communication* (pp. 593–608). Mahwah, NJ: Lawrence Erlbaum Associates.

Jordan, A. B. (2003). A family systems approach to examining the role of the Internet in the home. In J. Turow & A. L. Kavanaugh (Eds.) *The wired homestead: An MIT Press sourcebook on the Internet and the family* (pp. 141–60). Cambridge, MA: MIT Press.

Kaare, B. H., Brandtzæg, P. B., Heim, J., & Endestad, T. (2007). In the borderland between family orientation and peer culture: The use of communication technologies among Norwegian tweens. *New Media & Society, 9*(4), 603–24.

Kaiser Family Foundation (2003). *Zero to six: Electronic media in the lives of infants, toddlers and preschoolers.* Menlo Park, CA: Henry J. Kaiser Family Foundation.

——(2006). *The media family: Electronic media in the lives of infants, toddlers, preschoolers and their parents.* Menlo Park, CA: Henry J. Kaiser Family Foundation.

Lapierre, M., Piotrowski, J. T., & Linebarger, D. L. (2010). *Results from a nationally representative sample of American families.* Philadelphia, PA: Annenberg School for Communication, University of Pennsylvania.

Lee, S., & Chae, Y. (2007). Children's internet use in a family context: Influence on family relationships and parental mediation. *Cyberpsychology and Behavior, 10*(5), 640–44.

Lenhart, A. (2007a). *A timeline of teens and technology. Presentation made to the Policy & Advocacy in the Schools Meeting of the American Psychological Association.* San Francisco, CA. Retrieved from http://www.pewinternet.org/Presentations/2007/A-Timeline-of-Teens-and-Technology.aspx.

——(2007b). *Cyberbullying.* Washington, DC: Pew Internet & American Life. Retrieved from http://www.pewinternet.org/~/media//Files/Reports/2007/PIP%20Cyberbullying%20Memo.pdf.pdf.

——(2010). *Cell phones and American adults.* Washington, DC: Pew Internet & American Life. Retrieved from http://www.pewinternet.org/~/media//Files/Reports/2010/PIP_Adults_Cellphones_Report_2010.pdf.

Lenhart, A., Ling, R., Campbell, S., & Purcell, K. (2010). *Teens and mobile phones.* Washington, DC: Pew Internet & American Life. Retrieved from http://www.pewinternet.org/~/media//Files/Reports/2010/PIP-Teens-and-Mobile-2010-with-topline.pdf.

Lewin, T. (2003). A growing number of video viewers watch from crib. *The New York Times.* Retrieved from http://www.nytimes.com/2003/10/29/us/a-growing-number-of-video-viewers-watch-from-crib.html?pagewanted=1.

Ling, R. (2000). "We will be reached": The use of mobile telephony among Norwegian youth, *Information, Technology, & People, 13*(2), 102–20.

Macgill, A. (2007). *Parent and teen internet use.* Washington, DC: Pew Internet & American Life. Retrieved from http://www.pewinternet.org/~/media//Files/Reports/2007/PIP_Teen_Parents_data_memo_Oct2007.pdf.

McCall, R. B., Parke, R. D., Kavanaugh, R. D., Engstrom, R. Russell, J., & Wycoff, E. (1977). Imitation of live and televised models by children one to three years of age, *Monographs of the Society for Research in Child Development, 42*(5), 1–94.

Mesch, G. S. (2003). The family and the Internet: The Israeli case. *Social Science Quarterly, 84*(4), 1038–50.

——(2006). Family relations and the Internet: Exploring a family boundaries approach. *The Journal of Family Communication, 6,* 119–38.

——(2009). Parental mediation, online activities, and cyberbullying. *Cyber Psychology & Behavior, 12*(4), 387–93.

Mitchell, E. (1985). The dynamics of family interaction around home video games. In M. B. Sussman (Ed.), *Personal computers and the family* (pp. 121–36). New York: Haworth Press.

Nikken, P. & Jansz, J. (2006). Parental mediation of children's videogame playing: A comparison of the reports by parents and children. *Learning, Media, & Technology, 31*(2), 181–202.

Nikken, P., Jansz, J., & Schouwstra, S. (2007). Parents' interest in videogame ratings and content descriptors in relation to game mediation. *European Journal of Communication, 22*(3), 315–36.

The NPD Group. (2010). *Kids & consumer electronics.* Port Washington, NY: The NPD Group.

Plowman, L., McPake, J. & Stephen, C. (2010). The technologisation of childhood? Young children and technology in the home. *Children & Society, 24*, 63–74.

Prensky, M. (2001). Digital natives, digital immigrants Part 1, *On the Horizon, 9*(5), 1–6.

Ribak, R. (2009). Remote control, umbilical cord and beyond: The mobile phone as a transitional object. *British Journal of Developmental Psychology, 27*, 183–96.

Richards, R., McGee, R., Williams, S. M., Welch, D., & Hancox, R. J. (2010). Adolescent screen time and attachment to parents and peers. *Archives of Pediatrics & Adolescent Medicine, 164*(3), 258–62.

Rideout, V. J., Foehr, U. G., & Roberts, D. F. (2010). *Generation M²: Media in the lives of 8- to 18-year-olds.* Retrieved from http://www.kff.org/entmedia/upload/8010.pdf.

Roberts, D. F., Foehr, U. G., & Rideout, V. (2005). *Generation M: Media in the lives of 8- to 18-year-olds.* Retrieved from http://www.kff.org/entmedia/upload/Generation-M-Media-in-the-Lives-of-8-18-Year-olds-Report.pdf.

Shuler, C. (2009). *iLearn: A content analysis of the iTunes App Store's education section.* New York: The Joan Ganz Cooney Center at Sesame Workshop.

Stephen, C., McPake, J., Plowman, L., & Berch-Heyman, S. (2008). Learning from the children: Exploring preschool children's encounters with ICT at home. *Journal of Early Childhood Research, 6*(2), 99–117.

Thornton, C. (2009). Compete: Facebook tops MySpace in popularity in January. *PCWorld*, February 12. Retrieved from http://www.pcworld.com/article/159431/compete_facebook_tops_myspace_in_popularity_in_january.html.

Tinnell, C. S. (1985). An ethnographic look at personal computers in the family setting. In M. B. Sussman (Ed.), *Personal Computers and the Family* (pp. 59–69). New York: Haworth Press.

Valcke, M., Schellens, T., Van Keer, H., & Gerarts, M. (2007). Primary school children's safe and unsafe use of the Internet at home and at school: An exploratory study. *Computers in Human Behavior, 23*, 2838–50.

Vandewater, E. A., Bickham, D. S., Lee, J. H., Cummings, H. M., Wartella, E. A., & Rideout, V. J. (2005). When the television is always on: Heavy television exposure and young children's development. *American Behavioral Scientist, 48*(5), 562–77.

Vandewater, E. A., Bickham, D. S., & Lee, J. H. (2006). Time well spent? Relating television use to children's free-time activities. *Pediatrics, 117*(2), e181–91.

Vandewater, E. A., Rideout, V. J., Wartella, E. A., Huang, X., Lee, J. H., & Shim, M. (2007). Digital childhood: Electronic media and technology use among infants, toddlers, and preschoolers. *Pediatrics, 119*(5), e1006–15.

Wartella, E., Richert, R. A., & Robb, M. B. (2010). Babies, television, and videos: How did we get here? *Developmental Review, 30*, 116–27.

Watt, D., & White, J. M. (1999). Computers and the family life: A family development perspective. *Journal of Comparative Family Studies, 30*(1), 1–15.

Weisskirch, R. (2010). No crossed wires: Cell phone communication in parent-adolescent relationships, *Cyberpsychology, Behavior, and Social Networking*. Retrieved from http://www.liebertpub.com/contentframe.aspx?code=PTwO51UJtdLXj4PbCAd%2b9O61QLd6H8GZ41xAX4QUr60XXFuL5J4PBhXzkH8HkRY27oEZ3lftKxPpFPzhIIWKeUmYqZytBcNc9vU%2b8cVSO9c%3d.

Windows (2011). Retrieved from http://windows.microsoft.com/en-US/windows/history.

Wolak, J., Mitchell, K., & Finkelhor, D. (2006). *Online victimization: 5 years later.* Alexandra, VA: National Center for Missing and Exploited Children. Retrieved from http://www.missingkids.com/en_US/publications/NC167.pdf.

28

The Reciprocal Influence of Drug and Alcohol Abuse and Family Members' Communication

Ashley P. Duggan and Beth A. Le Poire Molineux

The family system can play a role in substance abuse treatment, as well as in family circumstances promoting continued alcohol and drug use (e.g., Haugland, 2003; Rangarajan & Kelly, 2006). About 9.4 percent of the total U.S. population of individuals age 12 and above were classified as substance dependent or substance abusive (SAMHSA, 2006). The National Institute on Drug Abuse (NIDA) estimates economic costs of substance abuse around $484 billion per year (NIDA, 2007). The consequences of substance abuse also involve family problems, including communication problems (Fals-Stewart & Birchler, 1998; Kelly, Halford, & Young, 2002), increased detachment (Carroll, Robinson, & Flowers, 2002), verbal aggressiveness (Straus & Sweet, 1992), and physical abuse (Testa, Quigley, & Leonard, 2003; Wekerle & Wall, 2002). Spouses of substance abusers are frequently affected in terms of both physical and mental health (e.g., Hurcom, Coppello, & Orford, 2000). Children of alcoholics are at greater risk for behavioral, psychological, cognitive, and neuropsychological deficits (Johnson & Leff, 1999). Parents of adolescent substance abusers may be perceived as more controlling and less loving (e.g., Pandina & Schuele, 1983), and family members may influence continued substance abuse (e.g., Copello, Velleman, & Templeton, 2005; Rotunda, West, & O'Farrell, 2004).

While these findings point to the need to study negative effects of substance abuse on the family, research also documents potential positive intervening effects of family communication on substance abuse. Recovery programs are now incorporating family members in substance abuse therapy and treatment (e.g., Mann, 2003; Osterman & Grubic, 2000), with some treatment programs involving the family throughout the treatment process (Saatcioglu, Erim, & Cakmak, 2006). Research documents positive outcomes from involving family members in treatment. Behavioral couples therapy with alcoholics and remission after individual alcoholism treatment have been associated with improved family functioning in the form of reduced family stressors, improved marital adjustment, reduced domestic violence and conflict, reduced risk of separation and divorce, reduced emotional distress in spouses, and improved cohesion and caring (O'Farrell & Feehan, 1999; O'Farrell, Murphy, Alter, & Fald-Stewart, 2010). Including families in substance abuse treatment can potentially improve health outcomes for family members and enable a stronger support network to further aid in the recovery process (Morgan & Crane, 2010).

Relational effects point to the need to study the reciprocal impact of family members and continued substance abuse. Family members play a role in initiating alcohol or drug use, in the choice of substances, in the intensity of substance use, and in the decision to use or abstain from substances (Gruber & Taylor, 2006). Family interventions can involve family members promoting substance abusive individuals to participate in treatment, joint involvement of family members in the treatment, and responding to the needs of family members (Copello, Velleman, & Templeton, 2005). This chapter provides an overview of the ramifications of substance abuse on various family members, including spouses, children, siblings, and parents of adolescent abusers. Based on research supporting the Inconsistent Nurturing as Control (INC) theory assertion that significant others (spouses/cohabitors) in relationships with substance abusive individuals unintentionally and subtly encourage substance abusive behavior through their well-intentioned efforts to curtail this behavior (Duggan, Dailey, & Le Poire, 2008; Le Poire, 1992; Le Poire, 1995; Le Poire & Cope, 1999; Le Poire, Erlandson, & Hallett, 1998; Le Poire Hallett, & Erlandson, 2000), this chapter explores the unique communication dynamics in sustaining or deterring family members' substance abuse.

Background

Spousal Relationships

Living with a substance abusive romantic partner poses demanding challenges. Spouses share the pain of the problems associated with substance abuse and the gain of recovery. Substance abuse problems are manifest in the ways spouses approach, maintain, and communicate about relationships. Spouses of heroin users describe lack of emotional support and an inability to cope effectively with stressful events (Lex, 1990). Couples with one drug-using partner have been described as conflict-prone and intimacy-avoidant (Winn, 1995). Alcohol-related problems and anger predict lower marital satisfaction (Johns, Newcomb, Johnson, & Bradbury, 2007). Alcohol abuse is described as both a predictor and a consequence of marital stress, spousal abuse, and separation and divorce (Amato & Previti, 2003). The way couples communicate about substance abuse may exacerbate the problem, or on the contrary, may lead to greater abstinence and improved family functioning (e.g., Mann, 2003; Osterman & Grubic, 2000). Spouses may enable drinking or drug using through learned behavioral responses that increase the probability of further substance use, such as drinking with the spouse or minimizing negative consequences (Rotunda, West, & O'Farrell, 2004).

Clinical work and research provide evidence that romantic partner responses to drinking and drugging may either facilitate or hinder treatment acceptance and recovery efforts. The role of the spouse in alcoholism has been a focus in the literature since the 1970s, when research described the predicament of wives of alcoholics (e.g., Edwards, Harvey, & Whitehead, 1973). Much of the literature on family members in treatment continues to focus on the role of the spouse in relationship to the substance abuser (e.g., O'Farrell & Fals-Stewart, 2000). The spouse is the focus of research and clinical work both because of the relational complications inherent in substance abusive marriages and because of the ways communication with the spouse becomes ingrained with ongoing substance use. The original notion of codependency, or co-alcoholic, refers to an individual sacrificing his or her own personal and/or psychological needs for the sake of continued participation in a relationship (e.g., O'Gorman, 1993). Behaviors indicative of codependency include simultaneously enmeshing and controlling the drug or alcohol use through attempts to dominate or to attempt to sabotage recovery attempts. Thus, this review of spouses of substance abusers begins with the notion of "codependency" and then considers the ways relational aspects of a romantic commitment to a substance abusive individual may encourage codependent tendencies. This approach proffers that relational paradoxes which exist in the substance abuser–spouse relationship make it very difficult for this partner to attempt to control the substance abuse effectively and takes blame away from the spouse, instead focusing on challenging relationship dynamics.

Overview of Codependency

An essential characteristic of codependency is investing self-esteem, identity, and self-worth in the ability to control and influence behavior and feelings in others even when faced with adverse consequences (Cowan, Bommersbach, & Curtis, 1995; Springer, Britt, & Schlenker, 1998). The codependent individual might subvert his or her own needs to cater to the relational partner and is likely to remain in, and even perpetuate, a painful relationship and to use denial, rationalization, and projection to reframe negative relational implications (Cermak, 1986, 1991). Codependency has been associated with partners of alcoholic and drug-abusing individuals in the clinical field for the past two decades, but neither definitions of codependency nor empirical evidence for codependency clearly differentiate codependency as an individual-level trait or a relational process. Controversy is grounded in distinctions between codependency as a dyadic tool, a psychological assessment, and a disease entity (Morgan, 1991). Some clinicians who refer to co-dependency imply that a consistent pattern of traits and behaviors is recognizable across individuals (Cermak, 1991). In counseling, codependency is identified as a syndrome of internalized traits, self-perceptions, and relational styles associated with an individual's having been reared in a dysfunctional home (Wright & Wright, 1999).

A consensus definition developed by the National Council on Codependence defines codependency as reliance on people and things outside the self that neglect and diminish one's own identity and suggests that the false self that emerges is expressed through compulsive habits, addictions, and other disorders that further increase alienation for the true identity and foster a sense of shame (Whitfield, 1989). Codependency may be observed in denial or delusion (distorted thinking), emotional repression (distorted feelings), and compulsions (distorted behavior) (Wegscheider-Cruse & Cruse, 1990). Similarly, the core symptom of codependency is described as other focus/self-neglect comprised of a combination of control and boundary issues that manifests as a compulsion to help or control events or people, sometimes also associated with growing up in a troubled family, low self-worth, using a positive front to repress negative feelings, and preoccupation with imagined health difficulties (Hughes-Hammer, Martsolf, & Zeller, 1998). Key concepts of codependency may be summarized into seven categories:

1 socialization/development factors
2 psychological-relational factors
3 emotional factors
4 cognitive factors

5   communicative factors
6   behavioral factors
7   consequences upon so called "failure."

(Le Poire, Hallett, & Giles, 1998)

The often-cited criticism of the conceptualizations of codependency is the inclusion of so many common characteristics as to be virtually fruitless with regard to treatment or clear diagnosis. The enabling dimension of codependency may be observed in focus outside the self and in changing emotions and behavior to accommodate to the substance abusive individual (Harkness, Manhire, Blanchard, & Darling, 2007). Most salient to the current argument is that spousal dysfunction is dependent drinking, and enabling behaviors are normal reactions to stress present in substance abusive families and may reflect the partner's desire to avoid hassles and conflicts with the drinker (Rotunda, West, & O'Farrell, 2004). In other words, individuals' mental health dysfunction is higher when their spouse drinks and lower when their spouse is abstinent. Partners of substance abusers may exhibit higher anxiety and depression *because* their partners are not in control of their substance abuse. Thus, the authors argue that that the unique dynamics of the relationship elicit the responses of both substance abusers and their spouses. Inconsistent nurturing as control theory provides a framework to interpret the relational dynamics of this ongoing pattern.

Competing Goals of Nurturing and Control and Family Communication

Inconsistent Nurturing as Control Theory

Spouses are often strong and caring individuals who are known to both nurture and control their partners simultaneously. Inconsistent Nurturing as Control theory is based on the assumption that functional partners (partners of substance abusers or individuals who otherwise engage in behaviors that interfere with everyday functioning) have competing goals of nurturing and controlling (see Le Poire, 1992, 1995 for review).[1] Le Poire (1995) argues that there are several paradoxical injunctions in relationships that include afflicted partners (e.g., drug abusers, physically abusive individuals, depressed individuals, eating-disordered individuals) and that these paradoxes ultimately impact expressions of control by the functional family member (i.e., the partner with no problem interfering with day to day functioning) in the relationship. The contradictory nature of the functional family member's nurturing and subsequently controlling behavior is at the heart of the most problematic paradox in the relationship. Specifically, simultaneously, functional family members wish to retain their relationship *while* they attempt to extinguish the undesirable behavior (e.g., Duggan & Le Poire, 2006; Prescott & Le Poire, 2002). In addition, it is possible that the afflicted individual maintains the relationship because the functional family member's nurturing behavior is highly rewarding, particularly during times of crisis (Le Poire, 1995). These assumptions lead to the paradoxical conclusion that if functional family members actually control the undesirable behavior, they also lose their ability to utilize their nurturing resource base in response to that undesirable behavior. Thus, functional family members who seek to curtail the negative behavior may ultimately be driven by fear that extinguishing the undesirable behavior will decrease the substance abuser's dependency on them. These competing goals could lead to the inconsistent use of reinforcement and punishment of the change attempts. This inconsistency is at the heart of INC theory and could lead to decreased effectiveness of control attempts.

Application to the Functional Family Member–Substance-Dependent Relationship

In learning theory terms, INC argues that the functional family members' initial nurturing behavior may *reinforce* the substance abusive individual's drug or alcohol use. In contradistinction to the goal of reducing substance abuse, inconsistent influence may actually increase ongoing substance abuse (Le Poire, 1995). Even more problematically, functional family members may *intermittently* reinforce substance abusive behaviors. When they become resentful of their role as nurturer (e.g., Wiseman, 1991), they may instead reinforce substance abuse. This intermittent reinforcement may ultimately strengthen abusive behavior because intermittent reinforcement produces more long-term nonextinguishable behavior than continuous reinforcement. The lack of caregiving on the functional individual's part is likely an attempt to *punish*, or extinguish the substance abuse. Similarly, spouses of alcoholics develop dominance as a response to failure of the alcoholic spouse to fulfill his or her roles fully within the family (Saatcioglu, Erim, & Cakmak, 2006) but may also resent their need to assume additional control. Thus, they may become frustrated with their attempts to control and may also resort to intermittent control behaviors. INC theory argues that similar to intermittent reinforcement, the intermittent nature of this punishing behavior should actually *increase* the substance abuse, as well. Thus, inconsistent nurturing may ultimately strengthen the likelihood of substance abusive behavior through the learning theory processes of both intermittent reinforcement and intermittent punishment.

Le Poire and her colleagues have conducted a number of studies supporting the notion that this suspected inconsistency manifests within communication behavior over the life span of the relationship. Le Poire, Hallett, and Erlandson (2000) interviewed partners of substance abusers to investigate the pattern of their strategy usage. Before labeling their partners as substance abusive, functional partners typically reinforced the substance abusive behavior of their partners (e.g., offering a drink when they got home from work or using substances with their partners). Subsequent to a significant event which promoted labeling of their partners as substance abusive (e.g., a car accident, partner missing for weeks, violence, etc.), partners dramatically shifted their behavior to punish their partners (e.g., calling the police, threatening to leave, removing substances from the house). In sum, this first study of INC theory found that functional partners (of both genders) changed their strategy usage over time so that they (a) reinforced substance dependent behavior more before their determination that the behavior was problematic than after; (b) punished substance dependent behavior more after they labeled the drinking/drugging behavior as being problematic, than before; and (c) upon frustration, reverted to a mix of reinforcing and punishing strategies, resulting in an overall pattern of inconsistent reinforcement and punishment. Thus, as expected by INC theory, reinforcement is followed by punishment, which in turn is followed by reinforcement mixed with punishment.

One further question regarding this patterning pertains to the effectiveness of the inconsistent strategies. For the theory to hold, greater inconsistency should be more predictive of relapse and less predictive of persuasive effectiveness. However, it is important to note that this patterning in and of itself was not found to be more predictive of greater relapse. In contrast, patterns of reinforcement and punishment were linked to persuasive outcomes (Le Poire et al., 2000). Partners who were more consistent in punishing substance abuse and reinforcing alternative behavior (e.g., encouraging attendance at AA meetings) had substance abusive partners who relapsed less. Moreover, more successful partners also reported less depression than those with partners who relapsed more. This suggests that partners of substance abusing individuals can aid in reduced recidivism, and this assistance can also translate into better mental health outcomes for the partners.

A follow-up study examined whether episodic versus steady alcoholics had partners who differentially reinforced and punished substance abuse (Le Poire & Cope, 1999). Given that steady drinking may provide more positive functioning for the family unit than less predictable episodic drinking (e.g., Jacob and Leonard, 1988), it was predicted that partners of episodic drinkers may be more motivated to stop the alcoholic behavior and thus may use more effective strategies than partners of steady drinkers. Contrary to the prediction, partners of episodic drinkers used less effective strategies (less consistency) while partners of steady drinkers used more effective strategies (greater reinforcement of alternative behavior) immediately following the alcoholism labeling. Following frustration with initially unsuccessful persuasive attempts however, alcoholism subtype did operate as expected in that partners of episodic drinkers used more effective strategies (greater consistency combined with more punishment of drinking behavior) than did partners of steady drinkers.

Because INC theory proved to be an important link to better understand interpersonal influence in relationships over time, the next studies were the first to examine INC theory during ongoing interpersonal influence episodes between substance abusive individuals and their romantic partners and explores the role of interpersonal communication in sustaining or deterring substance abuse in married or cohabiting couples including one substance abusive individual (Duggan, Dailey, & Le Poire, 2008). Previous work relied on interviews of substance abusers and their partners, but this extension examined actual conversations and analyzed nonverbal and verbal communication that reinforces or punishes substance abuse. Results reveal consistent verbal punishment of substance abuse (e.g., threats, nagging) predicted lower relapse, while verbal reinforcement (e.g., telling the partner they are more fun when they use) predicted higher relapse. With regard to nonverbal communication, vocalic punishment and vocalic reinforcement predicted relapse and persuasive effectiveness. Results suggest the combination of behaviors resemble intermittent reinforcement and punishment and should actually strengthen the substance abusive behavior the partner tries to curtail.

Overall patterns of reinforcement and punishment were associated with health outcomes, and the next studies examined individual and relational differences in reinforcement and punishment patterns of partners of depressed individuals (Duggan, 2007). Female partners of depressed individuals used more strategies to actively help their partners get well before labeling the behavior problematic and then reverted to a mixture of reinforcing depression and helping partners get well, but male partners actively helped partners get well after labeling the depressive behavior problematic and eventually decreased helping and instead contributed to depressive behaviors. For example, male partners contributed to depressive behaviors by telling partners that they too would feel depressed if they experienced such lack of motivation, weight gain, or job loss, and by escalating negativity in the household.

The next study investigated the contention that the unique dynamics of caregiver–recipient relationships invoke particular paradoxes in the ways individuals subvert their own needs to help curtail the negative health behavior of a relational partners or family member in ways that make it difficult to assist in changing behavior (Duggan, Le Poire, Prescott, & Baham, 2009). Four contexts of interpersonal influence were examined to explore relational dynamics in the reasons why communication behaviors result in less than effective persuasion attempts in reducing substance abuse, increasing eating behavior of anorexics, altering violent tendencies, and curtailing depression. This work brings to light the unique power dynamics of helping-type relationships and the ways relationship dynamics are shaped by the influence attempts. As predicted by INC theory, individuals across these four relationship types who tried to change their partners' behavioral patterns were often nurturer-controllers who believed that change would enhance overall mental and physical health and improve their relationships but ended up using helping and controlling behaviors simultaneously. These mixed messages frequently serve to inter-mittently reinforce and intermittently punish the substance abuse, eating disorders, violent behavior, and depression.

If relationship dynamics are shaped by negative behavior, then strategies to curtail the behavior should be similar across contexts. In order to examine this question, a qualitative analysis of communicative strategies partners use to control compulsive behaviors was conducted. This analysis suggests thematic similarities for partners of both substance abusive and depressed individuals (Duggan, Le Poire, & Addis, 2006). Specifically, partners of substance abusive individuals and partners of depressed individuals supported the compulsive behavior by giving up their own time needs to accommodate the partner; ignored or avoided the problem by withdrawal, denial, or avoidance; and attempted to help end undesirable behavior by involving professionals, offering advice, and setting relational boundaries. This research lends support to the claim that the paradoxical nature of the functional-afflicted relationship restricts the use of verbal references to the problem and cultivating a reliance on nonverbal strategies of control.

INC Application to Other Family Relationships

Substance abusers and their partners do not live in a vacuum, but rather, are continually surrounded by their children, their siblings, and their parents. Given this, it is of para-mount importance that researchers also study the ways in which other significant family members also attempt to assist their substance abusing family member in their struggle with substance abuse. Continued evidence of this strategy use patterning in other family rela-tionships (with parents, children, and siblings) would support the additional contention that family members intermittently reinforce and punish the behavior they are trying to extinguish. This theoretical contention has successfully been applied to mothers of eating disordered daughters, indicating that mothers of eating disordered daughters displayed similar patterns of reinforcement and punishment such that they reinforced eating disorders more before they labeled the behavior problematic but punished the eating disorders more after (Prescott & Le Poire, 2002). Further, results indicated that consistently reinforcing alternative behavior immediately following labeling of the eating disorder significantly predicted higher perceptions of the mothers' persuasive effectiveness, but reinforcing the eating disorder predicted higher relapse. The most important implication of these find-ings for the current treatment is that significant family members (i.e., mothers) use similar patterns of inconsistent reinforcement and punishment as do partners of substance abusers. What is still to be determined is the role of important family members in helping to deter future substance abuse. Evidence of this patterning of strategy usage in future studies would support the contention that other family members (in addition to spouses) intermittently reinforce and punish the behavior they are trying to extinguish.

Parent Influence on Adolescent Substance Abuse

Much research has examined the role of parents in adolescents' substance use and abuse. Exposure to adverse family environments, particularly family conflict early in life, can influence the risk trajectory for developing substance use disorders in adolescence (Skeer, McCormick, Normand, Buka, & Gilman, 2009). Studies of parent–adolescent relations and substance abuse support the inconsistent nurturing as control theory contention that both nurturing and control messages are important in predicting adolescents' substance abuse. For instance, explanations for adolescent substance abuse are described as maladaptive means of coping with stress induced by adverse family environments (Skeer et al., 2009). Family dynamics contribute to risk for developing alcohol and drug abuse problems, but the family can also provide protective and recovery factors (O'Farrell & Fals-Stewart, 2006). When adolescents abuse drugs or alcohol, most parents feel a sense of hopelessness and desperation, with helplessness leading to denial and desperation leading parents into battles for control (Fagan, 2006). Thus, parents may try to shield adolescents from fully experiencing the consequences of their behavior, or they may engage in a spirited battle for control over the adolescent's behavior (Fagan, 2006).

Similarly, parental alcohol use and dependence followed by offspring substance abuse is found to play a significant role in family aggregation of alcohol use and dependence (Hartman, Lessem, Hopfer, Crowley, & Stallings, 2006). Other research also provides evidence for parental behavior influencing adolescent substance abuse. Hall, Henggeler, Ferreira, and East (1992) found that adolescents' substance use was associated with family affection and parental control, while Pandina and Schuele (1983) found that higher adolescent substance abuse was associated with higher levels of perceived parental control and lower perceived parental love. Additionally, frequency of adolescent substance use increased with high parental expectations and bad social climate in the family (Hurrelmann, 1990), and problematic drinking behavior was associated with low levels of family social support and with dysfunctional coping strategies (Schor, 1996).

Messages of support and control can be perceived as contradictory and thus may lead to inconsistent findings with regard to control attempts and substance abuse outcomes for adolescents. Humes and Humphrey (1994) found that parents of substance abusing daughters communicated a conflictual message of both greater affirmation and condemnation of their daughters' autonomy. This could be explained by the INC contention that nurturing behaviors may actually promote substance abuse when inconsistently mixed with punishment. This inconsistency in the relationships between control, support, and decreased alcohol use points to the need to directly examine the strategies that parents use in attempts to control their adolescents' substance abuse in terms of their reinforcing and punishing natures. Given that many of the above studies also found that modeling of substance abuse by parents is an important factor (e.g., Orenstein & Ullman, 1996), parents' drug and alcohol use should also be considered.

Sibling Relationships

Studying sibling relationships with adolescent substance abusers would allow for understanding the whole family system. For instance, Hall et al. (1992) found that several aspects of sibling relations were linked with substance use, and in some cases, sibling relations measures (especially sibling conflict) accounted for significantly more variance in substance use than did family relations measures. While parents play an important role in adolescent substance abuse, older brother–younger brother relationships also have a significant impact on younger brother substance abuse (Brook, Brook, & Whiteman, 1999), and sibling completion of substance abuse treatment programs (Feigelman, 1987).

Most relevant to the current exploration, it has also been postulated that siblings may attempt to sabotage substance abuse recovery attempts (Huberty & Huberty, 1986). This is consistent with family systems theory as well in that non-substance abusing siblings may actually benefit by helping to maintain the impression that their sibling is the "identified patient" and thus take the spotlight off them during the adolescent years when less monitoring due to distracted parents may be desirable. Thus, from a family systems perspective, it is very important to try to understand the types of strategies that siblings of adolescent substance abusers use in an attempt to deter their sibling's substance abuse. It is possible that siblings use inconsistently reinforcing and subsequently punishing strategies as predicted by inconsistent nurturing as control theory. This inconsistency is likely to result in strengthened, as opposed to weakened, tendencies to abuse substances. This is especially likely to manifest relationships in which the older sibling abuses substances (Brook et al., 1999), and thus birth order should also be measured in research on the influence of siblings on substance abuse. The effects of modeling have been shown to be stronger from older to younger siblings, and older siblings rivalry with younger siblings may result in greater attempts to sabotage the "good" recovering behavior of the substance abuser so that the older sibling may shine by comparison.

Family Influence on Children Raised Amidst Substance Abuse

Children of substance abusers may also play a role in helping a parent recover from drug or alcohol abuse. The detrimental effects of being raised by a substance abusing parent have been documented (e.g., Mothersead, Kivlighan, & Wynkoop, 1998), ranging from increased maltreatment (e.g., Sheridan, 1995), and increased maladjustment (Rubio-Stipec, Bird, Canino, & Bravo, 1991) to increased probability of foster care (Dore, Doris, & Wright, 1995). Additionally, mothers recovering from an addiction are more likely to report greater parenting stress and greater use of problematic parenting behaviors (Harmer et al., 1999). Additionally, offspring of substance abusers show a higher incidence of anxiety disorders and substance disorders, as well as conduct disorder and depression (Hussong et al., 2007).

Other researchers caution that negative effects are not certain. Some studies have shown that parental alcoholism was not a significant predictor of differences in adult self-esteem or locus of control (Werner & Broida, 1991), nor of the majority of measures assessing multiple aspects of psychological well-being and personality development (Tweed & Ryff, 1991). Specifically, there may be an interaction between presence of substance abusing parents and supportive relationships with nonabusing parents and siblings and appropriate levels of parentification which permit the child of an alcoholic to have high self-esteem and adaptive capabilities while simultaneously lacking problematic substance use (Walker & Lee, 1998). In contradistinction, however, studies of the protective effects of sober parents found very little evidence of the buffering hypothesis (Curran & Chassin, 1996). Thus we should use caution, as research in this area has not yet produced a definitive or coherent picture (Hurcom et al., 2000).

Still other findings link children from homes in which one or both parents are labeled problem drinkers with alcohol disorders (e.g., Pihl, Peterson, & Finn, 1990; Sher, 1991), earlier onset of illicit substance use, higher rates of lifetime marijuana and cocaine use, and more frequent adolescent antisocial behavior (Windle, 1996). Failure to recognize the impact of parental alcohol or drug abuse may be due to multiple adaptation strategies, including assuming adult responsibilities, taking care of emotional needs of the family, or disruptive acting out (Scharff, Broida, Conway, & Yue, 2004).

Research also provides evidence that children of alcoholic parents develop parentifica-tion, where children take on parental roles within the family (Burnett, Jones, Bliwise, & Ross, 2006). Evidence of this abounds in ongoing therapy sessions with adult children of alcoholics who develop many strengths which actually bode them well in life, as they frequently become the structure providers within their own family or within organiza-tions, as individuals rely on them to be the steady state which they are so well equipped to do because of their early learning. This finding that adult children of alcoholics (and children of other parents who provide chaotic living environments due to mental health issues [e.g., depression, bi-polar disorder, or personality disorders including but not limited to borderline and paranoid personality disorders]) undergirds theorizing and research finding that these children have many interpersonal strengths which cause them to be highly responsive to others because they learned to attach to others through their caregiving behavior. This altercentrism allows these adults to be highly effective workers in that they tend to be very reliable and attract others to them who also need more struc-ture. Unfortunately, this often translates into nurturer–caregiving behavior as evidenced by many of the nonsubstance abusive individuals referenced here. Thus perpetuates the cycle of adult children of chaotic home environments continuing to be drained by the neediness of the new partners they are drawn too because of the similarity in how they learned to love.

Adult children of alcoholics (ACOAs) also are drawn to routine that is predictable and under their control, unlike the earlier chaotic environment in which they were raised. This is part of an overall system of control on the ACOA's part which may be perceived as overly managing relationships. According to psychoanalytic theorizing such as self-psychology, these children may develop an omnipotent feeling of power over others and themselves because their normal childhood belief that they were grandiose and all powerful never transmuted into appropriate perceptions of their actual abilities. In the world they grew up in as parentified children, they really did have inordinate and inappropriate amount of control, as the parents' relied on the children to make decisions out of their normal scope or capacity. This results in seemingly very mature children who are further reinforced through the school and other social systems as being very well-behaved and grounded children. Thus perpetuates the ACOA's belief that they *should* be able to control other's behavior (including their spouses). A potential outcome of the ongoing attempts at control is the spiraling into relationship difficulties with their partners and their children who often find them overly controlling and demanding.

It may be that the parent–adolescent relationship can be interpreted as reciprocal, where functional parents inconsistently reinforce and punish adolescent substance use, or where functional adolescents reinforce and punish their parents' substance abusive behavior. When parents drink and children feel frightened and helpless, they may care for their par-ents to bring some sense of control to an otherwise uncontrollable situation. Together these findings indicate a highly stressful situation for the child of the substance abuser. What is still to be understood are the ways in which children may attempt to deter their parents' future substance abuse episodes as they continue to live in this highly stressful situation. It is highly likely that children begin to understand the disruptive nature of their family life is linked to substance abuse and, therefore, that children will begin attempts to deter their parents' substance abuse in the future. In line with inconsistent nurturing as control theory, because children also love their parents and desire positive relations, it is likely that they will sometimes inadvertently do things which are nurturing and therefore reinforce the substance abusing behavior. Thus, future research should examine strategies that adult children of substance abusers employ in response to their parents' abusive episodes.

Implications for Treatment

Communication patterns identified in this chapter pose particular implications for treatment. Family behavior therapy for substance abuse incorporates ongoing components of involving the whole family in setting behavioral goals and implementing contingent rewards. Functional children of substance abusing parents may receive child-focused treatments that parallel adult treatments, both designed to increase and consistently reinforce desired behavior (Donohue et al., 2009). Behavioral therapy programs have developed since the 1970s to involve significant others and community support systems in the treatment plan, utilizing multiple behavioral therapies to address problems that contributed to alcohol or drug use. Developing behavioral goals and a treatment plan, addressing basic necessities, and stimulus control are core features of family behavior therapy (Donohue et al., 2009). Recent substance abuse interventions focus on behavioral couples therapy combined with individual counseling. Initial evidence suggests that behavioral family counseling for substance abuse, where family members are involved in treatment, predicts better retention of individuals in treatment, improved drug and alcohol abstinence, and improved relationship adjustment (O'Farrell, Murphy, Alter, & Fals-Stewart, 2010).

Couples or individual treatment for the partner of the substance abuser may also prove useful in "unhooking" the couple from the evidenced pattern of inconsistent nurturing and control surrounding the substance abuse. Specifically, therapists using the traditional domestic violence triangle of victim–perpetrator–rescuer can shine a light on this pattern, especially to the extent that nonsubstance abusive partners feel victimized by their partners' substance abuse and thereby punish this abusive behavior as a way to curtail their own victimization. Unfortunately, substance abusers will similarly feel victimized by the punishing behavior and blame the nonsubstance abusive partner for their substance abuse as being a result of the nonabuser's critical demanding behavior. This may translate into the stereotypical pattern of denial for substance abusers as they can blame their partner instead of accepting their own responsibility for their actions. Alcoholics Anonymous (AA) goes a long way to get abusers to accept responsibility for their own drinking, and may be affecting this relational process in a positive way.

Ironically, asking nonsubstance abusers to temporarily take the role of "rescuer" can unhook this pattern as lessening negativity and a more positive relational climate may result. Ultimately, both partners need to step off this triangle altogether to attempt to meet each other as adults where both are responsible for their own actions and no longer allowed to play the victim to the other's "bad behavior" (e.g., substance abuse or nagging controlling behavior). Here again, AA is wise to expect partners to both take responsibility for their own behavior. Recognizing the influence of both partners offers a way to break the pattern of abuse (this time substance abuse as opposed to violence) by weakening the strangle hold that the victim–perpetrator places on the types of communication behavior they are able to enact. By enacting responsible "adult" like choice driven behavior, they can break this pattern and discontinue the pattern of blaming and externalizing.

Research suggests that treating parental substance abuse also has positive secondary effects on children. In particular, interventions that reduce parental drinking and improve couple functioning may serve as an important preventive intervention for pre-adolescents, whereas adolescents may need more intensive interventions to address internalizing and externalizing symptoms (Kelley & Fals-Stewart, 2007). Families need to be prepared for the fact that the initial reaction to increased structure may be met with negativity, but that consistency is a key element to long-term behavior change. If families have tried to implement change in the past but were not able to be consistent in reinforcing positive behaviors and punishing negative behaviors, they should be encouraged about the potential effectiveness in long-term change with counseling intervention. The ability to maintain behavioral changes following an episode of treatment is critical, and the first year following substance abuse treatment is recognized clinically as a period of high risk for relapse (Clifford, Maisto, Stout, Mckay, & Tonigan, 2006).

Summary and Conclusions

The current chapter emphasizes the fact that all family members are influenced by substance abuse in the family environment regardless of whether the substance abusive family member is a spouse, a parent, an adolescent child, or sibling. When one individual in a family abuses drugs and alcohol, the whole family is affected. Similarly, each individual in the family can play a role in the manifestations of continued drug or alcohol use per se, and in the ways the substance abuse plays out in family relationships. Family members may unintentionally reinforce the substance abuse they desperately seek to curtail through their efforts to nurture the family member but control the drug or alcohol use. As important as the deleterious effects that substance abuse can have on family members are, this work also explored the potential positive intervening effects of family communication for continued substance abuse. Specifically, behavioral couples therapy has been associated with improved family functioning, abstinence, better family relations, and positive feelings about self. Further, Le Poire et al. (2000) found that consistently punishing substance abuse combined with consistently reinforcing alternative behavior was predictive of lesser relapse in a substance abusing sample, and consistency predicted persuasive effectiveness in ongoing conversation about decreasing substance abuse (Duggan, Dailey, & Le Poire, 2008). Through greater examination of all family members' use of inconsistent nurturing as control, we may better understand the mechanisms by which spouses can help each other, children can help their parents, parents can help their adolescent children, and siblings can help each other in the familial battle against substance abuse.

Note

1 This article was published with 1994 as the year on the cover page, but 1995 on all subsequent pages. The publication year was 1995.

References

Amato, P. R., & Previti, D. (2003). People's reasons for divorcing: Gender, social class, the life course, and adjustment. *Journal of Family Issues*, 24, 602–26.

Brook, J. S., Brook, D. W., & Whiteman, M. (1999). Older sibling correlates of younger sibling drug use in the context of parent–child relations. *Genetic, Social and General Psychology Monographs, 125*, 451–68.

Burnett, G., Jones, R. A., Bliwise, N. G., & Ross, L. T. (2006). Family unpredictability, parental alcoholism, and the development of parentification. *The American Journal of Family Therapy, 34*, 181–89.

Carroll, J. J, Robinson, B. E., & Flowers, C. (2002). Marital estrangement, positive feelings toward partners and locus of control: Female counselors married to alcohol-abusing and non-alcohol-abusing spouses. *Journal of Addictions & Offender Counseling, 23*, 30–40.

Cermak, T. L. (1986). *Diagnosing and treating co-dependence: A guide for professionals who work with chemical dependents, their spouses and children.* Minneapolis, MN: Johnson Institute books.

Cermak, T. (1991). Co-addiction as a disease. *Psychiatric Annals, 21*, 266–72.

Clifford, P. R., Maisto, S. A., Stout, R. L., Mckay, J. R., & Tonigan, J. S. (2006). Long-term posttreatment function among those treated for alcohol use disorders. *Alcoholsm: Clinical and Experimental Research, 30*, 311–19.

Copello, A. G., Velleman, D. B., & Templeton, L. J. (2005). Family interventions in the treatment of alcohol and drug problems. *Drug and Alcohol Reviews, 24*, 369–85.

Cowan, G., Bommersbach, M., & Curtis, S. R. (1995). Codependency, loss of self, and power. *Psychology of Women Quarterly, 19*, 221–36.

Curran, P. J., & Chassin, L. (1996). A longitudinal study of parenting as a protective factor for children of alcoholics. *Journal of Studies on Alcohol, 57*, 305–13.

Donohue, B., Azrin, N., Allen, D. N., Romero, V., Hill, H. H., Tracy, K., Lapota, H., Gorney, S., Abdel-al, R., Caldas, D., Herdzik, K., Valdez, R., & Van Hasselt, V. B. (2009). Family behavior therapy for substance abuse and other associated problems: A review of its intervention components and applicability. *Behavior Modification, 33*, 495–519.

Dore, M. M., Doris, J. M., & Wright, P. (1995). Identifying substance abuse in maltreating families: A child welfare challenge. *Child Abuse and Neglect, 19*, 531–43.

Duggan, A. P. (2007). Sex Differences in Communicative Attempts to Curtail Depression: An Inconsistent Nurturing as Control Perspective. *Western Journal of Communication, 71*, 114–35.

Duggan, A. P., Dailey, R., & Le Poire, B. A. (2008). Reinforcement and Punishment of Substance Abuse During Ongoing Interactions: A Conversational Test of Inconsistent Nurturing as Control Theory. *Journal of Health Communication, 13*, 417–33.

Duggan, A. P., & Le Poire, B. A. (2006). One down; two involved: An application and extension of inconsistent nurturing as control theory to couples including one depressed individual. *Communication Monographs, 73*, 379–405.

Duggan, A. P., Le Poire, B. A., & Addis, K. (2006). A qualitative analysis of communicative strategies used by partners of substance abusers and depressed individuals during recovery: Implications for inconsistent nurturing as control theory. In R. M. Dailey & B. A. Le Poire (Eds.), *Applied interpersonal communication matters: Family, health, and community relations* (pp. 150–74). New York: Peter Lang.

Duggan, A. P., Le Poire, B. A, Prescott, M., & Baham, C. S. (2009). Understanding the helper: The role of codependency in health care and health care outcomes. In D. E. Brashers & D. Goldsmith (Eds.), *Communicating to manage health and illness* (pp. 271–300). New York: Routledge.

Edwards, P., Harvey, C., & Whitehead, P. (1973). Wives of alcoholics, a critical review and analysis. *Quarterly Journal of Studies on Alcohol, 34*, 112–32.

Fagan, R. (2006). Counseling and treating adolescents with alcohol and other substance use problems and their families. *The Family Journal: Counseling and Therapy for Couples and Families, 14*, 326–33.

Fals-Stewart, W., & Birchler, G. R. (1998). Marital interactions of drug-abusing patients and their partners: Comparisons with distressed couples and relationship to drug-using behavior. *Psychology of Addictive Behaviors, 12*, 28–38.

Feigelman, W. (1987). Day-care treatment for multiple drug abusing adolescents: Social factors linked with completing treatment. *Journal of Psychoactive Drugs, 19*, 335–44.

Gruber, K. J., & Taylor, M. F. (2006). A family perspective for substance abuse: Implications from the literature. *Journal of Social Work Practice in the Addictions, 6*, 1–29.

Hall, J. A., & Henggeler, S. W., Ferreira, D. K., & East, P. L. (1992). Sibling relations and substance use in high-risk female adolescents. *Family Dynamics of Addiction Quarterly, 2*, 44–51.

Harkness, D., Manhire, S., Blanchard, J., & Darling, J. (2007). Codependent attitude and behavior: Moderators of psychological distress with alcohol and other drug (AOD) problems. *Alcoholism Treatment Quarterly, 25*, 39–52.

Hartman, C. A., Lessem, J. M., Hopfer, C. J., Crowley, T. J., & Stallings, M. C. (2006). The family transmission of adolescent alcohol abuse and dependence. *Journal of Studies on Alcohol, 67*, 657–64.

Harmer, A. L. M., Sanderson, J., & Mertin, P. (1999). Influence of negative childhood experiences on psychological functioning, social support, and parenting for mothers recovering from addiction. *Child Abuse and Neglect, 23*, 421–33.

Haugland, B. S. M. (2003). Parental alcohol abuse: Relationship between child adjustment, parental characteristics, and family functioning. *Child Psychiatry and Human Development, 34*, 127–46.

Huberty, D. J., & Huberty, C. E. (1986). Sabotaging siblings: An overlooked aspect of family therapy with drug dependent adolescents. *Journal of Psychoactive Drugs, 18*, 31–41.

Hughes-Hammer, C., Martsolf, D. S., & Zeller, R. A. (1998). Depression and codependency in women. *Archives of Psychiatric Nursing, 12*, 326–34.

Hussong, A. M., Wirth, R. J., Edwards, M. C., Curran, P. J., Chassin, L. A., & Zucker, R. A. (2007). Externalizing symptoms among children of alcoholic parents: Entry points for an antisocial pathway to alcoholism. *Journal of Abnormal Psychology, 116*, 529–42.

Humes, D. L., & Humphrey, L. L. (1994). A multimethod analysis of families with a polydrug-dependent or normal adolescent daughter. *Journal of Abnormal Psychology, 103*, 676–85.

Hurcom, C., Copello, A., & Orford, J. (2000). The family and alcohol: Effects of excessive drinking and conceptualizations of spouses over recent decades. *Substance Use and Misuse, 35*, 473–502.

Hurrelmann, K. (1990). Parents, peers, teachers and other significant partners in adolescence. *International Journal of Adolescence and Youth, 2*, 211–36.

Jacob, T., & Leonard, K. (1988). Alcoholic spouse interaction as a function of alcoholism subtype and alcohol consumption interaction. *Journal of Abnormal Psychology, 97*, 231–37.

Johns, A. L., Newcomb, M. D., Johnson, M. D., & Bradbury, T. N. (2007). Alcohol-related problems, anger, and marital satisfaction in monoethnic Latino, biethnic Latino, and European American newlywed couples. *Journal of Social and Personal Relationships, 24*(2), 255–75.

Johnson, J. L., & Leff, M. (1999). Children of substance abusers: Overview of research findings. *Pediatrics, 103*, 1085–99.

Kelley, M. L., & Fals-Stewart, W. (2007). Treating parental alcoholism with learning sobriety together: Effects on adolescent versus preadolescents. *Journal of Family Psychology, 21*, 435–44.

Kelly, A. B., Halford, W. K., & Young, R. M. (2002). Couple communication and female problem drinking: A behavioral observation study. *Psychology of Addictive Behaviors, 16*, 269–71.

Le Poire, B. A. (1992). Does the codependent encourage substance dependent behavior? Paradoxical injunctions in the codependent relationship. *The International Journal of the Addictions, 27*, 1465–74.

——(1995). Inconsistent nurturing as control theory: Implications for communication-based research and treatment programs. *Journal of Applied Communication Research, 23*, 1–15.

Le Poire, B. A., & Cope, K. (1999). Episodic versus steady state drinkers: Evidence of differential reinforcement patterns. *Alcoholism Treatment Quarterly, 17*, 79–90.

Le Poire, B. A., Erlandson, K. T., & Hallett, J. S. (1998). Punishing versus reinforcing strategies of drug discontinuance: The effect of persuaders' drug use on persuasive effectiveness and relapse. *Health Communication, 10*, 293–316.

Le Poire, B. A., Hallett, J. S., & Erlandson, K. T. (2000). An initial test of inconsistent nurturing as control theory: How partners of drug abusers assist their partners' sobriety. *Human Communication Research, 26*, 432–57.

Le Poire, B. A., Hallett, J. S., & Giles, H. (1998). Codependence: The paradoxical nature of the functional-afflicted relationship. In B. H. Spitzberg & W. R. Cupach (Eds.), *The dark side of close relationships* (pp. 153–76). Mahwah, NJ: Lawrence Erlbaum Associates.

Lex, B. W. (1990). Male heroin addicts and their female mates: Impact on disorder and recovery. *Journal of Substance Abuse, 2*, 147–275.

Mann, A. (2003). *Relationships matter: Impact of parental, peer factors on teen, young adult substance abuse*. National Institute on Drug Abuse, Vol. 18, No. 2. Retrieved from http://drugabuse.gov/NIDA_notes/NNVol18N2/Relationships.html.

Morgan, J. P. (1991). What is codependency? *Journal of Clinical Psychology, 47*(5), 720–29.

Morgan, T. B., & Crane, D. R. (2010). Cost-effectiveness of family-based substance abuse treatment. *Journal of Marital and Family Therapy, 36*, 486–98.

Mothersead, P. K., Kivlighan, D. M., & Wynkoop, T. F. (1998). Attachment, family dysfunction, parental alcoholism, and interpersonal distress in late adolescence: A structural model. *Journal of Counseling Psychology, 45*, 196–203.

National Institute on Drug Abuse (NIDA) (2007). Retrieved from www.nida.nih.gov.

O'Farrell, T. J., & Fals-Stewart, W. (2000). Behavioral couples therapy for alcoholism and drug abuse. *Journal of Substance Abuse Treatment, 18,* 51–54.

——(2006). *Behavioral couples therapy for alcoholism and drug abuse.* New York: Guilford Press.

O'Farrell, T. J., & Feehan, M. (1999). Alcoholism treatment and the family: Do family and individual treatments for alcoholic adults have preventive effects for children? *Journal of Studies on Alcohol, 13,* 125–29.

O'Farrell, T. J., Murphy, M., Alter, J., & Fals-Stewart, W. (2010). Behavioral family counseling for substance abuse: A treatment development pilot study. *Addictive Behaviors, 35,* 1–6.

O'Gorman, P. (1993). Codependency explored: A social movement in search of definition and treatment. *Psychiatric Quarterly, 64,* 199–212.

Orenstein, A., & Ullman, A. (1996). Characteristics of alcoholic families and adolescent substance use. *Journal of Alcohol and Drug Education, 41,* 86–101.

Osterman, F., & Grubic, V. N. (2000). Family functioning of recovered alcohol-addicted patients: A comparative study. *Journal of Substance Abuse Treatment, 19,* 475–79.

Pandina, R. J. & Schuele, J. A. (1983). Psychosocial correlates of alcohol and drug use of adolescent students and adolescents in treatment. *Journal of Studies on Alcohol, 44,* 950–73.

Pihl, R. O., Peterson, J., & Finn, P. R. (1990). An heuristic model for the inherited predisposition to alcoholism. *Psychology of Addicted Behavior, 4,* 12–25.

Prescott, M. E., & Le Poire, B. A. (2002). Eating disorders and the mother–daughter communication: A test of inconsistent nurturing as control theory. *Journal of Family Communication, 2,* 59–78.

Rangarajan, S., & Kelly, L. (2006). Family communication patterns, family environment, and the impact of parental alcoholism on offspring self-esteem. *Journal of Social and Personal Relationships, 23,* 655–71.

Rotunda, R. J., West, L., & O'Farrell, T. J. (2004). Enabling behavior in a clinical sample of alcohol-dependent clients and their partners. *Journal of Substance Abuse Treatment, 26,* 269–76.

Rubio-Stipec, M., Bird, H., Canino, G., & Bravo, M. (1991). Children of alcoholic parents in the community. *Journal of Studies on Alcohol, 52,* 78–88.

Saatcioglu, O., Erim, R., & Cakmak, D. (2006). Role of family in alcohol and substance use. *Psychiatry and Clinical Neurosciences, 60,* 125–32.

SAMHSA (2006). Overview of findings from the 2002 national survey on drug use and health. Retrieved from http://samhsa.gov/oas/oasftp.htm.

Scharff, J. L., Broida, J. P., Conway, K., & Yue, A. (2004). The interaction of parental alcoholism, adaptation role, and family dysfunction. *Addictive Behaviors, 29,* 575–81.

Schor, E. L. (1996). Adolescent alcohol use: Social determinants and the case for early family-centered intervention. *Bulletin of the New York Academy of Medicine, 73,* 335–55.

Skeer, M., McCormick, M. C., Normand, S. T., Buka, S. L., & Gilman, S. E. (2009). A prospective study of familial conflict, psychological stress, and the development of substance use disorders in adolescence. *Drug and Alcohol Dependence, 104,* 65–72.

Sher, K. J. (Ed.) (1991). *Children of alcoholics: A critical appraisal of theory and research.* Chicago, IL: University of Chicago Press.

Sheridan, M. J. (1995). A proposed intergenerational model of substance abuse, family functioning, and abuse/neglect. *Child Abuse and Neglect, 19,* 519–30.

Springer, C. A., Britt, T. W., & Schlenker, B. R. (1998). Codependency: Clarifying the construct. *Journal of Mental Health Counseling, 20,* 141–58.

Straus, M. A., & Sweet, S. (1992). Verbal/symbolic aggression in couples: Incidence rates and relationships to personal characteristics. *Journal of Marriage and the Family, 54,* 346–57.

Testa, M., Quigley, B. M., & Leonard, K. E. (2003). Does alcohol make a difference? Within-participants comparison of incidents of partner violence. *Journal of Interpersonal Violence, 18,* 735–43.

Tweed, S. H., & Ryff, C. D. (1991). Adult children of alcoholics: Profiles of wellness admidst distress. *Journal of Studies on Alcohol, 52,* 133–41.

Walker, J. P., & Lee, R. E. (1998). Uncovering strengths of children of alcoholic parents. *Contemporary Family Therapy, 20,* 521–38.

Wegscheider-Cruse, S., & Cruse, J. R. (1990). *Understanding codependency.* Deerfield Beach, FL: Health Communications, Inc.

Wekerle, C., & Wall, A. M. (Eds.) (2002). *The violence and addiction equation: Theoretical and clinical issues in substance abuse and relationship violence.* New York: Brunner-Routledge.

Werner, L. J., & Broida, J. P. (1991). Adult self-esteem and locus of control as a function of familial alcoholism and dysfunction. *Journal of Studies on Alcohol, 52,* 249–52.

Windle, M. (1996). On the discriminative validity of a family history of problem drinking index with a national sample of young adults. *Journal of Studies on Alcohol, 57,* 378–86.

Winn, M. E. (1995). Drawing upon the strengths of couples in the treatment of chronic drug addiction. *Journal of Family Psychotherapy, 6,* 33–54.

Whitfield, C. L. (1989). Co-dependence: Our most common addiction—Some physical, mental, emotional and spiritual perspectives. *Alcoholism Treatment Quarterly, 6,* 19–36.

Wiseman, J. P. (1991). *The other half: Wives of alcoholics and their social-psychology.* New York: De Gruyter.

Wright, P. H., & Wright, K. D. (1999). The two faces of codependent relating: A research-based perspective. *Contemporary Family Therapy: An International Journal, 21,* 527–43.

29

Charting Dangerous Territory

The Family as a Context of Violence and Aggression

René M. Dailey, Carmen M. Lee, and Brian H. Spitzberg

Every family is a journey of discovery, and each member's path through this journey holds both the promise of great joy and great pain. People find themselves with few maps to guide their journeys through the wilderness of family life. One of the more hazardous detours that often arises in these family journeys is the experience of violence and aggression. This chapter summarizes the research regarding aggressive and violent inter-actions in family relationships. We map out the prevalence and effects of abuse including some under-explored areas of family violence. We also chart some heuristic theoretical perspectives with an eye toward understanding the communicative nature of aggression and violence. In closing, we survey prevention and intervention strategies and suggest a course for future directions of research.

Mapping the Territory: Definitions and Prevalence of Family Violence and Aggression

A variety of efforts have been undertaken to explore the breadth and depth of family violence (e.g., Anderson, Umberson, & Elliott, 2004; Barnett, Miller-Perrin, & Perrin, 1997; Bergen, 1998). These efforts reveal the extensive interdisciplinary nature of research and theory in family violence as well as the challenges of delimiting the scope of the phenomenon. In addition, the political and ideological forces surrounding the evolving concept of what constitutes a "family" considerably compound the problems of defining family violence. Consensus in defining the nature of violence and its semantic family of concepts is unlikely, but it is incumbent upon serious scholarly inquiry into the topic to specify working definitions and the rationale underlying such choices.

Several stances need to be articulated in the process of defining violence. First, all definitional choices in regard to violence will inevitably run afoul of certain cultural, political, ideological or theoretical fault lines. What is viewed as abusive in one culture may be highly tolerated in another (e.g., Van Oudenhoven et al., 2008). Second, the progress of science requires a narrowing rather than a broadening of the meaning of key terms. Third, there is a family of terms associated with family violence that deserve consideration and articulation in relationship to one another. The list includes, but is not limited to: abuse (psychological, sexual), aggression, battering, bullying, coercion, harassment, incest, neglect, rape, sexual pressure, stalking, unwanted sex, and violence.

We highlight a few of these terms as they have been more recently used in the literature to specify the more general notion of abuse. First, *aggression* has been defined as any action that is unwanted by and injurious to the victim, whether physically or psychologically (Bandura, 1973; Baron & Richardson, 1994). *Violence* is often used synonymously with aggression, but it is also often viewed as a subset of aggression. Typically these terms refer to some combination of physical contact (e.g., hitting, choking) imposed involuntarily, received harms (e.g., damaging volume, painful punishment), or physical restraint, isolation, neglect or deprivation of sources of sustenance (e.g., restraint, starvation). More generally, *physical violence* (a) is enacted by another with the intent to harm, (b) is unwanted by the target(s), and (c) imposes physical short-term or long-term harm. In addition, what once was primarily referred to as "wife abuse" or "wife battering," and later as "domestic violence," has increasingly been studied under the more inclusive term of *intimate partner violence* (IPV).

In contrast to physical violence, communicative aggression may seek to injure, but it does so without, or in addition to, physical contact or restraint. All aggression and violence are forms of communication. Communicative or psychological forms of aggression, however, attempt their injury through a process that is interpretively and symbolically mediated. The terms "psychological abuse" and "communicative aggression" will be treated as synonymous for the purposes of this chapter. *Communicative aggression* (CA) is defined as "any recurring set of messages that function to impair a person's enduring preferred self-image" (Dailey, Lee, & Spitzberg, 2007, p. 303). CA represents a collection of messages that diminish a person's self-concept in undesirable ways (e.g., domination, denigration, withholding support, restriction of freedoms, or attempts to cause emotional distress).

Withdrawal, avoidance, ostracism, deprivation, or *neglect* more generally, can also occur physically or symbolically. It is not uncommon to define neglect as actions that result in a deficit in providing for a person's basic needs (Barnett et al., 1997). This term is most commonly applied to child neglect, but it seems functionally applicable to teen and adult relations as well. Various types of episode-based avoidance, such as the silent treatment, imposed isolation, or conflict withdrawal may be perceived as punitive or abusive (Williams, Shore, & Grahe, 1998).

Another set of concepts relevant to family violence includes sexual abuse, sexual assault, marital rape, incest, and the various terms related to sexual aggression (see Spitzberg, 1998). *Child sexual abuse* (CSA) has been defined in ways that range from *any* sexual interaction between adults and children, to conditional operationalizations such as whenever a significantly older person or person with substantially greater power engages in interaction with a child for the purpose of sexual stimulation for self or others (Barnett et al., 1997; Rind, Tromovitch, & Bauserman, 1998). *Incest,* in turn, involves sexual interaction among immediate family members that would be proscribed by law (Pagelow, 1984). *Sexual aggression* is the unwanted or societally prohibited imposition of harm or violation through the organs and activities associated with reproduction, ranging from sexual withholding to rape, with various forms of coerciveness in between (Spitzberg, 1998). Despite some similarities, the etiologies and effects of sexually oriented forms of aggression and abuse often appear relatively distinct from nonsexual forms of abuse (Basile, Arias, Desai, & Thompson, 2004; Vatnar & Bjørkly, 2008).

Each of these terms represents a contested site of scholarly and public policy debate (see e.g., Morgan & Wilson, 2005). Some scholars even suggest objective or standardized attempts to capture such phenomena are misguided, given the extent to which victimization itself is individually and socially constructed (Queen, Brackley, & Williams, 2009). Such cautionary admonitions suggest the extraordinary difficulty of mapping the territory (or territories) of violence in the family context.

Prevalence of Violence and Abuse

The precision of prevalence estimates depends heavily on operational and conceptual definitions, which makes claims about prevalence difficult. Whereas most of the estimates refer to lifetime experience, some studies assess repetitive or severe forms of aggression which results in considerably different prevalence rates. Table 29.1 reports a selective

Table 29.1 Summary of Selected Large-scale North American Family Violence Prevalence and Incidence Studies

Construct	Source	Sample	Estimate(s)
Child maltreatment	Fletcher (2010)	8,851 adolescents	20% neglect; 10% physical abuse
	McCarroll et al. (2008)	Incidence rate per 1,000 children of Army parents	All rates < 1%
	Anda et al. (2006)	17,337 health maintenance organization patients	Emotional: 10.6%; Physical: 28.3%Sexual: 20.7%
	Clément & Chamberland (2007)	3,148 mothers (Canada)	Psychological aggression: 6.9–75.9%; minor: 2.4–32.7%; severe: 0.3–4.8%
Childhood sexual abuse	Fletcher (2010)	8,851 adolescents	5%
	Rind et al. (1998)	13,704 (24 samples) males; 21,999 (45 samples) females	14% males, 27% females
	Stander et al. (2002)	5,226 females; 5,969 males	3% males; 18% females,
	Pereda et al. (2009)	37,904 males + 63,118 women	7.9% males; 19.7% females
Communicative aggression/	Greenwood et al. (2002)	2,881 men who have sex with men	34.0–36.2%
Psychological abuse	Follingstad & Edmundson (2010)	614 adults	77% perpetrated; 84% received
Intimate partner violence	Moracco et al. (2007)	1,800 women	23.4% females
	Fletcher (2010)	8,851 adolescents	30%
	Zlotnick et al. (2006)	Subsample of 3,173 women from national sample of 13,017	2.3% without injury, 1.4% with injury
	Reeves & O'Leary-Kelly (2007)	1,550 female; 823 male employees	21.2% males ; 28% females
	Greenwood et al. (2002)	2,881 men who have sex with men	22.0–24.0%

Table 29.1 (continued)

Construct	Source	Sample	Estimate(s)
	Breiding et al. (2008); Breiding et al. (2009)	70,156 participants	15.9% males; 26.4% females
	Caetano et al. (2008)	1,136 intact couples	8% mutual, 4% male-only perpetrated, 2% female-only perpetrated
	Kessler et al. (2001)	3,537 cohabiting or married adults (1,738 men, 1,799 women)	18.4% males; 17.4% females
	Tjaden & Thoennes (1998, 2000)	16,000 adults (8,000 males, 8,000 females)	7% males; 20.4% females
Intimate partner rape	Tjaden & Thoennes (1998, 2000)	16,000 adults (8,000 males, 8,000 females)	0.2% males; 4.5% females
	Basile (2002)	Subsample of 602 women of a sample of 1,108 adults	13%
Sexual aggression	Greenwood et al. (2002)	2,881 men who have sex with men	5.1-6.4%
	Basile et al. (2007)	4,877 females, 4,807 males	6.5% (10.6% women, 2.1% men). Note: The perpetrator of first forced sex was an intimate partner for 30.4% of females and 15.9% of males, and a non-intimate family member (parent, stepparent, grandparent, sibling, or other family relation) for 23.7% of females, and 17.7% of males.
Sexual coercion	Reeves & O'Leary-Kelly (2007)	1,550 female; 823 male employees	17.7% women; 0.9% men

assortment of prevalence estimates based on large-scale studies. In sum, the abuse of children ranges from 3 to 20 percent (child neglect: 20 percent; physical abuse: 10 percent; child sexual abuse: 3–27 percent). Incest, including intimate rape, intimate sexual aggression, and sexual coercion, ranges from 0.2 to 18 percent. Intimate partner violence ranges from 4 to 30 percent. Communicative aggression and psychological abuse ranges from 34 to 84 percent. When sex differences are reported, the majority of studies indicate that females are victimized at higher rates than males.

As research progresses, it will be possible to perform cross-sectional and cross-generational meta-analyses on prevalence estimates, which will enable the identification of various operational and theoretical moderators of these estimates. When estimates range from 1 percent to 30 percent and higher, it matters to science and society what the actual rates, and their moderators, are. Despite the need for precision, if these various forms of violence have broader deleterious effects, then even the lowest prevalence estimates indicate that the problem is serious and extensive.

Undesirable Destinations: Effects of Family Violence and Abuse

Research has strongly indicated that various forms of family violence are generally deleterious for most victims (for reviews, see Spitzberg, 2009, 2010). For much of the early stages of research on family violence, a relatively small domain of effects were examined, involving constructs such as depression, anxiety, self-esteem, divorce, post-traumatic stress syndrome (PTSD) and physical injury. As research and theory evolved, a broader typology of effects has been identified. Cupach and Spitzberg (2004) outline several individual level effects, which are all potentially interdependent. *General disturbance* represents diffuse trauma, such as changes in personality, PTSD, or sense of diminished quality of life. *Affective health* refers to emotional forms of trauma, including anger, anxiety, depression, fear, jealousy, and stress. *Cognitive health* includes mental trauma such as confusion, distrust, diminished self-esteem, suicide ideation, and sense of helplessness. *Physical health* effects reflect trauma to immune system, appetite, drug abuse, insomnia, nausea, physical illness, self-injury, and suicide. *Behavioral disturbance* is a category representing disruptions to overt activities, including changing behavioral routines, changing location, and changing work, school, residential, worship, or other activity patterns. *Social health* includes trauma to a victim's relationships with others, such as social isolation, relational cautiousness, and intimacy deterioration. *Resource health* effects represent disruptions of income, career, earning potential, lost time from work, or other forms of resource depletion. *Spiritual health* effects are revealed in the loss of faith, whether in a divine being, a religion, or other social institutions such as marriage, the law, or the justice system. A final set of potential effects has only recently garnered significant scholarly attention: *resilience* effects. Some victims experience some degree of strength, resurgence, renewed sense of self, greater confidence in relationships and family, or general optimism.

Child Adjustment

Children are generally considered the most innocent of victims, and the ones with the longest arc of potential consequences. Research indicates that at the individual developmental level, children who observe family violence are more likely to experience adult anxiety and depression (El-Sheikh, Cummings, Kouros, Elmore-Staton, & Buckhalt, 2008). Children who are the direct recipients of emotional, physical, or sexual abuse appear to have higher adult rates of panic reactions, depressed effect, anxiety, hallucinations, sleep disturbance, severe obesity, multiple somatic symptoms, substance abuse, early intercourse, promiscuity, sexual dissatisfaction, impaired childhood memory, perceived stress, anger management difficulties, and IPV perpetration (Anda et al., 2006). Victims of child sexual abuse also appear more likely to perpetrate sexual abuse as adults (Jespersen, Lalumiére, & Seto, 2009), and one study found female victims of CSA were at 25 times greater risk of adult IPV victimization (Vatnar & Bjørkly, 2008). The unique effects of child sexual abuse on adult adjustment, however, appear to be small and confounded with other family dysfunction processes (Rind et al., 1998; Ulrich, Randolph, & Acheson, 2005–6).

Adult Adjustment

The effects of IPV on adults are equally dismal. Communicative aggression victimization as an adult is associated with current poor health, chronic disease, injury, and depression (Coker et al., 2002). Longitudinal research found that IPV victimization was related to later depression, life satisfaction, self-esteem, and functional impairment for women (Zlotnick, Johnson, & Kohn, 2006). Current partner IPV, sexual violence, psychological aggression, and stalking are also significantly related to PTSD (Basile et al., 2004; Mechanic, Weaver, & Resick, 2008). At the physical level, women IPV victims report higher rates of using disability equipment, activity limitations, cholesterol, cardiovascular disease, joint disease, HIV/STD risk, smoking, heavy or binge alcohol use, and high body mass index; and men IPV victims reported higher rates of using disability equipment, arthritis, asthma, stroke, HIV/STD risk, smoking, and heavy or binge drinking (Black & Breiding, 2008). Of course, IPV is also related to direct physical injury (Tjaden & Thoennes, 1998) and death by partner homicide (Campbell et al., 2003).

Most research to date has been cross-sectional, and attempts to interpret developmental causation have relied heavily on retrospective reports. Many family dysfunctions co-exist and reinforce one another, and factors such as depression can be both a predictor and an outcome of IPV. Longitudinal research that attempts to correct for such methodological problems estimates that cross-sectional effect sizes may be inflated by as much as 20 to 60 percent even though the deleterious effects still appear enduring and significant (Fletcher, 2010).

Under-explored Regions of Violence and Aggression in the Family

Although partner/spousal abuse and parent-to-child abuse are the most researched, other forms of abuse are common and gaining deserved attention. Violence between siblings is in actuality the most common form of family aggression (Strauss & Gelles, 1990). Although sibling aggression may be considered more socially acceptable or even expected, this aggression can have deleterious effects when siblings show a repeated pattern of aggression with intent to harm, humiliate, and defeat (Eriksen & Jensen, 2008). Like abuse in other family relationships, sibling abuse includes psychological, physical, and sexual forms. Prevalence rates vary widely, particularly between measures that objectively assess violent acts (e.g., using the Conflict Tactics Scale (CTS), over 80 percent report psychological abuse and 53 percent report physical abuse) and measures that ask adults whether they label themselves as experiencing sibling violence (15 percent and 11 percent, respectively; Mackey, Fromuth, & Kelly, 2009). Similar effects in other family relationships are reported. For example, those who report experiencing psychological or emotional abuse from a sibling tend to report internalizing problems and lower self-esteem (Kiselica & Morrill-Richards, 2007). Despite these similarities, it is important to keep the unique features of this type of abuse in mind. Siblings use violence for different reasons at different ages (Kiselica & Morrill-Richards, 2007). In addition, siblings may be modeling aggressive interactions they are witnessing or experiencing in the home.

Children can also be abusive toward their parents (child-to-parent violence, CPV). This creates a complex problem given that parents still have the responsibility of caring for their children (Kennair & Mellor, 2007), and parents are not often willing to acknowledge being abused or to seek help (Pagani, Larocque, Vitaro, & Tremblay, 2003). CPV is more prevalent in single-parent families (up to 30 percent) than in two-parent families (up to 18 percent) and when parenting styles are extreme (Kennair & Mellor, 2007). CPV fortunately decreases with the age of the child (Ulman & Straus, 2003) suggesting that, even though they become physically stronger, children rely less on aggressive tactics as they become developmentally more complex. As with other types of abuse,

CPV occurs when there is more stress on the family, when other forms of violence occur in the home, and when children abuse substances.

Another largely hidden form of abuse is elder abuse. Both the abusers and abused tend to conceal the abuse due to shame (Choi & Mayer, 2000). Whereas elder abuse entails the common types (e.g., neglect, psychological, physical), elders are also subject to financial or material exploitation. Common risk factors of victims include older age and impairments or cognitive deficits. Risk factors for perpetrators include dependence on the abused, substance abuse, psychopathology, and caregiving stress or burden (Choi & Mayer, 2000; Lee, 2009; Yan & Tang, 2004). Effects similar to other types of abuse occur such as PTSD, negative emotions, depression as well as financial losses and poorer survival (Bonnie & Wallace, 2003; Choi & Mayer, 2000).

Studies have shown the prevalence of same-sex violence or sexual aggression is similar to heterosexual relationships (Tjaden, Thoennes, & Allison, 1999; Turell, 2000). Despite this, other societal factors may influence the attention to and intervention of aggression in same-sex relationships. For example, male-to-male violence is perceived as less severe and people are less willing to intervene to help victims of such violence (Seelau & Seelau, 2005). Further, victims of same-sex violence are less likely to seek help as well as receive help when they do report it to authorities (Potoczniak, Mourot, Crosbie-Burnett, & Potoczniak, 2003).

Although these types of abuse are largely similar in terms of victim and perpetrator profiles, facilitating factors, and effects, each type of abuse entails unique dynamics that likely require different theoretical explanations as well as different intervention strategies. For example, although power is typically involved in abuse, the power and control dynamics likely differ between sibling violence, CPV, and elder abuse. In addition, common societal views on sibling conflict and same-sex relationships may hamper efforts to treat these forms of aggression. Overall, even though these forms of abuse are not well plotted on the map of family aggression and violence, they are an important dimension of the phenomenon of family violence that impact the relationships therein.

Explaining the Process of Violence and Aggression: Navigational Tools

The study of violence and abuse within intimate relationships is not without structure. Although most of the investigation of this phenomenon focuses on the prevalence and effects such abuse has on individuals, there is a considerable amount of information that seeks to provide an overarching perspective for understanding violence and aggression within various intimate relations. Despite the multitude of different theoretical explanations, many researchers assert that intimate partner violence results from a combination of various biological, psychological, social, contextual, and interactional factors (see Crowell & Burgess, 1996; Little & Kaufman Kantor, 2002).

One way to examine the various theoretical perspectives of violence and abuse in interpersonal relationships is to organize them based on Spitzberg's (1998) Dispositional-Episodic theoretical continuum. Theories of interpersonal violence and aggression can be placed along a continuum from dispositional theories that attempt to identify genetic and evolutionary causes of violent behavior to episodic theories which examine specific contexts or interactional situations where violence is likely to occur (see Figure 29.1). Although all theories provide insights on the causes of violence and abuse (e.g., alcohol abuse, mental illness), we limit our discussion to theories that focus on the communicative or interactive nature of abuse.

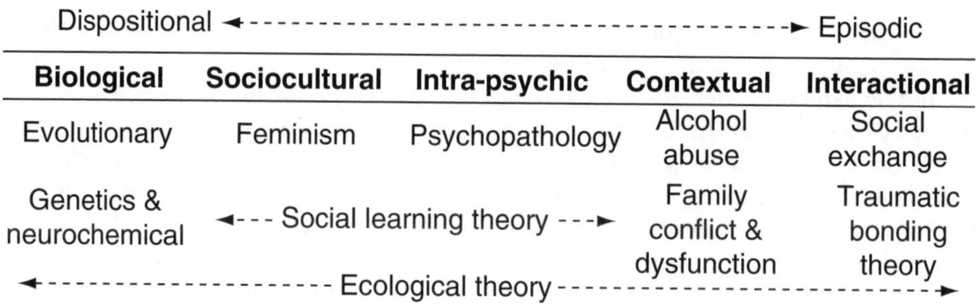

Biological	**Sociocultural**	**Intra-psychic**	**Contextual**	**Interactional**
Evolutionary	Feminism	Psychopathology	Alcohol abuse	Social exchange
Genetics & neurochemical	◄- - - Social learning theory - - -►		Family conflict & dysfunction	Traumatic bonding theory
◄- - - - - - - - - - - - - - - - - - - Ecological theory -►				

Figure 29.1 Theories of Intimate Partner Violence

Theories of Interpersonal Violence and Aggression

Socio-cultural Theoretical Models

Socio-cultural theories focus on the role of culture and how it socializes individuals in terms of how we think, feel, and behave. These theories include feminist theory and social learning theory.

Feminist theory. From a feminist perspective, violence and aggression toward women is a result of male dominance in the family and society (DeKeseredy, 2011; Johnson, 2011). While feminist theory has been effective at explaining the relationship between gender inequity in society and violence against women (see Graham, Rawlings, & Rimini, 1988), it has received criticism as well. Specifically, researchers have indicated that feminist theory fails to explain instances of female perpetrator–male victimization (Schneider, 1992), child abuse (Ashe & Cahn, 1993), and gay and lesbian domestic violence (Letellier, 1994).

Social learning theory. According to social learning theory (Bandura, 1977), individuals learn how to behave through observation and modeling the attitudes, values, and behaviors of others. When applied to family violence, this theory contends that, as children, individuals learn violence as it is modeled by adults or even social media (e.g., television) and then, in turn, use these learned violent behaviors in adulthood with their own significant others (Mihalic & Elliott, 1997) and children (Feshbach, 1980). Subsequently, this theoretical approach would explain why both men and women experience violence in intimate partner relationships. More specifically, it suggests men batter because they learned violence in their families, and women seek out violent men because they might have experienced or witnessed violence within their home.

Although a considerable amount of research utilizing social learning theory focuses on couple violence, research also indicates intimate partner violence is transmitted through generations. According to the intergenerational transmission of violence hypothesis (see Renner & Slack, 2006), mistreated children are more likely to grow up to become mistreating parents. In support of this, the majority of abusing parents were also found to be abused as children (see Pears & Capaldi, 2001).

Interactional Theoretical Models

Interactional theories of violence and aggression in families focus on the role of communication, both verbal and nonverbal messages, between and among family members. Spitzberg

(1998) suggested "biology, culture, society, cognition, and context become relevant only through interpersonal interaction, and it is the interaction that determines the outcome" (p. 199). Several key interactional theories include traumatic bonding theory, exchange/social control theory, and ecological theory.

Traumatic bonding theory. Dutton and Painter (1993), in their explanation of traumatic bonding theory, suggest that "powerful emotional attachments are seen to develop from two specific features of abusive relationships: power imbalances and intermittent good-bad treatment" (p. 105). Power imbalances are suggested to occur when individuals feel attachment toward a stronger (physical) person, which can result in feelings of power inequality over time. This often results in negative self-appraisal and feelings of being incapable of taking care of oneself. As a result, the individual relies more on the dominant person and develops a dependency. In regard to intermittent good–bad treatment, Dutton and Painter denote that while attachment theory would suggest that bonds are strengthened with consistent good treatment, bad behavior (e.g., physical, verbal, or psychological abuse) intermittently mixed in with good treatment also strengthens the bond between the abuser and the victim. Dutton and Painter further argue that this "paradoxical attachment" is consistent with previous findings indicating strong relationships between abused children and their parents as well as hostages' positive feelings toward their captors.

Exchange/social control theory. Perhaps the most applicable theoretical model for understanding the role of communication behavior as it relates to violence and aggression in intimate relations is the exchange/social control theory (Gelles, 1982). Gelles proposed two principles that help explain the occurrence of family violence. The first principle, based on exchange theory, is that violence will occur when perpetrators perceive that its rewards outweigh the costs of such violence. According to exchange theory, human behavior is guided by the need to obtain rewards while avoiding costs or punishment. When applied to family violence, Gelles suggests that husbands/fathers might use violence because it equalizes or gains power in the relationship, which is instrumental to goal achievement. The second principle, based on control theory, suggests that violence is utilized when people do not have social controls that restrain their behavior. Specifically, if family members feel that the likelihood of outside intervention (e.g., government, law, or social agencies) is low, violence is more likely to occur.

Ecological model. More and more researchers are utilizing an ecological theoretical perspective or model to examine violence in interpersonal relationships. According to DePanfilis (1998), an ecological model to examining intimate partner violence takes into consideration the interactions among individual, family, community, and societal factors. At the individual level, biological and personality characteristics are considered. At the familial level, parenting styles, parental substance use, and family interactions (e.g., with a specific parent or relatives) are considered. The community level factors in where the family resides as well as the social support that occurs from outside the family structure. Finally, the societal level considers governmental laws that are in place for victims of abuse (e.g., child neglect, maltreatment) (Little & Kaufman Kantor, 2002). Although difficult to examine in one study, an ecological model provides a more comprehensive approach to understanding and explaining violence in families.

Typologies of Intimate Partner Violence

In addition to the theoretical approaches utilized to explain why violence and abuse occur in various familial relations, researchers have derived typologies for understanding intimate partner violence. Although numerous typologies examining violent couples exist, a close examination of the research indicates considerable overlap in content. Two typologies in particular have received considerable attention across various disciplines: Holtzworth-Munroe and Stuart's (1994) male batterer typology and Johnson's (2008) intimate partner violence typology.

Holtzworth-Munroe and Stuart (1994) focus exclusively on the male as a perpetrator based on claims by researchers such as Hotaling and Sugarman (1986) who assert that the occurrence of violence in intimate relationships hinges on the actions of the male (see Herrera, Wiersma, & Cleveland, 2008). This typology is both theoretically and empirically derived and has been consistently supported by subsequent research (see Dixon & Browne, 2003; Johnson et al., 2006).

According to Holtzworth-Munroe and Stuart (1994), three dimensions distinguish types of male batterers:

1 severity (i.e., the frequency and breadth of types of abuse);
2 generality (i.e., whether family-only or extrafamilial);
3 the abuser's personality disorder or psychopathology.

Based on these three dimensions, male abusers can be distinguished as: (1) family-only, (2) dysphoric/borderline, or (3) generally violent/antisocial. Family-only batterers engage in less severe forms of marital violence, whether it is psychological or sexual in nature, and rarely engage in violence outside of the family or criminal behavior. Dysphoric/borderline batterers exhibit higher levels of marital violence, including psychological and sexual abuse, can be low or moderate in their extrafamilial violence, and may exhibit borderline personality disorder as well as consume alcohol or drugs and experience depression. Finally, generally violent/antisocial batterers tend to exhibit moderate to high levels of marital violence, including psychological and sexual abuse, higher levels of extrafamilial violence, and exhibit antisocial or psychopathic personal disorders. Generally violent/antisocial batterers tend also to be high drug/alcohol consumers but tend to experience little depression.

Unlike Holtworth-Munroe and Stuart's (1994) exclusive focus on the male as a perpetrator, Johnson's (1995, 2008) approach focuses on both males and females in terms of their violent behavior. Johnson's intimate partner violence typology focuses on individuals' motives for engaging in violence—to control the situation or to control their relational partner. Based on this, Johnson (2006) suggests there are four main types of intimate partner violence. Situational couple violence (SCV) involves a motive to control the situation through various violent tactics (e.g., an argument that escalates). In contrast, if the motive is to control the relational partner, Johnson (2006) suggests this can take one of three forms. Intimate terrorism (IT) is when the perpetrator uses violence to exert control over a relational partner, which is suggested to be perpetuated more by husbands than wives. Violent resistance (VR) focuses on the victim's use of violence in an effort to resist intimate terrorist attempts, which is more likely used by wives. Finally, mutual violent control (MVC) occurs when both relational partners use violence in an attempt to control one another.

Although Johnson (2008) contends that four types of intimate partner violence exist, the majority of research examines differences in IT and SCV. Research has found that IT and SCV differ in terms of: (a) severity, with IT associated with more severe, physical violence than SCV (Johnson & Leone, 2005; Leone, Johnson, Cohan & Lloyd, 2004); (b) victim outcomes, with IT victims reporting more depression and post-traumatic stress disorders as well as seeking more formal help (Leone, Johnson, & Cohan, 2007); and (c) relational types, with IT more likely to occur in marital relationships and SCV more likely to occur amongst cohabitating couples (Johnson, 2006, 2011). However, it should be noted that Brownridge (2010) found a lack of gender and relational asymmetry in terms of victims who experience SCV and IT.

Overall, examination of the various theoretical models and typologies suggests that no one approach is enough to understand the various factors that influence the occurrence of violence within intimate relationships. As presented in the ecological model, researchers need to consider the layering of various individual, family, community, and societal factors. Future research will need to consider the importance of each of these factors or levels as it contributes to violence so that prevention and intervention efforts can be focused. Finally, it was apparent that although communication and interaction are implicit in some theories (e.g., parenting style, modeling, how power and control are communicated), the role of communication in the process of abuse is rarely emphasized. As such, augmenting theories and models by incorporating the interactive nature of abuse may prove useful in future research.

Correcting the Course: Prevention and Interventions

Although an extensive review of intervention programs is beyond the scope of this chapter, a general description of what is being done to either treat or prevent these types of abuse is warranted. Many types of interventions exist, and they vary in the target (e.g., victim, per-petrator, couple, parents, children, family), structure (e.g., psychoeducation curriculum, cognitive-behavioral therapy, communication and problem-solving skills training, group versus individual sessions), and setting (e.g., in-home, schools or community centers, psychotherapist offices). Few rigorous, empirical evaluations of these programs have been conducted (Foshee, Luz, Reyes, & Wyckoff, 2009; Sullivan, 2006), and unfortunately, the data from these studies suggest the programs have either no impact, or small to moderate effects on the recidivism of abuse (e.g., Babcock, Green, & Robie, 2004; Gondolf, 2011).

To provide a picture of the types of intervention programs, we outline a few examples of the varying approaches that have been subjected to more empirical testing. The Duluth Domestic Abuse Intervention Project (DAIP or Duluth model; Pence & Paymar, 1993) is a common batterer intervention program (BIP) typically mandated by state authorities. It is a feminist-based, psychoeducational program that focuses on men's use of power and control over women. The goals of the program are to change men's attitudes and behaviors toward their partner, and research suggests this program can be effective (Babcock et al., 2004).

One of the more extensively tested child maltreatment programs is parent–child interaction therapy (PCIT). This intervention targets parents who have abused their young children and involves live-coaching, behavioral parent training that focuses on teaching parents to enact relationship enhancing and discipline skills to decrease negative responses and increase positive responses to child behavior (Herschell & McNeil, 2005). Whereas BIPs tend to have more standardized implementation, PCIT is more indivi-dualized to each parent. Research to date shows this program holds promise (e.g., Chaffin et al., 2004; Herschell & McNeil, 2005).

In preventing IPV, the Youth Relationship Project (YRP; Wolfe et al., 1996) targets adolescents who have been previously maltreated to prevent abuse in their subsequent relationships. YRP employs curriculum based on social learning, feminist, and attachment theories. It aims to educate participants about: power and its role in relationship violence, developing skills to build healthy relationships, and seeking help from community resources (Wolfe et al., 1997). Intervention participants indeed reported less frequent and severe abuse than those in a control group over two years (Wolfe et al., 2003).

Despite the lack of rigorous testing and limited effects of intervention programs, most researchers have similar suggestions for the construction and evaluation of abuse intervention programs. Researchers contend more integrated or ecological approaches (e.g., Whitaker et al., 2009; Wolfe et al., 1997) as well as programs that are individualized or tailored to the type of violence (e.g., Babcock, Canady, Graham, & Schart, 2007; Murphy, Meis, & Eckhardt, 2009) will be more effective. For instance, violence in which partners are mutually aggressive (e.g., situational couple violence; Johnson, 2008) should be treated in a different manner than violence perpetrated by only one partner (Babcock et al., 2007). In terms of evaluation, more rigorous, experimental, and large-scale studies are needed (Sullivan, 2006) that measure the enactment or experience of subsequent abuse rather than the typically assessed outcomes of attitude change, knowledge, or intentions (Foshee et al., 2009; Whitaker et al., 2006).

In addition, coordination among researchers and practitioners is needed. Given the various factors involved in abuse, interdisciplinary approaches in constructing these programs are necessary (e.g., psychologists, social workers, law enforcement, etc.). Specific to the field of communication, as Morgan and Wilson (2005) argue, communication researchers are particularly poised to provide recommendations on the communication involved in treating abuse. Indeed, many of the intervention programs include communication and skills training, and these programs can be enhanced by the work of communication researchers.

Conclusions

The attention family violence and abuse have garnered from researchers, mental health counselors, social organizations, and governmental agencies is a sign of progress. Research has yielded a strong foundation for describing the prevalence and effects of abuse, paths for explaining why abuse occurs, and preliminary methods for combatting abuse. Yet, much of the map of abuse and aggression needs further exploration and clarification. For example, we need to better explicate the *process* of abuse such as how abuse emerges in families and how families change abusive patterns. Additional research could also expand beyond the dyad and assess the systemic dynamics of violence in families. More generally, an ecological approach incorporating multiple levels of factors simultaneously would better elucidate the progression, outcomes, and interventions of abuse in the family context. Furthermore, the differences between families and individuals who experience resilient outcomes, versus those who experience greater trauma, need to be better understood. Although not a simple task, these are the important next steps in understanding and preventing this form of communication that has such deleterious effects on the individual family members and their relationships.

References

Anda, R. F., Felitti, V. J., Bremner, J. D., Walker, J. D., Whitfield, C., Perry, B. D., ... & Giles, W. H. (2006). The enduring effects of abuse and related adverse experiences in childhood: A convergence of evidence from neurobiology and epidemiology. *European Archives of Psychiatry and Clinical Neuroscience, 256*, 174–86.

Anderson, K. L., Umberson, D., & Elliott, S. (2004). Violence and abuse in families. In A. L. Vangelisti (Ed.), *Handbook of family communication* (pp. 629–45). Mahwah, NJ: Lawrence Erlbaum Associates.

Ashe, M., & Cahn, N. (1993). Child abuse: A problem for feminist theory. *Texas Journal of Women and the Law*, 2, 75–112.

Babcock, J. C., Canady, B. E., Graham, K., & Schart, L. (2007). The evolution of battering interventions: From the dark ages into the scientific age. In J. Hamel & T. L. Nicholls (Eds.), *Family interventions in domestic violence: A handbook of gender-inclusive theory and treatment* (pp. 215–44). New York: Springer.

Babcock, J. C., Green, C. E., & Robie, C. (2004). Does batterers' treatment work? A meta-analytic review of domestic violence treatment. *Clinical Psychology Review*, 23, 1023–53.

Bandura, A. (1973). *Aggression: A social learning analysis.* Englewood Cliffs, NJ: Prentice-Hall.

——(1977). *Social learning theory.* Englewood Cliffs, NJ: Prentice Hall.

Barnett, O. W., Miller-Perrin, C. L., & Perrin, R. D. (1997). *Family violence across the lifespan: An introduction.* Thousand Oaks, CA: Sage.

Baron, R. A., & Richardson, D. R. (1994). *Human aggression*, 2nd edn. New York: Plenum.

Basile, K. C. (2002). Prevalence of wife rape and other intimate partner sexual coercion in a nationally representative sample of women. *Violence and Victims*, 17, 511–24.

Basile, K. C., Arias, I., Desai, S., & Thompson, M. P. (2004). The differential association of intimate partner physical, sexual, psychological, and stalking violence and post-traumatic stress symptoms in a nationally representative sample of women. *Journal of Traumatic Stress*, 17, 413–21.

Basile, K. C., Chen, J., Black, M. C., & Saltzman, L. E. (2007). Prevalence and characteristics of sexual violence victimization among U.S. adults, 2001–3. *Violence and Victims*, 22, 437–48.

Bergen, R. K. (Ed.) (1998). *Issues in intimate violence.* Thousand Oaks, CA: Sage.

Black, M. C., & Breiding, M. J. (2008). Adverse health conditions and health risk behaviors associated with intimate partner violence—United States, 2005. *Journal of the American Medical Association*, 300, 646–47.

Bonnie, R. J., & Wallace, R. B. (2003). *Elder mistreatment: Abuse, neglect, and exploitation in an aging America.* Washington, DC: The National Academic Press.

Breiding, M. J., Black, M. C., & Ryan, G. W. (2008). Prevalence and risk factors of intimate partner violence in eighteen U.S. states/territories, 2005. *American Journal of Preventative Medicine*, 34, 112–18.

Breiding, M. J., Ziembroski, J. S., & Black, M. C. (2009). Prevalence of rural intimate partner violence in 16 US states, 2005. *Journal of Rural Health*, 25, 240–46.

Brownridge, D. A. (2010). Does the situational couple violence-intimate terrorism typology explain cohabitors' high risk of intimate partner violence? *Journal of Interpersonal Violence*, 25, 1264–83.

Caetano, R., Vaeth, P. A., & Ramisetty-Mikler, S. (2008). Intimate partner violence victim and perpetrator characteristics among couples in the United States. *Journal of Family Violence*, 23, 507–18.

Campbell, J. C., Webster, D., Koziol-McLain, J., Block, C., Campbell, D., Curry, M. A., ... & Laughon, K. (2003). Risk factors for femicide in abusive relationships: Results from a multisite case control study. *American Journal of Public Health*, 93, 1089–97.

Chaffin, M., Silovsky, J. F., Funderburk, B., Valle, L. A., Brestan, E. V., Balachova, T., ... & Bonner, B. L. (2004). Parent–child interaction therapy with physically abusive parents: Efficacy for reducing future abuse reports. *Journal of Consulting and Clinical Psychology*, 72, 500–10.

Choi, N. G., & Mayer, J. (2000). Elder abuse, neglect, and exploitation: Risk factors and prevention strategies. *Journal of Gerontological Social Work*, 33, 5–25.

Clément, M., & Chamberland, C. (2007). Physical violence and psychological aggression towards children: Five-year trends in practices and attitudes from two population surveys. *Child Abuse & Neglect*, 31, 1001–11.

Coker, A. L., Davis, K. E., Arias, I. A., Desai, S., Sanderson, M., Brandt, H. M., & Smith, P. H. (2002). Physical and mental health effects of intimate partner violence for men and women. *American Journal of Preventive Medicine*, 23, 260–68.

Crowell, N. A., & Burgess, A. W. (1996). *Understanding violence against women.* Washington, DC: National Academy Press.

Cupach, W. R., & Spitzberg, B. H. (2004). *The dark side of relationship pursuit: From attraction to obsession to stalking.* Mahwah, NJ: Lawrence Erlbaum Associates.

Dailey, R. M., Lee, C. M., & Spitzberg, B. H. (2007). Psychological abuse and communicative aggression. In B. H. Spitzberg & W. R. Cupach (Eds.), *The dark side of interpersonal communication*, 2nd edn (pp. 297–326). Mahwah, NJ: Lawrence Erlbaum Associates.

DeKeseredy, W. S. (2011). Feminist contributions to understanding woman abuse: Myths, controversies, and realities. *Aggression and Violent Behavior, 16*, 297–302.

DePanfilis, D. (1998). Intervening with families when children are neglected. In H. Dubowitz (Ed.), *Neglected children: Research, practice and policy* (pp. 211–36). Thousand Oaks, CA: Sage.

Dixon, L., & Browne, K. (2003). The heterogeneity of spouse abuse: A review. *Aggression and Violent Behavior, 8*, 107–30.

Dutton, D. G., & Painter, S. (1993). Emotional attachments in abusive relationships: A test of traumatic bonding theory. *Violence and Victims, 8*, 105–20.

El-Sheikh, M., Cummings, E. M., Kouros, C. D., Elmore-Staton, L., & Buckhalt, J. (2008). Marital psychological and physical aggression and children's mental and physical health: Direct, mediated, and moderated effects. *Journal of Consulting and Clinical Psychology, 76*, 138–48.

Eriksen, S., & Jensen, V. (2008). A push or a punch: Distinguishing the severity of sibling violence. *Journal of Interpersonal Violence, 24*, 183–208.

Feshbach, S. (1980). Child abuse and the dynamics of human aggression and violence. In G. Gerbner, C. J. Ross, & E. Zigler (Eds.), *Child abuse: An agenda for action* (pp. 48–60). Oxford: Oxford University Press.

Fletcher, J. (2010). The effects of intimate partner violence on health in young adulthood in the United States. *Social Science and Medicine, 70*, 130–35.

Follingstad, D. R., & Edmundson, M. (2010). Is psychological abuse reciprocal in intimate relationships? Data from a national sample of American adults. *Journal of Family Violence, 25*, 495–508.

Foshee, V. A., Luz, H., Reyes, M., & Wyckoff, S. C. (2009). Approaches to preventing psychological, physical, and sexual partner abuse. In K. D. O'Leary & E. M. Woodin (Eds.), *Psychological and physical aggression in couples: Causes and interventions* (pp. 165–89). Washington, DC: American Psychological Association.

Gelles (1982). An exchange/social control approach to understanding intrafamily violence. *Behavior Therapy, 5*, 5–8.

Gondolf, E. W. (2011). The weak evidence for batterer program alternatives. *Aggression and Violent Behavior, 16*, 347–53.

Graham, D. L. R., Rawlings, E., & Rimini, N. (1988). Survivors of terror: Battered women, hostages, and the Stockholm Syndrome. In K. Yllo & M. Bograd (Eds.), *Feminist perspectives on wife abuse* (pp. 217–33). Thousand Oaks, CA: Sage.

Greenwood, G. L., Relf, M. V., Huang, B., Pollack, L. M., Canchola, J. A., & Catania, J. A. (2002). Battering victimization among a probability based sample of men who have sex with men. *American Journal of Public Health, 92*, 1964–69.

Herrera, V. M., Wiersma, J. D., & Cleveland, H. H. (2008). The influence of individual and partner characteristics on the perpetration of intimate partner violence in young adult relationships. *Journal of Youth and Adolescence, 37*, 284–96.

Herschell, A. D., & McNeil, C. B. (2005). Theoretical and empirical underpinnings of parent–child interaction therapy with child physical abuse populations. *Education and Treatment of Children, 28*, 142–62.

Holtzworth-Munroe, A., & Stuart, G. L. (1994). Typologies of male batterers: Three subtypes and the differences among them. *Psychological Bulletin, 116*, 476–97.

Hotaling, G. T., & Sugarman, D. B. (1986). An analysis of risk markers in husband to wife violence: The current state of knowledge. *Violence and Victims, 1*, 101–24.

Jespersen, A. F., Lalumiére, M. L., & Seto, M. C. (2009). Sexual abuse history among adult sex offenders and non-sex offenders: A meta-analysis. *Child Abuse & Neglect, 33*, 179–92.

Johnson, M. P. (1995). Patriarchal terrorism and common couple violence: Two forms of violence against women. *Journal of Marriage and Family, 57*, 283–94.

——(2006). Violence and abuse in personal relationships: Conflict, terror, and resistance in intimate partnerships. In A. L. Vangelisti & D. Perlman (Eds.), *The Cambridge handbook of personal relationships* (pp. 557–76). Cambridge: Cambridge University Press.

——(2008). *A typology of domestic violence: Intimate terrorism, violent resistance, and situational couple violence*. Boston, MA: Northeastern University Press.

——(2011). Gender and types of intimate partner violence: A response to an anti-feminist literature review. *Aggression and Violent Behavior, 16*, 289–96.

Johnson, M. P., & Leone, J. M. (2005). The differential effects of intimate terrorism and situational couple violence: Findings from the National Violence Against Women Survey. *Journal of Family Issues*, 26, 322–49.

Johnson, R., Gilchrist, E., Beech, A. R., Weston, S., Takriti, R., & Freeman, R. (2006). A psychometric typology of U.K. domestic violence offenders. *Journal of Interpersonal Violence*, 21, 1270–85.

Kennair, N., & Mellor, D. (2007). Parent abuse: A review. *Child Psychiatry and Human Development*, 38, 203–19.

Kessler, R. C., Molnar, B. E., Feurer, I. D., & Appelbaum, M. (2001). Patterns and mental health predictors of domestic violence in the United States: Results from the national comorbidity study. *International Journal of Law and Psychiatry*, 24, 487–508.

Kiselica, M. S., & Morrill-Richards, M. (2007). Sibling maltreatment: The forgotten abuse. *Journal of Counseling and Development*, 85, 148–60.

Lee, M. (2009). A path analysis of elder abuse by family caregivers: Applying the ABCX model. *Journal of Family Violence*, 24, 1–9.

Leone, J. M., Johnson, M. P., & Cohan, C. L (2007). Victim help seeking: Differences between intimate terrorism and situational couple violence. *Family Relations*, 56, 427–39.

Leone, J. M., & Johnson, M. P., Cohan, C. L, & Lloyd, S. (2004). Consequences of domestic violence for low-income, ethnic minority women: A control-based typology of male partner violence. *Journal of Marriage and Family*, 66, 472–91.

Letellier, P. (1994). Gay and bisexual male domestic violence victimization: Challenges to feminist theory and responses to violence. *Violence and Victims*, 9, 95–106.

Little, L. & Kaufman Kantor, G. (2002). Using ecological theory to understand intimate partner violence and child maltreatment. *Journal of Community Health Nursing*, 19(3), 133–45.

Mackey, A. L., Fromuth, M. E., & Kelly, D. B. (2009). The association of sibling relationship and abuse with later psychological adjustment. *Journal of Interpersonal Violence*, 25, 955–68.

McCarroll, J. E., Fan, Z., Newby, J. H., & Ursano, R. J. (2008). Trends in US Army child maltreatment reports: 1990–2004. *Child Abuse Review*, 17, 108–18.

Mechanic, M. B., Weaver, T. L., & Resick, P. A. (2008). Mental health consequences of intimate partner abuse: A multidimensional assessment of four different forms of abuse. *Violence Against Women*, 14, 634–54.

Mihalic, S. W., & Elliott, D. (1997). A social learning theory model of marital violence. *Journal of Family Violence*, 12, 21–48.

Moracco, K. E., Runyan, C. W., Bowling, J. M., & Earp, J. A. (2007) Women's experiences with violence: A national study. *Women's Health Issues*, 17, 3–12.

Morgan, W. M., & Wilson, S. R. (2005). Nonphysical child abuse: A review of literature and challenge to communication scholars. In P. J. Kalbfleisch (Ed.), *Communication Yearbook* (Vol. 29, pp. 1–32). Mahwah, NJ: Lawrence Erlbaum Associates.

Murphy, C. M., Meis, L. A., & Eckhardt, C. I. (2009). Individualized services and individual therapy for partner abuse perpetrators. In K. D. O'Leary & E. M. Woodin (Eds.), *Psychological and physical aggression in couples: Causes and interventions* (pp. 211–31). Washington, DC: American Psychological Association.

Pagani, L., Larocque, D., Vitaro, F., & Tremblay, R. E. (2003). Verbal and physical abuse toward mothers: The role of family configuration, environment, and coping strategies. *Journal of Youth and Adolescence*, 32, 215–22.

Pagelow, M. D. (1984). *Family violence*. New York: Praeger.

Pears, K. C., & Capaldi, D. M. (2001). Intergenerational transmission of abuse: A two-generational prospective study of an at-risk sample. *Child Abuse & Neglect*, 25, 1439–61.

Pence, E., & Paymar, M. (1993). *Education groups for men who batter: The Duluth model*. New York: Springer.

Pereda, N., Guilera, G., Forns, M., & Gómez-Benito, J. (2009). The prevalence of child sexual abuse in community and student samples: A meta-analysis. *Clinical Psychology Review*, 29, 328–38.

Potoczniak, M. J., Mourot, J. T., Crosbie-Burnett, M., & Potoczniak, D. J. (2003). Legal and psychological perspectives on same-sex domestic violence: A multisystemic approach. *Journal of Family Psychology*, 17, 252–59.

Queen, J., Brackley, M. H., & Williams, G. B. (2009). Being emotionally abused: A phenomenological study of adult women's experiences of emotionally abusive intimate partner relationships. *Issues in Mental Health Nursing*, 30, 237–45.

Reeves, C., & O'Leary-Kelly, A. M. (2007). The effects and costs of intimate partner violence for work organizations. *Journal of Interpersonal Violence, 22*, 327–44.

Renner, L. M., & Slack, K. S. (2006). Intimate partner violence and child maltreatment: Understanding intra- and intergenerational connections. *Child Abuse & Neglect, 30*, 599–617.

Rind, B., Tromovitch, P., & Bauserman, R. (1998). A meta-analytic examination of assumed properties of child sexual abuse using college students. *Psychological Bulletin, 124*, 22–53.

Schneider, E. (1992). Particularity and generality: Challenges of feminist theory and practice in work on woman-abuse. *New York University Law Review, 67*, 520–68.

Seelau, S. M., & Seelau, E. P. (2005). Gender-role stereotypes and perceptions of heterosexual, gay, and lesbian domestic violence. *Journal of Family Violence, 20*, 363–71.

Spitzberg, B. H. (1998). Sexual coercion. In B. H. Spitzberg & W. R. Cupach (Eds.), *The dark side of close relationships* (pp. 179–232). Mahwah, NJ: Lawrence Erlbaum Associates.

——(2009). Aggression, violence, and hurt in close relationships. In A. L. Vangelisti (Ed.), *Feeling hurt in close relationships* (pp. 209–32). Cambridge: Cambridge University Press.

——(2010). Intimate partner violence and aggression: Seeing the light in a dark place. In W. R. Cupach & B. H. Spitzberg (Eds.), *The dark side of close relationships*, 2nd edn (pp. 327–80). New York: Routledge.

Stander, V. A., Olson, C. B., & Merrill, L. L. (2002). Self-definition as a survivor of childhood sexual abuse among navy recruits. *Journal of Consulting and Clinical Psychology, 70*, 369–77.

Straus, M. A., & Gelles, R. J. (1990). How violent are American families? Estimates from the National Family Violence Resurvey and other studies. In M. A. Straus & R. J. Gelles (Eds.), *Physical violence in American families: Risk factors and adaptations to violence in 8,145 families* (pp. 95–112). New Brunswick: NJ: Transaction.

Sullivan, C. M. (2006). Interventions to address intimate partner violence: The current state of the field. In J. R. Lutzker (Ed.), *Preventing violence: Research and evidence-based intervention strategies* (pp. 195–212). Washington, DC: American Psychological Association.

Tjaden, P., & Thoennes, N. (1998). *Prevalence, incidence, and consequences of violence against women: Findings from the National Violence Against Women Survey*. National Institute of Justice (NCJ 172837), November. Washington DC: U.S. Department of Justice.

——(2000). *Full report of the prevalence, incidence, and consequences of violence against women: Findings from the National Violence Against Women Survey* (NCJ 183781). Washington, DC: National Institute of Justice and Centers for Disease Control and Prevention.

Tjaden, P., Thoennes, N., & Allison, C. J. (1999). Comparing violence over the life span in samples of same-sex and opposite-sex cohabitants. *Violence and Victims, 14*, 413–25.

Turell, S. C. (2000). A descriptive analysis of same-sex relationship violence for a diverse sample. *Journal of Family Violence, 15*, 281–93.

Ulman, A., & Straus, M. A. (2003). Violence by children against mothers in relation to violence between parents and corporal punishment by parents. *Journal of Comparative Family Studies, 34*, 41–60.

Ulrich, H., Randolph, M., & Acheson, S. (2005–6). Child sexual abuse: A replication of the meta-analytic examination of child sexual abuse by Rind, Tromovitch and Bauserman (1998). *The Scientific Review of Mental Health Practice, 4*, 37–51.

Van Oudenhoven, J. P., de Raad, B., Askevis-Leherpeux, F., Boski, P., Brunborg, G. S., Carmona, C., & Woods, S. (2008). Terms of abuse as expression and reinforcement of cultures. *International Journal of Intercultural Relations, 32*, 174–85.

Vatnar, S. K. B., & Bjørkly, S. (2008). An interactional perspective of intimate partner violence: An in-depth semi-structured interview of a representative sample of help-seeking women. *Journal of Family Violence, 23*, 265–79.

Whitaker, D. J., Le, B., Hanson, R. K., Baker, C. K., McMahon, P. M., Ryan, G., ... & Rice, D. D. (2009). Risk factors for the perpetration of child sexual abuse: A review and meta-analysis. *Child Abuse & Neglect, 32*, 529–48.

Whitaker, D. J., Morrison, S., Lindquist, C., Hawkins, S. R., O'Neil, J. A., Nesius, A. M., ... & Reese, L. (2006). A critical review of interventions for the primary prevention of perpetration of partner violence. *Aggression and Violent Behavior, 11*, 151–66.

Williams, K. D., Shore, W. J., & Grahe, J. E. (1998). The silent treatment: Perceptions of its behaviors and associated feelings. *Group Processes and Intergroup Relations, 1*, 117–41.

Wolfe, D. A., Wekerle, C., Gough, R., Reitzel-Jaffe, D., Grasley, C., Pittman, A. L., & Stumpf, J. (1996). *The Youth Relationship Project manual: A group approach with adolescents for the prevention of woman abuse and the promotion of healthy relationships*. Thousand Oaks, CA: Sage.

Wolfe, D. A., Wekerle, C., Reitzel-Jaffe, D., Grasley, C., Pittman, A.-L. & MacEachran, A. (1997). Interrupting the cycle of violence: Empowering youth to promote healthy relationships. In D. A Wolfe, R. J. McMahon, & R. D. Peters (Eds.), *Child abuse: New directions in prevention and treatment across the lifespan* (pp. 102–29). Thousand Oaks, CA: Sage.

Wolfe, D. A., Wekerle, C., Scott, K., Straatman, A.-L., Grasley, C. ... & Reitzel-Jaffe, D. (2003). Dating violence prevention with at-risk youth: A controlled outcome evaluation. *Journal of Consulting and Clinical Psychology, 71*, 279–91.

Yan, E. C.-W., & Tang, C. S.-K. (2004). Elder abuse by caregivers: A study of prevalence and risk factors in Hong Kong Chinese Families. *Journal of Family Violence, 19*, 269–77.

Zlotnick, C., Johnson, D. M., & Kohn, R. (2006). Intimate partner violence and long-term psychosocial functioning in a national sample of American women. *Journal of Interpersonal Violence, 21*, 262–75.

30

Psychophysiological Methods in Family Communication Research

Kory Floyd, Colin Hesse, and Perry M. Pauley

We have been witness in the past decade to some extraordinary theoretic and methodological advances in the study of family communication, as many other chapters in this volume articulate. Among those with the greatest promise for transforming our understanding of family behavior is the collection of methods offered by psychophysiology. In 2004, Floyd articulated the potential of psychophysiological methods for illuminating family communication, as part of a special issue of *Journal of Family Communication* focused on innovative methodology. Today, psychophysiological research provides an unprecedented look at the connections between familial behavior, physiological response, and health, offering communication researchers multiple new avenues for effecting improvements in physical well-being via improvements in social well-being.

Our goal in this chapter is to introduce the theoretic principles of psychophysiology and to describe various research programs that are exploiting their advantages to improve our understanding of family communication processes. We conclude with recommendations for researchers interested in incorporating psychophysiological methods into their own research.

Psychophysiology as a Method for Understanding Family Communication

A principal assumption of psychophysiology is that cognitive, emotional, behavioral, and social events are all reflected in the body's physiological processes. Take, for example, the experience of fear, which is associated with a host of hormonal reactions, nervous system activities, and muscular responses that distinguish it from other emotional experiences, such as sadness or surprise. Falling in love likewise initiates neural and hormonal activities that differ systematically from those associated with falling out of love. Psychophysiological researchers focus attention on the multiple ways that social events—including communicative behaviors—interface with the body's physiological systems and influence health, disease, and wellness (Loving, Heffner, & Kiecolt-Glaser, 2006).

To appreciate the relevance of psychophysiological methods in the study of communication, it is necessary to recognize the somewhat counterintuitive assumption that *all communication acts are biological acts.* No social behavior, whether verbal or nonverbal, is possible without the direct intervention and interaction of multiple anatomical and physiological systems. Production of a spoken word, for example, requires intricate coordination between the cerebral cortex, the spinal cord, the respiratory system, the laryngeal complex, and the muscles of the soft palate, tongue, and lips. Decoding of the same word depends on equally intricate collaboration between the tympanic membrane, the ossicles and cochlea, the spinal cord, and the cerebral cortex.

Communicative behaviors not only make use of anatomical and physiological systems; they, in turn, act upon those systems. If the spoken word is one of anger, its decoding will likely induce muscular tension, temporary immunosuppression, and the elevation of stress hormones such as cortisol in the hearer. If the word instead conveys appreciation, it may cause the release of neurotransmitters such as dopamine or peptide hormones such as oxytocin, imparting sensations of reward to the receiver. Recognizing the link between communication and physiology does not deny that many interpersonal acts are also historical, cultural, religious, political, economic, and aesthetic. Those are pervasive influences on communicative behavior, and we would not argue otherwise. Our argument implies, however, that insight into family communication is greatly advanced by exploring and understanding its physiological components. To prime our discussion, we next review the major physiological systems adjudicated in biophysiological behavioral research.

Principal Physiological Systems

To appreciate the use of psychophysiological methods, it is useful to understand various physical systems and what they do. In this section, we briefly address those issues for the brain and nervous system, and the cardiovascular, endocrine, and immune systems, which are the focus of much psychophysiological research.

Brain and Nervous System

The brain is a mass of tissue and nerves that consumes approximately 20 percent of the body's energy and brain controls every bodily activity and function with the exception of certain reflex actions. Structurally, the brain comprises four major regions: the *cerebrum, diencephalon, brain stem,* and *cerebellum.* The cerebrum, composed of the frontal, parietal, occipital, and temporal lobes, governs memory and learning, language and communication, olfaction, sensory processing, and movement. The diencephalon contains the thalamus, the epithalamus, and hypothalamus, the latter of which is an important component of the *limbic system,* which manages emotional experiences. The brain stem consists of the midbrain, the pons, and the medulla oblongata and plays important roles in alertness, consciousness, pain sensitivity, and cardiovascular and respiratory control. The cerebellum coordinates muscle movement, regulates muscle tone, and maintains equilibrium.

The brain and spinal cord comprise the central nervous system, whose function is to coordinate all bodily activity. The spinal cord serves three primary functions. First, it relays information and instructions from the brain through spinal nerves to coordinate motor activity. Second, it relays sensory information from sensory organs (eyes, ears, tongue, nose, and skin) to the brain for processing. Finally, it coordinates various reflex actions (Maton et al., 1993).

Cardiovascular System

The cardiovascular system comprises the heart and the arteries, arterioles, capillaries, veins, and venules through which blood is circulated. The heart contracts continuously to pump oxygenated blood to the body. Deoxygenated blood returns from the body to the heart, where it is pushed through the pulmonary artery to the lungs for reoxigination. Newly oxygenated blood returns from the lungs to the heart's left atrium, where it is passed to the left ventricle for circulation via the aorta, the body's largest artery.

Endocrine System

The endocrine system comprises a network of ductless glands that produce and secrete *hormones*. Hormones are chemicals that bind to cells that contain receptor sites. Once bound, hormones alter the metabolic processes of their receptor cells.

Social science research has tended to focus primarily on the activities of particular glands, including the pituitary and adrenal glands and the gonads. The pituitary gland, located at the base of the brain, secretes eight hormones, four of which have been of interest to social scientists. *Oxytocin* stimulates uterine contractions and the let-down reflex in expectant mothers, and also plays a role in emotional bonding and attachment (Young & Wang, 2004). *Vasopressin* regulates water absorption by the kidneys and also facilitates pair bonding (Hammock & Young, 2006). *Prolactin* stimulates milk production in lactating women and is responsive to changes in emotion in both women (Turner et al., 2002) and men (Fleming, Corter, Stallings, & Steiner, 2002). Finally, *adrenocorticotropic hormone (ACTH)* initiates the one of the body's major stress responses (Aguilera, 1994).

The adrenal glands, located atop the kidneys, produce *cortisol*, a steroid hormone elevated in response to stress (Burke, Davis, Otte, & Mohr, 2005). The adrenal glands also produce small quantities of *androgens*, the male sex hormones, and *estrogens*, the female sex hormones (Rainey, Carr, Sasano, Suzuki, & Mason, 2002). Levels of androgens in females and estrogens in males are regulated by the adrenal glands. Most sex hormones, however, are secreted by the gonads. Female gonads, called ovaries, produce estrogens and *progesterone*, which govern secondary sex characteristics and regulate menstruation, and also appear to contribute to the onset and maintenance of maternal behavior (Rosenblatt, 2008). Male gonads, called testes, produce androgens (including *testosterone*), which produce secondary sex characteristics and regulate sperm production, and are also associated with aggression in both men (Dabbs, Frady, Carr, & Besch, 1987) and women (Dabbs, Ruback, Frady, Hopper, & Sgoutas, 1988).

Immune System

The body's immune system consists of a coordination of structures and processes that protects against disease by identifying and destroying tumor cells and pathogens, whether bacterial, viral, fungal, parasitic, or prionic (Klosterman, 2009). The immune system includes two separate but interrelated components: the *innate* immune response and the *adaptive* immune response. Innate immunity is a nonspecific response that humans share not only with other mammals but also with lower-order organisms such as sponges. The innate immune response includes three processes: (a) inflammation, produced by granulocytes and cytokines; (b) antibody response, produced by complement proteins; and (c) cellular response, facilitated by leukocytes and natural killer cells. The adaptive immune response is a pathogen-specific response that incorporates B and T lymphocytes (small white blood cells that identify foreign bodies for the immune system to attack) and immunoglobulins. Unlike the innate immune response, the adaptive immune response confers immunity, protecting the organism against future threats by the same pathogen.

Having now reviewed the fundamental principles of psychophysiology and the major physical systems it adjudicates, we turn our attention next to the broad and growing research literature on the physiological bases of family communication.

Applications to Family Communication

Thus far we have reviewed some of the major concepts, biological systems, and theoretic approaches used in biophysiological social science. Even though the importance of biology was emphasized years ago by interpersonal communication scholars such as Beatty and McCroskey (Beatty, McCroskey, & Heisel, 1998; McCroskey, 1997), Cappella (e.g., 1991, 1996), and others (e.g., Andersen, Garrison, & Andersen, 1979; Horvath, 1995), communication science lags behind many other social science disciplines (including psychology, sociology, family studies, bio-behavioral health) in terms of recognizing and implementing a biological approach. Several communication scholars have argued for quite some time that a focus on biology is the "wave of the future." In fact, Knapp, Miller, and Fudge (1994) argued in the *Handbook of Interpersonal Communication* that providing greater attention to biological correlates and influences was an important direction in interpersonal communication research. Much contemporary research in family and interpersonal communication suggests that their vision is finally being realized. Why has it taken so long for interpersonal communication scholars to begin to recognize the importance of biology? We can identify at least eight reasons why interpersonal communication scholars have only recently incorporated biology into their empirical studies:

1 the relative newness and smallness of the communication discipline;
2 a lack of knowledge about how to conduct biosocial research;
3 the belief that researchers must be biologists or neuroscientists to do physiological research;
4 a lack of understanding about the importance of biology for human behavior;
5 the logical barriers of cost, technology, and time;
6 a fear that validating the role of biology in human behavior somehow diminishes the study of behavior;
7 a concern on the part of institutional review boards and funding agencies that the communication discipline is unequipped to do such research;
8 a backlash to a misperceived deterministic approach in biosocial research.

Regardless of just how much of our communication is genuinely genetically directed, researchers have come a long way from using deterministic approaches to study biosocial processes. As Booth, Carver, and Granger (2000) noted, until relatively recently there were significant gaps in the understanding of the connections between physiological processes and human behavior. As those authors suggested, "the nature of many physiological processes was largely unknown, and the technology necessary to operationalize physiological variables was in its infancy" (p. 1018). Many researchers who conducted physiological research turned to rather simplistic, reductionistic explanations to understand the influence of biology on behavior (Booth et al., 2000). However, the introduction of noninvasive and relatively inexpensive measures of biological markers and the breaking of interdisciplinary boundaries has dramatically increased our knowledge of physiology in human behavior (Booth et al., 2000; Hellhammer, Wust, & Kudielka, 2009). Dynamic models that recognize the fluid interplay among contextual, behavior, and biological processes have replaced deterministic ones. Gottlieb (1991) contends that biology lays the foundation for individuals' ability to adapt to environmental challenges. However, environmental challenges simultaneously induce behavioral change that, in turn, affects biological responses such as hormone secretion and gene manifestation (Booth et al., 2000). Biological processes that predict a particular behavioral response, and behaviors that predict changes in biological processes, may be stimulated or attenuated by environmental challenges. Consequently, interpersonal communication and the environment that surrounds those communicative behaviors, play a considerable role in influencing, and being influenced by, physiological processes.

In this section, we highlight some of the physiological research in interpersonal communication while simultaneously drawing from research in other disciplines to inform our research. More specifically, we will examine biosocial research on speech anxiety and "trait-based" communication skills, attraction, affection, touch and social support, aggression and violence, emotions, and intrapersonal communication processes such as planning and imagined interactions.

Communicating Attraction: Pathways to Long-Term Pair Bonding

Several theorists in the fields of communication and psychology have argued that the formation of significant relational ties with others is an essential part of the human experience. Baumeister and Leary (1995) proposed that humans have a fundamental "need to belong," that is, an innate need to form long-term relationships with other individuals in the context of communities. Taylor et al. (2000) likewise argued that the need for long-term relationships is necessary for survival, particularly for the female members of a given species. Similarly, Floyd (2006) argued that the affection and support received from long-term relationships augments the overall health and well-being of individuals in these relationships.

Although each of these theorists offer a slightly different perspective on the significance of close relationships, all are unanimous in their assertion that the formation of long-term pair bonds confers certain strategic advantages on the members of these partnerships. For example, the belongingness hypothesis specifically notes that membership in a community provides individuals with greater access to important resources like food, shelter, water, protection, and potential mating partners (Baumeister & Leary, 1995). Tend-and-befriend theory (TBT; Taylor et al., 2000) posits that the protection provided within communities is an especially important factor in the formation of long-term relationships among female members of a species. Because female members of most mammalian species are physically smaller than their male counterparts and typically bear the primary responsibility of care for offspring, the typical fight-or-flight responses associated with the experience of stress are maladaptive insofar as they potentially place offspring at greater risk. As a result, parallel behavioral mechanisms that promote affiliation in the face of stress have evolved: tending and befriending. According to the theory (Taylor, 2006; Taylor et al., 2000), tending involves caring for, protecting, and soothing offspring during moments of stress whereas befriending involves the active solicitation of assistance from peers. In addition to many of the social benefits delineated in the aforementioned theories, Floyd's (2006) affection exchange theory (AET) argues that the communication of affection, a behavior that aids in the development and maintenance of close relationships, is physiologically rewarding for individuals. As such, individuals are encouraged to develop and foster significant relationships (especially affectionate romantic relationships) by biochemical reactions that occur within their own bodies (a review of studies investigating this claim follows). Given that these relationships are both psychologically and physiologically rewarding, people often invest considerable resources into the maintenance of these relationships. The theory further argues that, over the lifespan of the relationship, individuals tend to be highly selective when picking potential relational partners and utilize affection gestures to remain attuned to their partners' level of commitment to the relationship after it is established.

One of the claims of AET is that people are selective when choosing a potential long-term romantic partner, but what features are desirable when individuals try to identify suitable partners? One typology (McCroskey & McCain, 1972) identified three characteristics that individuals find particularly attractive in relational partners (including long-term pair-bond partners): physical attractiveness, social attributes, and task abilities. Physical attractiveness includes numerous aspects of physical appearance such as clothing and sexual attractiveness. Social attributes refer primarily to the friendship prospect that others pose; as such, items associated with this dimension of attractiveness refer to others' pleasantness and whether or not they are similar to/compatible with existing friends. Finally, task abilities refer to whether or not others are reliable, adept at solving problems, and focused on relevant tasks. In subsequent paragraphs, we will review research relevant to the first two of these characteristics.

Physical Attractiveness

Researchers from fields like evolutionary psychology and cultural anthropology have invested considerable effort into identifying physical traits that contribute to an individual's level of attractiveness. Although these studies have identified several traits that contribute to both men and women's levels of attractiveness (for review, see Gallup & Frederick, 2010), for the purpose of this review, we will focus on studies that have examined the role of facial attractiveness, body proportion and symmetry, and scent in assessments of attractiveness.

Although many people recite the adage "beauty is in the eye of the beholder," several studies have revealed that there are in fact several facial features that are universally attractive (e.g., facial symmetry, facial neotany). In a recent study, Gangestad, Thornhill, and Garver-Apgar (2010) examined whether or not men's facial masculinity, facial attractiveness, or intelligence moderated the relationship between the point of maximum fertility in their female partner's menstrual cycle and extra-dyadic attraction. Overall, results indicated a strong and consistent effect for facial masculinity such that low levels of facial masculinity were associated with relatively high levels of female partners' extra-dyadic attraction during ovulation. By comparison, men's facial attractiveness yielded a similar albeit weaker effect (partial ^{2} for masculinity = .25 and for attractiveness = .14) and men's levels of intelligence did not affect the relationship between fertility and extra-dyadic attraction.

Studies examining the role of body symmetry and scent have revealed that these characteristics tend to overlap quite significantly. The now-famous "T-shirt studies" (Gangestad & Thornhill, 1998; Thornhill & Gangestad, 1999) were among the first to evaluate the relationship between physical attractiveness and scent. In each of these studies, experimenters asked individuals to sleep in T-shirts for two nights then asked opposite-sex raters to evaluate the scent of the T-shirts on three criteria: pleasantness, sexiness, and intensity. Although men did not demonstrate a strong preference for particular female scents, women (particularly those who were ovulating during the assessment) consistently preferred the scent of men whose level of fluctuating asymmetry (FA) was low. These authors argue that one possible explanation for the relationship between scent and symmetry is that both are indicators of genetic fitness. Indeed, recent studies investigating the link between attractive scents and genetic fitness have identified the major histocompatibility complex (MHC) as a likely link between these two factors (Thornhill et al., 2003). The MHC is a highly polymorphic collection of genes that enables the immune system to differentiate between the body's own tissue and pathogens (Penn & Potts, 1999) meaning that animals (including humans) with heterogynous MHC genes are advantaged over their counterparts with relatively homogenous MHC genes. As a result, results from experimental studies indicate that individuals preferentially seek out mates whose MHC genes would benefit potential offspring. At least one experimental study has explored the relationship between scent, MHC variability, and body symmetry; Thornhill et al. (2003) determined that ovulating women's assessments of men's scent attractiveness were negatively associated with men's degree of FA ($r = -.29$) whereas men's MHC heterozygosity was positively associated with scent attractiveness ($r = .33$) despite the fact that FA and MHC heterozygosity were not directly related.

Social Attractiveness

Physical features like facial attractiveness, scent, and body symmetry often affect assessments of attractiveness at an unconscious level. In contrast, scholars in communication studies have identified several aspects of interaction that affect attraction at a conscious level. Burleson and colleagues (Burleson & Denton, 1992; Burleson & Samter, 1996) have examined the role that cognitive and communicative skills play in the process of attraction and the maintenance of ongoing relationships. Overall, the results of these studies reveal that one of the most important social aspects of both attraction and relationship maintenance is similarity in social skill levels. Whether seeking a friend or a spouse, individuals are attracted to others whose cognitive and social abilities match their own, and, once the relationship has been established, similarly matched pairs tend to foster satisfying interaction. Evidence for the matching effect is evident among dyads with differing levels of skills—Burleson and Denton (1992) reported that married couples consisting of two low-skilled communicators did not differ in reported levels of satisfaction from couples consisting of two highly skilled communicators.

Communicating Affection in the Family

For many couples that successfully navigate the attraction and courtship process, the next step in the progression of their relationship is marriage, a public pronouncement of their mutual affection as well as a legal relationship in which spouses agree to share their resources with one another. Indeed, empirical studies have confirmed that, compared to unmarried individuals and those in dissatisfying relationships, happily married individuals report higher levels of happiness and satisfaction, report lower levels of depression, experience decreased mortality risks, and exhibit reduced risk for cardiovascular diseases (for a full review, see Robles & Kiecolt-Glaser, 2003). Of the explanations that have been offered for the benefits of marriage, several scholars have argued that the provision of social support that occurs within these relationships provides satisfied spouses with the resources they need to maintain their health and well-being (Robles & Kiecolt-Glaser, 2003).

While it appears that spousal relationships can indeed be healthy, scholars are still developing theoretical explanations as to *why* supportive spousal relationships lead to positive health indicators. One possible explanation highlighted by our research group at Arizona State University lies in the ability of an individual to communicate and receive affection, defined as feelings of deep warmth and regard towards another (Floyd, 2006). In this section we will discuss the theoretical foundation of this premise, moving into the research on the benefits of both spousal and parental affection.

Affection Exchange Theory

Affection exchange theory (AET), initially developed a decade ago and subsequently elaborated (Floyd, 2006), is a neo-Darwinian perspective based on the theoretical premise that humans are driven towards the superordinate evolutionary goals of survival and reproduction. AET states that all humans are born with the innate capacity to give and receive affection, regardless of time, race, and culture. Since the inception of AET in the literature, a growing number of articles have supported the basic tenets of the theory. Floyd (2002) found a positive association between affection and a host of relational and psychological variables, including relational satisfaction, a secure attachment style, and the number of close relationships. These findings were replicated in a later study that additionally showed that the benefits existed for given affection *even after controlling for received affection* (Floyd et al., 2005). Research has also found that affection is associated with healthier levels of blood pressure, glycosylated hemoglobin, and total cholesterol (Floyd, Hesse, & Haynes, 2007; Floyd, Mikkelson, Hesse, & Pauley, 2007). We subsequently will discuss a multitude of studies showing the same health benefits in a family context.

Spousal Affection and the Stress Response. Studies examining the benefits of spousal communication of affection have examined the question from two basic avenues: whether levels of affection that are typical within ongoing partnerships or manipulated levels of spousal affection relate to health. Floyd and Riforgiate (2008) examined whether expressed affection in a spousal relationship was related to individual diurnal cortisol variation. A healthy diurnal variation contains a high peak in the morning and a large drop throughout the day, reaching the low point during near midnight (Kirschbaum & Hellhammer, 1989). As hypothesized, they found a strong linear relationship between levels of expressed affection by the spouse and participant diurnal cortisol variation, as well as waking cortisol levels and the ratio between cortisol and dehydroepiandrosterone-sulfate (DHEA-S) (Floyd & Riforgiate, 2008). Another study utilizing a sample of premenopausal women found an inverse relationship between self-reported levels of partner hugs and blood pressure. They also discovered a positive relationship between partner hugs and baseline levels of oxytocin, a hormone commonly linked to bonding and attachment (Light, Grewen, & Amico, 2005).

Several studies have examined the question of whether manipulated levels of spousal affection can impact physiological health. One research team has conducted work on the physiological benefits of warm contact (a ten-minute period of sitting in close proximity while holding hands and viewing a romantic film clip) in a spousal relationship (e.g., Grewen, Girdler, Amico, & Light, 2005). A recent study out of this line of research took married couples through a four-week intervention designed to teach couples how to support each other better through touch and massage. Oxytocin levels rose for the experimental group throughout the procedure, while the experimental group also experienced a significant drop in alpha amylase relative to controls (Holt-Lunstad, Birmingham, & Light, 2008). Another study found a relationship between oxytocin levels and nonverbal displays of romantic love such as Duchenne smiles and head nods (Gonzaga, Turner, Keltner, Campos, & Altemus, 2006). Our research team examined the benefits of kissing in a spousal relationship, instructing the experimental group to increase romantic kissing in their relationship over a six-week period, while a control group experienced no relational change. After the trial, the experimental group had a significant drop in total cholesterol, while the control group had no change (Floyd et al., 2009).

Parental Affection and the Stress Response. The amount of affection that parents show to their children can also have important attachment and biopsychosocial outcomes. Tend and befriend theory (TBT: Taylor et al., 2000) argues that one of the main behaviors exhibited by women in periods of high stress is tending to offspring while blending into the environment. The displays of affection thus mute the stress response from the child, giving the child maximum capacity to survive until adulthood. Taylor and colleagues review a plethora of research that supports the premise that affectionate communication from the mother leads to a healthier stress response from the child (Taylor et al., 2000). Other research has revealed that mothers' abilities to communicate affection to their children can be affected by their attachment style. One study of first-time mothers found a relationship between a secure attachment style and greater brain activation of several regions associated with reward while the mothers viewed images of their own infants. Mothers with a secure attachment style also experienced greater levels of oxytocin activation upon touching their infant than did those with an insecure attachment style (Strathearn, Fonagy, Amico, & Montague, 2009). Oxytocin has also been linked to the communication between fathers and infants, with a positive relationship between levels of synchronous effect between fathers and infants during a social interaction and levels of oxytocin (Gordon, Zagoory-Sharon, Leckman, & Feldman, 2010).

Parental affection can lead to several biopsychosocial outcomes for the children as well. Schrodt, Ledbetter, and Ohrt (2007) found that affection mediated the relationship between family communication patterns and young adult children's mental well-being (both perceived stress and mental health). Another study surveyed children over the span of several decades as they grew into adults, discovering an inverse relationship between levels of maternal affection that participants received at the age of eight months and levels of general distress for the same participants as adults (Maselko, Kubzansky, Lipsitt, & Buka, 2011). Children who received lower levels of parental affection were less able to regulate the stress response, with higher baseline cortisol levels and more sustained cortisol levels following a stressor (Wismer Fries, Shirtcliff, & Pollak, 2008).

The overarching conclusion from this body of research is that affection in the family is adaptive, helping spouses to connect, helping parents nurture offspring, and helping children respond to stress throughout their lifetime. Altough affection can lead to substantial health benefits, the communication of conflict can prove detrimental to several psychological and physiological markers, which we will now discuss.

Conflict in the Family

As previously outlined, a large body of research supports the conclusion that satisfying marital relationships lead to higher indices of psychological and physiological well-being for individuals compared to people who are single or even dating; however, a multitude of studies demonstrate that, as healthy as marriages can be, unhealthy marriages lead to very unhealthy consequences for those same individuals, including poor indices of cardiovascular health and immune functioning. (e.g., Denton, Burleson, Hobbs, Von Stein, & Rodriguez, 2001; Robles & Kiecolt-Glaser, 2003). In this section we will summarize studies that have examined marital conflict in couples, the links between physiology and divorce, and the impact of conflict and divorce on children.

Physiology and Marital Conflict

Research on the physiology of marital conflict has focused on both newlywed and long-term married couples. Several studies by the Kiecolt-Glaser research team from Ohio State have analyzed the physiological effects of marital conflict behaviors in newlywed couples. In one of their earlier studies, newlywed couples were instructed to undertake a 30-minute conflict discussion on a divisive topic. The researchers found that the individuals (especially women) who exhibited more negative behaviors during the conversation had significantly higher levels of adrenocorticotropic hormone (ACTH), epinephrine, and norepinephrine (Malarkey, Kiecolt-Glaser, Pearl, & Glaser, 1994). In a second study, wives' cortisol levels (indeed, all hormonal levels that were studied, including epinephrine and norepinephrine) rose in response to the conflict setting, and this was especially true when the wife would enact a negative behavior that prompted her husband to withdraw from the interaction (Kiecolt-Glaser et al., 1996). The husband's cortisol level, on the other hand, did not significantly change during the conflict setting. This was partially explained by the notion that women are generally more sensitive to negativity in the relationship than are men (Kiecolt-Glaser et. al., 1996).

Both studies also proposed an interaction between measures of immune functioning and the amount of negative communication strategies participants enacted during the conflict. Overall, the findings showed a strong interaction, as more negative participants had significantly greater variation in their immune system health when compared to positive participants. For example, compared to positive participants, negative participants were found to have lower levels of antibodies, evidence of a weaker immune system (Kiecolt-Glaser et al., 1993). Negative participants also had a higher amount of antibody titers produced for the Epstein-Barr virus (EBV), a latent herpes virus that is present in virtually everyone, suggesting that the cellular immune response of the negative group was less competent in controlling the latent virus (Kiecolt-Glaser et al., 1993). Overall, the negative participants showed a greater amount of immune down-regulation. As with the hormonal results, the effects of the conflict on the immune system were stronger for women than for men. Those findings support the claim that newlywed couples are physiologically impacted by marital conflict and strife.

To ensure that the high levels of happiness and relationship satisfaction typical of newlywed couples did not confound the results of the studies previously discussed, Kiecolt-Glaser and colleagues replicated the study using older married adults (Kiecolt-Glaser et al., 1997). The researchers gathered couples that had been married, on average, for 42 years (mean age of 61). As with the newlywed couples, negative behaviors and negative escalation (especially for wives) accounted for a significant proportion of the variance for cortisol production, as well as several immunological assays (e.g., EBV and lymphocyte production), supporting the claim that the relationship between physiology and marital conflict lasts throughout the life of the marriage.

Physiology and Divorce

Several studies claim that the longevity of a marriage can be predicted through individual physiological reactivity to marital conflict. Levenson and Gottman (1985) discovered a general relationship between physiological arousal during conflict and relational satisfaction over a three-year period. Three years after the couples engaged in conflict, all previous measures of physiological arousal were highly correlated with the husband's later marital satisfaction, even controlling for the initial levels. Levenson and Gottman continued this promising line of research by undertaking three more long-term studies of married couples (see review in Gottman, 1994). Overall, the husband's heart rate was found to be a predictor of marital satisfaction and relational dissolution in two of the three studies, while the wife's heart rate was a predictor in the middle study. Based on these findings, Gottman referred to this cardiovascular arousal as flooding in his later papers, arguing that the arousal leads to a cascading effect for a couple towards isolation, loneliness, and divorce (Gottman, 1994).

In 2003, Kiecolt-Glaser's research team decided to bring back their 1993 newlywed sample for a ten-year follow-up, seeking to understand whether conflict behavior and hormonal levels could predict future dissolution of the marriage (17 of the 90 couples had divorced in the interim). Basal levels of epinephrine and ACTH at Time 1 were markedly higher for the divorced group versus the married group (Kiecolt-Glaser et al., 2003). Norepinephrine spikes were significantly higher for those couples still married who classified themselves as dissatisfied as opposed to satisfied couples (Kiecolt-Glaser et al., 2003).

The toll that divorce takes on the physiological makers of health in distressed and recently divorced individuals has been well documented, but until recently, the physiological effects of divorce on the children of divorced and divorcing couples had received comparatively little attention. Indeed, research has confirmed that inter-parental conflict often spills over into parent–child interactions in the form of negative comments and inappropriate disclosures that reduce children's well-being (Afifi, McManus, Hutchinson, & Baker, 2007). Experimental studies examining the effect of marital distress on conversations between children and parents have confirmed that the discussion of inter-parental conflict is both psychologically and physiologically distressing to the children. Afifi, Afifi, Morse, and Hamrick (2008) found that the experience of divorce significantly contributed to children's feelings of being "caught" between their parents and that this feeling predicted both emotional and physiological distress during a discussion of the parents' relationship. Additional evidence suggests that young adult children of divorced parents experience hormonal changes that contribute to feelings of stress when engaged in a discussion of family conflict issues with a parent. When divorced parents make inappropriate disclosures to their young adult children, their children's α-amylase levels (a salivary enzyme linked to cardiovascular responses to stress; see Granger et al., 2006, for review) exhibit a marked reduction immediately following the conversation followed by a significant increase 20 minutes post-interaction (Afifi, Granger, Denes, Joseph, & Aldeis, 2011). The authors note that this pattern of delayed reaction is significant insofar as it provides speculative evidence for the burden that adult children from divorced families often experience. Whereas divorced and divorcing parents are often hesitant to disclose many details about their relationship to younger children, adult children frequently serve as a confidant for one or more of their parents. As such, the authors posit that they exhibit a somewhat blunted stress response during inappropriate parental disclosures but that their discomfort with the situation eventually provokes a "flight" response.

Although this review is far from exhaustive, it has identified multiple interpersonal communication topics toward which the principles of biophysiology have been applied. To conclude our chapter, we offer the following comments on the future uses of the evolutionary and biophysiological approach and some brief words of advice for researchers interested in pursuing that approach in their own work.

Incorporating Psychophysiological Methods in Family Communication Research

To conclude this chapter, we have elected to address some practical issues relevant for family communication researchers interested in incorporating physiological measures into their work. Those issues concern training requirements and requirements for facilities and instrumentation.

Training Requirements

We have surmised elsewhere (Floyd & Afifi, 2012; Floyd & Haynes, 2005) that psychophysiological methods could be more useful in many sub-fields of the communication discipline if only adequate training were available to graduate students and researchers. Indeed, a small handful of graduate programs in communication now offer such training, which incorporates the theoretic, physiological, and procedural aspects of psychophysiological research.

Theoretic Training

Applying physiological methods to the study of family communication requires fluency in the theoretic bases of psychophysiology, biological psychology, and the processes of natural selection. Those theories give researchers a basis for deriving testable hypotheses—such as, for instance, the hypothesis that marital conflict is physically stressful. Those theories are not overly complex, but they are infrequently incorporated into communication training at the undergraduate or graduate level, which instead relies heavily on learning theory models.

Physiological Training

Besides understanding the theories from which one might derive predictions regarding the physiological nature of communication acts, researchers must also understand the physiological systems and outcomes they are examining. To document the physical stress of marital conflict, for instance, one should be familiar with the structure of the endocrine system and the nature of stress hormones, in order to know which hormones to measure and when.

Procedural Training

Finally, as with any method, researchers must learn the procedures of psychophysiological research. Knowing which stress hormones should be elevated by marital stress—and why—are important first steps, but they are of limited use until one knows *how* to measure those hormones. Unlike attitudes, beliefs, or intentions, most physiological outcomes cannot be measured via self-report or unobtrusive observation; rather, they require a different skill set, which can be obtained via education and experience.

Facilities and Instrumentation

A second practical issue for communication researchers interesting in using psychophysiology is the need for adequate facilities and instruments. Here, we will address the importance of data collection facilities, data analysis facilities, and instrumentation separately.

Data Collection Facilities

Facility requirements for data collection vary substantially according to the type of physiological outcomes being measured. Simple cardiovascular measurements, such as blood pressure or pulse rate, can be made in most any facility where proper instrumentation is available. Taking immune and hormonal measurements, in contrast, often requires collecting blood samples, which must be done by trained personnel in a laboratory with an appropriate biohazard rating. Although most communication departments do not have such laboratories, communication researchers can often gain access to appropriate facilities by collaborating with scholars in other disciplines, such as nursing, clinical psychology, or exercise science.

Data Analysis Facilities

Many laboratories that are equipped to collect physiological samples—such as blood or saliva—are not equipped to analyze them. Communication researchers should investigate in advance their options for data analysis. Options include professional service laboratories that will analyze the samples on a fee basis and "wet labs" at the researchers' own school, which may be willing to conduct the analyses at cost.

Instrumentation

Finally, psychophysiological measures require appropriate instrumentation. Some instruments—such as a stethoscope and sphygmomanometer for blood pressure assessment—are relatively inexpensive and uncomplicated to operate. Other instrumentation—such as an electrocardiogram for heart rate assessment or an electroencephalogram for neurological assessment—are more expensive to buy and maintain, and come with greater training requirements. Again, communication researchers just beginning to use physiological methods often find it best to collaborate with colleagues who are trained to operate such instrumentation.

Communication researchers are fortunate to have a wide variety of theories and methods to bring to bear on understanding the family. In this chapter, we have articulated how the use of psychophysiology can illuminate aspects of family communication—and its implications for health and well-being—that are not well adjudicated by other methods.

References

Afifi, T. D., Afifi, W. A., Morse, C., & Hamrick, K. (2008). Adolescents' avoidance tendencies and physiological reactions to discussions about their parents' relationship: Implications for post-divorce and non-divorced families. *Communication Monographs*, 75, 290–317.

Afifi, T. D., Granger, D., Denes, A., Joseph, A., & Aldeis, D. (2011). Parents' communication skills and adolescents salivary amylase and cortisol response patterns. *Communication Monographs*, 78, 273–95.

Afifi, T. D., McManus, T., Hutchinson, S., & Baker, B. (2007). Parental divorce disclosures, the factors that prompt them, and their impact on parents' and adolescents' well-being. *Communication Monographs*, 74, 78–103.

Aguilera, G. (1994). Regulation of pituitary ACTH secretion during chronic stress. *Frontiers in Neuroendocrinology*, 15, 321–50.

Andersen, P. A., Garrison, J. P., & Andersen, J. F. (1979). Implications of a neurophysical approach for the study of nonverbal communication. *Human Communication Research*, 6, 74–89.

Baumeister, R. F., & Leary, M. R. (1995). The need to belong: Desire for interpersonal attachments as a fundamental human motivation. *Psychological Bulletin*, 117, 497–529.

Beatty, M. J., McCroskey, J. C., & Heisel, A. D. (1998). Communication apprehension as temperamental expression: A communibiological paradigm. *Communication Monographs*, 65, 197–219.

Booth, A., Carver, K., & Granger, D. (2000). Biosocial perspectives on the family. *Journal of Marriage and the Family*, 62, 1018–34.

Burke, H. M., Davis, M. C., Otte, C., & Mohr, D. C. (2005). Depression and cortisol responses to psychological stress: A meta-analysis. *Psychoneuroendocrinology*, 30, 846–56.

Burleson, B. R., & Denton, W. H. (1992). A new look at similarity and attraction in marriage: Similarities in social-cognitive and communication skills as predictors of attraction and satisfaction. *Communication Monographs*, 59, 268–87.

Burleson, B. R., & Samter, W. (1996). Similarity in the communication skills of young adults: Foundations of attraction, friendship, and relationship satisfaction. *Communication Reports*, 9, 127–39.

Cappella, J. (1991). The biological origins of automated patterns of human interaction. *Communication Theory*, 1, 4–35.

——(1996). Why biological explanation? *Journal of Communication*, 46, 4–7.

Dabbs, J. M., Frady, R. L., Carr, T. S., & Besch, N. F. (1987). Saliva testosterone and criminal violence in young adult prison inmates. *Psychosomatic Medicine*, 49, 174–82.

Dabbs, J. M., Ruback, R. B., Frady, R. L., Hopper, C. H., & Sgoutas D. S. (1988). Saliva testosterone and criminal violence among women. *Personality and Individual Differences*, 9, 269–75.

Denton, W. H., Burleson, B. R., Hobbs, B. V., Von Stein, M., & Rodriguez, C. P. (2001). Cardiovascular reactivity and initiate/avoid patterns of marital communication: A test of Gottman's psychophysiologic model of marital interaction. *Journal of Behavioral Medicine*, 24, 401–21.

Fleming, A. S., Corter, C., Stallings, J., & Stainer, M. (2002). Testosterone and prolactin are associated with emotional responses to infant cries in new fathers. *Hormones and Behavior*, 42, 399–413.

Floyd, K. (2002). Human affection exchange: V. Attributes of the highly affectionate. *Communication Quarterly*, 50, 135–52.

——(2004). An introduction to the uses and potential uses of physiological measurement in the study of family communication. *Journal of Family Communication*, 4, 295–318.

——(2006). *Communicating affection: Interpersonal behavior and social context*. Cambridge: Cambridge University Press.

Floyd, K., & Afifi, T. D. (2012). Biological and physiological perspectives on interpersonal communication. In M. L. Knapp & J. A. Daly (Eds.), *Handbook of interpersonal communication*, 4th edn (pp. 87–127). Thousand Oaks, CA: Sage.

Floyd, K., Boren, J. P., Hannawa, A. F., Hesse, C., McEwan, B., & Veksler, A. E. (2009). Kissing in marital and cohabiting relationships: Effects on blood lipids, stress, and relationship satisfaction. *Western Journal of Communication*, 73, 113–33.

Floyd, K., & Haynes, M. T. (2005). Applications of the theory of natural selection to the study of family communication. *Journal of Family Communication*, 5, 79–101.

Floyd, K., Hess, J., Miczo, L., Halone, K., Mikkelson, A. C., & Tusing, K. (2005). Human affection exchange: VIII. Further evidence of the benefits of expressed affection. *Communication Quarterly*, 53, 285–303.

Floyd, K., Hesse, C., & Haynes, M. T. (2007). Human affection exchange: XV. Metabolic and cardiovascular correlates of trait expressed affection. *Communication Quarterly, 55*, 79–94.

Floyd, K., Mikkelson, A. C., Hesse, C., & Pauley, P. M. (2007). Affectionate writing reduces total cholesterol: Two randomized, controlled trials. *Human Communication Research, 33*, 119–42.

Floyd, K., & Riforgiate, S. (2008). Affectionate communication received from spouses predicts stress hormone levels in healthy adults. *Communication Monographs, 75*, 351–68.

Gallup, G. G., & Frederick, D. A. (2010). The science of sex appeal: An evolutionary perspective. *Review of General Psychology, 14*, 240–50.

Gangestad, S. W., & Thornhill, R. (1998). Menstrual cycle variation in women's preferences for the scent of symmetrical men. *Proceedings of the Royal Society of London B, 265*, 927–33.

Gangestad, S. W., Thornhill, R., & Garver-Apgar, C. E. (2010). Men's facial masculinity predicts changes in their female partners' sexual interests across the ovulatory cycle, whereas men's intelligence does not. *Evolution and Human Behavior, 31*, 412–24.

Gonzaga, G. C., Turner, R. A., Keltner, D., Campos, B., & Altemus, M. (2006). Romantic love and sexual desire in close relationships. *Emotion, 6*, 163–79.

Gordon, I., Zagoory-Sharon, O., Leckman, J. F., & Feldman, R. (2010). Oxytocin and the development of parenting in humans. *Biological Psychiatry, 68*, 377–82.

Gottlieb, G. (1991). Experiential canalization of behavioral development: Theory. *Developmental Psychology, 27*, 4–13.

Gottman, J. (1994). *What predicts divorce? The relationship between marital processes and marital outcomes.* Hillsdale, NJ: Lawrence Erlbaum Associates.

Granger, D. A., Kivlighan, K. T., Blair, C., El-Sheikh, M., Mize, J., Lisonbee, J. A., Buckhalt, J. A., et al. (2006). Integrating the measurement of salivary α-amylase into studies of child health, development, and social relationships. *Journal of Social and Personal Relationships, 23*, 267–90.

Grewen, K. M., Girdler, S. S., Amico, J., & Light, K. C. (2005). Effects of partner support on resting oxytocin, cortisol, norepinephrine, and blood pressure before and after warm partner contact. *Psychosomatic Medicine, 67*, 531–38.

Hammock, E. A. D., & Young, L. J. (2006). Oxytocin, vasopressin and pair bonding: Implications for autism. *Philosophical Transactions of the Royal Society of London B: Biological Sciences, 361*, 2187–98.

Hellhammer, D. H., Wust, S., & Kudielka, B. M. (2009). Salivary cortisol as a biomarker in stress research. *Psychoneuroendocrinology, 34*, 163–71.

Holt-Lunstad, J., Birmingham, W. A., & Light, K. C. (2008). Influence of a "warm touch" support enhancement intervention among married couples on ambulatory blood pressure, oxytocin, alpha amylase, and cortisol. *Psychosomatic Medicine, 70*, 976–85.

Horvath, C. W. (1995). Biological origins of communicator style. *Communication Quarterly, 43*, 394–407.

Kiecolt-Glaser, J. K., Bane, C., Glaser, R., & Malarkey, W. B. (2003). Love, marriage, and divorce: Newlyweds' stress hormones foreshadow relationship changes. *Journal of Consulting and Clinical Psychology, 71*, 176–88.

Kiecolt-Glaser, J. K., Glaser, R., Cacioppo, J., MacCallum, R., Snydersmith, M., Kim, C., & Malarkey, W. (1997). Marital conflict in older adults: Endocrinological and immunological correlates. *Psychosomatic Medicine, 59*, 339–49.

Kiecolt-Glaser, J. K., Malarkey, W. B., Chee, M., & Newton, T. (1993). Negative behavior during marital conflict is associated with immunological down-regulation. *Psychosomatic Medicine, 55*, 395–409.

Kiecolt-Glaser, J. K., Newton, T., Cacioppo, J. T., MacCallum, R. C., Glaser, R., & Malarkey, W. B. (1996). Marital conflict and endocrine function: Are men really more physiologically affected than women? *Journal of Consulting and Clinical Psychology, 64*, 324–32.

Kirschbaum, C., & Hellhammer, D. H. (1989). Salivary cortisol in psychobiological research: An overview. *Neuropsychobiology, 22*, 150–69.

Knapp, M., Miller, G. R., & Fudge, K. (1994). Background and current trends in the study of interpersonal communication. In M. L. Knapp & G. R. Miller (Eds.), *Handbook of interpersonal communication*, 2nd edn (pp. 3–20). Thousand Oaks, CA: Sage.

Klosterman, L. (2009). *Immune system.* Tarrytown, NY: Marshall Cavendish Benchmark.

Levenson, R. W., & Gottman, J. M. (1985). Physiological and affective predictors of change in relationship satisfaction. *Journal of Personality and Social Psychology, 49*, 85–94.

Light, K. C., Grewen, K. M., & Amico, J. A. (2005). More frequent partner hugs and higher oxytocin levels are linked to lower blood pressure and heart rate in premenopausal women. *Biological Psychology, 69*, 5–21.

Loving, T. J., Heffner, K. L., & Kiecolt-Glaser, J. K. (2006). I've got you under my skin: Physiology and interpersonal relationships. In A. L. Vangelisti & D. Perlman (Eds.), *The Cambridge handbook of personal relationships* (pp. 385–408). Cambridge: Cambridge University Press.

Malarkey, W. B., Kiecolt-Glaser, J. K., Pearl, D., & Glaser, R. (1994). Hostile behavior during marital conflict alters pituitary and adrenal hormones. *Psychosomatic Medicine, 56,* 41–51.

Maselko, J., Kubzansky, L., Lipsitt, L., & Buka, S. L. (2011). Mother's affection at 8 months predicts emotional distress in adulthood. *Journal of Epidemiology and Community Health, 65,* 621–25.

Maton, A., Hopkins, J., McLaughlin, C. W., Johnson, S., Warner, M. Q., LaHart, D., & Wright, J. L. (1993). *Human biology and health.* Englewood Cliffs, NJ: Prentice Hall.

McCroskey, J. C. (1997). *Why we communicate the ways we do: A communibiological perspective.* The Carroll C. Arnold Distinguished Lecture presented at the annual convention of the National Communication Association convention, Chicago, IL, November.

McCroskey, J. C., & McCain, T. A. (1972). *The measurement of interpersonal attraction.* Paper presented at the annual meeting of the Western Speech Communication Association, Honolulu, HI, November.

Penn, D. J., & Potts, W. K. (1999). The evolution of mating preferences and major histocompatibility complex genes. *The American Naturalist, 153,* 145–64.

Rainey, W. E., Carr, B. R., Sasano, H., Suzuki, T., & Mason, J. I. (2002). Dissecting human adrenal androgen production. *Trends in Endocrinology and Metabolism, 13,* 234–39.

Robles, T. F., & Kiecolt-Glaser, J. K. (2003). The physiology of marriage: pathways to health. *Physiology & Behavior, 79,* 409–16.

Rosenblatt, J. S. (2008). Psychobiology of maternal behavior: Contribution to the clinical understanding of maternal behavior among humans. *Acta Paediatrica, 83,* 3–8.

Schrodt, P., Ledbetter, A. M., & Ohrt, J. K. (2007). Parental confirmation and affection as mediators of family communication patterns and children's mental well-being. *Journal of Family Communication, 7,* 23–46.

Strathearn, L., Fonagy, P., Amico, J., & Montague, P. R. (2009). Adult attachment predicts maternal brain and oxytocin response to infant cues. *Neuropsychopharmacology, 34,* 2655–66.

Taylor, S. E. (2006). Tend and befriend: Biobehavioral bases of affiliation under stress. *Current Directions in Psychological Science, 15,* 273–77.

Taylor, S. E., Klein, L. C., Lewis, B. P., Gruenewald, T. L., Gurung, R. A. R., & Updegraff, J. A. (2000). Biobehavioral responses to stress in females: Tend-and-befriend, not fight-or-flight. *Psychological Review, 107,* 411–29.

Thornhill, R., & Gangestad, S. W. (1999). The scent of symmetry: A human sex pheromone that signals fitness? *Evolution and Human Behavior, 20,* 175–201.

Thornhill, R., Gangestad, S. W., Miller, R., Scheyd, G., McCollough, J. K., & Franklin, M. (2003). Major histocompatibility complex genes, symmetry, and body scent attractiveness in men and women. *Behavioral Ecology, 14,* 668–78.

Turner, R. A., Altemus, M., Yip, D. N., Kupferman, E., Fletcher, D., Bostrom, A., Lyons, D. M., & Amico, J. A. (2002). Effects on emotion of oxytocin, prolactin, and ACTH in women. *Stress, 5,* 269–76.

Wismer Fries, A. B., Shirtcliff, E. A., & Pollak, S. D. (2008). Neuroendocrine dysregulation following early social deprivation in children. *Developmental Psychobiology, 50,* 588–99.

Young, L. J., & Wang, Z. (2004). The neurobiology of pair bonding. *Nature Neuroscience, 7,* 1048–54.

31

Mental Health

Chris Segrin

It would be nearly impossible to understand any mental health problem without some appreciation of the family processes that predated or aggravated the disorder. Scientists and clinicians are increasingly recognizing the role of family interaction patterns in the cause, course, and treatment of mental health problems. Toward that end, a great deal of sophisticated and ground breaking research has been conducted on family communication patterns and processes that are associated with mental health problems. The origins of this research and theorizing are far older than the field of communication itself and show just how consequential family communication can be to the mental health of family members. This research also shows how important family processes can be distorted and corrupted by the mental health problems of those in the family system. Perhaps due to the nature of the populations studied in this body of research, most studies on family communication and mental health are conducted by people whose formal employment may be outside of the communication field, but whose methods, constructs, and scholarship fall squarely within family communication research.

Research and theory on family interactions and mental health make up part of the larger interpersonal paradigm in mental health (see Horowitz & Strack, 2010; Segrin, 2001 for reviews). According to this perspective, both the maintenance and disruption of mental health are thought to be strongly influenced by the nature of one's interpersonal relationships. Naturally, family relationships occupy a prominent position in the interpersonal landscape of most individuals. As the research reviewed in this chapter will show, there is a strong connection between family interaction processes and family members' mental health.

In the service of brevity, the mental health problems featured in this chapter are only described in rudimentary form. Interested readers can find more detailed descriptions of these problems in the *Diagnostic and Statistical Manual of Mental Disorders* (4th edn, text revision) (American Psychiatric Association, 2000). Also, this chapter excludes analysis of substance use disorders as that is the topic of Chapter 28, and child abuse and neglect as major risk factors for a multitude of mental health problems as that is the topic of Chapter 29 of this volume.

Brief History of Research and Theory on Family Interaction and Mental Health

The recognition of dysfunctional family processes as both causes and consequents of mental health problems dates back well over 100 years. Freud (1966) wrote about the role of both parent–child interactions (family of origin) and marital problems (family of orientation) in precipitating mental health problems. The neo-Freudian Harry Stack Sullivan (1953) greatly expanded the thesis that family and other interpersonal relationships played a key role in maintaining or disrupting mental health. Publication of the book, *Pragmatics of Human Communication* (Watzlawick, Bavelas, & Jackson, 1967) was a milestone in scholarly inquiry into family communication and mental health. Communication scholars revered the book for its insightful conceptualizations of interpersonal communication processes. Clinical psychologists and psychiatrists were intrigued by the seductive hypothesis that double bind family communication played a vital role in schizophrenia. The "double bind hypothesis" was never empirically validated and was quickly abandoned as an explanation for schizophrenia. However, it was perhaps the crest of a wave of inquiry into family interactions and mental health problems, specifically schizophrenia, that was being aggressively pursued in the 1950s and 1960s. Since then, it would be fair to say that research and theorizing on family interactions and mental health has grown exponentially with each passing decade, and family processes are now recognized as major factors in the development, course, and treatment of many different mental health problems.

Pathogenic Family of Origin Interactions

At birth, the human psyche exists only in primitive form. Throughout the first two decades of life extraordinary development occurs in cognition, emotion regulation, language, and personality. The family of origin is the crucible of this psychosocial development. Unfortunately, some families exhibit and enact pathogenic processes that not only inhibit this development, but that damage the psychological well-being of the child. In some cases, these destructive family processes have relatively immediate consequences and manifestations in child mental health problems. However, the effects of some other insidious family processes build gradually over time, exhibiting a sleeper effect that is ultimately manifest in adult mental health problems. In the sections that follow, several distinct and dysfunctional interaction patterns in the family of origin are discussed for their form and function in disrupting mental health.

Parental Affectionless Control

One particularly noxious parent–child interaction pattern that has been linked to numerous mental health problems is often referred to as "affectionless control." This is a combination of parental overprotectiveness or excessive control coupled with low care, sometimes to the point of neglect. Affectionless control is a paradoxical pattern of behavior in that the parent seeks to strictly control the child, often without rationale, while at the same time showing little affection or genuine concern for the child's well-being.

Depression is one of the most pervasive mental health problems in the world. It is an affective disorder marked by sad effect, anhedonia (inability to experience pleasure), feelings of guilt and worthlessness, and numerous somatic symptoms (e.g., sleep and appetite disturbance). Low parental care coupled with overprotection is a common family of origin profile reported by people with depression (Parker, 1983; Sheeber, Hops, & Davis, 2001). Parker found depressed outpatients to be 3.4 times more likely than matched control subjects to have at least one parent who exhibited affectionless control. Others have found that exposure to affectionless control as a child is associated with a fivefold increase in the likelihood of having major depressive disorder 20 years later (Pilowsky, Wickramarantne, Nomura, & Weissman, 2006). Parental affectionless control appears to impart risk for depression in offspring by creating maladaptive cognitive patterns such as low self-esteem, self-criticism, and a self-blaming and defeating inferential style (Alloy, Abramson, Smith, Gibb, & Neeren, 2006). That is to say that children internalize this experience and it influences the way that they think about themselves and their world in such a way as to promote subsequent depression.

Presently, the American Psychiatric Association recognizes two categories of eating disorders as mental health problems, namely anorexia nervosa and bulimia nervosa (American Psychiatric Association, 2000). People with anorexia nervosa refuse to maintain an appropriate body weight and often have an intense fear of gaining weight, coupled with a distorted body image. Bulimia nervosa is defined by recurrent episodes of uncontrolled binge eating, inappropriate compensatory behaviors to control weight gain (e.g., self-induced vomiting), and an undue influence of body shape and weight on self-evaluations. Both concurrent and retrospective analyses point to affectionless control as a prominent feature of the family of origin of people with eating disorders (e.g., Latzer, Hochdorf, Bachar, & Canetti, 2002). For example, lack of parental care (Webster & Palmer, 2000), excessive parental overprotectiveness and intrusiveness (Rorty, Yager, Rossotto, & Buckwalter, 2000), alienation and detachment between mother and daughter (Cunha, Relvas, & Soares, 2009), and excessive parental control (Wonderlich, Ukestad, & Perzacki, 1994) are features of the family environment that go hand in hand with eating disorders. The paradox of affectionless control is nicely illustrated in findings showing that parents of anorexia patients were simultaneously more nurturing and comforting but also more ignoring and neglecting of their daughters in comparison to parents of healthy controls or bulimia patients (Humphrey, 1989). It is entirely reasonable to presume that the affectionless control parent–child interaction pattern has teleological significance in eating disorders. Eating disorders are often hypothesized to be a covert expression of the struggle for control between the patient and the overcontrolling parent.

In addition to depression and eating disorders, parental affectionless control also appears in the family background of people with certain personality disorders. One such example is borderline personality disorder. The core features of this mental health problem involve instability of interpersonal relationships, effect, and self-image. People with borderline personality disorder exhibit intense and variable mood, combined with more generally aberrant and aloof behavior, excessive daydreaming, a dissociated self-image, frantic efforts to avoid abandonment, impulsivity, suicidal behavior and threats, feelings of emptiness, and problems with anger control. Poor maternal and paternal caring, to the point of neglect, is often found in the family of origin background of those with borderline personality disorder (Nordahl & Stiles, 1997). This lack of parental caring is often coupled with a greater overprotectiveness (Links, 1992) similar to that reported by other psychiatric groups. The lack of parental care can be pronounced to the point of attacking and rejecting behavior from the parent to the child (Stern, Herron, Primavera, & Kakuma, 1997). Parental affectionless control has also been implicated in histrionic personality disorder. People with histrionic personality disorder exhibit a pervasive pattern of excessive emotionality and attention seeking. Their social interactions are characterized by inappropriately seductive or provocative behavior, rapidly shifting and shallow emotions, excessively impressionistic speech that is lacking in detail, and self-dramatization. Research has shown that parental overprotection coupled with low parental care is prevalent in the family backgrounds of people with cluster B personality disorders (i.e., antisocial, borderline, histrionic, and narcissistic) (Nordahl & Stiles, 1997). Related family processes that have been linked to histrionic personality disorder include high achievement orientation and high levels of parental control (Baker, Capron, & Azorlosa, 1996).

Affectionless control is extraordinarily corrosive to the fragile and developing psyche of a child. Adults who exhibit this pattern of parenting behavior are undoubtedly struggling with a pathological approach-avoidance conflict and have failed to effectively bond with their child in a way that allows for emotional support and availability. Affectionless control may confuse children and leave then wanting and disconnected from the security that is ordinarily found in a parental figure. Consequently a variety of mental health problems (e.g., depression, eating disorders, personality disorders) ensue. The common denominator of these particular problems is a less than favorable view of the self. This negative self-image, along with the efforts to compensate for it that are expressed in symptoms of these mental health problems, is cultivated from an early age by the intrusive and overcontrolling parent who otherwise fails to provide for the emotional needs of the child.

Family Adaptability and Cohesion

Systems-oriented researchers have emphasized adaptability and cohesion as two dimensions of family relationships that are crucial to healthy family functioning, provided that neither are too extreme (Olson, 2000). Adaptability refers to the family's ability to alter its power structure and roles to meet developmental demands and external stressors. Cohesion reflects the family's emotional bonding and sense of internal connection. Communication is the means by which families both express and adjust these two important processes. Extreme, and especially low, levels of adaptability and cohesion represent a profile of family dysfunction in which the atmosphere is ripe for offspring mental health problems.

People with eating disorders will often report low levels of cohesion in their family of origin (e.g., Latzer, Hochdorf, Bachar, & Canetti, 2002; Waller, Slade, & Calam, 1990). Although low family cohesion is often reported by young people with eating disorders as well as their parents (e.g., Waller et al., 1990), eating disordered children give lower ratings to their family's cohesiveness than their parents do (Hoste, Hewell, & le Grange, 2007). Regardless of which family member's perception is actually "correct," the fact that the parent and child with an eating disorder differ in their view of the family's cohesiveness says something in itself about these family relationships. Investigations of family adaptability in eating disorders have yielded less consistent results than those of cohesion. Some evidence indicates a negative association between family adaptability and symptoms of eating disorders (e.g., Vidovic, Jures, Begovac, Mahnik, & Tocilj, 2005; Waller et al., 1990). However, other investigations revealed more chaos, less organization, more inconsistent discipline, greater role reversal, and more poorly defined boundaries in families of girls with eating disorders or symptoms of eating disorders (e.g., Ross & Gill, 2002; Rowa, Kerig, & Geller, 2001). All of these patterns are suggestive of excessive adaptability. As in the case of cohesion, parents of young women with eating disorders do not feel that boundary violations are a problem in the family, in sharp contrast to perceptions of their daughters who readily report boundary problems (Rowa et al., 2001). In most studies, people with eating disorders seem to have been raised in a family that is marked by extreme levels of adaptability (either too much or too little), indicating potentially detrimental family relations.

Very low or very high levels of family cohesion, to the point of enmeshment, may also predispose people to develop depression (Jewell & Stark, 2003). Children in families with low cohesion often do not feel connected to, or cared for by, their parents. Low family cohesion has been documented as a particularly powerful predictor of adolescent depression in African American families (Herman, Ostrander, & Tucker, 2007). At the other extreme, in enmeshed families the emotional well-being of the parent and child are so strongly linked that issues that are upsetting to a parent invariably upset and distress the child. In some families enmeshment is expressed in the form of co-rumination (i.e., extensively discussing, rehashing, and speculating about problems), and this communication behavior is associated with increased symptoms of depression in adolescents (Waller & Rose, 2010).

Extreme family adaptability or cohesion are each associated with a number of other offspring mental health problems. These include social anxiety (Peleg-Popko & Dar, 2001), schizophrenia (Phillips, West, Shen, & Zheng, 1998), and the development of personality disorders (Gontag & Erickson, 1996). In some cases, the presence of a child with a significant mental health problem could alter the family's adaptability and cohesion. At the same time there is a compelling rationale, informed by both theory and empirical results, indicating that when these vital family processes reach extreme levels, child mental health deteriorates.

Communication Deviance

Communication deviance is a family interaction pattern that has been uniquely linked to the onset and course of schizophrenia. Schizophrenia is a formal thought disorder characterized by bizarre delusions, hallucinations, grossly disorganized or catatonic behavior, inability to initiate and persist in goal-directed activity, affective flattening, and impoverished and disorganized thinking evident in speech and language behavior. Early research on family interaction and schizophrenia revealed that patients' families often exhibited odd and unfocused styles of interacting with each other in which they experienced difficulty establishing and maintaining a shared focus of attention through their discourse (Miklowitz, 1994; Wynne, 1981). Topics of conversation will often drift or abruptly change direction with a lack of closure. Such interactions are marked by a blurred focus of attention and meaning. This characteristic style of family communication has been labeled "communication deviance" (Singer, Wynne, & Toohey, 1978). Wynne theorized that people learn to focus their attention and derive meaning from external stimuli through their interactions, particularly with parents, during the early years of life (Wynne, 1981). Odd and deviant styles of communication among the parents were presumed to interact with biological predispositions to contribute to thought and communication disturbances in children who were unable to relate to, and understand, their parents.

Communication deviance is often assessed through analysis of discourse during family problem solving discussions (e.g., Velligan, Funderburg, Giesecke, & Miller, 1995; Velligan et al., 1996). This technique, referred to as interactional communication deviance (ICD), codes the family's discourse into categories such as *idea fragments, contradictions and retractions*, and *ambiguous references*. A complete index of the categories and their definitions is provided in Table 31.1.

Communication deviance is more prevalent among parents of schizophrenia patients than it is in parents of either nonschizophrenic patients or healthy controls (e.g., Miklowitz, 1994; Subotnik, Goldstein, Nuechterlein, Woo, & Mintz, 2002). This unusual

Table 31.1 Interactional Communication Deviance Scoring System

ICD Code	Definition	Examples
Idea fragments	Speaker abandons ideas or abruptly ends comments without returning to them	"But the thing is as I said, there's got . . . you can't drive in the alley."
Unintelligible remarks	Comments are incomprehensible in the context of conversation	"Well, that's just probably a real closing spot."
Contradictions or retractions	Speaker contradicts earlier statements or presents mutually inconsistent alternatives	"No, that's right, she does."
Ambiguous references	Speaker uses sentences with no clear object of discussion	"Kid stuff that's one thing but something else is different too."
Extraneous remarks	Speaker makes off-task comments	"I wonder how many rooms they have like this?"
Tangential inappropriate responses	Non sequitur replies or speaker does not acknowledge others' statements	Patient: "Sometimes I work on the back yard." Mother: "Let's talk about your schoolwork."
Odd word usage or odd sentence construction	Speaker uses words in odd ways, leaves out words, puts words out of order, uses many unnecessary words	"It's gonna be up and downwards along the process all the while to go through something like this."

Source: Adapted from Miklowitz et al. (1991). Copyright 1991 by the American Psychological Association.

form of family communication can also predict the onset of schizophrenia among young people who have yet to fully develop the disorder (Goldstein, 1987). In one such study of families with a moderately disturbed teenager, high communication deviance in the parents was strongly associated with the appearance of schizophrenia-spectrum disorders in some of the family offspring at a 15-year follow-up (Goldstein, 1985). In a similar study, disturbed high-risk adolescents were followed over a period of five years (Doane, West, Goldstein, Rodnick, & Jones, 1981). By the end of the study, approximately 10 percent of those whose parents who were low or intermediate in communication deviance went on to develop schizophrenia, whereas 56 percent of those whose parents were high in communication deviance developed schizophrenia. Family communication deviance also appears to influence the course of schizophrenia. For example, Velligan et al. (1996) followed a group of schizophrenia patients and their parents for one year. During the study, slightly over 50 percent of the patients had experienced a relapse. Parental communication deviance at the time of the patient's discharge was significantly higher in the families of those who relapsed versus those who did not. As it turns out, the parents of those patients who relapsed exhibited a dramatic increase in their communication deviance over the course of the study. This investigation indicates that returning to a home with high communication deviance will increase the likelihood of relapse.

Parental communication deviance functions as a type of stressor that affects the course and outcome of schizophrenia. When parents' communication is particularly amorphous and peculiar, children may become confused and uncertain about even basic and fundamental social realities. This confusion undoubtedly has functional significance in the course of the schizophrenia as it is so central in the constellation of symptoms that make up the disorder. The discourse of communication deviance raises substantial questions about parents' own mental health. It is therefore understandable that when discharged into the care of such individuals, their offspring remain at risk for future relapse.

Expressed Emotion

Family expressed emotion (EE) is a pattern of criticism, overinvolvement, over-protectiveness, excessive attention, and emotional reactivity, usually communicated by parents toward their children, who are at risk as a result of the behavior. EE is assessed through the frequency of critical remarks, degree of hostility, and the degree of emotional overinvolvement expressed by a family member during an interview or family interaction. High family EE is a feature of several different mental health problems.

Perhaps the earliest research on family EE and mental health was conducted in the context of schizophrenia. EE was conceptualized as a combination of several behavioral characteristics: intrusiveness, anger and/or acute distress and anxiety, overt blame and criticism of the patient, and an intolerance of the patient's symptoms (Vaughn & Leff, 1981). One of Vaughn and Leff's early studies revealed that patients who returned to a home with high EE relatives had a nine-month relapse rate of 51 percent, whereas only 13 percent of those who returned to a low EE family relapsed (Vaughn & Leff, 1976). A review of 25 studies on family EE indicated a 50 percent relapse rate, over a period of 9–12 months, among schizophrenia patients discharged to a high EE family, but only 21 percent among those with low EE relatives (Bebbington & Kuipers, 1994). These findings indicate that the odds of relapse are increased by about 2.5 times for those patients discharged to high versus low EE relatives. In addition to being a useful and reliable predictor of relapse, EE may also be fruitfully understood as a familial risk indicator for schizophrenia (Miklowitz, 1994). Even people with no history of schizophrenia are at elevated risk for developing the disorder if reared in an environment characterized by high EE. In each case one could interpret the family EE as a stressor that promotes or exacerbates symptoms.

High family EE has also been implicated in bipolar disorder. The essential feature of bipolar disorder is an oscillation between manic and depressive affective states. A manic episode involves the experience of inflated self-esteem or grandiosity, minimal sleep, excessive and pressured speech, flight of ideas, inability to focus attention, distractibility, psychomotor agitation, and poor judgment that often takes the form of risky behaviors. Naturally, depressive episodes have most of the features of major depressive disorder. As with schizophrenia, family EE is a risk factor for relapse into bipolar episodes. Relapse rates for bipolar patients who return to high EE households have been found to be as high as 92 percent over the course of two years, compared to only 39 percent among those who returned to low EE households (Miklowitz, Simoneau, Sachs-Ericsson, Warner, & Suddath, 1996). The mean duration to relapse was only 34 weeks for those returning to high EE households compared to 52 weeks for those who lived in a low EE environment (Miklowitz et al., 1996). High EE parents of adolescents with bipolar disorder also report lower adaptability and cohesion, and higher conflict in the family environment than low EE parents (Sullivan & Miklowitz, 2010) which could also explain the ill effects of this family interaction style. It should also be noted that family EE tends to be a better predictor of depressive than manic symptoms, and can provoke symptoms when it comes from caregiving parents or a spouse (Miklowitz & Johnson, 2009).

Family expressed emotion appears to also be an important family process in the etiology and course of eating disorders (e.g., Hedlund, Fichter, Quadflieg, & Brandl, 2003). In their examination of some of the core features of EE, Kyriacou, Treasure, and Schmidt (2008) found emotional overinvolvement in 60 percent of the parents of anorexia nervosa patients, in contrast to 3 percent of control parents. They also found comparable rates of high criticism at 47 percent versus 15 percent for parents of patients versus controls, respectively. Maternal EE during family interactions with eating disordered patients is a powerful predictor of patients' eventual outcomes and responses to therapy (van Furth et al., 1996). Mothers' openly critical comments during a family interaction assessment were a better predictor of patients' outcomes than a host of other predictors such as body weight prior to onset of the disorder, duration of illness, body mass index, and age at onset (van Furth et al., 1996). Family expressed emotion may be problematic in part because it is associated with high levels of conflict and poorer levels of organization in families of people with eating disorders (Hedlund et al., 2003). The criticism element of expressed emotion appears to run rampant in families of young people with eating disorders. People at high risk for eating disorders tend to live with parents who are very critical and they are often teased by their parents and siblings about their weight (Polivy & Herman, 2002).

Family expressed emotion is a noxious and almost mean spirited communication behavior that can stress the delicate psychological landscape of a child or adolescent, or even an adult. It is evident in both the prodromal and clinical stages of various mental-health problems. Family EE clearly accelerates relapse into clinical episodes among remitted patients. High levels of family EE may be particularly troublesome because they reliably covary with other pathogenic family processes such as low adaptability and cohesion and high levels of family conflict.

Family of Orientation Antecedents and Concomitants

Family interactions continue to play a role in mental health long after most people leave their family of origin. Mental health problems can be disruptive to interactions within one's family of orientation. In some cases, dysfunctional patterns of interaction in the family of orientation can even precipitate episodes of mental illness. Research on family of orientation interactions and mental health has zeroed in on marital interaction and parenting as two classes of family of orientation relations that are disrupted by mental-health problems. In the sections that follow, dysfunctional marital interaction, emotional contagion, and parental failure are discussed as examples of family of orientation interaction processes that are associated with a variety of mental health problems.

Dysfunctional Marital Interaction

Maintaining a satisfying marriage requires good communication skills enacted with benevolent intentions, an agreeable temperament, and at least moderately positive perceptions of one's partner, among many other things. Not surprisingly, mental health problems appear to corrupt many of the fundamental components of marital quality. Although this suggests that mental health problems predate marital problems, at the same time, there is reason to believe that certain mental health problems, especially depression, could follow decreases in marital quality. In either case, there is a strong association between poor mental health and low marital quality.

Depression is the mental health problem most studied for its relationship with dysfunctional marital interaction (see Beach, 2001 for a review). Repeatedly, this research has shown that depression and marital distress go hand in hand. As depressive symptoms worsen or improve, so too does relationship quality with the spouse (Judd et al., 2000). The communication between depressed people and their spouses is often negative in tone and tends to generate negative effect in each spouse (Gotlib & Whiffen, 1989). In the context of marriage, depression is associated with poor communication during problem solving interactions (Basco, Prager, Pite, Tamir, & Stephens, 1992), verbal aggressiveness (Segrin & Fitzpatrick, 1992), and problems in establishing intimacy (Basco et al., 1992). A history of depression is associated with less positive reciprocity in marital interactions (Johnson & Jacob, 2000). Marital conflict is a key problem for depressed spouses. Depressed wives report more frequent arguments than nondepressed wives, and that their husbands do not understand or respect them (Coyne, Thompson, & Palmer, 2002). Their husbands report frequent arguments and complain that their depressed wives blamed them for everything that goes wrong, lacked ambition, and that their wives depended too much on them. During conflict resolution interactions, there are more negative messages sent from, and directed to, the person with depression than what is seen in nondepressed married couples (Sher & Baucom, 1993). The specific communication of depressed spouses during conflict includes a lot of self-complaints, sadness, slowed speech and monotone vocal cues, whining, and despondent expressions (Jackman-Cram, Dobson, & Martin, 2006). In marriage, at least part of the negative effect of depression on marital satisfaction comes through dysfunctional conflict patterns, specifically demand–withdrawal, avoidance, and lower levels of constructive communication (Heene, Buysse, & Van Oost, 2007).

A range of other mental health problems also appear to create difficulties for marriage. For example, spouses of people with schizophrenia report markedly lower marital satisfaction than spouses of healthy control subjects (Hooley, Richters, Weintraub, & Neale, 1987). Anxiety disorders also appear to be associated with lower spousal reports of relationship quality, especially on days when the person with the anxiety disorder is expressing a lot of symptoms (Zaider, Heimberg, & Iida, 2010). Patients with borderline personality disorder exhibit marital distress and disruption and this is at least partially explained by an increased perpetration of both minor and severe marital violence (Whisman & Schonbrun, 2009). Patients with bipolar disorder report lower marital quality to the extent that they experience depressive symptoms, however, their spouses' ratings of poor relationship functioning appear more strongly correlated with the patient's manic symptoms (Sheets & Miller, 2010). Whisman (2007) studied the association between mental health problems (anxiety disorders, mood disorders, and substance use disorders) and marital distress in a nationally representative sample of over 2,000 respondents. The problems that were most negatively associated with marital quality, as assessed with the Dyadic Adjustment Scale, were bipolar disorder, alcohol use disorders, generalized anxiety disorder, and post traumatic stress disorder. People with these problems were anywhere between 2.3 and 3.6 times more likely than healthy controls to have significant marital distress.

Mental health problems in one or both spouses make it very difficult to maintain marital satisfaction. Problems such as depression, schizophrenia, bipolar disorder, and generalized anxiety disorder are major risk factors for marital distress. Many of these problems may have their deleterious effect on marital quality through impaired communication processes (e.g., demand–withdrawal conflict patterns, intimate partner violence) that are otherwise known to be toxic to marriage.

Emotional Contagion

Theories of emotional contagion postulate that people will catch the intense emotional states of those with whom they interact through largely unconscious interpersonal processes (Hatfield, Cacioppo, & Rapson, 1994). This effect is predicated on the assumption and observation that people will mimic and synchronize their nonverbal behaviors with those of the people around them. This similarity in behavior is theorized to provide feedback that generates the same emotional experience as those people whose behaviors are being observed and matched. Although emotional contagion is most often observed in convergence of momentary emotional states during social interaction, there is some evidence to suggest that emotional contagion has more pronounced effects in family relationships, especially marriage. Naturally, in terms of mental health, these effects would be evident in the domain of affective disorders.

Symptoms of depression tend to be significantly and positively correlated in married couples (Benazon & Coyne, 2000; Segrin & Fitzpatrick, 1992). In couples dealing with a serious health problem or disability of one partner, symptoms of depression tend to be correlated (Goodman & Shippy, 2002), and the spouses often have symptoms of depression that are on par with those of the sick or disabled person (e.g., Segrin & Badger, 2010). Data from longitudinal investigations show that symptoms of depression in one spouse or partner predict a worsening of depression in the other partner (Joiner, 1994; Segrin et al., 2005). Comparable longitudinal studies reveal similar contagion effects for parent to child depressive symptoms (e.g., Abela, Zinck, Kryger, Zilber, & Hankink, 2009; Abela, Zuroff, Ho, Adams, & Hankin, 2006). These findings indicate that over time, the daily interactions that are part and parcel of close family relationships, especially marriages and parent–child relationships, can produce a significant exacerbation of depressive symptoms in one person as a result of those of the other.

Emotional contagion does not appear to be limited only to the experience of depression. In laboratory social interactions, emotional contagion has been documented for anxiety as well (Gump & Kulik, 1997). A longitudinal investigation of family members (mostly spouses) of women with breast cancer showed that higher levels of anxiety in the family member were predictive of a worsening of the breast cancer patients' anxiety over time (Segrin, Badger, Dorros, Meek, & Lopez, 2007). Therefore, in some situations, the anxiety of one family member can prompt increases in the anxiety of another family member.

Emotional contagion is a rather primitive process that may operate outside of human awareness. Nevertheless, there is evidence to suggest that people with symptoms of affective disorders, namely depression and anxiety, may have a deleterious influence on similar symptoms of their close family members. Presently, these contagion effects appear to operate in family relational contexts where there is otherwise a high degree of interdependence as in the case of married spouses or parents and their children.

Parental Failure

In its most effective form, parenting is a complex and skilled behavior that requires insight, patience, emotion control, and flexible communication styles to meet the ever-changing needs of developing children. Unfortunately, mental health problems can severely corrupt these and other processes, leading to poor parenting and ultimately to significant negative child outcomes. Research on parenting and mental health has major theoretical significance for understanding familial transmission and aggregation of mental health problems.

By far, the majority of research into parenting practices of people afflicted with mental health problems has focused on depression. This is undoubtedly due to the extraordinarily high incidence of depression in the general population as well as the pervasiveness of depression as an immediate consequent of childbirth. The experience of depression goes hand in hand with a variety of dysfunctional parenting behaviors. Chiariello and Orvaschel (1995) explained that depression interferes with parenting skills by corrupting parents' capacity to relate to their children. In general, the social behavior of depressed parents is characterized by similar negativity, hostility, complaining, and poor interpersonal problem solving that is associated with their other relationships. For instance, the communication between depressed mothers and their children is more negative and less positive than that of nondepressed mothers (Foster, Garber, & Durlak, 2008; Park, Garber, Ciesla, & Ellis, 2008). The same holds for depression in fathers— they exhibit fewer positive (e.g., affectionate, sensitive, supportive, positively accepting) and more negative (e.g., hostile, coercive, intrusive, restrictive, controlling, and critical) behaviors than nondepressed fathers do (Wilson & Durbin, 2010). Family interactions with a depressed father are also marked by positivity suppression; that is the tendency for a positive message (e.g., agree, approve, smile and laugh) by one family member to be met with either a negative (e.g., criticize, disagree, put down) or problem solving (e.g., question, command, solution) message by other family members (Jacob & Johnson, 2001). The unfortunate consequent of these dysfunctional parenting practices of people with depression is that their children evidence a number of negative psychosocial outcomes of their own, including depression. As Jacob and Johnson (2001) plainly stated, "family communication could be one of the channels promoting the increased risk of depression among children of depressed parents" (p. 39).

Parenting problems are not just limited to people with depression. It is apparent that other mental health problems are equally disruptive to parenting processes. For example, mothers who have schizophrenia exhibit even lower quality social interaction with their children than do mothers with affective disorders (Wan et al., 2007). The parent–child interactions studied by Wan et al. (2007) were marked by a lack of maternal sensitivity and responsiveness, and infant avoidance of the mother. In addition to being remote and insensitive toward their children, mothers with schizophrenia also appear more intrusive and self-absorbed when interacting with their child, in comparison to mothers with affective disorders (Riordan, Appleby, & Faragher, 1999). When interacting with their children, mothers with anxiety disorders exhibit more criticism, more conflict, less sensitivity, less warmth, and more overcontrol of their children, when compared to healthy mothers (Moore, Whaley, & Sigman, 2004; Schneider et al., 2009). Observations of mother–infant interactions reveal less sensitivity and less structure in the interaction, along with less child interest and eagerness, when mothers with borderline personality disorder were compared to control mothers (Newman, Stevenson, Bergman, & Boyce, 2007). Finally, parents with bipolar disorder report more negative communication styles and less expressiveness with their children than healthy parents do (Vance, Jones, Espie, Bentall, & Tai, 2008).

Conclusion

The research on family process and mental health has documented numerous communication patterns in the family of origin that appear to be risk factors for subsequent mental health problems in offspring. Parents who are unwilling or unable to create a supportive family environment and who instead exhibit pathogenic behaviors such as affectionless control, critical expressed emotion, and extreme adaptability or cohesion increase the risk of mental health problems in their offspring. Sometimes these problems are evident while the child is still living in the family of origin (e.g., eating disorders) and in other cases the mental health problems may be slower to develop and show up later in life (e.g., personality disorders). In either case, dysfunctional family communication patterns can be viewed as stressors that either interact with psychobiological predispositions to create the disorder or that have a direct effect on creating mental health problems. Adults with mental health problems, not surprisingly, often have concomitant interpersonal problems in their family of orientation relationships. It is difficult, if not impossible, to have a spouse, parent, or sibling with a major mental health problem while otherwise maintaining a harmonious and trouble-free family environment. Psychological problems have ripple effects that invariably affect the lives of other people who are in contact with the ill person.

One of the challenges for future research is explaining why one family stressor (e.g., affectionless control) culminates in different psychological problems (e.g., eating disorders, personality disorders, depression) in different people. Although family systems theorists described this phenomenon with the concept of multifinality, it has yet to be adequately explained in the domain of family processes and mental health. A related challenge will be explaining why some people who are exposed to stressful family interactions develop certain mental health problems and others do not. The study of resilience holds great promise for informing theories of mental health maintenance, not just mental health problems. Each of these goals is being actively pursued by researchers and clinicians and will further reinforce the fact that family interaction has a major influence on the mental health of its members, and family members' mental health has an equally major influence on the nature of their interactions.

References

Abela, J. R., Zinck, S., Kryger, S., Zilber, I., & Hankink, B. L. (2009). Contagious depression: Negative attachment cognitions as a moderator of the temporal association between parental depression and child depression. *Journal of Clinical Child and Adolescent Psychology*, 38, 16–26.

Abela, J. R. Z., Zuroff, D. C., Ho, M. R., Adams, P., & Hankin, B. L. (2006). Excessive reassurance seeking, hassles, and depressive symptoms in children of affectively ill parents: A multiwave longitudinal study. *Journal of Abnormal Child Psychology*, 34, 171–87.

Alloy, L. B., Abramson, L. Y., Smith, J. M., Gibb, B. E., & Neeren, A. M. (2006). Role of parenting and maltreatment histories in unipolar and bipolar mood disorders: Mediation by cognitive vulnerability to depression. *Clinical Child and Family Psychology Review*, 9, 23–64.

American Psychiatric Association (2000). *Diagnostic and statistical manual of mental disorders*, 4th edn. Washington, DC: Author.

Baker, J. D., Capron, E. W., & Azorlosa, J. (1996). Family environment characteristics of persons with histrionic and dependent personality disorders. *Journal of Personality Disorders*, 10, 82–87.

Basco, M. R., Prager, K. J., Pite, J. M., Tamir, L. M., & Stephens, J. J. (1992). Communication and intimacy in the marriages of depressed patients. *Journal of Family Psychology*, 6, 184–94.

Beach, S. R. H. (Ed.). (2001). *Marital and family processes in depression: A scientific foundation for clinical practice*. Washington, DC: American Psychological Association.

Bebbington, P., & Kuipers, L. (1994). The predictive utility of expressed emotion in schizophrenia: An aggregate analysis. *Psychological Medicine, 24*, 707–18.

Benazon, N. R., & Coyne, J. C. (2000). Living with a depressed spouse. *Journal of Family Psychology, 14*, 71–79.

Chiariello, M. A., & Orvaschel, H. (1995). Patterns of parent–child communication: Relationship to depression. *Clinical Psychology Review, 15*, 395–407.

Coyne, J. C., Thompson, R., & Palmer, S. C. (2002). Marital quality, coping with conflict, marital complaints, and affection in couples with a depressed wife. *Journal of Family Psychology, 16*, 26–37.

Cunha, A. I., Relvas, A. P., & Soares, I. (2009). Anorexia nervosa and family relationships: Perceived family functioning, coping strategies, beliefs, and attachment to parents and peers. *International Journal of Clinical and Health Psychology, 9*, 229–40.

Doane, J. A., West, K. L., Goldstein, M. J., Rodnick, E. H., & Jones, J. E. (1981). Parental communication deviance and affective style: Predictors of subsequent schizophrenia spectrum disorders. *Archives of General Psychiatry, 38*, 679–85.

Foster, C. J. E., Garber, J., & Durlak, J. A. (2008). Current and past maternal depression, maternal interaction behaviors, and children's externalizing and internalizing symptoms. *Journal of Abnormal Child Psychology, 36*, 527–37.

Freud, S. (1966). *Introductory lectures on psychoanalysis.* New York: W. W. Norton & Company. (Original work published in 1917.)

Goldstein, M. J. (1985). Family factors that antedate the onset of schizophrenia and related disorders: The results of a fifteen year prospective longitudinal study. *Acta Psychiatrica Scandinavica (Supplementum), 71*, 7–18.

——(1987). Family interaction patterns that antedate the onset of schizophrenia and related disorders: A further analysis of data from a longitudinal, prospective study. In K. Hahlweg & M. J. Goldstein (Eds.), *Understanding major mental disorder: The contribution of family interaction research* (pp. 11–32). New York: Family Process Press.

Gontag, R., & Erickson, M. T. (1996). The relationship between Millon's personality types and family system functioning. *The American Journal of Family Therapy, 24*, 215–26.

Goodman, C. R., & Shippy, R. A. (2002). Is it contagious? Affect similarity among spouses. *Aging and Mental Health, 6*, 266–74.

Gotlib, I. H., & Whiffen, V. E. (1989). Depression and marital functioning: An examination of specificity and gender differences. *Journal of Abnormal Psychology, 98*, 23–30.

Gump, B. B., & Kulik, J. A. (1997). Stress, affiliation, and emotional contagion. *Journal of Personality and Social Psychology, 72*, 305–19.

Hatfield, E., Cacioppo, J. T., & Rapson, R. L. (1994). *Emotional contagion.* Paris: Cambridge University Press.

Hedlund, S., Fichter, M. M., Quadflieg, N., & Brandl, C. (2003). Expressed emotion, family environment, and parental bonding in bulimia nervosa: A 6-year investigation. *Eating and Weight Disorders, 8*, 26–35.

Heene, E., Buysse, A., & Van Oost, P. (2007). An interpersonal perspective on depression: The role of marital adjustment, conflict communication, attributions, and attachment within a clinical sample. *Family Process, 46*, 499–514.

Herman, K. C., Ostrander, R., & Tucker, C. M. (2007). Do family environments and negative cognitions of adolescents with depressive symptoms vary by ethnic group? *Journal of Family Psychology, 21*, 325–30.

Hooley, J. M., Richters, J. E., Weintraub, S., & Neale, J. M. (1987). Psychopathology and marital distress: The positive side of positive symptoms. *Journal of Abnormal Psychology, 96*, 27–33.

Horowitz, L. M., & Strack, S. (Eds.) (2010). *Handbook of interpersonal psychology.* Hoboken, NJ: John Wiley & Sons.

Hoste, R. R., Hewell, K., & le Grange, D. (2007). Family interaction among white and ethnic minority adolescents with bulimia nervosa and their parents. *European Eating Disorders Review, 15*, 152–58.

Humphrey, L. L. (1989). Observed family interactions among subtypes of eating disorders using structural analysis of social behavior. *Journal of Consulting and Clinical Psychology, 57*, 206–14.

Jackman-Cram, S., Dobson, K. S., & Martin, R. (2006). Marital problem-solving behavior in depression and marital distress. *Journal of Abnormal Psychology, 115*, 380–84.

Jacob, T., & Johnson, S. L. (2001). Sequential interactions in the parent–child communications of depressed fathers and depressed mothers. *Journal of Family Psychology*, 15, 38–52.

Jewel, J. D., & Stark, K. D. (2003). Comparing the family environments of adolescents with conduct disorder or depression. *Journal of Child and Family Studies*, 12, 77–89.

Johnson, S. L., & Jacob, T. (2000). Sequential interactions in the marital communication of depressed men and women. *Journal of Consulting and Clinical Psychology*, 68, 4–12.

Joiner, T. E. (1994). Contagious depression: Existence, specificity to depressive symptoms, and the role of reassurance seeking. *Journal of Personality and Social Psychology*, 67, 287–96.

Judd, L. J., Akiskal, H. S., Zeller, P. J., Paulus, M., Leon, A. C., Maser, J. D., Endicott, J., Coryell, W., Kunovac, J. L., Mueller, T. I., Rice, J. P., & Keller, M. B. (2000). Psychosocial disability during the long-term course of unipolar major depressive disorder. *Archives of General Psychiatry*, 57, 375–80.

Kyriacou, O., Treasure, J., & Schmidt, U. (2008). Expressed emotion in eating disorders assessed via self-report: An examination of factors associated with expressed emotion in carers of people with Anorexia Nervosa in comparison to control families. *International Journal of Eating Disorders*, 41, 37–46.

Latzer, Y., Hochdorf, Z., Bachar, E., & Canetti, L. (2002). Attachment style and family functioning as discriminating factors in eating disorders. *Contemporary Family Therapy*, 24, 581–99.

Links, P. S. (1992). Family environment and family psychopathology in the etiology of borderline personality disorder. In J. F. Clarkin, E. Marziali, & H. Munroe-Blum (Eds.), *Borderline personality disorder: Clinical and empirical perspectives* (pp. 15–66). New York: Guilford Press.

Miklowitz, D. J. (1994). Family risk indicators in schizophrenia. *Schizophrenia Bulletin*, 20, 137–49.

Miklowitz, D. J., & Johnson, S. L. (2009). Social and familial factors in the course of bipolar disorder: Basic processes and relevant interventions. *Clinical Psychology*, 16, 281–96.

Miklowitz, D. J., Simoneau, T. L., Sachs-Ericsson, N., Warner, R., & Suddath, R. (1996). Family risk indicators in the course of bipolar affective disorder. In C. Mundt, M. J. Goldstein, K. Hahlweg, & P. Fiedler (Eds.), *Interpersonal factors in the origin and course of affective disorders* (pp. 204–17). London: Gaskell.

Miklowitz, D. J., Velligan, D. I., Goldstein, M. J., Nuechterlein, K. H., Gitlin, M. J., Ranlett, G., & Doane, J. A. (1991). Communication deviance in families of schizophrenic and manic patients. *Journal of Abnormal Psychology*, 100, 163–73.

Moore, P. S., Whaley, S. E., & Sigman, M. (2004). Interactions between mothers and children: Impacts of maternal and child anxiety. *Journal of Abnormal Psychology*, 113, 471–76.

Newman, L. K., Stevenson, C. S., Bergman, L. R., & Boyce, P. (2007). Borderline personality disorder, mother–infant interaction and parenting perceptions: preliminary findings. *Australian and New Zealand Journal of Psychiatry*, 41, 598–605.

Nordahl, H. M., & Stiles, T. C. (1997). Perceptions of parental bonding in patients with various personality disorders, lifetime depressive disorders, and healthy controls. *Journal of Personality Disorders*, 11, 391–402.

Olson, D. H. (2000). Circumplex model of marital and family systems. *Journal of Family Therapy*, 22, 144–67.

Park, I. J. K., Garber, J., Ciesla, J. A., & Ellis, B. J. (2008). Convergence among multiple methods of measuring positivity and negativity in the family environment: Relation to depression in mothers and their children. *Journal of Family Psychology*, 22, 123–34.

Parker, G. (1983). Parental "affectionless control" as an antecedent to adult depression. *Archives of General Psychiatry*, 40, 856–60.

Peleg-Popko, O., & Dar, R. (2001). Marital quality, family patterns, and children's fears and social anxiety. *Contemporary Family Therapy*, 23, 465–87.

Phillips, M. R., West, C. L., Shen, Q., & Zheng, Y. (1998). Comparison of schizophrenia patients' families and normal families in China, using Chinese versions of FACES-II and the Family Environment Scales. *Family Process*, 37, 95–106.

Pilowsky, D. J., Wickramarantne, P., Nomura, Y., & Weissman, M. M. (2006). Family discord, parental depression, and psychopathology in offspring: 20-year follow-up. *Journal of the American Academy of Child and Adolescent Psychiatry*, 45, 452–60.

Polivy, J., & Herman, C. P. (2002). Causes of eating disorders. *Annual Review of Psychology*, 53, 187–213.

Riordan, D., Appleby, L., & Faragher, B. (1999). Mother–infant interaction in post-partum women with schizophrenia and affective disorders. *Psychological Medicine*, 29, 991–95.

Rorty, M., Yager, J., Rossotto, E., & Buckwalter, G. (2000). Parental intrusiveness in adolescence recalled by women with a history of bulimia nervosa and comparison women. *International Journal of Eating Disorders, 28,* 202–8.

Ross, L. T., & Gill, J. L. (2002). Eating disorders: Relations with inconsistent discipline, anxiety, and drinking among college women. *Psychological Reports, 91,* 289–98.

Rowa, K., Kerig, P. K., Geller, J. (2001). The family and anorexia nervosa: Examining parent–child boundary problems. *European Eating Disorders Review, 9,* 97–114.

Schneider, S., Houweling, J. E. G., Gommlich-Schneider, S., Klein, C., Nundel, B., & Wolke, D. (2009). Effect of maternal panic disorder on mother–child interaction and relation to child anxiety and child self-efficacy. *Archives of Women's Mental Health, 12,* 251–59.

Segrin, C. (2001). *Interpersonal processes in psychological problems.* New York: Guilford Press.

Segrin, C., & Badger, T. A. (2010). Psychological distress in different social network members of breast and prostate cancer survivors. *Research in Nursing and Health, 33,* 450–64.

Segrin, C., Badger, T. A., Dorros, S. M., Meek, P., & Lopez, A. M. (2007). Interdependent anxiety and psychological distress in women with breast cancer and their partners. *Psycho-Oncology, 16,* 634–43.

Segrin, C., Badger, T., Meek, P., Lopez, A. M., Bonham, E., & Sieger, A. (2005). Dyadic interdependence on affect and quality of life trajectories among women with breast cancer and their partners. *Journal of Social and Personal Relationships, 22,* 673–89.

Segrin, C., & Fitzpatrick, M. A. (1992). Depression and verbal aggressiveness in different marital couple types. *Communication Studies, 43,* 79–91.

Sheeber, L., Hops, H., & Davis, B. (2001). Family processes in adolescent depression. *Clinical Child and Family Psychology Review, 4,* 19–35.

Sheets, E. S., & Miller, I. W. (2010). Predictors of relationship functioning for patients with bipolar disorders and their partners. *Journal of Family Psychology, 24,* 371–79.

Sher, T. G., & Baucom, D. H. (1993). Marital communication: Differences among maritally distressed, depressed, and nondistressed-nondepressed couples. *Journal of Family Psychology, 7,* 148–53.

Singer, M., Wynne, L., & Toohey, M. (1978). Communication disorders and the families of schizophrenics. In L. C. Wynne, R. L. Cromwell, & S. Matthysse (Eds.), *The nature of schizophrenia: New approaches to research and treatment* (pp. 499–511). New York: Wiley.

Stern, M. I., Herron, W. G., Primavera, L. H., & Kakuma, T. (1997). Interpersonal perceptions of depressed and borderline inpatients. *Journal of Clinical Psychology, 53,* 41–49.

Subotnik, K. L., Goldstein, M. J., Nuechterlein, K. H., Woo, S. M., & Mintz, J. (2002). Are communication deviance and expressed emotion related to family history of psychiatric disorders in schizophrenia? *Schizophrenia Bulletin, 28,* 719–29.

Sullivan, A. E., & Miklowitz, D. J. (2010). Family functioning with bipolar disorder. *Journal of Family Psychology, 24,* 60–67.

Sullivan, H. S. (1953). *The interpersonal theory of psychiatry.* New York: Norton.

van Furth, E. F., van Strien, D. C., Martina, L. M. L., van Son, M. J. M., Hendrickx, J. J. P., & van Engeland, H. (1996). Expressed emotion and the prediction of outcome in adolescent eating disorders. *International Journal of Eating Disorders, 20,* 19–31.

Vance, Y. H., Jones, S. H., Espie, J., Bentall, R., & Tai, S. (2008). Parental communication style and family relationships in children of bipolar parents. *British Journal of Clinical Psychology, 47,* 355–59.

Vaughn, C., & Leff, J. P. (1976). The measurement of expressed emotion in the families of psychiatric patients. *British Journal of Clinical and Social Psychology, 15,* 157–65.

Vaughn, C. E., & Leff, J. P. (1981). Patterns of emotional response in relatives of schizophrenic patients. *Schizophrenia Bulletin, 7,* 43–44.

Velligan, D. I., Funderburg, L. G., Giesecke, S. L., & Miller, A. L. (1995). Longitudinal analysis of communication deviance in the families of schizophrenic patients. *Psychiatry, 58,* 6–19.

Velligan, D. I., Miller, A. L., Eckert, S. L., Funderburg, L. G., True, J. E., Mahurin, R. K., Diamond, P., & Hazelton, B. C. (1996). The relationship between parental communication deviance and relapse in schizophrenia patients in the 1-year period after hospital discharge. *Journal of Nervous and Mental Disease, 184,* 490–96.

Vidovic, V., Jures, V., Begovac, I., Mahnik, M., Tocilj, G. (2005). Perceived family cohesion and adaptability and communication in eating disorders. *European Eating Disorders Review, 13,* 19–28.

Waller, E. M., & Rose, A. J. (2010). Adjustment trade-offs of co-rumination in mother-adolescent relationships. *Journal of Adolescence, 33,* 487–97.

Waller, G., Slade, P., & Calam, R. (1990). Family adaptability and cohesion: Relation to eating attitudes and disorders. *International Journal of Eating Disorders, 9,* 225–28.

Wan, M. W., Salmon, M. P., Riordan, D., Appleby, L., Webb, R., & Abel, K. M. (2007). What predicts mother–infant interaction in schizophrenia? *Psychological Medicine, 37,* 537–46.

Watzlawick, P., Bavelas, J. B., & Jackson, D. D. (1967). *Pragmatics of human communication.* New York: W. W. Norton & Company.

Webster, J. J., & Palmer, R. L. (2000). The childhood and family background of women with clinical eating disorders: A comparison with women with major depression and women without psychiatric disorder. *Psychological Medicine, 30,* 53–60.

Wilson, S., & Durbin, C. E. (2010). Effects of paternal depression on fathers' parenting behaviors: A meta-analytic review. *Clinical Psychology Review, 30,* 167–80.

Whisman, M. A. (2007). Marital distress and DSM-IV psychiatric disorders in a population-based national survey. *Journal of Abnormal Psychology, 116,* 638–43.

Whisman, M. A., & Schonbrun, Y. C. (2009). Social consequences of borderline personality disorder symptoms in a population-based survey: Marital distress, marital violence, and marital disruption. *Journal of Personality Disorders, 23,* 410–15.

Wonderlich, S., Ukestad, L., & Perzacki, R. (1994). Perceptions of nonshared childhood environment in bulimia nervosa. *Journal of the American Academy of Child and Adolescent Psychiatry, 33,* 740–47.

Wynne, L. C. (1981). Current concepts about schizophrenics and family relationships. *Journal of Nervous and Mental Disease, 169,* 82–89.

Zaider, T. I., Heimberg, R. G., & Iida, M. (2010). Anxiety disorders and intimate relationships: A study of daily processes in couples. *Journal of Abnormal Psychology, 119,* 163–73.

Part VII
Epilogue and Commentary

32

The Family of the Future

What Do We Face?

Kathleen M. Galvin

At the close of the 20th century, organizational development specialist Peter Vaill (1996) asserted that living in a world of "permanent white water," a complex, turbulent, competitive environment, necessitates lifelong learning. Fourteen years later he re-emphasized the ongoing need to manage surprising, novel, and obtrusive events (Vaill, Bunker & Santana, 2010). Twenty-first century family communication scholarship represents a shift from an early, extensive focus on marital interaction to a broad range of research questions. The rapidly evolving nature of families and their environments challenge communication scholars to continually explore new directions.

Relying on a slight variation of the framework printed in the handbook edition (2004), this chapter will update selected material, explore cutting edge family interaction research and provide informed speculation regarding future scholarship.

The family of the future will:

1 Reflect an increasing diversity of self-conceptions, evidenced through structural as well as cultural variations, that will challenge current family scholars to abandon their historical, nucleocentric biases, unitary cultural assumptions, and implied economic and religious assumptions.
2 Live increasingly within four and five generations of familial connection. Escalating longevity and changing birth rates will necessitate greater attention to developmental patterns of infants through centenarians, with a strong focus on patterns of multiple intergenerational contacts, generational reversals, and influence patterns within smaller families.
3 Function in a world of somatic concerns—influenced by health-related genetic discoveries and fast-paced medical advances. In earlier decades family studies foregrounded relational interactions while minimizing the focus on individuals. Breakthroughs in areas such as genetics and illness will necessitate greater understanding of individuals embedded within family systems.
4 Encounter rapidly changing environments due to unprecedented technological change. Family members will be faced with new issues and interaction patterns resulting from technological changes in areas such as telecommunications, medical

treatment, and education. These changes must be viewed through dual life course and developmental lenses.

5   Require new and innovative ways to protect and enhance family life, that specifically address the needs of multi-problem families and evolving family forms through the development of targeted intervention and prevention strategies. This necessitates attending to the role communication in supporting family resilience and family enrichment.

Each of the previous assertions, reflecting a "permanent white water" environment, continues to have significant implications for the future study of family interaction.

Family Conceptions

Increasingly families will define themselves through their interactions; communicative definitions of family are privileged over structural definitions (Whitchurch & Dickson, 1999). As families become more diverse, "their definitional processes expand exponentially, rendering their identity highly discourse dependent" (Galvin, 2006, p. 3). Thus communicative strategies manage external boundaries as well as internal family boundaries. Members need to explain or defend their family identity to outsiders and reinforce their family identity through narratives or discussion among insiders. As the concept of voluntary kin develops (Braithwaite et al., 2010) and conceptualizations of the family expand (Edwards & Graham, 2009), the concept of family is further problematized.

Structural Variations

Families no longer can be usefully categorized in unitary terms, such as blended, single parent, or adoptive, due to overlapping complexities of connection. Various family structures remain understudied from a communication perspective, although some scholars have addressed communication and the intentional family building processes of families formed through transracial/transnational adoption (Docan-Morgan, 2010, Harrigan, 2010). The growth of open adoption and same-sex partner adoption represent this change (Farr & Patterson, 2009) even as these categories display overlapping complexities. Few communication-oriented studies of the following family forms exist: foster parents (Patrick & Palladino, 2009), in-laws (Morr Serewicz, 2008; Rittenour & Soliz, 2009), and families with bisexual and transgendered members (Bilbarz & Savci, 2010).

Ethnic Variations

The nature of most marital research led to the claim that "The psychology of marriage as it exists is really a psychology of European American middle class marriage" (Flanagan et al., 2002, p. 109). Gudykunst and Lee (2001) called for studies "on identities and family communication among non-European American families that can be used to generate predictions for future research" (p. 80).

At the turn of the century a few scholars had explored competencies developed within African American families to prepare members for communicatively managing boundary issues and addressed the socialization of African American children through parental warnings about racial dangers and disappointments as well as fostering the development of communicative coping mechanisms for confronting discrimination.

Calls for research on preparing children to confront racial derogation (Daniel & Daniel, 1999; Ferguson, 1999) remain unheeded.

Future categorization of family race/ethnicity will change as marriage, adoption, and cohabitation increase the population of mixed ethnicity families. Interracial/interethnic marriages continue to rise, accounting for 14.6 percent marriages in 2008 (Passel, Wang & Taylor, 2010). Their gender patterns vary; 22 percent of all black male newlyweds and 9 percent of black female newlyweds marry outside their race. Some parents encounter confounding issues such as interactions with extended family members who love the child but refuse to acknowledge any biracial features (Root, 1999). Fortunately multiracial/ethnic families are receiving increasing attention from communication scholars (Soliz, Thorson, & Rittenour, 2009). Although research focused on families of color has increased, communication practices in Asian and East Asian families and Hispanic/ Latino families have received limited attention.

The Hispanic population reached 15.4 percent (American Community Survey, 2008) and Hispanic children are projected to reach 30 percent of all children by 2025 (Fry & Passel, 2009).[1] The majority of Latino children in the U.S.A. are "second generation" U.S. born children, while 37 percent are third generation or higher (Fry, 2009). In 2007, 34.5 million U.S. residents reported Spanish as the most commonly spoken language at home (Shin & Kominski, 2010). Many immigrants must overcome language barriers and adapt to new discourse patterns (Langdon 2009).

Characterized by *familism*, Hispanic families place family at the center of life, reflecting the influence of Catholicism and powerful intergenerational and extended family ties and maternal values (Clauss-Ehlers, 2007). Strong marriages are characterized by children, communication, and religion (Skogrand, Hatch, & Singh, 2008).

Mexicans' staggered pattern of immigration creates gender role challenges (Bush, Bohon, & Kim, 2010). Fathers usually migrate first, leaving mothers to function as single parents with relatives' support. Reunification necessitates role and relational reorganization, often traumatic for children (Glick, 2010). Extended family members provide nurturing, children's discipline, companionship, financial support, and problem solving (Falicov, 2005). Parents rely on indirect, implicit communication, consonant with Mexicans' focus on family harmony. Whereas positive emotional expressiveness is valued, assertiveness and open disagreement are discouraged.

Latino parents, especially those of Mexican origin, report less extensive parental communication about sexual issues than those of non-Mexican origins (Raffaelli & Green, 2003). Only 38 percent of immigrant youths reported discussing sex with their parents, compared to 63 percent for those in the second and third generation (Pew Hispanic Center, 2009). Given the growing Hispanic population, more family communication practices require scholarly attention.

Economic Variations

Although money can reflect family interpersonal dynamics (Jellinek & Beresin, 2008), family communication scholarship assumes a level of financial security. Recent economic reversals contributed to diminished family relational quality and disruption (Bartholomae & Fox, 2010). When families face economic reversals, conversation topics include closing out credit cards or living without health insurance (McKee-Ryan, Song, Wanberg, & Kinicki, 2005). Unemployment necessitates challenging conversations such as renegotiating breadwinner roles or work patterns thereby increasing emotional stress

(Gudmunson, Beutler, Israelsen, McCoy, & Hill, 2007). The strong association between economic pressure and emotional distress affects even supportive couples (Conger, Rueter, & Elder, 1999). Serious financial strain increases the incidence of couple's disagreements while decreasing couple's time together (Gudmunson et al., 2007). When facing ongoing financial stress, members benefit from learning communicative coping strategies (Wadsworth & Santiago, 2008). Little is known about financial conversations between middle aged adults and their parents, or parents and their young children.

In any economic climate, discussing family finances remains a critical communication task. Financial negotiations occur when adding a child, funding a college education, or supporting returning adult offspring. Work–family interaction research emphasizes links between economic pressures and family decision making; most work/family discussions involve financial considerations (Waite & Nielsen, 2001). Selected communication theories have the potential to contribute to understanding parent–child interactions about consumer finance (Allen, 2008).

Cultural variations in financial management impact couples. Collectivistic cultures view money as an extended family resource thereby creating conflict in multiethnic partnerships (Lincoln, 2007). Wealthy families experience unique needs for communication-related attention. Little is known about the "have/have not" divide's pressures on poor families and their communication patterns. Familial financial communication remains significantly understudied.

Religious/Spiritual/Sanctification Variations

Family researchers seldom address religion (Parke, 2001) even as U.S. religious affiliation is shifting. The PEW Forum on Religion & Public Life (2008) suggests significant changes in religious identification: 23.9 percent identify themselves as Catholic, 51 percent, Protestant, and 16 percent, no affiliation; spousal religious affiliation differs in 37 percent of couples. Although scholars argue that religion has the potential to help couples build marital intimacy and stimulate companionship (Fincham, Stanley, & Beach, 2007), few communication scholars address this area.

Religious affiliation impacts partner interactions, parenting styles, gender roles, and family/work decisions. Christian parents, primarily mothers, report discussing religious topics with children more than five times weekly (Boyatzis & Janicki, 2003). Parental public religiosity curbs the frequency of family conversations about sex and birth control (Regnerus, 2005). A meta-analytic review of links between religion, marriage, and parenting revealed some evidence linking religiousness with greater use of adaptive communication skills, collaboration in handling disagreements, positivity in family relationships, and parental coping (Mahoney, Pargament, Murray-Swank, & Murray-Swank, 2003). These researchers found an inverse relationship between religion and domestic violence or marital verbal conflict. Recent research emphasizes spirituality and *sanctification* or the process whereby "[a]n aspect of life is perceived as having divine character and significance" (Pargament & Mahoney, 2005, p. 228). The rise of sanctification and the growth of non-institutional religious worship create opportunities for family communication researchers

Interfaith couples experience more communication challenges than same-faith couples. Frequently they face conflicts moving toward marriage or encounter disagreements due to the lack of a shared religious social network. When partners with different religious orientations disagree over religious issues they are vulnerable to some types of demand–withdraw conflict patterns (Hughes & Dickson, 2006).

Finally, non-Western faith traditions remain a fertile field for family communication research. Understanding the influence of Islam, in which marriage is a family affair (Abudabbeh, 2005), would expand knowledge of families that value intensely emotional intimate relationships and strong identification with the reputation and honor of the family (Daneshpour, 1998). Taken together, the aforementioned points depict the varied conception of families and the evolving complexities impacting family members' interaction patterns.

Life Course and Evaluations

A futuristic perspective requires exploring developmental patterns within individual, generational, and historical time. A life course approach focuses on "how varying events and their timing in the lives of individuals affected families in particular historical contexts" (Aldous, 1990, p. 573). It recognizes that lives are influenced by changing contextual features such as poverty, race relations, or technological advances. Unique individual experiences may occur "off time" or "on time." Given current medical and technological advances, women may bear children "off time" in their 50s and the rural elderly may finish high school "off time" through online studies. Historical life course issues involve recognizing the impact of shared group experiences (Civil Rights Movement, September 11, 2001, Gulf of Mexico oil spill) on family development. Personal, unusual experiences, such as surviving a plane crash or losing both legs in battle, contribute to an individual's life course while also affecting other family members. Couples choosing to remain voluntarily child-free engage in unique intra-dyadic communication processes (Durham & Braithwaite, 2009). Family developmental stages must be framed within a life course context.

Increasingly, more families will experience four and five generations. Lifespan predictions for U.S. children are 78.9 years for those born in 2015 (males 76.4; females, 81.4) (U.S. National Center for Health Statistics, 2009). Researchers need to include great-grandparents and great-great-grandparents in studies of family interaction. Intergenerational issues will be easier to research in real life rather than through retrospective analyses. Due to increasing longevity and decreasing fertility, the population age structure in industrialized nations is shifting from a pyramid to an elongated rectangle, leaving older generations competing for connection to fewer grandchildren and great-grandchildren (Bengston, 2001). Increasingly communication scholars are focusing on grandparent–grandchild relationships (Soliz & Harwood, 2006; Fowler & Soliz, 2010) and step-grandparents (Soliz, 2007). Communication researchers need to address multiple elder roles, such as great-grandparents or great uncles and aunts. Multigenerational relationships in families with gay, lesbian, and transgendered members, cohabiting partners, never-married parents, and multicultural patterns require scholarly attention. Although communication research addresses multigenerational transmissions of family culture, usually from a downward influence model, few studies address bi-directional influences, especially across multiple generations (Saphir & Chaffee, 2002). Power and knowledge reversals impact families as youngsters develop technological skills and cultural knowledge unavailable to older family members (Palfrey & Gasser, 2008).

When immigrant adults lack English language fluency, an older child, frequently female, assumes the role of family language broker by translating, interpreting and occasionally mediating elders' interactions (Morales & Hanson, 2005). Starting about ages 8–12, children translate or interpret face-to-face interactions, transactions, forms, letters, and other materials (Weisskirch, 2006). Frequently this responsibility carries into adulthood.

Consequences of assuming this role vary. Benefits include a greater level of acculturation, higher academic achievement, increased self-confidence and expanded English facility (Trickett & Jones, 2007). Stronger bonds develop with parents (Morales & Hanson, 2005). Children experience an adult world by translating in medical settings, social security offices, or school conferences, serving parents and other relatives. However, costs include feeling embarrassed or overwhelmed by multiple demands as well as pressure to assume an adult role (Morales & Hanson, 2005). Some children worry about family finances or relatives' health, concerns they learn through translating. Language brokers may withhold information or selectively choose an appropriate response among competing options (Weisskirch, 2006).

Perceptions of this role vary. When asked to report their feelings, Mexican American college students' responses ranged from helpful, proud and useful, to ashamed, embarrassed and guilty (Weisskirch, 2006). More Anglo-oriented respondents reported greater difficulty with family relations and feeling forced to translate, whereas more Latino-oriented respondents reported more positive experiences. Little is known about how this role impacts relationships and interaction patterns. For example, higher amounts of Vietnamese teenage brokering were related to increased adolescent reports of family conflict, but higher levels of family adaptability (Trickett & Jones, 2007). Privacy management, message manipulation, conflict management, sibling interaction patterns and role negotiation in these families require scholarly attention.

Somatic Concerns

Historically many factors limited family communication scholars from incorporating biology into empirical studies but future research will reflect a strong biophysiological perspective (Floyd & Afifi, 2011). Traditionally family communication research foregrounded relational interaction while minimizing an individual focus. However, as incorporating physiological state gains prominence in psychology, more communication scholars will incorporate these data in relational studies. Recent research addresses the impact of family members' physiological state on interactional processes such as intimacy, conflict, or problem solving (Afifi, Afifi, Morse & Hamrick, 2008; Floyd & Riforgiate, 2009, Floyd & Afifi, 2011). The current focus on the impact of physiology, genetics, and evolution on interaction patterns emerged from renewed attention to biological contributions to individual communication practices and discussions of a communibiological paradigm (Beatty, McCroskey, & Valencic, 2001).

Growing evidence links psychological processes to physical health. For example, writing about personal topics influences measures of physical and mental health. According to Pennebaker and Chung (in press), "When individuals write or talk about personally upsetting experiences in the laboratory, consistent and significant health improvements are found" (p. 13). Family health communication involves: (a) the day-to-day health-related talk that affects members' interactions, choices, behaviors, and expectations; (b) members' interaction about health surrounding a particular illness; (c) the meaning of health and illness for members, particularly within the family's cultural or religious tradition; and (d) discussion of familial genetic history.

Valuable research models exist for understanding everyday health-related family conversations including issues such as the link between rule-related conversations and current offspring behavior or the impact of parental encouragement of health-promoting behaviors such as exercise or sun protection (Bylund, Baxter, Imes, & Wolf, 2010). A member with a chronic illness impacts family members' interaction with each other and extended family members. Smith & Soliday's (2001) study of the effects of parental chronic kidney disease on the family reveals an impact on: time together, quality of joint activities, and worries that create stress for all members. These impact immediate family members' interactions, as well as interactions with relatives and friends. Increasingly research links marriage with better health. Waite and Gallagher (2000) reported that marriage protects health, while Carr and Springer (2010) found "The protective effects of marriage for self-rated health, chronic conditions, functional limitations, and mortality were comparable across all income and age groups" (p. 749). Unhappy marriages do not produce such benefits. Communication-related marital health benefits involve having one spouse, usually the woman, who monitors both persons' health and nags the partner to engage in desirable health practices, and having a spouse with whom to discuss one's troubles. Weaker health benefits for cohabiting partners vary by gender and life course stage due to poorer relational quality, greater instability, and social selection (Carr & Springer, 2010). Future research needs to explore the health-related communication behaviors of cohabiting and same-sex partnerships. Other health-related concerns involve family members with a disability (Braithwaite & Thompson, 2000; Canary, 2008) or an addiction. Currently few family communication scholars are advancing these areas.

Personalized or predictive medicine, resulting from genome mapping, facilitates family discussion of heredity and its health implications. The impact of genetic advances depends heavily on whether family members talk about their genetic heritage since "The *best* genetic test is often family history. But that requires us to both know and tell" (Parrott, 2009, p. 149). Established family communication patterns and rules "influence and are influenced by the presence of a genetic condition or inherited health risk in a family" (Gaff & Bylund, 2010, p. xvii). Members need to disclose and discuss genetic conditions and recognize the problematic impact of withholding such information from relatives. Communication issues include enacting disclosure strategies, coping with the relatives' reactions, and continuing the conversations over years. Factors that impact disclosure include family structure, roles, gender, privacy rules, culture, timing, practical ethics and scientific knowledge; factors that affect ongoing discussion include family communication patterns, gender differences, and the disease's potential impact (Galvin & Grill, 2009). Research needs to address facilitating discussion about predictive genetic testing to increase the number of informed at-risk family members (Gaff, Collins, Symes & Halliday, 2005) as well as managing discussions over time and across generations.

Multiple family communication theories have the potential to influence research on initial disclosure and ongoing interactions. Researchers may examine how societal master narratives impact the construction of narrative frames or the process of framing a diagnosis (Trees, Koenig Kellas & Roche, 2010), or how members engage in privacy management to reveal or conceal genetic information (Petronio & Gaff, 2010). Future research should "inform the development of theoretically and empirically based practice to foster 'good' communication" (Gaff et al., 2007, p. 1).

Technological Advances

Multiple life course issues confront family members. Selected technological changes will serve as exemplars for countless technological developments impacting families.

Reproductive Technologies

Reproductive technologies provide biological parenthood to many who previously could not achieve it. Infertility impacts communication privacy management as women tend to experience shifting privacy boundaries over time when addressing this with others (Bute & Vik, 2010). When sperm or egg donors are involved in conception, parents face communication challenges related to decision making regarding technological assistance and eventual explanation to their children. Deciding to use reproductive technologies to conceive involves complicated conversations between partners and decisions about when and to whom this decision is revealed. Many parents report no plans to tell their children. In their study of the association between young adult offspring's perceptions of their parents' use of topic avoidance to maintain secrecy and family functioning, Paul and Berger (2007) found an inverse relationship between topic avoidance regarding donor assisted conception and family functioning. They concluded that use of donor conception should be shared with offspring and that parents should disclose the information jointly. Such technological issues raise critical communication issues of family privacy, parental infertility, and children's rights to genetic information. A study of 485 adults conceived through sperm donation revealed young adults experienced "profound struggles" with their origins and identities, although most affirmed a right to know the truth about their background (Marquardt, Glenn & Clark, 2010). Discussions may differ between two parent heterosexual couples and single women and lesbian mothers because the latter groups may confront the issues earlier when small children ask "Have I got a Daddy?" (Montuschi, 2006).

Media Technologies

The interface of family interactions and new technologies remains a critical research area. Of particular interest is how the Internet impacts the hierarchical communication structure as youngsters gain information and skills unfamiliar to their parents. The child's information power may create a generational reversal fraught with stress. Americans are more likely to construct discussion networks involving people from different, non-familial, backgrounds; Internet users are 38 percent less likely to rely exclusively on their spouses or partners as discussion confidants (Hampton, Sessions, Her, & Rainie, 2009). Many family members create family websites, research family history, share family photos or health-related news, and sustain relationships with extended family members; these practices remain understudied. Increasingly, older relatives send requests to "friend" younger relatives, not always a welcome message.

Individuals may be categorized as Digital Natives, or younger people continuously connected by technology who think and process information differently from previous generations, and Digital Settlers or Digital Immigrants, older persons who vary in their sophistication in use of technology but who also rely, heavily to slightly, on digital technology (Palfrey & Gasser, 2008). When adults discuss and monitor their children's online experiences, their offspring are less likely to engage in risky behaviors such as disclosing personal information or meeting up offline with online acquaintances. When parents are unprepared to discuss online experiences, such conversations do not occur (Palfrey & Gasser 2008).

Livingston & Helsper's (2008) study of parental mediation examined parental attempts to regulate their children's media use in order to maximize the advantages of the online environment by using strategies such as rule-making, restrictions, co-viewing, or co-using. They found that two-thirds of parents reported discussing Internet use with their children; almost half watched the computer screen and about a third remained physically close when a child is online.

Internet dangers include cyber-bulling and sexting, online communication practices not understood by some parents. Cyber-bulling includes harassment or posting false rumors (Whitaker & Bushman, 2009). In their study of 2000 middle school students Hinduja and Patchin (2009) reported that 20 percent of respondents indicated seriously thinking about attempting suicide; cyber-bulling victims were almost twice as likely to have attempted or considered suicide compared to youth who had not experienced cyber-bulling. Some adolescents engage in "sexting," or sending text messages with pictures of children or teens who are naked or engaged in sexual acts (American Academy of Pediatrics, 2009). Sexting creates serious problems for adolescents and their families, resulting in emotional pain, thoughts of suicide, and serious legal consequences. An online study of 1,247 respondents ages 14–24 reported that that three in ten young people have been involved in some type of naked texting; one in ten shared a naked image of themselves, and 29 percent reported receiving messages with sexual words or images through texting or on the Internet (A Thin Line, 2009). Few parents hold conversations about dangerous online behavior, leaving their children vulnerable. In some cases, older siblings or cousins go online to see what a younger relative is doing (Hinduja & Patchin, 2009). More research needs to assess the extent to which parents communicate about Internet dangers and the nature of those conversations. The Internet serves as an exemplar for other major technological innovations such as PDAs, cell phones, or videogames that have implications for family interaction.

Gerentechnology addresses issues regarding communication between elderly persons and their family members using digital-age assistive information and communication technologies that allow older individuals to maintain independence and improve mental health through behavior monitoring and maintaining connections to outside support networks (Blaschke, Freddolino & Mullen, 2009). Gerentechnology affects family communication by supporting the well-being of older members while reducing their isolation. For example, household sensors inform geographically distant adult children that the medicine cabinet and refrigerator doors have been opened indicating their father took his medicine and ate lunch. Webcams support intergenerational discussions of baseball scores or parental health. Such technology delays, or compensates for, the declines of aging while enhancing family interaction (Fozard, Rietsema, Bouma, & Graafmans, 2000). Although such gerontology advances attempt to keep relationships co-equal, monitoring involves role reversal, guilt, and occasional deception (Stout, 2010). Successful elder adaptation depends on ongoing parent–adult child discussion of issues. Research needs to address communicative processes by which such transitions occur and the ongoing impact of this mediated communication.

Family Lifestyles: Stress and Intervention/Prevention

Future families will need innovative ways to protect and improve members' lives congruent with a range of family forms and high stress circumstances. Life stresses, such as coping when a soldier returns from battle with devastating injuries, or maintaining family identity in a homeless shelter, present significant communication challenges.

Familial resilience, manifested through highly functional communication, undergirds stress management. Resilience, the process of "reintegrating from disruptions in life"

(Richardson, 2002, p. 309), remains understudied from a communication perspective. Interventions to support family resilience include attempts to identify "key interactional processes that enable families to withstand and rebound from disruptive life challenges" (Walsh, 2006, p. 3). Intervention efforts with families experiencing severe stresses aim to increase "members' abilities to clarify their crisis situation, to express and respond to each other's needs and concerns, and to negotiate system changes that meet new demands" (Walsh, 2006, p. 107) Communication processes involved in human resilience involve: "(a) crafting normalcy, (b) affirming identity anchors, (c) maintaining and using communication networks, (d) putting alternative logics to work, and (e) downplaying negative feelings while foregrounding positive emotions" (Buzzanell, 2010, p. 1).

Severe economic pressures, usually accompanied by concerns for physical space, safety, and employment, undermine partner, and parent–child interaction. Children living in poverty are more likely to suffer depression, social withdrawal and low self-esteem, all of which have implications for family interaction (Seccombe, 2000). Family life is compounded by unsafe neighborhoods, leaving many mothers depressed and children witnessing violence. Yet data from over 100,000 families revealed that routines and relationships enrich poor families; 73 percent of parents in poor families reported they can share ideas and talk well with their children, a finding quite similar to those in other income brackets (Valladares & Anderson Moore, 2009).

Intervention programs targeted at specific family issues produce limited benefits when they overlook how parents, children, and society connect within various community contexts and networks (Socha & Stamp, 2009). An ecological perspective necessitates understanding external social capital or "the extent to which the family system is embedded in an integrative network of people and institutions in the community that share common values" (Bowen, Richman, & Bowen, 2000, p. 121). Traditionally many studies of poor and urban communities focused on community deficiencies and problems, overlooking capacity-focused development. An asset-based and relationship driven strategy focuses on community strengths while rebuilding the relationships between and among local residents, associations and institutions (Kretzmann, McKnight, Dobrowolski & Puntenney, 2005).

When families experience breakdowns resulting from internal rather than external factors, communication knowledge and skills remain central features of enrichment and therapeutic approaches. Prevention and intervention efforts remain overlooked and under-researched from a communication perspective. The recent focus on positive aspects of marriage including trust, empathic forgiveness, social support, commitment, teamwork, and sacrifice (Flanagan, et al., 2002), reflects little involvement of communication scholars who need to be incorporated into communication-focused enrichment programs. Specific resilience-related communication skills include clarity, open emotional expression, and collaborative problem solving (Walsh, 2006).

Governmental initiatives have created online supports for marriage, including The National Healthy Marriage Resource Center, a clearinghouse of information and resources on healthy marriages including marital education and enrichment programs (Stanley, Markman, & Jenkins, 2008). It includes some additional resources for other family forms and culturally diverse and disadvantaged populations. Little communication scholarship appears among these outreach efforts.

Future research programs need to address the role of family communication in the management of devastating stresses and development of familial resilience. Family researchers must find ways to contribute to the revitalized area of marital and family enrichment through communication skills training and the development of family-focused prevention programs through communication-oriented research programs.

Conclusion

Family communication research matured dramatically over the past two decades. In order to increase its impact, more communication scholars need to partner with researchers in other disciplines such as economics, education, health, law, psychology or technology to incorporate other perspectives, address problems of greater magnitude and investigate family interactions within varying contexts.

The multiple research directions identified within this handbook are vast and complex. Yet family members will discover that Vaill's (1996) "permanent white water" predictions of the future continue to be accurate—turbulence is woven through all areas of relational life—and unanticipated circumstances and concerns will emerge with each passing year. Family communication scholars must recognize that avoiding the turbulent rapids is impossible. Surviving and thriving in permanent white water depends on more than individual skill and effort; it requires the concentrated efforts of ongoing research teams committed to long-term research programs. Both family members and family scholars need to develop the ability to forecast the upcoming swirling currents while negotiating the immediate ones. It continues to be a challenging ride!

Note

1 The terms "Hispanic" and "Latino" are contested and will be used interchangeably.

References

Abudabbeh, N. (2005). Arab families: An overview. In M. McGoldrick, J. Giordano, & N. Garcia-Preto (Eds.), *Ethnicity and family therapy*, 3rd edn (pp. 423–36). New York: Guilford Press.

Afifi, T. D., Afifi, W. A., Morse, C., & Hamrick, K. (2008). Adolescents' avoidance tendencies and physiological reactions to discussions about their parents' relationship: Implications for post-divorce and non-divorced families. *Communication Monographs, 75*, 290–317.

Aldous, J. (1990). Family development and the life course: Two perspectives on family change. *Journal of Marriage and the Family, 52*, 571–83.

Allen, M. W. (2008). Consumer finance and parent–child communication. In J. J. Xiao (Ed.), *Handbook of consumer finance research* (pp. 351–61). New York: Springer.

American Academy of Pediatrics (2009). Help kids with cell phones get the message: Say no to "sexting." *AAP News, 30*:26. Retrieved from http://aapnews.aappublications.org/ cgi/content/full/30/8/26-d.

American Community Survey (2008). Statistical portrait of Hispanics in the United States, 2008. Retrieved from http://pewhispanic.org/files/factsheets/hispanics2008/ Table%201.pdf.

A Thin Line (2009). AP-MTV Digital Abuse Study. Retrieved from http://www.athinline.org/ MTV-AP_Digital_Abuse_Study_Executive_Summary.pdf.

Bartholomae, S., & Fox, J. (2010). Economic stress and families. In S. J. Price, C. A. Price, & P. C. McKenry (Eds.), *Families & change: Coping with stressful events and transitions*, 4th edn (pp. 185–209). Los Angeles, CA: Sage.

Beatty, M. J., McCroskey, J. C., & Valencic, K. M. (2001). *The biology of communication: A communibiological perspective*. Cresskill, NJ: Hampton Press.

Bengston, V. L. (2001). Beyond the nuclear family: The increasing importance of multigenerational bonds. *Journal of Marriage and the Family, 63*, 1–16.

Bilbarz, T. J., & Savci, E. (2010). Lesbian, gay, bisexual, and transgender families. *Journal of Marriage and the Family, 72*, 480–97.

Blaschke, C. M., Freddolino, P. P., & Mullen, E. E. (2009). Ageing and technology: A review of the research literature. *British Journal of Social Work, 39*, 641–56.

Bowen, G. L., Richman, J. M., & Bowen, N. K. (2000). Families in the context of communication across time. In S. J. Price, P. C. McKenry, & M. J. Murphy (Eds.), *Families across time*, 4th edn (pp. 117–28). Los Angeles, CA: Roxbury Press.

Boyatzis, C. Y., & Janicki, D. L. (2003). Parent–child communication about religion: Survey and diary data on unilateral transmission and bio-directional reciprocity styles. *Review of Religious Research, 44*(3), 252–70.

Braithwaite, D. O. & Thompson, T. L. (2000). Communication and disability research: A productive past and a bright future. In D. O. Braithwaite & T. L. Thompson (Eds.), *Handbook of communication and people with disabilities* (pp. 507–15). Mahwah, NJ: Lawrence Erlbaum Associates.

Braithwaite, D. O., Bach, B. W., Baxter, L. A., DiVerniero, R., Hammonds, J. R., Hosek, A. M.,, & Wolf, B. M. (2010). Constructing family: A typology of voluntary kin. *Journal of Social and Personal Relationships, 27*, 388–407.

Bush, K. R., Bohon, S. A., & Kim, H. K. (2010). Adaptation among immigrant families: Resources and barriers. In S. J. Price, C. A. Price & P. C. McKenry (Eds.), *Families and change: Coping with stressful events and transitions*, 4th edn (pp. 285–310). Los Angeles, CA: Sage.

Bute, J. J. & Vik, A. (2010). Privacy management as unfinished business: Shifting boundaries in the context of infertility. *Communication Studies, 6*, 1–20.

Buzzanell, P. N. (2010). Resilience: Talking, resisting, and imagining new normalcies into being. *Journal of Communication, 60*, 1–14.

Bylund, C. L., Baxter, L. A., Imes, R. S., & Wolf, B. (2010). Parental rule socialization for preventive health and adolescent rule compliance. *Family Relations, 59*, 1–13.

Canary, H. E. (2008). Negotiating dis/ability in families: Constructions and contradictions. *Journal of Applied Communication Research, 36*, 437–58.

Carr, D., & Springer, K. W. (2010). Advances in families and health research in the 21st century. *Journal of Marriage and Family, 72*, 743–61.

Clauss-Ehlers, C. S. (2007). Extending work-family concepts to the lives of Latinas. *Encyclopedia.* February 27. Retrieved from http://wfnetwork.bc.edu/encyclopedia_entry.php?id=4238&area +All.

Conger, R. D., Rueter, M. A., & Elder, G. H. (1999). Couple resilience to economic pressure. *Journal of Personality and Social Psychology, 76*, 54–71.

Daneshpour, M. (1998). Muslim families and family therapy. *Journal of Marital and Family Therapy, 24*(5), 355–68.

Daniel, J. L. & Daniel, J. E. (1999) African-American childrearing: The context of a hot stove. In T. J. Socha & R. C. Diggs (Eds.), *Communication, race and family: Exploring communication in Black, White and biracial families* (pp. 25–43). Mahwah, NJ: Lawrence Erlbaum Associates.

Docan-Morgan, S. (2010). Korean adoptees' retrospective reports of intrusive interactions: Exploring boundary management in adoptive families. *Journal of Family Communication, 10*, 137–57.

Durham, W., & Braithwaite, D. O. (2009). Communication privacy management within the family-planning trajectories of voluntarily child-free couples. *Journal of Family Communication, 9*, 43–65.

Edwards, A. P., & Graham, E. E. (2009). The relationship between individuals' definitions of family and implicit personal theories of communication. *Journal of Family Communication, 9*, 191–208.

Falicov, C. J. (2005). Mexican families. In M. McGoldrick, J. Giordano, & N. Garcia-Preto (Eds.), *Ethnicity and family therapy*, 3rd edn (pp. 229–41). New York: Guilford Press.

Farr, R. H., & Patterson, C. J. (2009). Transracial adoption by lesbian, gay, and heterosexual couples: Who completes transracial adoptions and with what results? *Adoption Quarterly, 12*, 187–204.

Ferguson, I. B. (1999). African-American parent–child communication about racial derogation. In T. J. Socha & R. C. Diggs (Eds.), *Communication, race and family: Exploring communication in Black, White and biracial families* (pp. 45–67). Mahwah, NJ: Lawrence Erlbaum Associates.

Fincham, F. D., Stanley, S. M., & Beach, S. R. (2007). Transformative processes in marriage: An analysis of emerging trends. *Journal of Marriage and Family, 69*, 275–92.

Flanagan, K. M., Clements, M. L., Whitton, S. W., Portney, M. J., Randall, D. W., & Markman, H. J. (2002). Retrospect and prospect in the psychological study of marital and couple relationships. In J. P. McHale & W. S. Grolnick (Eds.), *Retrospect and prospect in the psychological study of families* (pp. 99–128). Mahwah, NJ: Lawrence Erlbaum Associates.

Floyd, K., & Afifi, T. D. (2011). Biological and physiological perspectives on interpersonal communication. In M. L. Knapp & J. A. Daly (Eds.), *The Sage handbook of interpersonal communication*, 4th edn (pp. 87–127). Thousand Oaks, CA: Sage.

Floyd, K. & Riforgiate, J. B. (2009). Principles of endocrine system measurement in communication research. In M. J. Beatty, J. C. McCroskey, & K. Floyd (Eds.), *Biological dimensions of communication: Perspectives, methods and research* (pp. 249–64). Cresskill, NJ: Hampton Press.

Fowler, C. A., & Soliz, J. (2010). Responses of young adult grandchildren to grandparent's painful self-disclosures. *Journal of Language and Social Psychology, 29,* 75–100.

Fozard, J. L., Rietsema, J., Bouma, H., & Graafmans, J. A. M. (2000). Gerontology: creating enabling environments for the challenges and opportunities of aging. *Educational Gerontology, 26,* 331–34.

Fry, R. (2009, May 28). Latino children: A majority are U.S.-born offspring of immigrants. Pew Hispanic Center. http://pewhispanic.org/reports.report.php?ReportID=110.

Fry, R. & Passel, J. (2009). *Latino children: A majority are U.S. born offspring of immigrants.* Pew Hispanic Center. http://pewhispanic.org/reports.report.php?ReportID=110.

Gaff, C. L., & Bylund, C. L. (2010). Introduction. In C. L. Gaff, & C. L. Bylund (Eds.), *Family communication about genetics: Theory and practice* (pp. xv–xx). Oxford: Oxford University Press.

Gaff, C. L., Clarke, A. J., Atkinson, P., Sivell, S., Elwyn, G., Iredale, R., & Edwards, A. (2007). Process and outcome in communication of genetic information within families: A systematic review. *European Journal of Human Genetics, 1*(13), 1–13.

Gaff, C. L., Collins, V., Symes, T., & Halliday, J. (2005). Facilitating family communication about predictive genetic testing: Probands' perceptions. *Journal of Genetic Counseling, 41*(2), 133–40.

Galvin, K. M. (2006). Diversity's impact on defining the family: Discourse-dependence and identity. In L. H. Turner & R. West (Eds.), *The family communication sourcebook* (pp. 3–19). Thousand Oaks, CA: Sage.

Galvin, K. M., & Grill, L. H. (2009). Opening up the conversation on genetic and genomics in families: The space for communication scholars. In C. S. Beck (Ed.), *Communication yearbook, 33* (pp. 213–57). New York: Routledge.

Glick, J. E. (2010). Connecting complex processes: A decade of research on immigrant families. *Journal of Marriage and the Family, 72,* 498–515.

Gudmunson, C. G., Beutler, I. F., Israelsen, C. L., McCoy, J. K., & Hill, E. J. (2007). Linking financial strain to marital instability: Examining the roles of emotional distress and marital interaction. *Journal of Family and Economic Issues, 28*(3), 357–76.

Gudykunst, W. B., & Lee, C. M. (2001). An agenda for studying ethnicity and family communication. *Journal of Family Communication, 1,* 75–86.

Hampton, K. N., Sessions, E. J., Her, E. J., & Rainie, L. (2009). Social isolation and new technology: How the Internet and mobile phones impact Americans' social networks. November 4. Pew Internet & American Life Project. Retrieved from http:/www.pewinternet.org/ Reports/ 2009/1.

Harrigan, M. M. (2010). Exploring the narrative process: An analysis of the adoption stories mothers tell their internationally adopted children. *Journal of Family Communication, 10,* 24–39.

Hinduja, S., & Patchin, J. W. (2009). Cyberbullying and suicide. Cyberbullying Research Center. Retrieved from www.cyberbullying.us.

Hughes, P. C., & Dickson, F. C. (2006). Relational dynamics in interfaith marriages. In L. H. Turner & R. West (Eds.), *The family communication sourcebook* (pp. 373–87). Thousand Oaks, CA: Sage.

Jellinek, M. S., & Beresin, E. (2008). Money talks: Becoming more comfortable with understanding a family's finances. *Journal of the American Academy of Child and Adolescent Psychiatry, 47*(3), 249–53.

Kretzmann, J. P., McKnight, J. L., Dobrowolski, S., & Puntenney, D. (2005). Discovering community power: A guide to mobilizing local assets and your organization's capacity. Asset-Based Community Development Institute, Northwestern University. Retrieved from http://www. northwestern.edu/ipr/abcd.html.

Langdon, H. W. (2009). Providing optimal special education services to Hispanic children and their families. *Communication Disorders Quarterly, 30,* 83–96.

Lincoln, K. D. (2007). Financial strain, negative interactions, and mastery: Pathways to mental health among older African Americans. *Journal of Black Psychology, 33,* 439–62.

Livingston, S., & Helsper, E. J. (2008). Parental mediation of children's internet use. *Journal of Broadcasting and Electronic Media*. Retrieved from http://www.allbuniness.com/society-social-families-children-family/11764547-1.

Mahoney, A., Pargament, K. I., Murray-Swank, A., & Murray-Swank, N. (2003). Religion and the sanctification of family relationships. *Review of Religious Research, 44*, 220–36.

Marquardt, E., Glenn, N. D., & Clark, K. (2010). My Daddy's name is Donor. Institute for American Values. Retrieved from http://familyscholars.org/my-daddys-name-is-donor.

McKee-Ryan, F. M., Song, Z., Wanberg, C. R., & Kinicki, A. J. (2005). Psychological & physical well-being during unemployment: A meta-analytic study. *Journal of Applied Psychology, 90*(1), 53–76.

Montuschi, O. (2006). Telling and talking about donor conception with 0–7 year olds: A guide for parents. April. Donor Conception Network. Retrieved from www.dcnetworks.org.

Morales, A., & Hanson, W. E. (2005). Language brokering: An integrative review of the literature. *Hispanic Journal of Behavioral Sciences, 27*, 471–503.

Morr Serewicz, M. C. (2008). Toward a triangular theory of the communication and relationships of in-laws: Theoretical proposal and social relations analysis of relational satisfaction and private disclosure in in-law triads. *Journal of Family Communication, 8*, 264–92.

Palfrey, J., & Gasser, U. (2008). *Born digital: Understanding the first generation of Digital Natives*. New York: Basic Books.

Pargament, K. L., & Mahoney, A. (2005). Sacred matters: Sanctification as a vital topic for the psychology of religion. *International Journal for the Psychology of Religion, 15*(3), 179–98.

Parke, R. D. (2001). Introduction to the special section of families and religion: A call for recoi. mitment by researchers, practitioners, and policymakers. *Journal of Family Psychology, 15*, 555–58.

Parrott, R. (2009). *Talking about health: Why communication matters*. Malden, MA.: Wiley Blackwell.

Passel, J. S., Wang, W., & Taylor, P. (2010). Marrying out. *Pew Research Center Publications*. Retrieved from http://pewresearch.org/pubs/1616/american-marriage-interracial-interethnic.

Patrick, D., & Palladino, J. (2009). The community interactions of gay and lesbian foster parents. In T. J. Socha & G. H. Stamp (Eds.), *Parents and children communicating with society: Managing relationships outside of home* (pp. 323–42). New York: Routledge.

Paul, M. S., & Berger, R. (2007). Topic avoidance and family functioning in families conceived with donor insemination. *Human Reproduction, 22*(9), 2566–71.

Pennebaker, J. & Chung, C. K. (in press). Expressive writing: Connections to mental and physical health. In H. S. Friedman (Ed.), *Oxford handbook of health psychology*. Oxford: Oxford University Press. Retrieved from http://homepage.psy.utexas.edu/homepage/faculty/pennebaker/reprints/Pennebaker&ChungFriedman_Chapter.pdf.

Petronio, S., & Gaff, C. L. (2010). Managing privacy ownership and disclosure. In C. L. Gaff & C. L. Bylund (Eds.), *Family communication about genetics: Theory and practice* (pp. 120–35). Oxford: Oxford University Press.

Pew Forum on Religion & Public Life (2008). U.S. Religious Landscape Survey. Pew Research Center, Washington D.C. February. Retrieved from http://www.religions.pewforum.org.

Pew Hispanic Center (2009). Between two worlds: How young Latinos come of age in America, Washington, DC. Retrieved from http://pewhispanic.org/reports/report.php?ReportID=117.

Raffaelli, M., & Green, S. (2003). Parent–adolescent communication about sex: retrospective reports by Latino college students. *Journal of Marriage and Family, 65*, 474–81.

Regnerus, M. D. (2005). Talking about sex: Religion and patterns of parent–child communication about sex and contraception. *The Sociological Quarterly, 46*, 79–105.

Richardson, G. E. (2002). The metatheory of resilience and resiliency. *Journal of Clinical Psychology, 58*(3), 301–21.

Rittenour, C. E., & Soliz, J. (2009). Communication and relational dimensions of shared family identity and relational intentions in mother-in-law/daughter-in-law relationships: Developing a conceptual model for mother-in-law/daughter-in-law research. *Western Journal of Communication, 71*, 67–90.

Root, M. P. P. (1999). Resolving "other" status: Identity development of biracial individuals. In S. Coontz, M. Parson & G. Raley (Eds.), *American Families: A Multicultural Reader* (pp. 439–54). New York: Routledge.

Saphir, M. N. & Chaffee, S. H. (2002). Adolescents' contributions to family communication patterns. *Human Communication Research, 28*(1), 86–108.

Shin, H. B. & Kominski, R. A. (2010). Language use in the United States: 2007. *American Community Survey Reports*, Washington, DC: U.S. Census Bureau.

Seccombe, K. (2000). Families in poverty in the 1990s: Trends, causes, consequences, and lessons learned. *Journal of Marriage and the Family*, 62, 1094–113.

Skogrand, L., Hatch, D., & Singh, A. (2008). Strong marriages in Latino cultures. In R. Dalla, J. DeFrain, J. Johnson, & D. Abbott (Eds.), *Strengths and challenges of new immigrant families: Implications for research, policy, education, and service* (pp. 117–34). Lanham, MD: Lexington Books.

Smith, S. R., & Soliday, E. (2001). The effects of parental chronic kidney disease on the family. *Family Relations*, 50, 171–77.

Socha, T. J., & Stamp, G. H. (Eds.) (2009). *Parents and children communicating with society: Managing relationships outside the home*. New York: Routledge.

Soliz, J. (2007). Communicative predictors of a shared family identity: Comparison of grand-children's perceptions of family-of-origin grandparents and stepgrandparents. *Journal of Family Communication*, 7, 177–94.

Soliz, J., & Harwood, J. (2006). Shared family identity, age salience, and intergroup contact: Investigation of the grandparent–grandchild relationship. *Communication Monographs*, 75(1), 87–107.

Soliz, J., Thorson, A. R. & Rittenour, C. E. (2009). Communicative correlates of satisfaction, family identity, and group salience in multiracial/ethnic families. *Journal of Marriage and Family*, 71, 819–32.

Stanley, S. M., Markman, H. J., & Jenkins, N. H. (2008). Marriage education and government policy: Helping couples who choose marriage achieve success. National Healthy Marriage Resource Center. Retrieved from www.healthymarriageinfo.org/docs/StanleyMarriage_Ed_and_Gov_Policy_5_08.pdf.

Stout, H. (2010). Monitoring Mom and Dad. *New York Times*, July 29, 2010, D1, D7.

Trees, A. R., Koenig Kellas, J., & Roche, M. I. (2010). Family narratives. In C. L. Gaff & C. L. Bylund (Eds.), *Family communication about genetics: Theory and practice* (pp. 68–86). Oxford: Oxford University Press.

Trickett, E. J., & Jones, C. J. (2007). Adolescent culture brokering and family functioning: A study of families from Vietnam. *Cultural Diversity and Ethnic Minority Psychology*, 13(2), 143–50.

U.S. National Center for Health Statistics, National Vital Statistics Reports (NVSR). (2009). *Deaths: Final Data for 2006*. Vol. 57, No. 14, April 17, 2009. Retrieved from http://www.census.gov/compendia/ stateb/2010/tables/10s0102.pdf.

Vaill, P. B. (1996). *Learning as a way of being*. San Francisco, CA: Jossey-Bass.

Vaill, P. with Bunker, K., & Santana, L. C. (2010). Interview with Peter Vaill. In K. A. Bunker & L. C. Santana (Eds.), *Extraordinary leadership: Addressing the gaps in senior executive development* (pp. 43–68). San Francisco, CA: Jossey-Bass.

Valladares, S., & Anderson Moore, K. (2009). The strengths of poor families. Child Trends Research Brief. Publication #2009–26, May. Washington, DC Retrieved from http://www.childtrends.org.

Wadsworth, M. E., & Santiago, C. D. (2008). Risk and resiliency processes in ethnically diverse families in poverty. *Journal of Family Psychology*, 22, 399–410.

Waite, L. J., & Gallagher, M. (2000). *The case for marriage*. New York: Doubleday.

Waite, L. J., & Nielsen, M. (2001). The rise of the dual earner family, 1963–97. In R. Hertz & N. K. Marshall (Eds.), *Working families: The transformation of the American home* (pp. 23–41). Berkeley, CA: University of California Press.

Walsh, F. (2006). *Strengthening family resilience*, 2nd edn. New York: The Guilford Press.

Weisskirch, R. S. (2006). Emotional aspects of language brokering among Mexican American adults. *Journal of Multilingual and Multicultural Development*, 27(4), 332–43.

Whitchurch, G. G., & Dickson, F. C. (1999). Family communication. In M. Sussman, S. K. Steinmetz & G. W. Peterson (Eds.), *Handbook of marriage and the family*, 2nd edn (pp. 687–704). New York: Plenum Press.

Whitaker, J. L. & Bushman, B. J. (2009). Online dangers: Keeping children and adolescents safe. *Washington & Lee Law Review*, 66, 1053–64.

Contributors

Tamara D. Afifi is a Professor in the Department of Communication at the University of California, Santa Barbara. Most of her research focuses on how family members cope communicatively with various challenges they face. When examining her research program, two primary themes emerge: (1) information regulation (privacy, secrets, disclosure, avoidance) in parent–child and dating relationships, and (2) communication processes related to uncertainty, loss, stress, and psychological health. She often incorporates a variety of methodological approaches (e.g., observations, field studies, lab studies, surveys, interviews, physiological data) to study a particular phenomenon. Professor Afifi's work is theoretical and applied, focusing on theories and concepts (such as her Theoretical Model of Communal Coping) as they apply to couples and families in real world situations, including divorce, refugee camps, wartime situations, natural disasters, and economic uncertainty.

Jeffrey J. Arnett is a Research Professor in the Department of Psychology at Clark University in Worcester, Massachusetts. He has also taught at the University of Missouri. During 2005 he was a Fulbright Scholar at the University of Copenhagen, Denmark. He is the Editor of the Journal of Adolescent Research and author of the book *Emerging Adulthood: The Winding Road from the Late Teens Through the Twenties*, published in 2004 by Oxford University Press. He is also author of one of the most widely used textbooks on adolescent development, *Adolescence and Emerging Adulthood: A Cultural Approach* (2012, Prentice Hall, 5th edn).

Brian R. Baucom is an Assistant Professor in the Department of Psychology at the University of Utah having completed his doctoral degree in Clinical Psychology at the University of California, Los Angeles. His research focuses on the assessment of dysfunctional behavioral and emotional processes during conflict in couples and families as well as on interventions for dysfunctional couple processes. His work makes use of standard observational coding methods as well as newly developed signal processing techniques for assessing behavior and emotion during interaction. His work has been funded by the National Institute of Child Health and Human Development, the National Science Foundation, and the Deutsche Forschungsgemeinschaft e.V.

John M. Beaton is an Associate Professor and Chair of the Department of Family Relations and Applied Nutrition, at the University of Guelph. He primarily has taught in the Couple and Family Therapy Program, training graduate students to be therapists. He is a clinical member and approved supervisor with the American Association of Marriage and Family Therapy. His research and clinical interests are primarily in the areas of men's health, fatherhood, and community intervention. He has a number of publications in social science journals in the areas of fatherhood, intergenerational family relationships, and community intervention. More recently, he has a passion for addressing men's and children's physical health issues with a community action research approach.

Kira Birditt is an Assistant Research Professor at the Institute for Social Research at the University of Michigan. Her research focuses on negative aspects of relationships and their implications for well-being across the lifespan.

Heather Bortfeld is an Associate Professor at the University of Connecticut. She completed her doctoral work at the State University of New York at Stony Brook (Experimental Psychology) and was a Postdoctoral Fellow in James Morgan's lab (Cognitive and Linguistic Sciences) at Brown University. Her research focuses on how preverbal infants begin to segment spoken language and how integration of the audio and visual aspects of speech supports this process. In her lab, she applies both behavioral and neurophysiological techniques to answer these questions.

Dawn O. Braithwaite is a Willa Cather Professor of Communication and Chairperson at the University of Nebraska-Lincoln. She studies how people in personal and family relationships interact and negotiate change and challenges. Her work is centered in discourse dependent and understudied families, authoring 90 articles and five edited books. Dr. Braithwaite was awarded the National Communication Association's Brommel Award for Outstanding Scholarship in Family Communication and the UNL Arts & Sciences Award for Outstanding Research in the Social Sciences. She is a past President of the National Communication Association and the Western States Communication Association and served on the board of the Consortium of Social Science Associations in Washington, DC.

Susan Branje is Professor in Dynamics of Socialization at the Research Centre Adolescent Development, Utrecht University, The Netherlands. She received her Ph.D. from the Radboud University Nijmegen in 2003. The general aim of her work is to understand the developmental changes in adolescents' relationships with parents, siblings, friends, and romantic partners, and the associations with adolescent psychosocial adjustment. She also studies the interplay between relational factors and individual characteristics on psychosocial adjustment. She conducted several longitudinal multi-informant, multi-method studies including questionnaire data, observational studies and diary studies. Professor Branje is Secretary of the European Association for Research on Adolescence and Associate Editor of *Personal Relationships* and *The Journal of Early Adolescence*, and she has co-authored over 60 papers in SSCI and SCI journals.

Molly R. Butterworth holds an M.S. in Clinical Psychology. She is a doctoral student in clinical psychology at the University of Utah and is completing her pre-doctoral internship at the University of Utah Counseling Center. Her clinical interests include working with LGBT individuals, trauma survivors, and relationship concerns. Her research interests include LGBT psychology, minority stress, and attachment. She is particularly interested in the close relationships of sexual minorities. Her Masters research examined the attachment hierarchies of polyamorous adults. Currently, she is exploring the impact of social marginalization, interpersonal behavioral, and relationships outcomes in same-sex and other-sex couples.

Daniel J. Canary is Professor in the Hugh Downs School of Human Communication at Arizona State University. He has authored or co-authored 10 books and over 70 articles and scholarly book chapters. Daniel's research interests include conflict communication, conversational argument, relational maintenance behaviors, and sex differences and similarities in communication. Former President of the International Network on Personal Relationships and the Western States Communication Association, Professor Canary is a member of several editorial boards. Daniel likes to travel, play guitar, and walk his dogs, Pepper and the Artful Dodger.

John P. Caughlin is Conrad Professorial Scholar, Professor, and Associate Head of Communication at the University of Illinois at Urbana-Champaign. His research focuses on the avoidance of communication in various contexts, such as when relational partners or families deal with health challenges. He has published recently in journals such as *Communication Monographs*, *Health Communication*, *Human Communication Research*, and the *Journal of Social and Personal Relationships*. His awards include the Brommel Award from the National Communication Association for contributions to family communication, the Garrison Award for the Analysis of Interpersonal Communication in Applied Settings, the Miller Early Career Achievement Award from the International Association for Relationship Research, the Arnold O. Beckman Research Award from the University of Illinois Research Board, and the Franklin H. Knower Article Award from the Interpersonal Communication Division of the National Communication Association.

W. Andrew Collins is a Morse-Alumni distinguished teaching Professor of Child Development and Psychology at the University of Minnesota. A graduate of Stanford University, Dr. Collins conducts research on parent and peer relationships and influences during adolescence and young adulthood. He is Principal Investigator of the Minnesota Longitudinal Study of Parents and Children, in which participants have been followed from birth to age 34. Currently Editor of the *Monographs of the Society for Research in Child Development*, he is a Fellow of both the American Psychological Association and the American Psychological Society. He served as President of the Society for Research on Adolescence from 2000 to 2002. Dr. Collins has edited or co-edited several books and monographs and has contributed numerous book and handbook chapters as well as articles in scholarly journals.

René M. Dailey is an Associate Professor at the University of Texas at Austin. Her research interests center on family and dating relationships. Her research regarding families focuses on how communication is associated with members' mental and physical health (e.g., psychosocial adjustment, weight management). Her research on dating relationships assesses the functioning and outcomes of on-again/off-again relationships. Her work has appeared in communication and personal relationships journals, and she co-edited *Applied Interpersonal Communication Matters: Family, Health, and Community Relations* (Peter Lang, 2006).

Amanda Denes is an Assistant Professor in the Department of Communication Sciences at the University of Connecticut. Amanda received her Ph.D. from the University of California, Santa Barbara in 2012, her M.A. from UCSB in 2009, and her B.A. from Boston College in 2007. She broadly studies interpersonal communication, disclosure, identity, and health.

Bella DePaulo, Visiting Professor of Psychology at the University of California, Santa Barbara, is the author of *Singled Out: How Singles Are Stereotyped, Stigmatized, and Ignored, and Still Live Happily Ever After* and *Singlism: What It Is, Why It Matters, and How to Stop It*. She also writes the "Living Single" blog for *Psychology Today*.

Nicole Depowski is a graduate student in Developmental Psychology at the University of Connecticut. She received her Bachelor of Arts in psychology from Albion College in 2010. Her research focuses on language outcomes in children with cochlear implants and how children integrate visual and verbal speech.

Lisa M. Diamond is Associate Professor of Psychology and Gender Studies at the University of Utah. She received her Ph.D. from Cornell University in 1999. Dr. Diamond studies the longitudinal development of sexuality, sexual orientation, and sexual identity, as well as the health implications of intimate relationships over the lifespan. Dr. Diamond is the author of *Sexual Fluidity* (2008, Harvard University Press), which describes variability in female sexuality from adolescence to young adulthood. Dr. Diamond has received numerous awards for her work from the American Association of University Women, the International Association for Relationship Research, the Society for the Psychological Study of Social Issues, and the American Psychological Association.

William J. Doherty is Professor of Family Social Science and Director of the Citizen Professional Center at the University of Minnesota. He is past President of the National Council on Family Relations. His academic interests include marriage, divorce prevention, fragile families, and fatherhood, and a main focus of his work is on democratic community initiatives to create healthy environments for children.

Kristin L. Drogos is a doctoral candidate in the Department of Communication at the University of Illinois. Broadly, she is interested in researching the ways that media impact youth. Her current dissertation explores the role that social network sites play in the identity formation process of adolescents.

Ashley P. Duggan is Associate Professor in the Communication Department at Boston College and adjunct faculty at Tufts University School of Medicine. Her research addresses the intersections of nonverbal and verbal communication processes, health, and relationships. She is currently working on projects examining interpersonal control tactics about health behavior, emotional experience and expression in provider–patient interactions, family communication about illness, and the influence of nonverbal behaviors in shaping conversations about physical and mental health. She is involved in traditional communication work and in interdisciplinary work on health outcomes.

Diana S. Ebersole earned her M.A. (2008) at the University of Texas at Austin, and her Ph.D. (2012) at Penn State University. Her research focuses on interpersonal and family communication with emphases on prevention and health.

Kathleen A. Eldridge is an Associate Professor at Pepperdine University in the Graduate School of Education and Psychology and a licensed clinical psychologist. She completed her doctoral degree in Clinical Psychology at the University of California, Los Angeles, and specializes in psychotherapy research, couple and family therapy, and relationship communication. Dr. Eldridge publishes research on couple therapy and relationship communication, particularly the demand–withdraw pattern, and presents the results of this research at national and international conferences. Dr. Eldridge also collaborates with students and faculty colleagues as co-Principal Investigator of the Pepperdine Applied Research Center, which bridges research and practice within the Community Counseling Centers at Pepperdine University. She has a private practice and has worked in clinical settings with diverse populations comprised of children, adolescents, college students, adults, couples, and families.

Judith A. Feeney is Associate Professor of Psychology at the University of Queensland. She has published five books and more than 100 journal articles and book chapters. Her research interests focus on couple and family relationships, particularly from the perspective of attachment theory.

Karen L. Fingerman is a Professor of Human Development and Family Sciences at the University of Texas, Austin. She studies adult development and old age. She has conducted research and published numerous scholarly articles on positive and negative emotions and social support in adults' family relationships. Her work has examined parents and children, grandparents and grandchildren, friends, acquaintances, and peripheral social ties. The National Institute on Aging funded her work on problematic social ties across the lifespan and currently funds her research on middle-aged adults, their grown children and aging parents. The Brookdale Foundation, the MacArthur Transitions to Adulthood, and the MacArthur Research Network Aging in Society groups also have funded her research. She received the Springer Award for Early Career Achievement in Research on Adult Development and Aging from Division 20 of the American Psychological Association in 1998 and the Margret Baltes Award for Early Career Achievement in Behavioral and Social Gerontology from the Gerontological Society of America in 1999.

Julie Fitness is Professor of Psychology at Macquarie University in Sydney, Australia. Her research interests include emotions, betrayal, revenge and forgiveness, with a particular focus on the experience and expression of emotions such as love, hate, anger and hurt in marital and familial relationships. She has also published on topics such as the emotionally intelligent marriage and the causes and consequences of familial rejection. She is a Fellow of the Association for Psychological Science and is a past Associate Editor of the journal *Psychological Science*. She is about to begin a four-year term as Editor of the journal *Personal Relationships*.

Mary Anne Fitzpatrick is the founding Dean of the College of Arts and Sciences at the University of South Carolina where she holds a position as a Carolina Distinguished Professor of Psychology. Prior to her move to South Carolina, Fitzpatrick held a number of faculty and administrative positions at the University of Wisconsin-Madison, including the WARF Kellett Professorship. A past President of the International Communication Association, Fitzpatrick received its 2001 Career Achievement Award. She was elected as a Fellow of the International Communication in 1993, and a Fellow of the American Association for the Advancement of Science in 2012. An internationally recognized authority on interpersonal communication, Fitzpatrick is the author of over 120 articles, chapters and books, and is often invited to give lectures and presentations in this country and abroad, and to consult with government and educational institutions.

Kory Floyd is Professor and Associate Director of the Hugh Downs School of Human Communication at Arizona State University. His research focuses on the communication of affection in personal relationships and on the intersections between communication, physiology, and health. He has published ten books and nearly 80 journal articles and book chapters related to family communication, nonverbal communication, and psychophysiology. He is the former Editor of *Journal of Family Communication* and former Chair of the Family Communication Division of the National Communication Association.

Stanley O. Gaines, Jr. is Senior Lecturer in Psychology, School of Social Sciences, Brunel University. Dr. Gaines authored the book, *Culture, Ethnicity, and Personal Relationship Processes* (Routledge, 1997), and he has written or co-written more than 80 additional publications in the fields of ethnic studies and close relationships. Dr. Gaines is especially interested in links among ethnic group membership, ethnic identity, and cultural values among African-descent persons in the U.S.A., the U.K., and throughout the African Diaspora.

Kathleen M. Galvin is a Professor in the Department of Communication Studies at Northwestern University. Her research interests focus on the social construction of families, particularly the discourse-dependent nature of families formed outside of full biological and traditional legal ties, and on family decision making in high stakes health situations involving minor children. She is the Senior Author of *Family Communication: Cohesion and Change*, in its eighth edition, and the Editor of *Making Connections: Readings in Relational Communication*, in its 5th edition. Kathleen M. Galvin teaches courses in relational communication, family communication and specialized courses in family diversity and family communication in health contexts.

Barbara Gruenbaum earned her Bachelor of Arts in Psychology from the University of Connecticut in May 2012. She was supported by a Summer Undergraduate Research Fund Award from the University of Connecticut while she conducted research on audio-visual integration in early development in Dr. Bortfeld's lab. She is currently pursuing graduate studies in School Psychology.

Trey D. Guinn is a doctoral candidate in the Department of Communication Studies at the University of Texas at Austin. Trey received both his M.S. and B.A. from Baylor University. His research and professional interests focuses on interpersonal relationships and communication effectiveness.

Lisa M. Guntzviller is a doctoral candidate in the Brian Lamb School of Communication at Purdue University. Her research focuses on interpersonal communication in underserved populations (e.g., low-income, low-education) and has been published in outlets such as *Journal of Health Communication*, *Patient Education & Counseling*, and *Journal of Aging & Health*. Her dissertation examines interaction goals, parenting styles, mother–child relationship satisfaction, and adolescent outcomes for Mexican-American language brokers (bilingual children who interpret for their Spanish-speaking parents) and their mothers.

Jake Harwood is Professor of Communication at the University of Arizona. He is Author of *Understanding Communication and Aging* (2007, Sage) and Co-Editor of *The Dynamics of Intergroup Communication* (2011, Peter Lang). His recent publications have appeared in *Personality and Social Psychology Bulletin*, *Journal of Applied Communication Research*, and the *British Journal of Social Psychology*. He was previously head of the Gerontology program at the University of Arizona.

Colin Hesse is an Assistant Professor at the Department of Communication at the University of Missouri-Columbia. He explores research related to the communication of affection, emotions, and the relationship between the way we communicate and build relationships and our mental and physical health. He has co-authored several journal articles, book chapters and one textbook, *The Biology of Human Communication* (2nd edn). He is the former editorial assistant of *Journal of Family Communication*

Erin K. Holmes is an Assistant Professor in the School of Family Life at Brigham Young University in Provo, Utah. She completed a Ph.D. in Human Development and Family Sciences from the University of Texas at Austin. Her research focuses on a systemic ecological approach to fathering and mothering, including not only processes inside families that influence parents (such as marital relationships, coparenting, or parental well-being), but also processes outside of families that influence parents (such as employment). Dr. Holmes recently won the National Council on Family Relations Best Article on Men in Families by a New Professional Award for her work in this area.

Ted L. Huston studies how and why intimate relationships change over time. Using data drawn from a 15-year longitudinal study funded by both the National Science Foundation and the National Institutes of Mental Health, his research has examined the role of disillusionment in divorce, the connection between problems that surface during courtship and later marital distress, the impact of parenthood on marriage, gender differences in interpersonal styles, and marital roles. Thirty-three Ph.D. students have completed their degrees under his supervision and taken positions both in universities and in the private sector. A recent survey placed Huston and four of his former students among the 35 most influential social scientists studying personal relationships in the world. Professor Huston served as the third President of the International Society for the Study of Personal Relationships, and he has received the society's award for Paper of the Year.

Nancy A. Jennings is an Associate Professor in the Department of Communication at the University of Cincinnati. She is also the Director of the Children's Education and Entertainment Research (CHEER) Lab and Co-Director of the Graduate Program in Communication. Her research focuses on children's cognitive and social development and their use of media through experimental study and evaluation of television content and media literacy promotion programs. Dr. Jennings has served on local and national taskforces for screen-time reduction, provides parent education programs on children's media use, and has published in numerous peer-reviewed journals. Dr. Jennings earned her M.B.A. in Marketing at DePaul University and her Ph.D. in Radio, TV, and Film at the University of Texas at Austin.

Jody Koenig Kellas is an Associate Professor of Communication Studies at the University of Nebraska Lincoln. She conducts research and teaches classes on interpersonal and family communication. Her main interest is in the ways in which people communicate to make sense of their relational lives. With this interest, her scholarship focuses on relational narratives, storytelling, accounts, attributions, and memorable messages. She conducts observational research with couples and families in order to understand how communicated sense-making and perspective-taking predict individual and relational health. Dr. Kellas' research has been published in *Communication Monographs*, *Human Communication Research*, *Journal of Social and Personal Relationships*, *Western Journal of Communication*, *Journal of Family Communication*, *Communication Quarterly*, *Narrative Inquiry*, and several edited volumes.

Ascan F. Koerner is an Associate Professor of Communication Studies. His research focuses mainly on family communication patterns and the cognitive representations of relationships and their influence on interpersonal communication, including message production and message interpretations. Secondary research interests include evolutionary psychology and interpersonal influence. His research has appeared in communication journals, such as *Communication Monographs*, *Communication Theory*, and *Human Communication Research*, and interdisciplinary journals, such as the *Journal of Marriage and Family*, and the *Journal of Social and Personal Relationships* and a number of edited volumes.

Brett Laursen is Professor of Psychology and Director of Graduate Training at Florida Atlantic University and Docent Professor of Social Developmental Psychology at the University of Jyvaskyla, Finland. Professor Laursen received his Ph.D. from the Institute of Child Development at the University of Minnesota and an honorary doctorate from Orebro University, Sweden. He is a Fellow of the American Psychological Association (Division 7) and a Fellow and Charter Member of the Association for Psychological Sciences. Professor Laursen has authored numerous papers on parent–child and peer relationships and edited several volumes on adolescent development and developmental methodology, the most recent being *Relationship Pathways: From Adolescence to Young Adulthood* (with Andy Collins) and *The Handbook of Developmental Research Methods* (with Todd Little and Noel Card).

Beth A. Le Poire Molineux was a full Professor of Communication (specializing in nonverbal and family communication) at the University of California Santa Barbara until 2005 when she went back to school to attain a Master's of Science in Counseling Psychology (2007). She has been a practicing therapist since 2006 and became a Licensed Marriage and Family Therapist (LMFT) in 2010. She has been practicing in the oncology and immunology outpatient clinics at Ventura County Medical Center since 2008 which allows her to utilize her health, family, and nonverbal specialties in a therapeutic setting.

Carmen M. Lee is an Assistant Professor in the School of Communication at San Diego State University. Her research interests focus on intercultural and interpersonal communication. Her intercultural interests focus on intercultural attraction and her interpersonal interests focus on communicative abuse in casual sexual relationships. She has presented at national and international conferences and has published in *Human Communication Research*, *International Journal of Intercultural Relations*, *Howard Journal of Communications*, and the *Journal of Family Communication*.

Mei-Chen Lin is an Associate Professor in the School of Communication Studies at Kent State University. Her research focuses on the ways in which individuals' social identities influence their perceptions of self and interaction with others. Specifically, she conducts research in communicative issues revolving around aging and older adulthood, such as intergenerational communication, older adults' age identity expression, and family communication about aging related issues.

Kristin D. Mickelson is an Associate Professor of Psychology at Kent State University. Her research focuses on psychosocial factors involved in the relation between stress and health, with special emphases on social support, communal coping, and socioeconomic status and gender.

Ashley V. Middleton is a doctoral candidate at the University of Illinois at Urbana-Champaign. Her research focuses on communication and coping in the context of alcohol and drug use. Her work has been published in *Communication Monographs*, *Health Communication*, *Journal of Social and Personal Relationships*, and *Qualitative Health Research*.

Elizabeth A. Munz is an Assistant Professor in the Department of Communication and Media at the State University of New York at New Paltz. Her research interests include the impact of parent–child communication on parents' and children's experiences during times of transition. In 2011, Dr. Munz received the Sandra Petronio Dissertation Excellence Award from the Family Communication Division of NCA for her dissertation exploring caregiver confirmation, child elaboration, and children's attachment security during the transition to kindergarten.

Patricia Noller is Emeritus Professor in the School of Psychology at the University of Queensland. She has published extensively in the area of personal relationships. She was founding Editor of the journal, *Personal Relationships*, and is a Fellow of the National Council on Family Relationships and of the Academy of the Social Sciences in Australia.

Jon Nussbaum is a Professor of Communication, Arts, & Sciences, and Human Development & Family Studies at Penn State University. He is the Past President of the International Communication Association and the International Society of Language and Social Psychology, former Editor of the *Journal of Communication*, a Fulbright Research Fellow in the U.K. (1991–92), the B. Aubrey Fisher mentor award winner (2010), a Fellow of the International Communication Association and a Fellow within the Adult Development and Aging Division of the American Psychological Association. Nussbaum has a well established publication record (13 books and over 80 journal articles and book chapters) studying communication behaviors and patterns across the lifespan including research on family, friendship and professional relationships with well and frail older adults. His current research centers on quality health care for older adults, health-care organizations and intimacy across the lifespan.

Perry M. Pauley is an Assistant Professor in the School of Communication at San Diego State University. His research examines the role that supportive and affectionate messages play in psychophysiological indices of health. His work has appeared in journals such as *Communication Studies*, *Communication Monographs*, and *Human Communication Research*.

Sandra Petronio is a Professor in the Department of Communication Studies at IUPUI and in the IU School of Medicine, a senior affiliate faculty in the Charles Warren Fairbanks Center for Medical Ethics, IU Health, an adjunct faculty in the IU Schools of Nursing and Informatics. Her areas of expertise are in health and family communication. She has published five books and numerous research articles. She studies privacy, disclosure, and confidentiality within family, health, and interpersonal contexts. She has developed, applied, and tested the evidenced-based theory of "Communication Privacy Management" in 2002 published, *Boundaries of Privacy: Dialectics of Disclosure* on this theory. This book won several national and international awards. Launched six years ago, Petronio continues to serve as the Director of the IUPUI "Translation into Practice" campus-wide initiative.

Jennifer S. Priem is Assistant Professor at Wake Forest University. Her research focuses on how communication affects biological stress. Specifically, she examines how message features during supportive interactions affect stress recovery in interpersonal relationships. Her work has also included studies that examine dyadic perceptions of support and the impact of perceptions and message features on stress reactions to hurtful interactions.

Rena L. Repetti is a Professor in the Department of Psychology at UCLA. She received her Ph.D. in 1985 from Yale University. Repetti studies how experiences outside of the family (primarily at work and at school) shape the patterning of family interactions and, ultimately, the emotional and social functioning of children and parents. Through the UCLA Center on Everyday Lives of Families, Repetti and her students have been involved in a microscopic investigation of a "week in the life" of families, including videotaping of the families both inside and outside of the home as they go about their daily lives.

Kendrick A. Rith is pursuing graduate training in Clinical Psychology at the University of Utah. His research interests center around relationship functioning within same-sex couples, including both psychological and biobehavioral processes, and support processes within the family-of-origin of sexual-minority youths. He plans to focus his clinical work on sexual-minority individuals confronting identity issues, minority stress, and families coping with their children's sexual identity transitions.

Christine E. Rittenour is an Assistant Professor in the Department of Communication Studies at West Virginia University. She researches the ways that family communication reflects and affects family members' various social and structural identities, value orientations, and pro/anti-social behaviors. She teaches courses in family communication, communication theory, and communication and aging. Her research is published in journals such as *Western Journal of Communication*, *Family Communication*, and *Communication Studies*.

Maria Schmeeckle is an Associate Professor of Sociology at Illinois State University. She studied life course sociology, intergenerational relationships, and family boundaries in stepfamilies while in graduate school at the University of Southern California. More recently, she has been researching the global contexts surrounding children who do not live with their parents. Her courses include American Family, Marriage, and Family, and Children in Global Perspective.

Paul Schrodt is the Philip J. & Cheryl C. Burguières Professor and an Associate Professor in the Department of Communication Studies at Texas Christian University. His research examines communication and family functioning, with a particular interest in behaviors that facilitate stepfamily functioning, stepparent–stepchild relationships, and mental well-being in family members. He is a former Chair of the Family Communication Division of the National Communication Association, as well as a past recipient of the Franklin Knower Article Award and the Early Career Award from the Interpersonal Communication Division of NCA. He has published articles recently in journals such as *Communication Monographs*, *Human Communication Research*, *Personal Relationships*, the *Journal of Social and Personal Relationships*, and the *Journal of Family Communication*.

Chris Segrin is a Professor in the Department of Communication at the University of Arizona. His research interests include marital and family relationships, mental-health problems, and communication and well-being. He is author of the books *Interpersonal Processes in Psychological Problems*, and *Family Communication*, and over 100 articles and chapters on interpersonal relationships, mental health, and communication skills. His research has been funded by the National Cancer Institute, the National Institute of Nursing Research, Oncology Nursing Foundation, the Lance Armstrong Foundation, and the American Cancer Society.

Kathleen E. Shaw is a graduate student in the Developmental Psychology program at the University of Connecticut. She received her Bachelor of Arts (Psychology) and Master of Arts (Cognitive Psychology) from Oregon State University. Her research focuses on audiovisual integration, spatial attention, and dyslexia.

Carolyn K. Shue is an Associate Professor of Communication Studies at Ball State University, Muncie, Indiana. Her family communication research focus examines the intersection of health and the family. She has done work with family members of individuals who have Alzheimer's disease and most recently examined family communication related to mealtime conversations as part of a community intervention focused on childhood obesity. Her work has been published in *Communication Education*, *Health Communication*, and various medical journals.

Alan L. Sillars is Professor of Communication Studies at the University of Montana. His research focuses on conflict and interpersonal perception, particularly in the context of family relationships. Sillars has published numerous articles and chapters on these topics and twice received the Franklin H. Knower article award from the National Communication Association for his work on family conflict.

Brian H. Spitzberg received his B.A. (1978) in Speech Communication at University of Texas at Arlington, and his M.A. (1980) and Ph.D. (1981) in Communication Arts and

Sciences at the University of Southern California. He is currently Senate Distinguished Professor in the School of Communication at San Diego State University. His areas of research include interpersonal competence, conflict, jealousy, courtship violence, sexual coercion, and stalking. He is Co-Author of several books and scholarly articles, and serves as a frequent reviewer for numerous scholarly journals. He also serves in an advisory capacity for the San Diego City Attorney's Domestic Violence unit and the San Diego District Attorney's intergovernmental Stalking Strike Force and is a member of the Association of Threat Assessment Professionals.

Susan Sprecher is a Professor of Sociology at Illinois State University, with a joint appointment in Psychology. She received her doctorate degree from the University of Wisconsin-Madison. Her research, which has spanned over 30 years, has focused on a number of issues about close relationships and sexuality, including the influence of social networks on dyadic relationships, compassionate love, sexuality, and attraction. She was an Editor of the journal *Personal Relationships* (2002–6) and has Co-Edited several books or handbooks, most recently, *The Encyclopedia of Human Relationships* (2009, Sage).

Laura Stafford is a Professor and Chair of the Department of Communication at the University of Kentucky. Her main areas of research and teaching are in long-distance relationships, relationship maintenance, and family communication.

Glen H. Stamp is Professor of Communication and Department Chair in Communication Studies at Ball State University, Muncie, Indiana. His interests include interpersonal and family communication. His research on transition to parenthood, defensive communication, and conflict has been published in such journals as *Communication Monographs*, *Communication Studies*, and *Communication Quarterly*.

Catherine A. Surra is Professor of Human Development and Family Studies, Penn State Harrisburg, and the Director of the School of Behavioral Sciences and Education. She is also Professor Emerita, University of Texas at Austin. She studies the development of marital and nonmarital romantic unions. Her research has examined how commitment evolves over time, the ways in which partners choose one another as mates, and the links between the selection process and the long-term health of heterosexual relationships. In recent work, she has developed and evaluated a website designed to foster healthy decisions about committing to relationships. Dr. Surra has received grants from The National Institute of Mental Health and the U.S. Department of Agriculture. She has served on the editorial board of *Personal Relationships* and the *Journal of Marriage and Family*. She is past Chair of the Research and Theory Section of the National Council on Family Relations, and is a founding member and held elected office in the International Association for Relationship Research, formerly the International Society for the Study of Personal Relationships.

April R. Trees, an Associate Professor at Saint Louis University, conducts research and teaches classes on interpersonal, family, and nonverbal communication. Her main research agenda focuses on how conversations and stories about difficult experiences can be beneficial for making sense of and managing stressors, particularly in the family. She also studies the ways in which identity concerns are managed in and shaped by communication practices. Within these research areas, she has an ongoing interest in the intersection of verbal and nonverbal communication in relational processes. Dr. Trees's research has been published in a number of different journals, including *Human Communication Research*, *Communication Monographs*, *Journal of Social and Personal Relationships*, and *Journal of Family Communication*.

Anita L. Vangelisti is the Jesse H. Jones Centennial Professor of Communication in the Department of Communication Studies at the University of Texas at Austin. Her work focuses on the associations between communication and emotion in the context of close, personal relationships. She has published numerous articles and chapters and has edited or authored several books including the *Handbook of Family Communication* and the *Handbook of Personal Relationships*. Vangelisti is Co-Editor of the Cambridge University Press book series on Advances in Personal Relationships, was Associate Editor of *Personal Relationships*, edited the *ISSPR Bulletin*, and has served on the editorial boards of over a dozen scholarly journals. She has received recognition for her research from the National Communication Association, the International Society for the Study of Personal Relationships, and the International Association for Relationship Research and served as President of the International Association for Relationship Research.

Shu-wen Wang is a doctoral candidate in Clinical Psychology at the University of California, Los Angeles, and will join the Psychology Department at Haverford College as an Assistant Professor in fall 2012. Her research interests are in the areas of stress, social support, social interaction, and family relationships. She also focuses on cultural factors that impact stress, support, and relationship processes. Wang is currently completing her clinical internship at the Veteran Affairs West Los Angeles Medical Center.

Ellen A. Wartella is Al-Thani Professor of Communication, Professor of Psychology, Professor of Human Development and Social Policy and Director of the Center on Media and Human Development at Northwestern University. She is a leading scholar of the role of media in children's development and serves on a variety of national and international boards and committees on children's issues. Dr. Wartella is a trustee of Sesame Workshop and serves on the PBS Advisory Board on children and television. She is a past member of the Board on Children, Youth and Families at the National Academy of Sciences and chaired the Committee on Examination of Front of Pack Nutrition Rating Systems and Symbols in 2011 at the Institute of Medicine. She is a member of the American Psychological Association, the Society for Research in Child Development and is past President of the International Communication Association.

Lisa M. Wenger is a Ph.D. candidate in the Department of Family Relations & Human Development at the University of Guelph. Drawing on a background as a community based health researcher, her current research interests primarily orient around the social and cultural dimensions of health and illness, with a particular focus on gender and health. Her dissertation research is a grounded theory examination of how men diagnosed with cancer subjectively experience and navigate health-related help seeking throughout the course of their illness.

Stacey L. Williams is an Assistant Professor of Psychology at East Tennessee State University. In her research she studies perceived self and public stigma associated with numerous identities and experiences. She is interested in understanding how stigma perceptions relate to psychosocial outcomes such as support exchanges and informal and formal service seeking. She also has interests in intimate partner violence and trauma.

Brian J. Willoughby is an Assistant Professor in the School of Family Life at Brigham Young University. He has published numerous articles on couple dynamics, parenting, and emerging adulthood in the leading family science, psychological and sociological journals. His research has been widely cited in the media, appearing in such outlets as *USA Today*, *MSNBC*, *Men's Health*, the *Washington Post*, and *ABC News*. Dr. Willoughby also serves on the international board of the Society for the Study of Emerging Adulthood as an expert on couple and family relationships.

Barbara J. Wilson is the Vice Provost of Academic Affairs at the University of Illinois at Urbana-Champaign (UIUC) and also the Kathryn Lee Baynes Dallenbach Professor in the Department of Communication at UIUC. Her areas of expertise include the social and psychological effects of the media, particularly on youth. She is Co-Author of *Children, Adolescents, and the Media* (Sage, 2nd edn, 2009) and three book volumes of the *National Television Violence Study* (Sage, 1997–98). She also Co-Edited the *Handbook of Children, Media, and Development* (Wiley-Blackwell, 2008), and has published over 100 articles, chapters, and technical reports on media effects and their implications for media policy.

Steven R. Wilson is Professor in the Brian Lamb School of Communication at Purdue University. He is author of *Seeking and Resisting Compliance: Why People Say What They Do When Trying to Influence Others* (Sage, 2002), Co-Editor of *New Directions in Interpersonal Communication Research* (Sage, 2010, with Sandi Smith), and author of 60 peer-review articles and scholarly chapters. His recent work explores parent–child control dynamics associated with child abuse as well as the impact of military deployment on children. He has served as an Associate Editor for *Personal Relationships* and received the NCA Bernard Brommel award for career contributions to family communication.

Index

Note: Page numbers in *italics* are for tables.